~ Favorite Brand Name ~

· Grandma's ·

OLD-FASHIONED

· Cookies ·

D1406898

Publications International, Ltd.

Pictured on the front cover: Peanut Butter Sensations *(page 8),* Original Nestlé® Toll House®
Chocolate Chip Cookies *(page 36),* Luscious Lemon Bars *(page 52),* Caramel-Layered Brownies
(page 62) and Linzer Sandwich Cookies *(page 90).*

Pictured on the back cover *(clockwise from top left):* Brandy Lace Cookies *(page 26),* Ultimate Sugar
Cookies *(page 20)* and Peanut Butter Bears *(page 70).*

Contents

Favorites

CHOCOLATE–DIPPED ALMOND HORNS

       1½ cups powdered sugar
        1 cup butter or margarine, softened
        2 egg yolks
       1½ teaspoons vanilla
        2 cups all-purpose flour
        ½ cup ground almonds
        1 teaspoon cream of tartar
        1 teaspoon baking soda
        1 cup semisweet chocolate chips, melted
          Powdered sugar

Preheat oven to 325°F. In large bowl, combine powdered sugar and butter. Beat at medium speed until creamy. Add egg yolks and vanilla; continue beating until well blended. Reduce speed to low. Add flour, almonds, cream of tartar and baking soda. Continue beating until well mixed. Shape into 1-inch balls. Roll balls into 2-inch ropes; shape into crescents. Place 2 inches apart on cookie sheets. Flatten slightly with bottom of glass covered in waxed paper. Bake for 8 to 10 minutes or until set. (Cookies do not brown.) Cool completely. Dip half of each cookie into chocolate; sprinkle remaining half with powdered sugar. Refrigerate until set.

Makes about 3 dozen cookies

OATMEAL APPLE COOKIES

¾ **CRISCO® Stick or ¾ cup CRISCO®
    All-Vegetable Shortening**
1¼ **cups firmly packed brown sugar**
  1 **egg**
  ¼ **cup milk**
1½ **teaspoons vanilla**
  1 **cup all-purpose flour**
1¼ **teaspoons ground cinnamon**
  ½ **teaspoon salt**
  ¼ **teaspoon baking soda**
  ¼ **teaspoon ground nutmeg**
  3 **cups quick oats (not instant or
       old-fashioned)**
  1 **cup peeled, diced apples**
  ¾ **cup raisins (optional)**
  ¾ **cup coarsely chopped walnuts (optional)**

1. Preheat oven to 375°F. Grease cookie sheet with shortening.

2. Combine shortening, sugar, egg, milk and vanilla in large bowl. Beat at medium speed of electric mixer until well blended.

3. Combine flour, cinnamon, salt, baking soda and nutmeg in small bowl. Mix into creamed mixture at low speed until just blended. Stir in, one at a time, oats, apples, raisins and nuts with spoon.

4. Drop rounded tablespoonfuls of dough 2 inches apart onto cookie sheet.

5. Bake at 375°F for 13 minutes or until set. Cool 2 minutes on cookie sheet. Remove to wire rack. Cool completely.   *Makes about 2½ dozen cookies*

PEANUT BUTTER SENSATIONS

½ **CRISCO® Stick or ½ cup CRISCO®
    All-Vegetable Shortening**
  1 **cup JIF® Creamy Peanut Butter**
  ¾ **cup granulated sugar**
  ½ **cup firmly packed brown sugar**
  1 **tablespoon milk**
  1 **teaspoon vanilla**
  1 **egg**
1¼ **cups all-purpose flour**
  ¾ **teaspoon baking soda**
  ½ **teaspoon baking powder**
  ¼ **teaspoon salt**

1. Preheat oven to 375°F.

2. Combine shortening, peanut butter, granulated sugar, brown sugar, milk and vanilla in large bowl. Beat at medium speed of electric mixer until well blended. Beat in egg.

3. Combine flour, baking soda, baking powder and salt in small bowl. Mix into creamed mixture at low speed until just blended. Drop rounded tablespoonfuls of dough 2 inches apart onto ungreased cookie sheet. Make crisscross pattern on dough with floured fork.

4. Bake at 375°F for 8 to 10 minutes. Cool 2 minutes on cookie sheet. Remove to wire rack. Cool completely.   *Makes about 2 dozen cookies*

Oatmeal Apple Cookies

COCOA SNICKERDOODLES

1 cup butter or margarine, softened
¾ cup firmly packed brown sugar
¾ cup plus 2 tablespoons granulated sugar, divided
2 eggs
2 cups uncooked rolled oats
1½ cups all-purpose flour
¼ cup plus 2 tablespoons unsweetened cocoa powder, divided
1 teaspoon baking soda
2 tablespoons ground cinnamon

Preheat oven to 375°F. Lightly grease cookie sheets or line with parchment paper. Beat butter, brown sugar and ¾ cup granulated sugar in large bowl until light and fluffy. Add eggs; mix well. Combine oats, flour, ¼ cup cocoa and baking soda in medium bowl. Stir into butter mixture until blended. Mix remaining 2 tablespoons granulated sugar, cinnamon and remaining 2 tablespoons cocoa in small bowl. Drop dough by rounded teaspoonfuls into cinnamon mixture; toss to coat. Place 2 inches apart on prepared cookie sheets. Bake 8 to 10 minutes or until firm in center. *Do not overbake.* Remove to wire racks to cool.

Makes about 4½ dozen cookies

SPICY PUMPKIN COOKIES

2 CRISCO® Sticks or 2 cups CRISCO® All-Vegetable Shortening
2 cups sugar
1 can (16 ounces) solid pack pumpkin
2 eggs
2 teaspoons vanilla
4 cups all-purpose flour
2 teaspoons baking powder
2 teaspoons ground cinnamon
1 teaspoon salt
1 teaspoon baking soda
1 teaspoon ground nutmeg
½ teaspoon ground allspice
2 cups raisins
1 cup chopped nuts

1. Preheat oven to 350°F.

2. Combine shortening, sugar, pumpkin, eggs and vanilla in large bowl; beat well.

3. Combine flour, baking powder, cinnamon, salt, baking soda, nutmeg and allspice in medium bowl. Add to pumpkin mixture; mix well. Stir in raisins and nuts. Drop rounded teaspoonfuls of dough, 2 inches apart, onto greased cookie sheet.

4. Bake at 350°F for 12 to 15 minutes. Cool on wire rack. If desired, frost with vanilla frosting.

Makes about 7 dozen cookies

Chocolate-Peanut Cookies (page 30),
Cocoa Snickerdoodles

RASPBERRY ALMOND SANDWICH COOKIES

1 package DUNCAN HINES® Golden Sugar Cookie Mix
1 egg
¼ cup CRISCO® Oil
1 tablespoon water
¾ teaspoon almond extract
1⅓ cups sliced natural almonds, broken
Seedless red raspberry jam

1. Preheat oven to 375°F.

2. Combine cookie mix, egg, oil, water and almond extract in large bowl. Stir until thoroughly blended. Drop half the dough by level measuring teaspoons 2 inches apart onto ungreased cookie sheets. (It is a small amount of dough but will spread during baking to 1½ to 1¾ inches.)

3. Place almonds on waxed paper. Drop other half of dough by level measuring teaspoons onto nuts. Place almond side up 2 inches apart on cookie sheets.

4. Bake both plain and almond cookies at 375°F for 6 minutes or until set but not browned. Cool 1 minute on cookie sheets. Remove to wire racks. Cool completely.

5. Spread bottoms of plain cookies with jam; top with almond cookies. Press together to make sandwiches. Store in airtight containers.

Makes 6 dozen sandwich cookies

OLD–FASHIONED OATMEAL COOKIES

¾ CRISCO® Stick or ¾ cup CRISCO® All-Vegetable Shortening
1¼ cups firmly packed brown sugar
1 egg
⅓ cup milk
1½ teaspoons vanilla
1 cup all-purpose flour
½ teaspoon baking soda
½ teaspoon salt
¼ teaspoon ground cinnamon
3 cups quick oats (not instant or old-fashioned)
1 cup raisins
1 cup coarsely chopped walnuts

1. Preheat oven to 375°F. Grease cookie sheet.

2. Combine shortening, sugar, egg, milk and vanilla in large bowl. Beat at medium speed of electric mixer until well blended.

3. Combine flour, baking soda, salt and cinnamon in small bowl. Mix into creamed mixture at low speed until just blended. Stir in oats, raisins and nuts with spoon.

4. Drop rounded tablespoonfuls of dough 2 inches apart onto cookie sheet.

5. Bake at 375°F for 10 to 12 minutes or until lightly browned. Cool 2 minutes on cookie sheet. Remove to wire rack. Cool completely.

Makes about 2½ dozen cookies

Raspberry Almond Sandwich Cookies

MOM'S BEST OATMEAL COOKIES

**1 CRISCO® Stick or 1 cup CRISCO®
All-Vegetable Shortening**
1½ cups firmly packed brown sugar
2 eggs
2 teaspoons vanilla
1½ cups all-purpose flour
1 teaspoon salt
1 teaspoon baking powder
1 teaspoon ground cinnamon
¼ teaspoon baking soda
**2 cups quick oats (not instant or
old-fashioned)**
1 cup chopped pecans
⅔ cup sesame seeds
⅔ cup flaked coconut

1. Preheat oven to 350°F.

2. Combine shortening and sugar in large bowl. Beat at medium speed of electric mixer until well blended. Beat in eggs and vanilla.

3. Combine flour, salt, baking powder, cinnamon and baking soda in small bowl. Mix into creamed mixture at low speed until blended. Stir in, one at a time, oats, nuts, sesame seeds and coconut with spoon. Drop rounded tablespoonfuls of dough 2 inches apart onto ungreased cookie sheet.

4. Bake at 350°F for 10 minutes or until lightly browned. Remove immediately to wire rack. Cool completely. *Makes about 6 dozen cookies*

GINGER SNAP OATS

**¾ CRISCO® Stick or ¾ cup CRISCO®
All-Vegetable Shortening**
1 cup firmly packed brown sugar
½ cup granulated sugar
½ cup molasses
2 teaspoons vinegar
2 eggs
1¼ cups all-purpose flour
1 tablespoon ground ginger
1½ teaspoo
½ teaspoo
¼ teaspoo
2¾ cups qu
old-f
1½ cups ra

1. Preheat o
shortening.

2. Combine
sugar, mola
Beat at me
blended.

3. Combir
and cloves
mixture a
raisins. D
inches ap

4. Bake
2 minute
Cool co

Top to bottom: Ginger Snap Oats, Mom's Best Oatmeal Cookies

VIENNESE HAZELNUT BUTTER THINS

- **1 cup hazelnuts**
- **1¼ cups powdered sugar**
- **1 cup butter, softened**
- **1 large egg**
- **1 teaspoon vanilla**
- **1¼ cups all-purpose flour**
- **¼ teaspoon salt**
- **1 cup semisweet chocolate chips**

1. Preheat oven to 350°F. Spread hazelnuts in single layer on baking sheet. Bake 10 to 12 minutes or until toasted and skins begin to flake off; let cool slightly. Wrap nuts in heavy kitchen towel; rub to remove as much of the skins as possible. Process nuts in food processor until nuts are ground, but not pasty.

2. Beat powdered sugar and butter in medium bowl with electric mixer at medium speed until light and fluffy. Beat in egg and vanilla. Gradually add flour and salt. Beat in nuts at low speed.

3. Place dough on sheet of waxed paper. Roll back and forth to form a log 12 inches long and 2½ inches wide. Wrap in plastic wrap and refrigerate until firm, 2 hours or up to 48 hours.

4. Preheat oven to 350°F. Cut dough with knife crosswise into ¼-inch-thick slices. Place cookies 2 inches apart on *ungreased* cookie sheets.

5. Bake 10 to 12 minutes or until edges are very lightly browned. Let cookies stand on cookie sheets 1 minute. Remove cookies with spatula to wire racks; cool completely.

6. Melt chocolate chips in 2-cup glass measure in microwave at HIGH 2½ to 3 minutes, stirring once. Dip each cookie into chocolate, coating half way up sides. Let excess chocolate drip back into cup. Transfer cookies to waxed paper; let stand at room temperature 1 hour or until set. Store tightly covered between sheets of waxed paper at room temperature or freeze up to 3 months.

Makes about 3 dozen cookies

RAISIN SPICE DROPS

- **¾ cup (1½ sticks) margarine, softened**
- **⅔ cup firmly packed brown sugar**
- **⅔ cup granulated sugar**
- **2 eggs**
- **1 teaspoon vanilla**
- **2½ cups QUAKER® Oats (quick or old-fashioned, uncooked)**
- **1¼ cups all-purpose flour**
- **1 teaspoon ground cinnamon**
- **½ teaspoon baking soda**
- **½ teaspoon salt (optional)**
- **¼ teaspoon ground nutmeg**
- **⅔ cup raisins**
- **½ cup chopped nuts**

Preheat oven to 350°F. In large bowl, beat margarine and sugars until fluffy. Blend in eggs and vanilla. Add remaining ingredients; mix well. Drop dough by rounded teaspoonfuls onto ungreased cookie sheet. Bake 8 to 10 minutes or until light golden brown. Cool on wire rack. Store tightly covered. *Makes about 4½ dozen cookies*

Viennese Hazelnut Butter Thins

SWISS MOCHA TREATS

2 ounces imported Swiss bittersweet chocolate candy bar, broken
½ cup plus 2 tablespoons butter, softened, divided
1 tablespoon instant espresso powder
1 teaspoon vanilla
1¾ cups all-purpose flour
½ teaspoon baking soda
½ teaspoon salt
¾ cup sugar
1 large egg
3 ounces imported Swiss white chocolate candy bar, broken

1. Melt bittersweet chocolate and 2 tablespoons butter in small, heavy saucepan over low heat, stirring often. Add espresso powder; stir until dissolved. Remove from heat; stir in vanilla. Let cool to room temperature.

2. Combine flour, baking soda and salt in medium bowl.

3. Beat remaining ½ cup butter and sugar in large bowl with mixer at medium speed until fluffy. Beat in bittersweet chocolate mixture and egg. Gradually add flour mixture. Beat at low speed until well blended. Cover; refrigerate 30 minutes or until firm.

4. Preheat oven to 375°F. Roll tablespoonfuls of dough into 1-inch balls; place 3 inches apart on *ungreased* cookie sheets. Flatten each ball into ½-inch-thick round with fork dipped in sugar.

5. Bake 9 to 10 minutes or until set (do not overbake or cookies will become dry). Immediately remove cookies to wire racks; cool completely.

6. Place white chocolate in small resealable plastic freezer bag; seal bag. Microwave at MEDIUM (50% power) 1 minute. Turn bag over; microwave at MEDIUM 1 minute or until melted. Knead until chocolate is smooth. Cut off tiny corner of bag; pipe or drizzle white chocolate onto cooled cookies. Let stand 30 minutes or until set. Store tightly covered at room temperature or freeze up to 3 months. *Makes about 4 dozen cookies*

WALNUT MACAROONS

2⅔ cups flaked coconut
1¼ cups coarsely chopped California walnuts
⅓ cup all-purpose flour
½ teaspoon ground cinnamon
¼ teaspoon salt
4 egg whites
1 teaspoon grated lemon peel
2 (1-ounce) squares semisweet chocolate, melted

Combine coconut, walnuts, flour, cinnamon and salt in large bowl. Mix in egg whites and lemon peel. Drop by teaspoonfuls onto lightly greased cookie sheets. Bake at 325°F for 20 minutes or until golden brown. Dip macaroon bottoms in melted chocolate. Place on waxed paper to set.
Makes about 3 dozen cookies

*Favorite recipe from **Walnut Marketing Board***

Swiss Mocha Treats

ULTIMATE SUGAR COOKIES

1¼ cups granulated sugar
1 CRISCO® Stick or 1 cup CRISCO®
   All-Vegetable Shortening
2 eggs
¼ cup light corn syrup or regular pancake
   syrup
1 tablespoon vanilla
3 cups all-purpose flour (plus
   4 tablespoons), divided
¾ teaspoon baking powder
½ teaspoon baking soda
½ teaspoon salt
   Granulated sugar or colored sugar
   crystals

1. Place sugar and shortening in large bowl. Beat at medium speed of electric mixer until well blended. Add eggs, syrup and vanilla; beat until well blended and fluffy.

2. Combine 3 cups flour, baking powder, baking soda and salt in medium bowl. Add gradually to shortening mixture, beating at low speed until well blended.

3. Divide dough into 4 equal pieces; shape each piece into disk. Wrap with plastic wrap. Refrigerate 1 hour or until firm.

4. Preheat oven to 375°F. Place sheets of foil on countertop for cooling cookies.

5. Sprinkle about 1 tablespoon flour on large sheet of waxed paper. Place disk of dough on floured paper; flatten slightly with hands. Turn dough over; cover with another large sheet of waxed paper. Roll dough to ¼-inch thickness. Remove top sheet of waxed paper. Cut into desired shapes with floured cookie cutters. Place 2 inches apart on ungreased cookie sheet. Repeat with remaining dough.

6. Sprinkle with granulated sugar.

7. Bake one cookie sheet at a time at 375°F for 5 to 7 minutes or until edges of cookies are lightly browned. *Do not overbake.* Cool 2 minutes on cookie sheet. Remove cookies to foil to cool completely.   *Makes about 3½ dozen cookies*

Ultimate Sugar Cookies

Cinnamon–Apricot Tart Oatmeal Cookies

½ **cup water**
1 **package (8 ounces) dried apricot halves, diced**
1 **CRISCO® Stick or 1 cup CRISCO® All-Vegetable Shortening**
1 **cup firmly packed brown sugar**
¼ **cup granulated sugar**
1 **egg**
2 **teaspoons vanilla**
1½ **cups all-purpose flour**
2 **teaspoons ground cinnamon**
1 **teaspoon baking soda**
1 **teaspoon salt**
1 **cup plus 2 tablespoons chopped pecans**
3 **cups quick oats (not instant or old-fashioned)**

1. Place ½ cup water in small saucepan. Heat to boiling. Place diced apricots in strainer over boiling water. Reduce heat to low. Cover. Steam for 15 minutes. Cool. Reserve liquid.

2. Preheat oven to 375°F. Grease cookie sheet. Combine shortening, brown sugar, granulated sugar, egg and vanilla in large bowl. Beat at medium speed of electric mixer until well blended.

3. Combine flour, cinnamon, baking soda and salt in small bowl. Mix into creamed mixture at low speed until just blended. Stir in nuts, apricots and reserved liquid from apricots. Stir in oats with spoon. Drop rounded tablespoonfuls of dough 2 inches apart onto cookie sheet.

4. Bake at 375°F for 10 to 11 minutes. Cool 2 minutes on cookie sheet. Remove to wire rack. Cool completely.   *Makes 3½ to 4 dozen cookies*

Easy Lemon Cookies

1 **package DUNCAN HINES® Moist Deluxe Lemon Cake Mix**
2 **eggs**
½ **cup CRISCO® Oil**
1 **teaspoon grated lemon peel**
Pecan halves, for garnish

1. Preheat oven to 350°F.

2. Combine cake mix, eggs, oil and lemon peel in large bowl. Stir until thoroughly blended. Drop by rounded teaspoonfuls 2 inches apart onto ungreased cookie sheets. Press pecan half in center of each cookie. Bake at 350°F for 9 to 11 minutes or until edges are light golden brown. Cool 1 minute on cookie sheets. Remove to wire racks. Cool completely. Store in airtight container.

Makes 4 dozen cookies

TIP: You may substitute whole almonds or walnut halves for the pecan halves.

Top to bottom: Chocolate-Orange Chip Cookies (page 34), Cinnamon-Apricot Tart Oatmeal Cookies

KENTUCKY BOURBON PECAN TARTS

Cream Cheese Pastry (recipe follows)
2 eggs
½ cup granulated sugar
½ cup KARO® Light or Dark Corn Syrup
2 tablespoons bourbon
1 tablespoon MAZOLA® Margarine, melted
½ teaspoon vanilla
1 cup chopped pecans
Powdered sugar (optional)

Preheat oven to 350°F. Prepare Cream Cheese Pastry. Divide dough in half; set aside one half. On floured surface, roll out pastry to ⅛-inch thickness. *If necessary, add small amount of flour to keep pastry from sticking.* Cut into 12 (2¼-inch) rounds. Press evenly into bottoms and up sides of 1¾-inch muffin pan cups. Repeat with remaining pastry. Refrigerate.

In medium bowl, beat eggs slightly. Stir in granulated sugar, corn syrup, bourbon, margarine and vanilla until well blended. Spoon 1 heaping teaspoon pecans into each pastry-lined cup; top with 1 tablespoon corn syrup mixture.

Bake 20 to 25 minutes or until lightly browned and toothpick inserted into center comes out clean. Cool in pans 5 minutes. Remove; cool completely on wire rack. If desired, sprinkle cookies with powdered sugar.

Makes about 2 dozen cookies

CREAM CHEESE PASTRY

1 cup all-purpose flour
¾ teaspoon baking powder
Pinch salt
½ cup MAZOLA® Margarine, softened
1 package (3 ounces) cream cheese, softened
2 teaspoons sugar

In small bowl, combine flour, baking powder and salt. In large bowl, mix margarine, cream cheese and sugar until well combined. Stir in flour mixture until well blended. Press firmly into ball with hands.

Prep Time: 45 minutes
Bake Time: 25 minutes, plus cooling

Top to bottom: Brandy Lace Cookies (page 26), Kentucky Bourbon Pecan Tarts

AUSTRIAN TEA COOKIES

1½ **cups sugar, divided**
½ **cup butter, softened**
½ **cup vegetable shortening**
1 **egg, beaten**
½ **teaspoon vanilla extract**
2 **cups all-purpose flour**
2 **cups ALMOND DELIGHT® Brand Cereal, crushed to 1 cup**
½ **teaspoon baking powder**
¼ **teaspoon ground cinnamon**
14 **ounces almond paste**
2 **egg whites**
5 **tablespoons raspberry or apricot jam, warmed**

In large bowl, beat 1 cup sugar, butter and shortening. Add egg and vanilla; mix well. Stir in flour, cereal, baking powder and cinnamon until well blended. Refrigerate 1 to 2 hours or until firm.

Preheat oven to 350°F. Roll dough out on lightly floured surface to ¼-inch thickness; cut into 2-inch circles with floured cookie cutter. Place on ungreased cookie sheet; set aside. In small bowl, beat almond paste, egg whites and remaining ½ cup sugar until smooth. With pastry tube fitted with medium-sized star tip, pipe almond paste mixture ½ inch thick on top of each cookie along outside edge. Place ¼ teaspoon jam in center of each cookie, spreading out to paste. Bake 8 to 10 minutes or until lightly browned. Let stand 1 minute before removing from cookie sheet. Cool on wire rack. *Makes about 3½ dozen cookies*

BRANDY LACE COOKIES

¼ **cup sugar**
¼ **cup MAZOLA® Margarine**
¼ **cup KARO® Light or Dark Corn Syrup**
½ **cup all-purpose flour**
¼ **cup very finely chopped pecans or walnuts**
2 **tablespoons brandy**
Melted white and/or semisweet chocolate (optional)

Preheat oven to 350°F. Lightly grease and flour cookie sheets.

In small saucepan, combine sugar, margarine and corn syrup. Bring to boil over medium heat, stirring constantly. Remove from heat. Stir in flour, pecans and brandy. Drop 12 evenly spaced half teaspoonfuls of batter onto prepared cookie sheets.

Bake 6 minutes or until golden. Cool 1 to 2 minutes or until cookies can be lifted but are still warm and pliable; remove with spatula. Curl around handle of wooden spoon; slide off when crisp. If cookies harden before curling, return to oven to soften. If desired, drizzle with melted chocolate. *Makes 4 to 5 dozen cookies*

Prep Time: 30 minutes
Bake Time: 6 minutes, plus curling and cooling

Austrian Tea Cookies

~ CLASSIC ~

Chips & Chunks

PEANUT BUTTER CHOCOLATE CHIPPERS

1 cup creamy or chunky peanut butter
1 cup firmly packed light brown sugar
1 large egg
¾ cup milk chocolate chips
Granulated sugar

1. Preheat oven to 350°F.

2. Combine peanut butter, brown sugar and egg in medium bowl with mixing spoon until well blended. Add chips; mix well.

3. Roll heaping tablespoonfuls of dough into 1½-inch balls. Place balls 2 inches apart on *ungreased* cookie sheets.

4. Dip table fork into granulated sugar; press criss-cross fashion onto each ball, flattening to ½-inch thickness.

5. Bake 12 minutes or until set. Let cookies stand on cookie sheets 2 minutes. Remove cookies with spatula to wire racks; cool completely. Store tightly covered at room temperature or freeze up to 3 months. *Makes about 2 dozen cookies*

CHOCOLATE CHIP SANDWICH COOKIES

COOKIES
1 package DUNCAN HINES® Chocolate Chip Cookie Mix
1 egg
⅓ cup CRISCO® Oil
3 tablespoons water

CREAM FILLING
1½ cups marshmallow creme
¾ cup butter or margarine, softened
2½ cups powdered sugar
1½ teaspoons vanilla extract

1. Preheat oven to 375°F.

2. For Cookies, combine cookie mix, egg, oil and water in large bowl. Stir until thoroughly blended. Drop by rounded teaspoonfuls 2 inches apart onto ungreased cookie sheets. Bake at 375°F for 8 to 10 minutes or until light golden brown. Cool 1 minute on cookie sheets. Remove to wire racks.

3. For Cream Filling, combine marshmallow creme and butter in large bowl. Add powdered sugar and vanilla extract, beating until smooth.

4. To assemble, spread bottoms of half the cookies with 1 tablespoon cream filling; top with remaining cookies. Press together to make sandwich cookies. Refrigerate to quickly firm the filling, if desired.

Makes about 24 sandwich cookies

TIP: After chilling the assembled cookies, wrap individually in plastic wrap. Store in the refrigerator until ready to serve.

CHOCOLATE–PEANUT COOKIES

1 cup butter or margarine, softened
¾ cup granulated sugar
¾ cup firmly packed light brown sugar
2 eggs
1 teaspoon vanilla
1 teaspoon baking soda
¼ teaspoon salt
2¼ cups all-purpose flour
2 cups chocolate-covered peanuts

Preheat oven to 375°F. Line cookie sheets with parchment paper or leave ungreased. Beat butter, granulated sugar, brown sugar, eggs and vanilla in large bowl with electric mixer until fluffy. Beat in baking soda and salt. Stir in flour to make stiff dough. Blend in chocolate-covered peanuts. Drop by rounded teaspoonfuls 2 inches apart onto cookie sheets. Bake 9 to 11 minutes or until just barely golden. *Do not overbake.* Remove to wire racks to cool.

Makes about 5 dozen cookies

Chocolate Chip Sandwich Cookies

OATMEAL SCOTCHIES

1¼ cups all-purpose flour
1 teaspoon baking soda
½ teaspoon salt
½ teaspoon ground cinnamon
1 cup (2 sticks) butter or margarine, softened
¾ cup granulated sugar
¾ cup packed brown sugar
2 eggs
1 teaspoon vanilla extract *or* grated peel of 1 orange
3 cups quick or old-fashioned oats
2 cups (12-ounce package) NESTLÉ® TOLL HOUSE® Butterscotch Flavored Morsels

COMBINE flour, baking soda, salt and cinnamon in small bowl. Beat butter, granulated sugar, brown sugar, eggs and vanilla in large mixing bowl until creamy. Gradually beat in flour mixture. Stir in oats and morsels. Drop by rounded tablespoons onto ungreased cookie sheets.

BAKE in preheated 375°F oven for 7 to 8 minutes for chewy cookies, 9 to 10 minutes for crisp cookies. Let stand for 2 minutes; remove to wire racks to cool completely.   *Makes 4 dozen cookies*

CHOCO–SCUTTERBOTCH

⅔ CRISCO® Stick or ⅔ cup CRISCO® All-Vegetable Shortening
½ cup firmly packed brown sugar
2 eggs
1 package DUNCAN HINES® Moist Deluxe Yellow Cake Mix
1 cup toasted rice cereal
½ cup milk chocolate chunks
½ cup butterscotch chips
½ cup semi-sweet chocolate chips
½ cup coarsely chopped walnuts or pecans

1. Preheat oven to 375°F.

2. Combine shortening and brown sugar in large bowl. Beat at medium speed of electric mixer until well blended. Beat in eggs.

3. Add cake mix gradually at low speed. Mix until well blended. Stir in cereal, chocolate chunks, butterscotch chips, chocolate chips and nuts with spoon until well blended. Shape dough into 1¼-inch balls. Place 2 inches apart on ungreased cookie sheet. Flatten slightly. Shape sides to form circle, if necessary.

4. Bake at 375°F for 7 to 9 minutes or until lightly browned around edges. Cool 2 minutes before removing to paper towels to cool completely.
        Makes about 3 dozen cookies

Oatmeal Scotchies

IVORY CHIP STRAWBERRY FUDGE DROPS

⅔ **CRISCO® Stick or ⅔ cup CRISCO® All-Vegetable Shortening**
1 **cup sugar**
1 **egg**
½ **teaspoon strawberry extract**
½ **cup buttermilk**
6 **tablespoons puréed frozen sweetened strawberries**
1¾ **cups all-purpose flour**
6 **tablespoons unsweetened cocoa powder**
¾ **teaspoon baking soda**
½ **teaspoon salt**
1½ **cups white chocolate baking chips**

1. Preheat oven to 350°F. Grease cookie sheet. Combine shortening, sugar, egg and strawberry extract in large bowl. Beat at medium speed of electric mixer until well blended. Beat in buttermilk and strawberry purée.

2. Combine flour, cocoa, baking soda and salt in medium bowl. Mix into creamed mixture at low speed of electric mixer until blended. Stir in white chocolate chips.

3. Drop rounded tablespoonfuls of dough 2 inches apart onto cookie sheet.

4. Bake 11 to 12 minutes or until tops spring back when pressed lightly. Remove immediately to wire rack. Cool completely.

Makes about 2½ dozen cookies

CHOCOLATE–ORANGE CHIP COOKIES

½ **CRISCO® Stick or ½ cup CRISCO® All-Vegetable Shortening**
1¼ **cups firmly packed brown sugar**
2 **squares (1 ounce each) unsweetened chocolate, melted and cooled**
1 **egg**
2 **tablespoons orange juice concentrate**
2 **tablespoons grated orange peel**
1 **teaspoon vanilla**
1½ **cups all-purpose flour**
¾ **teaspoon baking soda**
¼ **teaspoon salt**
1 **cup semi-sweet chocolate chips**
½ **cup blanched slivered almonds**

1. Preheat oven to 375°F. Combine shortening, sugar and melted chocolate in large bowl. Beat at medium speed of electric mixer until well blended. Beat in egg, concentrate, peel and vanilla.

2. Combine flour, baking soda and salt in small bowl. Mix into creamed mixture at low speed until well blended. Stir in chocolate chips and nuts.

3. Drop tablespoonfuls of dough 2 inches apart onto ungreased cookie sheet.

4. Bake at 375°F for 7 to 9 minutes or until set. Cool 2 minutes on cookie sheet. Remove to wire rack. Cool completely.

Makes about 3½ dozen cookies

Ivory Chip Strawberry Fudge Drops

ORIGINAL NESTLÉ® TOLL HOUSE® CHOCOLATE CHIP COOKIES

2¼ cups all-purpose flour
1 teaspoon baking soda
1 teaspoon salt
1 cup (2 sticks) butter, softened
¾ cup granulated sugar
¾ cup firmly packed brown sugar
1 teaspoon vanilla extract
2 eggs
2 cups (12-ounce package) NESTLÉ®
    TOLL HOUSE® Semi-Sweet Chocolate
    Morsels
1 cup chopped nuts

COMBINE flour, baking soda and salt in small bowl. Beat butter, granulated sugar, brown sugar and vanilla in large mixing bowl. Add eggs one at a time, beating well after each addition; gradually beat in flour mixture. Stir in morsels and nuts. Drop by rounded tablespoons onto ungreased cookie sheets.

BAKE in preheated 375°F oven for 9 to 11 minutes or until golden brown. Let stand for 2 minutes; remove to wire racks to cool completely.

Makes about 5 dozen cookies

COWBOY COOKIES

½ cup butter or margarine, softened
½ cup firmly packed light brown sugar
¼ cup granulated sugar
1 egg
1 teaspoon vanilla
1 cup all-purpose flour
2 tablespoons unsweetened cocoa
½ teaspoon baking powder
¼ teaspoon baking soda
1 cup uncooked rolled oats
1 cup (6 ounces) semisweet chocolate
    chips
½ cup raisins
½ cup chopped nuts

Preheat oven to 375°F. Lightly grease cookie sheets or line with parchment paper. Beat butter, brown sugar and granulated sugar in large bowl with electric mixer until blended. Add egg and vanilla; beat until fluffy. Combine flour, cocoa, baking powder and baking soda in small bowl; stir into creamed mixture with oats, chocolate chips, raisins and nuts. Drop dough by teaspoonfuls 2 inches apart onto prepared cookie sheets. Bake 10 to 12 minutes or until lightly browned around edges. Remove to wire racks to cool.

Makes about 4 dozen cookies

Original Nestlé® Toll House® Chocolate Chip Cookies

ULTIMATE CHOCOLATE CHIP COOKIES

¾ **CRISCO® Stick or ¾ cup CRISCO® All-Vegetable Shortening**
1¼ **cups firmly packed brown sugar**
2 **tablespoons milk**
1 **tablespoon vanilla**
1 **egg**
1¾ **cups all-purpose flour**
1 **teaspoon salt**
¾ **teaspoon baking soda**
1 **cup semi-sweet chocolate chips**
1 **cup coarsely chopped pecans***

*You may substitute an additional ½ cup semi-sweet chocolate chips for the pecans.

1. Preheat oven to 375°F.

2. Combine shortening, sugar, milk and vanilla in large bowl. Beat at medium speed of electric mixer until well blended. Beat in egg.

3. Combine flour, salt and baking soda in small bowl. Mix into creamed mixture at low speed until just blended. Stir in chocolate chips and nuts.

4. Drop rounded tablespoonfuls of dough 3 inches apart onto ungreased cookie sheet.

5. Bake at 375°F for 8 to 10 minutes for chewy cookies (they will look light and moist—*do not overbake*), 11 to 13 minutes for crisp cookies. Cool 2 minutes on cookie sheet. Remove to wire rack. Cool completely.   *Makes about 3 dozen cookies*

Variations for Ultimate Chocolate Chip Cookies

DRIZZLE: Combine 1 teaspoon CRISCO® All-Vegetable Shortening and 1 cup semi-sweet chocolate chips or 1 cup white melting chocolate, cut into small pieces, in microwave-safe measuring cup. Microwave at 50% (MEDIUM). Stir after 1 minute. Repeat until smooth (or melt on rangetop in small saucepan on very low heat). To thin, add a little more shortening. Drizzle back and forth over cookie. Sprinkle with nuts before chocolate hardens, if desired. To quickly harden chocolate, place cookies in refrigerator for a few minutes.

CHOCOLATE DIPPED: Melt chocolate as directed for Drizzle. Dip one end of cooled cookie halfway up in chocolate. Sprinkle with finely chopped nuts before chocolate hardens. Place on waxed paper until chocolate is firm. To quickly harden chocolate, place cookies in refrigerator for a few minutes.

Clockwise from top: Old-Fashioned Oatmeal Cookies (page 12), Peanut Butter Sensations (page 8), Ultimate Chocolate Chip Cookies

Bar Cookies

CHOCOLATE CHIP SHORTBREAD

½ cup butter, softened
½ cup sugar
1 teaspoon vanilla
1 cup all-purpose flour
¼ teaspoon salt
½ cup mini semisweet chocolate chips

Preheat oven to 375°F. Beat butter and sugar in large bowl with electric mixer at medium speed until light and fluffy. Beat in vanilla. Add flour and salt. Stir in chips.

Divide dough in half. Press each half into ungreased 8-inch round cake pan. Bake 12 minutes or until edges are golden brown. Score shortbread with sharp knife, taking care not to cut completely through shortbread. Make 8 wedges per pan.

Let pans stand on wire racks 10 minutes. Invert shortbread onto wire racks; cool completely. Break into wedges.

Makes 16 cookies

PEANUT BUTTER BARS

- ½ **CRISCO® Stick or ½ cup CRISCO® All-Vegetable Shortening**
- 1½ **cups firmly packed brown sugar**
- ⅔ **cup JIF® Creamy or Extra Crunchy Peanut Butter**
- 2 **eggs**
- 1 **teaspoon vanilla**
- 1½ **cups all-purpose flour**
- ½ **teaspoon salt**
- ¼ **cup milk**

1. Preheat oven to 350°F. Grease 13×9×2-inch baking pan.

2. Combine shortening, brown sugar and peanut butter in large bowl. Beat at medium speed of electric mixer until well blended. Beat in eggs and vanilla.

3. Combine flour and salt in small bowl. Add alternately with milk to creamed mixture at low speed. Beat until well blended. Spread in pan.

4. Bake 28 to 32 minutes or until golden brown and center is set. Cool in pan on wire rack. Top with frosting or glaze, if desired. Cut into 2¼×1½-inch bars.

Makes 32 bars

Frosting and Glaze Variations

CHOCOLATE DREAM FROSTING:

Combine 2 tablespoons CRISCO® All-Vegetable Shortening, 1 cup miniature marshmallows, 1 square (1 ounce) unsweetened chocolate and 3 tablespoons milk in medium microwave-safe bowl. Cover with waxed paper. Microwave at 50% (MEDIUM). Stir after 1 minute. Repeat until smooth (or melt on rangetop in medium saucepan on low heat). Stir in 1¾ cups powdered sugar. Beat until well blended. Spread over top. Sprinkle ¼ cup finely chopped peanuts over frosting. Set aside until frosting is firm. Cut into bars.

MICROWAVE CHOCOLATE CHIP GLAZE:

Combine 1 tablespoon CRISCO® All-Vegetable Shortening, ¼ cup semi-sweet chocolate chips and 3 tablespoons milk in medium microwave-safe bowl. Microwave at 50% (MEDIUM). Stir after 1 minute. Repeat until smooth (or melt on rangetop in small saucepan on very low heat). Add ½ cup powdered sugar and ¼ teaspoon vanilla. Stir until smooth. (Add small amount of hot milk if thinner consistency is desired.) Drizzle over top. Sprinkle ¼ cup finely chopped peanuts over glaze. Set aside until glaze is firm. Cut into bars.

Top to bottom: "Cordially Yours" Chocolate Chip Bars (page 44), Peanut Butter Bars

California Apricot Power Bars

2 cups California dried apricot halves, coarsely chopped (12 ounces)
2½ cups pecans, coarsely chopped (10 ounces)
1¼ cups pitted dates, coarsely chopped (8 ounces)
1¼ cups whole wheat flour
1 teaspoon baking powder
1 cup firmly packed brown sugar
3 large eggs
¼ cup apple juice or water
1½ teaspoons vanilla

Preheat oven to 350°F. Line 15½×10½×1-inch jelly-roll pan with foil. In large bowl, stir together apricots, pecans and dates; divide in half. In small bowl, combine flour and baking powder; add to half of fruit-nut mixture. Toss to coat. In medium bowl, combine brown sugar, eggs, apple juice and vanilla; stir into flour mixture until thoroughly moistened. Spread batter evenly into prepared pan. Lightly press remaining fruit-nut mixture on top.

Bake 20 minutes or until bars are golden and spring back when pressed lightly. Cool in pan 5 minutes. Turn out onto wire rack; cool 45 minutes. Peel off foil and cut into bars. Store in airtight container. Bars may be frozen.

Makes about 32 bars

*Favorite recipe from **California Apricot Advisory Board***

"Cordially Yours" Chocolate Chip Bars

¾ CRISCO® Stick or ¾ cup CRISCO® All-Vegetable Shortening
2 eggs
½ cup granulated sugar
¼ cup firmly packed brown sugar
1½ teaspoons vanilla
1 teaspoon almond extract
2 cups all-purpose flour
1 teaspoon baking soda
½ teaspoon ground cinnamon
1 can (21 ounces) cherry pie filling
1½ cups milk chocolate big chips
Powdered sugar

1. Preheat oven to 350°F. Grease 15½×10½×1-inch jelly-roll pan.

2. Combine shortening, eggs, granulated sugar, brown sugar, vanilla and almond extract in large bowl. Beat at medium speed of electric mixer until well blended.

3. Combine flour, baking soda and cinnamon in medium bowl. Mix into creamed mixture at low speed until just blended. Stir in pie filling and chocolate chips. Spread in pan.

4. Bake 25 minutes or until lightly browned and top springs back when lightly pressed. Cool completely in pan on wire rack. Sprinkle with powdered sugar. Cut into 2½×2-inch bars.

Makes 30 bars

California Apricot Power Bars

LAYERED CHOCOLATE CHEESE BARS

¼ **cup (½ stick) margarine or butter**
1½ **cups graham cracker crumbs**
¾ **cup sugar**
1 **package (4 ounces) BAKER'S®**
 GERMAN'S® Sweet Chocolate, melted
1 **package (8 ounces) PHILADELPHIA**
 BRAND® Cream Cheese, softened
1 **egg**
1 **cup BAKER'S® ANGEL FLAKE® Coconut**
1 **cup chopped nuts**

HEAT oven to 350°F.

MELT margarine in oven in 13×9-inch pan. Add graham cracker crumbs and ¼ cup of the sugar; mix well. Press into pan. Bake for 10 minutes.

COMBINE melted chocolate, the remaining ½ cup sugar, the cream cheese and egg. Spread over crust. Sprinkle with coconut and nuts; press lightly.

BAKE for 30 minutes. Cool; cut into bars.

Makes about 24 bars

Prep Time: 20 minutes
Baking Time: 40 minutes

BANANA SPLIT BARS

⅓ **cup margarine or butter, softened**
1 **cup sugar**
1 **egg**
1 **banana, mashed**
½ **teaspoon vanilla**
1¼ **cups all-purpose flour**
1 **teaspoon CALUMET® Baking Powder**
¼ **teaspoon salt**
⅓ **cup chopped nuts**
2 **cups KRAFT® Miniature Marshmallows**
1 **cup BAKER'S® Semi-Sweet Real**
 Chocolate Chips
⅓ **cup maraschino cherries, drained and**
 quartered

HEAT oven to 350°F.

BEAT margarine and sugar until light and fluffy. Add egg, banana and vanilla; mix well. Mix in flour, baking powder and salt. Stir in nuts. Pour into greased 13×9-inch pan.

BAKE for 20 minutes. Remove from oven. Sprinkle with marshmallows, chips and cherries. Bake 10 to 15 minutes longer or until toothpick inserted in center comes out clean. Cool in pan; cut into bars. *Makes about 24 bars*

Prep Time: 20 minutes
Baking Time: 30 to 35 minutes

Top plate (clockwise from top): Layered Chocolate Cheese Bar, Banana Split Bar, Chocolate Peanut Butter Bar (page 54)

PEACHY OATMEAL BARS

CRUMB MIXTURE
- 1½ **cups all-purpose flour**
- 1 **cup uncooked rolled oats**
- ¾ **cup margarine, melted**
- ½ **cup sugar**
- 2 **teaspoons almond extract**
- ½ **teaspoon baking soda**
- ¼ **teaspoon salt**

FILLING
- ¾ **cup peach or apricot preserves**
- ⅓ **cup flaked coconut**

Preheat oven to 350°F.

For Crumb Mixture, combine all crumb mixture ingredients in large bowl of electric mixer. Beat at low speed, scraping bowl often, until mixture is crumbly, 1 to 2 minutes. *Reserve ¾ cup crumb mixture;* press remaining crumb mixture onto bottom of greased 9-inch square baking pan.

For Filling, spread preserves to within ½ inch of edge of crust; sprinkle with reserved crumb mixture and coconut. Bake for 20 to 25 minutes or until edges are lightly browned. Cool completely. Cut into bars. *Makes about 24 bars*

STREUSEL STRAWBERRY BARS

- 1 **cup butter or margarine, softened**
- 1 **cup sugar**
- 2 **cups all-purpose flour**
- 1 **egg**
- ¾ **cup pecans, coarsely chopped**
- 1 **jar (10 ounces) strawberry or raspberry preserves**

Preheat oven to 350°F. Combine butter and sugar in large mixing bowl. Beat at low speed, scraping bowl often, until well blended. Add flour and egg. Beat until mixture is crumbly, 2 to 3 minutes. Stir in pecans. Reserve 1 cup crumb mixture; press remaining crumb mixture onto bottom of greased 9-inch square baking pan. Spread preserves to within ½ inch of edge of crust. Crumble reserved crumb mixture over preserves. Bake for 40 to 50 minutes or until lightly browned. Cool completely. Cut into bars. *Makes about 24 bars*

Top to bottom: Peachy Oatmeal Bars, Streusel Strawberry Bars

CHOCOLATE CARAMEL PECAN BARS

  2 cups butter, softened, divided
  ½ cup granulated sugar
  1 large egg
2¾ cups all-purpose flour
  ⅔ cup firmly packed light brown sugar
  ¼ cup light corn syrup
2½ cups coarsely chopped pecans
  1 cup semisweet chocolate chips

1. Preheat oven to 375°F. Grease 15×10-inch jelly-roll pan; set aside.

2. Beat 1 cup butter and granulated sugar in large bowl with electric mixer at medium speed until light and fluffy. Beat in egg. Add flour. Beat at low speed until blended. Pat dough into prepared pan.

3. Bake 20 minutes or until light golden brown.

4. While bars are baking, prepare topping. Combine remaining 1 cup butter, brown sugar and corn syrup in medium, heavy saucepan. Cook over medium heat until mixture boils, stirring frequently. Boil gently 2 minutes, without stirring. Quickly stir in pecans and spread topping evenly over base. Return to oven and bake 20 minutes or until dark golden brown and bubbling.

5. Immediately sprinkle chocolate chips evenly over hot caramel. Gently press chips into caramel topping with spatula. Loosen caramel from edges of pan with a thin spatula or knife.

6. Remove pan to wire rack; cool completely. Cut into 3×1½-inch bars. Store tightly covered at room temperature or freeze up to 3 months.

Makes 40 bars

ALMOND TOFFEE SQUARES

  1 cup (2 sticks) margarine or butter, softened
  1 cup firmly packed brown sugar
  1 egg
  1 teaspoon vanilla
  2 cups all-purpose flour
  ¼ teaspoon salt
  2 packages (4 ounces each) BAKER'S® GERMAN'S® Sweet Chocolate, broken into squares
  ½ cup toasted slivered almonds
  ½ cup lightly toasted BAKER'S® ANGEL FLAKE® Coconut

HEAT oven to 350°F.

BEAT margarine, sugar, egg and vanilla. Mix in flour and salt. Press into greased 13×9-inch pan.

BAKE for 30 minutes or until edges are golden brown. Remove from oven. Immediately sprinkle with chocolate squares. Cover with foil; let stand 5 minutes or until chocolate is softened.

SPREAD chocolate evenly over entire surface; sprinkle with almonds and coconut. Cut into squares while still warm. Cool on wire rack.

Makes about 26 squares

Chocolate Caramel Pecan Bars

LEMON NUT BARS

1⅓ **cups all-purpose flour**
½ **cup firmly packed brown sugar**
¼ **cup granulated sugar**
¾ **cup butter**
1 **cup old-fashioned or quick oats, uncooked**
½ **cup chopped nuts**
1 **(8-ounce) package PHILADELPHIA BRAND® Cream Cheese, softened**
1 **egg**
3 **tablespoons lemon juice**
1 **tablespoon grated lemon peel**

Preheat oven to 350°F. Stir together flour and sugars in medium bowl. Cut in butter until mixture resembles coarse crumbs. Stir in oats and nuts. Reserve 1 cup crumb mixture; press remaining crumb mixture onto bottom of greased 13×9-inch baking pan. Bake 15 minutes. Beat cream cheese, egg, juice and peel in small mixing bowl at medium speed with electric mixer until well blended. Pour over crust; sprinkle with reserved crumb mixture. Bake 25 minutes. Cool; cut into bars.   *Makes about 36 bars*

Prep Time: 30 minutes
Cook Time: 25 minutes

LUSCIOUS LEMON BARS

CRUST
½ **cup butter or margarine, softened**
½ **cup granulated sugar**
Grated peel of ½ SUNKIST® Lemon
1¼ **cups all-purpose flour**

LEMON LAYER
4 **eggs**
1⅔ **cups granulated sugar**
3 **tablespoons all-purpose flour**
½ **teaspoon baking powder**
Grated peel of ½ SUNKIST® Lemon
Juice of 2 SUNKIST® Lemons (6 tablespoons)
1 **teaspoon vanilla extract**
Powdered sugar

For Crust, in medium bowl, cream together butter, granulated sugar and lemon peel. Gradually stir in flour to form a soft crumbly dough. Press evenly into bottom of aluminum foil-lined 13×9×2-inch baking pan. Bake at 350° for 15 minutes.

For Lemon Layer, while crust is baking, in large bowl, whisk or beat eggs well. Stir together granulated sugar, flour and baking powder. Gradually whisk sugar mixture into eggs. Whisk in lemon peel, juice and vanilla. Pour over hot crust. Return to oven. Bake for 20 to 25 minutes or until top is lightly browned. Cool. Using foil on two sides, lift out cookie base. Gently loosen foil along all sides. With long wet knife, cut into bars or squares. Sprinkle tops with powdered sugar.
Makes about 3 dozen bars

Lemon Nut Bars

HEATH® BARS

- **1 cup butter, softened**
- **1 cup firmly packed brown sugar**
- **1 egg yolk**
- **1 teaspoon vanilla**
- **2 cups all-purpose flour**
- **18 to 19 Original HEATH® English Toffee Snack Size Bars, crushed, divided**
- **½ cup finely chopped pecans**

Preheat oven to 350°F. In large bowl, with electric mixer, beat butter well; blend in brown sugar, egg yolk and vanilla. By hand, mix in flour, ⅔ cup Heath® Bars and nuts. Press into ungreased 15½×10½-inch jelly-roll pan.

Bake 18 to 20 minutes or until browned. Remove from oven and immediately sprinkle remaining Heath® Bars over top. Cool slightly; cut into bars while warm. *Makes about 48 bars*

CHOCOLATE PEANUT BUTTER BARS

- **2 cups peanut butter**
- **1 cup sugar**
- **2 eggs**
- **1 package (8 ounces) BAKER'S® Semi-Sweet Chocolate**
- **1 cup chopped peanuts**

HEAT oven to 350°F.

BEAT peanut butter, sugar and eggs in large bowl until light and fluffy. Reserve 1 cup peanut butter mixture; set aside.

MELT four squares of the chocolate. Add to peanut butter mixture in bowl; mix well. Press into ungreased 13×9-inch pan. Top with reserved peanut butter mixture.

BAKE for 30 minutes or until edges are lightly browned. Melt the remaining 4 squares chocolate; spread evenly over entire surface. Sprinkle with peanuts. Cool in pan until chocolate is set. Cut into bars. *Makes about 24 bars*

Prep Time: 15 minutes
Baking Time: 30 minutes

Heath® Bars

Brownies

DECADENT BLONDE BROWNIES

½ cup butter or margarine, softened
¾ cup granulated sugar
¾ cup firmly packed light brown sugar
2 large eggs
2 teaspoons vanilla
1½ cups all-purpose flour
1 teaspoon baking powder
½ teaspoon salt
1 package (10 ounces) semisweet chocolate chunks
1 jar (3½ ounces) macadamia nuts, coarsely chopped

Preheat oven to 350°F. Beat butter, granulated sugar and brown sugar in large bowl with electric mixer at medium speed until light and fluffy. Beat in eggs and vanilla. Add combined flour, baking powder and salt. Stir until well blended. Stir in chocolate chunks and macadamia nuts. Spread evenly into greased 13×9-inch baking pan. Bake 25 to 30 minutes or until golden brown. Remove pan to wire rack; cool completely. Cut into 3¼×1½-inch bars.   *Makes about 2 dozen brownies*

RASPBERRY FUDGE BROWNIES

- ½ cup butter or margarine
- 3 squares (1 ounce each) bittersweet chocolate*
- 2 eggs
- 1 cup sugar
- 1 teaspoon vanilla
- ¾ cup all-purpose flour
- ¼ teaspoon baking powder
- Dash salt
- ½ cup sliced or slivered almonds
- ½ cup raspberry preserves
- 1 cup (6 ounces) milk chocolate chips

*Bittersweet chocolate is available in specialty food stores. One square unsweetened chocolate plus 2 squares semisweet chocolate may be substituted.

Preheat oven to 350°F. Butter and flour 8-inch square baking pan. Melt butter and bittersweet chocolate in small, heavy saucepan over low heat. Remove from heat; cool. Beat eggs, sugar and vanilla in large bowl until light. Beat in chocolate mixture. Stir in flour, baking powder and salt until just blended. Spread ¾ of batter in prepared pan; sprinkle almonds over top. Bake 10 minutes. Remove from oven; spread preserves over almonds. Carefully spoon remaining batter over preserves, smoothing top. Bake 25 to 30 minutes or just until top feels firm. Remove from oven; sprinkle chocolate chips over top. Let stand a few minutes, then spread evenly over brownies. Cool completely. When chocolate is set, cut into squares.

Makes 16 brownies

WHITE CHOCOLATE CHUNK BROWNIES

- 4 squares (1 ounce each) unsweetened chocolate, coarsely chopped
- ½ cup butter or margarine
- 2 large eggs
- 1¼ cups granulated sugar
- 1 teaspoon vanilla
- ½ cup all-purpose flour
- ½ teaspoon salt
- 1 white baking bar (6 ounces), cut into ¼-inch pieces
- ½ cup coarsely chopped walnuts (optional)
- Powdered sugar for garnish

Preheat oven to 350°F. Melt unsweetened chocolate and butter in small, heavy saucepan over low heat, stirring constantly; set aside. Beat eggs in large bowl; gradually add granulated sugar, beating at medium speed about 4 minutes until very thick and lemon colored. Beat in chocolate mixture and vanilla. Beat in flour and salt just until blended. Stir in baking bar pieces and walnuts. Spread evenly into greased 8-inch square baking pan. Bake 30 minutes or until edges begin to pull away from sides of pan and center is set. Remove pan to wire rack; cool completely. Cut into 2-inch squares. Sprinkle with powdered sugar, if desired.

Makes about 16 brownies

Raspberry Fudge Brownies

TOFFEE BROWNIE BARS

CRUST
- ¾ **cup butter or margarine, softened**
- ¾ **cup firmly packed brown sugar**
- 1 **egg yolk**
- ¾ **teaspoon vanilla extract**
- 1½ **cups all-purpose flour**

FILLING
- 1 **package (19.8 ounces) DUNCAN HINES® Fudge Brownie Mix**
- 1 **egg**
- ⅓ **cup water**
- ⅓ **cup CRISCO® Oil**

TOPPING
- 1 **package (12 ounces) milk chocolate chips, melted**
- ¾ **cup finely chopped pecans**

1. Preheat oven to 350°F. Grease 15½×10½×1-inch jelly-roll pan.

2. For Crust, combine butter, brown sugar, egg yolk and vanilla extract in large bowl. Stir in flour. Spread in pan. Bake 15 minutes or until golden.

3. For Filling, combine brownie mix, egg, water and oil in large bowl. Stir with spoon until well blended, about 50 strokes. Spread over hot crust. Bake 15 minutes or until surface appears set. Cool 30 minutes.

4. For Topping, spread melted chocolate on top of brownie layer; garnish with pecans. Cool completely in pan on wire rack. Cut into bars.

Makes about 48 brownies

EXTRA MOIST & CHUNKY BROWNIES

- 1 **(8-ounce) package cream cheese, softened**
- 1 **cup sugar**
- 1 **egg**
- 1 **teaspoon vanilla extract**
- ¾ **cup all-purpose flour**
- 1 **(4-serving size) package ROYAL® Chocolate or Dark 'n' Sweet Chocolate Pudding & Pie Filling**
- 4 **(1-ounce) semisweet chocolate squares, chopped**

MICROWAVE DIRECTIONS: In large bowl, with electric mixer at high speed, beat cream cheese, sugar, egg and vanilla until smooth; blend in flour and pudding mix. Spread batter in greased 8×8×2-inch microwavable dish; sprinkle with chocolate. Microwave on HIGH (100% power) for 8 to 10 minutes or until toothpick inserted in center comes out clean, rotating dish ½ turn every 2 minutes. Cool completely in pan. Cut into squares.

Makes 16 brownies

Toffee Brownie Bars

CARAMEL-LAYERED BROWNIES

  4 squares BAKER'S® Unsweetened
    Chocolate
  ¾ cup (1½ sticks) margarine or butter
  2 cups sugar
  3 eggs
  1 teaspoon vanilla
  1 cup all-purpose flour
  1 cup BAKER'S® Semi-Sweet Real
    Chocolate Chips
1½ cups chopped nuts
  1 package (14 ounces) caramels
  ⅓ cup evaporated milk

HEAT oven to 350°F.

MICROWAVE chocolate and margarine in large microwavable bowl on HIGH 2 minutes or until margarine is melted. **Stir until chocolate is completely melted.**

STIR sugar into melted chocolate mixture. Mix in eggs and vanilla until well blended. Stir in flour. Remove 1 cup of batter; set aside. Spread remaining batter in greased 13×9-inch pan. Sprinkle with chips and 1 cup of the nuts.

MICROWAVE caramels and milk in same bowl on HIGH 4 minutes, stirring after 2 minutes. Stir until caramels are completely melted and smooth. Spoon over chips and nuts, spreading to edges of pan. Gently spread reserved batter over caramel mixture. Sprinkle with the remaining ½ cup nuts.

BAKE for 40 minutes or until toothpick inserted into center comes out with fudgy crumbs. **Do not overbake.** Cool in pan; cut into squares.

Makes about 24 brownies

BLONDE BRICKLE BROWNIES

1⅓ cups all-purpose flour
  ½ teaspoon baking powder
  ¼ teaspoon salt
  2 eggs
  ½ cup granulated sugar
  ½ cup firmly packed brown sugar
  ⅓ cup butter or margarine, melted
  1 teaspoon vanilla
  ¼ teaspoon almond extract
  1 package (6 ounces) BITS 'O BRICKLE®,
    divided
  ½ cup chopped pecans (optional)

Preheat oven to 350°F. Grease 8-inch square baking pan. Mix flour with baking powder and salt; set aside. In large bowl, beat eggs well. Gradually beat in granulated sugar and brown sugar until thick and creamy. Add butter, vanilla and almond extract; mix well. Gently stir in flour mixture until moistened. Fold in ⅔ cup Bits 'O Brickle® and nuts. Pour into prepared pan.

Bake 30 minutes. Remove from oven; immediately sprinkle remaining Bits 'O Brickle® over top. Cool completely in pan on wire rack. Cut into squares.

Makes about 16 brownies

Blonde Brickle Brownies

CHOCOLATEY ROCKY ROAD BROWNIES

BROWNIES
- 1 cup butter or margarine
- 4 squares (1 ounce each) unsweetened chocolate
- 1½ cups granulated sugar
- 1 cup all-purpose flour
- 3 eggs
- 1½ teaspoons vanilla
- ½ cup salted peanuts, chopped

FROSTING
- ¼ cup butter or margarine
- 1 (3-ounce) package cream cheese
- 1 square (1 ounce) unsweetened chocolate
- ¼ cup milk
- 2¾ cups powdered sugar
- 1 teaspoon vanilla
- 2 cups miniature marshmallows
- 1 cup salted peanuts

For Brownies, preheat oven to 350°F. In 3-quart saucepan, combine 1 cup butter and 4 squares chocolate. Cook over medium heat, stirring constantly, until melted, 5 to 7 minutes. Add granulated sugar, flour, eggs and 1½ teaspoons vanilla; mix well. Stir in ½ cup chopped peanuts. Spread into greased 13×9-inch baking pan. Bake 20 to 25 minutes or until brownie starts to pull away from sides of pan. Cool completely.

For Frosting, in 2-quart saucepan, combine ¼ cup butter, cream cheese, 1 square chocolate and milk. Cook over medium heat, stirring occasionally, until melted, 6 to 8 minutes. Remove from heat; add powdered sugar and 1 teaspoon vanilla; beat with hand mixer until smooth. Stir in marshmallows and 1 cup peanuts. Immediately spread over cooled brownies. Cool completely; cut into bars. Store in refrigerator. *Makes about 4 dozen brownies*

Chocolatey Rocky Road Brownies

BROWNIE BON BONS

  2 jars (10 ounces each) maraschino cherries
       with stems
    Cherry liqueur (optional)*
  4 squares BAKER'S® Unsweetened
       Chocolate
  ¾ cup (1½ sticks) margarine or butter
  2 cups granulated sugar
  4 eggs
  1 teaspoon vanilla
  1 cup all-purpose flour
    Chocolate Fudge Filling (recipe follows)
  ½ cup powdered sugar

*For liqueur-flavored cherries, drain liquid from cherries. Do not remove cherries from jars. Refill jars with liqueur to completely cover cherries; cover tightly. Let stand at least 24 hours for best flavor.

HEAT oven to 350°F.

MICROWAVE chocolate and margarine in large microwavable bowl on HIGH 2 minutes or until margarine is melted. **Stir until chocolate is completely melted.**

STIR granulated sugar into melted chocolate mixture. Mix in eggs and vanilla until well blended. Stir in flour. Fill greased 1¾×1-inch miniature muffin cups ⅔ full with batter.

BAKE for 20 minutes or until toothpick inserted into center comes out with fudgy crumbs. **Do not overbake.** Cool slightly; loosen edges with tip of knife. Remove from pans. Turn each brownie onto wax paper-lined tray while warm. Make ½-inch indentation into top of each brownie with end of wooden spoon. Cool completely.

PREPARE Chocolate Fudge Filling. Drain cherries, reserving liquid or liqueur. Let cherries stand on paper towels to dry. Combine powdered sugar with enough reserved liquid to form a thin glaze.

SPOON or pipe about 1 teaspoon Chocolate Fudge Filling into indentation of each brownie. Gently press cherry into filling. Drizzle with powdered sugar glaze.   *Makes about 48 bon bons*

CHOCOLATE FUDGE FILLING
  1 package (3 ounces) PHILADELPHIA
       BRAND® Cream Cheese, softened
  1 teaspoon vanilla
  ¼ cup corn syrup
  3 squares BAKER'S® Unsweetened
       Chocolate, melted and cooled
  1 cup powdered sugar

BEAT cream cheese and vanilla in small bowl until smooth. Slowly pour in corn syrup, beating until well blended. Add chocolate; beat until smooth. Gradually add powdered sugar, beating until well blended and smooth.   *Makes about 1 cup*

Brownie Bon Bons

Delights

CHOCOLATE CHIP LOLLIPOPS

1 package DUNCAN HINES® Chocolate Chip Cookie Mix
1 egg
⅓ cup CRISCO® Oil
2 tablespoons water
Flat ice cream sticks
Assorted decors

1. Preheat oven to 375°F.

2. Combine cookie mix, egg, oil and water in large bowl. Stir until thoroughly blended. Shape dough into 32 (1-inch) balls. Place balls 3 inches apart on ungreased cookie sheets. Push ice cream stick into center of each ball. Flatten dough ball with hand to form round lollipop. Decorate by pressing decors onto dough. Bake at 375°F for 8 to 9 minutes or until light golden brown. Cool 1 minute on cookie sheets. Remove to wire racks. Cool completely. Store in airtight container.

Makes 2½ to 3 dozen cookies

PEANUT BUTTER BEARS

      1 **cup SKIPPY® Creamy Peanut Butter**
      1 **cup MAZOLA® Margarine, softened**
      1 **cup firmly packed brown sugar**
   ⅔ **cup KARO® Light or Dark Corn Syrup**
      2 **eggs**
      4 **cups all-purpose flour, divided**
      1 **tablespoon baking powder**
      1 **teaspoon ground cinnamon (optional)**
   ¼ **teaspoon salt**

In large bowl, with mixer at medium speed, beat peanut butter, margarine, brown sugar, corn syrup and eggs until smooth. Reduce speed; beat in 2 cups of the flour, the baking powder, cinnamon and salt. With spoon, stir in remaining 2 cups flour. Wrap dough in plastic wrap; refrigerate 2 hours.

Preheat oven to 325°F. Divide dough in half; set aside half. On floured surface, roll out half the dough to ⅛-inch thickness. Cut with floured bear cookie cutter. Repeat with remaining dough. Bake on ungreased cookie sheets 10 minutes or until lightly browned. Remove from cookie sheets; cool completely on wire rack. Decorate as desired.

Makes about 3 dozen bears

Prep Time: 35 minutes, plus chilling
Bake Time: 10 minutes, plus cooling

NOTE: Use scraps of dough to make bear faces. Make one small ball of dough for muzzle. Form 3 smaller balls of dough and press gently to create eyes and nose; bake as directed. If desired, use frosting to create paws, ears and bow ties.

MARSHMALLOW KRISPIE BARS

      1 **package (19.8 ounces) DUNCAN HINES®**
         Fudge Brownie Mix
      1 **package (10½ ounces) miniature**
         marshmallows
   1½ **cups semi-sweet chocolate chips**
      1 **cup JIF® Creamy Peanut Butter**
      1 **tablespoon butter or margarine**
   1½ **cups crisp rice cereal**

1. Preheat oven to 350°F. Grease bottom of 13×9×2-inch baking pan.

2. Prepare and bake brownies following package directions for original recipe. Remove from oven. Sprinkle marshmallows on hot brownies. Return to oven. Bake for 3 minutes longer.

3. Place chocolate chips, peanut butter and butter in medium saucepan. Cook on low heat, stirring constantly, until chips are melted. Add rice cereal; mix well. Spread mixture over marshmallow layer. Refrigerate until chilled. Cut into bars.

Makes 24 bars

Peanut Butter Bears

WATERMELON SLICES

1 **package DUNCAN HINES® Golden Sugar Cookie Mix**
1 **egg**
¼ **cup CRISCO® Oil**
1½ **tablespoons water**
12 **drops red food coloring**
5 **drops green food coloring**
Chocolate sprinkles

1. Combine cookie mix, egg, oil and water in large bowl. Stir until thoroughly blended; reserve ⅓ cup dough.

2. For red cookie dough, combine remaining dough with red food coloring. Stir until evenly tinted. On waxed paper, shape dough into 12-inch-long roll with one side flattened. Cover; refrigerate with flat side down until firm.

3. For green cookie dough, combine reserved ⅓ cup dough with green food coloring in small bowl. Stir until evenly tinted. Place between 2 layers of waxed paper. Roll dough into 12×4-inch rectangle. Refrigerate for 15 minutes.

4. Preheat oven to 375°F.

5. To assemble, remove green dough rectangle from refrigerator. Remove top layer of waxed paper. Trim edges along both 12-inch sides. Remove red dough log from refrigerator. Place red dough log, flattened side up, along center of green dough. Mold green dough up to edge of flattened side of red dough. Remove bottom layer of waxed paper. Trim excess green dough, if necessary.

6. Cut chilled roll with flat side down into ¼-inch-thick slices with sharp knife. Place 2 inches apart on ungreased cookie sheets. Sprinkle chocolate sprinkles on red dough for seeds. Bake at 375°F for 7 minutes or until set. Cool 1 minute on cookie sheets. Remove to wire racks. Cool completely. Store between layers of waxed paper in airtight container.   *Makes 3 to 4 dozen cookies*

TIP: To make neat, clean slices, use unwaxed dental floss.

Watermelon Slices

PEANUT BUTTER PIZZA COOKIES

1 package DUNCAN HINES® Peanut Butter Cookie Mix
1 egg
¼ cup CRISCO® Oil
1 tablespoon water
Sugar
1 container (16 ounces) DUNCAN HINES® Creamy Homestyle Chocolate Frosting
Cashews
Candy-coated chocolate pieces
Gumdrops, halved
Flaked coconut
½ bar (2 ounces) white chocolate baking bar
1½ teaspoons CRISCO® All-Vegetable Shortening

1. Preheat oven to 375°F.

2. Combine cookie mix, peanut butter packet from Mix, egg, oil and water in large bowl. Stir until thoroughly blended. Shape into 12 (2-inch) balls (about 3 level tablespoons each). Place balls 3½ inches apart on ungreased cookie sheets. Flatten with bottom of large glass dipped in sugar to make 3-inch circles. Bake at 375°F for 9 to 11 minutes or until set. Cool 1 minute on cookie sheets. Remove to wire racks. Cool completely.

3. Frost cookies with Chocolate frosting. Decorate with cashews, candy pieces, gumdrops and coconut. Melt white chocolate and shortening in small saucepan on low heat, stirring constantly, until smooth. Drizzle over cookies.

Makes 12 large cookies

CRUMBLE BARS

½ cup butter or margarine
1 cup all-purpose flour
¾ cup quick-cooking oats, uncooked
⅓ cup firmly packed light brown sugar
½ teaspoon salt
½ teaspoon baking soda
½ teaspoon vanilla extract
4 MILKY WAY® Bars (2.15 ounces each), each cut into 8 slices

Preheat oven to 350°F. Lightly grease 8×8×2-inch baking pan; set aside.

Melt butter in large saucepan. Remove from heat; stir in flour, oats, sugar, salt, baking soda and vanilla. Blend until crumbly. Press ⅔ of mixture into prepared pan. Arrange MILKY WAY® Bar slices in pan to within ½ inch from edges. Finely crumble remaining mixture over the MILKY WAY® Bars. Bake 20 to 25 minutes or until edges are golden brown. Cool in pan on wire rack. Cut into bars or squares to serve.

Makes 12 to 16 bars

Peanut Butter Pizza Cookies

Chocolatey Peanut Butter Goodies

COOKIES
- 1 CRISCO® Stick or 1 cup CRISCO® All-Vegetable Shortening
- 4 cups (1 pound) powdered sugar
- 1½ cups JIF® Extra Crunchy Peanut Butter
- 1½ cups graham cracker crumbs

FROSTING
- 1 tablespoon CRISCO® All-Vegetable Shortening
- 1⅓ cups semi-sweet chocolate chips

1. For Cookies, combine shortening, powdered sugar, peanut butter and crumbs in large bowl with spoon. Spread evenly on bottom of 13×9-inch baking pan.

2. For Frosting, combine shortening and chocolate chips in small microwave-safe bowl. Microwave at 50% (MEDIUM). Stir after 1 minute. Repeat until smooth (or melt on rangetop in small saucepan on very low heat). Spread over top of cookie mixture. Cool at least 1 hour or until chocolate hardens. Cut into 2×1½-inch bars.

Makes 3 dozen bars

P. B. Graham Snackers

- ½ CRISCO® Stick or ½ cup CRISCO® All-Vegetable Shortening
- 2 cups powdered sugar
- ¾ cup JIF® Creamy Peanut Butter
- 1 cup graham cracker crumbs
- ½ cup semi-sweet chocolate chips
- ½ cup graham cracker crumbs, crushed peanuts or chocolate sprinkles (optional)

1. Combine shortening, powdered sugar and peanut butter in large bowl. Beat at low speed of electric mixer until well blended. Stir in 1 cup crumbs and chocolate chips. Cover and refrigerate 1 hour.

2. Form dough into 1-inch balls. Roll in ½ cup crumbs, peanuts or sprinkles for a fancier cookie. Cover and refrigerate until ready to serve.

Makes about 3 dozen cookies

Top to bottom: P.B. Graham Snackers and Chocolatey Peanut Butter Goodies

OLD-WORLD Holiday Treats

GOLDEN KOLACKY

½ cup butter, softened
4 ounces cream cheese, softened
1 cup all-purpose flour
Fruit preserves

Combine butter and cream cheese in large bowl; beat until smooth. Gradually add flour to butter mixture, blending until soft dough forms. Divide dough in half; wrap each half in plastic wrap. Refrigerate until firm.

Preheat oven to 375°F. Roll out dough, ½ at a time, on floured surface to ⅛-inch thickness. Cut into 3-inch squares. Spoon 1 teaspoon preserves in center of each square. Bring up two opposite corners to center; pinch together tightly to seal. Fold sealed tip to one side; pinch to seal. Place 1 inch apart on ungreased cookie sheets. Bake for 10 to 15 minutes or until lightly browned. Remove to cooling racks; cool completely.

Makes about 2½ dozen cookies

WALNUT CHRISTMAS BALLS

 1 cup California walnuts
⅔ cup powdered sugar, divided
 1 cup butter or margarine, softened
 1 teaspoon vanilla
1¾ cups all-purpose flour
   Chocolate Filling (recipe follows)

Preheat oven to 350°F. In food processor or blender, process walnuts with 2 tablespoons sugar until finely ground. In large bowl, cream butter and remaining sugar. Beat in vanilla. Add flour and ¾ cup walnut mixture; beat until blended. Roll dough into about 3 dozen walnut-size balls. Place 2 inches apart on ungreased cookie sheets.

Bake 10 to 12 minutes or until just golden around edges. Remove to wire racks to cool completely. Prepare Chocolate Filling. Place generous teaspoonful of filling on flat side of half the cookies. Top with remaining cookies, flat side down, forming sandwiches. Roll chocolate edges of cookies in remaining ground walnuts.

Makes about 1½ dozen sandwich cookies

CHOCOLATE FILLING: Chop 3 squares (1 ounce each) semisweet chocolate into small pieces; place in food processor or blender with ½ teaspoon vanilla. In small saucepan, heat 2 tablespoons *each* butter or margarine and whipping cream over medium heat until hot; pour over chocolate. Process until chocolate is melted, turning machine off and scraping sides as needed. With machine running, gradually add 1 cup powdered sugar; process until smooth.

*Favorite recipe from **Walnut Marketing Board***

BANANA CRESCENTS

½ cup DOLE® Chopped Almonds, toasted
 6 tablespoons sugar, divided
½ cup margarine, cut into pieces
1½ cups plus 2 tablespoons all-purpose flour
⅛ teaspoon salt
 1 extra-ripe, medium DOLE® Banana, peeled
 2 to 3 ounces semisweet chocolate chips

Pulverize almonds with 2 tablespoons sugar in food processor.

Beat margarine, almond mixture, remaining 4 tablespoons sugar, flour and salt.

Puree banana; add to batter and mix until well blended.

Using 1 tablespoon batter, roll into log then shape into crescent. Place on ungreased cookie sheet. Bake in 375°F oven 25 minutes or until golden. Cool on wire rack.

Melt chocolate in microwavable dish at 50% power 1½ to 2 minutes, stirring once. Dip ends of cookies in chocolate. Refrigerate until chocolate hardens.

Makes 2 dozen cookies

Banana Crescents

GERMAN HONEY BARS

2¾ **cups all-purpose flour**
2 **teaspoons ground cinnamon**
1 **teaspoon baking powder**
½ **teaspoon baking soda**
½ **teaspoon salt**
½ **teaspoon ground cardamom**
½ **teaspoon ground ginger**
½ **cup honey**
½ **cup dark molasses**
¾ **cup firmly packed brown sugar**
3 **tablespoons butter, melted**
1 **large egg**
½ **cup chopped toasted almonds (optional)**
  Glaze (recipe follows)

1. Preheat oven to 350°F. Grease 15×10-inch jelly-roll pan; set aside.

2. Combine flour, cinnamon, baking powder, baking soda, salt, cardamom and ginger in medium bowl.

3. Combine honey and molasses in medium saucepan; bring to a boil over medium heat. Remove from heat; cool 10 minutes.

4. Stir brown sugar, butter and egg into honey mixture.

5. Place brown sugar mixture in large bowl. Gradually add flour mixture. Beat at low speed with electric mixer until dough forms. Stir in almonds with spoon. (Dough will be slightly sticky.)

6. Spread dough evenly into prepared pan. Bake 20 to 22 minutes or until golden brown and set. Remove pan to wire rack; cool completely.

7. Prepare Glaze. Spread over cooled cookie base. Let stand until set, about 30 minutes. Cut into 2×1-inch bars. Store tightly covered at room temperature or freeze up to 3 months.

Makes about 6 dozen bars

GLAZE
1¼ **cups sifted powdered sugar**
3 **tablespoons fresh lemon juice**
1 **teaspoon grated lemon peel**

Place all ingredients in medium bowl; stir with spoon until smooth.

German Honey Bars

DANISH RASPBERRY RIBBONS

COOKIES

1 cup butter, softened
½ cup granulated sugar
1 large egg
2 tablespoons milk
2 tablespoons vanilla
¼ teaspoon almond extract
2 to 2⅔ cups all-purpose flour, divided
6 tablespoons seedless raspberry jam

GLAZE

½ cup sifted powdered sugar
1 tablespoon milk
1 teaspoon vanilla

1. For Cookies, beat butter and granulated sugar in bowl with mixer at medium speed until fluffy. Beat in egg, 2 tablespoons milk, 2 tablespoons vanilla and almond extract until blended.

2. Gradually add 1½ cups flour. Beat at low speed until well blended. Stir in additional flour with spoon until stiff dough forms. Wrap in plastic wrap and refrigerate until firm, 30 minutes or overnight.

3. Preheat oven to 375°F. Cut dough into 6 pieces. Rewrap 3 pieces; refrigerate. With floured hands, shape each dough piece into 12-inch-long, ¾-inch-thick rope.

4. Place ropes 2 inches apart on *ungreased* cookie sheets. Make a ¼-inch-deep groove down center of each rope with handle of wooden spoon. (Ropes flatten to ½-inch-thick strips.)

5. Bake 12 minutes. Spoon 1 tablespoon jam along each groove. Bake 5 to 7 minutes longer or until strips are light golden brown. Cool strips 15 minutes on cookie sheets.

6. For Glaze, place powdered sugar, 1 tablespoon milk and 1 teaspoon vanilla in small bowl; stir until smooth. Drizzle Glaze over strips; let stand 5 minutes to dry. Cut strips at 45° angle into 1-inch slices. Cool cookies completely on wire racks. Repeat with remaining dough. Store tightly covered between sheets of waxed paper at room temperature.   *Makes about 5½ dozen cookies*

Danish Raspberry Ribbons

PEANUT BUTTER CUT–OUTS

½ cup **SKIPPY®** Creamy Peanut Butter
6 tablespoons **MAZOLA®** Margarine or butter, softened
½ cup firmly packed brown sugar
⅓ cup **KARO®** Light or Dark Corn Syrup
1 egg
2 cups all-purpose flour, divided
1½ teaspoons baking powder
1 teaspoon ground cinnamon (optional)
⅛ teaspoon salt

In large bowl, with mixer at medium speed, beat peanut butter, margarine, brown sugar, corn syrup and egg until smooth. Reduce speed; beat in 1 cup flour, baking powder, cinnamon and salt. With spoon, stir in remaining 1 cup flour.

Divide dough in half. Between two sheets of waxed paper on large cookie sheets, roll each half of dough to ¼-inch thickness. Refrigerate until firm, about 1 hour.

Preheat oven to 350°F. Remove top piece of waxed paper. With floured cookie cutters, cut dough into shapes. Place on ungreased cookie sheets. Bake 10 minutes or until lightly browned. *Do not overbake.* Let stand on cookie sheets 2 minutes. Remove from cookie sheets; cool completely on wire racks. Reroll dough trimmings and cut. Decorate as desired. *Makes about 5 dozen cookies*

NOTE: Use scraps of dough to create details on cookies.

BAVARIAN COOKIE WREATHS

3½ cups unsifted all-purpose flour
1 cup sugar, divided
3 teaspoons grated orange peel, divided
¼ teaspoon salt
1⅓ cups butter or margarine
¼ cup Florida orange juice
⅓ cup finely chopped blanched almonds
1 egg white beaten with 1 teaspoon water
Prepared frosting (optional)

Preheat oven to 400°F. In large bowl, mix flour, ¾ cup sugar, 2 teaspoons orange peel and salt. Using pastry blender, cut in butter and orange juice until mixture holds together. Knead few times and press into a ball.

Shape dough into ¾-inch balls; lightly roll each ball on floured board into a 6-inch-long strip. Using two strips, twist together to make a rope. Pinch ends of rope together to make a wreath; place on lightly greased baking sheet.

In shallow dish, mix almonds, remaining ¼ cup sugar and 1 teaspoon orange peel. Brush top of each wreath with egg white mixture and sprinkle with sugar-almond mixture.

Bake 8 to 10 minutes or until lightly browned. Remove to wire racks; cool completely. Frost, if desired. *Makes 5 dozen cookies*

*Favorite recipe from **Florida Department of Citrus***

Peanut Butter Cut-Outs

PECAN DATE BARS

CRUST
- ⅓ cup butter or margarine
- 1 package DUNCAN HINES® Moist Deluxe White Cake Mix
- 1 egg

TOPPING
- 1 (8-ounce) package chopped dates
- 1¼ cups chopped pecans
- 1 cup water
- ½ teaspoon vanilla extract
- Powdered sugar

1. Preheat oven to 350°F. Grease and flour 13×9-inch pan.

2. For Crust, cut butter into cake mix with a pastry blender or 2 knives until mixture is crumbly. Add egg; stir well (mixture will be crumbly). Press mixture into bottom of prepared pan.

3. For Topping, combine dates, pecans and water in medium saucepan. Bring to a boil. Reduce heat and simmer until mixture thickens, stirring constantly. Remove from heat. Stir in vanilla extract. Spread date mixture evenly over crust. Bake 25 to 30 minutes. Cool completely. Dust with powdered sugar.   *Makes about 32 bars*

BLACK RUSSIAN BROWNIES

- 4 squares (1 ounce each) unsweetened chocolate
- 1 cup butter
- ¾ teaspoon black pepper
- 4 eggs, lightly beaten
- 1½ cups sugar
- 1½ teaspoons vanilla
- ⅓ cup KAHLÚA®
- 2 tablespoons vodka
- 1⅓ cups all-purpose flour
- ½ teaspoon salt
- ¼ teaspoon baking powder
- 1 cup chopped walnuts or toasted sliced almonds
- Powdered sugar (optional)

Line bottom of 13×9-inch baking pan with waxed paper. Melt chocolate and butter with pepper in small saucepan over low heat. Remove from heat.

Combine eggs, sugar and vanilla in large bowl; beat well. Stir in cooled chocolate mixture, Kahlúa and vodka. Combine flour, salt and baking powder; add to chocolate mixture and stir until blended. Add walnuts. Spread in prepared pan.

Bake in 350°F oven just until toothpick inserted into center comes out clean, about 25 minutes. *Do not overbake.* Cool in pan on wire rack. Cut into bars. Sprinkle with powdered sugar, if desired.

Makes about 30 brownies

Pecan Date Bars

LINZER SANDWICH COOKIES

  1⅓ **cups all-purpose flour**
    ¼ **teaspoon baking powder**
    ¼ **teaspoon salt**
    ¾ **cup sugar**
    ½ **cup butter, softened**
    1 **large egg**
    1 **teaspoon vanilla**
      Seedless raspberry jam

1. Combine flour, baking powder and salt in small bowl.

2. Beat sugar and butter in medium bowl with electric mixer at medium speed until light and fluffy. Beat in egg and vanilla. Gradually add flour mixture. Beat at low speed until dough forms.

3. Form dough into 2 discs; wrap in plastic wrap and refrigerate 2 hours or until firm.

4. Preheat oven to 375°F. Working with 1 disc at a time, unwrap dough and place on lightly floured surface. Roll out dough with lightly floured rolling pin.

5. Cut dough into desired shapes with floured cookie cutters. Cut out equal numbers of each shape. (If dough becomes soft, cover and refrigerate several minutes before continuing.)

6. Cut 1-inch centers out of half the cookies of each shape. Gently press dough trimmings together; reroll and cut out more cookies. Place cookies 1½ to 2 inches apart on *ungreased* cookie sheets.

7. Bake 7 to 9 minutes or until edges are lightly browned. Let cookies stand on cookie sheet 1 to 2 minutes. Remove cookies with spatula to wire racks; cool completely. To assemble cookies, spread 1 teaspoon jam on flat side of whole cookies, spreading almost to edges. Place cookies with holes, flat-side down, on jam. Store tightly covered at room temperature or freeze up to 3 months.

Makes about 2 dozen cookies

WALNUT–BRANDY SHORTBREAD

    1 **cup butter, softened**
    ½ **cup firmly packed brown sugar**
    ⅛ **teaspoon salt**
    2 **tablespoons brandy**
    1 **cup all-purpose flour**
    1 **cup finely chopped toasted California**
       walnuts
      Granulated sugar

Cream butter with brown sugar and salt in large bowl; mix in brandy. Gradually add flour; stir in walnuts. Spread in ungreased 9-inch square pan. Refrigerate 30 minutes.

Pierce mixture all over with fork. Bake at 325°F about 55 minutes or until dark golden brown. If dough puffs up during baking, pierce again with fork. Sprinkle lightly with granulated sugar and cool. Cut into squares with sharp knife.

Makes 36 squares

Favorite recipe from **Walnut Marketing Board**

Linzer Sandwich Cookies

Acknowledgments

The publisher would like to thank the companies and organizations listed below for the use of their recipes and photos in this publication.

Best Foods, a Division of CPC International Inc.

California Apricot Advisory Board

Dole Food Company, Inc.

Florida Department of Citrus

Kahlúa Liqueur

Kraft Foods, Inc.

Leaf®, Inc.

M&M/MARS

Nabisco, Inc.

Nestlé Food Company

The Procter & Gamble Company

The Quaker Oats Company

Ralston Foods, Inc.

Sunkist Growers

Walnut Marketing Board

Index

INDEX

American Government

04/05

Thirty-Fourth Edition

EDITOR

Bruce Stinebrickner

DePauw University

Bruce Stinebrickner is the Frank L. Hall Professor of Political Science at DePauw University in Greencastle, Indiana, and has taught American politics at DePauw since 1987. He has also taught at Lehman College of the City University of New York (1974–1976), at the University of Queensland in Brisbane, Australia (1976–1987), and in DePauw programs in Argentina (1990) and Germany (1993). He earned his Ph.D. from Yale University in 1974. Having served two years as head of his department at the University of Queensland and nine years as chair of his department at DePauw, he began another term as department chair at DePauw in the 2002–2003 academic year.

Professor Stinebrickner is the coauthor (with Robert A. Dahl) of *Modern Political Analysis,* sixth edition (Prentice Hall, 2003). He has also served as editor for more than 25 editions of *Annual Editions: American Government* and for all 11 editions of *Annual Editions: State and Local Government,* which first appeared in McGraw-Hill/Dushkin's *Annual Editions* series in 1984. He has published articles on American local governments, the American presidential nomination and election process, the career patterns of Australian politicians, and freedom of the press. His current research interests focus on government policies involving children (e.g., schooling, adoption, and foster care). In both his teaching and his writing, Professor Stinebrickner applies insights on politics gained from living, teaching, and lecturing abroad.

McGraw-Hill/Dushkin

2460 Kerprer Bvld., Dubuque, IA 52001

Visit us on the Internet
http://www.dushkin.com

Credits

1. **Foundations of American Politics**
   Unit photo—C. Borland/PhotoLink/Getty Images
2. **Structures of American Politics**
   Unit photo—Jeremy Woodhouse/Getty Images
3. **Process of American Politics**
   Unit photo—S. Metzer/PhotoLink/Getty Images
4. **Products of American Politics**
   Unit photo—Peter Turnley/Copyright Corbis. All Rights Reserved.

Copyright

Cataloging in Publication Data
Main entry under title: Annual Editions: American Government. 2004/2005.
1. American Government—Periodicals. I. Stinebrickner, Bruce, *comp*. II. Title: American Government.
ISBN 0–07–286141–X   658'.05   ISSN 0891–3390

Thirty-Fourth Edition

Cover image © 2004 by Corbis
Printed in the United States of America   1234567890QPDQPD0987654   Printed on Recycled Paper

Editors/Advisory Board

Members of the Advisory Board are instrumental in the final selection of articles for each edition of ANNUAL EDITIONS. Their review of articles for content, level, currentness, and appropriateness provides critical direction to the editor and staff. We think that you will find their careful consideration well reflected in this volume.

To the Reader

As the *03/04* edition of this book went to press early in 2003, I wrote in the preface that "war with Iraq seems to be weeks, or at most months, away." Less than two months later, in March 2003, President Bush ordered the invasion of Iraq and U.S. forces quickly overthrew the regime of Saddam Hussein. Now, almost a year later, the prospects for genuine stability and self-governance in Iraq remain uncertain as violent resistance to the extensive U.S. presence there continues.

A year ago I also wrote that "the economic prosperity of the 1990s and the accompanying budgetary surpluses in the latter years of the Clinton presidency have disappeared into the past." In February 2004, government economists forecast a budgetary deficit of approximately 500 billion dollars in the next fiscal year and a string of deficits in the years to come. And a number of prominent individuals have begun to call renewed attention to the looming retirements of the baby boomer generation. They have noted with alarm that baby boomers' Social Security and Medicare entitlements will make unprecedented demands on the national treasury that must be taken into account *now*.

After a couple of years of very high presidential approval ratings and a sense that President Bush's re-election in November 2004 was almost a foregone conclusion, early 2004 has brought a change in the prevailing conventional wisdom. The early months of this year have seen the candidacy of an unlikely "frontrunner" for the Democratic presidential nomination, Howard Dean, collapse on the heels of unexpectedly weak showings in Iowa and New Hampshire. In turn, Senator John Kerry of Massachusetts emerged as the new frontrunner and as of this writing seems almost certain to be his party's presidential nominee. And the conventional wisdom now says that the November election between Republican Bush and Democrat Kerry will be closer and more hard fought than almost anyone would have thought only a few short months ago. On the other hand, continued Republican control of both the House of Representatives and the Senate after the November 2004 elections seems very likely.

Bruce Stinebrickner

Bruce Stinebrickner
Editor

Contents

UNIT 1
Foundations of American Politics

The thirteen selections in this unit outline the foundations of American politics. In addition to primary documents, there are discussions of contemporary political ideas and viewpoints as well as recent commentaries on constitutional issues.

The concepts in bold italics are developed in the article. For further expansion, please refer to the Topic Guide and the Index.

The concepts in bold italics are developed in the article. For further expansion, please refer to the Topic Guide and the Index.

UNIT 2
Structures of American Politics

Eighteen articles in this unit examine the structure and present status of the American presidency, Congress, the judiciary, and bureaucracy.

The concepts in bold italics are developed in the article. For further expansion, please refer to the Topic Guide and the Index.

The concepts in bold italics are developed in the article. For further expansion, please refer to the Topic Guide and the Index.

UNIT 3
Process of American Politics

In this unit, thirteen articles review how political parties, voters, election processes, interest groups, and the media work within the process of American politics.

The concepts in bold italics are developed in the article. For further expansion, please refer to the Topic Guide and the Index.

UNIT 4
Products of American Politics

Six selections in this unit examine the "products" of the American government: the domestic, economic, foreign, and defense policies that are generated by the administration and implemented by the bureaucracy.

The concepts in bold italics are developed in the article. For further expansion, please refer to the Topic Guide and the Index.

The concepts in bold italics are developed in the article. For further expansion, please refer to the Topic Guide and the Index.

Topic Guide

This topic guide suggests how the selections in this book relate to the subjects covered in your course. You may want to use the topics listed on these pages to search the Web more easily.

On the following pages a number of Web sites have been gathered specifically for this book. They are arranged to reflect the units of this *Annual Edition.* You can link to these sites by going to the DUSHKIN ONLINE support site at *http://www.dushkin.com/online/.*

ALL THE ARTICLES THAT RELATE TO EACH TOPIC ARE LISTED BELOW THE BOLD-FACED TERM.

Bureaucracy
28. Washington's Mega-Merger
29. Turkey Farm
31. Compete, or Else

Bush, George W.
14. The Return of the Imperial Presidency?
15. The Accidental Radical
16. Uncivil Liberties
17. Packaging the President
18. A Partner in Shaping an Assertive Foreign Policy
31. Compete, or Else

Campaign finance reform
40. A Better Way?
41. The Short, Unhappy Life of Campaign Finance Reform

Congress
2. The Constitution of the United States, 1787
3. The Size and Variety of the Union as a Check on Faction
14. The Return of the Imperial Presidency?
19. The State of Congress
20. The High Costs of Rising Incivility on Capitol Hill
21. Legislative Season Drawn in Solid Party Lines
22. On Their Own Terms
23. The Price of Power
24. John Dingell's Staying Power
27. One Branch Among Three

Constitution
2. The Constitution of the United States, 1787
3. The Size and Variety of the Union as a Check on Faction
4. Checks and Balances
10. Rights, Liberties, and Security: Recalibrating the Balance After September 11
11. Upon Further Review
12. Winks, Nods, Disguises—and Racial Preference
13. Guns and Tobacco: Government by Litigation
27. One Branch Among Three
39. The Redistricting Wars
40. A Better Way?

Declaration of Independence
1. The Declaration of Independence, 1776

Economic policy
6. The Death of Horatio Alger
45. The Tax-Cut Con

Elections and nominations
35. Running Scared
39. The Redistricting Wars
40. A Better Way?
41. The Short, Unhappy Life of Campaign Finance Reform

Electoral college
40. A Better Way?

Federalism
2. The Constitution of the United States, 1787
3. The Size and Variety of the Union as a Check on Faction
9. Federalism's Ups and Downs
39. The Redistricting Wars

Gender
22. On Their Own Terms

Globalization
5. Why Don't They Like Us?
48. The New Rome Meets the New Barbarians
49. The Compulsive Empire

Historic perspectives
1. The Declaration of Independence, 1776
2. The Constitution of the United States, 1787
3. The Size and Variety of the Union as a Check on Faction
4. Checks and Balances

Homeland and national security
5. Why Don't They Like Us?
14. The Return of the Imperial Presidency?
18. A Partner in Shaping an Assertive Foreign Policy
30. Time for a Rethink
48. The New Rome Meets the New Barbarians
49. The Compulsive Empire
50. No, It's Not Vietnam

Income distribution
6. The Death of Horatio Alger
46. Liberal Lessons From Welfare Reform
47. The O'Connor Project

Interest groups
3. The Size and Variety of the Union as a Check on Faction
37. Government's End
38. Associations Without Members

Judicial system
2. The Constitution of the United States, 1787
10. Rights, Liberties, and Security: Recalibrating the Balance After September 11
12. Winks, Nods, Disguises—and Racial Preference
13. Guns and Tobacco: Government by Litigation
25. Sandra's Day
27. One Branch Among Three

Media
17. Packaging the President
26. A Judge Speaks Out
42. Journalism and Democracy
43. The Making of a Movement: Getting Serious About Media Reform
44. Politics After the Internet

World Wide Web Sites

The following World Wide Web sites have been carefully researched and selected to support the articles found in this reader. The easiest way to access these selected sites is to go to our DUSHKIN ONLINE support site at *http://www.dushkin.com/online/*.

AE: American Government 04/05

The following sites were available at the time of publication. Visit our Web site—we update DUSHKIN ONLINE regularly to reflect any changes.

General Sources

The Federal Web Locator
http://www.infoctr.edu/fwl/

Use this site as a launching pad for the Web sites of U.S. federal agencies, departments, and organizations. It is well organized and easy to use for informational and research purposes.

John F. Kennedy School of Government
http://www.ksg.harvard.edu

Starting from Harvard University's KSG page, you will be able to click on a huge variety of links to information about American politics and government, ranging from political party and campaign data to debates of enduring issues.

Library of Congress
http://www.loc.gov

Examine this Web site to learn about the extensive resource tools, library services/resources, exhibitions, and databases available through the Library of Congress in many different subfields of government studies.

National Center for Policy Analysis
http://www.ncpa.org

Through this site access discussions on an array of topics that are of major interest in the study of American government, from regulatory policy and privatization to economy and income. The Daily Policy Digest is also available.

UNIT 1: Foundations of American Politics

American Studies Web
http://www.georgetown.edu/crossroads/asw/

This eclectic site provides links to a wealth of Internet resources for research in American studies, including agriculture and rural development, government, and race and ethnicity.

Federalism: Relationship Between Local and National Governments
http://www.infidels.org/~nap/index.federalism.html

Federalism versus states' rights has always been a spirited debate in American government. Visit this George Mason University site for links to many articles and reports on the subject.

National Archives and Records Administration (NARA)
http://www.nara.gov/nara/welcome.html

This official site, which oversees the management of all federal records, offers easy access to background information for students interested in the policy-making process, including a search of federal documents and speeches, and much more.

Opinion, Inc.: The Site for Conservative Opinion on the Web
http://www.opinioninc.com

Open this site for access to political, cultural, and Web commentary on a number of issues from a conservative political viewpoint. The site is updated frequently.

Scanned Originals of Early American Documents
http://www.law.emory.edu/FEDERAL/

Through this Emory University site you can view scanned originals of the Declaration of Independence, the Constitution, and the Bill of Rights. The transcribed texts are also available, as are *The Federalist Papers*.

Smithsonian Institution
http://www.si.edu

This site provides access to the enormous resources of the Smithsonian, which holds some 140 million artifacts and specimens in its trust for "the increase and diffusion of knowledge." Here you can learn about American social, cultural, economic, and political history from a variety of viewpoints.

UNIT 2: Structures of American Politics

Department of State
http://www.state.gov

View this site for understanding into the workings of a major U.S. executive branch department. Links explain exactly what the department does, what services it provides, and what it says about U.S. interests around the world, along with much more information.

Federal Reserve System
http://www.federalreserve.gov

Consult this page to learn the answers to FAQs about the Fed, the structure of the Federal Reserve System, monetary policy, and more. It provides links to speeches and interviews as well as essays and articles presenting different views on the Fed.

Supreme Court/Legal Information Institute
http://supct.law.cornell.edu/supct/index.html

Open this site for current and historical information about the Supreme Court. The LII archive contains many opinions issued since May 1990 as well as a collection of nearly 600 of the most influential decisions of the Court.

United States House of Representatives
http://www.house.gov

This Web page of the House of Representatives will lead you to information about current and past House members and agendas, the legislative process, and more. You can learn about events on the House floor as they happen.

United States Senate
http://www.senate.gov

This U.S. Senate Web page will lead to information about current and past Senate members and agendas, legislative activities, and committees.

UNIT 3: Process of American Politics

The Henry L. Stimson Center
http://www.stimson.org

The Stimson Center, a nonprofit and self-described nonpartisan organization, focuses on issues where policy, technology, and politics intersect. Use this site to find assessments of U.S. foreign and domestic policy and other topics.

www.dushkin.com/online/

Influence at Work
http://www.influenceatwork.com

This commercial site focuses on the nature of persuasion, compliance, and propaganda, with many practical examples and applications. Students of such topics as the roles of public opinion and media influence in policy making should find these discussions of interest. The approach is based on the research and methods of influence expert Dr. Robert Cialdini.

LSU Department of Political Science Resources
http://www.artsci.lsu.edu/poli/

This extensive site will point you to a number of resources for domestic and international political and governmental news, including LSU's Political Science WWW Server, which is maintained by a dedicated group of professionals.

NationalJournal.com
http://nationaljournal.com

This is a major site for information on American government and politics. There is discussion of campaigns, the congressional calendar, a news archive, and more for politicians and policy makers. Membership is required, however, to access much of the information.

Poynter Online
http://www.poynter.org

This research site of the Poynter Institute for Media Studies provides extensive links to information and resources about the media, including media ethics and reportage techniques. Many bibliographies and Web sites are included.

RAND
http://www.rand.org

RAND is a nonprofit institution that works to improve public policy through research and analysis. Links offered on this home page provide for keyword searches of certain topics and descriptions of RAND activities and major research areas.

UNIT 4: Products of American Politics

American Diplomacy
http://www.unc.edu/depts/diplomat/

American Diplomacy is an online journal of commentary, analysis, and research on U.S. foreign policy and its results around the world.

Cato Institute
http://www.cato.org/research/ss_prjct.html

The Cato Institute presents this page to discuss its Project on Social Security Privatization. The site and its links begin from the belief that privatization of the U.S. Social Security system is a positive goal that will empower workers.

Foreign Affairs
http://www.foreignaffairs.org

This home page of the well-respected foreign policy journal is a valuable research tool. It allows users to search the journal's archives and provides indexed access to the field's leading publications, documents, online resources, and more. Links to dozens of other related Web sites are possible from here.

The Gallup Organization
http://www.gallup.com

Open this Gallup Organization home page for links to an extensive archive of public opinion poll results and special reports on a variety of topics related to American society, politics, and government.

International Information Programs
http://usinfo.state.gov

This wide-ranging page offered by the State Department provides definitions, related documentation, and a discussion of topics of concern to students of American government. It addresses today's hot topics as well as ongoing issues that form the foundation of the field. Many Web links are provided.

STAT-USA
http://www.stat-usa.gov/stat-usa.html

This essential site, a service of the Department of Commerce, contains daily economic news, frequently requested statistical releases, information on export and international trade, domestic economic news and statistical series, and databases.

Tax Foundation
http://www.taxfoundation.org/index.html

Ever wonder where your taxes go? Consult the site of this self-described "nonprofit, nonpartisan policy research organization" to learn the history of "Tax Freedom Day," tax burdens around the United States, and other information about your tax bill or taxes in general.

We highly recommend that you review our Web site for expanded information and our other product lines. We are continually updating and adding links to our Web site in order to offer you the most usable and useful information that will support and expand the value of your Annual Editions. You can reach us at: *http://www.dushkin.com/annualeditions/.*

UNIT 1

Foundations of American Politics

Unit Selections

1. **The Declaration of Independence, 1776**, Thomas Jefferson
2. **The Constitution of the United States, 1787**, The Constitution of the U.S.
3. **The Size and Variety of the Union as a Check on Faction**, James Madison
4. **Checks and Balances**, James Madison
5. **Why Don't They Like Us?**, Stanley Hoffmann
6. **The Death of Horatio Alger**, Paul Krugman
7. **Coming Out Ahead: Why Gay Marriage is on the Way**, Ramesh Ponnuru
8. **Party On, Dudes! Ignorance Is the Curse of the Information Age**, Matthew Robinson
9. **Federalism's Ups and Downs**, Carl Tubbesing
10. **Rights, Liberties, and Security: Recalibrating the Balance After September 11**, Stuart Taylor Jr.
11. **Upon Further Review**, Ken Paulson
12. **Winks, Nods, Disguises—and Racial Preference**, Carl Cohen
13. **Guns and Tobacco: Government by Litigation**, Stuart Taylor Jr.

Key Points to Consider

- What do you think would surprise the Founders most about the values and ideals held by Americans today?

- Which ideals, ideas, and values seem likely to remain central to American politics, and which seem likely to erode and gradually disappear?

- To what "rights" do you think all Americans are entitled? How, if at all, has September 11 affected Americans' thinking on this matter?

- What makes constitutional interpretation and reinterpretation necessary in the American political system?

- Do you consider yourself a conservative, a liberal, a socialist, a reactionary, or what? Why?

 **Links: www.dushkin.com/online/**
These sites are annotated in the World Wide Web pages.

American Studies Web
http://www.georgetown.edu/crossroads/asw/

Federalism: Relationship Between Local and National Governments
http://www.infidels.org/~nap/index.federalism.html

National Archives and Records Administration (NARA)
http://www.nara.gov/nara/welcome.html

Opinion, Inc.: The Site for Conservative Opinion on the Web
http://www.opinioninc.com

Scanned Originals of Early American Documents
http://www.law.emory.edu/FEDERAL/

Smithsonian Institution
http://www.si.edu

This unit treats some of the less concrete aspects of the American political system—historic ideals, contemporary ideas and values, and constitutional and legal issues. These dimensions of the system are not immune to change. Instead, they interact with the wider political environment in which they exist, and they are modified accordingly. Usually this interaction is a gradual process, but sometimes events foster more rapid change.

Human beings can be distinguished from other species by their ability to think and reason at relatively high levels of abstraction. In turn, ideas, ideals, values, and principles can and do play important roles in politics. Most Americans value ideals such as democracy, freedom, equal opportunity, and justice. Yet the precise meanings of these terms and the best ways of implementing them are the subject of much dispute in the political arena. Such ideas and ideals, as well as disputes about their "real" meanings, are important elements in the practice of American politics.

Although the selections in this unit span more than 200 years, they are clearly related to one another. Understanding contemporary political viewpoints is easier if the ideals and principles of the past are also taken into account. In addition, we can better appreciate the significance of historic documents such as the Declaration of Independence and the Constitution if we are familiar with contemporary ideas and perspectives. The interaction of different ideas and values plays an important part in the continuing development of the "foundations" of the American political system.

The first section of this unit includes several historic documents from the eighteenth century. The first is the Declaration of Independence. Written in 1776, it proclaims the Founders' views of why independence from England was justified and, in so doing, identifies certain "unalienable" rights that "all men" are said to possess. The second document, the Constitution of 1787, re-

mains in effect to this day. It provides an organizational blueprint for the structure of American national government, outlines the federal relationship between the national government and the states, and expresses limitations on what government can do. Twenty-seven amendments have been added to the original Constitution in two centuries. In addition to the Declaration of Independence and the Constitution, the first section includes two selections from The Federalist Papers, a series of newspaper articles written in support of the proposed new Constitution. Appearing in 1787 and 1788, The Federalist Papers treated various provisions of the new Constitution and argued that putting the Constitution into effect would bring about good government.

The second section treats contemporary political ideas and viewpoints. As selections in this section illustrate, efforts to apply or act on political beliefs in the context of concrete circumstances often lead to interesting commentary and debate. "Liberal" and "conservative" are two labels often used in American political discussions, but political views and values have far more complexity than can be captured by these two terms.

Selections in the third section show that constitutional and legal issues and interpretations are tied to historic principles as well as to contemporary ideas and values. It has been suggested that throughout American history almost every important political question has at one time or another appeared as a constitutional or legal issue.

The historic documents and the other selections in this unit might be more difficult to understand than the articles in other units. Some of them may have to be read and reread carefully to be fully appreciated. But to grapple with the important material treated here is to come to grips with a variety of conceptual blueprints for the American political system. To ignore the theoretical issues raised would be to bypass an important element of American politics today.

The Declaration of Independence

WHEN in the Course of human events, it becomes necessary for one people to dissolve the political bands which have connected them with another, and to assume among the powers of the earth, the separate and equal station to which the Laws of Nature and of Nature's God entitle them, a decent respect to the opinions of mankind requires that they should declare the causes which impel them to the separation.—We hold these truths to be self-evident, that all men are created equal, that they are endowed by their Creator with certain unalienable Rights, that among these are Life, Liberty and the pursuit of Happiness.—That to secure these rights, Governments are instituted among Men, deriving their just powers from the consent of the governed.—That whenever any Form of Government becomes destructive of these ends, it is the Right of the People to alter or to abolish it, and to institute new Government, laying its foundation on such principles and organizing its powers in such form, as to them shall seem most likely to effect their Safety and Happiness. Prudence, indeed, will dictate that Governments long established should not be changed for light and transient causes; and accordingly all experience hath shewn, that mankind are more disposed to suffer, while evils are sufferable, than to right themselves by abolishing the forms to which they are accustomed. But when a long train of abuses and usurpations, pursuing invariably the same Object evinces a design to reduce them under absolute Despotism, it is their right, it is their duty, to throw off such Government, and to provide new Guards for their future security.—Such has been the patient sufferance of these Colonies; and such is now the necessity which constrains them to alter their former Systems of Government. The history of the present King of Great Britain is a history of repeated injuries and usurpations, all having in direct object the establishment of an absolute Tyranny over these States. To prove this, let Facts be submitted to a candid world.—He has refused his Assent to Laws, the most wholesome and necessary for the public good.—He has forbidden his Governors to pass Laws of immediate and pressing importance, unless suspended in their operation till his Assent should be obtained; and when so suspended, he has utterly neglected to attend to them.—He has refused to pass other Laws for the accommodation of large districts of people, unless those people would relinquish the right of Representation in the Legislature, a right inestimable to them and formidable to tyrants only.—He has called together legislative bodies at places unusual, uncomfortable, and distant from the depository of their public Records, for the sole purpose of fatiguing them into compliance with his measures.—He has dissolved Representative Houses repeatedly, for opposing with manly firmness his invasions on the rights of the people.—He has refused for a long time, after such dissolutions, to cause others to be elected; whereby the Legislative powers, incapable of Annihilation, have returned to the People at large for their exercise; the State remaining in the meantime exposed to all the dangers of invasion from without, and convulsions within.—He has endeavoured to prevent the population of these States; for that purpose obstructing the Laws for Naturalization of Foreigners; refusing to pass others to encourage their migrations hither, and raising the conditions of new Appropriations of Lands.—He has obstructed the Administration of Justice, by refusing his Assent to Laws for establishing Judiciary powers.—He has made Judges dependent on his Will alone, for the tenure of their offices, and the amount and payment of their salaries.—He has erected a multitude of New Offices, and sent hither swarms of Officers to harass our people, and eat out their substance. He has kept among us, in times of peace, Standing Armies without the Consent of our legislatures.—He has affected to render the Military independent of and superior to the Civil power.—He has combined with others to subject us to a jurisdiction foreign to our constitution, and unacknowledged by our laws; giving his Assent to their Acts of pretended Legislation:—For quartering large bodies of armed troops among us:—For protecting them, by a mock Trial, from punishment for any Murders which they should commit on the Inhabitants of these States:—For cutting off our Trade with all parts of the world:—For imposing Taxes on us without our Consent:—For depriving us in many cases, of the benefits of Trial by Jury:—For transporting us beyond Seas to be tried for pretended offences:—For abolishing the free System of English Laws in a neighboring Province, establishing therein an Arbitrary government, and enlarging its Boundaries so as to render it at once an example and fit instrument for introducing the same absolute rule into these Colonies:—For taking away our Charters, abolishing our most valuable Laws and altering fundamentally the Forms of our Governments:—For suspending our own Legislatures, and declaring themselves invested with power to legislate for us in all cases whatsoever.—He has abdicated Government here, by declaring us out of his Protection and waging War against us.—He has plundered our seas, ravaged our Coasts, burnt our towns, and destroyed the lives of our people.—He is at this time transporting large Armies of foreign Mercenaries to compleat the works of death, desolation and tyranny, already begun with circumstances of Cruelty & perfidy scarcely paralled in the most barbarous ages, and totally unworthy the Head of a civilized nation.—He has constrained our fellow Citizens taken Captive on the high Seas to bear Arms against their Country, to become the executioners of their friends and Brethren, or to fall themselves by their Hands.—He has excited domestic insurrections amongst us, and has endeavoured to bring on the inhabitants of our frontiers, the merciless Indian Savages, whose known rule of warfare, is an undistinguished destruction of all ages, sexes and conditions. In every stage of these Oppressions We have Petitioned for Redress in the most humble terms: Our repeated Petitions have been answered only by repeated injury. A Prince, whose character is thus marked by every act which may define a Tyrant, is unfit to be the ruler of a free people. Nor have We been wanting in attentions to our British brethren. We have warned them from time to time of attempts by their legislature to extend an unwarrantable jurisdiction over us. We have reminded them of the circumstances of our emigration and settlement here. We have appealed to their native justice and magnanimity, and we have conjured them by the ties of our common kindred to disavow these usurpations, which would inevitably interrupt our connections and correspondence. They too have been deaf to the voice of justice and of consanguinity. We must, therefore, acquiesce in the necessity, which denounces our Separation, and hold them, as we hold the rest of mankind, Enemies in War, in Peace Friends.—

WE, THEREFORE, the Representatives of the UNITED STATES OF AMERICA, in General Congress, Assembled, appealing to the Supreme Judge of the world for the rectitude of our intentions, do, in the Name, and by Authority of the good People of these Colonies, solemnly publish and declare, That these United Colonies are, and of Right ought to be FREE AND INDEPENDENT STATES; that they are Absolved from all Allegiance to the British Crown, and that all political connection between them and the State of Great Britain, is and ought to be totally dissolved; and that as Free and Independent States, they have full Power to levy War, conclude Peace, contract Alliances, establish Commerce, and to do all other Acts and Things which Independent States may of right do.—And for the support of this Declaration, with a firm reliance on the protection of divine Providence, we mutually pledge to each other our Lives, our Fortunes and our sacred Honor.

The History of The Constitution of the United States

CONSTITUTION OF THE UNITED STATES. The Articles of Confederation did not provide the centralizing force necessary for unity among the new states and were soon found to be so fundamentally weak that a different political structure was vital. Conflicts about money and credit, trade, and suspicions about regional domination were among the concerns when Congress on February 21, 1787, authorized a Constitutional Convention to revise the Articles. The delegates were selected and assembled in Philadelphia about three months after the call. They concluded their work by September.

The delegates agreed and abided to secrecy. Years afterward James Madison supported the secrecy decision writing that "no man felt himself obliged to retain his opinions any longer than he was satisfied of their propriety and truth, and was open to the force of argument." Secrecy was not for all time. Madison, a delegate from Virginia, was a self-appointed but recognized recorder and took notes in the clear view of the members. Published long afterward, Madison's Journal gives a good record of the convention.

The delegates began to assemble on May 14, 1787, but a majority did not arrive until May 25. George Washington was elected President of the Convention without opposition. The lag of those few days gave some of the early arrivals, especially Madison, time to make preparations on substantive matters, and Gov. Edmund Jennings Randolph presented a plan early in the proceedings that formed the basis for much of the convention deliberations. The essentials were that there should be a government adequate to prevent foreign invasion, prevent dissension among the states, and provide for general national development, and give the national government power enough to make it superior in its realm. The decision was made not merely to revise the articles but to create a new government and a new constitution.

One of the most crucial decisions was the arrangement for representation, a compromise providing that one house would represent the states equally, the other house to be based on popular representation (with some modification due to the slavery question). This arrangement recognized political facts and concessions among men with both theoretical and practical political knowledge.

Basic Features. Oliver Wendell Holmes, Jr., once wrote that the provisions of the Constitution were not mathematical formulas, but "organic living institutions [*sic*] and its origins and growth were vital to understanding it." The constitution's basic features provide for a supreme law—notwithstanding any other legal document or practice, the Constitution is supreme, as are the laws made in pursuance of it and treaties made under the authority of the United States.

The organizational plan for government is widely known. Foremost is the separation of powers. If the new government were to be limited in its powers, one way to keep it limited would have been executive, legislative, and judicial power [given] to three distinct and non-overlapping branches. A government could not actually function, however, if the separation meant the independence of one branch from the others. The answer was a design to insure cooperation and the sharing of some functions. Among these are the executive veto and the power of Congress to have its way if it musters a super-majority to override that veto. The direction of foreign affairs and the war power are both dispersed and shared. The appointing power is shared by the Senate and the president; impeaching of officers and financial controls are powers shared by the Senate and the House.

A second major contribution by the convention is the provision for the judiciary, which gave rise to the doctrine of judicial review. There is some doubt that the delegates comprehended this prospect but Alexander Hamilton considered it in *Federalist* No. 78: "The interpretation of the laws is a proper and peculiar province of the Courts.... Wherever a particular statute contravenes the Constitution, it will be the duty of the judicial tribunals to adhere to the latter and disregard the former."

Another contribution is the federal system, an evolution from colonial practice and the relations between the colonies and the mother country. This division of authority between the new national government and the states recognized the doctrine of delegated and reserved powers. Only certain authority was to go to the new government; the states were not to be done away with and much of the Constitution is devoted to insuring that they were to be maintained even with the stripping of some of their powers.

It is not surprising, therefore, that the convention has been called a great political reform caucus composed of both revolutionaries and men dedicated to democracy. By eighteenth-century standards the Constitution was a democratic document, but standards change and the Constitution has changed since its adoption.

Change and Adaptation. The authors of the Constitution knew that provision for change was essential and provided for it in Article V, insuring that a majority could amend, but being restrictive enough that changes were not likely for the "light and transient" causes Jefferson warned about in the Declaration of Independence.

During the period immediately following the presentation of the Constitution for ratification, requiring assent of nine states to be effective, some alarm was expressed that there was a major defect: there was no bill of rights. So, many leaders committed themselves to the presentation of constitutional amendments for the purpose. Hamilton argued that the absence of a bill of rights was not a defect; indeed, a bill was not necessary. "Why," he wrote, in the last of *The Federalist Papers*, "declare things that shall not be done which there is no power to do?" Nonetheless, the Bill of Rights was presented in the form of amendments and adopted by the states in 1791.

Since 1791 many proposals have been suggested to amend the Constitution. By 1972 sixteen additional amendments had been adopted. Only one, the Twenty-first, which repealed the

Eighteenth, was ratified by state conventions. All the others were ratified by state legislatures.

Even a cursory reading of the later amendments shows they do not alter the fundamentals of limited government, the separation of powers, the federal system, or the political process set in motion originally. The Thirteenth, Fourteenth, Fifteenth, and Nineteenth amendments attempt to insure equality to all and are an extension of the Bill of Rights. The others reaffirm some existing constitutional arrangements, alter some procedures, and at least one, the Sixteenth, states national policy.

Substantial change and adaptation of the Constitution beyond the formal amendments have come from national experience, growth, and development. It has been from the Supreme Court that much of the gradual significant shaping of the Constitution has been done.

Government has remained neither static nor tranquil. Some conflict prevails continually. It may be about the activities of some phase of government or the extent of operations, and whether the arrangement for government can be made responsive to current and prospective needs of society. Conflict is inevitable in a democratic society. Sometimes the conflict is spirited and rises to challenge the continuation of the system. Questions arise whether a fair trial may be possible here or there; legislators are alleged to be indifferent to human problems and pursue distorted public priorities. Presidents are charged with secret actions designed for self-aggrandizement or actions based on half-truths. Voices are heard urging revolution again as the only means of righting alleged wrongs.

The responses continue to demonstrate, however, that the constitutional arrangement for government, the allocation of powers, and the restraints on government all provide the needed flexibility. The Constitution endures.

Adam C. Breckenridge, University of Nebraska-Lincoln

The Constitution of the United States

We the People of the United States, in Order to form a more perfect Union, establish Justice, insure domestic Tranquility, provide for the common defence, promote the general Welfare, and secure the Blessings of Liberty to ourselves and our Posterity, do ordain and establish this Constitution for the United States of America.

ARTICLE. I.

SECTION. 1. All legislative Powers herein granted shall be vested in a Congress of the United States, which shall consist of a Senate and House of Representatives.

SECTION. 2. The House of Representatives shall be composed of Members chosen every second Year by the People of the several States, and the Electors in each State shall have the Qualifications requisite for Electors of the most numerous Branch of the State Legislature.

No Person shall be a Representative who shall not have attained to the age of twenty five Years, and been seven Years a Citizen of the United States, and who shall not, when elected, be an Inhabitant of that State in which he shall be chosen.

Representatives and direct Taxes shall be apportioned among the several States which may be included within this Union, according to their respective Numbers, which shall be determined by adding to the whole Number of free Persons, including those bound to Service for a Term of Years, and excluding Indians not taxed, three fifths of all other Persons. The actual Enumeration shall be made within three Years after the first Meeting of the Congress of the United States, and within every subsequent Term of ten Years, in such Manner as they shall by Law direct. The Number of Representatives shall not exceed one for every thirty Thousand, but each State shall have at Least one Representative; and until such enumeration shall be made, the State of New Hampshire shall be entitled to chuse three, Massachusetts eight, Rhode-Island and Providence Plantations one, Connecticut five, New York six, New Jersey four, Pennsylvania eight, Delaware one, Maryland six, Virginia ten, North Carolina five, South Carolina five, and Georgia three.

When vacancies happen in the Representation from any State, the Executive Authority thereof shall issue Writs of Election to fill such Vacancies.

The House of Representatives shall chuse their Speaker and other Officers; and shall have the sole Power of Impeachment.

SECTION. 3. The Senate of the United States shall be composed of two Senators from each State, chosen by the Legislature thereof, for six years; and each Senator shall have one Vote.

Immediately after they shall be assembled in Consequence of the first Election, they shall be divided as equally as may be into three Classes. The Seats of the Senators of the first Class shall be vacated at the Expiration of the second Year, of the second Class at the Expiration of the fourth Year, and of the third Class at the Expiration of the sixth Year, so that one third may be chosen every second year; and if Vacancies happen by Resignation, or otherwise, during the Recess of the Legislature of any State, the Executive thereof may make temporary Appointments until the next Meeting of the Legislature, which shall then fill such Vacancies.

No Person shall be a Senator who shall not have attained to the Age of thirty Years, and been nine Years a Citizen of the United States, and who shall not, when elected, be an Inhabitant of that State for which he shall be chosen.

The Vice President of the United States shall be President of the Senate, but shall have no Vote, unless they be equally divided.

The Senate shall chuse their other Officers, and also a President pro tempore, in the Absence of the Vice President, or when he shall exercise the Office of President of the United States.

The Senate shall have the sole Power to try all Impeachments. When sitting for that Purpose, they shall be on Oath or Affirmation. When the President of the United States is tried the Chief Justice shall preside: And no Person shall be convicted without the Concurrence of two thirds of the Members present.

Judgment in Cases of Impeachment shall not extend further than to removal from Office, and disqualification to hold and enjoy any Office of honor, Trust or Profit under the United States: but the Party convicted shall nevertheless be liable and subject to Indictment, Trial, Judgment and Punishment, according to Law.

SECTION. 4. The Times, Places and Manner of holding Elections for Senators and Representatives, shall be prescribed in each State by the Legislature thereof; but the Congress may at any time by Law make or alter such Regulations, except as to the Places of chusing Senators.

The Congress shall assemble at least once in every Year, and such Meeting shall be on the first Monday in December, unless they shall by Law appoint a different Day.

SECTION. 5. Each House shall be the Judge of the Elections, Returns and Qualifications of its own Members, and a Majority of each shall constitute a Quorum to do Business; but a smaller Number may adjourn from day to day, and may be authorized to compel the Attendance of absent Members, in such Manner, and under such Penalties as each House may provide.

Each House may determine the Rules of its Proceedings, punish its Members for disorderly Behaviour, and, with the Concurrence of two thirds, expel a Member.

Each House shall keep a Journal of its Proceedings, and from time to time publish the same, excepting such Parts as may in their Judgment require Secrecy; and the Yeas and Nays of the Members of either House on any question shall, at the Desire of one fifth of those Present, be entered on the Journal.

Neither House, during the Session of Congress, shall, without the Consent of the other, adjourn for more than three days, nor to any other Place than that in which the two Houses shall be sitting.

SECTION. 6. The Senators and Representatives shall receive a Compensation for their Services, to be ascertained by Law, and paid out of the Treasury of the United States. They shall in all Cases, except Treason, Felony and Breach of the Peace, be privileged from Arrest during their Attendance at the Session of their respective Houses, and in going to and returning from the same; and for any Speech or Debate in either House, they shall not be questioned in any other Place.

No Senator or Representative shall, during the Time for which he was elected, be appointed to any civil Office under the Authority of the United States, which shall have been created, or the Emoluments whereof shall have been encreased during such time; and no Person holding any Office under the United States, shall be a Member of either House during his Continuance in Office.

SECTION. 7. All Bills for raising Revenue shall originate in the House of Representatives; but the Senate may propose or concur with amendments as on other Bills.

Every Bill which shall have passed the House of Representatives and the Senate, shall, before it become a Law, be presented to the President of the United States; If he approve he shall sign it, but if not he shall return it, with his Objections to that House in which it shall have originated, who shall enter the Objections at large on their Journal, and proceed to reconsider it. If after such Reconsideration two thirds of that House shall agree to pass the Bill, it shall be sent, together with the Objections, to the other House, by which it shall likewise be reconsidered, and if approved by two thirds of that House, it shall become a Law. But in all such Cases the Votes of both Houses shall be determined by Yeas and Nays, and the Names of the Persons voting for and against the Bill shall be entered on the Journal of each House respectively. If any Bill shall not be returned by the President within ten Days (Sundays excepted) after it shall have been presented to him, the Same shall be a Law, in like Manner as if he had signed it, unless the Congress by their Adjournment prevent its Return, in which Case it shall not be a Law.

Every Order, Resolution, or Vote to which the Concurrence of the Senate and House of Representatives may be necessary (except on a question of Adjournment) shall be presented to the President of the United States; and before the Same shall take Effect, shall be approved by him, or being disapproved by him, shall be repassed by two thirds of the Senate and House of Representatives, according to the Rules and Limitations prescribed in the Case of a Bill.

SECTION. 8. The Congress shall have Power To lay and collect Taxes, Duties, Imposts and Excises, to pay the Debts and provide for the common Defence and general Welfare of the United States; but all Duties, Imposts and Excises shall be uniform throughout the United States;

To borrow Money on the credit of the United States;

To regulate Commerce with foreign Nations, and among the several States, and with the Indian Tribes;

To establish an uniform Rule of Naturalization, and uniform Laws on the subject of Bankruptcies throughout the United States;

To coin Money, regulate the Value thereof, and of foreign Coin, and fix the Standard of Weights and Measures;

To provide for the Punishment of counterfeiting the Securities and current Coin of the United States;

To establish Post Offices and post Roads;

To promote the Progress of Science and useful Arts, by securing for limited Times to Authors and Inventors the exclusive Right to their respective Writings and Discoveries;

To constitute Tribunals inferior to the supreme Court;

To define and punish Piracies and Felonies committed on the high Seas, and Offences against the Law of Nations;

To declare War, grant Letters of Marque and Reprisal, and make Rules concerning Captures on Land and Water;

To raise and support Armies, but no Appropriation of Money to that Use shall be for a longer Term than two Years;

To provide and maintain a Navy;

To make Rules for the Government and Regulation of the land and naval Forces;

To provide for calling forth the Militia to execute the Laws of the Union, suppress Insurrections and repel Invasions;

To provide for organizing, arming, and disciplining, the Militia, and for governing such Part of them as may be employed in the Service of the United States, reserving to the States respectively, the Appointment of the Officers, and the Authority of training the Militia according to the discipline prescribed by Congress;

To exercise exclusive Legislation in all Cases whatsoever, over such District (not exceeding ten Miles square) as may, by Cession of Particular States, and the Acceptance of Congress, become the Seat of the Government of the United States, and to exercise like Authority over all Places purchased by the Consent of the Legislature of the State in which the Same shall be, for the Erection of Forts, Magazines, Arsenals, dock-Yards, and other needful Buildings;—And

To make all Laws which shall be necessary and proper for carrying into Execution the foregoing Powers, and all other Powers vested by this Constitution in the Government of the United States, or in any Department or Officer thereof.

SECTION. 9. The Migration or Importation of such Persons as any of the States now existing shall think proper to admit, shall not be prohibited by the Congress prior to the Year one thousand eight hundred and eight, but a Tax or duty may be imposed on such Importation, not exceeding ten dollars for each Person.

The Privilege of the Writ of Habeas Corpus shall not be suspended, unless when in Cases of Rebellion or Invasion the public Safety may require it.

No Bill of Attainder or ex post facto Law shall be passed.

No Capitation, or other direct, Tax shall be laid, unless in Proportion to the Census or Enumeration herein before directed to be taken.

No Tax or Duty shall be laid on Articles exported from any State.

No Preference shall be given by any Regulation or Commerce or Revenue to the Ports of one State over those of another; nor shall Vessels bound to, or from, one State, be obliged to enter, clear or pay Duties in another.

No Money shall be drawn from the Treasury, but in Consequence of Appropriations made by Law; and a regular Statement and Account of the Receipts and Expenditures of all public Money shall be published from time to time.

No Title of Nobility shall be granted by the United States: And no Person holding any Office of Profit or Trust under them, shall, without the Consent of the Congress, accept of any present Emolument, Office, or Title, of any kind whatever, from any King, Prince, or foreign State.

SECTION. 10. No State shall enter into any Treaty, Alliance, or Confederation; grant Letters of Marque and Reprisal; coin Money; emit Bills of Credit; make any Thing but gold and silver Coin a Tender in Payment of Debts; pass any Bill of Attainder, ex post facto Law, or Law impairing the Obligation of Contracts, or grant any Title of Nobility.

No State shall, without the Consent of the Congress, lay any Imposts or Duties on Imports or Exports, except what may be absolutely necessary for executing its inspection Laws: and the net Produce of all Duties and Imposts, laid by any State on Imports or Exports, shall be for the Use of the Treasury of the United States; and all such Laws shall be subject to the Revision and Controul of the Congress.

No state shall, without the Consent of Congress, lay any Duty of Tonnage, keep Troops, or Ships of War in time of Peace, enter into any Agreement or Compact with another State, or with a foreign Power, or engage in War, unless actually invaded, or in such imminent Danger as will not admit of delay.

ARTICLE. II.

SECTION. 1. The executive Power shall be vested in a President of the United States of America. He shall hold his Office during the Term of four Years, and, together with the Vice President, chosen for the same Term, be elected as follows

Each State shall appoint, in such Manner as the Legislature thereof may direct, a Number of Electors, equal to the whole Number of Senators and Representatives to which the State may be entitled in the Congress: but no Senator or Representative, or Person holding an Office of Trust or Profit under the United States, shall be appointed an Elector.

The Electors shall meet in their respective States, and vote by Ballot for two Persons, of whom one at least shall not be an Inhabitant of the same State with themselves. And they shall make a List of all the persons voted for, and of the Number of Votes for each; which List they shall sign and certify, and transmit sealed to the Seat of Government of the United States, directed to the President of the Senate. The President of the Senate shall, in the Presence of the Senate and House of Representatives, open all the Certificates, and the Votes shall then be counted. The Person having the greatest Number of Votes shall be the President, if such Number be a Majority of the whole Number of Electors appointed; and if there be more than one who have such Majority, and have an equal Number of Votes, then the House of Representatives shall immediately chuse by Ballot one of them for President; and if no Person have a Majority, then from the five highest on the List the said House shall in like Manner chuse the President. But in chusing the President, the Votes shall be taken by States, the Representation from each State having one Vote; a quorum for this Purpose shall consist of a Member or Members from two thirds of the States, and a Majority of all the States shall be necessary to a Choice. In every Case, after the Choice of the President, the Person having the greatest Number of Votes of the Electors shall be the Vice President. But if there should remain two or more who have equal Votes, the Senate shall chuse from them by Ballot the Vice President.

The Congress may determine the Time of chusing the Electors, and the Day on which they shall give their Votes; which Day shall be the same throughout the United States.

No Person except a natural born Citizen, or a Citizen of the United States, at the time of the Adoption of this Constitution, shall be eligible to the Office of President; neither shall any person be eligible to that Office who shall not have attained to the Age of thirty five Years, and been fourteen Years a Resident within the United States.

In Case of the Removal of the President from Office, or of his Death, Resignation, or Inability to discharge the Powers and Duties of the said Office, the Same shall devolve on the Vice President, and the Congress may by Law provide for the Case of Removal, Death, Resignation or Inability, both of the President and Vice President, declaring what Officer shall then act as President, and such Officer shall act accordingly, until the Disability be removed, or a President shall be elected.

The President shall, at stated Times, receive for his Services, a Compensation, which shall neither be encreased nor diminished during the Period for which he shall have been elected, and he shall not receive within that period any other Emolument from the United States, or any of them.

Before he enter on the Execution of his Office, he shall take the following Oath or Affirmation:—"I do solemnly swear (or affirm) that I will faithfully execute the Office of President of the United States, and will to the best of my Ability, preserve, protect and defend the Constitution of the United States."

SECTION. 2. The President shall be Commander in Chief of the Army and Navy of the United States, and of the Militia of the several States, when called into the actual Service of the United States; he may require the Opinion, in writing, of the principal Officer in each of the executive Departments, upon any Subject relating to the Duties of their respective Offices, and he shall have Power to grant Reprieves and Pardons for Offences against the United States, except in Cases of Impeachment.

He shall have Power, by and with the Advice and Consent of the Senate, to make Treaties, provided two thirds of the Senators present concur; and he shall nominate, and by and with the Advice and Consent of the Senate, shall appoint Ambassadors, other public Ministers and Consuls, Judges of the supreme Court, and all other Officers of the United States, whose Appointments are not herein otherwise provided for, and which shall be established by Law: but the Congress may by Law vest the Appointment of such inferior Officers, as they think proper, in the President alone, in the Courts of Law, or in the Heads of Departments.

The President shall have Power to fill up all Vacancies that may happen during the Recess of the Senate, by granting Commissions which shall expire at the End of their next Session.

SECTION. 3. He shall from time to time give to the Congress Information of the State of the Union, and recommend to their Consideration such Measures as he shall judge necessary and expedient; he may, on extraordinary Occasions, convene both Houses, or either of them, and in Case of Disagreement between them, with Respect to the Time of Adjournment, he may adjourn them to such Time as he shall think proper; he shall receive Ambassadors and other public Ministers; he shall take Care that the Laws be faithfully executed, and shall Commission all the Officers of the United States.

SECTION. 4. The President, Vice President and all civil Officers of the United States, shall be removed from Office on Impeachment for, and Conviction of, Treason, Bribery, or other high Crimes and Misdemeanors.

ARTICLE. III.

SECTION. 1. The judicial Power of the United States, shall be vested in one supreme Court, and in such inferior Courts as the Congress may from time to time ordain and establish. The Judges, both of the supreme and inferior Courts, shall hold their Offices during good Behaviour, and shall, at stated Times, receive for their Services, a Compensation, which shall not be diminished during their Continuance in Office.

SECTION. 2. The judicial Power shall extend to all Cases, in Law and Equity, arising under this Constitution, the Laws of the United States, and Treaties made, or which shall be made, under their Authority;—to all Cases affecting Ambassadors, other public Ministers and Consuls;—to all Cases of admiralty and maritime Jurisdiction;—to Controversies to which the United States shall be a Party;—to Controversies between two or more States;—between a State and Citizens of another State;—between Citizens of different States;—between Citizens of the same State claiming Lands under Grants of different States, and between a State, or the Citizens thereof, and foreign States, Citizens or Subjects.

In all Cases affecting Ambassadors, other public Ministers and Consuls, and those in which a State shall be Party, the supreme Court shall have original Jurisdiction. In all the other Cases before mentioned, the supreme Court shall have appellate Jurisdiction, both as to Law and Fact, with such Exceptions, and under such Regulations as the Congress shall make.

The Trial of all Crimes, except in Cases of Impeachment, shall be by Jury; and such Trial shall be held in the State where the said Crimes shall have been committed; but when not committed within any State, the Trial shall be at such Place or Places as the Congress may by Law have directed.

SECTION. 3. Treason against the United States, shall consist only in levying War against them, or in adhering to their Enemies, giving them Aid and Comfort. No Person shall be convicted of Treason unless on the Testimony of two Witnesses to the same overt Act, or on Confession in open Court.

The Congress shall have Power to declare the Punishment of Treason, but no Attainder of Treason shall work Corruption of Blood, or Forfeiture except during the Life of the Person attained.

ARTICLE. IV.

SECTION. 1. Full Faith and Credit shall be given in each State to the public Acts, Records, and judicial Proceedings of every other State. And the Congress may by general Laws prescribe the Manner in which such Acts, Record and Proceedings shall be proved, and the Effect thereof.

SECTION. 2. The Citizens of each State shall be entitled to all Privileges and Immunities of Citizens in the several States.

A Person charged in any State with Treason, Felony, or other Crime, who shall flee from Justice, and be found in another State, shall on Demand of the executive Authority of the State from which he fled, be delivered up, to be removed to the State having Jurisdiction of the Crime.

No Person held to Service or Labour in one State, under the Laws thereof, escaping into another, shall, in Consequence of any Law or Regulation therein, be discharged from such Service or Labour, but shall be delivered up on Claim of the Party to whom such Service or Labour may be due.

SECTION. 3. New States may be admitted by the Congress into this Union; but no new State shall be formed or erected within the Jurisdiction of any other State; nor any State be formed by the Junction of two or more States, or Parts of States, without the Consent of the Legislatures of the States concerned as well as of the Congress.

The Congress shall have Power to dispose of and make all needful Rules and Regulations respecting the Territory or other Property belonging to the United States; and nothing in this Constitution shall be so construed as to Prejudice any Claims of the United States, or of any particular State.

SECTION. 4. The United States shall guarantee to every State in this Union a Republican Form of Government, and shall protect each of them against Invasion; and on Application of the Legislature, or of the Executive (when the Legislature cannot be convened) against domestic Violence.

ARTICLE. V.

The Congress, whenever two thirds of both Houses shall deem it necessary, shall propose Amendments to this Constitution, or, on the Application of the Legislature of two thirds of the several States, shall call a Convention for proposing Amendments, which, in either Case, shall be valid to all Intents and Purposes, as Part of this Constitution, when ratified by the Legislatures of three fourths of the several States, or by Conventions in three fourths thereof, as the one or the other Mode of Ratification may be proposed by the Congress; Provided that no Amendment which may be made prior to the Year One thousand eight hundred and eight shall in any Manner affect the first and fourth Clauses in the Ninth Section of the first Article; and that no State, without its Consent, shall be deprived of its equal Suffrage in the Senate.

ARTICLE. VI.

All Debts contracted and Engagements entered into, before the Adoption of this Constitution, shall be as valid against the United States under this Constitution, as under the Confederation.

This Constitution, and the Laws of the United States which shall be made in Pursuance thereof; and all Treaties made, or which shall be made, under the Authority of the United States, shall be the supreme Law of the Land; and the Judges in every State shall be bound thereby, any Thing in the Constitution or Laws of any State to the Contrary notwithstanding.

The Senators and Representatives before mentioned, and the Members of the several State Legislatures, and all executive and judicial Officers, both of the United States and of the several States, shall be bound by Oath or Affirmation, to support this Constitution; but no religious Test shall ever be required as a Qualification to any Office or public Trust under the United States.

ARTICLE. VII.

The Ratification of the Conventions of nine States, shall be sufficient for the Establishment of this Constitution between the States so ratifying the Same.

Done in Convention by the Unanimous Consent of the States present the Seventeenth Day of September in the Year of our Lord one thousand seven hundred and Eighty seven and of the Independence of the United States of America the Twelfth In witness whereof We have hereunto subscribed our Names,

Go. WASHINGTON—Presidt. and deputy from Virginia

New Hampshire	JOHN LANGDON NICHOLAS GILMAN
Massachusetts	NATHANIEL GORHAM RUFUS KING
Connecticut	Wm. SAML JOHNSON ROGER SHERMAN
New York...	ALEXANDER HAMILTON
New Jersey	WIL: LIVINGSTON DAVID BREARLEY Wm. PATERSON JONA: DAYTON
Pennsylvania	B FRANKLIN THOMAS MIFFLIN ROBt MORRIS GEO. CLYMER THOs. FITZSIMONS JARED INGERSOLL JAMES WILSON GOUV MORRIS
Delaware	GEO: READ GUNNING BEDFORD jun JOHN DICKINSON RICHARD BASSETT JACO: BROOM
Maryland	JAMES McHENRY DAN OF St THOs. JENIFER DANL CARROLL
Virginia	JOHN BLAIR JAMES MADISON Jr.
North Carolina	Wm. BLOUNT RICHd. DOBBS SPAIGHT HU WILLIAMSON
South Carolina	J. RUTLEDGE CHARLES COTESWORTH PINCKNEY CHARLES PINCKNEY PIERCE BUTLER
Georgia	WILLIAM FEW ABR BALDWIN

In Convention Monday, September 17th 1787.

Present The States of

New Hampshire, Massachusetts, Connecticut, Mr. Hamilton from New York, New Jersey, Pennsylvania, Delaware, Maryland, Virginia, North Carolina and Georgia.

Resolved,

That the preceeding Constitution be laid before the United States in Congress assembled, and that it is the Opinion of this Convention, that it should afterwards be submitted to a Convention of Delegates, chosen in each State by the People thereof, under the Recommendation of its Legislature, for their Assent and Ratification; and that each Convention assenting to, and ratifying the Same, should give Notice thereof to the United States in Congress assembled. Resolved, That it is the Opinion of this Convention, that as soon as the Conventions of nine States shall have ratified this Constitution, the United States in Congress assembled should fix a Day on which Electors should be appointed by the States which shall have ratified the same, and a Day on which the Electors should assemble to vote for the President, and the Time and Place for commencing Proceedings under this Constitution. That after such Publication the Electors should be appointed, and the Senators and Representatives elected: That the Electors should meet on the Day fixed for the Election of the President, and should transmit their Votes certified, signed, sealed and directed, as the Constitution requires, to the Secretary of the United States in Congress assembled, that the Senators and Representatives should convene at the Time and Place assigned; that the Senators should appoint a President of the Senate, for the sole Purpose of receiving, opening and counting the Votes for President; and, that after he shall be chosen, the Congress, together with the President, should, without Delay, proceed to execute this Constitution.

By the Unanimous Order of the Convention

Go. WASHINGTON—Presidt.

W. JACKSON Secretary.

RATIFICATION OF THE CONSTITUTION

State	Date of ratification
Delaware	Dec 7, 1787
Pennsylvania	Dec 12, 1787
New Jersey	Dec 19, 1787
Georgia	Jan 2, 1788
Connecticut	Jan 9, 1788
Massachusetts	Feb 6, 1788
Maryland	Apr 28, 1788
South Carolina	May 23, 1788
New Hampshire	June 21, 1788
Virginia	Jun 25, 1788
New York	Jun 26, 1788
Rhode Island	May 29, 1790
North Carolina	Nov 21, 1789

ARTICLES IN ADDITION TO, AND AMENDMENT OF, THE CONSTITUTION OF THE UNITED STATES OF AMERICA, PROPOSED BY CONGRESS, AND RATIFIED BY THE SEVERAL STATES, PURSUANT TO THE FIFTH ARTICLE OF THE ORIGINAL CONSTITUTION.

AMENDMENT I.

Congress shall make no law respecting an establishment of religion, or prohibiting the free exercise thereof; or abridging the freedom of speech, or of the press; or the right of the people peaceably to assemble, and to petition the Government for a redress of grievances.

AMENDMENT II.

A well regulated Militia, being necessary to the security of a free State, the right of the people to keep and bear Arms, shall not be infringed.

AMENDMENT III.

No Soldier shall, in time of peace be quartered in any house, without the consent of the Owner, nor in time of war, but in a manner to be prescribed by law.

AMENDMENT IV.

The right of the people to be secure in their persons, houses, papers, and effects, against unreasonable searches and seizures, shall not be violated, and no Warrants shall issue, but upon probable cause, supported by Oath or affirmation, and particularly describing the place to be searched, and the persons or things to be seized.

AMENDMENT V.

No person shall be held to answer for a capital, or otherwise infamous crime, unless on a presentment or indictment of a Grand Jury, except in cases arising in the land or naval forces, or in the Militia, when in actual service in time of War or public danger; nor shall any person be subject for the same offence to be twice put in jeopardy of life or limb; nor shall be compelled in any criminal case to be a witness against himself, nor be deprived of life, liberty, or property, without due process of law; nor shall private property be taken for public use, without just compensation.

AMENDMENT VI.

In all criminal prosecutions, the accused shall enjoy the right to a speedy and public trial, by an impartial jury of the State and district wherein the crime shall have been committed, which district shall have been previously ascertained by law, and to be informed of the nature and cause of the accusation; to be confronted with the witnesses against him; to have compulsory process for obtaining witnesses in his favor, and to have the Assistance of Counsel for his defence.

AMENDMENT VII.

In Suits at common law, where the value in controversy shall exceed twenty dollars, the right of trial by jury shall be preserved, and no fact tried by a jury, shall be otherwise re-examined in any Court of the United States, than according to the rules of the common law.

AMENDMENT VIII.

Excessive bail shall not be required, nor excessive fines imposed, nor cruel and unusual punishments inflicted.

AMENDMENT IX.

The enumeration in the Constitution, of certain rights, shall not be construed to deny or disparage others retained by the people.

AMENDMENT X.

The powers not delegated to the United States by the Constitution, nor prohibited by it to the States, are reserved to the States respectively, or to the people.

AMENDMENT XI.

(Adopted Jan. 8, 1798)
The Judicial power of the United States shall not be construed to extend to any suit in law or equity, commenced or prosecuted against one of the United States by Citizens of another State, or by Citizens or Subjects of any Foreign State.

AMENDMENT XII.

(Adopted Sept. 25, 1804)
The Electors shall meet in their respective states and vote by ballot for President and Vice-President, one of whom, at least, shall not be an inhabitant of the same state with themselves; they shall name in their ballots the person voted for as President, and in distinct ballots the person voted for as Vice-President, and they shall make distinct lists of all persons voted for as President, and of all persons voted for as Vice-President, and of the number of votes for each, which lists they shall sign and certify, and transmit sealed to the seat of the government of the United States, directed to the President of the Senate;—The President of the Senate shall, in the presence of the Senate and House of Representatives, open all the certificates and the votes shall then be counted;—The person having the greatest number of votes for President, shall be the President, if such number be a majority of the whole number of Electors appointed; and if no person have such majority, then from the persons having the highest numbers not exceeding three on the list of those voted for as President, the House of Representatives shall choose immediately, by ballot, the President. But in choosing the President, the votes shall be taken by states, the representation from each state having one vote; a quorum for this purpose shall consist of a member or members from two-thirds of the states, and a majority of all the states shall be necessary to a choice. And if the House of Representatives shall not choose a President whenever the right of choice shall devolve upon them, before the fourth day of March next following, then the Vice-President shall act as President, as in the case of the death or other constitutional disability of the President.—The person having the

greatest number of votes as Vice-President, shall be the Vice-President, if such number be a majority of the whole number of Electors appointed, and if no person have a majority, then from the two highest numbers on the list, the Senate shall choose the Vice-President; a quorum for the purpose shall consist of two-thirds of the whole number of Senators, and a majority of the whole number shall be necessary to a choice. But no person constitutionally ineligible to the office of President shall be eligible to that of Vice-President of the United States.

AMENDMENT XIII.

(Adopted Dec. 18, 1865)

SECTION 1. Neither slavery nor involuntary servitude, except as a punishment for crime whereof the party shall have been duly convicted, shall exist within the United States, or any place subject to their jurisdiction.

SECTION 2. Congress shall have power to enforce this article by appropriate legislation.

AMENDMENT XIV.

(Adopted July 28, 1868)

SECTION 1. All persons born or naturalized in the United States and subject to the jurisdiction thereof, are citizens of the United States and of the State wherein they reside. No State shall make or enforce any law which shall abridge the privileges or immunities of citizens of the United States; nor shall any State deprive any person of life, liberty, or property, without due process of law; nor deny to any person within its jurisdiction the equal protection of the laws.

SECTION 2. Representatives shall be apportioned among the several States according to their respective numbers, counting the whole number of persons in each State, excluding Indians not taxed. But when the right to vote at any election for the choice of electors for President and Vice President of the United States, Representatives in Congress, the Executive and Judicial officers of a State, or the members of the Legislature thereof, is denied to any of the male inhabitants of such State, being twenty-one years of age, and citizens of the United States, or in any way abridged, except for participation in rebellion, or other crime, the basis of representation therein shall be reduced in the proportion which the number of such male citizens shall bear to the whole number of male citizens twenty-one years of age in such State.

SECTION 3. No person shall be a Senator or Representative in Congress, or elector of President and Vice President, or hold any office, civil or military, under the United States, or under any State, who, having previously taken an oath, as a member of Congress, or as an officer of the United States, or as a member of any State legislature, or as an executive or judicial officer of any State, to support the Constitution of the United States, shall have engaged in insurrection or rebellion against the same, or given aid or comfort to the enemies thereof. But Congress may by a vote of two-thirds of each House, remove such disability.

SECTION 4. The validity of the public debt of the United States, authorized by law, including debts incurred for payment of pensions and bounties for services in suppressing insurrection or rebellion, shall not be questioned. But neither the United States nor any State shall assume or pay any debt or obligation incurred in aid of insurrection or rebellion against the United States, or any claim for the loss or emancipation of any slave; but all such debts, obligations and claims shall be held illegal and void.

SECTION 5. The Congress shall have power to enforce, by appropriate legislation, the provisions of this article.

AMENDMENT XV.

(Adopted March 30, 1870)

SECTION 1. The right of citizens of the United States to vote shall not be denied or abridged by the United States or by any State on account of race, color, or previous condition of servitude.

SECTION 2. The Congress shall have power to enforce this article by appropriate legislation.

AMENDMENT XVI.

(Adopted Feb. 25, 1913)

The Congress shall have power to lay and collect taxes on incomes, from whatever source derived, without apportionment among the several States, and without regard to any census or enumeration.

AMENDMENT XVII.

(Adopted May 31, 1913)

The Senate of the United States shall be composed of two Senators from each State, elected by the people thereof, for six years; and each Senator shall have one vote. The electors in each State shall have the qualifications requisite for electors of the most numerous branch of the State legislatures.

When vacancies happen in the representation of any State in the Senate, the executive authority of such State shall issue writs of election to fill such vacancies: Provided, That the legislature of any State may empower the executive thereof to make temporary appointments until the people fill the vacancies by election as the legislature may direct.

This amendment shall not be so construed as to affect the election or term of any Senator chosen before it becomes valid as part of the Constitution.

AMENDMENT XVIII.

(Adopted Jan. 29, 1919)

SECTION 1. After one year from the ratification of this article the manufacture, sale or transportation of intoxicating liquors within, the importation thereof into, or the exportation thereof from the United States and all territory subject to the jurisdiction thereof for beverage purposes is hereby prohibited.

SECTION 2. The Congress and the several States shall have concurrent power to enforce this article by appropriate legislation.

SECTION 3. This article shall be inoperative unless it shall have been ratified as an amendment to the Constitution by the legislatures of the several States, as provided in the Constitution, within seven years from the date of the submission hereof to the States by the Congress.

AMENDMENT XIX.

(Adopted Aug. 26, 1920)

The right of citizens of the United States to vote shall not be denied or abridged by the United States or by any State on account of sex.

Congress shall have power to enforce this article by appropriate legislation.

AMENDMENT XX.

(Adopted Feb. 6, 1933)

SECTION 1. The terms of the President and Vice President shall end at noon on the 20th day of January, and the terms of Senators and Representatives at noon on the 3d day of January, of the years in which such terms would have ended if this article had not been ratified; and the terms of their successors shall then begin.

SECTION 2. The Congress shall assemble at least once in every year, and such meeting shall begin at noon on the 3d day of January, unless they shall by law appoint a different day.

SECTION 3. If, at the time fixed for the beginning of the term of the President, the President elect shall have died, the Vice President elect shall become President. If a President shall not have been chosen before the time fixed for the beginning of his term, or if the President elect shall have failed to qualify, then the Vice President elect shall act as President until a President shall have qualified; and the Congress may by law provide for the case wherein neither a President elect nor a Vice President elect shall have qualified, declaring who shall then act as President, or the manner in which one who is to act shall be selected, and such person shall act accordingly until a President or Vice President shall have qualified.

SECTION 4. The Congress may by law provide for the case of the death of any of the persons from whom the House of Representatives may choose a President whenever the right of choice shall have devolved upon them, and for the case of the death of any of the persons from whom the Senate may choose a Vice President whenever the right of choice shall have devolved upon them.

SECTION 5. Sections 1 and 2 shall take effect on the 15th day of October following the ratification of this article.

SECTION 6. This article shall be inoperative unless it shall have been ratified as an amendment to the Constitution by the legislatures of three-fourths of the several States within seven years from the date of its submission.

AMENDMENT XXI.

(Adopted Dec. 5, 1933)

SECTION 1. The eighteenth article of amendment to the Constitution of the United States is hereby repealed.

SECTION 2. The transportation or importation into any State, Territory, or possession of the United States for delivery or use therein of intoxicating liquors, in violation of the laws thereof, is hereby prohibited.

SECTION 3. This article shall be inoperative unless it shall have been ratified as an amendment to the Constitution by conventions in the several States, as provided in the Constitution, within seven years from the date of the submission hereof to the States by the Congress.

AMENDMENT XXII.

(Adopted Feb. 27, 1951)

SECTION 1. No person shall be elected to the office of the President more than twice, and no person who has held the office of President, or acted as President, for more than two years of a term to which some other person was elected President shall be elected to the office of the President more than once. But this Article shall not apply to any person holding the office of President when this Article was proposed by the Congress, and shall not prevent any person who may be holding the office of President, or acting as President, during the term within which this Article becomes operative from holding the office of President or acting as President during the remainder of such term.

SECTION 2. This Article shall be inoperative unless it shall have been ratified as an amendment to the Constitution by the legislatures of three-fourths of the several States within seven years from the date of its submission to the States by the Congress.

AMENDMENT XXIII.

(Adopted Mar. 29, 1961)

SECTION 1. The District constituting the seat of Government of the United States shall appoint in such manner as the Congress may direct:

A number of electors of President and Vice President equal to the whole number of Senators and Representatives in Congress to which the District would be entitled if it were a State, but in no event more than the least populous State; they shall be in addition to those appointed by the States, but they shall be considered, for the purposes of the election of President and Vice President, to be electors appointed by a State; and they shall meet in the District and perform such duties as provided by the twelfth article of amendment.

SECTION 2. The Congress shall have power to enforce this article by appropriate legislation.

AMENDMENT XXIV.

(Adopted Jan. 23, 1964)

SECTION 1. The right of citizens of the United States to vote in any primary or other election for President or Vice President, for electors for President or Vice President, or for Senator or Representative in Congress, shall not be denied or abridged by the United States or any State by reason of failure to pay any poll tax or other tax.

SECTION 2. The Congress shall have the power to enforce this article by appropriate legislation.

AMENDMENT XXV.

(Adopted Feb. 10, 1967)

SECTION 1. In case of the removal of the President from office or of his death or resignation, the Vice President shall become President.

SECTION 2. Whenever there is a vacancy in the office of the Vice President, the President shall nominate a Vice President who shall take the office upon confirmation by a majority vote of both houses of Congress.

SECTION 3. Whenever the President transmits to the President pro tempore of the Senate and the Speaker of the House of Representatives his written declaration that he is unable to discharge the powers and duties of his office, and until he transmits to them a written declaration to the contrary, such powers and duties shall be discharged by the Vice President as Acting President.

SECTION 4. Whenever the Vice President and a majority of either the principal officers of the executive departments or of such other body as Congress may by law provide, transmit to the President pro tempore of the Senate and the Speaker of the House of Representatives their written declaration that the President is unable to discharge the powers and duties of his office, the Vice President shall immediately assume the powers and duties of the office as Acting President.

Thereafter, when the President transmits to the President pro tempore of the Senate and the Speaker of the House of Representatives his written declaration that no inability exists, he shall resume the powers and duties of his office unless the Vice President and a majority of either the principal officers of the executive department or of such other body as Congress may by law provide, transmit within four days to the President pro tempore of the Senate and the Speaker of the House of Representatives their written declaration that the President is unable to discharge the powers and duties of his office. Thereupon Congress shall decide the issue, assembling within forty-eight hours for that purpose if not in session. If the Congress within twenty-one days after receipt of the latter written declaration, or, if Congress is not in session, within twenty-one days after Congress is required to assemble, determines by two-thirds vote of both Houses that the President is unable to discharge the powers and duties of his office, the Vice President shall continue to discharge the same as Acting President; otherwise, the President shall resume the powers and duties of his office.

AMENDMENT XXVI.

(Adopted June 30, 1971)

SECTION 1. The right of citizens of the United States, who are 18 years of age or older, to vote shall not be denied or abridged by the United States or by any state on account of age.

SECTION 2. The Congress shall have the power to enforce this article by appropriate legislation.

AMENDMENT XXVII.

(Adopted May 7, 1992)

No law, varying the compensation for the services of the Senators and Representatives, shall take effect, until an election of Representatives shall have intervened.

THE SIZE AND VARIETY OF THE UNION AS A CHECK ON FACTION

FEDERALIST NO. 10

(MADISON)

To the People of the State of New York:

AMONG the numerous advantages promised by a well-constructed Union, none deserves to be more accurately developed than its tendency to break and control the violence of faction. The friend of popular governments never finds himself so much alarmed for their character and fate, as when he contemplates their propensity to this dangerous vice. He will not fail, therefore, to set a due value on any plan which, without violating the principles to which he is attached, provides a proper cure for it. The instability, injustice, and confusion introduced into the public councils, have, in truth, been the mortal diseases under which popular governments have everywhere perished; as they continue to be the favorite and fruitful topics from which the adversaries to liberty derive their most specious declamations. The valuable improvements made by the American constitutions on the popular models, both ancient and modern, cannot certainly be too much admired; but it would be an unwarrantable partiality, to contend that they have as effectually obviated the danger on this side, as was wished and expected. Complaints are everywhere heard from our most considerate and virtuous citizens, equally the friends of public and private faith, and of public and personal liberty, that our governments are too unstable, that the public good is disregarded in the conflicts of rival parties, and that measures are too often decided, not according to the rules of justice and the rights of the minor party, but by the superior force of an interested and overbearing majority. However anxiously we may wish that these complaints had no foundation, the evidence of known facts will not permit us to deny that they are in some degree true. It will be found, indeed, on a candid review of our situation, that some of the distresses under which we labor have been erroneously charged on the operation of our governments; but it will be found, at the same time, that other causes will not alone account for many of our heaviest misfortunes; and, particularly, for that prevailing and increasing distrust of public engagements, and alarm for private rights, which are echoed from one end of the continent to the other. These must be chiefly, if not wholly, effects of the unsteadiness and injustice with which a factious spirit has tainted our public administrations.

By a faction, I understand a number of citizens, whether amounting to a majority or minority of the whole, who are united and actuated by some common impulse of passion, or of interest, adverse to the rights of other citizens, or to the permanent and aggregate interests of the community.

There are two methods of curing the mischiefs of faction: the one, by removing its causes; the other, by controlling its effects.

There are again two methods of removing the causes of faction: the one, by destroying the liberty which is essential to its existence; the other, by giving to every citizen the same opinions, the same passions, and the same interests.

It could never be more truly said than of the first remedy, that it was worse than the disease. Liberty is to faction what air is to fire, an aliment without which it instantly expires. But it could not be less folly to abolish liberty, which is essential to political life, because it nourishes faction, than it would be to wish the annihilation of air, which is essential to animal life, because it imparts to fire its destructive agency.

The second expedient is as impracticable as the first would be unwise. As long as the reason of man continues fallible, and he is at liberty to exercise it, different opinions will be formed. As long as the connection subsists between his reason and his self-love, his opinions and his passions will have a reciprocal influence on each other; and the former will be objects to which the latter will attach themselves. The diversity in the faculties of men, from which the rights of property originate, is not less an insuperable obstacle to a uniformity of interests. The protection of these faculties is the first object of government. From the protection of different and unequal faculties of acquiring property, the possession of different degrees and kinds of property immediately results; and from the influence of these on the sentiments and views of the respective proprietors, ensues a division of the society into different interests and parties.

The latent causes of faction are thus sown in the nature of man; and we see them everywhere brought into different degrees of activity, according to the different circumstances of civil society. A zeal for different opinions concerning religion, concerning government, and many other points, as well of speculation as of practice; an attachment to different leaders ambitiously contending for pre-eminence and power; or to persons of other descriptions whose fortunes have been interesting to the human passions, have, in turn, divided mankind into parties, inflamed them with mutual animosity, and rendered them much more disposed to vex and oppress each other than to co-operate for their common good. So strong is this propensity of mankind to fall into mutual animosities, that where no substantial occasion presents itself, the most frivolous and fanciful distinctions have been sufficient to kindle their unfriendly passions and excite their most violent conflicts. But the most common and durable source of factions has been the various and unequal distribution of property. Those who hold and those who are without property have ever formed distinct interests in society.

Those who are creditors, and those who are debtors, fall under a like discrimination. A landed interest, a manufacturing interest, a mercantile interest, a moneyed interest, with many lesser interests, grow up of necessity in civilized nations, and divide them into different classes, actuated by different sentiments and views. The regulation of these various and interfering interests forms the principal task of modern legislation, and involves the spirit of party and faction in the necessary and ordinary operations of the government.

No man is allowed to be a judge in his own cause, because his interest would certainly bias his judgment, and, not improbably, corrupt his integrity. With equal, nay with greater reason, a body of men are unfit to be both judges and parties at the same time; yet what are many of the most important acts of legislation, but so many judicial determinations, not indeed concerning the rights of single persons, but concerning the rights of large bodies of citizens? And what are the different classes of legislators but advocates and parties to the causes which they determine? Is a law proposed concerning private debts? It is a question to which the creditors are parties on one side and the debtors on the other. Justice ought to hold the balance between them. Yet the parties are, and must be, themselves the judges; and the most numerous party, or, in other words, the most powerful faction must be expected to prevail. Shall domestic manufactures be encouraged, and in what degree, by restrictions on foreign manufactures? are questions which would be differently decided by the landed and the manufacturing classes, and probably by neither with a sole regard to justice and the public good. The apportionment of taxes on the various descriptions of property is an act which seems to require the most exact impartiality; yet there is, perhaps, no legislative act in which greater opportunity and temptation are given to a predominant party to trample on the rules of justice. Every shilling with which they overburden the inferior number, is a shilling saved to their own pockets.

It is in vain to say that enlightened statesmen will be able to adjust these clashing interests, and render them all subservient to the public good. Enlightened statesmen will not always be at the helm. Nor, in many cases, can such an adjustment be made at all without taking into view indirect and remote considerations, which will rarely prevail over the immediate interest which one party may find in disregarding the rights of another or the good of the whole.

The inference to which we are brought is, that the *causes* of faction cannot be removed, and that relief is only to be sought in the means of controlling its *effects*.

If a faction consists of less than a majority, relief is supplied by the republican principle, which enables the majority to defeat its sinister views by regular vote. It may clog the administration, it may convulse the society; but it will be unable to execute and mask its violence under the forms of the Constitution. When a majority is included in a faction, the form of popular government, on the other hand, enables it to sacrifice to its ruling passion or interest both the public good and the rights of other citizens. To secure the public good and private rights against the danger of such a faction, and at the same time to preserve the spirit and the form of popular government, is then the great object to which our inquiries are directed. Let me add that it is the great desideratum by which this form of government can be rescued from the opprobrium under which it has so long labored, and be recommended to the esteem and adoption of mankind.

By what means is this object attainable? Evidently by one of two only. Either the existence of the same passion or interest in a majority at the same time must be prevented, or the majority, having such coexistent passion or interest, must be rendered, by their number and local situation, unable to concert and carry into effect schemes of oppression. If the impulse and the opportunity be suffered to coincide, we well know that neither moral nor religious motives can be relied on as an adequate control. They are not found to be such on the injustice and violence of individuals, and lose their efficacy in proportion to the number combined together, that is, in proportion as their efficacy becomes needful.

From this view of the subject it may be concluded that a pure democracy, by which I mean a society consisting of a small number of citizens, who assemble and administer the government in person, can admit of no cure for the mischiefs of faction. A common passion or interest will, in almost every case, be felt by a majority of the whole; a communication and concert result from the form of government itself; and there is nothing to check the inducements to sacrifice the weaker party or an obnoxious individual. Hence it is that such democracies have ever been spectacles of turbulence and contention; have ever been found incompatible with personal security or the rights of property; and have in general been as short in their lives as they have been violent in their deaths. Theoretic politicians, who have patronized this species of government, have erroneously supposed that by reducing mankind to a perfect equality in their political rights, they would, at the same time, be perfectly equalized and assimilated in their possessions, their opinions, and their passions.

A republic, by which I mean a government in which the scheme of representation takes place, opens a different prospect, and promises the cure for which we are seeking. Let us examine the points in which it varies from pure democracy, and we shall comprehend both the nature of the cure and the efficacy which it must derive from the Union.

The two great points of difference between a democracy and a republic are: first, the delegation of the government, in the latter, to a small number of citizens elected by the rest; secondly, the greater number of citizens, and greater sphere of country, over which the latter may be extended.

The effect of the first difference is, on the one hand, to refine and enlarge the public views, by passing them through the medium of a chosen body of citizens, whose wisdom may best discern the true interest of their country, and whose patriotism and love of justice will be least likely to sacrifice it to temporary or partial considerations. Under such a regulation, it may well happen that the public voice, pronounced by the representatives of the people, will be more consonant to the public good than if pronounced by the people themselves, convened for the purpose. On the other hand, the effect may be inverted. Men of factious tempers, of local prejudices, or of sinister designs, may, by intrigue, by corruption, or by other means, first obtain the suffrages, and then betray the interests, of the people. The question resulting is, whether small or extensive republics are more favorable to the election of proper guardians of the public weal; and it is

clearly decided in favor of the latter by two obvious considerations:

In the first place, it is to be remarked that, however small the republic may be, the representatives must be raised to a certain number, in order to guard against the cabals of a few; and that, however large it may be, they must be limited to a certain number, in order to guard against the confusion of a multitude. Hence, the number of representatives in the two cases not being in proportion to that of the two constituents, and being proportionally greater in the small republic, it follows that, if the proportion of fit characters be not less in the large than in the small republic, the former will present a greater option, and consequently a greater probability of a fit choice.

In the next place, as each representative will be chosen by a greater number of citizens in the large than in the small republic, it will be more difficult for unworthy candidates to practise with success the vicious arts by which elections are too often carried; and the suffrages of the people being more free, will be more likely to centre in men who possess the most attractive merit and the most diffusive and established characters.

It must be confessed that in this, as in most other cases, there is a mean, on both sides of which inconveniences will be found to lie. By enlarging too much the number of electors, you render the representative too little acquainted with all their local circumstances and lesser interests; as by reducing it too much, you render him unduly attached to these, and too little fit to comprehend and pursue great and national objects. The federal Constitution forms a happy combination in this respect; the great and aggregate interests being referred to the national, the local and particular to the State legislatures.

The other point of difference is, the greater number of citizens and extent of territory which may be brought within the compass of republican than of democratic government; and it is this circumstance principally which renders factious combinations less to be dreaded in the former than in the latter. The smaller the society, the fewer probably will be the distinct parties and interests composing it; the fewer the distinct parties and interests, the more frequently will a majority be found of the same party; and the smaller the number of individuals composing a majority, and the smaller the compass within which they are placed, the more easily will they concert and execute their plans of oppression. Extend the sphere and you take in a greater variety of parties and interests; you will make it less probable that a majority of the whole will have a common motive to invade the rights of other citizens; or if such a common motive exists, it will be more difficult for all who feel it to discover their own strength, and to act in unison with each other. Besides other impediments, it may be remarked that, where there is a consciousness of unjust or dishonorable purposes, communication is always checked by distrust in proportion to the number whose concurrence is necessary.

Hence, it clearly appears, that the same advantage which a republic has over a democracy, in controlling the effects of faction, is enjoyed by a large over a small republic,—is enjoyed by the Union over the States composing it. Does the advantage consist in the substitution of representatives whose enlightened views and virtuous sentiments render them superior to local prejudices and to schemes of injustice? It will not be denied that the representation of the Union will be most likely to possess these requisite endowments. Does it consist in the greater security afforded by a greater variety of parties, against the event of any one party being able to outnumber and oppress the rest? In an equal degree does the increased variety of parties comprised within the Union, increase this security. Does it, in fine, consist in the greater obstacles opposed to the concert and accomplishment of the secret wishes of an unjust and interested majority? Here, again, the extent of the Union gives it the most palpable advantage.

The influence of factious leaders may kindle a flame within their particular States, but will be unable to spread a general conflagration through the other States. A religious sect may degenerate into a political faction in a part of the Confederacy; but the variety of sects dispersed over the entire face of it must secure the national councils against any danger from that source. A rage for paper money, for an abolition of debts, for an equal division of property, or for any other improper or wicked project, will be less apt to pervade the whole body of the Union than a particular member of it; in the same proportion as such a malady is more likely to taint a particular county or district, than an entire State.

In the extent and proper structure of the Union, therefore, we behold a republican remedy for the diseases most incident to republican government. And according to the degree of pleasure and pride we feel in being republicans, ought to be our zeal in cherishing the spirit and supporting the character of Federalists.

PUBLIUS

Federalist No. 10 from THE FEDERALIST papers, 1787.

CHECKS AND BALANCES

FEDERALIST NO. 51

(MADISON)

To the People of the State of New York:

To what expedient, then, shall we finally resort, for maintaining in practice the necessary partition of power among the several departments, as laid down in the Constitution? The only answer that can be given is, that as all these exterior provisions are found to be inadequate, the defect must be supplied, by so contriving the interior structure of the government as that its several constituent parts may, by their mutual relations, be the means of keeping each other in their proper places. Without presuming to undertake a full development of this important idea, I will hazard a few general observations, which may perhaps place it in a clearer light, and enable us to form a more correct judgment of the principles and structure of the government planned by the convention.

In order to lay a due foundation for that separate and distinct exercise of the different powers of government, which to a certain extent is admitted on all hands to be essential to the preservation of liberty, it is evident that each department should have a will of its own; and consequently should be so constituted that the members of each should have as little agency as possible in the appointment of the members of the others. Were this principle rigorously adhered to, it would require that all the appointments for the supreme executive, legislative, and judiciary magistracies should be drawn from the same fountain of authority, the people, through channels having no communication whatever with one another. Perhaps such a plan of constructing the several departments would be less difficult in practice than it may in contemplation appear. Some difficulties, however, and some additional expense would attend the execution of it. Some deviations, therefore, from the principle must be admitted. In the constitution of the judiciary department in particular, it might be inexpedient to insist rigorously on the principle: first, because peculiar qualifications being essential in the members, the primary consideration ought to be to select that mode of choice which best secures these qualifications; secondly, because the permanent tenure by which the appointments are held in that department, must soon destroy all sense of dependence on the authority conferring them.

It is equally evident, that the members of each department should be as little dependent as possible on those of the others, for the emoluments annexed to their offices. Were the executive magistrate, or the judges, not independent of the legislature in this particular, their independence in every other would be merely nominal.

But the great security against a gradual concentration of the several powers in the same department, consists in giving to those who administer each department the necessary constitutional means and personal motives to resist encroachments of the others. The provision for defence must in this, as in all other cases, be made commensurate to the danger of attack. Ambition must be made to counteract ambition. The interest of the man must be connected with the constitutional rights of the place. It may be a reflection on human nature, that such devices should be necessary to control the abuses of government. But what is government itself, but the greatest of all reflections on human nature? If men were angels, no government would be necessary. If angels were to govern men, neither external nor internal controls on government would be necessary. In framing a government which is to be administered by men over men, the great difficulty lies in this: you must first enable the government to control the governed; and in the next place oblige it to control itself. A dependence on the people is, no doubt, the primary control on the government; but experience has taught mankind the necessity of auxiliary precautions.

This policy of supplying, by opposite and rival interests, the defect of better motives, might be traced through the whole system of human affairs, private as well as public. We see it particularly displayed in all the subordinate distributions of power, where the constant aim is to divide and arrange the several offices in such a manner as that each may be a check on the other—that the private interest of every individual may be a sentinel over the public rights. These inventions of prudence cannot be less requisite in the distribution of the supreme powers of the State.

But it is not possible to give to each department an equal power of self-defence. In republican government, the legislative authority necessarily predominates. The remedy for this inconveniency is to divide the legislature into different branches; and to render them, by different modes of election and different principles of action, as little connected with each other as the nature of their common functions and their common dependence on the society will admit. It may even be necessary to guard against dangerous encroachments by still further precautions. As the weight of the legislative authority requires that it should be thus divided, the weakness of the executive may require, on the other hand, that it should be fortified. An absolute negative on the legislature appears, at first view, to be the natural defence with which the executive magistrate should be armed. But perhaps it would be neither altogether safe nor alone sufficient. On ordinary occasions it might not be exerted with the requisite firmness, and on extraordinary occasions it might be perfidiously abused. May not this defect of an absolute negative be supplied by some qualified connection between this weaker department and the weaker branch of the stronger department, by which the latter may be led to support the constitutional rights of the former, without being too much detached from the rights of its own department?

If the principles on which these observations are founded be just, as I persuade myself they are, and they be applied as a criterion to the several State constitutions, and to the federal Constitution, it will be found that if the latter does not perfectly correspond with them, the former are infinitely less able to bear such a test.

There are, moreover, two considerations particularly applicable to the federal system of America, which place that system in a very interesting point of view.

First. In a single republic, all the power surrendered by the people is submitted to the administration of a single government; and the usurpations are guarded against by a division of the government into distinct and separate departments. In the compound republic of America, the power surrendered by the people is first divided between two distinct governments, and then the portion allotted to each subdivided among distinct and separate departments. Hence a double security arises to the rights of the people. The different governments will control each other, at the same time that each will be controlled by itself.

Second. It is of great importance in a republic not only to guard the society against the oppression of its rulers, but to guard one part of the society against the injustice of the other part. Different interests necessarily exist in different classes of citizens. If a majority be united by a common interest, the rights of the minority will be insecure. There are but two methods of providing against this evil: the one by cre-

ating a will in the community independent of the majority—that is, of the society itself; the other, by comprehending in the society so many separate descriptions of citizens as will render an unjust combination of a majority of the whole very improbable, if not impracticable. The first method prevails in all governments possessing an hereditary or self-appointed authority. This, at best, is but a precarious security; because a power independent of the society may as well espouse the unjust views of the major, as the rightful interests of the minor party, and may possibly be turned against both parties. The second method will be exemplified in the federal republic of the United States. Whilst all authority in it will be derived from and dependent on the society, the society itself will be broken into so many parts, interests and classes of citizens, that the rights of individuals, or of the minority, will be in little danger from interested combinations of the majority. In a free government the security for civil rights must be the same as that for religious rights. It consists in the one case in the multiplicity of interests, and in the other in the multiplicity of sects. The degree of security in both cases will depend on the number of interests and sects; and this may be presumed to depend on the extent of country and number of people comprehended under the same government. This view of the subject must particularly recommend a proper federal system to all the sincere and considerate friends of republican government, since it shows that in exact proportion as the territory of the Union may be formed into more circumscribed Confederacies, or States, oppressive combinations of a majority will be facilitated; the best security, under the republican forms, for the rights of every class of citizens, will be diminished; and consequently the stability and independence of some member of the government, the only other security, must be proportionally increased. Justice is the end of government. It is the end of civil society. It ever has been and ever will be pursued until it be obtained, or until liberty be lost in

the pursuit. In a society under the forms of which the stronger faction can readily unite and oppress the weaker, anarchy may as truly be said to reign as in a state of nature, where the weaker individual is not secured against the violence of the stronger; and as, in the latter state, even the stronger individuals are prompted, by the uncertainty of their condition, to submit to a government which may protect the weak as well as themselves; so, in the former state, will the more powerful factions or parties be gradually induced, by a like motive, to wish for a government which will protect all parties, the weaker as well as the more powerful. It can be little doubted that if the State of Rhode Island was separated from the Confederacy and left to itself, the insecurity of rights under the popular form of government within such narrow limits would be displayed by such reiterated oppressions of factious majorities that some power altogether independent of the people would soon be called for by the voice of the very factions whose misrule had proved the necessity of it. In the extended republic of the United States, and among the great variety of interests, parties, and sects which it embraces, a coalition of a majority of the whole society could seldom take place on any other principles than those of justice and the general good; whilst there being thus less danger to a minor from the will of a major party, there must be less pretext, also, to provide for the security of the former, by introducing into the government a will not dependent on the latter, or, in other words, a will independent of the society itself. It is no less certain than it is important, notwithstanding the contrary opinions which have been entertained, that the larger the society, provided it lie within a particular sphere, the more duly capable it will be of self-government. And happily for the *republican cause,* the practicable sphere may be carried to a very great extent, by a judicious modification and mixture of the *federal principle.*

PUBLIUS

Federalist No. 51 from *THE FEDERALIST papers,* 1787.

Why Don't They Like Us?

How America Has Become the Object of Much of the Planet's Genuine Grievances—and Displaced Discontents

BY STANLEY HOFFMANN

It wasn't its innocence that the United States lost on September 11, 2001. It was its naïveté. Americans have tended to believe that in the eyes of others the United States has lived up to the boastful clichés propagated during the Cold War (especially under Ronald Reagan) and during the Clinton administration. We were seen, we thought, as the champions of freedom against fascism and communism, as the advocates of decolonization, economic development, and social progress, as the technical innovators whose mastery of technology, science, and advanced education was going to unify the world.

Some officials and academics explained that U.S. hegemony was the best thing for a troubled world and unlike past hegemonies would last—not only because there were no challengers strong enough to steal the crown but, above all, because we were benign rulers who threatened no one.

But we have avoided looking at the hegemon's clay feet, at what might neutralize our vaunted soft power and undermine our hard power. Like swarming insects exposed when a fallen tree is lifted, millions who dislike or distrust the hegemon have suddenly appeared after September 11, much to our horror and disbelief. America became a great power after World War II, when we faced a rival that seemed to stand for everything we had been fighting against—tyranny, terror, brainwashing—and we thought that our international reputation would benefit from our standing for liberty and stability (as it still does in much of Eastern Europe). We were not sufficiently marinated in history to know that, through the ages, nobody—or almost nobody—has ever loved a hegemon.

Past hegemons, from Rome to Great Britain, tended to be quite realistic about this. They wanted to be obeyed or, as in the case of France, admired. They rarely wanted to be loved. But as a combination of high-noon sheriff and proselytizing missionary, the United States expects gratitude and affection. It was bound to be disappointed; gratitude is not an emotion that one associates with the behavior of states.

THE NEW WORLD DISORDER

This is an old story. Two sets of factors make the current twist a new one. First, the so-called Westphalian world has collapsed. The world of sovereign states, the universe of Hans Morgenthau's and Henry Kissinger's Realism, is no longer. The unpopularity of the hegemonic power has been heightened to incandescence by two aspects of this collapse. One is the irruption of the public, the masses, in international affairs. Foreign policy is no longer, as Raymond Aron had written in *Peace and War*, the closed domain of the soldier and the diplomat. Domestic publics—along with their interest groups, religious organizations, and ideological chapels—either dictate or constrain the imperatives and preferences that the governments fight for. This puts the hegemon in a difficult position: It often must work with governments that represent but a small percentage of a country's people—but if it fishes for public support abroad, it risks alienating leaders whose cooperation it needs. The United States paid heavily for not having had enough contacts with the opposition to the shah of Iran in the 1970s. It discovers today that there is an abyss in Pakistan, Saudi Arabia, Egypt, and Indonesia between our official allies and the populace in these countries. Diplomacy in a world where the masses, so to speak, stayed indoors, was a much easier game.

The collapse of the barrier between domestic and foreign affairs in the state system is now accompanied by a disease that attacks the state system itself. Many of the "states" that are members of the United Nations are pseudo-states with shaky or shabby institutions, no basic consensus on values or on procedures among their heterogeneous components, and no sense of national identity. Thus the hegemon—in addition to suffering the hostility of the government in certain countries (like Cuba, Iraq, and North Korea) and of the public in others (like, in varying degrees, Pakistan, Egypt, and even France)—can now easily become both the target of factions fighting one another in disintegrating countries and the pawn in their quarrels (which range over such increasingly borderless issues as drug trafficking, arms trading, money laundering, and other criminal enterprises). In addition, today's hegemon suffers from the volatility and turbulence of a global system in which ethnic, religious, and ideological sympathies have become transnational and in which groups and individuals uncontrolled by states can act on their own. The world of the nineteenth century, when hegemons could impose their order, their institutions, has been supplanted by the world of the twenty-first century: Where once there was order, there is now often a vacuum.

What makes the American Empire especially vulnerable is its historically unique combination of assets and liabilities. One has to go back to the Roman Empire to find a comparable set of resources. Britain, France, and Spain had to operate in multipolar systems; the United States is the only superpower.

But if America's means are vast, the limits of its power are also considerable. The United States, unlike Rome, cannot simply impose its will by force or through satellite states. Small "rogue" states can defy the hegemon (remember Vietnam?). And chaos can easily result from the large new role of nonstate actors. Meanwhile, the reluctance of Americans to take on the Herculean tasks of policing, "nation building," democratizing autocracies, and providing environmental protection and economic growth for billions of human beings stokes both resentment and hostility, especially among those who discover that one can count on American presence and leadership only when America's material interests are gravely threatened. (It is not surprising that the "defense of the national interest" approach of Realism was developed for a multipolar world. In an empire, as well as in a bipolar system, almost anything can be described as a vital interest, since even peripheral disorder can unravel the superpower's eminence.) Moreover, the complexities of America's process for making foreign-policy decisions can produce disappointments abroad when policies that the international community counted on—such as the Kyoto Protocol and the International Criminal Court—are thwarted. Also, the fickleness of U.S. foreign-policy making in arenas like the Balkans has convinced many American enemies that this country is basically incapable of pursuing long-term policies consistently.

NONE OF THIS MEANS, OF COURSE, THAT THE UNITED STATES has no friends in the world. Europeans have not forgotten the liberating role played by Americans in the war against Hitler and in the Cold War. Israel remembers how President Harry Truman sided with the founders of the Zionist state; nor has it forgotten all the help the United States has given it since then. The democratizations of postwar Germany and Japan were huge successes. The Marshall Plan and the Point Four Program were revolutionary initiatives. The decisions to resist aggression in Korea and in Kuwait demonstrated a commendable far-sightedness.

But Americans have a tendency to overlook the dark sides of their course (except on the protesting left, which is thus constantly accused of being un-American), perhaps because they perceive international affairs in terms of crusades between good and evil, endeavors that entail formidable pressures for unanimity. It is not surprising that the decade following the Gulf War was marked both by nostalgia for the clear days of the Cold War and by a lot of floundering and hesitating in a world without an overwhelming foe.

STRAINS OF ANTI-AMERICANISM

The main criticisms of American behavior have mostly been around for a long time. When we look at anti-Americanism today, we must first distinguish between those who attack the United States for what it does, or fails to do, and those who attack it for what it is. (Some, like the Islamic fundamentalists and terrorists, attack it for both reasons.) Perhaps the principal criticism is of the contrast between our ideology of universal liberalism and policies that have all too often consisted of supporting and sometimes installing singularly authoritarian and repressive regimes. (One reason why these policies often elicited more reproaches than Soviet control over satellites was that, as time went by, Stalinism became more and more cynical and thus the gap between words and deeds became far less wide than in the United States. One no longer expected much from Moscow.) The list of places where America failed at times to live up to its proclaimed ideals is long: Guatemala, Panama, El Salvador, Chile, Santo Domingo in 1965, the Greece of the colonels, Pakistan, the Philippines of Ferdinand Marcos, Indonesia after 1965, the shah's Iran, Saudi Arabia, Zaire, and, of course, South Vietnam. Enemies of these regimes were shocked by U.S. support for them—and even those whom we supported were disappointed, or worse, when America's cost-benefit analysis changed and we dropped our erstwhile allies. This Machiavellian scheming behind a Wilsonian facade has alienated many clients, as well as potential friends, and bred strains of anti-Americanism around the world.

A second grievance concerns America's frequent unilateralism and the difficult relationship between the United States and the United Nations. For many countries, the United Nations is, for all its flaws, the essential agency of cooperation and the protector of its members' sovereignty. The way U.S. diplomacy has "insulted" the UN system—sometimes by ignoring it and sometimes by rudely imposing its views and policies on it—has been costly in terms of foreign support.

Third, the United States' sorry record in international development has recently become a source of dissatisfaction abroad. Not only have America's financial contributions for narrowing the gap between the rich and the poor declined since the end of the Cold War, but American-dominated institutions such as the International Monetary Fund and the World Bank have often dictated financial policies that turned out to be disastrous for developing countries—most notably, before and during the Asian economic crisis of the mid-1990s.

Finally, there is the issue of American support of Israel. Much of the world—and not only the Arab world—considers America's Israel policy to be biased. Despite occasional American attempts at evenhandedness, the world sees that the Palestinians remain under occupation, Israeli settlements continue to expand, and individual acts of Arab terrorism—acts that Yasir Arafat can't completely control—are condemned more harshly than the killings of Palestinians by the Israeli army or by Israeli-sanctioned assassination squads. It is interesting to note that Israel, the smaller and dependent power, has been more successful in circumscribing the United States' freedom to maneuver diplomatically in the region than the United States has been at getting Israel to enforce the UN resolutions adopted after the 1967 war (which called for the withdrawal of Israeli forces from then-occupied territories, solving the refugee crisis, and establishing inviolate territorial zones for all states in the region). Many in the Arab world, and some outside, use this state of affairs to stoke paranoia of the "Jewish lobby" in the United States.

ANTIGLOBALISM AND ANTI-AMERICANISM

Those who attack specific American policies are often more ambivalent than hostile. They often envy the qualities and institutions that have helped the United States grow rich, powerful, and influential.

The real United States haters are those whose anti-Americanism is provoked by dislike of America's values, institutions, and society—and their enormous impact abroad. Many who despise America see us as representing the vanguard of globalization—even as they themselves use globalization to promote their hatred. The Islamic fundamentalists of al-Qaeda—like Iran's Ayatollah Khomeini 20 years ago—make excellent use of the communication technologies that are so essential to the spread of global trade and economic influence.

We must be careful here, for there are distinctions among the antiglobalist strains that fuel anti-Americanism. To some of our detractors, the most eloquent spokesman is bin Laden, for whom America and the globalization it promotes relentlessly through free trade and institutions under its control represent evil. To them, American-fueled globalism symbolizes the domination of the Christian-Jewish infidels or the triumph of pure secularism: They look at the United States and see a society of materialism, moral laxity, corruption in all its forms, fierce selfishness, and so on. (The charges are familiar to us because we know them as an exacerbated form of right-wing anti-Americanism in nineteenth- and twentieth-century Europe.) But there are also those who, while accepting the inevitability of globalization and seem eager to benefit from it, are incensed by the contrast between America's promises and the realities of American life. Looking at the United States and the countries we support, they see insufficient social protection, vast pockets of poverty amidst plenty, racial discrimination, the large role of money in politics, the domination of the elites—and they call us hypocrites. (And these charges, too, are familiar, because they are an exacerbated version of the left-wing anti-Americanism still powerful in Western Europe.)

On the one hand, those who see themselves as underdogs of the world condemn the United States for being an evil force because its dynamism makes it naturally and endlessly imperialistic—a behemoth that imposes its culture (often seen as debased), its democracy (often seen as flawed), and its conception of individual human rights (often seen as a threat to more communitarian and more socially concerned approaches) on other societies. The United States is perceived as a bully ready to use all means, including overwhelming force, against those who resist it: Hence, Hiroshima, the horrors of Vietnam, the rage against Iraq, the war on Afghanistan.

On the other hand, the underdogs draw hope from their conviction that the giant has a heel like Achilles'. They view America as a society that cannot tolerate high casualties and prolonged sacrifices and discomforts, one whose impatience with protracted and undecisive conflicts should encourage its victims to be patient and relentless in their challenges and assaults. They look at American foreign policy as one that is often incapable of overcoming obstacles and of sticking to a course that is fraught with high risks—as with the conflict with Iraq's Saddam Hussein at the end of the Gulf War; as in the flight from Lebanon after the terrorist attacks of 1982; as in Somalia in 1993; as in the attempts to strike back at bin Laden in the Clinton years.

Thus America stands condemned not because our enemies necessarily hate our freedoms but because they resent what they fear are our Darwinian aspects, and often because they deplore what they see as the softness at our core. Those who, on our side, note and celebrate America's power of attraction, its openness to immigrants and refugees, the uniqueness of a society based on common principles rather than on ethnicity or on an old culture, are not wrong. But many of the foreign students, for instance, who fall in love with the gifts of American education return home, where the attraction often fades. Those who stay sometimes feel that the price they have to pay in order to assimilate and be accepted is too high.

WHAT BRED BIN LADEN

This long catalog of grievances obviously needs to be picked apart. The complaints vary in intensity; different cultures, countries, and parties emphasize different flaws, and the criticism is often wildly excessive and unfair. But we are not dealing here with purely rational arguments; we are dealing with emotional responses to the omnipresence of a hegemon, to the sense that many people outside this country have that the United States dominates their lives.

Complaints are often contradictory: Consider "America has neglected us, or dropped us" versus "America's attentions corrupt our culture." The result can be a gestalt of resentment that strikes Americans as absurd: We are damned, for instance, both for failing to intervene to protect Muslims in the Balkans and for using force to do so.

But the extraordinary array of roles that America plays in the world—along with its boastful attitude and, especially recently, its cavalier unilateralism—ensures that many wrongs caused by local regimes and societies will be blamed on the United States. We even end up being seen as responsible not only for anything bad that our "protectorates" do—it is no coincidence that many of the September 11 terrorists came from America's protégés, Saudi Arabia and Egypt—but for what our allies do, as when Arabs incensed by racism and joblessness in France take up bin Laden's cause, or when Muslims talk about American violence against the Palestinians. Bin Laden's extraordinary appeal and prestige in the Muslim world do not mean that his apocalyptic nihilism (to use Michael Ignatieff's term) is fully endorsed by all those who chant his name. Yet to many, he plays the role of a bloody Robin Hood, inflicting pain and humiliation on the superpower that they believe torments them.

Bin Laden fills the need for people who, rightly or not, feel collectively humiliated and individually in despair to attach themselves to a savior. They may in fact avert their eyes from the most unsavory of his deeds. This need on the part of the poor and dispossessed to connect their own feeble lot to a charismatic and single-minded leader was at the core of fascism and of communism. After the failure of pan-Arabism, the fiasco of nationalism, the dashed hopes of democratization, and the fall of Soviet communism, many young people in the Muslim world who might have once turned to these visions for succor turned instead to Islamic fundamentalism and terrorism.

One almost always finds the same psychological dynamics at work in such behavior: the search for simple explanations—and what is simpler and more inflammatory than the machinations of the Jews and the evils of America—and a highly selective approach to history. Islamic fundamentalists remember the promises made by the British to the Arabs in World War I and the imposition of British and French imperialism after 1918 rather than the support the United States gave to anticolonialists in French North Africa in the late 1940s and in the 1950s. They remember British opposition to and American reluctance toward intervention in Bosnia before Srebrenica, but they forget about NATO's actions to save Bosnian Muslims in 1995, to help Albanians in Kosovo in 1999, and to preserve and improve Albanians' rights in Macedonia in 2001. Such distortions are manufactured and maintained by the controlled media and schools of totalitarian regimes, and through the religious schools, conspiracy mills, and propaganda of fundamentalism.

WHAT CAN BE DONE?

Americans can do very little about the most extreme and violent forms of anti-American hatred—but they can try to limit its spread by addressing grievances that are justified. There are a number of ways to do this:

- First—and most difficult—drastically reorient U.S. policy in the Palestinian-Israeli conflict.
- Second, replace the ideologically market-based trickle-down economics that permeate American-led development institutions today with a kind of social safety net. (Even *New York Times* columnist Thomas Friedman, that ur-celebrator of the global market, believes that such a safety net is indispensable.)
- Third, prod our allies and protégés to democratize their regimes, and stop condoning violations of essential rights (an approach that can only, in the long run, breed more terrorists and anti-Americans).
- Fourth, return to internationalist policies, pay greater attention to the representatives of the developing world, and make fairness prevail over arrogance.
- Finally, focus more sharply on the needs and frustrations of the people suffering in undemocratic societies than on the authoritarian regimes that govern them.

America's self-image today is derived more from what Reinhold Niebuhr would have called pride than from reality, and this exacerbates the clash between how we see ourselves and foreign perceptions and misperceptions of the United States. If we want to affect those external perceptions (and that will be very difficult to do in extreme cases), we need to readjust our self-image. This means reinvigorating our curiosity about the outside world, even though our media have tended to downgrade foreign coverage since the Cold War. And it means listening carefully to views that we may find outrageous, both for the kernel of truth that may be present in them and for the stark realities (of fear, poverty, hunger, and social hopelessness) that may account for the excesses of these views.

Terrorism aimed at the innocent is, of course, intolerable. Safety precautions and the difficult task of eradicating the threat are not enough. If we want to limit terrorism's appeal, we must keep our eyes and ears open to conditions abroad, revise our perceptions of ourselves, and alter our world image through our actions. There is nothing un-American about this. We should not meet the Manichaeanism of our foes with a Manichaeanism of self-righteousness. Indeed, self-examination and self-criticism have been the not-so-secret weapons of America's historical success. Those who demand that we close ranks not only against murderers but also against shocking opinions and emotions, against dissenters at home and critics abroad, do a disservice to America.

STANLEY HOFFMANN *is the Paul and Catherine Buttenwieser University Professor at Harvard University.*

The Death of Horatio Alger

OUR POLITICAL LEADERS ARE DOING EVERYTHING THEY CAN TO FORTIFY CLASS INEQUALITY

by PAUL KRUGMAN

The other day I found myself reading a leftist rag that made outrageous claims about America. It said that we are becoming a society in which the poor tend to stay poor, no matter how hard they work; in which sons are much more likely to inherit the socioeconomic status of their father than they were a generation ago.

The name of the leftist rag? *Business Week*, which published an article titled "Waking Up From the American Dream." The article summarizes recent research showing that social mobility in the United States (which was never as high as legend had it) has declined considerably over the past few decades. If you put that research together with other research that shows a drastic increase in income and wealth inequality, you reach an uncomfortable conclusion: America looks more and more like a class-ridden society.

And guess what? Our political leaders are doing everything they can to fortify class inequality, while denouncing anyone who complains—or even points out what is happening—as a practitioner of "class warfare."

Let's talk first about the facts on income distribution. Thirty years ago we were a relatively middle-class nation. It had not always been thus: Gilded Age America was a highly unequal society, and it stayed that way through the 1920s. During the 1930s and '40s, however, America experienced what the economic historians Claudia Goldin and Robert Margo have dubbed the Great Compression: a drastic narrowing of income gaps, probably as a result of New Deal policies. And the new economic order persisted for more than a generation: Strong unions; taxes on inherited wealth, corporate profits and high incomes; close public scrutiny of corporate management—all helped to keep income gaps relatively small. The economy was hardly egalitarian, but a generation ago the gross inequalities of the 1920s seemed very distant.

Now they're back. According to estimates by the economists Thomas Piketty and Emmanuel Saez—confirmed by data from the Congressional Budget Office—between 1973 and 2000 the average real income of the bottom 90 percent of American taxpayers actually fell by 7 percent. Meanwhile, the income of the top 1 percent rose by 148 percent, the income of the top 0.1 percent rose by 343 percent and the income of the top 0.01 percent rose 599 percent. (Those numbers exclude capital gains, so

they're not an artifact of the stock-market bubble.) The distribution of income in the United States has gone right back to Gilded Age levels of inequality.

Never mind, say the apologists, who churn out papers with titles like that of a 2001 Heritage Foundation piece, "Income Mobility and the Fallacy of Class-Warfare Arguments." America, they say, isn't a caste society—people with high incomes this year may have low incomes next year and vice versa, and the route to wealth is open to all. That's where those commies at *Business Week* come in: As they point out (and as economists and sociologists have been pointing out for some time), America actually is more of a caste society than we like to think. And the caste lines have lately become a lot more rigid.

The myth of income mobility has always exceeded the reality: As a general rule, once they've reached their 30s, people don't move up and down the income ladder very much. Conservatives often cite studies like a 1992 report by Glenn Hubbard, a Treasury official under the elder Bush who later became chief economic adviser to the younger Bush, that purport to show large numbers of Americans moving from low-wage to high-wage jobs during their working lives. But what these studies measure, as the economist Kevin Murphy put it, is mainly "the guy who works in the college bookstore and has a real job by his early 30s." Serious studies that exclude this sort of pseudo-mobility show that inequality in average incomes over long periods isn't much smaller than inequality in annual incomes.

It is true, however, that America was once a place of substantial intergenerational mobility: Sons often did much better than their fathers. A classic 1978 survey found that among adult men whose fathers were in the bottom 25 percent of the population as ranked by social and economic status, 23 percent had made it into the top 25 percent. In other words, during the first thirty years or so after World War II, the American dream of upward mobility was a real experience for many people.

Now for the shocker: The *Business Week* piece cites a new survey of today's adult men, which finds that this number has dropped to only 10 percent. That is, over the past generation upward mobility has fallen drastically. Very few children of the lower class are making their way to even moderate affluence. This goes along with other studies indicating that rags-to-riches stories have become vanishingly rare, and that the correlation between fathers' and sons' incomes has risen in recent decades. In modern America, it seems, you're quite likely to stay in the social and economic class into which you were born.

Business Week attributes this to the "Wal-Martization" of the economy, the proliferation of dead-end, low-wage jobs and the disappearance of jobs that provide entry to the middle class. That's surely part of the explanation. But public policy plays a role—and will, if present trends continue, play an even bigger role in the future.

Put it this way: Suppose that you actually liked a caste society, and you were seeking ways to use your control of the government to further entrench the advantages of the haves against the have-nots. What would you do?

One thing you would definitely do is get rid of the estate tax, so that large fortunes can be passed on to the next generation. More broadly, you would seek to reduce tax rates both on corporate profits and on unearned income such as dividends and capital gains, so that those with large accumulated or inherited wealth could more easily accumulate even more. You'd also try to create tax shelters mainly useful for the rich. And more broadly still, you'd try to reduce tax rates on people with high incomes, shifting the burden to the payroll tax and other revenue sources that bear most heavily on people with lower incomes.

Meanwhile, on the spending side, you'd cut back on health-care for the poor, on the quality of public education and on state aid for higher education. This would make it more difficult for people with low incomes to climb out of their difficulties and acquire the education essential to upward mobility in the modern economy.

And just to close off as many routes to upward mobility as possible, you'd do everything possible to break the power of unions, and you'd privatize government functions so that well-paid civil servants could be replaced with poorly paid private employees.

It all sounds sort of familiar, doesn't it?

Where is this taking us? Thomas Piketty, whose work with Saez has transformed our understanding of income distribution, warns that current policies will eventually create "a class of rentiers in the U.S., whereby a small group of wealthy but untalented children controls vast segments of the US economy and penniless, talented children simply can't compete." If he's right—and I fear that he is—we will end up suffering not only from injustice, but from a vast waste of human potential.

Goodbye, Horatio Alger. And goodbye, American Dream.

Paul Krugman, an economics professor at Princeton and a columnist at the New York Times, *is the author, most recently*, of The Great Unraveling: Losing Our Way in the New Century (*Norton*).

Coming out ahead:
Why Gay Marriage is on the way.

by Ramesh Ponnuru

For social conservatives, it seems that the battle over gay rights is nearing an end before it has even fairly begun. It is true that a small majority of the American public continues to believe, as the poll question puts it, that "sexual relations between two adults of the same sex" are "always wrong." It is true, as well, that a slightly larger majority believes that persons of the same sex should not be allowed to marry.

But public opinion has been moving with stunning rapidity. In the 1970s and '80s, the percentage of Americans who believed gay sex was "always wrong" barely budged. The National Opinion Research Center found that 73 percent held that belief in 1973, and 76 percent did in 1990. By 2000, that number had fallen by 16 points. It fell another 6 in the next two years. In 1996, Gallup found that 26 percent of the public supported same-sex marriage. In late June of this year, 39 percent did. Young people support it more than their elders. The trend lines favor gay marriage.

So do legal developments, as Gerard V. Bradley explains (page 26). Elite, including legal-elite, opinion favors gay rights more than public opinion does. Still, public opinion influences the courts. If courts had imposed gay marriage in 1990, there would have been a substantial public backlash. Now the idea looks less radical. If the courts move this year, or two years from now, there may yet be a backlash — but perhaps not one large enough to be effective. Three decades after Roe, almost three years after Bush v. Gore, no one is shocked when the courts make the weightiest political decisions.

Another shift in public sentiment is less easily captured in poll numbers: the rise of what one might call an "anti-anti-gay" bloc. People in this group may have qualms about homosexuality and may not support gay marriage. But they are at least as uncomfortable with anything that strikes them as

hostile to gay people, with rhetoric that singles them out for criticism, with political figures who seem to spend too much time worrying about them. It is this group — more than gays themselves or even unequivocal supporters of gay rights — that has caused the Bush White House to take a moderate line on gay issues.

President Bush opposes gay marriage, "hate crimes" legislation, and even the Employment Non-Discrimination Act. But he has also appointed openly gay officials, refrained from picking fights with the gay lobby, and generally frustrated social-conservative groups. In March, Marc Racicot, then-leader of the Republican National Committee, met with a liberal gay organization and assured them that bigotry in his party was fading. In April, when Sen. Rick Santorum was being pilloried, Bush expressed support for him — but too tepidly for social conservatives. Some of them warned that traditionalist voters would stay home in 2004. But Bush is responding to political circumstances that run far deeper than today's tactical jockeying and that social conservatives, thus far, have been powerless to change.

The change in public attitudes toward homosexuality has several causes, but three in particular bear mentioning: the effects of the sexual revolution, the changed focus of gay activism in the 1990s, and the ineffectiveness of social-conservative organizations.

Because of the sexual revolution among heterosexuals, social conservatives may have lost on gay marriage as soon as they started debating it. In the 1990s, as liberal journalist E. J. Graff has written in the Boston Globe, "the religious right barnstormed the nation warning against 'gay marriage' — with an odd result. For both straight and gay folks, the phrase was transformed from an oxymoron into a real possibility."

Again, most people continue to agree with social conservatives that marriage should be reserved for heterosexual couples. But they do not agree with the premises that underlie that conclusion. The traditional moral argument against homosexual sex has been part of a larger critique of non-marital sex — and, classically, of sex that is not oriented toward procreation within marriage. Social conservatives need no instruction on how the links among sex, procreation, and marriage have been weakened among heterosexuals. They know that many people have adopted what might be called a privatized view of marriage, as an institution whose contours are plastic, whose purpose is to provide emotional satisfaction to the persons concerned, and whose terms are negotiable (and revocable). But they have been slow to see some of the political effects of these social changes.

The logic of the argument against homosexuality now implicates the behavior of a lot of heterosexuals. If the argument is made openly, and cast as a case for traditional sexual morals in general, a large part of the public will flinch. If the argument is made so as to single out gays, the logic vanishes. Social conservatives begin to look as though they are motivated not by principle but by the desire to persecute a minority. If no effective public argument can be made, the prohibition on gay marriage must survive based on tradition and unarticulated reasons. These are weak defenses in a rationalistic and sexually liberated era.

By the mid 1990s, social conservatives increasingly relied on the dialectical argument against gay marriage: the claim that acceptance of it logically requires acceptance of polygamy as well. That argument, as far as I can tell, is sound, and it may be effective in the short run. (In the long run it is as likely to increase support for polygamy as it is to decrease support for gay marriage.) But whatever its effectiveness, resorting to the dialectical argument was a sign of political weakness. It meant that gay marriage was not self-evidently objectionable, but had to be condemned because it would lead to other, more objectionable things. It meant that the argument from definition no longer worked.

At the same time that social conservatives were reaching this dead end, the agenda of gay-rights organizations was changing, too. What, after all, have been gays' great demands in recent years? They have asked for the opportunity to serve in the armed forces, to lead Boy Scout troops, to marry and adopt. Social-conservative rhetoric on homosexuality remained stuck in the 1970s, presenting gays as sexual radicals. Social conservatives were really the last squares. Homosexual groups also embraced the quintessential conservative idea of a fixed human nature. Indeed, they pushed an exaggerated form of that idea: genetic determinism. Many people who would otherwise be disposed to object to homosexuality came to believe that gays and lesbians were "born that way." Gay activists had to be ambivalent about this development, given the subtext: Who would choose to be that

way? A mildly "homophobic" sentiment was recruited to the side of gay rights.

It has been a powerful ally. Genetic determinism has erased the distinction between being and doing — between, that is, identity and behavior. No space has been left in which to love the sinner and hate the sin; objection is discrimination. Justice Scalia's recent attempt to maintain the distinction, to say that a ban on gays' sexual behavior does not discriminate against people on the basis of their (putatively innate) desires, was widely regarded as both hair-splitting and demeaning.

The most effective gay strategy was not a political strategy at all. It was the choice of individuals to identify themselves openly as homosexuals. Scores of millions of Americans now have friends and relatives whom they know are gay. Perhaps as a strict matter of logic, that should not have affected their views on sexual morality. But logic and eros have never been easy bedfellows, have they?

It was perhaps impossible for social conservatives to resist a tide so strong. But their failure was partly of their own making. They were simultaneously too loving and too hateful. The second point is familiar enough to everyone. For the reasons outlined above, persuasive social-conservative rhetoric on gay rights is difficult to devise. But the rhetoric the social Right actually adopted had the additional burden of lending itself to easy caricature as spiteful, harsh, and obsessive — in part because it was not infrequently all of those things. The Religious Right's love for gays, meanwhile, was not the sort that homosexuals could recognize. It took the form of wanting to save their souls. What religious conservatives wanted was for gays to become ex-gays. The unspoken wish of many other conservatives was for gays to re-closet themselves. Neither had any chance of happening in large numbers.

The proposed marriage amendment to the Constitution nicely illustrates the folly and weakness of organized social conservatism. The amendment will probably fail — most proposed constitutional amendments do. But it may very well be the only way to prevent the incremental judicial imposition of gay marriage. One would think that social-conservative groups would be working as hard as they could to enact it. Yet the Catholic bishops' conference is divided about the amendment. The Family Research Council came out against it, and then declared itself neutral. The council objects to the amendment because, among other things, it would not bar a state legislature from creating same-sex civil unions. The failure of judgment here should be an object lesson for students of politics for ages to come.

When the Massachusetts supreme court brings full-fledged gay marriage to an American state for the first time, the issue will heat up. Anyone who expects President Bush's storied quest for the Catholic vote to strengthen the hand of social conservatives has not been looking at the survey data. Catholic World Report recently commissioned a survey that suggested that students at Catholic colleges became more liberal during their time on campus. The freshmen were pro-life, and the seniors pro-choice. What was even more interesting was that a majority of Catholic-college freshmen already favored gay marriage when they got to campus. I suspect that even conservative Catholics who oppose gay marriage are especially sensitive to rhetoric that seems intolerant toward gays as persons.

After Massachusetts, will Republicans find a way to object forcefully to gay marriage and to push for the marriage amendment, without looking intolerant? That would be a tall order even for people who thought deeply about these matters. Social conservatives have not yet lost this battle, and their defeat is not quite inevitable. But that is the way to bet.

PARTY ON, DUDES!

IGNORANCE IS THE CURSE OF THE INFORMATION AGE

BY MATTHEW ROBINSON

Almost any look at what the average citizen knows about politics is bound to be discouraging. Political scientists are nearly unanimous on the subject of voter ignorance. The average American citizen not only lacks basic knowledge, but also holds beliefs that are contradictory and inconsistent. Here is a small sample of what Americans "know":

Nearly one-third of Americans (29 percent) think the Constitution guarantees a job. Forty-two percent think it guarantees health care. And 75 percent think it guarantees a high school education.

Forty-five percent think the communist tenet "from each according to his abilities, to each according to his needs" is part of the U.S. Constitution.

More Americans recognize the Nike advertising slogan "Just Do It" than know where the right to "life, liberty and the pursuit of happiness" is set forth (79 percent versus 47 percent).

Ninety percent know that Bill Gates is the founder of the company that created the Windows operating system. Just over half (53 percent) correctly identified Alexander Hamilton as a Founding Father.

Fewer than half of adults (47 percent) can name their own representative in Congress.

Fewer than half of voters could identify whether their congressman voted for the use of force in the Persian Gulf War.

Just 30 percent of adults could name Newt Gingrich as the congressman who led Republican congressional candidates in signing the Contract with America. Six months after the GOP took congress, 64 percent admitted they did not know.

A 1998 poll by the Pew Research Center for the People and the Press showed that 56 percent of Americans could not name a single Democratic candidate for president; 63 percent knew the name "Bush," but it wasn't clear that voters connected the name to George W. Bush.

According to a January 2000 Gallup poll, 66 percent of Americans could correctly name Regis Philbin when asked who hosts *Who Wants to Be a Millionaire,* but only 6 percent could correctly name Dennis Hastert when asked

to name the speaker of the House of Representatives in Washington.

Political scientists Michael X. Delli Carpini and Scott Keeter studied 3,700 questions surveying the public's political knowledge from the 1930s to the present. They discovered that people tend to remember or identify trivial details about political leaders, focusing on personalities or simply latching onto the politics that the press plays up. For example, the most commonly known fact about George Bush while he was president was that he hated broccoli, and during the 1992 presidential campaign, although 89 percent of the public knew that Vice President Quayle was feuding with the television character Murphy Brown, only 19 percent could characterize Bill Clinton's record on the environment.

Their findings demonstrate the full absurdity of public knowledge: More people could identify Judge Wapner (the long-time host of the television series *The People's Court*) than could identify Chief Justice Warren Burger or William Rehnquist. More people had heard of John Lennon than of Karl Marx. More Americans could identify comedian-actor Bill Cosby than could name either of their U.S. senators. More people knew who said "What's up, Doc;" "Hi ho, Silver;" or "Come up and see me sometime" than "Give me liberty or give me death;" "The only thing we have to fear is fear itself;" or "Speak softly and carry a big stick." More people knew that Pete Rose was accused of gambling than could name any of the five U.S. senators accused in the late 1980s of unethical conduct in the savings and loan scandal.

In 1986, the National Election Survey found that almost 24 percent of the general public did not know who George Bush was or that he was in his second term as vice president of the United States. "People at this level of inattentiveness can have only the haziest idea of the policy alternatives about which pollsters regularly ask, and such ideas as they do have must often be relatively innocent of the effects of exposure to elite discourse," writes UCLA political science professor John R. Zaller.

All of this would appear to be part of a broader trend of public ignorance that extends far beyond politics. Lack of knowledge on simple matters can reach staggering levels. In a 1996 study by the National Science Foundation, fewer than half of American adults polled (47 percent) knew that the earth takes one year to orbit the sun. Only about 9 percent could describe in their own words what a molecule is, and only 21 percent knew what DNA is.

Esoteric information? That's hard to say. One simple science-related question that has grown to have major political importance is whether police ought to genetically tag convicted criminals in the hopes of linking them to unsolved crimes. In other words, should police track the DNA of a convicted burglar to see if he is guilty of other crimes? Obviously, issues of privacy and government power are relevant here. Yet how can a poll about this issue make sense if the citizenry doesn't understand the scientific terms of debate? Asking an evaluative question seems pointless.

The next generation of voters—those who will undoubtedly be asked to answer even tougher questions about politics and science—are hardly doing any better on the basics. A 2000 study by the American Council of Trustees and Alumni found that 81 percent of seniors at the nation's 55 top colleges scored a D or F on high school-level history exams. It turns out that most college seniors—including those from such elite universities as Harvard, Stanford and the University of California—do not know the men or ideas that have shaped American freedom. Here are just a few examples from *Losing America's Memory: Historical Illiteracy in the 21st Century,* focusing on people's lack of knowledge about our First Citizen—the man whose respect for the laws of the infant republic set the standard for virtue and restraint in office.

Barely one in three students knew that George Washington was the American general at the battle of Yorktown—the battle that won the war for independence.

Only 42 percent could identify Washington with the line "First in war, first in peace, first in the hearts of his countrymen."

Only a little more than half knew that Washington's farewell address warned against permanent alliances with foreign governments.

And when it comes to actually explaining the ideas that preserve freedom and restrain government, the college seniors performed just as miserably.

More than one in three were clueless about the division of power set forth in the U.S. Constitution.

Only 22 percent of these seniors could identify the source of the phrase "government of the people, by the people, and for the people" (from Lincoln's Gettysburg Address).

Yet 99 percent of college seniors knew the crude cartoon characters Beavis and Butthead, and 98 percent could identify gangsta rapper Snoop Dogg.

Apparent ignorance of basic civics can be especially dangerous. Americans often "project" power onto institutions with little understanding of the Constitution or the law. Almost six of 10 Americans (59 percent) think the president, not Congress, has the power to declare war. Thirty-five percent of Americans believe the president has the power to adjourn Congress at his will. Almost half (49 percent) think he has the power to suspend the Constitution (49 percent). And six in 10 think the chief executive appoints judges to the federal courts without the approval of the Senate.

Some political scientists charge that American ignorance tends to help institutions and parties in power. That is hardly the active vigilance by the citizenry that the founders advocated. Political scientists continue to debate the role of ignorance and the future of democracy when voters are so woefully ignorant. As journalist Christopher Shea writes, "Clearly, voter ignorance poses problems for democratic theory: Politicians, the representatives of the people, are being elected by people who do not know their names or their platforms. Elites are committing the nation to major treaties and sweeping policies that most voters don't even know exist."

Professors Delli Carpini and Keeter discovered, for example, that most Americans make fundamental errors on some of the most contested and heavily covered political questions. "Americans grossly overestimate the average profit made by American corporations, the percentage of the U.S. population that is poor or homeless, and the percentage of the world population that is malnourished," they write. "And, despite 12 years of anti-abortion administrations, Americans substantially underestimate the number of abortions performed every year."

With most voters unable to even name their congressperson or senators during an election year, the clear winner is the establishment candidate. Studies by Larry Bartels at Princeton University show that mere name rec-

ognition is enough to give incumbents, a 5-percentage-point advantage over challengers: Most voters in the election booth can't identify a single position of the incumbent, but if they've seen the candidate's name before, that can be enough to secure their vote. (In many cases, voters can't even recognize the names of incumbents.)

Media polls are typically searching in vain for hard-nosed public opinion that simply isn't there. Polls force people to say they are leaning toward a particular candidate, but when voters are asked the more open-ended question "Whom do you favor for the presidency?" the number of undecided voters rises. The mere practice, in polling, of naming the candidates yields results that convey a false sense of what voters know. When Harvard's "Vanishing Voter Project" asked voters their presidential preferences without giving the names of candidates, they routinely found that the number of undecided voters was much higher than in media polls. Just three weeks before the 2000 election, 14 percent of voters still hadn't made up their minds.

Even when polling covers subjects on which a person should have direct knowledge, it can yield misleading results because of basic ignorance. The nonpartisan Center for Studying Health System Change (HSC) found that how people rate their health care is attributable to the type of plan they *think* they are in, more than their actual health insurance. The center asked 20,000 privately insured people what they thought of their coverage, their doctor and their treatment. But instead of just taking their opinions and impressions, the center also looked at what coverage each respondent actually had.

Nearly a quarter of Americans mis-identified the coverage they had. Eleven percent didn't know they were in an HMO, and another 13 percent thought they were in an HMO but were *not*. Yet when people believed they were in a much-maligned HMO (even when they actually had another kind of insurance), their perceived satisfaction with their health care was lower than that of people who believed they had non-HMO coverage (even when they were in an HMO). Similarly, on nearly all 10 measures studied by the center, those HMO enrollees who thought they had a different kind of insurance gave satisfaction ratings similar to those who actually had those other kinds of insurance.

Once center researchers adjusted for incorrect self-identification, the differences between HMO and non-HMO enrollees nearly vanished. Even on something as personal as health care, citizens display a striking and debilitating ignorance that quietly undermines many polling results.

After looking at the carnage of polls that test voter knowledge rather than impressions, James L. Payne concluded in his 1991 book *The Culture of Spending:*

> Surveys have repeatedly found that voters are remarkably ignorant about even simple, dramatic features of the political landscape. The

vast majority of voters cannot recall the names of congressional candidates in the most recent election; they cannot use the labels "liberal" and "conservative" meaningfully; they do not know which party controls Congress; they are wildly wrong about elementary facts about the federal budget; and they do not know how their congressmen vote on even quite salient policy questions. In other words, they are generally incapable of rewarding or punishing their congressman for his action on spending bills.

Ignorance of basic facts such as a candidate's name or position isn't the only reason to question the efficacy of polling in such a dispiriting universe. Because polls have become "players in the political process," their influence is felt in the policy realm, undercutting efforts to educate because they assume respondents' knowledge and focus on the horse race. Is it correct to say that Americans oppose or support various policies when they don't even have a grasp of basic facts relating to those policies? For instance, in 1995, Grass Roots Research found that 83 percent of those polled underestimated the average family's tax burden. Taxes for a four-person family earning $35,000 are 54 percent higher than most people think. Naturally, when practical-minded Americans look at political issues, their perceptions of reality influence which solutions they find acceptable. If they perceive that there are fewer abortions or lower taxes than there really are, these misperceptions may affect the kinds of policy prescriptions they endorse. They might change their views if introduced to the facts. In this sense, the unreflective reporting on public opinion about these policy issues is deceptive.

The Wall Street Journal editorial page provides another example of how ignorance affects public debate. Media reports during the 1995 struggle between the Republicans in Congress and the Clinton White House continually asserted that the public strongly opposed the GOP's efforts to slow the growth of Medicare spending. A poll by Public Opinion Strategies asked 1,000 Americans not what they felt, but what they actually *knew* about the GOP plan. Twenty-seven percent said they thought the GOP would cut Medicare spending by $4,000 per recipient. Almost one in four (24 percent) said it would keep spending the same. Another 25 percent didn't know. Only 22 percent knew the correct answer: The plan would increase spending to $6,700 per recipient.

Public Opinion's pollsters then told respondents the true result of the GOP plan and explained: "[U]nder the plan that recently passed by Congress, spending on Medicare will increase 45 percent over the next seven years, which is twice the projected rate of inflation." How did such hard facts change public opinion about Medicare solutions? Six of 10 Americans said that the GOP's proposed Medicare spending was too *high*. Another 29 percent said it was about right. Only 2 percent said it was too *low*.

Indeed polling and the media may gain their ability to influence results from voter ignorance. When a polling question introduces new facts (or any facts at all), voters are presented with a reframed political issue and thus may have a new opinion. Voters are continually asked about higher spending, new programs, and the best way to solve social ills with government spending. But how does the knowledge base (or lack of knowledge) affect the results of a polling question? That is simply unknown. When asked in a June 2000 *Washington Post* poll how much money the federal government gives to the nation's public schools, only 31 percent chose the correct answer. Although only 10 percent admitted to not knowing the correct answer, fully 60 percent of registered voters claimed they knew, but were wrong. Is there any doubt that voters' knowledge, or lack thereof, affects the debate about whether to raise school spending to ever higher levels?

Reporters often claim that the public supports various policies, and they use such sentiment as an indicator of the electoral prospects of favored candidates. But this, too, can be misleading. Take, for instance, the results of a survey taken by The Polling Company for the Center for Security Policy about the Strategic Defense Initiative. Some 54 percent of respondents thought that the U.S. military had the capability to destroy a ballistic missile before it could hit an American city and do damage. Another 20 percent didn't know or refused to answer. Only 27 percent correctly said that the U.S. military could not destroy a missile.

What's interesting is that although 70 percent of those polled said they were concerned about the possibility of ballistic missile attack, the actual level of ignorance was very high. The Polling Company went on to tell those polled that "government documents indicate that the U.S. military cannot destroy even a single incoming missile." The responses were interesting. Nearly one in five said they were "shocked and angry" by the revelation. Another 28 percent said they were "very surprised," and 17 percent were "somewhat surprised." Only 22 percent said they were "not surprised at all." Finally, 14 percent were "skeptical because [they] believe that the documents are inaccurate."

Beyond simply skewing poll results, ignorance is actually amplified by polling. Perhaps the most amazing example of the extent of ignorance can be found in Larry Sabato's 1981 book *The Rise of Political Consultants*. Citizens were asked: "Some people say the 1975 Public Affairs Act should be repealed. Do you agree or disagree that it should be repealed?" Nearly one in four (24 percent) said they wanted it repealed. Another 19 percent wanted it to remain in effect. Fifty-seven percent didn't know what should be done. What's interesting is that there was no such thing as the 1975 Public Affairs Act. But

for 43 percent of those polled, simply asking that question was enough to create public opinion.

Ignorance can threaten even the most democratic institutions and safeguards. In September 1997, the Center for Media and Public Affairs conducted one of the largest surveys ever on American views of the Fourth Estate. Fully 84 percent of Americans are willing to "turn to the government to require that the news media give equal coverage to all sides of controversial issues." Seven-in-10 back court-imposed fines for inaccurate or biased reporting. And just over half (53 percent) think that journalists should be licensed. Based on sheer numbers—in the absence of the rule of law and dedication to the Bill of Rights—there is enough support to put curbs on the free speech that most journalists (rightly) consider one of the most important bulwarks of liberty.

In an era when Americans have neither the time nor the interest to track politics closely, the power of the pollster to shape public opinion is almost unparalleled when united with the media agenda.

For elected leaders, voter ignorance is something they have to confront when they attempt to make a case for new policies or reforms. But for the media, ignorance isn't an obstacle. It's an opportunity for those asking the questions—whether pollster or media polling director—to drive debate. As more time is devoted to media pundits, journalists and pollsters, and less to candidates and leaders, the effect is a negative one: Public opinion becomes more important as arbiter for the chattering classes. But in a knowledge vacuum, public opinion also becomes more plastic and more subject to manipulation, however well intentioned.

Pollsters often try to bridge the gap in public knowledge by providing basic definitions of terms as part of their questions. But this presents a new problem: By writing the questions, pollsters are put in a position of power, particularly when those questions will be used in a media story. The story—if the poll is the story—is limited by the questions asked, the definitions supplied, and the answers that respondents are given to choose from.

The elevation of opinion without context or reference to knowledge exacerbates a problem of modern democracies. Self-expression may work in NEA-funded art, but it robs the political process of the communication and discussion that marries compromise with principle. Clearly "opinion" isn't the appropriate word for the mélange of impressions and sentiment that is presented as the public's belief in countless newspaper and television stories. If poll respondents lack a solid grasp of the facts, surveys give us little more than narcissistic opinion.

As intelligent and precise thinking declines, all that remains is a chaos of ideologies in which the lowest human appetites rule. In her essay "Truth and Politics," historian Hannah Arendt writes: "Facts inform opinions, and opinions, inspired by different interests and passions, can differ widely and still be legitimate as long as they respect factual truth. Freedom of opinion is a farce unless factual information is guaranteed and facts themselves are not in dispute."

If ignorance is rife in a republic, what do polls and the constant media attention to them do to deliberative democracy? As Hamilton put it, American government is based on "reflection and choice." Modern-day radical egalitarians—journalists and pollsters who believe that polls are the definitive voice of the people—may applaud the ability of the most uninformed citizen to be heard, but few if any of these champions of polling ever write about or discuss the implications of ignorance to a representative democracy. This is the dirtiest secret of polling.

Absent from most polling stories is the honest disclosure that American ignorance is driving public affairs. Basic ignorance of civic questions gives us reason to doubt the veracity of most polls. Were Americans armed with strongly held opinions and well-grounded knowledge of civic matters, they would not be open to manipulation by the wording of polls. This is one of the strongest reasons to question the effect of polls on representative government.

Pollsters assume and often control the presentation of the relevant facts. As a blunt instrument, the pollster's questions fail to explore what the contrary data may be. This is one reason that public opinion can differ so widely from one poll to another. When the citizens of a republic lack basic knowledge of political facts and cannot process ideas critically, uninformed opinion becomes even more potent in driving people. Worse, when the media fail to think critically about the lines of dispute on political questions, polls that are supposed to explore opinion will simplify and even mislead political leaders as well as the electorate.

When the media drives opinion by constant polling, the assumption of an educated public undermines the process of public deliberation that actually educates voters. Ideas are no longer honed, language isn't refined, and debate is truncated. The common ground needed for compromise and peaceful action is eroded because the discussion about facts and the parameters of the question are lost. In the frenzy to judge who wins and who loses, the media erodes what it is to be a democracy. Moments of change become opportunities for spin, not for new, bold responses to the exigencies of history.

Not only are polls influenced, shaped, and even dominated by voter ignorance, but so is political debate. The evidence shows that ignorance is being projected into public debate because of the pervasiveness of polls. Polls are leading to the democratization of ignorance in the public square by ratifying ill-formed opinions, with the march of the mob instigated by an impatient and unreflective media. Polls—especially in an age marked by their proliferation—are serving as broadcasting towers of ignorance.

Political science professor Rogan Kersh notes, "Public ignorance and apathy toward most policy matters have been constant (or have grown worse) for over three decades. Yet the same period has seen increasing reliance on finely tuned instruments for measuring popular opinion and more vigorous applications of the results in policy making." And here is the paradox in the Age of Polls: Pollsters and political scientists are still unclear about the full consequences of running a republic on the basis of opinion polls. The cost of voter ignorance is high, especially in a nation with a vast and sprawling government that, even for the most plugged-in elites, is too complicated to understand. Media polling that does not properly inform viewers and readers of its limitations serves only to give the façade of a healthy democracy, while consultants, wordsmiths and polling units gently massage questions, set the news agenda and then selectively report results. It is like the marionette player who claims (however visible the strings) that the puppet moves on his own.

This article is adapted from Mobocracy: How the Media's Obsession with Polling Twists the News, Alters Elections and Undermines Democracy, *by Matthew Robinson.*

Matthew Robinson is managing editor of Human Events.

Federalism's Ups and Downs

It's pretty much agreed that devolution has waned, and there are considerable pressures for centralization. What's not clear, is why.

By Carl Tubbesing

Cable TV Program Note

Debate on the Federalism Channel has intensified over erosion of state authority. In last night's program, Alexander Hamilton argued that one necessary consequence of the war on terrorism—or any war—is centralization of power with the national government. "Balderdash," retorted a panelist looking eerily like Franklin Roosevelt. "It's the economy, stupid. The federal government has to take charge when the economy falters." Benjamin Franklin argued that the trend toward weakening of state authority is systemic and was well under way before the terrorism attacks or the recession.

The Federalism Channel has gradually expanded its niche viewership with use of stand-ins for historical figures, state capitol "Jeopardy" and live auctions of Thomas Jefferson and John Adams bobble head dolls. Tonight's programming will be highlighted by a rare, behind-the-scenes look at the presidency of Millard Fillmore, the only president, according to '60's humorist Stan Freeberg, who was born with a clock in his stomach.

Which of our historical talking heads is right? What accounts for the recent slippage of the states in the federalism standings? Is it Alexander Hamilton, our founding father's staunchest advocate for a strong, national government? What about Franklin Roosevelt, who, by most accounts, had to overcome his own caution about central-

izing power before launching the New Deal and shifting the federalism center of gravity toward Washington, D.C.? Or is it Benjamin Franklin, renowned early American curmudgeon and contrarian? Let's take a look at some recent history first, and then we'll look at our panelists' arguments.

Two more recent figures—Bill Clinton and Newt Gingrich—are helpful in understanding current federalism history. Bill Clinton was elected president in 1992. As Arkansas governor, he had been a leader in the National Governors' Association and a believer in state innovation and experimentation. Like many state legislators and governors during the late 1980s and early 1990s, Clinton bristled at the implied arrogance of one-size-fits-all federal solutions. And like other state officials, he railed against unfunded federal mandates and cost shifts from federal to state governments.

In his first months as president, Clinton met frequently with state legislators and governors and was sympathetic to their pleas about restoring balance in the federal system. In October 1993, the president issued an executive order that told federal agencies to stop imposing unfunded mandates on state and local governments. That action proved to be the first of several steps taken during the 1990s that freed states to craft their own solutions to policy challenges.

The next steps followed the Republican takeover of Congress in 1994. Congressman Newt Gingrich and other Republican strategists orchestrated a national campaign around the Contract with America, a public relations gem, that, among other things, promised to end federal unfunded mandates and to devolve power to state governments.

The combination of a Republican congressional majority committed to devolution, a New Democrat, former governor as president and the lobbying clout of NCSL [National Conference of State Legislatures] and other state and local groups resulted in a series of new laws that dramatically shifted responsibilities to state governments.

This devolution litany included the Unfunded Mandate Reform Act, the welfare reform act, a major revision of the safe drinking water act, surface transportation legislation, a new children's health law, changes to Medicaid and protection of tobacco settlement funds. State legislatures assured their prominent role in devolution by securing language in several 1990s laws that guarantees legislatures the ability to appropriate federal block grant money.

Our three stand-in panelists, though, appear to accept the premise that devolution has waned—or, at least, that there are still considerable pressures for centralization. Secretary Hamilton, President Roosevelt and Ambassador Franklin differ, though, in their explanations. It's a bit audacious, but let's see if we can figure out who is correct.

WAR AS THE CENTRALIZING FORCE

Our Alexander Hamilton impersonator bases his claim on history. When the United States has gone to war, power has gravitated dramatically toward the federal government. The federal government did not just mobilize the armed forces for World War II, it mobilized the country. It established gasoline and tire rationing. It established wage and price controls. Congress found a major source of revenue and power when it used the income tax to finance World War I.

President Truman seized the steel mills during the Korean conflict. President Lincoln suspended writs of habeas corpus during the Civil War.

The war on terrorism, though, is being waged not just in Afghanistan. It's being fought in our own country as well with its well-established federalism structure and recent history of devolution and with hundreds of law enforcement agencies at all levels of government being enlisted in the war for homeland security. There has not been as much centralization as Mr. Hamilton would expect.

Actions so far have, in fact, shown some, though not complete, deference to state and local governments. The new aviation security law allows states to use grant money for airport security. That is greater flexibility than they had before. The aviation security law federalizes baggage and passenger screening. It also provides for demonstration projects at five airports to let state and local law enforcement agencies or private companies handle security. Major proposed legislation on bioterrorism in the Senate would use block grants to states as its funding mechanism—the no-strings-attached approach that state legislators normally prefer.

Anti-terrorism bills that would directly preempt state laws so far have not passed. At the end of last year, the House was considering legislation to protect insurance companies against losses caused by terrorist attacks. That bill would also preempt some state tort law provisions and some of their authority to regulate insurance, both traditional areas of state purview.

Tom Ridge, director of Homeland Security, has called for a strong state-federal partnership to combat terrorism. Officials at all levels point out the need for greater coordination among law enforcement agencies. The U.S. Conference of Mayors, for example, has endorsed legislation that would enable the FBI and other federal agencies to share more information with state and local police officials. "America is under attack," says New Orleans Mayor Marc Morial, "and our nation's police forces must be fully integrated into our national homeland defense effort."

New York Senator Steve Saland, NCSL's president, supports these calls for greater cooperation and puts them in a federalism context. "We have a law enforcement network that works reasonably well. Our approach is really reflective of our federal system and the sharing of responsibilities among the three levels of government. No one is now advocating centralization of law enforcement with the federal government. What is needed is better coordination."

Panelist Hamilton probably won't concede his point. But he might admit that his case is not as strong regarding this war on terrorism as it has been in previous wars. The country is mobilized in the war against terrorism. It would appear, though, to be a cooperative effort, rather than one in which the federal government's authority is enhanced at the expense of the states.

THE RECESSION AND FEDERALISM

Panelist Roosevelt, always an imposing personality, says he knows why the states' influence has waned recently.

When the economy slows, he argues, the federal government has to step in to get it back on track. The federal government has many tools to do this. It can lower interest rates; it can cut taxes; and it can spend money. The states are more constrained in what they can do to help. In fact, the requirements that states have balanced budgets often forces them into policy decisions that actually exacerbate the economic downturn. They may have to raise taxes when cutting them could help the economy. They may have to cut funding just when more spending might create jobs and encourage economic activity.

Congressional and administration proposals to stimulate the economy surfaced immediately after the terrorist attacks. Debate, posturing and negotiations over the proposals dragged well into December and eventually broke down. The conflict over economic stimulus revealed classic, philosophical fissures between Republicans and Democrats. But the debate, less conspicuously perhaps, also demonstrated tensions in the federal system.

"State legislators understood that some of the recovery proposals were better for the states than others," notes Saland. "Some, in fact, would actually be harmful. Good intentions at the national level do not necessarily translate into benefits for the states."

One major proposal that would have been included in a final package would have done considerable harm to the states. Negotiators rejected several proposals that state officials had advanced.

The economic stimulus proposal most damaging for states was an accelerated depreciation schedule for business investments. Supported by both Republicans and Democrats in Congress and the administration, this proposal would actually have caused revenue losses for state governments as high as $15 billion over the next three years—at a time when their budgets are already reeling from the recession. The reason? Most states tie their business depreciation to the federal schedule. A change in the federal structure means a change in state schedules.

Most of the proposals that would have been sensitive to state concerns were not included in 11th hour negotiations. State officials liked those that freed them of financial obligations, made tax changes without affecting states or sent new federal money in their direction. NCSL, for example, supported a plan offered by New Mexico Senator Pete Domenici that would have created a month-long federal payroll tax holiday. For a month, employees and employers would stop making their FICA (Social Security) contributions. Employers—including state governments—would save money and employees would have bigger paychecks. Both outcomes would generate economic activity. Negotiators flirted with the Domenici proposal, but eventually dropped it.

The National Governors Association made changes in Medicaid matching rates its biggest economic stimulus priority. The governors' organization likened reductions in state Medicaid spending to revenue sharing. The Bush administration and congressional negotiators rejected this plan as cumbersome, expensive and politically unfeasible.

NCSL leaders argued for tax rebates for individuals instead of permanent changes to the income tax code. Negotiators, instead, opted for a reduction in one of the middle income tax brackets—a change that would substantially reduce revenues in states that link their income tax system to the federal one.

Panelist No. 2, our FDR look-alike, claims he has won the argument—that is that the center of federalism gravity moves toward the national government when the economy is weak. "What would the states have gotten out of that stimulus package?" he wonders. "Not much. If anything, their budgets would have been in worse shape because of the changes in the federal tax code." He's willing, though, to give Ben Franklin a chance.

IT'S NOT THE WAR, IT'S NOT THE RECESSION

Remember, the Federalism Channel's Ben Franklin asserts that the recent waning of state authority was well under way before the economy faltered and the nation went to war against terrorism.

"It doesn't take Poor Richard to figure out that we created a system in Philadelphia that was always going to be in tension. The states made great progress in the mid-'90s. I loved devolution! But even then, there were pressures in the other direction. The economy has changed. Technology has changed. Politics have changed. Unfunded mandates are making a comeback; and preemption never went away." Hold on to your lorgnette, Mr. Roosevelt. Ambassador Franklin may have a point.

One of Congress's last major actions of 2001 was to approve the conference agreement on reauthorization of the Elementary and Secondary Education Act. The year began with President Bush and Congress making education reform their top priority. Passage of the ESEA legislation, the vehicle for the reform proposals, gave Congress and the president, Republicans and Democrats, a major accomplishment unrelated to either the war on terrorism or economic recovery. The new law, though, is not without detractors, including state legislators who worry about its assertion of an imposing, new role for the federal government in an area traditionally reserved for the states.

"It's a federalism double-whammy," claims Virginia Delegate Jim Dillard. "The bill preempts state laws on accountability, standards, testing and data collection. And it threatens to be a huge unfunded mandate."

State legislators were particularly disappointed that House conferees thwarted an amendment that would have forced the federal government finally to live up to a 1976 agreement to fund 40 percent of the costs of special education.

NCSL calls this a $16 billion unfunded federal mandate that remains the single most intractable education issue states face in their attempt to improve the performance of their schools.

State legislators were not alone in their disappointment. Vermont Senator Jim Jeffords left the Republican party earlier this year over a dispute about special education funding. His response to the ESEA conference agreement? "The resources are not there to make this bill work."

Last spring—before Sept. 11, before the recession—Congress and the president agreed to a $1.35 trillion tax cut package. Repeal of the federal estate tax was a key feature. The bargain struck over the tax also eliminated the state pick-up tax, a long-standing provision of the tax code that lets states take a dollar-for-dollar credit against the federal liability for state estate taxes paid. The new law gradually repeals the federal estate tax over 10 years. Yet it eliminates the state estate tax credit by FY 2005.

"This sounds harmless," notes California Senator Jim Costa. "The effect on state revenues, though, isn't. States will lose as much as $65 billion because of this change."

One important congressional battle of 2001 was fought to a federalism draw. State and local officials had worked for more than a year with members of the Senate, including North Dakota Senator Byron Dorgan and Wyoming Senator Mike Enzi, to craft legislation that would allow state and local governments to collect taxes on Internet sales. Their intent was to link this authorization to legislation that would extend a moratorium on taxation of Internet access fees.

When negotiations faltered, state legislators, led by Tennessee Representative Matt Kisber and Illinois Senator Steve Rauschenberger, choreographed an alternative that extends the moratorium on taxation of access fees for two years.

"This extension carries with it the implicit understanding and hope that the states themselves can finalize their own system for collecting taxes on Internet sales," says Kisber.

"Though not ideal by any means," Rauschenberger says, "this alternative was far preferable to the federally imposed solution that had been developed."

Preoccupation with terrorism and economic recovery delayed consideration of several other bills with significant implications for federalism. The patients' bill of rights that stalled in conference committee would preempt numerous state laws that govern managed care.

Proposed energy bills would preempt the states' authority to locate transmission lines. Another bill under consideration at the end of the session could preempt state and local authority to regulate new broadband technology.

IS BEN FRANKLIN RIGHT?

Although the session produced a few clear successes for state governments—including pension portability legislation and House approval of election reform legislation that NCSL helped develop—the overall report card for 2001 gives considerable support to Mr. Franklin's argument. There are substantial pressures right now in our federal system for centralization—pressures that had surfaced well before the terrorist attacks and the recession.

Before we let Mr. Franklin celebrate, though, we should caution him to remember the insight of another well-known aphorist: "It ain't over 'til it's over." States will be tested again this year as Congress and the president take up unfinished business, such as election reform and broadband legislation, and as they move on to other significant issues, including welfare reform and surface transportation reauthorization. It promises a year full of lively debate and entertainment on the Federalism Channel. Stay tuned.

Carl Tubbesing, NCSL's deputy executive director, heads the Washington, D.C., office.

Rights, Liberties, AND Security

Recalibrating the Balance after September 11

by Stuart Taylor, Jr.

When dangers increase, liberties shrink. That has been our history, especially in wartime. And today we face dangers without precedent: a mass movement of militant Islamic terrorists who crave martyrdom, hide in shadows, are fanatically bent on slaughtering as many of us as possible and—if they can—using nuclear truck bombs to obliterate New York or Washington or both, without leaving a clue as to the source of the attack.

How can we avert catastrophe and hold down the number of lesser mass murders? Our best hope is to prevent al-Qaida from getting nuclear, biological, or chemical weapons and smuggling them into this country. But we need be unlucky only once to fail in that. Ultimately we can hold down our casualties only by finding and locking up (or killing) as many as possible of the hundreds or thousands of possible al-Qaida terrorists whose strategy is to infiltrate our society and avoid attention until they strike.

The urgency of penetrating secret terrorist cells makes it imperative for Congress—and the nation—to undertake a candid, searching, and systematic reassessment of the civil liberties rules that restrict the government's core investigative and detention powers. Robust national debate and deliberate congressional action should replace what has so far been largely ad hoc presidential improvisation. While the USA-PATRIOT Act—no model of careful deliberation—changed many rules for the better (and some for the worse), it did not touch some others that should be changed.

Carefully crafted new legislation would be good not only for security but also for liberty. Stubborn adherence to the civil liberties status quo would probably damage our most fundamental freedoms far more in the long run than would judicious modifications of rules that are less fundamental. Considered congressional action based on open national debate is more likely to be sensitive to civil liberties and to the Constitution's checks and balances than unilateral expansion of executive power. Courts are more likely to check executive excesses if Congress sets limits for them to enforce. Government agents are more likely to respect civil liberties if freed from rules that create unwarranted obstacles to doing their jobs. And preventing terrorist mass murders is the best way of avoiding a panicky stampede into truly oppressive police statism, in which measures now unthinkable could suddenly become unstoppable.

This is not to advocate truly radical revisions of civil liberties. Nor is it to applaud all the revisions that have already been made, some of which seem unwarranted and even dangerous. But unlike most in-depth commentaries on the liberty-security balance since September 11—which argue (plausibly, on some issues) that we have gone too far in expanding government power—this article contends that in important respects we have not gone far enough. Civil libertarians have underestimated the need for broader investigative powers and exaggerated the dangers to our fundamental liberties. Judicious expansion of the government's powers to find suspected terrorists would be less dangerous to freedom than either risking possibly preventable attacks or resorting to incarceration without due process of law—as the Bush administration has begun to do. We should worry less about being wiretapped or searched or spied upon or interrogated and more about seeing innocent people put behind bars—or about being blown to bits.

Recalibrating the Liberty-Security Balance

The courts, Congress, the president, and the public have from the beginning of this nation's history demarcated the scope of protected rights "by a weighing of competing interests... the public-safety interest and the liberty interest," in the words of Judge Richard A. Posner of the U.S. Court of Appeals for the Seventh Circuit. "The safer the nation feels, the more weight judges will be willing to give to the liberty interest."

During the 1960s and 1970s, the weight on the public safety side of the scales seemed relatively modest. The isolated acts of violence by groups like the Weather Underground and Black Panthers—which had largely run their course by the mid-1970s—were a minor threat compared with our enemies today. Suicide bombers were virtually unheard of. By contrast, the threat to civil liberties posed by broad governmental investigative and detention powers and an imperial presidency had been dramatized by Watergate and by disclosures of such ugly abuses of power as FBI Director J. Edgar Hoover's spying on politicians, his wiretapping and harassment of the Rev. Martin Luther King, Jr., and the government's disruption and harassment of antiwar and radical groups.

To curb such abuses, the Supreme Court, Congress, and the Ford and Carter administrations placed tight limits on law enforcement and intelligence agencies. The Court consolidated and in some ways extended the Warren Court's revolutionary restrictions on government powers to search, seize, wiretap, interrogate, and detain suspected criminals (and terrorists). It also barred warrantless wiretaps and searches of domestic radicals. Congress barred warrantless wiretaps and searches of suspected foreign spies and terrorists—a previously untrammeled presidential power—in the 1978 Foreign Intelligence Surveillance Act. And Edward Levi, President Ford's attorney general, clamped down on domestic surveillance by the FBI.

> We are stuck in habits of mind that have not yet fully processed how dangerous our world has become or how ill-prepared our legal regime is to meet the new dangers.

As a result, today many of the investigative powers that government could use to penetrate al-Qaida cells—surveillance, informants, searches, seizures, wiretaps, arrests, interrogations, detentions—are tightly restricted by a web of laws, judicial precedents, and administrative rules. Stalked in our homeland by the deadliest terrorists in history, we are armed with investigative powers calibrated largely for dealing with drug dealers, bank robbers, burglars, and ordinary murderers. We are also stuck in habits of mind that have not yet fully processed how dangerous our world has become or how ill-prepared our legal regime is to meet the new dangers.

Rethinking Government's Powers

Only a handful of the standard law-enforcement investigative techniques have much chance of penetrating and defanging groups like al-Qaida. The four most promising are: infiltrating them through informants and undercover agents; finding them and learning their plans through surveillance, searches, and wiretapping; detaining them before they can launch terrorist attacks; and interrogating those detained. All but the first (infiltration) are now so tightly restricted by Supreme Court precedents (sometimes by mistaken or debatable readings of them), statutes, and administrative rules as to seriously impede terrorism investigators. Careful new legislation could make these powers more flexible and useful while simultaneously setting boundaries to minimize overuse and abuse.

Searches and Surveillance

The Supreme Court's case law involving the Fourth Amendment's ban on "unreasonable searches and seizures" does not distinguish clearly between a routine search for stolen goods or marijuana and a preventive search for a bomb or a vial of anthrax. To search a dwelling, obtain a wiretap, or do a thorough search of a car or truck, the government must generally have "probable cause"—often (if incorrectly) interpreted in the more-probable-than-not sense—to believe that the proposed search will uncover evidence of crime. These rules make little sense when the purpose of the search is to prevent mass murder.

Federal agents and local police alike need more specific guidance than the Supreme Court can quickly supply. Congress should provide it, in the form of legislation relaxing for terrorism investigations the restrictions on searching, seizing, and wiretapping, including the undue stringency of the burden of proof to obtain a search warrant in a terrorism investigation.

Search and seizure restrictions were the main (if widely unrecognized) cause of the FBI's famous failure to seek a warrant during the weeks before September 11 to search the computer and other possessions of Zacarias Moussaoui, the alleged "20th hijacker." He had been locked up since August 16, technically for overstaying his visa, based on a tip about his strange behavior at a Minnesota flight school. The FBI had ample reason to suspect that Moussaoui—who has since admitted to being a member of al-Qaida—was a dangerous Islamic militant plotting airline terrorism.

Congressional and journalistic investigations of the Moussaoui episode have focused on the intelligence agencies' failure to put together the Moussaoui evidence with other intelligence reports that should have alerted them that a broad plot to hijack airliners might be afoot. Investigators have virtually ignored the undue stringency of the legal restraints on the government's powers to investigate suspected terrorists. Until these are fixed, they will seriously hobble our intelligence agencies no matter how smart they are.

From the time of FDR until 1978, the government could have searched Moussaoui's possessions without judicial permission, by invoking the president's inherent power to collect intelligence about foreign enemies. But the 1978 Foreign Intelligence Security Act (FISA) bars searches of suspected foreign spies and terrorists unless the attorney general could obtain a warrant from a special national security court (the FISA court). The warrant application has to show not only that the target is a foreign terrorist, but also that he is a member of some international terrorist "group."

Coleen Rowley, a lawyer in the FBI's Minneapolis office, argued passionately in a widely publicized letter last May 21 to FBI Director Robert S. Mueller III that the information about Moussaoui satisfied this FISA requirement. Congressional investigators have said the same. FBI headquarters officials have disagreed, because before September 11 no evidence linked Moussaoui to al-Qaida or any other identifiable terrorist group. Unlike their critics, the FBI headquarters officials were privy to any relevant prior decisions by the FISA court, which cloaks its proceedings and decisions in secrecy. In addition, they were understandably gun-shy about going forward with a legally shaky warrant application in the wake of the FISA court's excoriation of an FBI supervisor in the fall of 2000 for perceived improprieties in his warrant applications. In any event, even if the FBI had done everything right, it was and is at least debatable whether its information about Moussaoui was enough to support a FISA warrant.

More important for future cases, it is clear that FISA—even as amended by the USA-PATRIOT Act—would not authorize a warrant in any case in which the FBI cannot tie a suspected foreign terrorist to one or more confederates, whether because his confederates have escaped detection or cannot be identified or because the suspect is a lone wolf.

Congress could strengthen the hand of FBI terrorism investigators by amending FISA to include the commonsense presumption that any foreign terrorist who comes to the United States is probably acting for (or at least inspired by) some international terrorist group. Another option would be to lower the burden of proof from "probable cause" to "reasonable suspicion." A third option—which could be extended to domestic as well as international terrorism investigations—would be to authorize a warrantless "preventive" search or wiretap of anyone the government has reasonable grounds to suspect of preparing or helping others prepare for a terrorist attack. To minimize any temptation for government agents to use this new power in pursuit of ordinary criminal suspects, Congress could prohibit the use in any prosecution unrelated to terrorism of any evidence obtained by such a preventive search or wiretap.

The Supreme Court seems likely to uphold any such statute as consistent with the ban on "unreasonable searches and seizures." While the Fourth Amendment says that "no warrants shall issue, but upon probable cause," warrants are not required for many types of searches, are issued for administrative searches of commercial property without probable cause in the traditional sense, and arguably should never be required. Even in the absence of a warrant or probable cause, the justices have upheld searches based on "reasonable suspicion" of criminal activities, including brief "stop-and-frisk" encounters on the streets and car

stops. They have also upheld mandatory drug-testing of certain government employees and transportation workers whose work affects the public safety even when there is no particularized suspicion at all. In the latter two cases, the Court suggested that searches designed to prevent harm to the public safety should be easier to justify than searches seeking evidence for criminal cases.

Exaggerated Fear of Big Brother

Proposals to increase the government's wiretapping powers awaken fears of unleashing Orwellian thought police to spy on, harass, blackmail, and smear political dissenters and others. Libertarians point out that most conversations overheard and e-mails intercepted in the war on terrorism will be innocent and that the tappers and buggers will overhear intimacies and embarrassing disclosures that are none of the government's business.

Such concerns argue for taking care to broaden wiretapping and surveillance powers only as much as seems reasonable to prevent terrorist acts. But broader wiretapping authority is not all bad for civil liberties. It is a more accurate and benign method of penetrating terrorist cells than the main alternative, which is planting and recruiting informers—a dangerous, ugly, and unreliable business in which the government is already free to engage without limit. The narrower the government's surveillance powers, the more it will rely on informants.

Moreover, curbing the government's power to collect information through wiretapping is not the only way to protect against misuse of the information. Numerous other safeguards less damaging to the counterterrorism effort—inspectors general, the Justice Department's Office of Professional Responsibility, congressional investigators, a gaggle of liberal and conservative civil liberties groups, and the news media—have become extremely potent. The FBI has very little incentive to waste time and resources on unwarranted snooping.

To keep the specter of Big Brother in perspective, it's worth recalling that the president had unlimited power to wiretap suspected foreign spies and terrorists un-

til 1978 (when FISA was adopted); if this devastated privacy or liberty, hardly anyone noticed. It's also worth noting that despite the government's already-vast power to comb through computerized records of our banking and commercial transactions and much else that we do in the computer age, the vast majority of the people who have seen their privacy or reputations shredded have not been wronged by rogue officials. They have been wronged by media organizations, which do far greater damage to far more people with far less accountability.

Nineteen years ago, in *The Rise of the Computer State*, David Burnham wrote: "The question looms before us: Can the United States continue to flourish and grow in an age when the physical movements, individual purchases, conversations and meetings of every citizen are constantly under surveillance by private companies and government agencies?" It can. It has. And now that the computer state has risen indeed, the threat of being watched by Big Brother or smeared by the FBI seems a lot smaller than the threat of being blown to bits or poisoned by terrorists.

The Case for Coercive Interrogation

The same Zacarias Moussaoui whose possessions would have been searched but for FISA's undue stringency also epitomizes another problem: the perverse impact of the rules—or what are widely assumed to be the rules—restricting interrogations of suspected terrorists.

"We were prevented from even attempting to question Moussaoui on the day of the attacks when, in theory, he could have possessed further information about other co-conspirators," Coleen Rowley complained in a little-noticed portion of her May 21 letter to Mueller. The reason was that Moussaoui had requested a lawyer. To the FBI that meant that any further interrogation would violate the Fifth Amendment "*Miranda* rules" laid down by the Supreme Court in 1966 and subsequent cases.

It's not hard to imagine such rules (or such an interpretation) leading to the loss of countless lives. While interrogating Moussaoui on September 11 might not have yielded any useful information, suppose that he had been part of a team planning a second wave of hijackings later in September and that his resistance could have been cracked. Or suppose that the FBI learns tomorrow, from a wiretap, that another al-Qaida team is planning an imminent attack and arrests an occupant of the wiretapped apartment.

We all know the drill. Before asking any questions, FBI agents (and police) must warn the suspect: "You have a right to remain silent." And if the suspect asks for a lawyer, all interrogation must cease until the lawyer arrives (and tells the suspect to keep quiet). This seems impossible to justify when dealing with people suspected of planning mass murder. But it's the law, isn't it?

Actually, it's not the law, though many judges think it is, along with most lawyers, federal agents, police, and cop-show mavens. You do *not* have a right to remain silent. The most persuasive interpretation of the Constitution and the Supreme Court's precedents is that agents and police are free to interrogate any suspect without *Miranda* warnings; to spurn requests for a lawyer; to press hard for answers; and—at least in a terrorism investigation—perhaps even to use hours of interrogation, verbal abuse, isolation, blindfolds, polygraph tests, death-penalty threats, and other forms of psychological coercion short of torture or physical brutality. Maybe even truth serum.

The Fifth Amendment self-incrimination clause says only that no person "shall be compelled in any criminal case to be a witness against himself." The clause prohibits forcing a defendant to testify at his trial and also making him a witness against himself indirectly by using compelled pretrial statements. It does not prohibit compelling a suspect to talk. *Miranda* held only that in determining whether a defendant's statements (and information derived from them) may be used against him at his trial, courts must treat all interrogations of arrested suspects as inherently coercive unless the warnings are given.

Courts typically ignore this distinction because in almost every litigated case the issue is whether a criminal defendant's incriminating statements should be suppressed at his trial; there is

no need to focus on whether the constitutional problem is the conduct of the interrogation, or the use at trial of evidence obtained, or both. And as a matter of verbal shorthand, it's a lot easier to say "the police violated *Miranda*" than to say "the judge would be violating *Miranda* if he or she were to admit the defendant's statements into evidence at his trial."

> You do *not* have a right to remain silent. The Fifth Amendment self-incrimination clause does not prohibit compelling a suspect to talk; it limits what can be used at trial.

But the war against terrorism has suddenly increased the significance of this previously academic question. In terrorism investigations, it will often be more important to get potentially life-saving information from a suspect than to get incriminating statements for use in court.

Fortunately for terrorism investigators, the Supreme Court said in 1990 that "a constitutional violation [of the Fifth Amendment's self-incrimination clause] occurs only at trial." It cited an earlier ruling that the government can obtain court orders compelling reluctant witnesses to talk and can imprison them for contempt of court if they refuse, if it first guarantees them immunity from prosecution on the basis of their statements or any derivative evidence. These decisions support the conclusion that the self-incrimination clause "does not forbid the forcible extraction of information but only the use of information so extracted as evidence in a criminal case," as a federal appeals court ruled in 1992.

Of course, even when the primary reason for questioning a suspected terrorist is prevention, the government could pay a heavy cost for ignoring *Miranda* and using coercive interrogation techniques, because it would sometimes find it difficult or impossible to prosecute extremely dangerous terrorists. But terrorism investigators may be

able to get their evidence and use it too, if the Court—or Congress, which unlike the Court would not have to wait for a proper case to come along—extends a 1984 precedent creating what the justices called a "public safety" exception to *Miranda*. That decision allowed use at trial of a defendant's incriminating answer to a policeman's demand (before any *Miranda* warnings) to know where his gun was hidden.

Those facts are not a perfect parallel for most terrorism investigations, because of the immediate nature of the danger (an accomplice might pick up the gun) and the spontaneity of the officer's question. And as Rowley testified, "In order to give timely advice" about what an agent can legally do, "you've got to run to a computer and pull it up, and I think that many people have kind of forgotten that case, and many courts have actually limited it to its facts."

But when the main purpose of the interrogation is to prevent terrorist attacks, the magnitude of the danger argues for a broader public safety exception, as Rowley implied in her letter.

Congress should neither wait for the justices to clarify the law nor assume that they will reach the right conclusions without prodding. It should make the rules as clear as possible as soon as possible. Officials like Rowley need to know that they are free to interrogate suspected terrorists more aggressively than they suppose. While a law expanding the public safety exception to *Miranda* would be challenged as unconstitutional, it would contradict no existing Supreme Court precedent and—if carefully calibrated to apply only when the immediate purpose is to save lives—would probably be upheld.

Would investigators routinely ignore *Miranda* and engage in coercive interrogation—perhaps extorting false confessions—if told that the legal restraints are far looser than has been supposed? The risk would not be significantly greater than it is now. Police would still need to comply with *Miranda* in almost all cases for fear of jeopardizing any prosecution. While that would not be true in terrorism investigations if the public safety exception were broadened, extreme abuses such as beatings and torture would violate the due process clause of the Fifth Amendment (and of the Fourteenth Amendment as well), which has been construed as barring interrogation techniques that "shock the conscience," and is backed up by administrative penalties and the threat of civil lawsuits.

Bringing Preventive Detention inside the Law

Of all the erosions of civil liberties that must be considered after September 11, preventive detention—incarcerating people because of their perceived dangerousness even when they are neither convicted nor charged with any crime—would represent the sharpest departure from centuries of Anglo-American jurisprudence and come closest to police statism.

But the case for some kind of preventive detention has never been as strong. Al-Qaida's capacity to inflict catastrophic carnage dwarfs any previous domestic security threat. Its "sleeper" agents are trained to avoid criminal activities that might arouse suspicion. So the careful ones cannot be arrested on criminal charges until it is too late. And their lust for martyrdom renders criminal punishment ineffective as a deterrent.

Without preventive detention, the Bush administration would apparently have no solid legal basis for holding the two U.S. citizens in military brigs in this country as suspected "enemy combatants"—or for holding the more than 500 noncitizens at Guantanamo Bay. Nor would it have had a solid legal basis for detaining any of the 19 September 11 hijackers if it had suspected them of links to al-Qaida before they struck. Nor could it legally have detained Moussaoui—who was suspected of terrorist intent but was implicated in no provable crime or conspiracy—had he had not overstayed his visa.

What should the government do when it is convinced of a suspect's terrorist intent but lacks admissible evidence of any crime? Or when a criminal trial would blow vital intelligence secrets? Or when ambiguous evidence makes it a tossup whether a suspect is harmless or an al-Qaidan? What should it do with suspects like Jose Padilla, who was arrested in Chicago and is now in military detention because he is suspected of (but not charged with) plotting a radioactive "dirty-bomb" attack on Washington, D.C.? Or with a (hypothetical) Pakistani graduate student in chemistry, otherwise unremarkable, who has downloaded articles about how terrorists might use small planes to start an anthrax epidemic and shown an intense but unexplained interest in crop-dusters?

Only four options exist. Let such suspects go about their business unmonitored until (perhaps) they commit mass murders; assign agents to tail them until (perhaps) they give the agents the slip; bring prosecutions without solid evidence and risk acquittals; and preventive detention. The latter could theoretically include not only incarceration but milder restraints such as house arrest or restriction to certain areas combined with agreement to carry (or to be implanted with) a device enabling the government to track the suspect's movements at all times.

As an alternative to preventive detention, Congress could seek to facilitate prosecutions of suspected "sleepers" by allowing use of now-inadmissible and secret evidence and stretching the already broad concept of criminal conspiracy so far as to make it almost a thought crime. But that would have a harsher effect on innocent terrorism suspects than would preventive detention and could weaken protections for all criminal defendants.

As Alan Dershowitz notes, "[N]o civilized nation confronting serious danger has ever relied exclusively on criminal convictions for past offenses. Every country has introduced, by one means or another, a system of preventive or administrative detention for persons who are thought to be dangerous but who might not be convictable under the conventional criminal law."

The best argument against preventive detention of suspected international terrorists is history's warning that the system will be abused, could expand inexorably—especially in the panic that might follow future attacks—and has such terrifying potential for infecting the entire criminal justice system and undermining our Bill of Rights that we should never start down that road. What is terrorist intent, and how may it be proved? Through a suspect's advocacy of a terrorist group's cause? Association with its members or sympathizers? If preventive detention is okay for people suspected of (but not charged with) terrorist intent, what about people suspected of homicidal intent, or violent proclivities, or dealing drugs?

These are serious concerns. But the dangers of punishing dissident speech, guilt by association, and overuse of preventive detention could be controlled by careful legislation. This would not be the first exception to the general rule against preventive detention. The others have worked fairly well. They include pretrial detention without bail of criminal defendants found to be dangerous, civil commitment of people found dangerous by reason of mental illness, and medical quarantines, a practice that may once again be necessary in the event of bioterrorism. All in all, the danger that a preventive detention regime for suspected terrorists would take us too far down the slippery slope toward police statism is simply not as bad as the danger of letting would-be mass murderers roam the country.

In any event, we already have a preventive detention regime for suspected international terrorists—three regimes, in fact, all created and controlled by the Bush administration without congressional input. First, two U.S. citizens—Jose Padilla, the suspected would-be dirty bomber arrested in Chicago, and Yaser Esam Hamdi, a Louisiana-born Saudi Arabian captured in Afghanistan and taken first to Guantanamo—have been in military brigs in this country for many months without being charged with any crime or allowed to see any lawyer or any judge. The administration claims that it never has to prove anything to anyone. It says that even U.S. citizens arrested in this country—who may have far stronger grounds than battlefield detainees for denying that they are enemy combatants—are entitled to no due process whatever once the government puts that label on them. This argument is virtually unprecedented, wrong as a matter of law, and indefensible as a matter of policy.

Second, Attorney General John Ashcroft rounded up more than 1,100 mostly Muslim noncitizens in the fall of 2001, which involved preventive detention in many cases although they were charged with immigration violations or crimes (mostly minor) or held under the material witness statute. This when-in-doubt-detain approach effectively reversed the presumption of innocence in the hope of disrupting any planned followup attacks. We may never know whether it succeeded in this vital objective. But the legal and moral bases for holding hundreds of apparently harmless detainees, sometimes without access to legal counsel, in conditions of unprecedented secrecy, seemed less and less plausible as weeks and months went by. Worse, the administration treated many (if not most) of the detainees shabbily and some abusively. (By mid-2002, the vast majority had been deported or released.)

Third, the Pentagon has incarcerated hundreds of Arab and other prisoners captured in Afghanistan at Guantanamo, apparently to avoid the jurisdiction of all courts—and has refused to create a fair, credible process for determining which are in fact enemy combatants and which of those are "unlawful."

These three regimes have been implemented with little regard for the law, for the rights of the many (mostly former) detainees who are probably innocent, or for international opinion. It is time for Congress to step in—to authorize a regime of temporary preventive detention for suspected international terrorists, while circumscribing that regime and specifying strong safeguards against abuse.

Civil Liberties for a New Era

It is senseless to adhere to overly broad restrictions imposed by decades-old civil-liberties rules when confronting the threat of unprecedented carnage at the hands of modern terrorists. In the words of Harvard Law School's Laurence H. Tribe, "The old adage that it is better to free 100 guilty men than to imprison one innocent describes a calculus that our Constitution—which is no suicide pact—does not impose on government when the 100 who are freed belong to terrorist cells that slaughter innocent civilians, and may well have access to chemical, biological, or nuclear weapons." The question is not whether we should increase governmental power to meet such dangers. The question is how much.

Stuart Taylor, Jr., is a senior writer for National Journal.

Upon Further Review

**Support for the First Amendment has rebounded as time has elapsed
since the shock of the September 11 attacks.**

By Ken Paulson

Two years after the terrorist attacks in New
York and Washington, D.C., our nation appears to have caught
its breath—and regained some perspective.

Those horrific assaults took a tremendous toll, in lives as
well as on our collective psyche. How could we prevent such attacks from happening again? Did we need to limit liberties in
the interest of security? Were we too free to be truly safe?

That sense of freedom as an obstacle to the war on terrorism
was reflected last year in our annual survey gauging public support for First Amendment freedoms (see "Too Free?" September 2002). For the first time in our polling, 49 percent of
respondents said they believed the First Amendment gives us
too much freedom.

While reaction to fear is largely reflexive, the passage of time allows us to be reflective. The 2003 State of the First Amendment
survey—conducted by the First Amendment Center in collaboration with AJR—suggested that public support for First Amendment freedoms may be returning to pre-9/11 levels. About
60 percent of respondents indicated overall support for First
Amendment freedoms, while 34 percent said First Amendment
freedoms go too far.

While First Amendment advocates certainly can't regard it
as a victory that one-third of Americans have misgivings about
these fundamental freedoms, there are other signs that most
Americans continue to embrace freedom of speech and religion.
While respondents displayed less enthusiasm for freedom of the
press, they did give high marks to the news media for their work
during the war in Iraq.

Among the key findings:

- The least popular First Amendment right continued to be freedom of the press—46 percent said the press in America has
  too much freedom to do what it wants, up from 42 percent
  last year.
- Sixty-five percent of those surveyed said they favor the policy
  of embedding U.S. journalists into individual combat units,

and 68 percent said the news media did an excellent or good
job in covering the war.

- Despite the positive perception of war coverage, more than
  two out of three surveyed said the government should be able
  to review in advance journalists' reports directly from combat zones.
- Americans indicated a hunger for more information about the
  war on terrorism. Forty-eight percent of those surveyed said
  they believe that Americans have too little access to information
  about the federal government's efforts to combat terrorism—up
  from 40 percent last year.
- When asked whether they believe the media have too much
  freedom to publish or whether there's too much government
  censorship, response was split: Forty-three percent said
  there's too much media freedom, and 38 percent said there's
  too much government censorship.

One area spurring fierce debate over the last year
has been the Federal Communications Commission's move to
loosen media ownership restrictions. As had been long anticipated, the FCC in June voted to let networks own more television stations and to let media companies own a newspaper and
TV and radio stations in the same market.

The public's unease with extensive media ownership by
large corporations and conglomerates was reflected in the
survey. The majority of respondents said the quality of
news reporting has deteriorated and opposed the removal of
limits on how many media outlets may be owned by a single
company:

- Fifty-two percent of those surveyed said media ownership by
  fewer corporations has meant a decreased number of viewpoints available to the public. Fifty-three percent said the
  quality of information also has suffered.

The First Amendment is part of the U.S. Constitution. Can you name any of the specific rights that are guaranteed by the First Amendment?

	1999	2000	2001	2002	2003
freedom of the press	12%	12%	14%	14%	16%
freedom of speech	44%	60%	59%	58%	63%
freedom of religion	13%	16%	16%	18%	22%
right to petition	2%	2%	1%	2%	2%
right of assembly	8%	9%	10%	10%	11%
other	6%	12%	14%	19%	21%
don't know/refused to answer	N/A	37%	36%	35%	37%

The First Amendment says: "Congress shall make no law respecting an establishment of religion, or prohibiting the free exercise thereof; or abridging the freedom of speech, or of the press, or the right of the people peaceably to assemble, and to petition the Government for a redress of grievances." Based on your own feelings, please tell whether you agree or disagree with the following statement: The First Amendment goes too far in the rights it guarantees.

	1999	2000	2001	2002	2003
strongly agree	16%	10%	29%	41%	19%
mildly agree	12%	12%	10%	8%	15%
mildly disagree	22%	26%	19%	15%	18%
strongly disagree	45%	48%	39%	32%	42%
don't know/refused	5%	5%	3%	3%	7%

Overall, how would you rate the job that the American educational system does in teaching students about the First Amendment?

	2001	2002	2003
excellent	5%	5%	6%
good	25%	26%	25%
fair	39%	35%	33%
poor	24%	28%	29%
don't know/refused	7%	6%	7%

A significant percentage of radio stations, television stations and newspapers today are owned by just a few corporations. Has this development led to an increased number of viewpoints available to the public, a decreased number, or has the number of viewpoints been affected?

	2003
increased	17%
decreased	52%
unaffected	24%
don't know/refused	7%

Has the ownership of a significant percentage of radio stations, television stations and newspapers by just a few corporations increased the quality of information available to citizens, decreased the quality, or has the quality of information not been affected?

	2003
increased	19%
decreased	53%
unaffected	24%
don't know/refused	4%

To what extent do corporate owners influence news organizations' decisions about which stories to cover or emphasize?

	2003
a great deal	44%
a fair amount	34%
not very much	15%
not at all	4%
don't know/refused	3%

The federal government has adopted a policy removing most limits on how many radio, television and newspaper outlets may be owned by a single company. Do you favor or oppose such a policy?

	2003
strongly favor	19%
mildly favor	19%
mildly oppose	23%
strongly oppose	31%
don't know/refused	7%

Because a significant percentage of radio stations, television stations and newspapers are owned by just a few corporations, some have proposed that the government increase its regulation of the operation of those news media outlets. Do you favor or oppose such a policy?

	2003
strongly favor	17%
mildly favor	24%
mildly oppose	25%
strongly oppose	25%
don't know/refused	8%

- Almost eight Americans in 10 said owners exert substantial influence over news organizations' newsgathering and reporting decisions. Only 4 percent said they believed there is no tampering with story selection or play.
- Fifty-four percent said they favor maintaining federal limits on how many radio, television and newspaper outlets may be owned by a single company, but one in two said they opposed any increased regulation.

Overall, the 2003 State of the First Amendment survey suggests some special challenges for America's news media.

While most respondents gave the press positive reviews for Iraq war coverage and said they count on the news media to provide more information about the war on terrorism, they also said the press has too much freedom and indicated suspicion of those who own the nation's newspapers and broadcast stations.

Fortunately, Americans also recognize responsible and responsive news coverage when they see it. For all of the skepticism about news media ownership and excesses, the nation's journalists remain uniquely positioned to win support for a free press—and the First Amendment as a whole—by living up to the watchdog role envisioned by the founding fathers.

At a time when many remain tempted to roll back civil liberties in the name of security, a free press plays a crucial role.

The nation's news media truly honor the First Amendment when they ask the tough questions, fight to keep the public's business public and provide the kind of thorough and balanced reporting that is the lifeblood of a democracy.

Even though the U.S. Constitution guarantees freedom of the press, government has placed some restrictions on it. Overall, do you think that Americans have too much press freedom, too little press freedom, or is the amount about right?

	1999	2000	2001	2002	2003
too much freedom	31%	40%	36%	33%	36%
too little freedom	17%	14%	13%	13%	13%
about right	49%	43%	47%	51%	48%
don't know/refused	4%	3%	4%	2%	2%

Overall, do you think the press in America has too much freedom to do what it wants, too little freedom to do what it wants, or is the amount about right?

	1999	2000	2001	2002	2003
too much freedom	42%	51%	46%	42%	46%
too little freedom	8%	7%	8%	8%	9%
about right	48%	41%	42%	49%	43%
don't know/refused	3%	2%	3%	1%	1%

Newspapers should be allowed to publish freely without government approval of a story.

	1999	2000	2001	2002	2003
strongly agree	38%	54%	53%	43%	48%
mildly agree	27%	22%	22%	26%	22%
mildly disagree	14%	9%	10%	16%	13%
strongly disagree	18%	11%	13%	11%	15%
don't know/refused	3%	3%	2%	3%	3%

Some people believe that the media has too much freedom to publish whatever it wants. Others believe there is too much government censorship. Which of these beliefs lies closest to your own?

	2001	2002	2003
too much media freedom	41%	42%	43%
too much gov. censorship	36%	32%	38%
neither	12%	15%	10%
both	7%	8%	4%
don't know/refused	4%	4%	5%

Newspapers should be allowed to freely criticize the U.S. military about its strategy and performance.

	2002	2003
strongly agree	33%	32%
mildly agree	24%	22%
mildly disagree	18%	14%
strongly disagree	24%	30%
don't know/refused	1%	1%

How concerned are you that corporations which own a significant percentage of radio stations may decide to restrict their employees from playing on the air the music of performers who make controversial statements?

	2003
very concerned	33%
somewhat concerned	33%
not too concerned	19%
not concerned at all	14%
don't know/refused	1%

Are you more or less likely to purchase a CD by a musician who has made controversial political remarks in public that do not reflect your own views, or does it make no difference?

	2003
more likely	4%
less likely	39%
makes no difference	54%
don't know/refused	3%

Are you more or less likely to purchase a CD by a musician who has made controversial political remarks in public that are in agreement with your own views, or does it make no difference?

	2003
more likely	17%
less likely	10%
makes no difference	71%
don't know/refused	2%

Are you more or less likely to attend a performance by an entertainer who has made controversial political remarks in public that do not reflect your own views, or does it make no difference?

	2003
more likely	3%
less likely	38%
makes no difference	57%
don't know/refused	2%

Are you more or less likely to attend a performance by an entertainer who has made controversial political remarks in public that are in agreement with your own views, or does it make no difference?

	2003
more likely	18%
less likely	9%
makes no difference	72%
don't know/refused	2%

Even though the U.S. Constitution guarantees freedom of speech, government has placed some restrictions on it. Overall, do you think Americans have too much freedom to speak freely, too little freedom to speak freely, or is the amount about right?

	1999	2000	2001	2002	2003
too much freedom	12%	11%	12%	10%	12%
too little freedom	26%	25%	26%	21%	23%
about right	59%	62%	61%	67%	63%
don't know/refused	3%	2%	2%	1%	2%

Do you agree or disagree with the following statements? People should be allowed to express unpopular opinions.

	1999	2000	2001	2002	2003
strongly agree	58%	69%	74%	67%	74%
mildly agree	28%	26%	19%	27%	21%
mildly disagree	8%	2%	3%	4%	3%
strongly disagree	5%	3%	2%	2%	2%
don't know/refused	1%	0%	1%	0%	1%

People should be allowed to say things in public that might be offensive to religious groups.

	2000	2001	2002	2003
strongly agree	22%	25%	29%	26%
mildly agree	24%	22%	28%	23%
mildly disagree	15%	16%	14%	14%
strongly disagree	38%	35%	28%	36%
don't know/refused	1%	3%	2%	1%

Musicians should be allowed to sing songs with lyrics that others might find offensive.

	1999	2000	2001	2002	2003
strongly agree	27%	32%	34%	31%	35%
mildly agree	29%	27%	27%	26%	26%
mildly disagree	15%	12%	9%	14%	10%
strongly disagree	26%	28%	28%	27%	26%
don't know/refused	4%	2%	2%	2%	3%

People should be allowed to say things in public that might be offensive to racial groups.

	1999	2000	2001	2002	2003
strongly agree	8%	15%	16%	14%	18%
mildly agree	13%	17%	18%	20%	20%
mildly disagree	16%	15%	15%	16%	14%
strongly disagree	62%	52%	49%	48%	47%
didn't know/refused	1%	1%	2%	1%	1%

People should be allowed to display in a public place art that has content that might be offensive to others.

	1999	2000	2001	2002	2003
strongly agree	17%	22%	24%	22%	22%
mildly agree	24%	24%	26%	24%	22%
mildly disagree	24%	17%	16%	22%	20%
strongly disagree	33%	34%	31%	30%	35%
don't know/refused	2%	4%	3%	2%	1%

How would you rate the job the news media did in covering the 2003 war in Iraq?

	2003
excellent	28%
good	40%
fair	21%
poor	8%
don't know/refused	3%

During the 2003 war in Iraq, the U.S. military adopted a policy of "embedding" American journalists into individual combat units. Do you favor or oppose this policy?

	2003
favor strongly	37%
favor mildly	28%
oppose mildly	12%
oppose strongly	19%
don't know/refused	4%

As part of the war on terrorism, law enforcement agencies should be allowed to monitor which books or other materials patrons check out of public libraries.

	2003
strongly agree	16%
mildly agree	14%
mildly disagree	19%
strongly disagree	48%
don't know/refused	2%

The government should be able to review in advance what journalists report directly from military combat zones.

	2003
strongly agree	44%
mildly agree	23%
mildly disagree	15%
strongly disagree	15%
don't know/refused	3%

As part of the war on terrorism, the government should be able to monitor religious groups even if that means infringing upon the religious freedom of those groups' members.

	2003
strongly agree	27%
mildly agree	23%
mildly disagree	18%
strongly disagree	27%
don't know/refused	5%

Individuals should be allowed to protest in public against America's involvement in war during a period of active military combat.

	2003
strongly agree	38%
mildly agree	29%
mildly disagree	9%
strongly disagree	22%
don't know/refused	1%

Any group that wants to should be allowed to hold a rally for a cause or issue even if it may be offensive to others in the community.

	1999	2000	2001	2002	2003
strongly agree	30%	34%	40%	33%	34%
mildly agree	32%	32%	25%	34%	33%
mildly disagree	16%	12%	11%	13%	15%
strongly disagree	20%	19%	22%	18%	15%
don't know/refused	3%	4%	2%	2%	3%

In light of the government's war on terrorism in response to the World Trade Center attacks, some people think that the government should have more power to monitor the activities of Muslims legally living in the United States than it has to monitor other religious groups. Others say that monitoring Muslims more closely than others would violate the Muslims' right to free exercise of their religion. Which of these comes closest to your own opinion?

	2002	2003
government should have more power to monitor Muslims than others	42%	39%
treating Muslims differently violates their free exercise rights	50%	52%
don't know/refused	8%	9%

Do you agree or disagree with this statement: "In covering the war on terrorism, the American press has been too aggressive in asking government officials for information."

	2002	2003
strongly agree	29%	23%
mildly agree	19%	15%
mildly disagree	23%	29%
strongly disagree	26%	29%
don't know/refused	3%	3%

Do you think Americans have too much, too little, or just about the right amount of access to information about the federal government's war on terrorism?

	2002	2003
too much	16%	12%
too little	40%	48%
just about the right amount	38%	38%
don't know/refused	6%	2%

Public school officials should be allowed to prohibit high school students from expressing their opinions about the war on school property during a period of active military combat.

	2003
strongly agree	19%
mildly agree	14%
mildly disagree	27%
strongly disagree	38%
don't know/refused	3%

Public school officials should be allowed to prohibit high school students from wearing T-shirts, armbands or other insignia expressing opinions about the war on school property during a period of active military combat.

	2003
strongly agree	31%
mildly agree	17%
mildly disagree	19%
strongly disagree	31%
don't know/refused	3%

Overall, do you think that students in public schools have too much freedom to express themselves, too little freedom, or just about the right amount while at school?

	2003
too much	13%
too little	28%
just about the right amount	54%
don't know/refused	4%

Even though the U.S. Constitution guarantees freedom of religion, government has placed some restrictions on it. Overall, do you think Americans have too much religious freedom, too little religious freedom, or is the amount about right?

	1999	2000	2001	2002	2003
too much freedom	8%	5%	4%	6%	8%
too little freedom	26%	29%	32%	20%	24%
about right	63%	63%	62%	70%	66%
don't know/refused	3%	3%	2%	4%	3%

Overall, do you think that students in public schools have too much religious freedom, too little religious freedom, or just about the right amount while at school?

	2001	2002	2003
too much	3%	3%	4%
too little	53%	53%	46%
just about the right amount	40%	40%	45%
don't know/refused	4%	4%	5%

Many public schools require teachers to lead students in recitation of the Pledge of Allegiance, which includes the phrase "One Nation Under God," although students are generally permitted to opt out for reciting the pledge if they so chose. Does that school practice violate the Constitutional principle of separation of church and state?

	2003
yes	26%
no	68%
don't know/refused	5%

The government's use of the phrase "in God we trust" on U.S. money and coins violates the Constitutional principle of separation of church and state.

	2003
strongly agree	10%
mildly agree	9%
mildly disagree	21%
strongly disagree	57%
don't know/refused	3%

Government officials should be allowed to post the Ten Commandments inside government buildings.

	2002	2003
strongly agree	52%	44%
mildly agree	18%	18%
mildly disagree	12%	13%
strongly disagree	16%	22%
don't know/refused	2%	3%

Parents should have the option of sending their children to non-public schools, including those with a religious affiliation, using vouchers or credits provided by the federal government that would pay some or all of the costs.

	2003
strongly agree	40%
mildly agree	22%
mildly disagree	12%
strongly disagree	23%
don't know/refused	4%

When you say or hear the Pledge of Allegiance, which includes the phrase "One Nation Under God," do you think of that phrase primarily as a religious statement, or as primarily a statement related to the American political tradition?

	2003
primarily a religious statement	18%
primarily a statement related to the Am. political tradition	73%
both	5%
neither	1%
don't know/refused	2%

Do you favor or oppose allowing the government to give money to religious institutions or churches to help them run drug abuse prevention programs, even if the religious institutions would be allowed to include a religious message as part of their program?

	2003
strongly favor	34%
mildly favor	26%
mildly oppose	15%
strongly oppose	21%
don't know/refused	4%

Some people feel that the U.S. Constitution should be amended to make it illegal to burn or desecrate the American flag as a form of political dissent. Others disagree. Do you think the U.S. Constitution should or should not be amended to prohibit burning or desecrating the American flag?

	1999	2000	2001	2002	2003
should not	48%	51%	59%	51%	55%
should*	51%	46%	39%	46%	44%
don't know/refused	1%	3%	2%	2%	2%

*(For those who responded "should"): If an amendment prohibiting burning or desecrating the American flag were approved, it would be the first time any of the freedoms in the First Amendment have been amended in over 200 years. Knowing this, would you still support an amendment to prohibit burning or desecrating the American flag?

	1999	2000	2001	2002	2003
yes	90%	87%	81%	83%	87%
no	8%	12%	15%	15%	12%
don't know/refused	2%	1%	4%	2%	1%

Ken Paulson is executive director of the First Amendment Center in Nashville, Tennessee.

The First Amendment Center/AJR Poll on the First Amendment was conducted by the center for Survey Research and Analysis at the University of Connecticut. A random national sample of 1,000 adults 18 years old and over was conducted by telephone between June 3 and June 15, 2003. The sampling error is + or - 3.1 percent at the 95 percent confidence level. The sample error is larger for sub-groups. Totals may not equal 100 percent due to rounding. Not all questions are asked every year.

From the *American Journalism Review*, August/September 2003, pp. 60-65. © 2003 by the Philip Merrill College of Journalism at the University of Maryland, College Park, MD 20742-7111.

Winks, Nods, Disguises—and Racial Preference

Carl Cohen

TWENTY-FIVE years ago, when the case of *Bakke* v. *University of California* arrived before the U.S. Supreme Court, it was widely anticipated that the Justices would at last resolve an issue that had been bedeviling the country for years: the permissibility of preference by race in university admissions. It did not happen. To the contrary, the internal divisions of the Court at that time, as reflected in six tangled opinions, left the matter in more muddled condition than it already was. True, Allan Bakke, the white applicant who had been turned down by the University of California in favor of less qualified minority candidates, won his suit; naked racial preference was thrown out. But what *other* sorts of racial and ethnic preferences might be permitted was left quite uncertain.

The chief muddler in 1978 was Justice Lewis Powell, a decent man and an honorable judge who found racial discrimination appalling and unconstitutional and yet also felt that he had to permit some wiggle room for college admissions officers to attend to race under some circumstances. In his long and convoluted opinion, notorious for the confusion to which it subsequently gave rise, Powell held that it would be reasonable for a university to take into consideration the race of particular applicants for the sake of achieving intellectual "diversity" in the student body. To treat people in general differently because of their color, Powell said, was plainly a violation of the equal-protection clause of the Fourteenth Amendment. But to allow the race of individual applicants to weigh in their favor for the sake of diversity did not amount to such a violation.

No other Justice joined Powell in his confused and rather fanciful homage to the concept of diversity. And yet his principle took root. This was in part because, in a Court divided between two parties of four, his had been the deciding voice. For the universities, the problem with *Bakke* was that it unambiguously rejected preferences for the sake of remedying past injustices committed against racial minorities—precisely the defense that, until then, many universities had been relying upon. If they were determined to go on giving preference, as for the most part they were, they would henceforth have to lean upon the weak reed of

Powell's speculations concerning diversity. And this, for the next quarter-century, they proceeded to do.

But would the "diversity defense" withstand renewed constitutional challenge? That central question was presented to the Supreme Court in two cases involving the University of Michigan and finally decided this past June: *Gratz* v. *Bollinger,* concerning the admissions practices of Michigan's undergraduate college, and *Grutter* v. *Bollinger,* concerning the admissions practices of its law school. ("Bollinger" is Lee Bollinger, formerly the president of the university.) Though the two cases differed significantly in their particulars, in each case the university justified its practice of using racial preferences on the grounds not of remediation but of diversity.

One would have thought—I certainly thought—that the university would have an extremely tough time of it. For any state to treat people differently by race is an odious practice, presumptively unconstitutional and hence subject to the rigorous standard of "strict scrutiny" applied to any putative exceptions to the rule. That standard has two prongs. To win the day, the university would need five of the nine Justices to agree both that racial diversity was a "compelling" need of the state of Michigan and that the system of preference it was using had been "narrowly tailored" to meet that compelling need.

How could it do that? It seemed eminently plain that the state's need for racial diversity in its university, if it had any such need at all, was not compelling under any ordinary meaning of that term. Moreover, the two Michigan systems giving preference, so far from being narrowly tailored, were (as one federal judge had earlier put it) more like a chain saw than a sewing machine in their mode of operation. Success for the University of Michigan thus seemed very unlikely indeed.

So confident was I that five Supreme Court votes could not be gathered to support a view plainly concocted only to pass muster under Powell's 1978 opinion that two years ago I came as close as the editors of COMMENTARY would permit me to predicting certain defeat for the university ("Race Preferences & the Universities—A Final Reckoning?," September 2001). As I saw it, *no* judge, taking seriously the standard of strict scrutiny, could possibly approve diversity as a state need compelling enough to justify deliberate racial discrimination. Right and left, I wagered steak dinners with every soft-headed supporter of the diversity principle who would allow his political passions to overrule his good sense.

I am buying many steaks these days.

In *Gratz* v. *Bollinger,* the Supreme Court of the United States did hold that the numerical admissions system used by Michigan's undergraduate college, in which a given number of points was awarded to all applicants in certain ethnic categories, violated the equal-protection clause of the Fourteenth Amendment as well as the Civil Rights Act of 1964. But on the same day, in *Grutter* v. *Bollinger,* the Court held that "the educational benefits that flow from a diverse student body" were indeed, in the context of higher education, a compelling state interest. Moreover, the particular form of deliberate racial discrimination practiced by the law school of the University of Michigan was found to be *consistent* with the constitutional guarantee of equal protection of the laws.

The diversity principle, even if only in one context, and with heavy restrictions, has thus been embedded in law; Powell's weak reed has become a mighty limb. In the meantime, in the tension between these two latest decisions, what was muddy in *Bakke* has become muddier still.

Much damage has been inflicted on the standard of strict scrutiny itself. As the four dissenting opinions in *Grutter* (the law-school decision) make vividly, even bitterly, clear, the need of the state of Michigan for diversity of skin colors in its university admissions was hardly "compelling." Even the maintenance of a law school by the state of Michigan, as Justice Clarence Thomas pointed out, although surely a good thing, is not a compelling need; many states thrive without one. Nor, for that matter, has the university's program delivered on its promise: exhaustive research has shown that its purported benefits (i.e., the promotion of tolerance and understanding for the views of "diverse" others) have been in scant evidence. No genuinely "compelling" educational need is being served.

As for the second prong of the standard of strict scrutiny—the requirement that, even if some compelling state need has been identified, the use of racial classifications must be narrowly tailored to the fulfillment of that need—the race preferences given by the law school, no less than the rejected admissions system of Michigan's undergraduate college, likewise failed to satisfy it. Demonstrating this failure formed the nub of Chief Justice Rehnquist's dissenting opinion in *Grutter,* in which he was joined by Justices Clarence Thomas, Antonin Scalia, and Anthony Kennedy. It has not been widely understood.

According to the University of Michigan, the educational benefits of diversity were said to flow from the creation of a "critical mass" of minority representatives in the student body: a number sufficiently large that the members of a given minority in a given class would not feel themselves "isolated" in that class. The racial instrument used in law-school admissions was, the university held, narrowly tailored to this end. Unlike the practice in the undergraduate college, the law school, in

evaluating applicants, claimed not to rely on some fixed numerical value mechanically awarded to every member of certain ethnic groups. Instead, the critical masses needed for the three designated minorities—African-Americans, Native Americans, and Hispanics—were said to have been artfully assembled through the use of highly sensitive reviews of each individual applicant.

Indeed, in the earlier, district-court trial of *Grutter,* as in the university's written arguments for the Supreme Court, the law school had gone to great lengths to avoid any mention whatsoever of numbers or percentages. And for good reason: any open confession of this kind would have exposed the school to the same condemnation received by the undergraduate college in *Gratz.* But the entire law-school system was a deception. The dissenting opinion of the Chief Justice proved this.

In any given class of students, a "critical mass," whatever it is, cannot be greatly different in size for African-Americans from what it is for other minorities; nor can it differ greatly in one year from what it was three years earlier, at least if the class itself has not changed in size. In fact, however, the numbers of the several minorities admitted to the Michigan law school in order to form their respective "critical masses" differed very greatly from minority to minority and, for each minority, from year to year. Calling attention to this starkly revealing feature of the school's admissions over a period of many years, and inserting numerical tables into his opinion to render the matter incontrovertible, Justice Rehnquist showed that the number of those admitted in each minority closely tracked the *number of applications* by members of that minority.

The figures themselves are worth examining. In recent years, the Michigan law school has offered admission each year, on average, to sixteen Native Americans, 51 Hispanics, and 100 African-Americans. If what had really been sought was a critical mass of each minority—that is, a number sufficiently large to ward off feelings of isolation within the class—and if the yield of 50 offers was enough to achieve that in the case of Hispanics, it cannot be the case (as the Chief Justice pointed out) that the yield of 100 offers was needed among some other minority, or that the yield of sixteen offers would be sufficient in the case of still another.

How did the numbers themselves come about? Rehnquist described the process. When, in 1995, 9.7 percent of the applicant pool was African-American, 9.4 percent of those admitted were African-Americans. Five years later, when 7.5 percent of the applicant pool was African-American, 7.3 percent of those admitted were African-Americans. A similar pattern was manifest throughout.

This "tight correlation between the percentage of applicants and admittees of a given race," Rehnquist wrote, devastatingly, could

only be the result of very careful race-based planning.... *We are bound to conclude that the law school has managed its admission program, not to achieve a "critical mass," but to extend offers of admission to members of selected minority groups in proportion to their statistical representation in the applicant pool.* [emphasis added]

Despite the law school's repeated protestations to the contrary, the statistics demonstrate that it was seeking some proportional representation of minorities in its entering classes. Its real objective was not critical mass—this, in Rehnquist's words, was "simply a sham"—but racial balance. But it could not have proclaimed this obvious truth, contending forthrightly that such proportionality would serve as its achievement of "diversity," for the simple reason that the admission of persons simply to achieve certain percentages of various ethnic groups is "patently unconstitutional." Justice Powell had made that point crisply in *Bakke* decades ago, and the same proposition was affirmed by the majority in *Grutter* without reservation. Instead, the law school engaged in a sham.

The *Grutter* majority accepted the sham whole hog. Baldly asserting that student-body ethnic diversity was a compelling state need, it found this end narrowly served by a process in which, allegedly, ethnicity was considered as no more than a "plus factor" in the files of "particular applicants," all the attributes of each applicant being "holistically" appraised and "all pertinent elements of diversity considered in light of the particular qualifications of each applicant" in the quest for a critical mass. (The language is that of Justice Sandra Day O'Connor in her majority opinion.) On this reading, the fact that, of two law-school applicants with identical academic credentials, a black applicant's chances of admission were in fact *hundreds* of times greater than those of a white applicant must be regarded as no more than a coincidence.

If this is strict scrutiny, the term is without meaning.

THANKS TO the Court's decision, still worse is now to come. The law-school system, a sham in reality, has been elevated to the status of a model—and not only for law schools. As we have seen, Michigan's use of race in *undergraduate* admissions, which did not pretend to be "individualized" or "holistic," was on that account found to be flatly unconstitutional. But henceforth, Michigan and many other universities will formulate their undergraduate preferential schemes in phrases echoing the language of the law-school program. Beginning now, "individualized review," "holistic," "critical mass," "plus factor," "a particular applicant's file," and the like will appear ubiquitously and talismanically in the description of admission systems from coast to coast.

Of course, it will be far easier to profess such highly individualized review systems than to realize them. And so a second-level sham will be explicitly invited: a fraud imitating a fraud.

Consider: the law school at Michigan enrolls some 350 new students each year. Of the several thousand who apply, a good number are speedily disqualified, with many of the remaining applicants interviewed in person and the complete file of every admitted applicant examined by a single person, the assistant dean for admissions. Even though, at the Michigan law school, the real goal has been racial balancing, the requisite process of "individualization," as approved by the Court, is conceivably doable, if with some strain.

The undergraduate college at Michigan is a rather different affair. It receives more than *25,000* applications for admission each year. Picture a gymnasium in which those fat application files are stacked in piles six feet high; there will be some 350 of these piles, or more, pretty nearly stuffing the gymnasium to the gills. Now imagine that each application is to be evaluated comparatively, with race and many other factors given varying and appropriate weights in the assessment of each candidate. Remember, *no* numerical value for ethnicity is to be assigned, no quantitative system applied.

How, in the name of reason, is the comparison of these 25,000 applicants to be carried out? Even for an army of admissions officers, the exercise would be hopeless. It is utterly impossible for the University of Michigan—not to speak of universities in Minnesota and Ohio and other states where undergraduate colleges are substantially larger still—to review all the particular qualifications of tens of thousands of applicants, weighing race as but one factor, without using some numerical calculus. Any future claim to that effect is *guaranteed* to be a deception.

IN ITS written argument defending the mechanical award of points for race in undergraduate admissions, the University of Michigan granted candidly that "the volume of applications and the presentation of applicant information make it impractical for [the undergraduate college] to use the … admissions system" of the law school. Of course. That is why the university argued, in effect, that since the racial results it sought could only be achieved using a system of numerical weights, such a system must be permissible, for there is no other way to achieve the approved aim of diversity.

No! responded the Court in *Gratz.* The use of race is permitted in some ways, but it is not urged, and you are certainly not entitled to do whatever you think is required. The Court's strictures were not to be bypassed: a university may not "employ whatever means it desires to achieve the stated goal of diversity without regard to the limits imposed by our strict-scrutiny analysis." Nor did "the fact that the implementation of a program providing individualized consideration might present administrative challenges … render constitutional an otherwise problematic system." So, under *Gratz,* the university has been forbidden to do what it asserts it must do in order to achieve the racial objective it asserts it must pursue and which, under *Grutter,* has now been found "compelling." Here, in the pull of the two decisions against each other, is indeed a recipe for still more pervasive obfuscation and more shameful hypocrisy.

Justice Ruth Ginsburg, who dissented from the majority in *Gratz,* saw this clearly. Writing in support of the now-unlawful point system, she frankly acknowledged that universities have already been deceitful and sly in this arena, resorting to "camouflage" by encouraging minority applicants and their supporters to convey their ethnic identification deviously and backhandedly in personal essays and letters of recommendation. Justice Ginsburg then concluded: "If honesty is the best policy, surely Michigan's accurately described, fully disclosed college affirmative-action program is preferable to achieving similar numbers through winks, nods, and disguises." Narrow tailoring need not be faked; instead, in Ginsburg's view, it could simply be ignored. A non-individualized program, assigning a fixed number of points for skin color, was the answer. Unless we permitted it, the result would be widespread cheating.

She was certainly right about the cheating. But cheating is already endemic, and is now bound to spread further. For those bent on racial preference, the "winks, nods, and disguises" decried by Ginsburg have now, thanks to her and her likeminded colleagues in *Grutter,* been made a practical necessity.

In a footnote to the opinion striking down the undergraduate point system, Chief Justice Rehnquist called Ginsburg's observations "remarkable," and answered them sharply:

> First, they suggest that universities—to whose academic judgment we are told in *Grutter* will pursue their affirmative-action programs whether or not they violate the United States Constitution. Second, they recommend that these violations should be dealt with, not by requiring the universities to obey the Constitution, but by changing the Constitution so that it conforms to the conduct of the universities.

THIS FOOTNOTE, destined to become famous, goes to the heart of the two cases. Conduct that is plainly wrong and ugly if confronted openly has been condoned by five members of the Supreme Court if carefully hidden and deliberately misdescribed. The unconscionable deceptions of years past are now enshrined and soon to be compounded. Duplicity is encouraged to run amok.

To be sure there are some signs of judicial distress. Even Justice O'Connor, who in *Grutter* found race preference tolerable, reluctantly acknowledged that "there are serious problems of justice connected with the idea of preference itself." These are precisely the problems that will saddle universities, and American society, for years to come.

How many years? The Court accepted the assurances of the University of Michigan that the racial discrimination it now practices must some day end. The firmly expressed expectation of the Court is that this will happen within 25 years (a piety to which Justice Thomas retorted that the principle of equality ought not have to wait a quarter of a century to be vindicated). In the meantime, what lies ahead is the agony of a long chain of public disputes. For one thing, there will be no end of quarreling over the systems of preference being given. Although the universities will claim the protection of the words used in *Grutter,* it will be very hard to hide the reality of their practices, and these will be subjected to continuing adverse scrutiny. We may thus be reasonably certain that Michigan and those of its sister institutions likewise relying upon allegedly nonquantified diversity as the justification for preferences will be back in court again and again.

But the controversy will also move from the courtroom to the ballot box. If the Supreme Court has found that, in the interest of diversity, race preference may be given, it remains for the people of the several states to decide for themselves whether, in their state, race preference is to be forbidden. In Michigan, for example, every effort will be made by the time of the presidential election of 2004 to place on the ballot a Michigan Civil Rights Initiative—an equivalent of California's Proposition 209. The operative sentence in that proposition, now incorporated in the California constitution, is nearly identical to a critical passage of the Civil Rights Act of 1964, with the addition of five words that appear here in emphasis. It reads:

> The state shall not discriminate against, *or grant preferential treatment to,* any individual or group on the basis of race, sex, color, ethnicity, or national origin in the operation of public employment, public education, or public contracting.

Once the matter is on the ballot, it will also become more difficult for legislators and political candidates to dodge this controversy as they have so often done in the past. Will they urge their constituents to vote *against* a proposition forbidding race preference? If so, must we not conclude that they *support* race preference?

The decision of the U.S. Supreme Court in *Grutter* v. *Bollinger* is disheartening in the extreme. But the governing rule in this matter will come ultimately from the citizenry, and we must trust that the large majority of Americans, as reported in survey after survey and confirmed in election after election, continues to find racism of every sort disgusting. I was wrong about the outcome of the battle in court; now the war must move to other fronts.

GUNS AND TOBACCO: GOVERNMENT BY LITIGATION

Stuart Taylor Jr.

"The legal fees alone are enough to bankrupt the industry."

—John Coale, one of the private lawyers suing gunmakers on behalf of municipalities, as quoted in *The Washington Post* after the March 17 settlement in which Smith & Wesson agreed to adopt various safety measures that have stalled in Congress.

In its March 21 ruling that the Clinton Administration lacked authority to regulate the tobacco industry, no matter how great the need for regulation, the Supreme Court reaffirmed the broad principle that the power to set national policy on such hotly contested issues belongs to Congress. But the Justices have taken little note of other bold efforts to bypass Congress—and short-circuit the judicial process to boot—by using the threat of ruinous litigation to impose de facto regulation and taxation on targeted industries, including guns and tobacco. As *The Wall Street Journal* observed, the gun lawsuits could bring about "a more sweeping round of gun regulation than any single piece of legislation in 30 years."

And the far larger tobacco companies, which seem to have been sued by almost everyone alive, could be bankrupted by litigation, including a pending class action by smokers in Florida and a Clinton Administration lawsuit that invokes far-

fetched legal theories to seek many billions of dollars to compensate the government for the cost of treating smokers covered by Medicare. Also in the dock are HMOs, companies that sold lead paint more than 40 years ago, and makers of latex gloves. Later may come purveyors of liquor, beer, fatty foods, and, someday, maybe even fast cars and violent videos.

THE FOUNDERS CREATED CONGRESS TO SET NATIONAL POLICY. THEY DIDN'T INTEND FOR POLICY TO BE FASHIONED BY LAWSUITS.

(For a fuller taste of these and other peculiar workings of our legal system, with copious links to news reports, check out an amusingly depressing Web site called *Overlawyered.com,* created and edited by Walter K. Olson of the conservative-libertarian Manhattan Institute.)

The alliance of would-be lawmakers behind many of these broad legal assaults includes the Clinton Administration, state attorneys general, and municipalities, working closely with public interest activists and wealthy pri-

vate lawyers who started it all. Their incentives to sue variously include hopes of raising vast new revenues, bringing unpopular industries to heel, protecting public health and safety, and reaping billions of dollars in fees for the lawyers, who also tend to be big campaign contributors.

This public-private alliance's most recent triumph illustrates the combination of policy-making ambitions and financial incentives that drives such litigation. The triumph was the March 17 decision by British-owned Smith & Wesson, the nation's largest maker of handguns, to abide by a long list of restrictions on gun sales demanded by the Clinton Administration. Smith & Wesson entered the agreement to extricate itself from some or all of the lawsuits against the industry by 29 cities, counties, and other plaintiffs.

The gun lawsuits were bankrolled by contingent-fee lawyers who are also prominent in the more-lucrative tobacco wars and have lots of money to invest in multifront attacks on other industries. They recruited municipalities as clients by dangling the prospect of imposing previously unimagined liability on gunmakers for selling unnecessarily dangerous guns, and selling them to the wrong people, thus allegedly contributing to governmental costs associated with murders, accidental shootings, and other gun violence. Every shooting by a spouse, a child, an armed robber, or a drug dealer is at least theoretically a potential source of liability to the gunmakers. Seizing on the fact that many such shootings occur in federally subsidized housing projects, President Clinton and Housing and Urban Development Secretary Andrew Cuomo jumped in by pressing the gun companies to accept new restrictions or face "death by a thousand cuts," as Cuomo put it.

The plaintiffs have never had to prove their flimsy theories of liability in court. Indeed, judges have dismissed some of the lawsuits. But in this era of astronomical jury awards, a few losses could bankrupt the gun companies even if they win most of their cases. And the legal fees alone are potentially crushing, given the plaintiffs' strategy of deploying massive firepower on multiple fronts, the better to force the companies to settle.

This strategy forced Smith & Wesson to raise the white flag. The restrictions drafted by Administration officials and agreed to by the company require it to develop "smart gun" technology within three years, so that only authorized users can fire new handguns; to limit bulk purchases; to bar dealers from selling at gun shows unless the buyers have passed background checks; to include trigger locks with all new handguns (which Smith & Wesson was already doing); and more. Others may be driven to make similar concessions.

If the plaintiffs' divide-and-conquer strategy forces the rest of the industry to fall into line, the effect would be the de facto imposition of new, nationwide gun-control rules much like those that President Clinton has urged but that Congress has refused to pass. This is reminiscent of the far richer tobacco industry's $246 billion in settlements with state attorneys general in 1998: The intent, and effect, was to finance the payments (and the billions in legal fees) by sharply raising cigarette prices, in what

was the functional equivalent of a new nationwide tax on smokers—a tax that neither Congress nor state legislatures had voted to impose.

Will restrictions like those in the Smith & Wesson settlement reduce the number of shooting deaths? There's great dispute about that. Even some advocates of more-radical controls such as banning all handguns worry that "smart gun" technology might increase total gun deaths by stimulating the sale of tens of millions more guns to people who mistakenly think them safe. The National Rifle Association and other, more scholarly opponents of the new gun controls sought by the Administration argue that they would not have prevented the rash of highly publicized shootings since the Littleton, Colo., massacre last year, and that "smart guns" might fail when most needed for legitimate self-defense.

I suspect that restrictions such as those agreed to by Smith & Wesson would save some lives, and so I would like to see Congress pass most, or all, of the Administration's proposals. But with scholarly experts, detailed empirical studies, and millions of people on all sides of the issue, I can't be sure.

One thing I am sure of is that the Framers of the Constitution created Congress—and assigned to it "all legislative powers herein granted"—to set policy for the nation on such complex questions of social engineering. They also made it hard to enact legislation unless backed by a fairly broad national consensus. That's a far cry from what's going on now, with the Clinton Administration and its allies boasting of using lawsuits to bypass partisan gridlock in Congress.

Do the ends justify the means? After all, these lawsuits represent just the latest in a succession of mushrooming theories

of liability, expansive constitutional doctrines, and other trends that have led to deep intrusions by the judicial and executive branches into what was once the province of Congress. Why stop now, when so much needs to be done, and Congress is so unhelpful?

But the gun litigation represents a deeply disturbing way of making public policy. It was started by private lawyers and municipalities with big financial interests at stake. The courts have largely been bystanders as the Clinton Administration and its allies have sought to bludgeon gunmakers into settling before trial. And in the words of Robert B. Reich, Clinton's former Labor Secretary, in *The American Prospect*: "If I had my way, there'd be laws restricting cigarettes and handguns. [But] the White House is launching lawsuits to succeed where legislation failed. The strategy may work, but at the cost of making our frail democracy even weaker.... You might approve the outcomes in these two cases, but they establish a precedent for other cases you might find wildly unjust."

After the Supreme Court's 5–4 ruling that the federal Food and Drug Administration lacks the power to regulate tobacco without new legislation, President Clinton appropriately stressed that the Justices had been unanimous in asserting that "tobacco use... poses perhaps the single most significant threat to public health in the United States." He also called on Congress to pass a new law incorporating the now-voided FDA rule. Senate Majority Leader Trent Lott, R-Miss., immediately announced his opposition. It will be a bitter election-year struggle, with all players attending closely to how the voters will react to whatever they do.

That's called democracy. It's not always the quickest or easiest way to get things done. But it's the best way.

UNIT 2

Structures of American Politics

Unit Selections

Key Points to Consider

- Read Articles I, II, and III of the U.S. Constitution to get a picture of the legislative, executive, and judicial branches as painted by the words of the Framers. How does that picture compare with the reality of the three branches as they operate today?

- How might the presidency and Congress change in the next 100 years? What about the judicial branch?

- What advantages and disadvantages do each of the following have for getting things done: The president? The vice president: A cabinet member? The Speaker of the House of Representatives? The Senate majority leader? The chief justice? A top-ranking bureaucrat in an executive branch agency? A congressional aide?

- Which position in American government would you most like to hold? Why?

 **Links: www.dushkin.com/online/**
These sites are annotated in the World Wide Web pages.

Department of State
http://www.state.gov

Federal Reserve System
http://www.federalreserve.gov

Supreme Court/Legal Information Institute
http://supct.law.cornell.edu/supct/index.html

United States House of Representatives
http://www.house.gov

United States Senate
http://www.senate.gov

James Madison, one of the primary architects of the American system of government, observed that the three-branch structure of government created at the Constitutional Convention of 1787 pitted the ambitions of some individuals against the ambitions of others. Nearly two centuries later, political scientist Richard Neustadt wrote that the structure of American national government is one of "separated institutions sharing powers." These two eminent students of American politics suggest an important proposition: the very design of American national government contributes to the struggles that occur among government officials who have different institutional loyalties and potentially competing goals.

This unit is divided into four sections. The first three treat the three traditional branches of American government and the last one treats the bureaucracy. One point to remember when studying these institutions is that the Constitution provides only a bare skeleton of the workings of the American political system. The flesh and blood of the presidency, Congress, judiciary, and bureaucracy are derived from decades of experience and the shared expectations of today's political actors.

A second relevant point is that the way a particular institution functions is partly determined by the identities of those who occupy relevant offices. The presidency operates differently with George W. Bush in the White House than it did when Bill Clinton was president. Similarly, Congress and the Supreme Court function differently according to who serve as members and who hold leadership positions within the institutions. There were significant changes in the House of Representatives after Republican Newt Gingrich succeeded Democrat Tom Foley as Speaker in 1995 and again when fellow Republican Dennis Hastert took over from Gingrich in 1999. In the Senate, between January 2001 and January 2003, majority leader Trent Lott, a Republican, was succeeded by Democrat Tom Daschle, who was in turn succeeded by Republican Bill Frist. These changes in leadership brought obvious changes in the operation of the Senate.

The first section of this unit contains articles on the presidency. After twelve straight years of Republican presidents (Ronald Reagan and the elder George Bush), Democrat Bill Clinton assumed the presidency in 1993. For the first two years of his presidency, Democrats also held a majority of seats in both the House of Representatives and the Senate. But in the 1994 congressional elections, Republicans won control of the House and Senate, a development that inevitably led to changes in the way that Clinton functioned as president for the rest of his term in office. When George W. Bush became president in 2001, Republicans held a narrow majority in the House of Representatives and the Senate was split 50–50 between Republicans and Democrats. In May 2001, Senate Democrats gained a working majority. These changes in membership and leadership in both the executive and legislative branches necessarily affected the operation of the Bush presidency.

The September 11, 2001, terrorist attacks on the World Trade Center and the Pentagon abruptly transformed the context in which President Bush was operating. Americans rallied around President Bush in his efforts to respond decisively to the attacks. In the fall of 2002, amid growing signs that the United States would soon be at war with Iraq, President Bush campaigned effectively for Republican candidates. The president's party increased its margin of control in the House and regained majority control of the Senate. The functioning of the Bush presidency shifted accordingly.

The second section in this unit addresses Congress. The legislative branch underwent substantial changes in the last half century under mostly Democratic control. Reforms in the seniority system and the budgetary process in the 1970s brought an unprecedented degree of decentralization and, according to some observers, chaos to Capitol Hill. In addition, during the 1970s and 1980s, both the number of staff and special-interest caucuses in Congress increased. The unexpected Republican takeover of the House of Representatives as a result of the 1994 congressional elections brought even more changes to that body. The new Republican speaker, Newt Gingrich, reduced the power of committees, imposed term limits on committee chairs, consolidated power in the Speaker's office, and became a prominent figure on the national scene. But 1998 brought the downfall of Gingrich as a result of the November congressional elections and, for the second time in history, the impeachment of a president. The 2000 congressional elections narrowed the Republican majority in the House to a handful of seats and resulted in a historic 50–50 split of Democrats and Republicans in the Senate. Republican Trent Lott became Senate majority leader in January 2001, only to give way to Democrat Tom Daschle in midyear when Senator Jim Jeffords left the Republican Party and became an independent. Although Lott expected to return to the leadership position in January 2003 because of Republican victories in the November 2002 Senate elections, he instead had to resign his Republican leadership position amid a controversy that harked back to the 1948 presidential candidacy of segregationist Strom Thurmond. Republican Senator Bill Frist of Tennessee replaced Lott and inevitably brought more changes to the operation of the Senate.

The Supreme Court sits at the top of the U.S. legal system and is the main focus of the third section in this unit. The Court is not merely a legal institution; it is a policymaker whose decisions can affect the lives of millions of citizens. The Court's decisive role in determining the outcome of the 2000 presidential election showed its powerful role in the American political system. Like all people in high government offices, Supreme Court justices have policy views of their own, and observers of the Court pay careful attention to the way the nine justices interact with one another in shaping decisions of the Court. Membership of the nine-member Court—and, in turn, operation of the institution as a whole—has been unusually stable in the past decade, with no vacancies occurring since 1994.

The bureaucracy of the national government, the subject of the fourth and last section in this unit, is responsible for carrying out policies determined by top-ranking officials. The bureaucracy is not merely a neutral administrative instrument, and it is often criticized for waste and inefficiency. On the other hand, government bureaucracies must be given credit for many of the accomplishments of American government.

As a response to the September 11 terrorist attacks, Congress in 2002 passed a bill establishing the Department of Homeland Security, the biggest reorganization of the executive branch since the Department of Defense was founded in the aftermath of World War II. In addition, parts of the national government bureaucracy, most notably the FBI and the CIA, have been scrutinized and criticized as a result of the failure of U.S. government intelligence to detect and prevent the September 11 attacks. It is clear that the functioning of particular parts of the bureaucracy has become a prominent concern since the World Trade Center was destroyed.

The Return of the *Imperial Presidency?*

One lesson of American politics since September 11 is that some tensions between presidents and Congress spring from a deeper source than the partisan passions of the moment.

by Donald R. Wolfensberger

Moments after President George W. Bush finished his stirring antiterrorism speech before Congress last September, presidential historian Michael Beschloss enthusiastically declared on national television that "the imperial presidency is back. We just saw it."

As someone who began his career as a Republican congressional staff aide during the turbulence of Vietnam and Watergate in the late 1960s and early 1970s, I was startled by the buoyant tone of Beschloss's pronouncement. To me, "imperial presidency" carries a pejorative connotation closely tied to those twin nightmares. Indeed, *Webster's Unabridged Dictionary* bluntly defines *imperial presidency* as "a U.S. presidency that is characterized by greater power than the Constitution allows."

Was Beschloss suggesting that President Bush was already operating outside the Constitution in prosecuting the war against terrorism, or did he have a more benign definition in mind? Apparently it was the latter. As Beschloss went on to explain, during World War II and the Cold War, Congress deferred to presidents, not just on questions of foreign policy and defense, but on domestic issues as well. Whether it was President Dwight D. Eisenhower asking for an interstate highway system or President John F. Kennedy pledging to land a man on the moon, Congress said, "If you ask us, we will." Without such a galvanizing crisis, the president would not be able to define the national interest so completely. "Now," continued Beschloss, "George Bush is at the center of the American solar system; that was not true 10 days ago." In fact, just nine months earlier Beschloss had described Bush as "the first post-imperial president" because, for the first time since the Great Depression, "we were not electing a president under the shadow of an international emergency like the Cold War or World War II or an economic crisis." Then came September 11.

Still, it's hard to join in such a warm welcome for the return of an idea that was heavily burdened just a generation ago with negative associations and cautionary experiences. Presidential scholars understandably become admirers of strong presidents and their presidencies. But a focus on executive power can become so narrow as to cause one to lose sight of the larger governmental system, with its checks and balances. To invest the idea of the imperial presidency with an aura of legitimacy and approbation would be a serious blow to America's constitutional design and the intent of the Framers.

It was historian Arthur M. Schlesinger, Jr., who popularized the term *imperial presidency* in his 1973 book by that title. Schlesinger, who had earlier chronicled the strong presidencies of Andrew Jackson and Franklin D. Roosevelt in admiring terms, admits in *The Imperial Presidency* his own culpability in perpetuating over the years "an exalted conception of presidential power":

American historians and political scientists, this writer among them, labored to give the expansive theory of the Presidency historical sanction. Overgeneralizing from the [pre-World War II] contrast between a President who was right and a Congress which was wrong, scholars developed an uncritical cult of the activist Presidency.

The view of the presidency as "the great engine of democracy" and the "American people's one authentic trumpet," writes Schlesinger, passed into the textbooks and helped shape the national outlook after 1945. This faith of the American people in the presidency, coupled with their doubts about the ability of democracy to respond adequately to the totalitarian challenge abroad, are what gave the postwar presidency its pretensions and powers.

"By the early 1970s," Schlesinger writes, "the American President had become on issues of war and peace the most absolute monarch (with the possible exception of Mao Tse Tung of China) among the great powers of the world." Moreover, "the claims of unilateral authority in foreign policy soon began to pervade and embolden the domestic presidency."

Uniforms redolent of imperial pomp briefly appeared on White House guards in the Nixon administration, only to vanish after a public outcry.

The growth of the imperial presidency was gradual, and occurred "usually under the demand or pretext of an emergency," Schlesinger observes. Further, "it was as much a matter of congressional abdication as of presidential usurpation." The seeds of the imperial presidency were sown early. Schlesinger cites as examples Abraham Lincoln's 1861 imposition of martial law and his suspension of habeas corpus, and William McKinley's decision to send 5,000 American troops to China to help suppress the Boxer Rebellion of 1900. It is a measure of how much things have changed that Theodore Roosevelt's 1907 decision to dispatch America's Great White Fleet on a tour around the world was controversial because he failed to seek congressional approval. Then came Woodrow Wilson's forays into revolutionary Mexico, FDR's unilateral declaration of an "unlimited national emergency" six months before Pearl Harbor, and Harry Truman's commitment of U.S. troops to the Korean War in 1950, without congressional authorization, and his 1952 seizure of strike-threatened steel mills.

In 1973, the year *The Imperial Presidency* was published, Congress moved to reassert its war-making prerogatives during non-declared wars by enacting the War Powers Resolution over President Nixon's veto. The following year, prior to Nixon's resignation under the imminent threat of impeachment, Congress enacted two more laws aimed at clipping the wings of the imperial presidency and restoring the balance of power between the two branches. The Congressional Budget and Impoundment Control Act of 1974 was designed to enable Congress to set its own spending priorities and prohibit the president from impounding funds it had appropriated. The Federal Election Campaign Act of 1974 was supposed to eliminate the taint of big money from presidential politics. Subsequent years witnessed a spate of other statutes designed to right the balance between the branches. The National Emergencies Act (1976) abolished scores of existing presidential emergency powers. The Ethics in Government Act (1978) authorized, among other things, the appointment of special prosecutors to investigate high-ranking executive branch officials. The Senate, in 1976, and the House, in 1977, established intelligence committees in the wake of hearings in 1975 revealing widespread abuses; and in 1980 the Intelligence Oversight Act increased Congress's monitoring demands on intelligence agencies and their covert operations.

Since those Watergate-era enactments, presidential scholars have decried the way Congress has emasculated the presidency. As recently as January of last year, political scientist Richard E. Neustadt, author of the classic *Presidential Power* (1964), lamented that "the U.S. presidency has been progressively weakened over the past three decades to the point where it is probably weaker today than at almost any time in the preceding century." Neustadt cited congressional actions as one of several causes of the decline.

As one who worked in the House of Representatives from 1969 to 1997, I have long been puzzled by such complaints. They have never rung true. What I witnessed during those years was the continuing decline of the legislative branch, not its ascendancy. Even Congress's post-Watergate efforts to reassert its authority look rather feeble in the harsh light of reality. The War Powers Resolution has been all but ignored by every president since Nixon as unconstitutional. They have abided by its reporting requirements, but presidential military forays abroad without explicit congressional authority continue unabated. Bosnia, Kosovo, Haiti, Somalia, and Serbia come readily to mind.

The congressional budget act has been used by every president since Ronald Reagan to leverage the administration's priorities by using budget summits with Congress to negotiate the terms of massive reconciliation bills on taxes and entitlements. The independent counsel act has been allowed to expire twice—though, in light of the unbridled power it gives counsels and the potential for abuse, this may have been wise. Federal funding of presidential campaigns has not stopped campaign finance abuses. And congressional oversight of perceived executive abuses has met with mixed results at best.

In the meantime, presidents have been relying more heavily than before on executive agreements to avoid the treaty ratification process, and on executive orders (or memorandums) of dubious statutory grounding in other areas. Administrations have defied Congress's requests for information with increasing frequency, dismissing the requests as politically motivated. And they have often invoked executive privilege in areas not previously sanctioned by judicial judgments.

The most recent example is Vice President Richard Cheney's refusal, on grounds of executive privilege, to turn over to the General Accounting Office (GAO), an arm of Congress, information about meetings between the president's energy task force and energy executives. The controversy took on added interest with the collapse of Enron, one of the energy companies that provided advice to the task force. Vice President Cheney, who served as President Gerald R. Ford's White House chief of staff, said his action was aimed at reversing "an erosion of the powers" of the presidency over the last 30 to 35 years resulting from "unwise compromises" made by past Administrations. President Bush backed Cheney's claim of executive privilege, citing the need to maintain confidentiality in the advice given to a president.

It is revealing in this case that the congressional requests for information came not through formal committee action or subpoenas but more indirectly from the GAO, at the prompting of two ranking minority committee Democrats in the House, even though their Senate party counterparts are committee chairmen with authority to force a vote on subpoenas. The committee system, which should be the bulwark of congressional policy-making and oversight of the executive branch, has been in steady decline since the mid-1970s. Not the least of the causes is the weakening of committee prerogatives and powers by Congress itself, as a response to members' demands for a more participatory policy process than the traditional committee system allowed. Party leaders eventually replaced committee leaders as the locus of power in the House, a shift that was not altered by the change in party control of Congress in 1995.

Another contributing factor has been the shift in the Republican Party's base of power to the South and West, which has given a more populist and propresidential cast to the GOP membership on Capitol Hill.

Even with recent promises by Speaker of the House Dennis Hastert (R-Ill.) and Senate Majority Leader Tom Daschle (D-S.D.) to "return to the regular order" by giving committees greater flexibility and discretion in agenda setting and bill drafting, Congress is hamstrung by self-inflicted staff cuts and three-day legislative workweeks that make deliberative lawmaking and careful oversight nearly impossible. The "permanent campaign" has spilled over into governing, diminishing the value members see in committee work and encouraging partisan position taking and posturing. (It also makes members eager to get back to their districts for the serious work of campaigning, which explains the three-day work week in Washington.) It is easier to take a popular campaign stand on an unresolved issue than make a painful policy choice and explain it to the voters.

Bill Clinton had the common touch— and an imperial taste for sending U.S. troops abroad without congressional approval.

Is it any wonder that even before the current emergency the executive was in a stronger position than Congress? Such power alone is not necessarily a sign of an imperial presidency. But testing the limits of power seems to be an inborn trait of political man, and presidents are no exception. Even presidential power proponent Richard Neustadt, who sees the presidency at the beginning of this 21st century as the weakest it's been in three decades, concedes that none of the formal limits on presidential powers by Congress or the courts have managed to eliminate those powers of greatest consequence, including the "plentitude of prerogative power" (a Lockean concept of acting outside the

constitutional box to save the nation) that Lincoln assumed during the Civil War.

Both presidents George H. W. Bush and George W. Bush, to their credit, sought authorization from Congress for the use of force against Iraq and international terrorists, respectively, before committing troops to combat. Yet both also claimed they bad inherent powers as president to do so to protect the national interest. (The younger Bush was on firmer ground since even the Framers explicitly agreed that the president has authority to repel foreign invasions and respond to direct attacks on the United States.)

The presidency is at its strongest at the outset of a national crisis or war. Just as President Franklin D. Roosevelt was encountering public and congressional wariness over his depression-era policies in the late 1930s, along came World War II and a whole new lease on the throne. Presidential power tends to increase at the expense of Congress. Alexander Hamilton put it succinctly in *The Federalist* 8: "It is of the nature of war to increase the executive at the expense of the legislative authority."

One way to gauge this balance of power is to look at the extent to which Congress deliberates over policy matters and the extent to which it gives the president most of what he requests with minimal resistance. Two weeks after Congress passed a $40 billion emergency spending bill and a resolution authorizing the president to use force against those behind the World Trade Center attacks, Senator Robert S. Byrd (D-W.Va.) rose in a nearly empty Senate chamber to remind his colleagues of their deliberative responsibilities. "In the heat of the moment, in the crush of recent events," Byrd observed, "I fear we may be losing sight of the larger obligations of the Senate."

> Our responsibility as Senators is to carefully consider and fully debate major policy matters, to air all sides of a given issue, and to act after full deliberation. Yes, we want to respond quickly to urgent needs, but a speedy response should not be used as an excuse to trample full and free debate.

Byrd was concerned in part about the way in which language relating to the controversy over adhering to the 1972 antiballistic missile treaty had been jettisoned from a pending defense authorization bill in the interest of "unity" after the terrorist attacks. But he was also disturbed by the haste with which the Senate had approved the use-of-force resolution "to avoid the specter of acrimonious debate at a time of national crisis." Byrd added that he was not advocating unlimited debate, but why, he asked, "do we have to put a zipper on our lips and have no debate at all?" Because of the "paucity of debate" in both houses, Byrd added, there was no discussion laying a foundation for the resolution, and in the future "it would be difficult to glean from the record the specific intent of Congress."

A review of the *Congressional Record* supports Byrd's complaint. Only Majority Leader Daschle and Minority Leader Trent Lott (R-Miss.) spoke briefly before the Senate passed the emergency spending bill and the use-of-force resolution. The discussion was truncated chiefly because buses were waiting to take senators and House members to a memorial service at the National Cathedral.

The House, to its credit, did return after the service for five hours of debate on the resolution, which it passed 420 to 1. Some 200 members spoke for about a minute each—hardly the stuff of a great debate. At no time did any member raise a question about the breadth, scope, or duration of the authority granted by the resolution. The closest some came were passing references to the way in which President Lyndon B. Johnson had used the language of the 1964 Gulf of Tonkin Resolution as authority to broaden U.S. involvement in Vietnam.

To the credit of Congress, a small, bipartisan leadership group had earlier negotiated a compromise with the White House to confine the resolution's scope to "those nations, organizations or persons" implicated in the September 11 attacks. The original White House proposal was much broader, extending the president's authority "to deter and pre-empt any future acts of terrorism or aggression against the United States." The language change is significant. If President Bush cannot demonstrate that Iraq was somehow involved in the September 11 attacks but decides to take military action against it, he will have to decide whether to seek additional authority from Congress or act without it, as President Bill Clinton did before him.

In times of war or national emergency, presidents have always acted in what they thought to be the national interest. That is not to say that Congress simply becomes a presidential lap dog. While it tends to defer to the commander in chief on military matters once troops have been committed to combat, it continues to exercise oversight and independence on matters not directly affecting the war's outcome. For example, President Bush was forced to make drastic alterations in his economic stimulus package by Senate Democrats who disagreed with his tax relief and spending priorities. And even in the midst of the war on terrorism, the House and Senate intelligence committees launched a joint inquiry into why our intelligence services were not able to detect or thwart the September 11 terrorist plot. In the coming months, moreover, Congress is sure to have its own ideas on how the federal budget can best be allocated to meet the competing demands for defense, homeland security, and domestic social-welfare programs.

Is the imperial presidency back? While at this writing the White House has not overtly exercised any extraconstitutional powers, the imperial presidency has been with us since World War II, and it is most likely to be re-energized during times of national crisis. Every president tends to test the limits of his power during such periods in order to do what he deems necessary to protect national security. To the extent that Congress does not push back and the public does not protest, the armor of the imperial presidency is further fortified by precedent and popular support against future attacks.

What is the danger in a set of powers that have, after all, evolved over several decades into a widely recognized reality without calamitous consequences for the Republic? As James Madison put in *The Federalist* 51, "The separate and distinct exercise of the different powers of government... is admitted on all hands to be essential to the preservation of liberty." The "great security against a gradual concentration of power in the same department," he went on, is to provide each department with the "necessary constitutional means and personal motives to resist.... Ambition must be made to counteract ambition."

The Constitution's system of separated powers and checks and balances is not a self-regulating machine. Arthur M. Schlesinger, Jr., observed in *The Imperial Presidency*, that what kept a strong presidency constitutional, in addition to the president's own appreciation of the Framers' wisdom, was the vigilance of the nation. "If the people had come to an unconscious acceptance of the imperial presidency," he wrote, "the Constitution could not hold the nation to ideals it was determined to betray." The only deterrent to the imperial presidency is for the great institutions of our society—Congress, the courts, the press, public opinion, the universities, "to reclaim their own dignity and meet their own responsibilities."

Donald R. Wolfensberger *is director of the Congress Project at the Wilson Center and the author of* Congress and the People: Deliberative Democracy on Trial *(2000). He retired as chief of staff of the House Rules Committee in 1997 after a 28-year career on the staff of the U.S. House of Representatives.*

From *The Wilson Quarterly*, Spring 2002, pp. 36–41. © 2002 by the Woodrow Wilson International Center for Scholars in Washington, DC.

The Accidental Radical

GEORGE W. BUSH COULD END UP REALIGNING PARTISAN LOYALTIES AND REDEFINING WHAT HIS PARTY STANDS FOR. SOUND FAMILIAR?

By Jonathan Rauch

"I was a lightweight trading on a famous name, they said." That was George W. Bush, then still governor of Texas, writing in his 1999 book, *A Charge to Keep*. He might have been pleased to know that "they," the purveyors of conventional wisdom, had said the same of Franklin Delano Roosevelt. "A pleasant man," the pundit Walter Lippmann famously called Roosevelt, "who, without any important qualifications for the office, would very much like to be president." H.L. Mencken dismissed him as "Roosevelt Minor."

When he sought the presidency, FDR had been governor of New York for all of four years. In that brief time, he had used his natural amiability to good effect, working the state's political machinery to pass some modest but significant reforms, but he had also taken care not to be seen as radical. In the presidential race, his views appeared to be eclectic bordering on confused. "He seemed to have no clear philosophy," wrote Michael Barone in 1990, in *Our Country: The Shaping of America from Roosevelt to Reagan*. In early 1933, no one in America, including Franklin Roosevelt, imagined how Roosevelt would govern as president.

Quite early in his presidency, as it became clear that Roosevelt would press the powers of his office to the limit and beyond, Mencken's condescension would turn to hatred, an enmity that many Americans shared. In today's era of Saint FDR, people forget that Roosevelt was, in his own day, a bitterly polarizing figure. To his adversaries, he seemed no ordinary opponent but a larger kind of menace, a radical whose determination to aggrandize Washington and himself portended an American dictatorship. Behind the mask of geniality, they saw a ruthless partisan who intended not to govern alongside the Republicans but to obliterate them.

The alarmists misunderstood FDR, as many misunderstand President Bush today, but they did not underrate his significance. By the time he was finished, FDR had greatly enlarged the federal government (from 3 percent of gross domestic product in 1930 to 10 percent in 1940), launched the welfare state, invented the modern regulatory state, and turned a provincial nation into a superpower. He had seized the Progressives' centralizing agenda, thrust it upon what had been a dourly Jeffersonian party, and used it to weld together the coalition—unionists, farmers, Northern blacks, Southern populists, and urban liberals—that brought the Democrats to dominance for a generation.

George W. Bush has been compared to a number of other presidents, such as Ronald Reagan, Harry Truman, and even William McKinley. It may say something, however, that at the White House Correspondents' Association Dinner earlier this year, when *National Journal*'s Carl Cannon brought up the topic of former presidents, Bush expressed singular admiration for FDR. "He was a strong wartime leader, and a very strong commander-in-chief," Bush remarked.

Had he pursued the subject, Bush might have found further parallels. Not the least is that Bush, like Roosevelt, is an accidental radical. He is an amiable establishmentarian who finds himself with the opportunity to effect transformational change, and who is seizing that opportunity and pushing the system to its limits. Or beyond.

GOODBYE, BARRY GOLDWATER

Suppose, as seems quite possible, that Bush will sign a Medicare prescription drug benefit into law before the year is out. Then suppose, as a thought experiment, that Bush's presidency were to end next January, on the third anniversary of his inaugural. Bush would have done enough in three years to make an ambitious two-term president happy. On the domestic side:

- **Taxes.** He cut them, not once but annually. He did this despite the fact that, after the first tax cut, it became clear that he was, with the slow economy's help, creating fiscal deficits as far as the eye could see. Bush's tax cuts, as they emerged seriatim, proved to be aimed not just at reducing the government's revenue but also at changing the structure of the tax code to reduce personal rates and, especially, to reduce taxes on capital accumulation.

  Grover Norquist, a prominent Republican activist, claims that Bush will come back for a tax cut every year. White House officials I talked to would neither confirm nor deny this—probably because they don't yet know whether it's true—but they make no secret of Bush's commitment to both cutting and reforming taxes. "I think the president thinks the tax code has a lot of problems when it comes to the way it treats individuals and small businesses," says one White House aide.

- **Spending.** At the same time he cut taxes, Bush increased spending, and not just a little. "He's the biggest-spending president we've had in a generation," says Stephen Moore, the president of the Club for Growth, a conservative anti-tax group. Moore noted that Bush has increased federal spending more in his first three years than President Clinton did in eight. "We passed the biggest farm bill, the biggest education bill, and we're about to pass the biggest expansion in an entitlement since the Great Society," says Moore. And an upcoming energy bill might be more of the same. "His fiscal record is appalling," Edward H. Crane, the president of the libertarian Cato Institute, recently told *The New York Times*.

- **Federal activism.** Barry Goldwater, the father of modern small-government conservatism, argued that the federal government should have no education policies at all. Bush jettisoned that tenet and made Washington a force in education as never before. Bush boasts of "record levels of expenditure for elementary and secondary education programs." His No Child Left Behind Act has increased the federal government's share of education spending and used those dollars to establish annual testing and achievement standards in all 50 states, with the states driving but Washington supervising. Meanwhile, with the establishment of a muscular new Homeland Security Department, Bush has embarked on the most sweeping and centralizing reform of the federal government since at least President Truman's day. Goodbye, Barry Goldwater.

- **"Competitive sourcing."** Commonly and undeservedly overlooked is the Bush administration's drive to open hundreds of thousands of federal jobs to private-sector competition. (*See NJ, 7/12/03, p. 2228.*) The Clinton White House began this process within the Pentagon, "but outside the Defense Department, job competitions were virtually unknown," reports the June 2003 issue of *Government Executive* magazine. Bush has expanded so-called "competitive sourcing" by orders of magnitude. A 1998 inventory conducted by the Clinton administration found 850,000 federal employees doing jobs deemed commercial in nature. The Bush administration intends to "compete" fully half of those jobs. This can be done administratively, without Congress's approval, and it's now well under way.

- **Health.** "If a prescription drug bill passes this year, the administration will have promoted and passed a significant expansion of the welfare state in each of its first three years," writes Kevin A. Hassett, an economist with the American Enterprise Institute, in the July 14 issue of *National Review* magazine. The education and farm bills increased the federal government's power, but the effects of the new prescription drug benefit would overshadow them both. "The biggest expansion of government health benefits since the Great Society," Nancy-Ann DeParle, President Clinton's Medicare administrator, called it in *The Washington Post*. "Disaster" was the conservative Heritage Foundation's more succinct characterization.

Bush would cut an imposing figure had he accomplished only two or three of those things. And the White House has yet to roll out potential changes in Social Security. "We're not fin-

ished yet," one administration official says. "Before he's done, I think Social Security will be there." Bush will likely make private Social Security accounts an issue in the 2004 presidential race and then use his (as he hopes) strong electoral showing as a mandate for reform in 2005. Resetting FDR's crown jewel would, of course, be a momentous change, and note that any politically viable change would entail spending money, probably a lot of money, further widening the fiscal breach.

THROWING OUT THE RULE BOOK

"If you can get fundamental reform," the administration official says, "he's willing to put up the dollars to get it." That about sums up the Bush approach to domestic policy. It also describes the president's approach to foreign affairs, where the policy shift is even greater, but where Bush is spending not primarily cash but diplomatic capital and international goodwill. Consider:

- **Treaties.** On coming to office, Bush promptly rejected a series of international agreements. The best-known was the Kyoto global-warming treaty, but out the window with it went a small-arms agreement, a biological weapons agreement, the Comprehensive Test Ban Treaty, and the International Criminal Court. He then withdrew the United States from the Anti-Ballistic Missile Treaty, a cornerstone of the Cold War order. Most of that was *before* September 11.

- **Pre-emption.** After 9/11, Bush dynamited the very foundation of Cold War diplomacy when he repudiated the doctrine of containment. "After September 11, the doctrine of containment just doesn't hold any water, as far as I'm concerned," he said earlier this year, with typical bluntness. "We must deal with threats before they hurt the American people again." Not content to act pre-emptively in Iraq, he went so far as to announce a doctrine of pre-emption, thus speaking loudly while carrying a big stick. Bush was well aware that he was knocking over furniture and shocking the world. He didn't mind. He seemed to feel that the world needed a paradigm change and that quiet incrementalism was not going to produce one.

- **The Middle East.** Beginning with a speech on June 24 of last year, Bush likewise upended five decades of Middle East policy. Since the 1940s, the United States had refrained from calling for a Palestinian state and had accepted Arab authoritarianism as a given. Bush not only reversed both policies but yoked the two reversals together by conditioning Palestinian independence on Palestinian democratization. "Throwing out the rule book," is how Daniel Pipes, a prominent Middle East scholar, described Bush's actions, in a recent *New York Post* article. "It could well be the most surprising and daring step of his presidency," wrote Pipes—a step, he added, that did not emerge from the usual process of consensus-building in Washington but that instead "reflects the president's personal vision."

Underlying all of Bush's foreign-policy departures is a little-noted shift that may be the most fundamental of the bunch. Unlike foreign-policy realists (including his father), Bush does not believe that states should be regarded as legitimate just because they are stable and can be dealt with. And unlike internationalists (including his predecessor), he does not believe that states should be regarded as legitimate just because they are internationally recognized. He believes that legitimacy comes only from popular sovereignty and civilized behavior.

President Reagan horrified realists and internationalists alike by declaring that the Soviet Union was not a legitimate state. He would deal with the Soviet regime but never accept it. He aimed at regime change. Realists argued that Reagan's naivete would destabilize the world order, and internationalists feared that it would threaten hard-won human-rights agreements, but Reagan insisted—perhaps not so naively—that only freedom could produce stability and protect human rights.

Bush embraces Reagan's notion and extends it worldwide. He will deal with Saddam Hussein's Iraq, or Kim Jong Il's North Korea, or Yasir Arafat's Palestinian Authority, or Charles Taylor's Liberia, if he must, but he will not accept such a regime as entitled to exist and, one way or another, he will try to change it. Against such regimes, the use of force may be impractical or unwise, but it is certainly not illegitimate. Indeed, for Bush, the real puzzle is why anyone would object, in principle, to the toppling of a regime such as Saddam Hussein's, or why anyone would regard the United Nations, which no one ever voted for, as morally relevant.

And so Bush, like Reagan but more so, does not accept the world as he finds it. He regards the existing world order as unacceptably dangerous. The existing world order, returning the compliment, regards him the same way.

DEMAND-SIDE CONSERVATISM

Onlookers find it hard to get a bead on this man. That he is audacious is obvious, but to what end? As was true of Roosevelt, Bush acts with a unifying style—energetic, daring, even radical in the sense of starting from scratch—but not with an evident philosophical unity. As was also true of Roosevelt, the lack of an evident governing principle gives rise to suspicions. Perhaps the only principle is to win.

Perhaps, but it seems probable that Bush is aiming at something more, both politically and substantively. Politically, he aims, as FDR did, to realign partisan loyalties. Substantively, he aims to redefine conservatism.

"The Republican Party in 1994 tested a proposition," says a White House aide: "that people wanted government to be radically reduced. And they found out that people didn't want government to be radically reduced." Bush saw this, and he saw that the anti-government conservatism of Goldwater and Reagan had reached a dead end; and if there is a single characteristic that distinguishes Bush, it is his willingness to meet a dead end with a bulldozer. In 2002, "he really did set out to have the Republican Party stand for something different," says Michael Gerson, who signed on with Bush in 1999 and is now his chief speechwriter.

Bush's view, expressed in his book and in the 2000 campaign, is that government curtails freedom not by being large or active but by making choices that should be left to the people. Without freedom of choice, people feel no responsibility, and Bush insists again and again, as he put it in the book: "I want to usher in a responsibility era."

If one way to give people more choices is to shrink government, fine. But if another way is to reform government—also fine. And if he needs to expand government to deliver more

choices—well, he can live with that. For Bush, individual responsibility and Big Government are not necessarily opposed to each other, any more than global stability and regime change are necessarily opposites. Moreover, small-government conservatism was root-canal politics, but the new approach is a political winner. If you spend more money, people like you. If you give them more choices, they like you. But if you spend more money giving them more choices, they *really* like you.

And so, in the Bush paradigm, education reform buys tests and standards and public-school choice, and all of that helps parents judge and choose schools. The prescription drug benefit buys alternatives to one-size-fits-all, single-payer Medicare. Competitive sourcing buys alternatives to government bureaucrats. Social Security reform buys individual accounts. And so forth.

Many of these initiatives will make the federal government bigger or stronger, but, for Bush, that is beside the point, which is to change government's structure, not its size. The question is not how much government spends; it's *how* government spends. Conservatives have been obsessed with reducing the supply of government when instead they should reduce the demand for it; and the way to do that is by repudiating the Washington-knows-best legacy of the New Deal. Republicans will empower the people, and the people will empower Republicans.

"Twenty years from now," Norquist says, "who's demanding extra government if I have a 401(k) medical savings account, I've pre-saved for my old age, I have control over where I send my kids to school? Investing in smaller demand for state power down the road is a rational position."

So that is the sense in which the Bush paradigm is conservative, or at least imagines itself to be conservative. Besides, tax cuts dry up future Democratic spending initiatives; competitive sourcing weakens public employees unions; education reform weakens teachers unions; litigation reform weakens the trial lawyers; trade liberalization, another Bush priority, weakens private-sector unions. "The Democratic Party—trial lawyers, labor union leaders, the two wings of the dependency movement (people on welfare, people who manage welfare), the coercive utopians (people who tell us our cars should be teeny), government employees—all the parts of that coalition shrink," Norquist says, "and our coalition grows, every time you make one of these reforms."

THE PROGRESSIVE PRESUMPTION

The plan, therefore, has both tactical and strategic elements. In the short run, give people things they want; in the longer run, weaken the Democrats' base while creating, program by program, a new constituency of Republican loyalists who want the government to help them without bossing them around. Most important of all, however, is what might be thought of as the meta-strategy.

Essential to FDR's success in capturing the loyalty of two generations—first the New Deal generation, then the Great Society one—was his success in capturing the mantle of progressive reform for the Democrats. Woodrow Wilson, a Democrat, had been a reformer, but so was Theodore Roosevelt, a Republican. FDR's hyperactive reformism decisively resolved the ambiguity. Regardless of what one thought of particular New Deal programs, as a group they established the Democrats as the party of progress. From that day to this, Republicans have been stereotyped as backward-looking and nay-saying—the stick-in-the-mud party, the perennial advocate of "turning back the clock."

The identification of liberals and Democrats with progressivism is essential to the Democrats' political appeal and, especially, their self-confidence. When all else fails, they remain the party of enlightenment, not least in their own minds. Thus, in his new book, *The Clinton Wars,* Sidney Blumenthal, a former Clinton aide, characterizes Bush as attempting "to repeal the progressive policies of the 20th century." Progressive presidents (meaning Clinton) "are elected because they stand for the idea that the old ways will not work—and should not work," he writes, whereas conservative presidents (meaning Bush) "preserve their power through inertia... The allies of conservative presidents are indifference, passivity, and complacency. Nostalgia is the emotion that underlies many conservative sentiments—a magical belief that if little is done, a simpler, happier time can be restored and a world of change kept at bay."

Conservatives, for their part, believe that today they are the ones who stand for progressive change, in the face of "reactionary liberalism," but they have never been able to convince the public. That is what Bush seeks to do, both by rejecting the mantra of minimal government and by passing reform after reform. Never mind how you feel about any one of his initiatives; as a group, they seek to establish that it is Republicans who now "stand for the idea that the old ways will not work." If the Democrats dig in their heels and fall back on stale rants against greed, inequality, and privatization, so much the better. The voters will know whom to thank for the empowering choices that Republicans intend to give them. As for which is the "party of nostalgia," the voters will also remember who defended, until the last dog died, single-payer Medicare, one-size-fits-all Social Security, schools without accountability, bureaucratic government monopolies, static economics, and Mutually Assured Destruction.

Reagan, the other conservative reformer among recent presidents, made important changes, but his agenda was more about undoing (Big Government, inflation, detente) than doing. He also had to deal with a Democratic Congress and a predominantly Democratic country. Bush, by contrast, can reasonably expect to enjoy eight years in office with Republican majorities in Congress and, effectively, on the Supreme Court. Republican and Democratic voter-registration numbers are now about even.

"In a certain way, a president who's willing to take on the way things are has to be presented with a historic opportunity," Gerson says. "The president has been presented with very significant economic challenges, the elements of a war, and the elements of a cold war, all at once. And that's given him both the opportunity and, in foreign policy, the requirement to do some new thinking." No president has been in that kind of position since Roosevelt.

So, will it work? It might. It might not.

LOOKING BACK ON BUSH

In January 2019, 10 years after George W. Bush left the White House and retired from politics, a noted historian looked back on the Bush presidency.

"That it was a seminal administration is not in doubt. Bush set out to be a president who mattered, and this he achieved. He proved to be a risk taker like few the office has ever seen, and

through his first term, difficult though this is to credit now, he seemed invincible.

"Again and again, he gambled and won. His critics said that withdrawal from the ABM Treaty would cause a dangerous rift with the Russians, that his war in Iraq would cause a permanent rift with Europe, and that his refusal to deal with Yasir Arafat would merely enhance Arafat's standing. Yet Russia accepted the ABM decision mildly, Europe moved toward Bush's position on intervention against rogue states, and a new Palestinian prime minister came to power.

"But the bets he had placed were large, and the positions he had taken were exposed, and in time what had looked like victories began to sour.

"The war in Iraq went well, but the occupation afterward deteriorated into a slow bloodletting. Military personnel disliked and resented serving in Iraq; their families protested; the steady toll of casualties discouraged the public. Re-enlistment rates sagged and the military was pinned down—all at a time when Bush was multiplying U.S. commitments. By the middle of his second term, American forces were spread thinner and scattered more widely than ever before, but readiness and morale were declining. In 2006, Bush was forced to float the idea of a military draft. His prestige never fully recovered from the ensuing backlash.

"America was weaker, yet the threat had grown. Bush's preemption policy was read, first by North Korea and Iran, and then by other troublesome states, as an invitation to arm up with nuclear weapons before Bush could stop them. One member of the 'axis of evil' (Saddam Hussein's Iraq) had been defeated, but by 2006 the other two had become nuclear powers, and other nations were rushing to follow. With so much nuclear proliferation on so many fronts, the administration found itself with few options but to downplay the very threats that it had once painted so starkly.

"The European Union, though fitfully cooperative, had grown alarmed by America's power and its own helplessness. Its new defense force, a pipe dream when Bush came to power, was deployed and active by the time he left. Alas, it was too weak to do much good against any determined adversary but strong enough to trip up the United States. That became clear when, to the Bush administration's chagrin, the Europeans dispatched military forces to independent Palestine.

"Palestine had been intended as a democratic seed in the authoritarian Middle East, but it was a failed state from the beginning. Born prematurely and unable to control its militants, it had degenerated into a haven for terrorists, who turned their suicide-bombing skills not just against Israel but also against U.S. interests. When Israel threatened war, Europe stepped in as 'trustee.' Predictably, Europe's forces were neither able nor willing to confront and disarm the Palestinian militants, but by blocking Israeli and American action, they became shields for a new rogue state—one that Bush himself had helped to create.

"Bush's opponents charged that the world was now more dangerous than before, and America's strategic position weaker. The charge, not unfounded, resonated with voters, whose confidence both in Bush and in American power was rapidly waning. First in the 2006 congressional campaign and then in the 2008 presidential election, the new call for 'strategic disengagement' caught hold. Left-wing pacifism and right-wing isolationism, both fringe movements when Bush took office, found new strength with mainstream voters. America, assertive and confident when Bush took over, had become gun-shy and inward-looking.

"Bush's domestic policies brought their own share of unintended consequences. Bush had argued that his dramatic expansion of Medicare contained new elements of competition that, over time, could be built upon to modernize the program; but interest-group politics ensured that nothing of the sort happened. Competition remained the small tail of a very large dog, a dog that developed a voracious appetite for tax dollars.

"There were no tax dollars to feed it. The demands of an overstretched military and an aging population, combined with Bush's tax cuts, had created a permanent fiscal crisis. Nor had the economy grown as hoped. Bush had let federal spending soar, both for the military and for entitlement programs, and the initial stimulative effects were more than offset by the economic drag of a burgeoning public sector. America was not Argentina, but by late in Bush's tenure it was clear that the alternative to becoming Argentina was to raise taxes painfully or cut benefits painfully or, more likely, do both. Voters felt angry and betrayed.

"As Medicare costs soared, it was only a matter of time until Washington imposed price controls on prescription drugs. That was what some liberals had wanted from the start; conservatives had counted on Bush to stand in the way, but the fiscal crisis and predictable demagoguery against 'Big Pharma' made resistance impossible. By the turn of the decade, America had established one of the world's most elaborate systems of drug price controls, and the leadership in pharmaceutical innovation had passed to Asia.

"Bush's most fervent wish had been to raise educational quality, but schools had not improved. States had quickly learned to design tests and standards that imposed no pain. From Washington's requiring standards to its actually setting them was but a small step, one that Congress took in 2007. That year the Education Department announced America's first national curriculum.

"The Republican coalition, united behind Bush in his days of early success, splintered and then fractured as his fortunes waned. The Reagan-Goldwater wing abhorred the centralization and carefree spending; business deplored the fiscal crisis and price controls; hawks were dispirited by the country's inward turn. Weary voters grew nostalgic for the Clinton era, with its prosperity and moderation. They wanted a change. In the Democratic landslide of 2008, they got it. The window for a Republican political alignment, open when Bush took office, had closed, probably for a generation.

"In 2009, George W. Bush retired to his ranch in Texas. His nation and his party were not reluctant to let him go. Today he lives in relative isolation, a figure in equal parts imposing and tragic. Bush, like Woodrow Wilson and Lyndon Johnson, had aimed high and achieved much. But, like them, he had let his impatience and impetuousness get the better of him. He was energetic and assertive, admirably so, but, like more than a few politicians before him, he mistook boldness for sustainability. He pushed the system and the public too hard. He had campaigned originally as a 'humble' man, and in the end humility was forced upon him."

'MY FAITH FREES ME'

When Antonio de Mendoza, Spain's great first viceroy of Mexico, left office in 1550, he left behind advice for his successor. The secret of good government, he said, was "to do little and do it slowly."

Even before the 2000 election, Bush made it clear to anyone who bothered to read his book that he would not be Mendoza's sort of leader—or, for that matter, the sort his father was. "I learned a great deal from my dad's presidency and campaigns," the younger Bush wrote in *A Charge to Keep*. "I learned you must spend political capital when you earn it, or it withers and dies." His father, he noted ruefully, "never spent the capital he earned from the success of Desert Storm."

In the book, Bush returns again and again to his theory of political capital. Page 123: "I believe you have to spend political capital or it withers and dies. And I wanted to spend my capital on something profound." Page 218: "I had earned political capital… Now was the time to spend that capital on a bold agenda." His aversion to hoarding approval seems to flow as much from his personality as from his political experience. On page 2 he recounts hearing a sermon that "changed my life." It was, he writes, "a rousing call to make the most of every moment, discard reservations, throw caution to the wind, rise to the challenge." A few pages later: "I live in the moment, seize opportunities, and try to make the most of them."

Bush's mentality seems more like that of an entrepreneurial CEO than of a conventional politician: He tends to look for strategies that cut to the heart of the problem at hand, rather than strategies that minimize conflict. "He doesn't like 'small ball'—that's his term," one of his aides says.

"My faith frees me," Bush writes, early in his book. "Frees me to make the decisions that others might not like. Frees me to try to do the right thing, even though it may not poll well. Frees me to enjoy life and not worry about what comes next." He clearly is not a man who fears failure. Neither was Franklin Roosevelt, though FDR was freed not by faith but by a national crisis in which all the risks were on the side of doing too little.

The point of this article is not to predict failure for George W. Bush, much less to wish it. The point is to dramatize the stakes he is playing for. He is risking his presidency, his nation's fiscal and geopolitical strength, and the conservative movement. If he wins, he is FDR. If he loses, he is LBJ.

Uncivil Liberties

Remember Bush's promise to "change the tone"? There are six reasons why it hasn't happened.

By Carl M. Cannon

George W. Bush sought the presidency while saying little about foreign policy and presenting a modest domestic agenda consisting primarily of three major issues—or, to be precise, two issues and a theme. The issues were cutting taxes and improving public education. The theme, which Bush applied only to Washington, was restoring good manners to the conduct of the government's business.

Bush's proposed tax cuts are now law; an ambitious education measure is on the books as well. A terrorist attack and a war that none of the candidates saw coming has enveloped Bush's presidency. But this war has brought into focus the elusive quality of Bush's great promise to "change the tone" in Washington, a line that still crops up in Bush's stock political speeches.

In his first public address after wrapping up the Republican nomination, Bush spoke of ending "the arms race of anger" in American politics and restoring civility and integrity to Washington. Dissecting the "excessive partisanship" of the previous eight years, Bush blamed not only President Clinton and Vice President Gore but also Republican congressional leaders. "Both parties share some of the blame," he said in that April 26, 2000, speech. "It does not have to be this way. I will set a different tone. I will restore civility and respect to our national politics."

"I don't have a lot of things that come with Washington," Bush said in his acceptance speech in Philadelphia. "I don't have enemies to fight. And I have no stake in the bitter arguments of the last few years. I want to change the tone of Washington to one of civility and respect."

Bush returned to this theme repeatedly, and when he gave a victory statement after the long Florida recount, he spoke graciously of Gore and his running mate, Sen. Joe Lieberman of Connecticut. "Tonight I chose to speak from the chamber of the Texas House of Representatives, because it has been a home to bipartisan cooperation," Bush said that night. "The spirit of cooperation I have seen in this hall is what is needed in Washington, D.C."

Bush's views on the utility of cross-party civility had been forged in Austin, where, when he was governor, his close working relationship with Democratic Lt. Gov. Bob Bullock helped create a rare atmosphere of comity. It didn't hurt Bush personally, either. With Bullock's endorsement, Bush went to win re-election with nearly 70 percent of the vote, a victory that helped stamp him as the man to beat for the Republican presidential nomination.

Bush's bipartisan image, however, lost some of its luster during the primary campaign, mainly because of the Bush camp's brutish attacks on Sen. John McCain, R-Ariz., in the South Carolina primary. After Bush wrapped up the nomination, his advisers concluded from focus groups that Gore's appeal with swing voters declined whenever Gore went on the attack. This left an opening on the high road, where Bush performed better anyway. Even at his inauguration on January 20, 2001, Bush took time to laud his predecessors. "As I begin, I thank President Clinton for his service to our nation," he said. "And I thank Vice President Gore for a contest conducted with spirit and ended with grace."

But more than two and a half years later, the harsh rhetoric of the Democratic candidates who would replace Bush seems to suggest that grace is in short supply in American politics. *National Journal* put the question to several prominent Republicans: Did Bush change the tone in Washington? Yes, they say. He did his part, but the Democrats have refused to meet him halfway.

And the Democrats' view? Bush has indeed changed the tone in Washington—for the worse.

The partisan venting obscures some realities. One is just how difficult a proposition it is to usher in an era of civility. Another is how rare such a thing would be. In some ways, it would be alien to the rough-and-tumble spirit of elective democracy, especially in wartime.

"Sharp partisan differences serve the nation by giving Americans clear choices between issue positions," says Democratic political consultant Brad Bannon. "The Founding Fathers wanted civility in politics and government, but the campaign between Adams and Jefferson in 1800 makes Campaign 2004 look like a love-fest. Basically we live in a 50-50 nation, and politics will be partisan and shrill until one party has a clear advantage and builds a national consensus."

Bannon's argument is a good jumping-off point for examining six reasons why the tone of American politics has not changed appreciably in Bush's first three years in office.

1. Politics Ain't Beanbag

This is especially true of presidential politics. Only 43 men have been president. Two of them, Andrew Johnson and Bill Clinton, were impeached, although they managed to avoid conviction in the Senate. A third, Richard Nixon, resigned to avoid impeachment and almost certain removal. Four American presidents, Abraham Lincoln, James A. Garfield, William McKinley, and John F. Kennedy, were assassinated in office. Six others—Andrew Jackson, Theodore and Franklin Roosevelt, Harry Truman, Gerald Ford, and Ronald Reagan—were shot at (it happened to Ford twice). TR and Reagan were wounded.

Verbal assaults and insults also come with the job. Many liberal Yale faculty members affronted George W. Bush by boycotting his commencement address at his alma mater. Eight years earlier, military veterans conspicuously turned their backs on Clinton when he appeared at the Vietnam Veterans Memorial during his first Memorial Day as commander-in-chief. Clinton tended to blame Rush Limbaugh for his troubles, but such rabble-rousers have always been part of the American landscape. Thomas Jefferson was christened "Mad Tom" by the opposition newspapers of his day; Lincoln was routinely lampooned as a baboon and an ape. Before Clinton was dubbed "Slick Willie" by a home-state newspaperman, California liberals coined the oniker "Tricky Dick" for Richard Nixon.

Long before conservatives chose to pillory Hillary, they made an indoor sport of abusing Eleanor. The wives of Grover Cleveland's Cabinet officers were asked at social functions about (fabricated) rumors that the president beat his wife while drunk. Cattiness toward Mrs. Cleveland was presaged by truly nasty—and published—attacks on Mary Todd Lincoln. In Lyndon Johnson's second term, his daughter Luci could hear demonstrators' chants of "LBJ, LBJ, how many kids have you killed today?" from her bedroom windows in the White House. Johnson came to office because of the death of a popular—but also widely reviled—American president. Neither JFK's charisma, nor his medals for valor in the Pacific while serving in the Navy, spared him the vitriol. In Georgia, the marquee of a movie theater showing *PT 109*, the movie about Kennedy's exploits, read, "See how the Japs almost got Kennedy."

It was ever thus. During a 1793 Cabinet meeting, Secretary of War Henry Knox showed George Washington a newspaper cartoon lampooning America's first president—it depicted him on the guillotine—for supposedly longing to be king. An infuriated Washington launched into a spectacular tirade that left the Cabinet members speechless. "There was a pause," Jefferson noted later. "Some difficulty in resuming our question."

Perhaps fearful of a similar performance in front of his own Cabinet, another president named George, the current chief executive, says he avoids editorial cartoons and editorials altogether. At a dinner earlier this year, President Bush confided that it wouldn't be constructive for him to get steamed up about opinion journalists who laid into him. "I've got to stay positive," he explained.

2. Florida on Their Minds

It is axiomatic in politics that voters don't cotton to candidates who look back. But these days, many Democratic activists remain obsessed with the 2000 election. Tipper Gore has repeatedly described the election as the time "when we won, but the Supreme Court decided we couldn't serve." Her frustration is understandable, but party professionals who ought to know better sound no different. "Gore … beat the other guy. The election was stolen," former Democratic nominee Michael Dukakis said publicly.

"We won that election, and they stole that election," Democratic Party chief Terence McAuliffe said in a 2001 speech to the Democratic National Committee. "President Bush tells us to get over it. Well, we're not going to get over it."

Leading liberal lights have taken this cue and run with it. "Bush is not our elected president," Gloria Steinem insists on the college lecture circuit. "He took office due to fraud in Florida. … He should be impeached." Filmmaker Michael Moore, in interviews following his anti-Bush tirade at the 2003 Oscar ceremony, echoed this theme. "The majority of Americans never elected this guy in the White House. And I'll keep saying that until he's out of there."

There is a performance-art feel to such outbursts, but in venting this way, prominent Democrats have unleashed passions they couldn't control even if they wanted to. Liberal Internet sites and letters-to-the-editor columns have repeated this "stolen election" formulation for nearly three years now, with no signs of abating.

The immediate upshot is that this reservoir of anti-Bush passion has produced a surge of grassroots support for former Vermont Gov. Howard Dean, the outsider who quickly came to be seen as the candidate who would give Bush the most hell in an election that many activists see as a kind of recall election of Bush. The Dean boom, in turn, has created a rhetorical arms race in anti-Bush invective among the other Democratic candidates. Sen. John Kerry, D-Mass., tells democrats it's time for "regime change" in Washington, while Sen. John Edwards, D-N.C., has termed Bush's budget policies "the most radical and dangerous economic theory to hit our shores since socialism." Rep. Dick Gephardt, D-Mo., who gave Bush visible support at the outset of the Iraq war, now pronounces the president "a miserable failure on foreign policy and on the economy." In a September 9 debate among the Democratic candidates, Bush and his policies were dubbed "outrageous," "abominable," and "a nightmare."

After the debate, Republican National Committee Chairman Ed Gillespie complained that the attacks constituted "a continuing patter of political hate speech." Or perhaps just a particularly spirited presidential campaign.

3. A Polarized Congress

That Bush might tread lightly after assuming power without winning the popular vote seems never to have entered the thinking of the White House brain trust. In terms of projecting an aura of effectiveness, this made sense. Privately, many congressional Democrats took their hats off to Bush for his self-confident approach. But that was before he began governing as though he'd carried, say, 49 states and won 60 percent of the popular vote.

"The reason why Bush is so polarizing is because he has pursued the most radical conservative agenda in modern history," says David Sirota, a veteran Capitol Hill legislative aide who now works for the Center for American Progress, a new liberal think tank.

Former White House press secretary Ari Fleischer counters that neither he nor current White House spokesman Scott McClellan has taken shots at opposition members of Congress, something that was common from the podium in the White House briefing room during Clinton's tenure. "Howard Dean criticizes Bush every day, but when he made that stumble on Israel, we stayed out of it," Fleischer said. "I mean, he served us up a softball on a tee—we could have whacked it out of the park. But Bush won't let us." Adds McClellan, "He really discourages personal criticism."

Democrats acknowledge the basic truth of this assertion, but point out that however polite Bush is, he is still maddening to them. "The polarity of Washington does not have much to do with Bush's personality; it has to do with his political program," Sirota says. "He ran as a right-of-center politician, and instead what we have is a right-of-the-Radical-Right president."

In other words, Bush doesn't get much credit from Democrats for refraining from personal invective during legislative fights because he is doing something they find almost as bad: namely, ignoring them, which means ignoring something like half of the country. They say this does not represent much of a change in tone. "About a month ago, I was meeting someone in the reception room near the House floor, and the devil incarnate—Newt Gingrich—was there," Bannon recalled. "And I thought to myself how little things had changed since he gave up his command."

Perhaps surprisingly, the "devil incarnate" does not really disagree with the Democrats' assessment. "There are profound differences in power—and in values—and these things have consequences," Gingrich said in an interview. "Bush's priorities are so far at odds with the lib-

eral wing of the Democratic Party, it's going to engender a reaction—and it has. He's pretty pleasant about it, but he's a guy who doesn't compromise much. He just calmly and purposely does what he does."

"Bush is a radical," adds Texas A&M presidential scholar George C. Edwards III. "That is not necessarily bad, but it is polarizing." Edwards ticks off the issues on which Bush has taken bold, conservative stands: tax-cutting in wartime, sweeping federal mandates on local education, defense reorganization, the pre-emptive national security strategy, partial privatization of Social Security. "They are major departures and likely to irritate a lot of people," Edwards said.

Norman Ornstein of the American Enterprise Institute noted that Bush "started with at least some promise of a new beginning, twinning the tough partisan approach on tax cuts to the work-with-liberals approach on education." But, he added, "education was not repeated. For the next eight months, we saw only partisan bills emerging, especially in the House, where Democrats felt utterly powerless and humiliated."

It's also true that when Democrats controlled the House, they oversaw the same smash-mouth, winner-take-all system. But Democrats insist that if Bush was serious about changing the tone in politics, he'd have had a man-to-man talk with majority leader and fellow Texan Tom DeLay.

"A president is the only one who can change the tone," says Bruce Reed, president of the centrist Democratic Leadership Council. "Only a president has the political capital to reach across party lines." Reed, who was Clinton's top domestic policy adviser, says Bush carries a "special burden" to do this, because he ran on it. "I believe that Bush's failure to change the tone in Washington is one of the great disappointments of his presidency, and a real vulnerability for Republicans in 2004 and beyond," Reed said. "Some Democrats are so angry, they don't see this and are tempted to look for a fierce partisan of our own."

Congress is so polarized ideologically that reaching consensus would be difficult for any president. Gerrymandering has left the generic Democratic House member far more liberal than the nation as a whole, while making the average Republican member far more conservative. Compounding the problem are the single-issue interest groups, which have never been better organized or more influential.

"One of the byproducts of having so many interest groups demanding policy, and doing so from perches in Washington where they interact daily with elected officials, is that there is less give in the system," says political scientist Martha Joynt Kumar of Towson State University. "Groups don't want to compromise, and they have multiple routes to influencing policy, including passing their information to reporters to try to prevent backsliding by officials who otherwise might compromise on their policy interests."

packaging the President

What the public sees of the nation's chief executive is carefully manipulated by the spin doctors at the White House

By Todd S. Purdum

A somber, dark-suited President George W. Bush cuts through row on row of stark white crosses in Normandy, France. He stands so close to that other George's carved-rock face at Mount Rushmore that he seems already immortalized there. In China, the most populous nation on earth, he and his wife, Laura, smile all alone on the Great Wall.

The pictures are striking—and no accident. If you've ever wondered why photographs of the President turn out so much better than the ones in your family scrapbook, it may be because the Bush White House—like its predecessors—works overtime to guarantee the most flattering images possible.

In fact, these pictures have a special name. They're not just photos. They're "photo opportunities," photo-ops for short, a term coined more than 30 years ago by Ron Ziegler, press secretary for President Richard M. Nixon, whose staff institutionalized the practice.

WHEN REALITY WASN'T VIRTUAL

Once upon a time, news photographers had the kind of access to Presidents and other politicians that let them capture spontaneous reality (even if they often protected their subjects in exchange). Franklin D. Roosevelt, who led the country through the Great Depression and World War II, was paralyzed from the waist down by polio and needed a wheelchair or heavy leg braces to move around. But most of the public never knew, because the press never showed them.

Some Presidents just couldn't avoid the camera's unflattering glare. Lyndon B. Johnson, who was President during the Vietnam War, once decided to prove his health by pulling up his shirt to show off the scar from gall-bladder surgery. In the mid-1970s, President Gerald R. Ford managed to trip in public just often enough to give a young comedian named Chevy Chase and a new TV program called *Saturday Night Live* lots of good material.

CHOOSING THE VIEW

Gradualy, however, through a combination of heightened security concerns and determined effort to control what the public sees, presidential aides have penned up photographers in smaller spaces, all but guaranteeing that they will use the camera angle and backdrop the White House wants.

That usually means big flags, majestic mountains, beautiful beaches, smiling children, uniformed troops, helmeted firefighters, soaring skyscrapers, and a blue-and-white Boeing 747 better known as *Air Force One*. Nine times out of 10, the tactic works, because it produces such terrific pictures.

Every White House has at least one person whose main job is to worry about such things. Josh King, had the impressive title "director of production for presidential events" under Bill Clinton, and worried about camera angles from the Grand Tetons to the World War II beaches of France.

FINDING THE RIGHT SPOT

"The world sees your candidate through the lens of a TV or still camera, filtered by the folks laying out the paper or editing the package," King says. "So you always try to think from their perspective and provide a tableau to match their needs. And then you manage the geometry of the exact spot you designate for the cameras and the line between that spot, your candidate, and the things that are happening around and behind him or her. The result should be a newsworthy composition."

Every so often an unflattering image still crops up. In 1992, the first President Bush vomited and fainted at a state dinner in Japan, and the episode was captured on videotape. The video was taken by a stationary camera that was supposed to tape the dinner speeches and the toasts—but nothing else. When a technician viewing a monitor in another room saw chaos erupting in the ballroom, he turned on the recorder and preserved a bit of history that the White House would have liked to forget.

TODD S. PURDUM is a Washington correspondent for *The New York Times*.

A Partner in Shaping an Assertive Foreign Policy

By ELISABETH BUMILLER

WASHINGTON, Jan. 6 — Condoleezza Rice, President Bush's national security adviser, stood in front of Mr. Bush's desk in the Oval Office last summer and tried to coax the president into something he did not want to face.

She suggested, carefully, that the White House begin repairing the rupture with the allies over Iraq by reaching out to Germany, whose chancellor, Gerhard Schröder, had infuriated the president by campaigning for re-election on an antiwar platform. Mr. Bush, simply put, did not trust him.

"I can't do it with Schröder," Mr. Bush told Ms. Rice, according to a senior administration official who witnessed the exchange. Ms. Rice, who had not directly suggested that Mr. Bush meet with Mr. Schröder, rushed to reassure. "No, no, no, we won't make you do it with Schröder," she said. But Mr. Bush seemed to know what Ms. Rice had in mind. "Wait a minute, you'll get me back with Schröder, I know what you're trying to do," the president said, the official recounted.

Soon enough, a meeting to begin defrosting relations was set up between Mr. Bush and Mr. Schröder at the session last September of the United Nations General Assembly. "'I knew that was going to happen,'" Mr. Bush laughingly told Ms. Rice after the meeting was scheduled, the senior administration official said. Ms. Rice gently bantered back, the official said, but then concluded, " 'Now, look, it's the right time to do it.' "

Condoleezza Rice began her relationship with George W. Bush as the foreign policy tutor who educated the little-traveled 2000 presidential candidate in the complexities of a world more dangerous than either of them knew. Now, three years, two wars and countless crises later, the relationship between the president and Ms. Rice has evolved into a partnership that has shaped one of the most assertive foreign policies in recent American history.

Like a number of earlier relationships between national security advisers and their bosses, including Henry Kissinger's association with Richard Nixon and Zbigniew Brzezinski's work with Jimmy Carter, Ms. Rice's interactions with Mr. Bush have developed into a fulcrum for the development of foreign policy. But even more than those earlier collaborations, Ms. Rice's relationship with Mr. Bush has been closely guarded.

Now, as Ms. Rice heads into what she insists will be her last year of service in the White House, she and other top Bush advisers have begun to lift the veil of secrecy about her relationship with the president, with whom she spends an extraordinary amount of time— long days at the White House, summer walks at the president's Texas ranch, weekends of gym workouts, football games on television and jigsaw puzzles with the president and first lady at Camp David. There, Ms. Rice has a cabin to herself on the wooded grounds.

"I sit with my reading and my cup of coffee, and especially if it's winter, I make a fire," Ms. Rice said in one of two recent interviews in her spacious West Wing office. "It's really not tough duty. But, of course, I look forward to having control of my life."

Ms. Rice is hardly the only important foreign policy adviser to Mr. Bush in a sometimes contentious inner circle that includes Vice President Dick Cheney, Defense Secretary Donald H. Rumsfeld and Secretary of State Colin L. Powell. Mr. Cheney, who lunches alone with Mr. Bush once a week and maintains his own national security staff, has had an especially large role in policy making, including the decision to go to war with Iraq.

Competing Viewpoints

In Washington, Ms. Rice has faced increasing criticism that while she has done a good job as the president's friend and cheerleader, she has done a bad job of managing the president's frequently warring foreign policy team.

Her inability to rein in other powerful advisers, critics say, has helped lead to little planning for the occupation in Baghdad, stalled negotiations between the Israelis and Palestinians, and no success in stopping North Korea from making nuclear weapons.

"She has a problem that I didn't have," said Brent Scowcroft, who was national security adviser to Mr. Bush's father and a longtime mentor to Ms. Rice. "Everyone then was facing in the same direction, but she's got people facing in opposite directions. And that's really hard."

Ms. Rice discounts the criticism, and several senior advisers to Mr. Bush said it was in fact the president who demanded the open debate. "The president has never said, 'I want only one opinion presented in the Oval Office,'" said Andrew H. Card Jr., the White House chief of staff. Ms. Rice, he said, "does not run around affixing muzzles to our faces."

Either way, no other adviser spends as much time with the president as Ms. Rice. "He takes Cheney seriously, obviously," said a senior administration official, "but she's the last person to talk him through it."

In short, Ms. Rice has become a germination point for Bush foreign policy, from the war in Iraq to sidelining Yasir Arafat to the policy of pre-emption. As a Russia specialist and a former provost of Stanford University, she says she has melded her realism — the view that great powers act in their own self-interest — with what she calls Mr. Bush's idealism, or what his critics say is his naïve belief in a "moral" American foreign policy that can spread democracy throughout the world.

In this equation, Ms. Rice is the unsentimental academic who focuses on facts and history, while Mr. Bush starts with a set of big-picture principles rooted in his Christian faith, along with a politician's sense about other leaders and the pressures that drive them. Ms. Rice said that she saw her job as translating the president's instincts into policy, and that he now influenced her as much as she influenced him.

"This president has a very strong anchor and compass about the direction of policy, about not just what's right and what's wrong, but what might work and what might not work," Ms. Rice said. The president likes to focus "on this issue of universal values and freedom," and after Sept. 11, she said, "I found myself seeing the value of that."

It is not, she added, "the orientation out of which I came."

Mr. Bush declined to be interviewed for this article, but as a presidential candidate in 2000 he gave a reporter a hint of his chemistry with Ms. Rice. "She's fun to be with," Mr. Bush said. "I like lighthearted people, not people who take themselves so seriously." Besides, he said, "She's really smart!"

A Friend to the Family

To the Bushes, Ms. Rice, 49, is almost a surrogate daughter, a charming, reassuring and — in private — sardonic presence who can explain Middle East policy in five digestible bites. She is also, like the president's mother and another influential adviser, Karen P. Hughes, a tough-minded woman brimming with self-confidence.

To Ms. Rice, an only child who has never married and whose parents have died, the Bushes are some of the closest friends she has. Just about the only time she spends away from her job, and the

Bushes, is on Sunday afternoons, when Ms. Rice, who trained as a concert pianist, returns from Camp David and practices with a chamber music group.

"We are all in one way or another close to the family, but she is especially close to the family because of the time she spends with the president," said Mr. Powell, who was national security adviser to Ronald Reagan. "This is not unusual, but at the same time, a little unusual."

Ms. Rice, a former Democrat turned ardent, hawkish Republican, has no trouble making her views known to the president. Last summer, along with Mr. Powell, she urged Mr. Bush to intervene militarily in the civil war in Liberia, over the opposition of the Pentagon. Mr. Bush eventually approved sending a contingent of 200 marines.

"And what he would challenge me on is, 'All right, if we send X number of marines, and they're at the airport, and they are characterized in a particular way, what's that going to do to our central premise that this is an African peacekeeping effort, not an American one?'" Ms. Rice said.

More recently, she told Mr. Bush she was concerned about developments in Russia, where the man Mr. Bush calls a trusted friend, President Vladimir V. Putin, has jailed the country's richest businessman.

"Then, usually, there's a conversation: 'Well, how do we communicate that?'" Ms. Rice said. In this case, she said, the president raised his unease in a conversation with Mr. Putin, "in a broad sense of just saying," Ms. Rice said, " 'O.K., everybody is concerned about this.'"

Making Arguments

Ms. Rice is the first to say that the president does not always take her advice, and that one of the biggest misperceptions about him is that he is captive to the competing views of his foreign policy advisers.

"I don't talk the president into almost anything, all right?" Ms. Rice said. "I just want that understood. You can't do that with the president. What you can do with the president is make your arguments."

In Northern Ireland this past April, Mr. Bush and Ms. Rice had a tense dis-

agreement about a phrase that Mr. Bush planned to use in a joint news conference with Prime Minister Tony Blair of Britain. With American and British forces making quick gains in Iraq, Mr. Bush wanted to say that the United Nations would have a "vital role" in an American-led occupation. Mr. Blair and Mr. Powell agreed. But Ms. Rice, according to a senior administration official, was under pressure from officials in Mr. Cheney's office who disliked the United Nations and thought "vital" was going too far.

The president used the word anyway — not once, but nine times. Afterward, the senior administration official said, Ms. Rice was "fussing about it a bit because she was afraid she might have some explaining to do back here in order to cover all of our various constituencies. And after a while, the president got annoyed about it."

The president, the official said, then cut off Ms. Rice, curtly telling her, the official recounted, "I did it, and that's it." The two nearly made a scene, the official said. "They almost had to go off for a minute to sort it out," the official recounted. "And then it blew over."

But Ms. Rice worked hand in hand with Mr. Bush on translating into policy his belief that democracy has a chance in the Middle East — now a central goal of his administration. In the spring of 2002, when violence raged between the Israelis and Palestinians, Ms. Rice said the president began to question not whether we "were pushing this party hard enough or that party hard enough," but "Did we have some fundamental problems here?"

Mr. Bush concluded that they did, and that Mr. Arafat had to be marginalized so that a democratic Palestinian state might emerge.

"When you think about the way people had thought about the Middle East, it was just about land," Ms. Rice said. "And the innovation here, and it was the president's innovation, was to take this sense that these values are universal, and that democratic states are different, and to apply that to the Middle East."

Since then, Ms. Rice has taken considerable control of the Middle East policy through Elliott Abrams, the fiercely pro-Israel director of Middle East Affairs at the National Security Council, whom Ms. Rice hired a year ago. Although Mr. Powell has been the administration's longtime point person on the negotiations, Ms. Rice traveled to the Middle East with Mr. Abrams last spring, and through him has enforced Mr. Bush's insistence that the United States not deal with Mr. Arafat.

Ms. Rice was in similar lock step with Mr. Bush, and Mr. Cheney, on going to war with Iraq, senior advisers to the president said, and served as an implementer of the president's wishes. Richard Haass, the former director of policy planning at the State Department who is now the president of the Council on Foreign Relations, recalls going to see Ms. Rice in July 2002, well before the president began making a public case for ousting Mr. Hussein, to discuss with Ms. Rice "the pros and cons" of making Iraq a priority.

"Basically she cut me off and said, 'Save your breath — the president has already decided what he's going to do on this,'" Mr. Haass said.

In the same way, Ms. Rice has worked to carry out Mr. Bush's demand for six-party talks, rather than direct American negotiations, to try to get North Korea to dismantle its nuclear weapons program. She shows no patience with other agencies that wanted a different approach.

"I'm not going to spend time trying to manage what level four at State and Defense think about our North Korea policy," Ms. Rice said, referring to lower-level officials.

Similarly, Ms. Rice and Mr. Bush decided last August at the president's ranch to bring the management of the administration's Iraq policy to the White House, after the Pentagon managed the war, under the purview of Ms. Rice and a new Iraq Stabilization Group.

It is unclear what has changed in the administration of Iraq policy since then. Ms. Rice will only say that her group "is really kind of the traditional role for the N.S.C. adviser" — a point made more sharply by Mr. Rumsfeld, the perceived loser in the switch.

At the time, Mr. Rumsfeld said he had "no idea" why Ms. Rice sent him a memorandum on the subject — an unusual public breach in a relationship that some in the administration liken to that of a cantankerous uncle with a take-charge niece. Ms. Rice is intimidated, some critics say, by the combative Mr. Rumsfeld.

"Really?" Ms. Rice said, pointedly. "I wonder if Don Rumsfeld would think that. I don't think so." Mr. Rumsfeld, she said, "has a kind of a bluntness that I actually like. We're able to be direct with each other, but we're friends, and have been for years."

She has managed men older than herself for years, she said. "I was the provost of Stanford University at 38, O.K.?" she said.

Ultimately, she added, she will look back on her job as that of a pianist in a chamber music group.

"The pianist is always facing the fact that this beast that is the grand piano can just overwhelm in sound and volume and drama any string, or all of the strings together," she said. "So you want your playing to have personality, but you don't want it to be front and center, overwhelming. It has to be part of the team."

The State of Congress

The legislative process is a mess, in the view of increasingly alarmed critics. But a *National Journal* analysis finds that both parties share responsibility.

By Richard E. Cohen, Kirk Victor, and David Baumann

For many Democrats, the way that Republicans pushed the Medicare bill to enactment late last year is Exhibit A in "What's Wrong With Congress." After each chamber approved Medicare legislation in June, a handful of senior Republican lawmakers dispensed with the formality of a House-Senate Conference committee and rewrote much of the bill during months of closed-door negotiations last fall. The Republicans excluded most of the Democratic conferees, except for two key centrist Senate Democrats who supported the legislation to begin with.

Then on November 22, Republican leaders held open the House vote on the Medicare conference report for an unprecedented three hours, beginning at 3 a.m., while they struggled to round up the necessary votes. One retiring Republican who opposed the bill even charged that GOP leaders attempted to pressure him by tying his vote to future financial and political support for his son's congressional campaign. Finally, following phone calls from President Bush, two junior Republicans switched their votes and backed the bill just before 6 a.m.

Immediately after that showdown, Democrats expressed outrage at the Republicans' tactics. "This vote was stolen from us by the Republicans," House Minority Leader Nancy Pelosi, D-Calif., said in a statement. "We won it fair and square, so they stole it by hook or crook." She added: "If there was ever an argument to be made for why Republicans are not fit to be in the majority in this House and why they

must be defeated at the polls next year, one need only look at their conduct on the floor of this House tonight. It brought dishonor to this institution."

For his part, Senator Minority Leader Tom Daschle, D-S.D., told reporters, "This was the most egregious violation of the rules of the institution that I've seen in 25 years. It's horrendous. It's reprehensible. It is very, very regrettable. I think that we've seen a diminution of respect for the rule of law. And that's abhorrent."

Two weeks later, as Congress prepared to leave town for the holidays, Pelosi and Daschle were still seething. In fact, at a December 9 press conference, they issued a harsh condemnation of the entire first session of the 108th Congress. "There is a very, very heavy hand of partisanship prevailing," Pelosi said, adding later that the situation "has gone so far beyond what the American people expect and deserve, and so far beyond what our Founding Fathers gave their lives, liberty, and sacred honor for."

Daschle said he was "very deeply disappointed" with "the extraordinary partisan way with which a lot of this work was resolved, without our involvement and participation, virtually against all the rules of the Congress." He called it "the single most partisan session of Congress that I participated in."

For many months, Pelosi, Daschle, and other Democrats had been ramping up their criticism of the way the Republicans were running Congress since assuming control of both chambers last January. A

turning point came in the summer, when House Ways and Means Committee Chairman Bill Thomas, R-Calif., set off a furor by calling the Capitol Police to evict Democrats from an adjacent room while the committee was debating a pension bill. Democrats were also angered when Republicans prevented them from fully participating in conference committees on the energy bill and on legislation reauthorizing the Federal Aviation Administration.

On October 29, Daschle told reporters that excluding Democrats from conferences "makes a mockery of the legislative process, and it certainly minimizes the role of every United States senator." On November 4, he reiterated his objections: "I believe whenever you lock out Democrats, whenever we don't have a full and open debate on issues of this import, the country suffers."

Pelosi told reporters on October 21, "I think the Republicans have turned everything on its ear. The regular order has gone by the bye." And on November 6, she declared that Republicans "have abused the rules, they burned the book on the rules.... It's fundamental to our democracy that 130 million people's representatives be heard at the table."

In numerous reviews of the year in Congress, journalists picked up on the Democratic critiques at least as much as they emphasized the Republicans' accomplishments. Congressional editor Charles Babington of *The Washington Post* wrote a piece in the Sunday Outlook section that began, "Congress's minority parties have suffered indignities for decades, but few could top the insult that Republicans dealt to Democrats this fall." He concluded that the increased partisan bitterness is "like drinking too much on New Year's Eve: It feels good at the time, but there's hell to pay later."

In a year-end wrap-up, headlined "Us vs. Them Rules American Politics," *Wall Street Journal* reporter Jackie Calmes's first paragraph read, "'Partisan' only begins to describe the air in the Capitol these days. Especially in the House, says Sen. John Breaux, where 'people genuinely hate each other.'" And reporter Carl Hulse wrote in *The New York Times* that Congress departed "with a final burst of partisan recriminations over the conduct of a session that produced Medicare changes, tax cuts, and hard feelings certain to spill over into the 2004 campaign."

The articles were flush with hand-wringing quotes about Congress from political scientists and other congressional experts, including especially dire commentary from Thomas Mann, a senior fellow at the liberal-leaning Brookings Institution. In an interview with *National Journal,* Mann voiced similarly serious concerns. "I have never seen Congress at such a low ebb in my 35 years in Washington," he said. "It's incredibly discouraging to someone who cares about Congress as an institution."

"I believe that we have seen the demise of regular order in Congress," Mann said. "It is not just one thing; it is a dozen things. Basically, what I see is a fragile, unified Republican-majority government, the first since Eisenhower, and the first with any prospect of substantial control of government, going back to the early part of the 19th century. [This] has led to a situation in which producing the party program trumps any institutional concerns. There is no one tending to the institutional maintenance of Congress."

Likewise, Steven Smith, a political science professor at Washington University in St. Louis, also described significant problems with the legislative process. "Essentially, one-half of Congress is left out of the action," Smith said in an interview: "I really am very worried about process in Congress." Hamilton ac-

knowledged, "If you're in control, you take advantage of your power to get what you want," but he added that rather than just focusing on short-term victories, Republicans should worry about the good of the institution.

Republican leaders brush aside many of the characterizations from Democrats and outside critics. After all, following years of broken promises and failed attempts by politicians of both parties, Republicans were finally able to pass legislation providing prescription drug benefits to senior citizens. House Speaker Dennis Hastert, R-Ill., called the enactment of the Medicare bill "important history" in which "common sense prevailed and Medicare was saved."

Republicans list what they see as significant legislative accomplishments—including the passage of the Medicare bill, tax cuts to stimulate the economy, and funding for the Iraq war and recovery efforts—as evidence that Congress did its job in 2003, and did it quite productively, despite the fact that their party holds only narrow majorities in the House and Senate.

"We accomplished a great deal this year," Senate Majority Whip Mitch McConnell, R-Ky., said in a hallway interview on November 25, the day the Senate completed the Medicare bill. "Those who lost are kind of upset, and they are always pointing to process when they are upset."

And Senate Republican Conference Chairman Rick Santorum, R-Pa., asked whether the legislative process is broken, responded: "No. The fact of the matter is that we have been able to get major accomplishments done this year in the face of a very, very closely divided Senate and House."

Some Republicans concede that they made a mistake by resorting to excessive partisanship in some instances last year, such as calling the Capitol Police to Ways and Means. "The problem in this business is that people put off problems," a veteran House Republican committee aide said. "In the long view, our slights of Democrats have been short-sighted and unnecessary."

Still, having gained complete control of Congress and the White House for two years for the first time in a

half-century, Republicans see this as their historic moment, and they say that any resulting institutional problems can be fixed later. "The public wants solutions, not gridlock," said House Republican Conference Chairwoman Deborah Pryce, R-Ohio. "We have learned a lot, and we delivered."

House Rules Committee Chairman David Dreier, R-Calif., said that the Republicans' task has been all the more challenging because "we are living with the narrowest majority" in the House and Senate. "We now understand much more of what's involved with being in the majority," he added. "I don't want to be dismissive of the Democrats' concerns. But I do believe that they are overstated."

Besides, as Republicans are quick to point out, Democrats had their own legislative and managerial shortcomings when they held the majorities before being ousted in the 1994 elections. GOP spokesmen cite, for example, the scandals of the early 1990s, after the disclosures of widespread overdrafts by lawmakers at the House Bank and various irregularities at the House Post Office.

When the Republicans were in the minority, they complained loudly about their legislative mistreatment by the Democrats. And Republicans vowed that if given the opportunity, they would manage Congress better than the Democrats did. In fact, Rep. Newt Gingrich, R-Ga., rose to fame in the late 1980s and early '90s with his late-night special-orders speeches on the House floor decrying the heavy-handed tactics of the "Imperial Congress" run by the Democratic majority. An examination of some of Gingrich's statements shows that he issued many of the same complaints—and with as much vitriol—as have Pelosi and Daschle in recent months.

"The Democratic Party has had a monopoly since 1954 in the House," Gingrich said in a House floor speech on April 11, 1988. "Lord Acton warned us that power tends to corrupt, and absolute power corrupts absolutely. The Founding Fathers never intended any one group of people, any one faction, to have power for 34 years. The Founding Fathers would have, I think, prophesied and expected that any group that had power for 34 years without challenge would in fact protect itself, would strengthen itself, would ensure that in its hands, more and more power was presented."

Gingrich went on to ask: "Do the 60 percent of the American people, the 49 states, that voted against the Left in the presidency, deserve active, vigorous support in the Congress? Do they deserve an institutional commitment to honesty in the House?"

During a January 1989 interview on PBS's *MacNeil/Lehrer News-Hour,* Gingrich pulled out all the stops. "It is my honest belief as a citizen that you now have Tammany Hall on Capitol Hill," he declared. "That it is a sick institution, and that it has no legitimate authority, has enormous power, but it has no legitimate authority; it does not represent the constitutional government. It is, in fact, a subversion of the process of free elections."

Two months later, on the day that he was elected House minority whip in March 1989, Gingrich was back on PBS. "We [Republicans] don't ask for the right to automatically win every vote. We ask for the right to have every vote; and as the alternative party in this House, we deserve fair respect, and we deserve to be treated on a professional basis as peers," he said. "For many years in the House, Republicans got the crumbs, and were told they should pretend they've been at the feast.... We have to have respect for the institution of the House."

In subsequent years, Gingrich oversaw the crafting of the Contract With America, the sweeping campaign platform that brought Republicans elected success in 1994. In the contract, Republicans criticized 40 years of one-party control and pledged institutional reforms "to restore the bonds of trust between the people and their elected representatives."

These days, Democrats accuse Republicans of having forgotten such promises. Republicans have now controlled both chambers for nine years, except for when the Democrats held a 50-49-1 Senate majority from June 2001 through December 2002. Democratic leaders hotly deny that they ever treated the minority party as badly as they say the Republicans are treating them now.

At a November 6 press conference, a reporter asked Pelosi to respond to Republican charges that the Democrats treated the GOP "a lot worse before 1995." She replied: "Not so. First of all, when Newt Gingrich became the speaker, he pulled up all the ladders that got him to that place. He tightened the rules considerably [to strengthen the leadership's power]. The record will show that is simply not the case.... It's simply not so."

Other Democratic insiders concede, however, that their party isn't entirely innocent. "House Democrats were pretty heavy-handed, so I don't fault House Republicans," said a Senate Democratic aide who has spent nearly two decades on the Hill. "That's the way the House works."

NOT BY THE BOOK

To assess the true state of Congress, *National Journal* looked in-depth at a dozen institutional trends. Many congressional insiders—regardless of their party affiliation—and outside experts would agree that these trends represent the way the modern-day legislative branch works. They include:

- The disintegration of the committee process;
- The greater concentration of power in the hands of House leaders;
- The increasing use of the House rules to deny the minority a full debate or votes on its views;
- The increasing use of filibusters, amendments, and holds to clog up the legislative works in the Senate;
- The lack of true debate in the Senate;
- The breakdown of the budget process;
- The heavy reliance on riders to the must-pass appropriations bills as a crutch to act on significant policy issues;
- The refusal by appropriators to fully fund authorization bills;
- The tendency toward government-by-CR;
- The majority party's abuse of the conference committee;
- The lack of true bipartisanship and the polarization of Congress;
- The inability or unwillingness of Congress to make thorough use of its oversight powers to keep the executive branch in check.

National Journal's analysis found that in some cases, these institutional trends have been exacerbated or have accelerated since 1995, when Republicans took over Congress. But the GOP isn't entirely to blame. Many of these institutional trends have been building over several decades, at least, and were well evident during the years of Democratic control. And a few of these developments in Congress merely reflect broad shifts in society or in the electorate. Moreover, in some respects, rank-and-file Republicans and Democrats are equally complicit in contributing to the state of affairs on a daily basis. In other words, both parties bear considerable responsibility for the state of Congress.

One thing is clear: The way that Congress operates these days bears little resemblance to the models described in the social-studies textbooks and civics primers of days gone by. Take the 80-page pamphlet, *How a Bill Becomes a Law: Congress in Action.* The guide was written in 1948 by two senior Senate aides, apparently for school children, and was published by the private National Capitol Publishers. Its pages feature cartoons of lawmakers debating politely, for the most part, while the text describes the legislative process in high-minded tones.

"The amount of misinformation given to the public about Congress is amazing," the authors, George H.E. Smith and Floyd M. Riddick, wrote in their introduction. "Such comments give the impression congressional lawmaking is dominated by political or special interests, and that the welfare of all the people is not strongly represented.... Whatever he may think of the law when it is finally in operation, no one who follows the step-by-step description of its progress can fail to gain a profound understanding and respect for representative government in a free republic."

Even today, lawmakers, academics, and reporters who cover Congress all too often use such textbook models to describe the legislative process. Take the official primer, *How Our Laws Are Made,* that members of Congress distribute to constituents—more than 6 million copies in 23 printings since 1953. The latest version, published in 2003, was au-

"GENTLEMEN, HEARINGS WILL NOW OPEN ON S.1..."

How a bill becomes a law . . .

CONGRESS IN ACTION

75 CENTS

by
GEORGE H. E. SMITH
and
FLOYD M. RIDDICK

NATIONAL

AN IDEALISTIC VIEW: This 1948 pamphlet extolled a "respect for representative government in a free republic."

thored by the House Parliamentarian and published by the Government Printing Office. The booklet describes a straightforward process in which "the open and full discussion provided under our Constitution often results in the notable improvement of a bill by amendment before it becomes law or in the eventual defeat of an inadvisable proposal."

The reality, of course, is now otherwise. Indeed, some might argue that the Civics 101 model of Congress has rarely, if ever, truly existed. In *How Congress Evolves,* a book published this month, Nelson Polsby, a University of California (Berkeley) political science professor, who has studied Congress for more than 40 years, describes the highly turbulent House of the mid-1930s through the early 1960s.

The House was "an increasingly difficult place to do business, as the coalition between Republicans and Southern Democrats solidified on a wide variety of domestic programs," Polsby writes of that era. "Liberal advocates of party responsibility in the population at large tore their hair over the 'deadlock of democracy,' the inability of Democratic presidents to redeem their campaign promises in an arena—the

House of Representatives—nominally controlled by Democrats."

From that perspective, today's problems in Congress may not look quite so bad. "I am no fan of the last few years, or maybe last 20 years, of legislative politics," said Burdett Loomis, a political science professor at the University of Kansas who has written widely about the contemporary Congress. "But I think you go back to, Are we better off now than we were in the 1950s with a 'conservative coalition,' where you couldn't even bring the major problem of the era—race—up legislatively?"

These days, "the electorate is polarized, and the legislature reflects that. I think the legislature is in troubled times," Loomis added. "I do think that it risks some of its legitimacy when it puts together a bill like the energy bill. The legislation was based, as far as I can see, purely on deals, and not on principle or deliberation or good policy ideas, whatever they might be. It would take a lot for me to think the legislative process is broken. Is it limping along? Yeah, I think it is."

Hamilton—who in 1993 and '94 co-chaired with Dreier the Joint Committee on the Organization of Congress, a House-Senate panel that explored possible congressional re-

forms but failed to take final action—said that Congress tends to go through cycles in which the process and civility are problems. Congress may be in one such cycle now. But whether a surge of reform efforts will follow is unclear.

For Congress to make internal reforms requires the support—and usually the initiative—of the majority party. So far, few Hill Republicans have publicly voiced unhappiness with congressional operations. But keep your eye on a group of 15 mostly junior House Republican conservatives, who late last year voted against both the Medicare bill and the fiscal 2004 omnibus appropriations bill as too costly.

The House GOP leadership remains mindful that in 1997, a group of junior conservatives instigated the unsuccessful coup attempt against Gingrich that rocked the party and led to the speaker's downfall a year later. Those conservative members and their successors continue to act independently from time to time. As the federal deficit has ballooned, they have called for budget process reforms, but have generated little support thus far. Because of the House Republicans' continuing narrow majority, however, party leaders hoping to stem further defections among their ranks may begin to see a new imperative for reforms.

Following the ugly battles late last year, Dreier sent a letter to all House members in December inviting recommendations on "maintaining civility in the House." Pelosi announced at the Democratic leaders' year-end press conference that she "soon will be proposing to the speaker some suggestions that I hope we could both agree to—win, lose, or draw in the next election—that are about bipartisanship, about communication, about respect of the minority in the House."

At the same time, Democrats are warning that they will extend the Medicare debate into this year's election campaign, and will hold supporters of the new law accountable. The Democrats' electoral challenge is to duplicate the GOP's 1994 victory by successfully running against Congress. But that may be easier said than done.

House Minority Whip Steny Hoyer, D-Md., conceded, "The public is not very animated by process" discussions. Other Democrats agreed that the public has low expectations for how Congress works in any case. And a veteran House Democratic aide said, "Compared to what it takes to win the majority," such as campaign fundraising and candidate recruiting, "most of these procedural complaints are howling into the wind."

Still, another Democratic strategist maintained that the controversial Medicare vote could backfire against many Republicans. "The public doesn't care that Republicans have been undemocratic in running the House, because most people know little about how the House operates," this Democrat said. "But they do understand that the environment is bad, and that prescription drugs cost a lot of money."

But whatever time it takes for one party or the other to gain political mileage from the current conflicts may have little connection to when members of Congress get serious about addressing—or even acknowledging—some of their internal problems.

The High Costs of Rising Incivility on Capitol Hill

By SHERYL GAY STOLBERG

WASHINGTON—EVER since Thomas Jefferson presided over the United States Senate as vice president, the chamber has had not only a tradition of civility but rules requiring it. So there were more than a few raised eyebrows earlier this month when the Senate's No. 2 Democrat, Harry Reid of Nevada, marched up to the crowded press gallery and, in a fit of pique at Senate Majority Leader Bill Frist of Tennessee, declared, "I've never seen such amateur leadership in all the time I've been in Congress, 21 years."

Mr. Reid's remark, uttered in frustration over the Republicans' all-night marathon attacking Democrats for blocking several judicial appointments, was yet another signal that, in 2003, the words civil and Congress may no longer belong in the same sentence.

"Civility and incivility run in cycles in Congress, and this is one of the low points," said Ross Baker, a political scientist at Rutgers University. "Benjamin Franklin once said that Congress should be a mirror image of the American people, and it is, in the sense that Americans are terribly divided and their elected representatives are unable to transcend those divisions."

Partisanship is a fact of political life, and every generation on Capitol Hill complains that it's worse than it used to be. But as recently as the 1980's, partisanship and civility seemed able to coexist. Today, in the House, Democrats and Republicans barely talk to each other, and some say the Senate, which Jefferson famously described as the "saucer" that would cool the passions of the House, is not far behind.

Republican leaders in both chambers shut their Democratic counterparts out of talks on the two biggest legislative initiatives, the Medicare prescription drug measure and the energy bill.

And scholars who study Congress say Americans are the worse for such behavior.

"The problem," said Burdett Loomis, a University of Kansas political scientist who has written about civility and deliberation in the Senate, "is that even a bill like Medicare is essentially a package of partisan compromises rather than something that actually gets talked about and deliberated. You get the sense that it's deal-making for partisan advantage, rather than trying to come to some approximation of good policy."

Both parties, Mr. Loomis said, are resorting to procedural tactics to win, like the Democratic filibuster of several of President Bush's judicial appointments, which only inflames passions further.

In the House earlier this year, Representative Bill Thomas of California, the chairman of the House Ways and Means Committee, evicted committee Democrats from a library where they had been gathering, prompting an extraordinary round of recriminations that led Mr. Thomas to apologize on the House floor. More recently, Republican leaders extended the customary voting period from 15 minutes to nearly three hours to give themselves enough time to twist the arms necessary to win the vote on the Medicare bill.

"There seems to be almost no shame," Mr. Loomis said. "Everyone is just completely righteous right now."

Aside from policy, such spectacles also lower the public's opinion of Congress as an institution, which is reflected in low voter turnout and the difficulties both parties face in recruiting candidates to run. As Mr. Baker said, "They don't want to serve in an institution in which life is so unpleasant."

History, of course, is replete with examples of unpleasantness—and worse—on Capitol Hill. One 19th century senator once referred to another as "a sniveling political Pecksniff." Lawmakers have, at various times, brandished pistols at one another and come to blows. In 1856, a dispute about slavery led a cane-wielding House member to whack Senator Charles Sumner, a Massachusetts abolitionist, over the head, badly injuring him.

In 1801, Jefferson, recognizing the dangers of this sort of behavior, wrote some rules on civility, according to which senators were not to attack one another by name, impugn one another's motives or disparage one another's states. Those who violate the code may be censured, as was Senator Joseph R. McCarthy, the Wisconsin Republican and anti-Communist, who was cited in 1954 for "conduct unbecoming a senator," in part for his behavior toward other lawmakers.

History shows, however, that partisanship need not breed incivility. Stories are legendary about the close personal ties between Thomas P. O'Neill Jr., the Democratic speaker of the House from 1977 to 1986, and Representative Robert H. Michel of Illinois, the Republican leader from 1981 to 1994. The two men would fight bitterly on the House floor during the week, then play golf together on the weekends.

Today, such cross-party friendships are increasingly rare. Most lawmakers don't stay in Washington over weekends; they head home to their districts, which gives them little time to socialize. More important, according to people on both sides of the political aisle, is that the old social order of the House was overturned in 1994, when Republicans, led by Representative Newt Gingrich of Georgia, wrested control of the chamber from Democrats after 40 years.

"There was a great deal of civility when Bob Michel was in the minority and Democrats were in the majority," said Grover G. Norquist, president of Americans for Tax Reform, a conservative advocacy group. "Every day Bob Michel got up and lost and didn't mind, and the Democrats won and they didn't mind.

"Gingrich," Mr. Norquist went on, "was the guy who said, 'I don't think it's okay to get up this morning and lose. I decided to get up this morning and figure out how to win, and I'm not going to settle for being the ranking member.' That's the beginning of incivility."

House Democrats have been chafing under Republican control ever since, and the tensions spread to the Senate as House members trained in Mr. Gingrich's bare-knuckles style won election there.

Things got so bad that in 1997 House members held the first of a series of bipartisan civility retreats outside Washington (fewer than half the members attended). The same year, the House Rules Committee held a hearing on civility. Its chairman, David Dreier, Republican of California, cited "evidence of a decline in debate decorum generally" that he said hindered legislation and "sets an undesirable tone" for discussion.

Partisan passions flared in 1998, when the House voted to impeach President Bill Clinton, and again in 2000, when the Supreme Court stepped in to settle the outcome of the presidential contest between George W. Bush and Al Gore. So by the time Republicans regained control of the Senate in 2002, the relations between Democrats and Republicans on Capitol Hill were strained almost beyond repair.

"I think what is distinct about this period is the failure to really listen to the other side," said John Podesta, who served as President Clinton's chief of staff and is now president of the Center for American Progress, a research organization. "There is no attempt to work in the center and find a kind of bipartisan middle."

That makes life on Capitol Hill especially difficult for centrists. In a recent interview, Senator Olympia Snowe, a moderate Republican from Maine, lamented the change. "More than anything else, I have been in the middle," she said, adding, "I've seen over time that there are fewer and fewer people in that position. Hence the polarization and the partisanship that has engulfed the institution. That deeply concerns me."

Some, including Senator Frist, see hopeful signs. Aides to Dr. Frist cite the Medicare bill, which was opposed by 9 Republicans but supported by 11 Democrats, as an example of the "bipartisan middle." And Senator Charles E. Schumer, Democrat of New York, said personal relations between senators were not as bad as they seem.

"It's much better behind the scenes than it is in public," said Mr. Schumer. On Monday night, the night before the Medicare vote, Dr. Frist served Tennessee barbecue in his office. "There were about an equal number of Democrats and Republicans there," Mr. Schumer reported, "and I noticed that the groups talking to one another were mixed, so to speak."

Mr. Baker is not convinced. "I think it may have to get worse," he said, "before it gets better. Something much nastier is going to have to happen, and then people will come to their senses and realize that this is no way for a legislature in the most important country of the world to be acting."

Legislative Season Drawn In Solid Party Lines

Senate takes the lead in fierce partisanship as nation remains evenly divided

By John Cochran

For the last three years, the margins of power in Congress have been so narrow that the parties have been screaming at each other, fighting over those last few seats that could tip the majority one way or another. Members of Congress and those who work with them say the atmosphere is more divided than ever.

They are right — the voting record now confirms it. In 2003, Congress as a whole was indeed more polarized than it has been in the five decades that Congressional Quarterly has been analyzing annual "party unity votes."

With both Democrats and Republicans looking ahead to the 2004 elections, the parties sought to highlight their differences on health care, education and other major issues, rather than seek broad consensus. They sharpened and intensified their conflicts in hopes of breaking the 50-50 partisan stalemate at the polls that has kept them close to parity in Congress, without a clear mandate to govern.

It was all about getting the public "off the dime," said William Connelly Jr., a political scientist at Washington and Lee University, and the polarization could be a precursor to a political realignment that tips the country in one direction or the other. It also may foreshadow a difficult and relatively unproductive legislative year ahead as the two parties continue to battle for the attention and favor of vot-

ers before the presidential and congressional elections. (*2004 outlook, p. 12*)

On roll call votes that pitted a majority of one party against a majority of the other — a party unity vote as defined by CQ — Democrats and Republicans in both chambers stuck tightly together throughout 2003.

House Democrats were more unified than at any time since 1960. On party unity votes, the average House Democrat toed the party line 87 percent of the time, according to CQ's analysis.

In the Senate, where President Bush's agenda was most in danger of being blocked by a powerful Democratic minority, it was Republicans who showed the tightest party discipline. On average, they voted with their party 94 percent of the time — their all-time high party unity score.

The Senate, historically the chamber where the parties have been most willing to cooperate, was the most polarized of all, at least statistically. Two out of every three Senate roll call votes divided the chamber down partisan lines.

Both in the raw number of party unity votes and the percentage of total roll calls that split the parties, the Senate has been more sharply divided only once in the half century that CQ has been tracking that percentage: in 1995, when the GOP took control of both sides of the Capitol for the first time in 40 years. (*1995 Almanac, p. 1–3*)

In the House, where the percentage is deflated by many routine, non-controversial votes, a little more than half of all roll calls were party unity votes. Major issues — the war in Iraq, Medicare legislation, education, the budget — most often triggered partisan votes in the House, as in the Senate.

The Great Divide

Whether the divisions between the parties are deepening because of the polarization of the electorate or vice versa is one of the great unknowns of the country's current political climate. A report released in November by the Pew Research Center for the People and the Press found that the electorate is almost evenly divided politically and, more important, further apart than ever in its political values.

"Political polarization is now as great as it was prior to the 1994 midterm elections that ended four decades of Democratic control in Congress," said the study's authors, who interviewed more than 2,500 voters about the core beliefs that shape their opinions on a range of topics. "But now, unlike then, Republicans *and* Democrats have become more intense in their political beliefs."

Over the past four years, for example, Democrats have become more critical of business and much stronger advocates of the social safety net — and their differences with Republicans on those issues

Party Unity — *Frequency of Partisan Voting by Chamber*

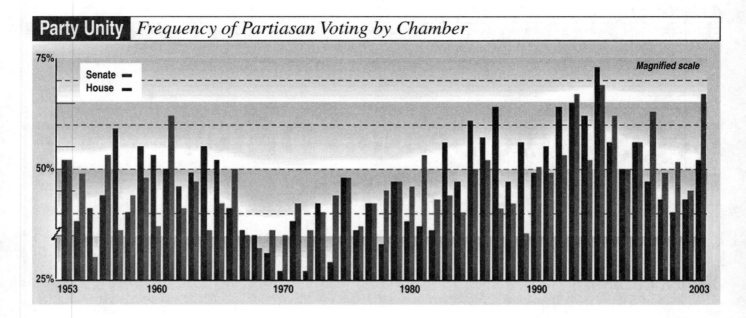

have widened, the Pew report said. Differences over national security policy have grown also as Democrats become increasingly angry and disenchanted with the war in Iraq.

Sharpened rhetoric and partisan battles have often preceded a period of realignment in the body politic, Connelly said. And the combat often centers on an overarching question about the role of government.

That was true in 1932, when Republican President Herbert Hoover and Democrat Franklin Delano Roosevelt fought over whether a larger, more active federal government could help pull the nation out of the Depression, Connelly said.

Whether the debate in Washington today is building toward just such a realignment is anyone's guess. One of the biggest bills of 2003, the Medicare prescription drug measure (PL 108-173), was meant at least in part to blur the differences between the parties, to allow Bush and the GOP to claim a victory on an issue that Democrats have owned for years.

At the same time, however, both sides have worked to sharply distinguish their positions on the Medicare bill, and the arguments they make cut directly to their differing views of government.

Democrats in particular are attempting to frame the issue as just the sort of

2003 Data			
	Partisan Votes	Total Votes	Percentage
Senate	306	459	66.7
House	349	675	51.7

For More Information

fundamental debate about the proper role of government that Roosevelt used to his advantage in 1932. They argue that the Republicans' ultimate goal is to dismantle Medicare, a program that tens of millions of seniors have come to depend on.

Republicans assert that their plan will improve Medicare by bringing market competition to the program, offering seniors more choices, not fewer.

Tipping the Electorate

Leaders of both parties in Congress spent much of the session bemoaning the heightened partisanship—and blaming the other side for it. One bad turn justified the next.

Senate Majority Leader Bill Frist, R-Tenn., complained that Democratic partisanship was holding up Bush's judicial nominees and other business even as he was enraging Democrats by shutting them out of the conference committees negotiating the Medicare drug bill and other high-profile measures. (*2003 CQ Weekly, p. 2761*)

Reviewing the year at a news conference last month, the two top Democrats — House Minority Leader Nancy Pelosi of California and Senate Minority Leader Tom Daschle of South Dakota — presented their list of "Republican failures" on a chart headlined, "Too much partisanship, too little progress." (*2003 CQ Weekly, p. 3066*)

But when a reporter asked Daschle what he expected could get accomplished in the second session of the 108th Congress, his quick first response was this: "Realistically, the most important thing we can get done next year is elect a Democratic majority in November."

Both the Republican and Democratic parties have been losing their moderate wings over time. Democrats have lost their Southern conservatives as the South trends increasingly Republican. The GOP has lost many of its Northeastern moderates.

But the more immediate factor driving the dynamics last year was the tighter margins, Connelly and other congressional observers say. When the parties are so closely balanced in Congress — and in the country as a whole — the imperative for political leaders on both sides is to play up differences, not find commonalities, in hope of tipping the closely balanced electorate their way, they said.

Final victory is so close for both parties that they are more reluctant to back down or settle for half measures..

Party Unity | *Parties Set Record for Partisanship*

Number of unanimous party votes in both chambers since 1962. Aggregates unanimous votes by Republicans and Democrats.

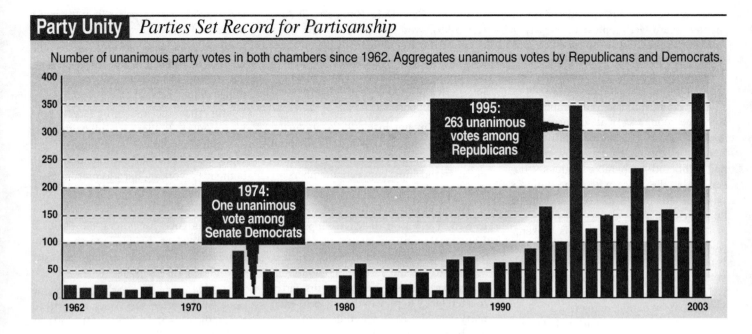

1974: One unanimous vote among Senate Democrats

1995: 263 unanimous votes among Republicans

Narrow margins also produce a rationale for the rank and file to stay in line. Republicans, who control both houses of Congress and the White House, are driven together by loyalty to their president, pressure to produce legislation and the prospect of strengthening their hold on power.

Democrats, meanwhile, have been tantalizingly close, at least in the Senate, to claiming the majority and all that goes with it — the right to claim choice committee spots, to control what legislation comes to a vote, to direct federal spending. That provides a powerful incentive for members to subsume their individual differences and stick together behind the party. (*Senate Democrats, p. 41*)

There is less willingness, too, to give the other party a share of the credit on major policy, like Medicare drugs, said Michael Malbin, a political scientist at the State University of New York in Albany. The narrow margins of power have "made both parties pay more attention to their bases and to developing a national message" in hope of winning a clear majority, Malbin said.

Unity as a Message

Pelosi, for one, has been aiming to highlight the differences between the parties in the starkest possible terms. She fought hard all year to persuade her caucus to stand together against the GOP, and she succeeded to a considerable degree.

She argued that unity is in itself a message, showing the public that Democrats are confident and excited about their agenda.

On the Nov. 22 vote to pass Medicare drug legislation, for example, all but 16 Democrats voted against the bill. Even members of the Blue Dog Coalition, moderate Democrats who often vote with Republicans, largely stayed with Pelosi on that vote. (*2003 CQ Weekly, p. 2960*)

In the Senate, where individual members wield considerable power and are more likely to go their own way, Daschle was somewhat less successful holding his membership together on Medicare and other big votes. Still, the average party unity score for Senate Democrats — how often they vote with the majority of their party against a majority of the other party — was 85 percent, close to their all-time high since 1960 of 89 percent, reached in 2001 and 1999.

Meanwhile, House Republicans tied their own top unity score of 91 percent, hit in 2001 and 1995. House Speaker J. Dennis Hastert, R-Ill., and his lieutenants put a premium on keeping the party together, and they leaned hard on their members to stay behind the party's agenda.

The most dramatic display of GOP command and control came with the Medicare vote: With Pelosi pushing to hold on to her own rank and file, Hastert kept the vote open for almost three hours just before dawn while he pushed

enough votes into line to get the legislation through. (*2003 CQ Weekly, p. 2962*)

In the Senate, both Democrats and Republicans ginned up votes and amendments designed at least partly to highlight differences between the parties — on abortion, education, drug pricing and other issues.

With Democrats holding up a handful of Bush nominees to the federal bench, Frist worked to call attention to the standoff by holding vote after vote to try to break the filibusters.

On one nominee alone — Miguel A. Estrada, one of Bush's picks for the U.S. Court of Appeals for the D.C. Circuit — Frist held seven separate "cloture" votes through the spring and summer to try to cut off the debate. (*2003 CQ Weekly, p. 2140*)

Such efforts were aimed in large part at the motivated base of each party. Interest groups on both sides were pushing senators to be confrontational

The Sensitive Senate

Indeed, the recent political dynamic has led some political scientists to speculate that it is the Senate today that may be most responsive to shifts in public mood.

The House, designed by the Founding Fathers to turn over frequently and be more sensitive to the popular will, has been made stable by partisan redistricting aimed at keeping districts safe for one party or the other. Statewide Senate races cannot be so gerrymandered thus a greater share are contested. Nearly a third of the Senate seats up for election in 2004 — 10 out of 34 — are rated highly competitive by CQ. By contrast, less than a tenth of House races — 30 out of 435 — are now considered competitive.

Some congressional observers are worried about the partisanship in the Senate, traditionally the slow-moving and deliberative chamber famously described as the place where the nation's passions are meant to cool, as hot tea cools in a saucer.

"It may be that the saucer is broken," said Ross Baker, a former Senate aide who is now a political scientist at Rutgers University. "If the saucer is in trouble, than we're in trouble. We've counted on the Senate to exert a moderating force."

Senators from both parties have observed that the chamber is becoming more like the House has traditionally been — fractious, partisan, quick-tempered — and they decry the change. Some old hands blame the change in part on former House members who moved to the Senate and brought hardball tactics and sharp rhetoric with them. (*2003 CQ Weekly, p. 3069*)

Former Sen. Dale Bumpers, D-Ark. (1975-99), was distressed by the decisions of the Republican leadership last year to lock Democrats out of important conference committees. The Senate "is less collegial" today than when he first arrived, Bumpers said.

"And I'm not just talking about the legislation," he said. "I'm talking about the whole aura. There aren't as many close friendships between members of the parties."

David Hoppe, who was chief of staff to Sen. Trent Lott of Mississippi when Lott was Republican leader, also said the Senate has grown less collegial, less willing to debate issues in good faith across party lines. He ascribes this partly to a tendency to play to the edges of each party, passing over a middle viewed as apathetic and uninvolved.

He offers one remedy: force senators who want to block legislation to put up or shut up by making them filibuster the old-fashioned way. Today's quiet filibuster — with cloture votes but no "talk-athon" — makes obstructionism too easy, Hoppe said. If filibusters were difficult, senators would be more likely to

try to work across party lines to make progress, he said.

"I'm convinced it will lessen the number of filibusters and force the Senate to find ground where you can get things done," he said.

But others see something largely positive at work. Rather than unhealthy partisanship, political scientists see vigorous debate and participation, with both sides working hard to present clear policy alternatives to sway a closely balanced electorate.

That is good for voters, they said. It gives them clear choices, something substantive to chew over as they consider their choices at the polls.

If 2004 is not the year that hands one party or the other the wider majority it seeks, the virtual deadlock will surely be broken eventually, Connelly and other political scientists said.

"I do not think the nation is comfortable where it is," said Gary Copeland, director of the Carl Albert Congressional Research and Studies Center at the University of Oklahoma. "In terms of public policy, every thing seems to hang in the balance by a few thousand votes every election."

WOMEN in POWER

On Their Own Terms

By Martha Angle

Power red. Electric blue. Canary yellow. In a blue and gray sea, the bold primary colors of the women of Congress all but demand attention—a second look, a closer scrutiny.

These are not the somberly garbed, soft-spoken widows and place-warmers of an earlier era. There is not a "Silent" Hattie Caraway in the bunch. The women of the 108th Congress, outspoken and ambitious, for the most part got here the same way their male colleagues did: They won on their own, after building careers in local and state government, in law practices, in business and as congressional aides. Now they are moving from the back benches to the front ranks. Some have climbed the seniority ladder to grab the gavels of House and Senate committees or subcommittees. Others have won the votes of their colleagues for party leadership posts. And still others are leaders without portfolio who wield influence among particular segments of their respective parties.

Nancy Pelosi of California, who began the 107th Congress as just another Democrat of middling clout but arching ambition, will be the House minority leader in the 108th—the highest congressional leadership position ever occupied by a woman. Across the aisle, Deborah Pryce of Ohio will chair the Republican Conference, the first woman to reach such a lofty position in the GOP since Sen. Margaret Chase Smith of Maine held the equivalent post three decades ago. Across the Capitol, Kay Bailey Hutchison, R-Texas, and Barbara A. Mikulski, D-Md., will serve as vice chairman and secretary, respectively, of their party caucuses.

In the entire history of the Senate, only two women have chaired standing committees, one of them the famously reticent Caraway, an Arkansas Democrat (1931–45) who presided over the obscure Committee on Enrolled Bills. In 2003, there will be two at once, and both are from Maine: Olympia J. Snowe on Small Business, and Susan Collins, her GOP colleague, on Governmental Affairs.

For all their gains within the institution, however, women remain grossly under-represented in Congress. Although they constitute 52 percent of the voting-age population, women make up just 14 percent of Congress—59 voting members of the House and 14 senators, including recently appointed Lisa Murkowski, R-Alaska.

It has taken nearly a century to reach that figure, and the gains have not come in a straight line, as Karen Foerstel and Herbert N. Foerstel noted in their 1996 book "Climbing the Hill: Gender Conflict in Congress." Following the 1916 election to the House of Montana Republican Jeannette Rankin, the first woman ever to serve in Congress, it was 40 years before the roster of women climbed to 20. That proved a temporary high-water mark; by 1969, just 11 women remained. The tide began to turn in the 1970s, and there have been no further notable reversals. But neither has there been exponential progress. There are still five states—Delaware, Iowa, Mississippi, New Hampshire and Vermont—that have never sent a woman to Congress.

Though few in number—a total of just 33 in the Senate and 189 in the House—women have left an indelible mark on Congress. Rankin cast the only votes against entering both World War I and World War II. "As a woman I can't go to war, and I refuse to send anyone else," she declared in 1941. That vote cost her the next election, but she remained an anti-war crusader until her death in 1973. Republican Rep. Frances Bolton of Ohio (1940–69) turned Rankin's position upside down, championing equal rights for women—including the obligation to serve in the military. Smith, the first woman elected to both chambers of Congress (House, 1940–49; Senate, 1949–73), demonstrated a different kind of courage as one of the earliest critics of a Republican colleague in the Senate, Wisconsin's Joseph R. McCarthy (1947–57), and his attacks on a wide range of prominent Americans as communist sympathizers. "I speak as a Republican. I speak as a woman. I speak as a United States senator. I don't want to see the Republican Party ride to a political victory on the four horsemen of calumny: fear, ignorance, bigotry and smear." She was virtually alone in challenging McCarthy in that 1950 speech, and he rampaged on for four more years before he was censured by the Senate.

Marcy Kaptur of Ohio, first elected in 1982, is the senior Democratic woman in the House. In her 1996 book,

"Women of Congress: A Twentieth-Century Odyssey," Kaptur paid tribute to those female lawmakers who went before her. "As a member of Congress at the dawn of the 21st century, I regard myself and my female colleagues as second-wave pioneers, descendants of the original trail-blazers who opened new vistas on America's political horizons," she wrote. "Like all pioneers, the women who served in Congress shattered convention. Many decided to run for the office they had held briefly as widows; others, especially more recently, ran on their own. For each, deciding to seek elected office also meant resolving to step away from the traditional cultural roles defined by gender alone."

> Call them women of substance in today's Congress. As lawyers, experienced legislators and business executives, they trod a path to higher office well-worn by their male colleagues. In the 108th, these women will have a firm grip on the levers of power as committee chairmen and party leaders. Still, their numbers fall far short in reflecting their gender among the populace.

Kaptur sees several reasons why women have been slow to reach the upper levels of leadership in Congress, including the fact that most did not run until their children were grown. That has left them less time in their professional lifetimes to accumulate seniority, she noted, and thus limited their access to committee chairmanships.

There are still relatively few women at the Capitol with young children, although the number is growing. Pryce, for one, can attest to the lingering suspicion that some male members harbor toward those mothers. She lost a daughter to cancer in 1999 and was divorced soon thereafter. Earlier this year, she adopted an infant girl. To win the conference chairmanship this fall, she had to overcome the whispered doubts of some of her fellow Republicans about how well she could do the demanding job given the competing tug on her time and attention from her new baby.

Like their male counterparts, the women who have risen to leadership roles in Congress span the ideological spectrum, from the assertive liberalism of California Sen. Barbara Boxer to the steadfast conservatism of North Carolina Rep. Sue Myrick. Like the men, women in Congress have pursued a wide array of legislative interests. None are focused purely on "women's issues," such as education, health care, children's nutrition and the like. In fact, several—such as Republican Rep. Ileana Ros-Lehtinen of Florida and Republican Sen. Kay Bailey Hutchison of Texas—have developed expertise and influence in the supposedly male arenas of foreign and defense policy. Pelosi in the 107th Congress was the top Democrat on the House Select Intelligence Committee, and before that held her party's top spot on the Foreign Operations Appropriations Subcommittee.

For all the disparity in their backgrounds and legislative focus, most of the women have a shared bond as mothers—a life-altering experience that invariably has shaped their views. "Having my daughter will only make me a better conference chairwoman," Pryce said when her commitment was questioned. "It will make me better able to serve real Americans and understand their problems."

Many women now in Congress, like those before them, have experienced some form of overt or subtle bias in their efforts to establish careers in politics—and before then. Describing her time as a House member from New York (1969–83), Democrat Shirley Chisholm said, "Of my two 'handicaps,' being female put more obstacles in my path than being black." The women of today know what she meant. Hutchison could not get a job after graduating from the University of Texas School of Law in 1967. Patty Murray was dismissed as "just a mom in tennis shoes" when she first got involved in politics in Washington state. Mary L. Landrieu, a Democratic colleague of Murray's in the Senate, was derisively labeled "Little Mary" by some of her colleagues when she was elected to the Louisiana legislature.

Their shared experiences have created a common bond among many women in Congress—especially those in the Senate, where Mikulski, the longest-serving woman, has mentored all those of both parties who have arrived since she joined the Senate in 1987. Those in office in the 106th Congress collaborated on a book, "Nine and Counting," that cemented their sense of solidarity. During the campaign season at the end of that Congress, Landrieu announced that she would not work for the defeat of any woman senator, regardless of party. This fall, Landrieu won the last and one of the most fiercely contested Senate races—a Dec. 7 runoff against another woman, Republican Suzanne Haik Terrell.

From *CQ Weekly*, December 28, 2002 by Martha Angle. © 2002 by CQ Quarterly Inc. Reprinted by permission.

THE PRICE OF POWER

The Bill Frist of his own creation is an antipolitician, a heroic surgeon with a reputation for purity. But you don't become master of the Senate by keeping your hands clean.

By David Grann

On July 24, 1998, a long gunman entered the United States Capitol. He wore a green fedora and carried a .38 Smith & Wesson, with extra bullets in his pockets. He was not a particularly good shot, but he had the rare clarity of mind of someone propelled by delusion, including the firm belief that there was a "ruby satellite system" in the Capitol that could reverse time. At the front door, he drew his pistol only inches from a Capitol Police officer's head and shot him, point-blank. He then turned near a statue of Abraham Lincoln and began shooting at another officer. In the exchange of gunfire, a tourist was hit in the face. As the intruder approached the office of Representative Tom DeLay, a detective named John M. Gibson yelled for everyone to get down. Staff members hid under their desks. Gibson opened fire, hitting the gunman again and again before collapsing himself.

"They got John!" one of the DeLay's aides yelled. "They got John!"

Only moments earlier, William Harrison Frist, then an unheralded Republican senator from Tennessee, was on the other side of the Capitol, out of earshot of the gunfire, speaking on the patient's bill of rights. "As a practicing physician," he stated, "I am absolutely convinced that health care is delivered best when that relationship between the doctor and the patient is given the very highest priority." When he finished, the onetime heart and lung transplant surgeon adjourned the Senate and headed to the airport. But as he climbed in his aide's car, the Capitol physician's office called and said, "We have men down."

Frist drove as close to the scene as he could. He took off his coat and ran past the police barricade. "I'm Senator Frist," he told an officer, flashing his ID. "I'm a doctor."

The police, still fearing there was more than one shooter, ushered him down a long marble corridor that smelled of gunpowder. He knelt by the first victim, checking his wounds and inserting a breathing tube. He lifted him on a stretcher and assisted paramedics as they wheeled him into an ambulance. But before they could close the door, the patient went into cardiac arrest. Although Frist helped to shock back his heartbeat, he was certain the man would die from his injuries.

A medic yelled that there were more victims inside, and Frist rushed back into the building to treat another of the wounded, a slight man who was lying on the carpet and bleeding heavily. An artery in his chest was severed, and Frist concentrated on stemming the flow of blood. He then rode along with him in the ambulance, keeping him alive by forcing oxygen into his lungs. Only as they approached the hospital did he learn that the man he had rescued was the accused gunman, Russell Weston Jr. "You're not a judge; you're not a jury," Frist later explained. "You're a physician."

The scene, like so many in the life of Bill Frist (only months ago he rescued a family in a car accident while driving through Florida on vacation), has helped to elevate him above the ranks of the ordinary politician. Last December, when he stepped in to replace the Senate majority leader, Trent Lott, in the wake of Lott's racially charged remarks, he was hailed by his colleagues not as an astute politician but as a citizen legislator, known less for his voting record than for his "healing touch." At a time when the Senate was increasingly ridiculed as obstructionist and out of touch—"a cruel joke," as one historian called it— Frist was seen as someone who could master not only the institution behind closed doors but its image in front of the public as well. Though he had less political experience than any other Senate leader in history, he represented the G.O.P.'s ideal vision of itself: someone who saves lives not through doling out government aid but through his own daring acts. "He's our messiah," a Republican aide proclaimed after he was chosen.

At his first news conference as majority leader, Frist fueled the impression that even his ideology was rooted in the purity of medicine. He said that his training allowed him "to listen very, very closely, to diagnose, to treat and, yes, to heal." He accepted his new responsibility, he added, "with a profound sense of humility very similar to placing that heart into a dying woman or a child or a man."

Rather than being hailed as a messiah, he was, only a few weeks ago, denounced by members of his own party as a betrayer, a double-dealing politician who negotiated what they called 'a secret deal 'on the president's tax cut.

It is, of course, common to see politics through the prism of your experiences. Plato thought that philosophers should rule as kings. And while it is true that medicine and politics often share the goal of aiding others, in practice they are quite different. Indeed, where medicine is supposed to be clinical and dispassionate, democratic politics often requires unseemly compromise and a certain ruthlessness. It is less about saving lives than serving them through tedious, incremental steps.

After barely 100 days as majority leader, Frist has found himself caught between these two forces, between the vision of himself as a savior and his own political ambitions. Rather than being hailed as a messiah, he was, only a few weeks ago, denounced by members of his own party as a betrayer, a double-dealing politician who negotiated what they called "a secret deal" on the president's tax cut. And the story of how Frist has tried to reconcile these competing visions of himself—and in the process to emerge as the heir to George Bush in 2008—is not just about the power of healing but also about the price of power.

One day not long ago, I went to meet Frist in his office. In the arcane world of the Senate, where nearly everything is meted out according to station (there are separate elevators and subway cars reserved for senators), the size and location of your office is perhaps the most visible measure of influence. While junior members are relegated to basements in distant buildings, Frist's main office is in the oldest part of the Capitol, just off the Senate floor. Lott had cleared away his belongings, and Frist's name was not stenciled on the large mahogany door in gold. Rather than "Senator," however, he had added the letters "M.D."

As I waited in his reception area, I glimpsed what Howard Baker, another majority leader from Tennessee, had called "the second-greatest view in Washington: the Washington Monument and the Mall." After a while, Frist hurried in wearing an elegant dark blue suit with a light blue tie. He has been called "the new face of the Republican Party," and up close he has immaculate features and thick brown hair. But there is something slightly mechanical about his manner, as if after years of performing surgery, he has learned to hold himself perfectly still. "I'm Dr. Frist," he said, extending his hand.

As several aides vied for his attention, he led me through a series of doors until we reached his private office. It was unusually spare. There was a desk and a couch and, in place of the traditional wall of photos with presidents and dignitaries, only two paintings. "They're from my son," he said of the artwork. "I don't want all that other stuff that people put up."

On his bookshelf was "Master of the Senate," the third volume of Robert A. Caro's epic biography on Lyndon Johnson. "People ask me if I've read it," Frist told me, "and the answer is yes. But I don't want to be like him. I want to be just the opposite. That's the last leader I want to become."

While Senate majority leader is one of the most coveted positions in Washington, it was not created by the Constitution but by other senators and thus has little power of decree, which is why it has been famously—or infamously—occupied by masters of the art of the deal. ("I'm a compromiser and a maneuverer," Johnson once said.) It is a job that previous senate leaders have likened to "herding cats" and "trying to push a wet noodle." And though in December Frist was seen by the White House as the ideal man for the job—an untarnished and loyal ally who would carry its water—he has increasingly struggled to move the Republican agenda with only a one-seat majority and little experience. Even on his first day, after hours of negotiating a deal on extending unemployment benefits, the Democratic minority threatened at the last minute to undermine him. "After a lot of hard work, I'm obviously disappointed, because this is the first move out for me, ..." Frist declared on the Senate floor in exasperation. "But I guess that is what I can come to expect." Unlike the speaker of the House, he could not ram through legislation simply by using parliamentary rules. A single senator, using a filibuster, could impede him; a single defector from his ranks could stop him cold. After Republicans boasted that they needed only one vote to pass Bush's plan to drill for oil in the Arctic National Wildlife Refuge in Alaska, Frist spent days trying to use his influence to find that vote. By the end of his first 100 days, he was still looking.

But this morning, before Frist set out on his schedule, he walked over to an antique cabinet. Inside was his medical bag. "I always keep it right here," he said. He carried it to the center of the room and began to go through it. "This is basically everything you need." He pulled out a series of long, slender tubes. "I can use these to breathe in someone." He tilted his head back, exposing the white of his neck, and outlined with his fingers where he would make an incision. "There's a little piece of cartilage that you can cut and then slip the tube into." After a brief demonstration, he dropped the tube and held up what appeared to be a mask. "This is for mouth to mouth," he said, "and this is an endotracheal tube, like the one I used in the Capitol shooting." He removed a strange L-shaped tool. "Come here," he said to one of his aides, who was trying to usher him to his next appointment. "Open your mouth." His startled subject took a step back. "I won't stick it in," Frist assured him. "This is called a laryngoscope." He had applied one during the recent car accident in Florida. "I told the paramedic, 'Get away, 'and I used this one, because you can get a little more leverage." He continued to go through the items, checking the batteries, unscrewing tops, examining syringes. "Oh, yeah," he exclaimed, pointing to a defibrillator. "This is if you were to drop dead. The first guy I resuscitated over here in the Dirksen Building, I had to shock him seven times to get him back. But I got him back."

He paused and looked at all the items spread on the couch. "I can keep anyone alive," he said. "I don't care what their problem is. This is all you need."

"THE ICONOGRAPHY of the healer," as Bill Frist calls it, began in his family long before the senator was born. It accumulated the power of myth on Feb. 3, 1914, when the Mobile & Ohio passenger train was approaching the station in Meridian, Miss., where Bill Frist's grandfather, Jacob Chester Frist, worked as the stationmaster. As he peered down from the platform, Jacob Frist saw several pedestrians crossing the tracks in front of the speeding train and broke into a run, shouting for them to get out of the way. Everyone jumped back except for an elderly woman who was holding her grandchild, a 3-year-old who was crippled from a previous spine injury and encased in a full body cast. "I was helping … keep the people out of danger, …" the station porter later recalled, "when I saw Stationmaster Frist hurl himself ahead of the moving train." As Frist pushed the woman and child out of the way, the train slammed into him, throwing him at least 15 feet in the air. "If Stationmaster Frist had not hurled himself … against this woman and child," another witness told authorities, they would "undoubtedly have been killed."

Jacob Frist, meanwhile, lay on the ground, his head severely traumatized, his leg shattered. For nearly a year he was confined to his house. After an account of his heroism appeared in The Meridian Star, people from across the country deluged him with letters, including one that said, "Your brave act was such as our Savior would have us do."

In March 1915, President Woodrow Wilson awarded him a medal and commendation. In a note expressing his thanks, Jacob Frist wrote: "I shall hand them down to my children and hope that my boys will do the same thing when they grow to be men should they ever have occasion to be placed in a like position. I think it the duty of every man, when women and children are in danger of being killed to try and save them."

Nearly five years after he was injured, Jacob Frist died from a cerebral hemorrhage, which was attributed to the accident. Bill Frist's father, Thomas, was only 8 years old. The accident was the last thing, he said, he remembered of his father.

Raised in a boarding house, Thomas Frist eventually became a doctor, which, as his son later observed, "offered him the two things he most needed—a way to ensure that his family was well provided for and a way to validate the selfless generosity that lay behind his father's impulsive sacrifice." In 1968, with the owner of Kentucky Fried Chicken, he helped found the Hospital Corporation of America, one of the first private hospital chains in the country. "He was this incredibly odd combination," one of the family's friends confided. "On the one hand, he was this old-fashioned doctor who made everyone feel at ease, and on the other, this kind of hustler." As his business dealings transformed the Frists into one of the richest families in America, he continued to preach the power of his calling, especially to his children. His first son, Thomas Jr., who helped his father start H.C.A., initially became a surgeon. And his second son, Robert, also became a surgeon. Of all the children, though, nearly everyone agreed that Billy Frist was the most

like his father. He had the old man's courtly charm, his missionary spirit and, what's more, he had the same ambition.

In "Transplant: A Heart Surgeon's Account of the Life-and-Death Dramas of the New Medicine," an unusually candid memoir that Frist wrote before he ran for office, he said of his childhood: "I longed to be first in everything, to be king of the hill, the grammar school capo di capo. I imagine I was quite insufferable." He sought out younger boys, he said, "who could look up to me, admire me…. I found it a virtual sin against nature when one of my young friends, though smaller, could kick a ball farther than I could. I resented anyone my age who was more popular, bigger, faster or smarter. I was jealous of them. I feared them. They might take over." By high school, he was among other things, class president, quarterback and voted most likely to succeed. Printed under his yearbook photo was his nickname: Mr. President.

When Frist arrived at Princeton in 1970, with aviator glasses and short hair, he quickly signed up for pre-med courses. "Having people come up to my father and say, 'Thank you for saving the life of my mother,'" Frist told me, "that became a part not just of his identity but my identity." He rarely slept and was often seen in his room, late at night, poring over his books. "In those days, there were groupies who would come in after class and want to continue the discussion," Uwe E. Reinhardt, the noted health economist who became Frist's close friend and mentor, told me. "And Billy Frist was always there."

On one final exam, Reinhardt asked his students to come up with a corrupt accounting scheme to show how companies could legally commit fraud. "I do remember he gave the most ingenious answer I had ever seen," Reinhardt said. "It was wholly corrupt."

After graduating cum laude, Frist set out, at last, to medical school at Harvard, which offered him, as he put it, a chance to "help others, to do good, while reaping most of the benefits our society can bestow—prestige, power and wealth."

During his second year at Harvard, he saw his first heart. "I stared at it cradled in my hand, spellbound," he said. Later, he spent days and nights in the lab, dissecting the hearts of cats for a research project, convinced he was on the verge of a scientific breakthrough. But with only six weeks to complete his project, he ran out of specimens. Though he was an animal lover, he went to shelters, collecting cats as pets, before sacrificing them in the interest of science. It was, he acknowledged in "Transplant," "a heinous and dishonest thing to do, and I was totally schizoid about the entire matter. By day, I was little Billy Frist, the boy who … had decided to become a doctor because of his gentle father. … By night, I was Dr. William Harrison Frist, future cardiothoracic surgeon, who was not going to let a few sentiments about cute, furry little creatures stand in the way of his career."

Within the world of medicine, cardiothoracic surgeons are generally considered a breed unto themselves: they are stereotypically the most driven, intrepid and emotionally detached. Frist, who taught himself to fly at 16, seemed much less removed than many other surgical residents. Patients recall Frist leaning into them, attuned to their needs and fears. But he also maintained an ability to separate himself that sometimes startled even his friends. "People would get close to Bill, and then the wall would suddenly come up," his college roommate, Rob Mowrey, said.

Consumed by his training to be a heart transplant surgeon, the one person he allowed in was his high-school sweetheart, who also planned to become a doctor. After dating for 10 years, they finally got engaged. But weeks before the wedding, increasingly filled with doubts, he met another young woman, named Karyn, who came into the emergency room with a sprained wrist. "I felt as if I'd known her all my life," he said later. Two days before the wedding, after being up for 48 hours on call, Frist flew to Nashville, still in his hospital whites. They sat at his fiancée's house, surrounded by gifts. "I explained that nothing was right with my life," he wrote. "With me. With me and her. I cried. And she cried, and I stayed an hour, and I flew back to Boston the next morning.... I headed straight to the hospital from the airport. My next shift was starting."

One day in the late 80's, after he had married Karyn and started his own transplant center at Vanderbilt University, Frist got a call in the middle of the night. A colleague said, "I think we've got a heart."

Frist took out the three-by-five card that he always carried with him. It was before the days of organ registries, and on it was a list of all his patients waiting for a donor. There were not enough hearts for all of them, and he knew that whomever he chose, another on the list would most likely die. A doctor had once asked him, "How can you play God like that?"

Frist now went down the list and reluctantly made his choice. "I would always be worried about the person who had just died," his wife told me. "But Bill wouldn't think about that. He couldn't. He would only think about retrieving the heart and the patient he was going to give it to."

As he raced to catch a plane, Frist carried two pairs of scissors, scrubs, tubing, six bags of saltwater and a red-and-white Igloo cooler. When he arrived at the hospital, he stood over the body, cutting open the donor's chest with a scalpel and scissors. He took out the heart and held it up. It weighed only about 10 ounces. He packed it in ice and placed it in the Igloo. Then he raced back to Tennessee, where his patient was already waiting in the operating room.

"You take what people regard as the soul of life outside the body," he told me, as he sometimes had other reporters, while we were walking through the Senate. "Then you take another heart, and it's sitting in a bucket like a piece of meat, and you carefully lower it in." As he demonstrated, he held out his hand motionless, as if it were a heart. "Then, bang, it starts beating again."

He often worked for days on end; on vacations he would take his beeper, prepared at any moment to harvest a heart. He enclosed on the back page of "Transplant" an organ donor card for readers to fill out. "I pursued every vehicle I could," he explained.

In 1993, he was appointed by Ned McWherter, the governor of Tennessee, to head a commission on the state's $3 billion Medicaid program. The governor told Frist that based on his findings he was going to take the $3 billion and put it into a total managed-care system.

Frist was startled. "How can you do that? You're just one person."

The governor laughed. "That's what politics is all about."

"At that point the light clicked," Frist told me. "The power … of *one* individual."

Then that same year, as his old friend Professor Reinhardt accompanied him on a plane trip to harvest a heart, Frist had his head buried in a large ring binder. "I was teasing him," Reinhardt said, "about looking up in a manual where the heart is." Frist lifted his head and shouted over the roar of the engine, "This is campaign literature." Later, after he had removed the heart, he said, "This is my last transplant."

The announcement that Frist intended to run in 1994 for the United States Senate against Jim Sasser, an 18-year incumbent in line to become the next Democratic majority leader, initially stunned most of his family and friends. Frist was so consumed with medicine that he hadn't even voted until 1988. Yet what surprised some people even more than his decision to run was the party with which he chose to align himself. "I always assumed he was a Democrat," said Dr. Norman Shumway, the renowned transplant surgeon who trained him at Stanford. Reinhardt assumed the same thing: "I thought he was naturally a Democrat."

At Princeton, Frist had worked as an intern for a Democratic congressman. His mother was a staunch liberal who liked to tell friends, "I'll die before I vote for a Republican." His oldest brother, Thomas Jr., had donated to Democrats throughout the state, including Sasser. Even Bill Frist's father, who often voted Republican, had recently contributed to the Democratic National Committee.

And while Bill Frist hadn't registered to vote until 1988, when he did, he donated $1,000 to the Democratic presidential candidate, Al Gore, the only politician whom he praised in "Transplant." And in 1993, when he made his first foray into public policy and led the state Medicare commission, it was for McWherter, a lifelong Democrat.

Several friends told me that Frist had confided that he wasn't sure whether he should run as a Democrat or as a Republican. "I said, 'What are you?'" McWherter recalled asking him at one point. "He said, 'Well, I'm not sure.' I said: 'Well, you got to make up your mind. This is a two party system.'"

According to some friends, before he chose, he even did "research" to see if he had a better chance of being elected as a Democrat or Republican. "They looked at the east of Tennessee and decided he had a better chance getting elected as a Republican," one friend told me.

Frist voted for reducing Medicare growth and minimizing the role of government in health care, though a close friend said that before running for office Frist had expressed a desire for a universal health care system like Canada's.

When I asked Frist about his ideological evolution, he said, "I just didn't change; those are my values." He denied doing any kind of polling, but acknowledged that he had told people he didn't know which party to join. "The pattern in my life is to systematically address an issue, and that was just another issue. I made a list of 20 people and said, 'I want to do something that is beyond saving people one on one.' I went around and talked to everybody, everyone I knew in politics, and said, 'What is the real difference between Democrat and Republican?'"

And if there was any ideological ambivalence—"That party stuff doesn't matter to me," he had initially told Reinhardt—once he made his decision he showed little evidence of it. It was a year in which Democrats were in trouble throughout the country, a year of a massive anti-incumbent revolt led by Newt Gingrich, and Frist seized on the backlash with fervor. After vowing to the state party chairman, "I will be the best student you will ever meet," he prepared 16, 17, 24 hours a day—and longer, staying up three nights straight, then napping for an hour and going another three days in a row, including Sundays. He sought advice from the masters of the art, most notably Karl Rove, who would later steer George Bush into the White House and who traveled with Frist briefly at the outset of the campaign. "I've never spoken about it before," Frist said when I asked about it. "But it did have an impact. The fact that this guy had come in, and no one thought I could win. And he said, 'You could do this thing.'"

And as his main tutor Frist hired Tom Perdue, a brilliant and ruthless campaign manager who only a few years earlier had settled a $400,000 libel suit for accusing an opponent of bribery and who now helped devise a strategy that would serve as a blueprint for Frist's entire career. While Frist attacked Sasser endlessly as an ignoble Washington insider—his commercials featured "The Ballad of Liberal, Taxing, Two-Faced Jim"—Frist portrayed himself as the quintessential outsider, a noble doctor. His unofficial campaign slogan was "Listen, diagnose and fix."

Drawing on more than $3.7 million of his own estimated $20 million fortune, much of which had been earned from stock in his father's and brother's company H.C.A., he dispatched Perdue to unleash a barrage of negative attacks. One commercial showed Sasser's face on Mount Rushmore alongside Dan Rostenkowski, the Democratic congressman recently indicted for corruption. His campaign also tried to link Sasser to Joycelyn Elders, the black surgeon general who had spoken controversially about masturbation, and Marion Barry, the black mayor of Washington who had been caught smoking crack cocaine with a former girlfriend. "We'd never seen anything like it," Sasser told me. "I'd been in the Senate 18 years, and I'd never seen a campaign so vicious. Handbills would mysteriously appear in redneck areas showing me with Joycelyn Elders. He'd say while he was saving lives as a heart surgeon, I was busy sending Tennessee dollars to Marion Barry. It was clearly a racist attack. The slanders went on and on and on."

In the end, Frist achieved one of the most stunning upsets in electoral history—"a political earthquake," as he proclaimed at his victory party. Or, as one newspaper exclaimed with a hint of disbelief, "Is There a Doctor in the Senate?"

"I JUST WANT TO PUT another log on the fire," Frist said, standing in his office one winter afternoon. He went out of the room and came back with several logs bundled in his arms and placed them in the fireplace.

As he sat down at a long wooden conference table, he clapped his hands and said, "So what are we going to do?"

I said I wanted to talk about how he had transformed himself from a doctor into a senator. "It's been pretty seamless," he said. "The learning curve in medicine is much steeper and more arduous. This comes naturally." He paused, as if he had said something he regretted. "So if you say that, it's like you're a natural politician. But I do like people, so it's not hard."

As he spoke, an aide came in the room. He nodded toward me. "This is my psychoanalyst here," Frist joked. Then, comparing his new role with his old one, he continued, "Addressing the big issues—life-and-death things—I think that can apply to the political end of it."

That same day, amid hours of meeting with advisers trying to break a Democratic filibuster of a Bush judicial nominee, Miguel Estrada, Frist appeared on the Senate floor and said he wanted to "put my physician hat on for one second." The terrorist threat had recently gone up from yellow to orange.

"This is a time of stress," he said. "In talking to my colleagues and their families, I sense that when we go to this high alert … people do not sleep as well. Some people eat more.… Some people develop back pain." He listed several things that people could do to cope. "Again, as a doctor—and then I will take my doctor hat off—exercise regularly, eat well and get a good night's rest."

When he returned to his office, he asked me: "Did you hear my talk on the floor? Me just talking about it will help in these life-and-death issues." Later he held a private conference call with a group of Senate spouses, who had expressed growing alarm over the senators' physical safety.

Frist told everyone to get out pencils and paper. "No. 1," he said, "during an attack cellphones won't work. No. 2, local phones may go out as well, so you need an out-of-state contact."

"I have a question about iodine," one senator's wife asked.

"If you're near a nuclear reaction," Frist explained, "it [protects the thyroid, but it doesn't protect the rest of the body."

What about duct tape?

The junior senator said he had a small favor to ask of Frist: a major Republican donor was seeking a minor ambassadorship. 'I don't even know what the hell it is,' the junior senator said, 'but he wants it.' Frist thought about it for a moment. 'He has lots of dollar figures down there?' 'That's exactly right. And he did raise a chunk of money for me.' 'All right,' Frist said. 'You're a good man.'

"Karyn Frist, do we have duct tape in the house?" he asked his wife, who was also on the phone. He said he only advocated it for high-risk scenarios, and he told them not to worry about their spouses. If anything ever happened at the Capitol, he said, "I will act with no hesitation. … That's what I did for a living before I came here."

Afterward, while the two of us sat by the fire, he seemed pleased with the call. "To me, the mission is no different" between a doctor and a senator, he said, sipping from a cup that said "Senate Majority Leader." "So it's not a matter of changing; it's a matter of adapting and compromising. There's much more negotiation in this business. In medicine, there is no room for compromise, and in this, there is much more negotiation to reach one's goals." Then, as he stood to go, he added, "The danger is if you adapt too much you can never recover."

WHEN FRIST FIRST ARRIVED in the Senate in 1994, he quickly discovered what every new member did—that despite holding one of the highest offices in the land, he had little influence within the institution. Ranked No. 99 out of 100 in seniority, Frist wasn't even initially given permanent office space. After the first State of the Union address, his wife recalled: "We just stood there by ourselves. No one came up to him, and I felt so bad. I wanted to go out and grab one of these reporters, and say: 'Please talk to my husband. He's a senator from Tennessee.'"

Until then, there were primarily only two routes to power within the institution: one, which had prevailed for centuries, was through the back alleys of the institution; the other, which had become more prevalent in recent years with the advent of cable news channels and C-Span, was by building up a base of power outside the institution—by, in effect, running against its tradition of horse trading, as someone like John McCain had. But while the former route could take years and taint your image, the latter never allowed you to truly dominate the institution. And Frist, who had become one of the quickest studies in politics, seemed to pursue a different path, one that had rarely, if ever, been tried. "I don't have time to pay my dues, to the congressman, a cabinet member, another senator," he said.

At first, it appeared that he intended to rise only by adhering to tradition, by bending to the will of his party patrons. Where he had once expressed doubts about his party allegiance, he now voted, with rare exceptions, the party line. He voted against gay employment rights and the Endangered Species Act. He voted for Bill Clinton's impeachment and against campaign finance reform. He voted for reducing Medicare growth and minimizing the role of government in health care, though a close friend told me that before running for office Frist had expressed a desire for a universal health care system like Canada's. And though other friends told me that they were certain Frist was for abortion rights, he voted steadfastly anti-abortion. (Even on one of the few occasions that he bucked his party and voted for Henry Foster as surgeon general, it seemed more personal than political. Foster, whom conservatives opposed because he had performed abortions as an obstetrician, was from Frist's home state and an old medical colleague.)

Before long, Frist's voting record was nearly indistinguishable first from Bob Dole's and then Lott's. Each told colleagues privately that Frist had the makings to one day be majority leader. And while Lott promoted him as the "resident doctor," Frist began his own crusades not just to serve people but also to save them—to rescue thousands of Americans dying from lack of organ donations and millions decimated by AIDS in Africa. But when his initiatives clashed with the entrenched powers in his party, he nearly always tailored them to appease his Republican patrons. After the Bush administration objected to his provision to increase emergency spending on AIDS to $500 million in 2002, he withdrew it at the last minute, cutting the initiative by more than half for that year. "It was devastating," said Dr. Paul Zeitz, executive director of the Global AIDS Alliance. "He had the right instincts, but he refused to stand by his own policy."

While Frist told Zeitz and others to be patient—that he would eventually prevail by working within the system—he also spoke of the competing instincts within him. "There is this tension between two forces I am engaged in," he once told The Boston Globe, "between raw political power versus what is probably a little more deeply inside of me, the real quest, the real drive for substantive issues, of really changing things for these few years I am in the United States Senate."

After he joined anti-abortion conservatives and opposed creating human embryos for research, many in the medical establishment complained that he had finally turned his back on his own profession—denying patients the best chance for a cure for diabetes and Parkinson's disease. Charles Barnett, a Tennessee doctor, told National Journal: "Bill Frist is the biggest disappointment to me. … He took this political stand not to help people, but to pay off the far right so nobody would get mad at him."

Frist said to me: "Are there things I've done—or have I voted certain ways—that if I could, I'd take them over and go back and redo them? The answer is yes." When I asked him for examples, he cited only one: the farm bill.

Finally in 2000, after six years of accumulating the goodwill of his Senate leaders, Frist started to construct his own political machine with the help of a new powerful patron: George Bush. Already connected to Karl Rove, Frist took several unheralded jobs—including Senate liaison to the campaign—that cemented his ties to the Bush team, which soon put him on the short list of vice-presidential candidates. During his own Senate re-election bid that year, Frist even coordinated his advertising with Bush—a little noticed gesture that helped deliver Gore's home state to Bush.

More important, Frist decided in 2000 to take the largest political gamble since he ran for office and to assume the chairmanship of the National Republican Senatorial Campaign Committee, which controls every race across the country by recruiting candidates and disbursing millions of dollars. "Most of my colleagues advised me not to do it," Frist explained. "Most said, You're a policy maker, you pull people together. Then all of a sudden you're a raw political figure. You're out there with the harshest political rhetoric. You have to be shrill and tear into the guts of people."

As he had in 1994, he immediately showed how aggressive he could be, releasing a series of attack ads that exploited Bush's popularity on the war on terrorism. "That comes from Frist," said his old mentor, Perdue, who at the time was running the Senate campaign of Saxby Chambliss in Georgia. "That was not just one day, 'Let's use the president.' That was well thought out." He added: "Frist didn't do that without a tacit approval. He would never violate his relationship with the president, and that was a very good strategy."

While some Democrats claimed that Frist was calling into question their patriotism, Frist relies again on Perdue, who unleashed what was considered the most devastating ad of the cycle: it showed a picture of Osama bin Laden and Saddam Hussein that eventually faded into the Democratic incumbent, Max Cleland, a Vietnam war hero who lost both his legs and his right arm in battle. Perdue told me that he sent each commercial he made to Frist and his staff to "let them be another focus group," and "they never told us not to do anything."

Hunkered down at his campaign headquarters, Frist spent hours recruiting candidates with Rove, with whom he communicated on his BlackBerry, and raising money. Just as he had once found a way to legally circumvent the accounting system on his college exam, he now found loopholes in the campaign finance system. Rather than divest his stocks from his family's company, which in 1994 merged with another company and was later fined $1.7 billion for the most massive health care fraud in history, he simply kept his stocks in a blind trust. And while the company still donated to his own campaign and to the Senate campaign committee, Frist specifically targeted pharmaceutical companies for donations—and in particular Eli Lilly, which along with its employees gave more than $400,000 to the senatorial war chest during the election cycle. The company went so far as to buy 5,000 copies of Frist's new book, "When Every Moment Counts: What You Need to Know About Bioterrorism From the Senate's Only Doctor," which it distributed to doctors around the country. In contrast to Jim Wright, the former speaker of the House who had to resign over selling his book to lobbyists, Frist made sure he didn't receive any financial remuneration and instead gave the profits to charity. Meanwhile, Frist offered his own boost to the company—introducing a provision that, among other things, protected Eli Lilly from lawsuits over a vaccine that thousands of parents maintained caused autism in their children. After the bill stalled, the same exact language mysteriously appeared in the Homeland Security Bill and consequently passed. (Representative Dick Armey belatedly took credit for inserting the language several weeks after his retirement, though few believe he acted alone. In January, Frist honored a deal brokered by Lott to remove it. But after he tried to reintroduce the bill again this year, angry families declared in a press release, "Frist tries to move under the veil of war.") By the eve of the 2002 election, Frist had raised more money than any G.O.P. senatorial campaign chairman in history. "All of a sudden, he became a natural," Perdue said.

What is striking is not that Frist has increasingly mastered the art of politics—after all, he is in a profession that demands it—but that unlike other politicians, he has mastered the art of seeming above it. Rather than act like a consummate insider, he maintained the glow of a noble outsider. Once, while other senators were in committee meetings, he resuscitated a tourist dying of a heart attack. Another time he ran from a leadership meeting to rescue Senator Strom Thurmond after he collapsed on the

Senate floor. Unlike John Glenn or John McCain, who entered politics as heroes, he had become a hero while *in* politics.

By the time he defied all expectations and delivered the Senate back to Republicans in the fall election, he had quietly amassed one of the most formidable political machines in Washington, commanding the loyalty not only of the senators he had brought into power but the entire G.O.P. caucus and the White House as well. When Lott's status as majority leader came under siege barely a month later, Frist emerged as the most likely candidate for a job that most spend their entire careers seeking. "He was tough enough to make it happen," Bob Dole told me of Frist's positioning himself to be a potential majority leader. "I think he knew there might be an opportunity when he was ready."

Frist had already conferred with his advisers about running for president in 2008, and some of his allies cautioned him that being majority leader could damage his presidential hopes—that the Senate had become increasingly ungovernable, a place that sank the higher ambitions of all those who tried to preside over it. Lott, who was once seen as a rising star, had been vanquished, and Dole, who had abandoned the position to run for president, could never fully escape his reputation as a wizard of Byzantine transactions. Frist had even once told his wife: "Don't ever let me become majority leader. What majority leader has ever been a great legislator?" But for all its risks, the position seemed to hold an even greater lure—overnight it would transform the doctor into one of the most dominant and recognizable politicians in America.

Frist soon began to organize behind the scenes. "He believes there was a divine sense in this," his friend Dr. Thomas Nesbitt Jr. explained. "He believes that God had his hand in this."

Speaking to me of his campaign for majority leader, Frist said, "It's a little like driving down the road in Florida and seeing people dying and responding."

Though more experienced members tried to outflank him, none had reputations that could counter the damage to the party's image. More significant, none had the invisible hand of the White House behind them. Reinhardt, who like many of Frist's friends and allies says he believes Frist will use his power to become a historic leader, explained the relationship this way: "Part of this came from the White House, which said this is a good guy we can use, and part of it came from his side. I would be very shocked if Billy wasn't thinking of the presidency in 2008, and he feels that being in that camp at this time is useful for his career."

Finally, on Dec. 19, Frist sent out a simple statement: "If it is clear that a majority of the Republican Caucus believes a change in leadership would benefit the institution of the United States Senate, I will likely step forward for that role." The next day his old benefactor Lott stepped down.

NOT LONG AGO, Frist was sitting in his new office when a senator he had just helped elect returned his call. Frist put him on speakerphone. "Did I get you out of the most important meeting now?" Frist said, his accent rising slightly.

"Well, I'll tell you what, if I had to sit there any longer and listen to Leahy and Schumer [expletive] and moan...."

Frist joked about life in the big city, and then asked the member for a small favor: he needed him to recite a speech in the old Senate chamber—a ritual that usually fell to the lowest person on the Senate totem poll. "It's an annual tradition … to have a senator read it," he said, noting he had done it, too. "You got C-Span with you in the room, watching you."

"I don't have to wear a wig, do I?"

Frist smiled. "I'd really encourage you to do it," he said.

The newly elected senator hesitated for a moment. "That'll be neat."

"Good. … I'll put you down."

Before hanging up, the other senator said he had a small favor to ask of Frist, too: a major Republican donor was seeking an ambassadorship to some overseas economic development organization. "I don't even know what the hell it is," the junior senator said, "but he wants it."

Frist thought about it for a moment. "He has lots of dollar figures down there?"

"That's exactly right. And he did raise a chunk of money for me."

"All right," Frist said. "You're a good man."

The exchange, which took place while I was sitting in the room, offered a glimpse not just of the Senate business but also of the business of the Senate. Early on, Frist used his newfound leverage—maneuvering and compromising—to pass the appropriation bills and legislation outlawing partial-birth abortions. But before long, even more than his predecessors, he found himself unable to control the unruly cloakrooms of the Senate. He failed to enact much of Bush's heralded faith-based initiative or find the one vote he needed for drilling in the Alaskan wildlife refuge or overcome the Democrats' filibuster of Estrada. Lott had told The Times of his old disciple: "I guess I just have a different view of how to get things done. They used to criticize me for moving the trains, but after all, what's the main goal here?"

Then only a few weeks ago, when he tried to broker an old-fashioned deal and move the trains on the president's most important domestic initiative—a $726 billion tax cut—he made what he acknowledged was a critical "mistake." Unable to muster enough votes to pass a budget that would accommodate such a large figure, he approved a pact with two moderate Senate Republicans to reduce the tax cut by more than half, which was not, given his slim majority, an unreasonable compromise. But in a move that reflected his inexperience—Dole had cautioned him that "the only thing you have up there is your word"—he failed to mention the agreement to G.O.P. leaders or to the administration, which was determined to stick to a higher figure. And in an extraordinary step, many Republicans, who had only months earlier championed him, publicly rebuked him.

"You just feel very betrayed, very frankly," Representative Sue Myrick of North Carolina told The Washington Times. "We were just furious, and we're still furious." Senator Lindsey Graham of South Carolina, whom Frist had just helped elect, told The Washington Post, "The way to lose everyone over time is have people feel you are not dealing straight up." Anonymous White House aides even let it be known that Rove had tracked down Frist while he was on a trip in Asia and told him he had disappointed the president.

Rather than rescue the institution, he seemed on the verge of becoming just another product of it. Where he had come to power promising to be "a healer"—to avoid the kind of rhetoric and divisiveness of Lott—only a few weeks ago he chose to support a key conservative ally, Senator Rick Santorum, who likened homosexuality to incest and polygamy. And after barely 100 days, there were reports that Frist was "losing control of his troops" and "off to a rocky start." It was as if he had achieved what he had always wanted, only to find it came at an unforeseeable cost.

Once, on the night of Bush's State of the Union address, while I was waiting in his office lobby, an aide told me that the senator wanted to see me right away. When I entered his office, Frist was leaning over his desk, his face slightly flushed. "The White House just called," he said. The president, he explained, was going to champion in his speech a proposal that Frist had been working on for years—to triple financing to $15 billion over five years for the fight against AIDS in Africa. "This is big," Frist said. He started to pace in the room. "This is big," he said again. Later, after the speech, he said, "I told the president, 'You just saved hundreds of thousands of lives,' and he looked at me and said, 'We just saved a lot more than that.'"

It was after midnight, but Frist lingered in his empty office. "This is why I went into politics," he said. "This is it! This is it!"

But within days it emerged that the White House had found the money for the proposal, in part, by slashing other health financing. And after Frist bowed to many of Bush's conditions that caused the various financing proposals to founder in Congress, a leading AIDS organization put out a news release saying, "Senator Frist Sabotages Key AIDS Initiatives." Protesters soon appeared outside Frist's Washington home at 6 a.m., blaring sirens, while others stormed into his Senate office hours later, yelling, "Frist is being a doctor of rhetoric instead of a doctor of action."

When a photo of Frist appeared in the paper, looking ashen, his friend Reinhardt told me: "Poor Billy. I've never seen him look so beleaguered."

Recently, just before his 51st birthday, Frist took a break from the Senate and visited his alma mater, Princeton. He had composed a speech called "The Floor of the U.S. Senate: Is Transplanting Ideas Any Different From Transplanting Hearts?" Addressing the packed auditorium, he talked about his vision of merging medicine and politics, of saving lives, an ideal that still seemed to captivate him. Then Frist paused and looked out at the crowd. "Majority leader sounds good, …" he said, "But people assume you've got a lot of power. … There is no power to it. You learn quickly that there's no power."

David Grann is a frequent contributor to the magazine. He wrote most recently about the baseball player Barry Bonds.

Congress

JOHN DINGELL'S STAYING POWER

BY BRODY MULLINS

When Rep. John D. Dingell, D-Mich., arrived at the White House earlier this month to discuss energy legislation, President Bush greeted him with a friendly jab. "You're the biggest pain in the ass on Capitol Hill," joked the President. "Thank you for a high compliment," responded Dingell, who was first elected to Congress in 1955, right around the time that Bush began playing Little League. "I've worked 47 years for that reputation, and I'd hate to see it dissipate in one afternoon."

The exchange between the rookie President and the House's most senior member underscores the influence that Dingell still wields in his 24th term on Capitol Hill. During Bush's first six months in office, Dingell has schooled him in what nine Presidents, scores of agency heads, and hundreds of members of Congress learned before: He is a lawmaker who can thwart a President's priorities, muscle his own initiatives through Congress, and otherwise be a major-league pain to the White House, congressional Republicans, and even his fellow congressional Democrats.

> ## JOHN DINGELL: "I just work like hell, and good things seem to happen."

This month alone, Dingell has exploited his leverage as the ranking Democrat on the House Energy and Commerce Committee to wedge himself into a handful of key issues. He riled the While House by sparking a General Accounting Office investigation into the energy-policy task force that Vice President Dick Cheney put together earlier this year. He annoyed congressional Republicans by co-sponsoring popular bipartisan patients' rights leg-

islation in the House that goes further than Bush prefers. He distressed senior Democrats by cutting a deal with Republicans that allows major elements of the President's energy plan to move forward. And he may anger members on both sides of the aisle by pushing broadband Internet legislation through the House before the August recess.

Of course, it's not unusual for Dingell to be in the middle of so many fights. He has long been known as one of Capitol Hill's most powerful and effective committee chairmen ever, thanks to his tenure at the helm of Energy and Commerce from 1981–95, and he has played a central role in many of the major laws enacted in the past half-century. Over the years, Dingell has also masterfully asserted Congress's right to oversee the executive branch. He once helped to throw a Reagan Administration official in jail for obstructing a committee investigation.

What is unusual is that after all his time in Congress, including the past six and a half years in the minority, the 75-year-old Dingell still has the fire and the wherewithal to continue to boldly make his mark. Dingell, after all, is in more than a few ways Capitol Hill's version of Cal Ripken—and Ripken is retiring this year. Elected in December 1955 to replace his father, Dingell has served more consecutive years than any other current member of Congress. He has even surpassed 98-year-old Sen. Strom Thurmond, R-S.C., who was elected in 1954 but took a few months off in 1956. Dingell is the only member of the House elected in the 1950s, and one of five elected before 1970. Nearly 20 percent of his current House colleagues were born after he first entered the chamber.

What's the secret to Dingell's longevity? Even in this era of poll-tested soundbites, he still counts on old-fashioned hard work and smarts to do the job. He takes the time to master the substance of legislation, with the help of one of the most experienced staffs in Congress, and he relies on his unmatched knowledge of the institution that he has honed since working as a congressional page in 1937. As Dingell himself said in a recent interview: "I just work like hell, and good things seem to happen."

Dingell's colleagues say that perhaps most important to his resilience, he has shrewd political instincts that allow him to build the coalitions needed to move legislation. "He understands which issues he absolutely has to solve to get the majority he is seeking," said Rep. Rich Boucher, D-Va., the ranking member of the committee's Energy and Air Quality Subcommittee. "That knowledge only comes with experience." Added Rep. W. J. "Billy" Tauzin, R-La., the current chairman of the Energy and Commerce Committee: "I've learned one thing in my years under Dingell—know what's do-able and what's not."

And Dingell isn't ready to quit yet. If anything, he seems more energized this year than in the recent past. Michigan's Republican-controlled Legislature has completed a redistricting plan that would put him in the same district as fellow Democratic Rep. Lynn Rivers, but Dingell has pledged to run for a 25th term next year, even though some senior members might take the opportunity to retire. "I expect," Dingell said without hesitation, "to be re-elected."

LEARNING FROM THE GROUND UP

The son of Polish Catholic immigrants, Dingell developed values and a work ethic that were ingrained during a dozen years of Jesuit education. The priests at Georgetown Prep and Georgetown University taught him to try to help others. But his true inspiration is his father, the late Rep. John Dingell Sr., a 12-term New Deal Democrat from Detroit who sponsored Social Security, the first interstate highway bill, and national health care legislation. "John still to this day loves his father," said Dingell's wife, Debbie, an executive at General Motors Corp., in an interview. "He is motivated by the kind of public servant his father was—that's what drives him."

In part because his father died of tuberculosis as a young man, Dingell each year faithfully reintroduces a bill to provide Americans with universal health care. Dingell said he remains "intensely proud" of his father. "I regard him as a giant," he said, although he adds: "I am not my father. I think for myself."

As Dingell made his way through Georgetown law school in the early 1950s, he worked as the Capitol's chief elevator operator—a job he got because of his dad's position in the House—and he literally learned from the ground up. When his father died in 1955, the 29-year-old Dingell was elected to replace him.

Two decades later, Dingell grabbed the reins of power for the first time when he and Rep. John Moss, D-Calif., organized a rebellion against the apathetic chairman of the Energy and Commerce Committee, Rep. Harley Staggers, D-W.Va. The pair launched the modern-day committee by boosting its budget and empowering sub-committee chairmen to pursue aggressive agendas. As his booty, Dingell claimed the gavel at the Energy and Power Subcommittee.

He took over at a perfect time. A few years later, a major energy crisis threatened the country, and Dingell soon proved he could produce. After a series of hearings, he drafted a far-reaching energy conservation bill and muscled it through his subcommittee in a legendary 1977 markup that lasted 17 straight days.

But Dingell also earned a reputation as a bully. With his broad new powers, he became fond of strong-arming opponents and burying their legislative priorities. After he was elected chairman of the full Energy and Commerce panel in 1981, he cemented his standing by preventing the committee's second-ranking Democrat, Rep. James Scheuer of New York, from chairing a subcommittee. "The day they passed out subcommittee chairs was known as 'Passover' in Scheuer's office," quipped a former committee aide.

Those close to Dingell say he never forgave Scheuer for breaking his word years earlier during some undisclosed dispute. But Dingell maintains he had nothing to do with his colleague's "misfortune." When asked why Scheuer never got a subcommittee chairmanship, Dingell replied: "The answer is simple: He never could get elected." He added smugly: "I never really worked hard to kill him. He did a fine job doing that himself."

Over the course of his 14-year reign as chairman, Dingell amassed quite a fiefdom. His committee managed to capture jurisdiction over nearly everything that moved. On a wall in the committee's cloakroom, Dingell hung a framed picture of the Earth. He said it represented the panel's jurisdiction.

During that time, Dingell developed another advantage often overlooked by his colleagues: a well-trained and experienced staff. Dingell paid his aides generously by congressional standards, gave them responsibility, and relied on their expertise. As a result, he was armed with some of the best talent on Capitol Hill. "That means that when he goes into battle, he has way more knowledge than anyone else," says John Arlington, a committee aide from 1987–91.

Dingell's staff recalls the peculiar occasions in the late 1980s when Bush Administration officials at the Environmental Protection Agency would enlist the help of Dingell aide Dick Frandsen to locate information about the agency that Dingell himself had requested. "Frandsen knew more about the EPA than they did," a former aide reminisced. Another aide, David Finnegan, worked for Dingell for so long that the two disagree on when they met. One thought 1958, the other 1960.

DOWNS AND UPS

The mid-1990s brought setbacks for Dingell. First, the Republicans took control of the House in 1995 and pried the chairman's gavel from Dingell's clutch. Then, they stripped a chunk of the panel's jurisdiction. Soon after, rumors began spreading that Dingell would retire. Instead, he adjusted to his new role as ranking member under then-Chairman Tom Bliley, R-Va. Though Bliley pursued a less-active agenda than his tireless predecessor, Dingell contributed to approving major reforms of the telecommunications and financial services industries.

Though he no longer was chairman, Dingell's mastery of the procedural rules gave him strength. His favorite tactic: forcing the committee clerk to read aloud, line by line, 100-page bills that he objected to. If the clerk skipped a single word, he asked the reading to start all over again.

Then, in December 1999, Dingell fainted at a reception and an ambulance rushed him to the hospital. When a priest arrived at his bedside, Dingell was in good spirits. "Father, I hate to disappoint you, but I don't need you tonight," he reportedly said. The episode turned out to be a simple case of dehydration after a long day and a stiff martini, which Dingell says he enjoys shaken, not stirred.

But that was not the last of Dingell's health problems. Early last year, a stubborn ankle injury forced him to hobble around the House on crutches. When a metal screw in his ankle snapped, Dingell was consigned to the same kind of motorized scooter that ushers 79-year-old Sen. Jesse Helms, R-N.C., through his final years in Congress. The nagging injury seemed to lower Dingell's spirits. A distinguished career was thought to be on its last legs. If the Democrats won back control of the House in November 2000, a few aides whispered around election time, Dingell would face a Democratic challenge for the committee gavel.

IN THE THICK OF IT: Dingell's teaming with Republicans Greg Ganske and Charlie Norwood on patients' rights legislation has aggravated House GOP leaders.

Yet when Democrats failed to win control of the House, Senate, or White House, Dingell startled observers by returning to Capitol Hill in January fully energized. He junked the crutches, ditched his motor scooter, and took on an aggressive schedule. "A few years ago, the end was near," said one lobbyist. "I don't know what the hell he did, but he is being effective again."

Part of the credit goes to Tauzin, who took over as Energy and Commerce chairman in January. He's a former Democrat who learned how to run the panel during 14 years under Dingell, and he has revitalized the committee by modeling it after Dingell's reign. To do so, Tauzin has reached out to Dingell by giving him a larger budget, additional staff, and more sway over committee business.

Soon after Tauzin took over the committee, for example, he worked with Dingell on legislation to increase broadband Internet service. That measure—the ubiquitous "Tauzin-Dingell" bill—passed the committee earlier this year and could come to the House floor as early as next week.

More recently, when Tauzin needed to move Bush's energy policy through the committee, he sat down with Dingell over the Fourth of July recess and together they crafted a bill they both supported. As part of the deal, Dingell delivered Democratic votes for the Republican bill, and Tauzin headed off a large increase in automobile fuel-efficiency standards—a major concern to automakers in Dingell's Detroit-area district. The Energy and Commerce Committee approved the energy bill, 50-5, on July 19, and House Republicans plan to bring it to a floor vote next week.

But Dingell continues to cause trouble for Republicans on health care legislation. His latest effort on patients' rights legislation—which he is co-sponsoring with Republican Reps. Charlie Norwood of Georgia and Greg Ganske of Iowa—elicited a veto threat from Bush. Republican leaders hope to defeat the Dingell-Norwood-Ganske bill and pass a narrower alternative bill.

Meantime, the fact that the White House has gone Republican has invigorated Dingell's oversight activities. Although he has never been easy on Democratic Administrations (he once called President Clinton's Kyoto treaty "the most asinine treaty I've ever seen"), Dingell clearly enjoys pestering Republican Presidents. "Dingell understands that Congress is a separate branch of government, and he has fiercely asserted its prerogatives," said Rep. David R. Obey, D-Wis.

Earlier this year, Dingell launched a GAO investigation to find out which oil and gas company lobbyists helped the White House shape its energy policy. Dingell has also slammed the Administration for routinely responding to his requests for information with computer-generated form letters. In a biting speech on the House floor on June 7, Dingell sarcastically credited the White House's "remarkable, automated, and superbly efficient computer system" for "moving forward the science of communications to new and higher levels." He added: "Each time I have written to President Bush, I have received an identical response from this amazing computer... each faithfully signed by the President's aide, Nicholas Calio."

THE 16TH DISTRICT OF DINGELL

Michigan Democrats are challenging the Republicans' redistricting map in court. But if Dingell is forced into a redistricting-induced election contest against fellow Democratic Rep. Rivers in November 2002, he is the heavy favorite to win. "Michigan is Dingell country," said one Democratic lawmaker. "He would cream her," Dingell has faced only token election opposition since the 1960s, and Rivers, according to Michigan insiders, is weighing a run for the Statehouse.

Even some Michigan Republicans want to see the generally liberal Dingell remain in the House, because of the considerable clout he has to help the state. "If a Democrat is going to be in that district, it might as well be John Dingell," said Paul Welday, an aide to Rep. Joseph Knollenberg, R-Mich.

Though the redistricting plan does not appear to pose a threat to Dingell, it may complicate plans to keep his House seat in his family. Insiders believe that Dingell would like to bestow the seat once held by his father on his son, Christopher, or on his wife, Debbie. But Christopher, a term-limited state senator, plans to run for a seat on the Wayne County circuit court. "Chris is not interested in running [for the House]," John Dingell said. Deb-

bie, meanwhile, says she is focused on the corporate world. "I'm still climbing the ladder at GM," she said. "There is still a glass ceiling that needs to be broken here."

Dingell, for his part, disputed that he could hand his seat to a family member. "This is not something that can be passed around like a country club membership or a seat on the stock exchange. It has to be earned," he said. "The seat and the job all belong to the people. If you do a good job, they'll reward you with another two years."

Still, after nearly a half-century in the House, Dingell will not hold the seat forever. Asked how long he would serve in the House, Dingell responded: "Till I get tired of this—or the people get tired of me."

Brody Mullins is a reporter for National Journal's Congress-Daily.

SANDRA'S *Day*

Why the Rehnquist Court has been the O'Connor Court, and how to replace her (should it come to that)

by Ramesh Ponnuru

CONSERVATIVES have never much cared for Justice Sandra Day O'Connor. They viewed her nomination to the Supreme Court as the result of Ronald Reagan's ill-advised, because gratuitous, 1980 campaign pledge to appoint the first female justice. During her confirmation hearings in 1981, some conservatives argued that her record as a state legislator in Arizona made it unlikely that she would vote against *Roe* v. *Wade*. Her subsequent votes confirmed that suspicion: She reaffirmed *Roe* in *Planned Parenthood* v. *Casey* (1992) and even divined a kind of constitutional right to partial-birth abortion in *Stenberg* v. *Carhart* (2000). Conservative activists tend to regard her as a "moderate," or even "liberal," justice, and say that President Bush should avoid appointing another justice like her.

The standard conservative picture of Justice O'Connor is, at best, an oversimplification. She is, in truth, both better and worse than they think she is. Some conservative Court-watchers fear that the Right's confusion could cost it dearly if there is a nomination fight later this year.

The conservative case for O'Connor is that she has voted reasonably well. While she has become a reliable vote for social liberalism at the Court, she has also sided with conservatives on many occasions. The conservative heroes on the Court have been Clarence Thomas, Antonin Scalia, and, to a lesser extent, the chief justice, William Rehnquist. O'Connor has generally voted with them on racial preferences, the death penalty, crim-

inal procedure, and other issues. She also sided with them in *Bush* v. *Gore*.

The Rehnquist Court is known for two great doctrinal innovations. Instead of continuing to insist on strict secularism, the Court now merely requires governmental neutrality among religions. The Court has also embarked on a so-called "federalism revolution" that limits the power of Congress while protecting the prerogatives of the states. O'Connor has played a leading role in both areas. Eugene Volokh, a law professor at UCLA who once clerked for her, concludes, "She's a woman of the center-right on a lot of the really important issues that have come before the Supreme Court."

Have conservatives damaged their own cause by taking an excessively negative view of O'Connor? Washington is rife with speculation that Rehnquist, O'Connor, or both will retire this summer. In one scenario, Rehnquist leaves and Bush elevates O'Connor to chief justice. If O'Connor leaves, however, the conservatives may have lowered the bar for her replacement. Alberto Gonzales, the White House counsel, is often mentioned as a potential Bush nominee. He is a moderate, and possibly to the left of O'Connor on some issues, such as racial preferences. But so hostile are conservatives to O'Connor that the White House could tell them that he is an improvement. If, on the other hand, Bush nominates a true-blue (true-red?) conservative to replace O'Connor, liberals will say that he is tilting the Court far to the right—and by exaggerating her liberalism, the conservatives will have lent that claim credibility.

ON THE O'CONNOR COURT

The difficulty conservatives have in getting a fix on O'Connor is a function of the bifurcation in their view of the Supreme Court. Conservative lawyers and law professors care a lot about issues such as affirmative action and federalism, on which O'Connor often votes the way they want. But social conservatives are the only mass constituency on the right that pays attention to the Court; and while they are usually allied with the conservative legal community, their priorities are different. The activists tend to disdain O'Connor because of her votes on abortion and, to a lesser extent, gay rights. The conservative lawyers tend to disagree with her decisions on those issues, but are less hostile to her because of her other votes. Another way of saying this is that how happy a conservative is with Justice O'Connor is a reflection on how happy he is with the Rehnquist Court.

Actually, the O'Connor Court might be a better label for it. Justice O'Connor gets her way more often than the chief justice does. As the "swing vote" on the Court, O'Connor is in the majority more often than any of her colleagues. Legal briefs in important cases are written to appeal, above all, to her. As a result of her position at the center of the Court, she can be a powerful voice for conservatives when she is with them. When the Court upheld school choice last year, it was her unqualified endorsement of the decision in a concurring opinion, as much as the majority opinion itself, that conferred solidity to the ruling. But it is disturbing to reflect that, given the power the Supreme Court has assumed, O'Connor has become the most powerful woman in America. Excluding foreign policy, indeed, one could even say that she is the most powerful *person* in America.

O'Connor's style of judging has increased that power. The justice is famous for issuing narrow rulings that turn on the particular facts of the case rather than rulings that articulate broad principles. Applying this common-law approach to constitutional cases preserves her freedom of action in future cases. But it also, and necessarily, undermines the predictability of the law and aggrandizes the judicial role. This is the principal critique that conservative lawyers—including Justice Scalia, in many opinions—make of O'Connor. She may often vote with Scalia and Thomas, says a former Rehnquist clerk, but "she is not driven by … legal arguments in the sense that a conservative jurist should be."

In the 1995 *Adarand* case, for example—concerning racial preferences in federal contracting—O'Connor voted with the conservatives. But she refused to say that racial preferences in federal contracting were always impermissible, or to expound some other rule that made it clear which preferences were okay. Instead she said that such preferences would receive "strict scrutiny" from the Court. "Strict scrutiny" is the highest degree of scrutiny in the Court's equal-protection jurisprudence; traditionally, a legislative or bureaucratic classification is subjected to strict scrutiny as a prelude to being found impermissible. Justice O'Connor, however, went out of her way to explain that while the program at issue in the case had to go, in future cases

strict scrutiny would not necessarily be "fatal in fact." So which preferences should stay and which go? The Clinton administration's response to this uncertain guidance was to preserve all existing federal preference programs except the one at issue and another that fell in court. To this day the Court's position with regard to other contracting preferences remains unclear.

O'Connor has ruled (or rather not ruled) similarly in racial-gerrymandering cases. Jeffrey Rosen, an influential legal commentator, has said that the upshot of those cases is that congressional district lines cannot be drawn with regard to race if the results offend Justice O'Connor's aesthetic sensibilities. Or take abortion. From her earliest days on the Court, O'Connor has argued that restrictions should be upheld so long as they do not impose an "undue burden" on the right to procure abortions. In *Casey*, Justices O'Connor, Anthony Kennedy, and David Souter adopted this standard for the Court. It is a standard, not a rule—in the parlance of the law profs—because its application depends on subjective judgments. In *Stenberg*, Justice O'Connor and four of her colleagues decided that a ban on partial-birth abortion imposed an "undue burden" on the abortion right; Justice Kennedy apparently felt that it was a "due burden," since he dissented from the judgment. Justice Scalia, also in dissent, noted that the only effect of the standard was to turn the Supreme Court into a veto board for abortion regulations.

In *Bush* v. *Gore*, the Court said that the doctrine underlying its decision was "limited to the present circumstances" and would not govern future cases. Critics have seized on the line as the epitome of the decision's lawlessness. But the Court has been making good-for-one-ticket-only decisions for some time, thanks in large part to O'Connor. Volokh, the former clerk for O'Connor, notes that in some areas of the law she has been willing to defend "bright-line rules" and that other justices also adopt vague, subjective standards on some occasions. This observation should be taken as a qualification, rather than a refutation, of a valid generalization: Justice O'Connor practices "one case at a time" judging more often, and with greater consequence, than her colleagues.

THE FEDERALISM REVOLUTION

Conservative lawyers consider the federalism revolution the most valuable part of the Rehnquist Court's legacy. O'Connor's record on federalism is not without the ambiguities one would expect from the rest of her jurisprudence. She has sometimes held the revolution back—as in *U.S.* v. *Lopez*, a 1995 case that is something of a landmark. The Constitution gives Congress the power to regulate commerce among the states. In *Lopez*, the Court ruled that the Gun-Free School Zones Act was not a legitimate exercise of this authority. The Court had not imposed a limit on congressional power under the commerce clause in six decades. O'Connor, the swing vote, joined a concurring opinion that appeared to weaken the Court's conclusion and left the law unsettled.

Notwithstanding such episodes, O'Connor can fairly be said to have not only participated in but even led the revolution. Her strong dissent from the federal drinking-age case in 1987 was a harbinger of it. And one of its signal accomplishments was the doctrine, announced by Justice O'Connor in *Gregory* v. *Ashcroft* (1991), that federal law will not be read to compromise the sovereignty of state governments unless the law includes a clear statement to that effect.

Unfortunately, the Court's federalism revolution isn't all it's cracked up to be by legal conservatives. Michael Greve of the American Enterprise Institute has noted that the Court's federalist decisions partake of romanticism about "states' rights." These decisions contain many references to the "dignity" of states. The Court's assumption is that it can protect federalism by protecting state governments. As a consequence, the Court has been inattentive to the "horizontal" dimension of federalism: to the constitutional provisions that promote competition and accountability among state governments by constraining *their* power. If Eliot Spitzer wants to nationalize American industries from the New York attorney general's office, the Supreme Court is not going to stop him. The O'Connor Court's federalism is not that of the Founders.

How legal conservatives convinced themselves that federalism could be restored by the federal judiciary is one of the minor mysteries of the age. The O'Connor Court is itself a significant offender against federalism, just as its predecessors, the Warren and Burger courts, were. When the voters of Colorado passed an amendment to the state constitution opposing certain gay-rights laws, the Court's response was to slap them down. On abortion, the Court—O'Connor very much included—is "hysterically nationalist," as Robert Nagel argues in *The Implosion of American Federalism*. When seen against this backdrop, the "federalism revolution" starts to look less like a readjustment of state-federal relations and more like a transfer of power from Congress to the Court.

A highly developed institutional *amour propre* may be the most striking feature of the O'Connor Court. It is present in the plurality opinion in *Casey*, which O'Connor joined. The *Casey* Court reaffirmed *Roe* in large part out of a reluctance to give in to the Court's critics. Appearing to capitulate would compromise the Court's ability to "speak before all others" for the nation's constitutional ideals. It is this self-regard that brings together O'Connor's penchant for finicky edicts, the O'Connor Court's marked reluctance to overturn the activist precedents of the Warren and Burger courts, the Court's racial cases, and its intervention in the 2000 election. There is an authoritarian streak in this jurisprudence that Justice O'Connor does not, in all likelihood, perceive.

Should O'Connor either retire or be nominated to chief justice, fixing her position in the conservative-liberal spectrum more precisely may be important in the political battles that follow. But her most important legacy is not as a liberal, moderate, or conservative justice. It might be best expressed in the title of Kenneth Starr's book on the O'Connor Court—*First Among Equals*—except that the title is two words too long. There is little evidence that O'Connor or her Court regards other governmental authorities as equals.

From the *National Review*, June 30, 2003, pp. 35-37. © 2003 by National Review, Inc., 215 Lexington Avenue, New York, NY 10016. Reprinted by permission.

'WE ALL (PARTICULARLY POLITICIANS AND THE MEDIA) NEED A CIVICS LESSON.'

A Judge Speaks Out

H. LEE SAROKIN

Democracy in America today faces many seemingly intractable problems—inequality, corruption, political disengagement—but is equally threatened by discrete official acts that eat away at its core institutions. Jesse Helms autocratically denies William Weld a hearing to be ambassador to Mexico. Janet Reno stubbornly drags her feet on appointing an independent counsel on campaign finance abuses. House majority whip Tom DeLay callously calls for impeachment of federal judges who heed a legal "technicality" called the Bill of Rights. These actions feed mistrust of government and must be loudly condemned, as they often are. But in the case of the assault on judicial independence by DeLay, Senator Orrin Hatch and others—which was ramped up during the 1996 elections and continues in an unprecedented stonewalling of President Clinton's nominees to the federal bench—the people who could fight back most eloquently, the judges themselves, are bound by a code of silence.

Judges should be loath to enter the fray, but there are extraordinary circumstances where their rebuttals are warranted, even necessary. When Bob Dole and Newt Gingrich threatened Judge Harold Baer with impeachment in March 1996 because of his decision to suppress evidence in a routine drug case (a decision that, under pressure, he later rescinded), it was inspiring to see four appellate judges publicly proclaim that the criticism had gone too far.

Now, we have the first riposte from one who was a target. Judge H. Lee Sarokin, a courageously independent federal trial and appellate judge for seventeen years in Newark, was for years a favorite scapegoat of those on the right. Last year, battered by increasingly malicious and distorted assault, Sarokin left the bench, saying he no longer wanted his rulings to be fodder for their twisted campaign. While we regretted his decision, we respected it and urged him to break the silence and explain just how corrosive these attacks have become [see "Gavel-to-Gavel Politics," July 1, 1996]. Here is his response.

—The Editors

I retired from the federal bench not because my opinions were being criticized but in protest over the politicization (what I characterized as the "Willie Hortonizing") of the federal judiciary. Politicians increasingly mischaracterize judicial opinions and then use them against those who nominated, appointed or voted to confirm the judges involved (like blaming a governor for crimes committed by a paroled prisoner). Not only do such tactics threaten the independence of the judiciary but, more important, they have a corrosive effect on the public's confidence in our judicial system and those who implement it. This is the toll when respected persons in high office constantly contend that judges are not following the law but rather are pursuing their own private agenda. I thought that by stepping down from the court and making my concerns public, I would convey the gravity of this dangerous course.

Now, a year later, I concede that my grand gesture was a complete fizzle, and indeed, rather than dissuade the practice, seems to have emboldened it, since it has been followed by demands, led by Representatives Tom DeLay and Bob Barr, to impeach judges for unpopular decisions. Although the election has ended, the political rhetoric attacking the judiciary has not.

The validity of a judicial opinion cannot rest on popularity. Resisting pressure to please the majority is judicial strength, not weakness.

Admittedly, from time to time there will be judicial decisions with which many will not agree. All too often that disagreement arises from the mischaracterization of the opinion and focuses on its result rather than its reasoning. But the validity of a judicial opinion cannot rest on its popularity. Resisting the pressure to please the majority is the strength of the judiciary, not its weakness. Judges who invoke the Constitution to protect the rights of people charged with crimes are not "soft on crime." Judges who declare that a statute or a public referendum violates the constitution are not "legislating" from the bench or "thwarting the will of the majority." They are carrying out their oath of office and following the rule of law.

The verdict in the Oklahoma City bombing trial may have restored some confidence in our judicial system. But a different scenario might illustrate the dangers of the current political vilification of judges and the resulting erosion of respect for our judicial system. Assume that prison guards, angered over the 168 deaths caused by the bombing of the Murrah Federal Building and frustrated by the lack of cooperation from those arrested, decided to beat one of those charged in order to obtain a confession.* As a result, they obtained a statement with sufficient detail so that there could be no doubt as to the knowledge and guilt of the confessor. Furthermore, these details led to the gathering of additional evidence regarding the source of the materials utilized in the making of the bomb, how they were transported, where they were stored, how the bomb was made and how it was ultimately delivered and detonated and by whom.

There are those who would argue, quite reasonably, that the guards should be punished, but that the evidence should be utilized. However, there are some protections that we view as so precious that nothing can be gained from their violation. Under existing law, the confession would not be admissible. In all probability, neither would any of the details, evidence and corroboration obtained as a result. Indeed, the taint of the illegally obtained confession and the fruits thereby gained might have led to an acquittal or dismissal of the charges. One can well imagine and understand the public outrage at such a result. Conservative politicians would be elbowing one another aside to reach microphones to lambaste the "liberal judge" who made such a ruling and decry the use of the "technicality" that made it possible—another example of a judicial system run amok, although there probably is not a judge in the country who would rule otherwise.

But suppose we were to change the above hypothetical scenario as follows: The guilty person beaten by law-enforcement officers was not the first but the tenth. Seven did not confess, because they were not guilty; two others did, even though they were not, just to bring the beatings to an end. One can imagine and hope for an equally vociferous outcry. If public confidence is essential to the maintenance of our judicial system—and it is—what lesson is to be drawn from these two hypothetical instances? What people really desire is two sets of rules and rights: one for the guilty and one for the innocent. People do not want criminals to gain advantage from the assertion of constitutional rights. On the other hand, they want those rights available to and enforced for the innocent. The problem with such an approach is that the determination of constitutional violations is frequently made by a judge before there is a determination of guilt or innocence. Furthermore, for the presumption of innocence to have any meaning, a determination of guilt must await a final verdict.

So if it is impossible or impractical to preserve the Bill of Rights for the innocent and deny it to the guilty, should the constitutional protections extended to those accused of crimes be repeated? Has crime become so prevalent and the need to combat it so great that we are willing to sacrifice some of our fundamental rights in order to win this battle? For both practical and principled reasons, the answer should be "no," even if the present atmosphere makes such amendments to the Constitution seem politically possible.

First, we all (and particularly the politicians and the media) need a civics lesson. Have we forgotten our history? The Fifth Amendment is not a "technicality." The right against self-incrimination was considered fundamental and essential to our freedom. Likewise, the restriction on searches and other government intrusions into our private lives was of sufficient importance that our forefathers were prepared to die for it.

Even if one is unmoved by the historical significance of these rights, their enforcement has virtually no impact on crime in this country. If the Bill of Rights were repealed tomorrow, insofar as its protections extend to those accused of crimes, it would not make the slightest ripple in the amount or nature of crime in this country. Law-enforcement officials themselves have repeatedly stated that enforcement of the Bill of Rights has not impeded them, and criminals hardly sit around a kitchen table and say: "If we are apprehended we can invoke our right against self-incrimination, and thus we shall go ahead and rob the corner candy store." They may be street-smart and "know their rights," but that knowledge is neither the catalyst nor cause of their unlawful activity. It probably never enters their thinking, assuming that there is much forethought given to the commission of most crimes.

Most significant, and contrary to the vision portrayed by conservative politicians and media, there is not a group of loony liberal judges out there leaping at the chance to set criminals free. The idea that any judge relishes ruling in favor of a person charged with a crime in the face of evidence of guilt, and particularly after a finding of guilt, is utter nonsense. Those rulings are made with great reluctance, but done because the law compels it. The suppression of the confession referred to earlier in this article would have to be made by any and every judge confronted with those facts. Furthermore, the number of such rulings is minuscule. Roughly, between 5 and 10 percent of all criminal cases are actually tried. In those that are tried, motions to suppress evidence are routinely denied every day, in every court in every state in this country. A dismissal of charges following the granting of a motion to suppress evidence is as rare an event as Senator Orrin Hatch recommending a liberal for a seat on the Supreme Court.

When motions to suppress are granted, those who wish to capitalize on such rulings invariably discuss the heinous nature of the crime or the long criminal history of the defendant, if one exists, neither of which is relevant to the question of whether the defendant's constitutional rights have been violated. Here again, we do not and cannot have two sets of rules—one for bad crimes and criminals and another for those less offensive. The exercise I posed above was chosen because there has been no more horrific crime in the history of this country than the Oklahoma City bombing; but the rights afforded by the Constitution cannot be reduced as the severity of the crime increases.

The law and those who administer it are not perfect. Mistakes are made. That is why we have courts of appeal. But it is essential that the public understand that in large measure the guilty are convicted (indeed, most plead guilty), the innocent are protected and the judicial system and its judges are devoted and dedicated to fairness and justice. Criticism has its place, but truth must have some role in the dialogue. (My nomination to the Court of Appeals was opposed on the basis that I "had a long history of freeing criminals in disregard of the rights of their victims." In fifteen years on the bench two people are free as a result of my rulings—Rubin "Hurricane" Carter, a decision affirmed by the Court of Appeals and left standing by the U.S. Supreme Court after review, and James Landano, who is still awaiting retrial while on bail—hardly a "long history of freeing criminals.") Indeed, granting a writ of habeas corpus orders a new trial and does not free the petitioner unless the state elects not to retry.

The Bill of Rights is meant to protect us all. If in the process a criminal benefits, we must decide whether that detriment outweighs the benefits and freedoms we all enjoy. It is ironic that the criticism leveled at the Bill of Rights and the frequent characterization of its parts as "technicalities" come from conservatives, since the rights enunciated are the embodiment of the conservative philosophy. They codify the fundamental conservative principle of excluding unwanted and unwarranted government intrusion in the private lives of citizens.

Although the critics of "judicial activism" insist that neither the result nor the identity of the judge is what motivates them, the evidence suggests otherwise. There are many former prosecutors who now sit on the judicial benches of this country who were strong advocates of the death penalty. When they rule in favor of capital punishment, none of these critics claim that the judges involved are "activists carrying out their own agendas"; but the personal motives or background of those who vote against the death penalty in a given case invariably becomes relevant. When the Chief Justice of the United States wrote an opinion declaring unconstitutional an act of Congress that prohibited guns within 1,000 feet of schools, there was no cry of "thwarting the will of the people"; if I had authored that opinion, *The Wall Street Journal* editorial world have read: "Sarokin Rules Schoolchildren Can Have Guns!"

The independence of the judiciary is essential to our democracy. Those who seek to tamper with it to gain a momentary political victory for themselves will cause a greater and more lasting loss to the public, and to the confidence in our judicial system, without which the rule of law cannot survive.

---

* There is no suggestion that any guard would engage in such conduct. The discussion is for illustrative purposes only.

H. Lee Sarokin is a retired judge of the United States Court of Appeals.

One Branch Among Three

The courts should not be so powerful—and they don't have to be

RAMESH PONNURU

PITY Alfred Goodwin. The judge has been vilified from coast to coast for ruling that it's unconstitutional to force schoolkids to listen to the words "under God" in the Pledge of Allegiance. The words "wacko," "stupid," "ridiculous," and "just nuts" have all been applied, either to the decision or to the judge himself. Except for Judge Stephen Reinhardt, who voted with him, almost nobody seems to be on Goodwin's side. Even the ACLU has been uncharacteristically quiet in its support for him. After a day of criticism, Goodwin felt moved to stay the implementation of his own decision as a matter of (in his words) "damage control."

Goodwin and Reinhardt deserve better. In the context of the church-state case law that the Supreme Court has built up over the last 55 years, their ruling was, at the very least, defensible. The Court has frequently held that there is a constitutional obligation for governments—state governments and the federal government alike—to avoid the appearance of endorsing religious views. It has ruled that public schools, in particular, must avoid actions that may generate social pressure for children to express support for such views. It's hard to reconcile the common public-school practice of reciting the Pledge with the Court's rulings.

What Goodwin and Reinhardt did was take orthodox liberal church-state jurisprudence to its logical conclusions. Only political prudence, or residual common sense, has kept their fellow judges from doing the same.

The decision can, of course, be faulted for exhibiting a certain judicial arrogance. The judges forbade a widespread, long-accepted practice, implying that the Supreme Court, state legislatures, and schools had all been constitutionally derelict and oppressive in letting the Pledge be recited all these years. But here again, Judge Goodwin's ruling is not so much more egregious than other judicial edicts. A week before it, the Supreme Court had ruled that it is unconstitutional for states to impose the death penalty on mentally retarded convicts. It thus overruled the judgment of 20 states, with no greater constitutional justification than that "evolving standards of decency" had left those states behind.

Unlike the Pledge decision, moreover, the death-penalty decision will have negative real-world consequences, as Death Row convicts start gaming the intelligence tests.

THE SLUMBER OF OUTRAGE

In both of these cases and many others, the worst damage done by the courts is to the constitutional structure: to self-government, federalism, and the rule of law. In such cases, the federal judiciary steps beyond its constitutional powers at the expense of local elected officials. But judicial self-aggrandizement as such does not seem to outrage the public. People grow angry only when judicial power is used for ends to which they object emotionally—like the removal of "God" from the Pledge.

It would be nice if the American people were more jealous of their constitutional prerogatives as a matter of principle. As things stand, it is incumbent on political leaders who *are* concerned about constitutional ideals to use moments of public agitation to restore those prerogatives.

Political leaders failed in this task the last time the courts presented them with an opportunity. In 1989, the Supreme Court ruled Texas's ban on flag-burning unconstitutional. The immediate issue, as in today's Pledge case, was less than earth-shattering. Also as in the present case, there was nonetheless an eruption of popular anger at the decision, and politicians reflected this mood in denouncing it. There were other parallels as well. Although states had long protected the flag without the raising of a constitutional question—just as schools for decades had asked children to recite the words "under God" in the Pledge—the ruling that doing so was unconstitutional was plausibly based on precedents that had drawn little notice from the public. (Those precedents classed various forms of expression, such as nude dancing, as "speech" deserving a certain level of constitutional protection. And whereas the First Amendment stipulates that "Congress" shall make no law abridging freedom of speech, the Court had extended the protection of free speech to apply against the states as well.)

Congress's response to the controversy was to pass a federal version of the Texas statute. The Court promptly, and predictably, struck the federal law down. Then congressmen started pushing for a constitutional amendment to ban flag burning. This effort served narrow political purposes, since it forced liberal congressmen to vote to allow flag-burning. But its chances of actual success in undoing the Court's ruling were always slim: The Constitution, quite properly, makes itself difficult to amend by elected officials. To many people, it also seemed a bit grotesque to amend the Constitution to deal with an issue that was, in itself, so picayune. One wouldn't want to clutter the Constitution with clarifications every time the courts misread it.

The congressional response to Judge Goodwin's ruling has been even more pathetic than the response to the flag-burning decision. Politicians have been content to take to the floor of Congress to recite the Pledge and denounce the ruling—and to vote for a resolution declaring themselves pro-Pledge. There has been enough mindless posturing to make anyone wonder, for a moment, whether judicial rule is all that much worse than representative democracy.

But perhaps the congressmen should not be judged too harshly. Most of them are unaware of any more constructive action they can take in the face of unconstitutional judicial actions. Our political culture contemplates two methods of correcting errant courts: amending the Constitution to override them, and appointing successor judges who will rule differently.

The amendment strategy, as mentioned, is very hard to pull off. (Even at that, it's under ideological challenge from prominent academics who regard corrective amendments as, in the words of Stanford Law School dean Kathleen Sullivan, "mutiny against the authority" of the courts.) The appointments strategy is hardly easier. Presidents Reagan and Bush I tried to improve the composition of the federal judiciary, but their success might be described, with charity, as mixed—and they were able to make five Supreme Court appointments. A set of conventions has also arisen around the judicial-selection process that inhibits presidents and senators from discovering either the scope of a nominee's view of his prospective constitutional powers or the uses to which he would likely put those powers.

Occasionally, someone will suggest that judges who regularly exceed their constitutional mandates should be impeached. Tom DeLay said this a few years ago, and was treated as a dangerous madman as a result. He shouldn't have been. In *Federalist* Number 81, Alexander Hamilton prescribes exactly that remedy for judicial usurpation. But modern legal scholars generally glance past those words in embarrassment. (Chief Justice William Rehnquist, acting in his sometime role as the head of the judges' union, has made a singularly unconvincing case that Hamilton's views have been made obsolete.) Should constitutionalists devote their energies to making the case that impeachment is not an extreme remedy for usurper-judges? Probably not. Any such educational campaign might end up teaching the wrong lesson—that the problem with the judiciary is a few bad apples, not a structural imbalance of power.

We treat the Constitution as though it were whatever the Court says it is. Such power, effectively unchecked, is bound to be abused.

Judicial errors are so hard to correct—and the potential remedies are now so weakened—because we have come to hold an inflated view of judicial authority. We think it natural that judges should have the last word on constitutional matters. We habitually treat the Constitution as though it were whatever the Supreme Court says it is. We assume that the Court has the job of determining the limits of everyone else's powers, which means, of course, that it has more power than everyone else. Such power, effectively unchecked, is bound to be abused.

HOW TO CHECK THE COURT

There is, however, a way to start changing these assumptions. The Constitution grants Congress the power to limit the jurisdiction of the federal courts. Article III, Section 2, explicitly gives Congress the power to limit the appellate jurisdiction of the Supreme Court ("the supreme Court shall have appellate Jurisdiction, both as to Law and Fact, with such Exceptions, and under such Regulations as the Congress shall make"). The power of Congress to limit the jurisdiction of the lower federal courts is implied. Article III, Section 1, grants Congress the power to create the "inferior Courts," which has to include the power to establish the scope and limits of their jurisdiction. (The Constitution spells out Congress's ability to limit the jurisdiction of the Supreme Court because the Constitution, rather than Congress, establishes that court.)

A simple majority of Congress and a presidential signature can regulate, or establish exceptions to, the jurisdiction of the federal courts. A constitutional amendment is not required. Such a bill would reduce the power of the judiciary—rather than merely recall a few judges (as impeachment would) or make an impotent gesture of defiance to the courts (as the congressional flag-burning statute did). In addition, the effort to pass a bill would be educational even if it failed to pass, since it would challenge prevailing misconceptions about the proper division of interpretive power over the Constitution.

So, for instance, Congress could pass a bill making it impossible for the lower federal courts to take up challenges to the constitutionality of schools' use of the Pledge of Allegiance—a bill that Republican congressman Todd Akin of Missouri has introduced. Judge Goodwin's decision would be effectively nullified, since neither he nor other federal judges would be able to enforce it.

If the bill starts to gain steam, there will be no shortage of criticisms of it. (Anthony Lewis may come out of retirement to denounce it.) People will call it an overreaction to one bad decision that the courts are already correcting. They will say that it is not the place of Congress to do the correcting, that it is the job of the courts alone to interpret the Constitution.

Some conservatives will be among the critics. Many of them accept judicial supremacy, criticizing how the Supreme Court rules us rather than the fact that it rules us. In some cases, they want to use judicial power for conservative ends. They may not be familiar with the constitutional basis for regulating the jurisdiction of the federal courts.

Even conservatives who *are* familiar with it sometimes raise the objection that reining in the federal courts would only empower the state courts, which are in many cases even worse. Pass Akin's bill, for example, and a California court could issue an anti-Pledge ruling. The objection is not persuasive. When state courts overstep their mandates, opponents in the state have political recourses available to them. In many states, they can vote out the offending judges at reelection. They can impeach the judges; they can amend state statutes and constitutions. It may be difficult to accomplish these things, of course, but they are not even theoretical possibilities when a federal court moves against a state. A state is practically powerless in such situations.

In the normal course of things, it's not the federal government's concern when a state court runs amok. When a federal court wrongly diminishes state autonomy, however, a branch of the federal government is acting as a rogue agent and should be restrained by the other branches. It is worth noting that the state courts are as riotous as they are because the legal culture has been influenced by decades of federal-court usurpations unchecked by any effective political response. Perhaps the Akin bill or something like it would inspire similar efforts at the state level.

Another argument against limiting the jurisdiction of the federal courts merits serious consideration. It is that it would set a dangerous precedent. Congress would soon start passing bills to undo sound judicial decisions merely because they are unpopular with the public or with congressmen. Of course, any power can be abused. But the present system—in which it is easy for federal judges to amend the Constitution by fiat, but difficult for

their amendments to be undone—is far more open to abuse than one that checks the judges would be.

Hamilton points to an enduring truth about judicial overreach: Its continuation depends on the acquiescence of the other branches.

Hamilton famously remarked that the judiciary is "the least dangerous" branch of the federal government because it has "no influence over either the sword or the purse." These words are often cited ruefully by conservatives, who think that Hamilton underestimated the dangers the federal judiciary could pose. But those words point to an enduring truth about judicial overreach: Its continuation depends on the acquiescence of the other branches.

Under our Constitution, self-government is not merely an option; it is an obligation. Passive acquiescence in judicial rule—a failure to resist it—does not legitimize it. The Congress is full of politicians who have been reciting the Pledge of Allegiance. But they take an oath to defend the Constitution, too. If they look, they will find in it the means for its reclamation.

The new Department of Homeland Security

Washington's mega-merger

America is about to get its long-promised Department of Homeland Security. How much will that help?

IT WILL be one of the biggest mergers ever. The newly consolidated business will have an annual turnover of $37 billion and 169,000 employees. The chief executive is babbling about synergies, benefits of rationalisation and economies of scale. The track record of ordinary mergers, involving two companies, is poor—and this one consolidates 22 units from 12 different companies. Meanwhile, in the background, the shareholders—or their representatives—are bickering and the unions are suspicious. If this were a real corporate merger, Wall Street would already be discounting the share price.

So the first question to ask about America's new Department of Homeland Security is whether the basic design (see chart) is the right one. It will bring most of the main functions of domestic security under one roof. Huge agencies will be seized from other departments—the Immigration and Naturalisation Service (39,500 employees) from Justice, the Coast Guard (43,600) from Transportation, the Customs Service (21,700) from the Treasury. Other independent entities—like the Federal Emergency Management Agency (5,100)—will be gobbled up whole. Yet the new department will not be omnivorous: it is not eating up some 100 departments and agencies that remain on its patch.

There are still people who think it should have been bigger or smaller. In 2001 a commission chaired by former senators Gary Hart and Warren Rudman proposed an even more sweeping reorganisation that would have also shaken up the Defence Department and the National Security Council (NSC), which are both basically untouched by the new entity. George Bush initially did not want a new department at all, merely a coordinating office in the White House, with the operational divisions left in different departments.

In fact, there is a lot to be said for the compromise agreed upon this week. To have folded everything into one giant department would have been logical but administratively impractical. As Richard Falkenrath, the policy director for the Office of Homeland Security, told a panel at the Brookings Institution, the job "requires specialisation and expertise. There's also a fair bit going on in the rest of the world which the NSC needs to stay focused on."

But leaving agencies scattered around would have been no good either. Consider two examples. If there were a chemical or biological attack now, health advice would come from no fewer than 12 federal agencies, to say nothing of local government ones. If there were an attack on a nuclear power plant, one agency would distribute anti-radiation treatment if you live within 10 miles. A different one distributes it if you live outside that circle. A third controls the drug stockpile. And a fourth takes over if the attack also happens to be within 10 miles of a nuclear-weapons facility.

So it is not surprising that the president came round to seeing the benefits of rationalisation. With such an immense job of coordination to do, having a single department with budgetary control looked necessary. An advisory White House office could never bang heads together.

The bill approved this week does more than merely move bureaucratic boxes into one place: it vests the powers of the various units in the new secretary (likely to be Tom Ridge, now head of the White House Office of Homeland Security), in order to eliminate duplication or enforce the adoption of common standards. He can delegate authority back to the bits as he sees fit, and he also has the power to take 5% of the budget of any one bit of his empire and move it around.

In other words, the bill vests a lot of administrative discretion in one person. That may be risky. Democrats also argued that it was unconstitutional, and trampled over employment rights. These were the issues that held up approval of the homeland-security bill for months over the summer and autumn. But it is probably just as well the administration won the fight: much discretionary power will be required to overcome bureaucratic inertia.

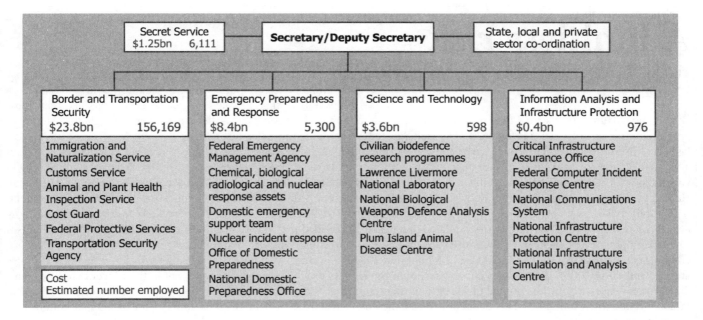

Secret Service $1.25bn 6,111	**Secretary/Deputy Secretary**	State, local and private sector co-ordination

Border and Transportation Security $23.8bn 156,169	Emergency Preparedness and Response $8.4bn 5,300	Science and Technology $3.6bn 598	Information Analysis and Infrastructure Protection $0.4bn 976
Immigration and Naturalization Service Customs Service Animal and Plant Health Inspection Service Cost Guard Federal Protective Services Transportation Security Agency	Federal Emergency Management Agency Chemical, biological radiological and nuclear response assets Domestic emergency support team Nuclear incident response Office of Domestic Preparedness National Domestic Preparedness Office	Civilian biodefence research programmes Lawrence Livermore National Laboratory National Biological Weapons Defence Analysis Centre Plum Island Animal Disease Centre	Critical Infrastructure Assurance Office Federal Computer Incident Response Centre National Communications System National Infrastructure Protection Centre National Infrastructure Simulation and Analysis Centre

Cost
Estimated number employed

Two reforms look particularly promising. First, the new department will gather together all the border and transport agencies into one place. At the moment, people entering America fill in one form for immigration officials and another one for customs, and they may have to see Department of Agriculture officers. That will now be rationalised—a no-brainer, admittedly, but this is by far the largest section of the new department, with 156,200 of the 169,000 employees.

The second reform concerns "information analysis". For the first time, America will have a central clearing house for assessing the vulnerabilities of, and threats to, Americans at home. At present, the Energy Department supervises security at power stations, the Transportation Department looks at roads and bridges, and so on. Bringing these things together will not guarantee better intelligence, but it should be easier to spot trends and connections.

For now, the new department will merely analyse intelligence gathered by others. But several figures, including Richard Shelby, the senior Republican on the Senate Intelligence Committee, and a commission chaired by Jim Gilmore, the former governor of Virginia, have argued that America needs a proper domestic intelligence-gathering operation, like Britain's MI5. At the moment, the gathering is done by the FBI, whose director, Robert Mueller, vigorously opposes any idea to split off spying from policing, even though most spooks insist that spying and policing are often contradictory things.

That battle is for the future, but similar vested interests are bound to make Mr Ridge's nice draft design extremely hard to put into practice. One cautionary tale comes from the Transportation Security Administration, the division which supplies the baggage screeners that went to work this week and which, at full strength, will be the second largest single part of the new department. The TSA was set up last year with congressional goodwill, a tough boss and an ambitious programme. But it lost the confidence of Congress and airport managers. It failed to get baggage-screening devices delivered on time. It could not resolve the competing claims of security and airport efficiency. And its first boss was sacked.

From this perspective, it is worrying that the new department does not really begin with firm political backing. Although the Senate voted 90 to nine this week to set up the department, that was only after months of squabbling. And the new department faces four challenges that may cost it more support.

- **The transition.** The new department is supposed to be up and running a year after the president signs the bill (which may be next week). It took 40 years and several congressional interventions to get the last comparable government reorganisation right, the establishment of the Department of Defence. It would be a disaster if the bureaucratic effort to set up the new department distracts from the real job of protecting the homeland.

- **Sporadic shortages of money.** Proposed spending on homeland security has roughly doubled since September 11th (though not all the promised money has materialised). Still there are holes. The Coast Guard has one of the oldest fleets in the world and no amount of reorganisation will provide enough money to buy new ships.

- **Civil liberties.** Even in its pre-MI5 incarnation, the department's domestic snoops are likely to come into conflict with civil libertarians. Privacy watchdogs are up in arms about a new "office of information awareness" which, they say, could put all e-mails, credit-card transactions, drug prescriptions and every bit of electronic information you generate on to one vast, Orwellian database. This nightmare idea has been floated by the Defence Department, and may come to nothing. But the fracas carries a warning to the Homeland Security Department.

- **The private sector.** Many of America's most vulnerable targets, such as chemical factories, are privately owned and guarded. Any Republican government will be reluctant to wade in and impose new federal regulations on private firms.

Terrorism insurance

A limitless risk

The government, it seems, was bound to bail out the industry

Why did Congress take such a long time to approve a federal programme for terrorist-risk insurance? Ever since September last year, insurers and their customers have been clamouring for a bill to make the government an insurer of last resort for terrorist attacks. Yet it was not until November 19th that it finally cleared the Senate, having passed the House a week earlier.

The bill makes available as much as $100 billion over the next three years to cover 90% of the losses related to terrorism. The federal programme kicks in when industry losses are greater than a certain sum ($10 billion in 2003, $12.5 billion in 2004 and $15 billion in 2005). If the losses do not reach that figure, the insurers' losses will still be limited to 7% of their premiums in 2003, rising to 15% in 2005. This deductible aside, the government will pay the rest.

Insurers argue that the logic for calling in the government is compelling. The industry managed to swallow a loss of around $50 billion from September 11th; but many big insurers would go under if another such loss occurred. So the government would have to become the insurer of last resort by default.

This year most insurers and reinsurers either refused to write terrorism insurance (which 45 states and the District of Columbia allowed them to do), or they demanded exorbitant prices that many businesses refused to pay. Today more than half America's businesses have no cover for terrorism; another quarter have only meagre cover. The cost of general insurance has risen, on average, by around 30% since the attacks. There have also been lawsuits related to bank covenants: for instance, the owners of the Condé Nast tower in New York are in dispute with their mortgage holders over the lack of terror cover for their building on Times Square.

With so many lobbyists in a panic, few politicians opposed the concept of a federal backstop. The main sticking point between Democrats and Republicans was a proposal by the House to bar victims of terrorist attacks from seeking punitive damages in lawsuits against private companies. Democrats and their most munificent benefactors, the trial lawyers, thought this was an attempt to introduce tort reform.

Now a compromise has been reached. Victims of terrorism can sue private companies for punitive damages, though only in federal courts, which are less accommodating to plaintiffs than certain state courts. They cannot sue the federal government. The White House, which had backed the House plan, has now decided that the bill is about "jobs, not tort reform", and says it will help stimulate the economy.

Insurers will now start writing terror cover again, and prices should fall dramatically—but not to their level before September 11th, which was close to zero. Before the attacks, terrorism insurance in America was simply part of blanket commercial cover—at no additional charge. That world has gone.

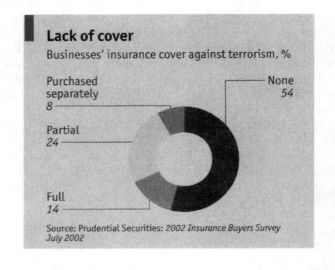

Lack of cover
Businesses' insurance cover against terrorism, %

Purchased separately 8
None 54
Partial 24
Full 14

Source: Prudential Securities: *2002 Insurance Buyers Survey July 2002*

But what if private security is not enough? Mr Ridge could well find himself battling against several huge industries.

In short, the new department is a step forward, but just a step. Eventually, it should make America's borders safer and improve domestic intelligence. But those are only parts of the picture. It is a top-down reform to improve security at a time when the most useful form of protection comes from the bottom up—from a security guard noticing something strange at a power plant, from a customs officer following up a hunch, from passengers overpowering a shoe bomber. Even after the new mega-merger, those are the people who will keep the homeland secure.

Turkey Farm

*The government can't afford to keep ignoring the case
for reforming civil service tenure*

By Robert Maranto

Jim worked in a Defense Department office with an employee whose lack of productivity was matched only by his hostile attitude. Eventually, a good manager with the patience of Job, a mastery of detail to match, and the help of higher management took the time to record, day by day, the offender's record of non-work. After developing improvement plans for the employee and thoroughly documenting his failure to meet them for many months, the incompetent worker was actually fired. Then, the employee appealed before the Merit Systems Protection Board (MSPB). Two years into the appeal, when it looked as if the government would finally win, MSPB threw out the case when one of the team, moving to dismiss the employee, made an offhand remark that "even the people in his neighborhood association think he's unstable." The employee was reinstated with back pay. The agency went through the process all over again. By this time Jim had become boss. With the benefits of hindsight and existing records, the final try took only one more year of work!

Jim's predicament is faced by thousands of hardworking federal employees who must suffer a small number of lazy, incompetent, and, occasionally, dangerous co-workers. For the past three years, I taught high level federal managers at the Federal Executive Institute (FEI). Despite the stereotypes about bureaucrats, the vast majority of federal managers are capable people who take pride in their work. In dedication and smarts, the government bureaucrats I've worked with are more than a match for the college professors I taught alongside during 15 years in the academy. Unfortunately, these good people are thoroughly frustrated by a personnel system which forces them to work alongside (and get the same raises as) a small number of turkeys.

A Broken Personnel System

One of my games in the civil service was to ask a lunch table full of federal managers whether it was possible to fire low-performing employees. Save for the ever optimistic personnel specialists, the usual consensus was that it was possible, but hardly ever worth the effort. My informal focus groups mirrored public employee surveys.

While career civil servants and political appointees do not always see eye to eye, mail surveys I conducted in the mid-1990s found that each side did agree that the federal personnel system is broken, at least when it comes to separating non-performers. Eighty-eight percent of Clinton political appointees and 83 percent of career managers agreed that "personnel rules make it too difficult to fire personnel"—more than half of each group strongly agreed. This dovetails with the findings of University of Georgia political scientist Hal Rainey. Reviewing years of survey data, Rainey reports that "[r]oughly 90 percent of the public managers agreed that their organization's personnel rules make it hard to fire poor managers and hard to reward good managers with higher pay, while 90 percent of the business managers disagreed."

Since courts have ruled that federal employees have property rights in their jobs, they can only be terminated after lengthy due process and multiple venues of appeal. As a result, managers who decide to use official means to deal with turkeys may face the prospect of spending all their time managing that one person, to the detriment of the rest of the office. As one of my informants, a manager in a regional office, recalled of his one (eventually successful) effort to separate an employee who was both unproductive and breaking the law: "As the year went on, it took more and more of my time and became all consuming. I had to spend a lot of time explaining why I was doing this." Similarly, when asked if he had ever fired a nonperformer, one manager told me that he had no intention of becoming like the one person in his agency who had fired several people and "wears that as a badge of honor, but he has no time to do his real work!"

Not only is firing a government employee time-consuming for managers, it is also dangerous. Managers who move against problem employees take serious risks. As Carolyn Ban details in *How Do Public Managers Manage?*, low performers facing personnel actions need not go gentle into that good night. They can make life difficult for months or years. They can take their case to the Merit Systems Protection Board (MSPB). They can file a grievance if they are covered by a union contract. Or if they belong to a protected class (by sex, race, age, or handicap), they can file an Equal Employment Opportunity complaint. Some bring their cases to the Office of the Special Counsel, claiming that they are being fired or otherwise harassed because they are whistle-blowers.

The problem of "low performing whistle-blowers" is particularly vexing for many federal managers, who, on the word of a single employee, can be subjected to prolonged investigations worthy of an independent counsel. Imagine having colleagues and subordinates questioned for months about whether you have ever used the long-distance line for personal calls or have padded the expense account. While the investigations go on, little work gets done and communication between co-workers stops, since everyone is afraid that a random remark could lead to a grand jury. Even when the boss is exonerated, a bad reputation can linger for years. And of course, if all else fails, the employee can simply sue his or her manager.

Not surprisingly, managers who have fired someone describe the process as traumatic. As one of the officials quoted above recalls, "here it is years later, the person has long since left the state, and I still don't want to talk about that sorry episode. It has an impact upon both the office and the family life of the individuals involved. It's something you only do once."

With the deck stacked against them, federal managers tend to avoid using official means of dealing with their turkeys. Phone surveys of managers by the U.S. Office of Personnel Management (OPM), reported in *Poor Performers in Government: A Quest for the True Story*, found that only 7.5 percent of the managers of low performing employees moved to reassign, demote, or remove them, and 77.8 percent of those managers reported that the efforts had no effect. While OPM gives a rough estimate of around 65,000 poor performers in government, from September 1997 to September 1998, only 159 federal employees were removed by performance based personnel actions, with another 1,693 removed for issues other than performance, such as breaking the law. Federal managers suffer low performers or act informally to improve their work and never use the federal personnel system, or only use it as a last resort.

Not infrequently, federal managers use two traditional means of shedding non-performers. By writing glowing letters of recommendation, a boss can get a turkey promoted to a different office. Fortunately, most civil servants are too ethical to use such tactics, and anyway, you can only do that once or twice before your credibility in the bureaucracy is shot. More typically, bosses place non-performers in "turkey farms," "dead pools," or (if it is a single person) "on the shelf." By quarantining non-performers, a good manager can save the rest of the organization from their influence.

The relative inability to act against a small number of poor performers has the effect of making that small number vexing to managers, who are people more used to solving problems than ignoring them. Managers don't like using turkey farms, but many feel they have no choice. At least, when downsizing comes, known turkeys make good candidates for reductions-in-force.

The Costs of Tenure

The sad part is that the vast majority of federal personnel do a good job. OPM's *Poor Performers in Government* report estimates that under 4 percent of federal civil servants are non-performers. One can quibble with OPM's methodology. I suspect that the real figure is a bit higher, but still, the poor performer problem is not nearly as bad as most Americans think. So why deal with it at all?

Aside from inefficiency, there are four huge costs of the federal government's inability to kick turkeys off the farm. First, non-performers themselves never get the message that they have to shape up or ship out and never get the chance for a new start. Instead, they often use the system to pursue old grudges for years. Second, good employees like Jim are forced to work alongside, do the work of, and often get the same raises as a small number of turkeys—a real morale killer.

Third, the low performance problem undermines the image and self-image of the bureaucracy. Business people have no tenure and look down on their government cousins who do. Military officers have an "up or out" promotion system—at key points in their careers officers either get promoted or get discharged. This makes the officer corps, at least at higher levels, a turkey-free zone, giving the brass a certain swagger in their dealings with their protected cousins in the civil service.

Most important, a tenured civil service undermines the legitimacy of the bureaucracy in the eyes of the public. After all, very few voters have tenure, so it is hard to tell citizens why their public servants cannot be fired. It is not surprising that college professors, public school teachers, and government bureaucrats have all come under attack in recent years. The very existence of tenure protects a small number of losers and leads the public to suspect the existence of a large number of low performers in government—a suspicion shared by many public managers.

Originally, the federal merit system was set up in 1884 to keep political parties from using government jobs to reward supporters. Patronage was seen as particularly onerous after President Garfield was assassinated by an insane "disappointed office seeker." Presumably, government would work better if run by technical experts than by political hacks. But on the federal level, at least, the spoils system got a bum rap. Even in the 19th century, a new president and Congress kept most of the incumbent civil servants in place, and only rarely replaced those with special expertise. Politicians have never relished the unpopular task of firing old employees to replace them with political supporters. As politicians have long lamented, each new political appointment provides 10 enemies who themselves wanted the job and one ingrate who got it. Besides, for perfectly sound electoral reasons, politicians cared (and still care) about the efficient management of government. As political scientist Michael Nelson has pointed out, even in the 19th century, more voters sent mail than delivered it. A party that replaces all the mail carriers disrupts service—not a good way to win re-election.

The temptation to "politicize" a bureaucracy in search of pork is even less apparent today. In the old days, political campaigns were won by precinct workers who might welcome a federal job. Today, politicians depend on big kickbacks from campaign contributors rather than small ones from government employees. More important, the greater size and expertise of modern government makes it less susceptible to political takeovers. In the old days, it may have made some sense for politicians to hire friends to deliver the mail, but imagine if a modern president hired precinct workers to run the Pentagon and NIH? To think that politicians would raid the civil service, you have to assume that they have an incredible capacity for both venality and stupidity, and the time to exercise both. In fact, modern presidents can hardly handle the 3,000 political appointments they have now. How could they place more? Sure, presidential political appointments have grown in number since 1960, but not nearly enough to match the growth in congressional staffs, interest groups, and reporters—the people appointees deal with on behalf of their agencies. Unless we downsize the rest of the Washington political class—something not likely to happen—we can't downsize political appointments.

Because of constant scrutiny by opponents, politicians in Washington do not have the sort of vast appointment powers they might have in some states and cities. Presidents are in fact very constrained in who they can appoint to government jobs and how many appointments they can make. *The Washington Post* test ("How will it look in *The Post*?") limits what they can do. Congressional scrutiny limits what they can do. Inter- and intra-party battles limit what they can do. Not surprisingly, the worst abuses under spoils were in states and localities with little political competition, not in a two-party, hyperpluralist Washington.

Rebuilding Public Service

To its credit, the Clinton administration has at least acknowledged the non-performer problem, and has begun to act on it. In accord with the *Poor Performer* study, OPM issued a CD-ROM guide to help managers, *Addressing and Resolving Poor Performance*. This is more than previous administrations dared try, but probably too little, too late. Not surprisingly, as the longtime guardian of the merit system, OPM's basic inclination is to save a system that should probably be buried. Real change in the merit system requires legislation to simplify procedures, followed by years of culture change inside government, along the lines of the National Performance Review's reforms of government procurement. The White House considered introduc-ing a bill to overhaul the civil service earlier this year but dropped it in deference to public employee unions, an important constituency in the 2000 presidential primaries.

Real change is occurring on an ad hoc basis, however, in the agencies. Currently, the Federal Aviation Administration and Internal Revenue Service are creating their own alternatives to the traditional merit system. The Pentagon and Department of Housing and Urban Development have floated trial balloons proposing to replace most tenured civil servants with contractors and fixed-term employees who can be separated with relative ease—something that is happening incrementally all over government. Further, the rise of Performance Based Organizations, called for by Vice President Gore's *Reinventing Government* reports, is likely to erode tenure by tying organization budgets and staffing levels to results. Indeed, on all levels of government, the reinventing movement is in part a way to use market mechanisms to get around civil service tenure. Declining demands for an organization's outputs force reductions in force, which in turn push marginal performers out the door.

Many of the most exciting changes are happening in the states. More than 30 states now have serious proposals to reform their civil service systems, but Georgia has gone the farthest. In 1996 Georgia removed tenure from new employees in state agencies. A detailed evaluation of the Georgia experiment does not yet exist, but early work by political scientist Steve Condrey suggests that removing tenure has increased the ability of public managers to manage for accountability. A single Georgia state agency reported terminating nearly 200 employees for cause in the first 20 months after the law came into effect—with no reported challenges or cases of impropriety. Notably, the Georgia civil service reform was developed and pushed through the legislature not by anti-government Republicans but by then Governor Zell Miller, a pro-government New Democrat who sees ending tenure as one way to restore the legitimacy of government.

In short, for the first time in decades, real civil service reform is beginning to happen. For historic context, it took 20 years from 1864 to 1883 to build political support for the original federal merit system, and another 40 years to put it in place. It may take another decade to reform the federal merit system, but tenure now lacks public legitimacy, and the first steps at reform have already been taken. This excites those of us who want to turn "civil service" from an epithet for cumbersome personnel rules into a public service ethic.

ROBERT MARANTO *is a visiting scholar at the Curry School of Education at the University of Virginia and co-editor most recently of* School Choice in the Real World: Lessons from Arizona Charter Schools.

America's intelligence services

Time for a rethink

Just when they are most needed, America's spies are in a mess. But reform will happen only if George Bush wants it

WASHINGTON, DC

IMAGINE a huge $30-billion conglomerate. It operates in one of the few businesses that might genuinely be described as cutthroat. Its competitors have changed dramatically, and so have its products and technologies. But its structure is the same as when it was founded, in 1947. Nobody leads this colossus (there is just an honorary chairman) and everyone exploits it. Demoralised and bureaucratic, it has just endured its biggest-ever loss. The response: the firm has been given even more money, and nobody has been sacked.

Soon, the intelligence committees from the two houses of Congress will begin a special joint review of America's spies. The joint chairmen, Congressman Porter Goss and Senator Bob Graham, both insist that reform is possible. But structural change depends on the administration, and George Bush has already backed George Tenet, the Director of Central Intelligence (DCI), who staggeringly refuses to admit that September 11th was a failure. "Failure", says Mr Tenet, "means no focus, no attention, no discipline—and those were not present in what either we or the FBI did here and around the world."

The best protection for the intelligence services is that so few people understand what they do. Most Americans associate espionage with the Central Intelligence Agency and the DCI, the most conspicuous creations of the 1947 National Security Act. In fact, the "intelligence community" contains 13 federal organisations, and the CIA accounts for only around a tenth of the intelligence budget of $30 billion. Most of the real money goes to high-tech military

agencies, such as the National Reconnaissance Office (NRO), which runs the satellites, and the National Imagery and Mapping Agency (NIMA). The biggest, the National Security Agency (NSA), once so secret that it was referred to as No Such Agency, employs 30,000 eavesdroppers. By contrast, the CIA's Directorate of Operations—its human spying bit—has only around 4,000 people.

Some critics argue that the true cost of intelligence-gathering is closer to $50 billion, and the number of agencies dealing with the subject is closer to 45 (or even 100). They count in various bits of the FBI (which oversees counter-intelligence at home), parts of the new Office of Homeland Security, and sundry military and diplomatic organisations. Generally speaking, the system gets more convoluted the lower down you go, eventually becoming a blur of incompatible computer systems, different chains of command and an obtuse budgeting system.

Above all, there is the question of responsibility. Mr Tenet, as DCI, is both boss of the CIA and also director of all America's intelligence-gathering. He has a "community management staff" to assist him, but his real clout is small. Most of the intelligence budget is controlled by proper departments, whose bosses sit in the cabinet. Jim Woolsey, a former DCI, recalls that his predecessor, Bob Gates, warned him that his position was like the king's in medieval France: the nobles all swear fealty to you, but do not fear you.

Blown to pieces

Many people think this tangled structure (see chart) caused the failures around September 11th. Others point to mismanage-

ment, culture and even the American way of life. Who is right?

The mismanagement school of critics, which wants Mr Tenet's head, can only be buttressed by the pig-headed refusal of the seventh floor at Langley to admit to any failure. The excuses proffered vary. Some pass the buck around the labyrinth: CIA people point out that it was the FBI's job to trail terrorists at home. Others point to the list of atrocities that have been averted, which is fair enough, though at least one of the examples, the capture of a bomber with Los Angeles airport as his target, owed more to an observant customs official than to good intelligence.

Al-Qaeda, America's spymasters tried to claim, was peculiarly difficult to infiltrate, since it was open only to kinsmen of members. That notion was blown apart by the appearance of John Walker Lindh, a Californian airhead, in Osama bin Laden's trenches. As one former CIA boss puts it, "Al-Qaeda was an evangelical organisation: it wanted members. We never suggested any."

Enough. By any reasonable definition, the fact that 19 terrorists could slaughter 3,000 people should count as a monumental failure of intelligence—the worst since Pearl Harbour. Besides, as one senior Bush adviser argues, "it is not as if there were not enough clues to be picked up for our $30 billion a year." The World Trade Centre was a known target; al-Qaeda people had plotted to fly aircraft into buildings before; a suspect had been picked up having flying lessons; and so on.

Those who point to gross mismanagement are, however, currently less influential than the "culture" critics. According to these, Mr Tenet is less culpable than symp-

Simplicity itself
America's intelligence apparatus

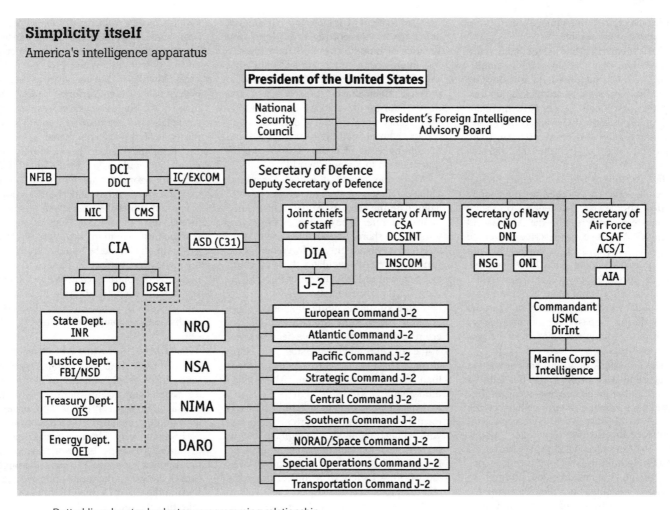

-------- Dotted line denotes budgetary programming relationship

ACS/I	Assistant Chief of staff/Intelligence	FBI	Federal Bureau of Investigation
AIA	Air Intelligence Agency	IC/EXCOM	Intelligence Community Executive Committee
CIA	Central Intelligence Agency		
CMS	Community Management Staff	INSCOM	Intelligence and Security Command
CNO	Chief of Naval Operations	INR	Bureau of Intelligence and Research
CSA	Chief of Staff, US Army	J–2	Joint Staff Intelligence
DARO	Defence Airborne Reconnaissance Office	NIC	National Intelligence Council
DCI	Director Central Intelligence	NIMA	National Imagery and Mapping Agency
DDCI	Deputy Director Central Intelligence	NRO	National Reconnaissance Office
DI	Directorate of Intelligence	NSD	National Security Division
DIA	Defence Intelligence Agency	NSG	Naval Security Group
DNI	Director of Naval Intelligence	OEI	Office of Energy Intelligence
DO	Directorate of Operations	OIS	Office of Intelligence Support
DS&T	Directorate of Science and Technology	USMC	United States Marine Corps

Source: William Oden, "Modernising Intelligence", National Institute for Public Policy, Jan 2002

tomatic of an intelligence community that has been in steady decline, held back by political correctness and an over-reliance on technology. Crucially, this explanation fits the political agenda of both the spies and the Bush administration.

Reined-in and risk-averse
Some trace the decline to the 1970s, when, after a series of scandals, the CIA was reined in by Congress. Many Republicans prefer to start with Bill Clinton, who, they claim, was

unwilling to wage war on terrorism. In 1996, in the wake of the murder of a Guatemalan by a CIA informant, officers were told to contact Langley before "establishing a relationship with an individual who has committed serious crimes or human-rights abuses or other repugnant acts." Nobody has been turned down under these guidelines. But they cannot have encouraged CIA people to make friends with, say, drug-smugglers.

The idea that the Directorate of Operations became risk-averse has been widely

promoted by frustrated ex-case-officers. In "See No Evil" (Crown, 2002), Robert Baer recalls how in Tajikistan in the early 1990s he asked for Dari and Pushtu speakers to interrogate Afghan refugees. He was first told that the CIA no longer collected data on Afghanistan, then offered a four-person sexual-harassment briefing team. Even defenders of the spy system admit it has a job-for-life mentality. John Gannon, a CIA analyst who has just moved to the private sector, says that he has fired more people in the past eight months than during his entire career in the service.

Yet daredevilry has never been more needed. During the cold war, an intelligence system that relied on intercepting Soviet military signals and picking up diplomatic gossip made sense. Now there are no ponderous tank divisions to track; and you are unlikely to meet your opposite number from al-Qaeda at the Brazilian ambassador's cocktail party.

In last July's *Atlantic Monthly*, Reuel Marc Gerecht, who worked for the agency in the Middle East, labelled America's counter-terrorism effort in the Arab world "a myth". An active spy describes coverage of Iran as "embarrassing" (America has not had an embassy there since 1979). A Bush adviser furiously says that "the White House has discovered more about *madrassas* [fundamentalist Islamic schools] in the papers during the past three months than we got from the intelligence system in the previous six years."

The sheer lack of American knowledge about some areas of the world has led to a form of poker game between its allies. For instance, European intelligence services that know the Arab world have been keen to balance information that Israel "spoonfeeds" to America. (All the spies, however, grudgingly admire Israel's masterly exposure of an Iranian-financed attempt to smuggle weapons to the Palestinians, which ensured Iran's insertion in the "axis of evil" speech and Mr Arafat's temporary excommunication by Mr Bush.)

There are "cultural" problems at home, too. America has no equivalent of MI5, Britain's domestic intelligence agency. The FBI is a law-enforcement agency: it looks for people breaking the law and arrests them. Intelligence-gathering is based on watching people, regardless of whether they break the law, and arresting them is often counter-productive.

Needless to say, there is not much love lost between the FBI and the CIA. Indeed, turf-consciousness spreads throughout the many domestic agencies that should play some part in intelligence-collection: witness the lousy sharing of information about the September 11th hijackers between the FBI, the Immigration and Naturalisation Service and local cops. The coordinating Office of Homeland Security has had little impact.

No James Bonds

Many spooks think the most important cultural barrier is a startlingly simple one: Americans do not like spying. There is no local equivalent of James Bond; in fiction, spies are mostly portrayed as right-wing lunatics or bungling fools. Americans are less interested in going overseas than other people are, and they stick out more when they do. Even during the CIA's mythical heyday during the cold war, nearly all its best agents were freedom- or cash-loving traitors who offered their services without prompting. And the agency has never been that good on the Islamic world.

More important, at home Americans value privacy more than most other people. They hate the security cameras that Europeans tolerate. They have opposed attempts to share knowledge about, say, suspicious movements of foreigners. One former CIA chief speculates that you could call September 11th "the failure of the ideology of the open society".

Some of these cultural shortcomings are now being addressed. Rules about recruiting dubious people have been relaxed. Some of the language gaps are being closed. The CIA alone has received more than 60,000 job applications. Many spies think that this will be enough.

That seems wrong in at least two fundamental ways. First, the current obsession with human intelligence downplays the importance of its technological equivalent. Here, though America unquestionably leads the world, a variety of technical problems still need to be fixed.

The NSA, for instance, has far too many old, incompatible computer systems, and finds it difficult to eavesdrop on fibre-optic cables. There is a row about whether the NRO should buy ever bigger, ever more expensive satellites, as the defence industry wants, or whether surveillance could be better achieved by smaller systems, not all of them space-based. At NIMA, there is the challenge of making imagery systems three-dimensional.

General William Odom, a former head of the NSA, says the intelligence community has received as much new technology as big companies like IBM, but has undergone none of the structural reforms of the sort seen in the private sector. The technical agencies are also struggling to deal with the huge amount of "open-source" information now available. At present, the technology often works best as a retrospective tool rather than a forward-looking one. After September 11th, all sorts of details were tracked down in America's digital vaults, but only once people knew the names to look for.

Telling the satellites and phone-taps where to look is also getting ever harder. Mr Gannon points back to 1998. Before the year began, he allocated the CIA's analytic resources to the priorities that had been established with the White House. In fact, more than 50% of the actual crises that year occurred in "lower-priority areas", and many of the biggest ones, such as the global financial crisis, the Kosovo war and India's nuclear test, were unanticipated.

Technology aside, the view that more manpower will make up the intelligence deficit is wrong for another reason. Structural problems often underlie the cultural ones. At the micro level, analysts are moved around too quickly. Mr Gerecht suggests that the best way to improve human intelligence rapidly would be to move spies out of the embassies. Above all, there is the question of who controls what. When the CIA's spy satellites missed India's nuclear test, this was surely because the satellites were run by generals interested in tanks.

The chief spook and his enemies

"Reforming" America's intelligence services is not simply a matter of getting better people and giving them more money and a slightly freer hand. The structure needs modernising from top to bottom.

Like anybody who has been copiously rewarded for doing bad work, America's intelligence services seem strangely caught between paranoia and arrogance. Staff at the CIA's Counter-Terrorist Centre joke that the only way they can spend the hundreds of millions of dollars they now have is to upgrade themselves on trips from business class to first class. Mr Tenet seems to have ridden the storm, and has even collected the odd plaudit for the spies' current work in Afghanistan.

His supporters point out that the former Senate intelligence staffer is more than just a political hack. His five-year reign has brought stability, and he has both the president's ear and political *nous* (he named the CIA's headquarters after Mr Bush's father). Moreover, Mr Tenet, who is said even by his detractors to be adept at covering his back, warned the Bush administration several times during the summer about the possibility of a bin Laden attack. Cynical spies point out that, had he been sacked, Mr Tenet might have contradicted the Bush administration's claim that it has always been more vigilant than its predecessor—something that does not seem to have been true before September 11th.

Recently, a commission chaired by Brent Scowcroft, a former national security adviser, came up with a proposal to put the three main technical agencies (NSA, NRO and NIMA) under Mr Tenet's control. The first reaction of the defence secretary, Donald Rumsfeld, was to squash this. It was not just a matter of turf-protection: military men point out that the vast majority of signals intercepts and imaging will always be for the Pentagon. On the other hand, the current system plainly puts the intelligence services second.

Few in Washington expect radicalism from the new joint congressional committee. Congressman Goss is a former CIA man; so is the staff director of the inquiry, who also used to work for Mr Tenet in his Senate committee days. More generally, Senator Graham talks gloomily about intelligence reform running into an iron triangle of the executive agency, its departmental backer and outside interests.

The idea of a cumbersome bureaucracy limping on simply because nobody can face reforming it is depressingly unAmerican. The grounds for hope begin with some of the people involved. Messrs Graham and Goss are generally respected by their peers. Ask either man how he might redesign the intelligence system, if he had a

free hand, and both come up with radical solutions. Others whisper that Mr Rumsfeld, who is known to be appalled by the chaos, might be willing to support dramatic reform providing there was a comprehensive plan. Even Mr Tenet has a vested interest in reform: at present, he risks a place in history as the captain who did not go down with his sinking ship.

Wholesale reform would be relatively easy to enforce. Most changes could be brought about by an executive order from the president. Mr Tenet also has far more room to be brutal: spies' jobs are theoretically less well protected than those of other bureaucrats.

Out of Langley

What should be done? Given the fact that nothing has really changed for 50 years, the list is long. Two big jobs, however, stick out. The first is that the intelligence community needs a proper chief executive—not another token tsar, but one with real budgetary power over the technical military agencies (and with far more power over who runs them). As a corollary, this new *über*-DCI should be taken out of Langley, and a separate person should run the CIA. One reason

why reform has always failed is that it has usually been seen in the Defence Department as a power-grab by the CIA.

One difficult question is how much of the actual analysis needs to be centred around this new DCI. Some duplication is inevitable—every general wants to have his own intelligence analysis. And the sheer number of agencies may be less of a problem than the fact that most of them act as vertical "stovepipes"—an insane idea for a community that is supposed to be collecting information. Congress should be less interested in how much money is being spent at NIMA than in how much is being spent fighting bioterrorism.

The other priority is to break down the artificial barrier between intelligence-gathering at home and abroad. Any thought of increased surveillance at home will annoy Americans and increase their worries about civil liberties. That is why it will need political bravery from Mr Bush. But September 11th illustrated the shortcomings of a 50-year-old intelligence system. Senator Graham argues that it is basic Darwinism: "If you don't understand changes in your habitat, you will die."

Compete, *or Else*

President Bush wants to remake the bureaucracy
so that government workers routinely vie with
private contractors for their jobs.

By John Maggs

One aspect of every president's legacy is all but over-looked in the history books—his impact on the form and function of the government. Ronald Reagan confronted the Soviet Union, helped revive the economy, and left a huge budget deficit. The debate continues about the nature of his achievements. Yet probably Reagan's greatest legacy to Washington and its leading industry is represented at the intersection of 12th Street and Constitution Avenue. The building still bears the name of the Interstate Commerce Commission, but its cavernous offices are now filled with a hodgepodge of other agencies. It once housed one of the most powerful and sprawling parts of the government, but the ICC doesn't exist anymore. The agency fell to Reagan's sweeping deregulation program, which also cut back government oversight of airlines, petroleum, telecommunications, antitrust health and safety, shipping, and international trade. Reagan didn't close down as many agencies as he had promised to, but his commitment to deregulation changed the Washington landscape more than did the huge new federal building that bears his name.

The early money says that George W. Bush's primary legacy to the federal government will be his creation of the Department of Homeland Security, the largest reorganization of government resources in 50 years. Even though the government's top law enforcement agency, the FBI, was left out, and even though the department's pieces won't become an effective whole for many years, the stitching together of the Homeland Security Department is reshaping Washington—again.

But in a decade or two, the verdict on Bush's legacy to government might well be a little different. Not because the creation of Homeland Security will seem less important, but because another Bush initiative promises to remake the government in even more fundamental ways. The president's radical aim is to eventually make upwards of 850,000 federal workers—nearly half of the civil-ian workforce now protected by bureaucratic tradition and civil service rules—compete against private contractors for their jobs every three to five years. So far, Bush has demanded that 425,000 face competition in the next few years, but he's also said that number won't be a ceiling for his administration. The administration seeks both to reduce the federal workforce by hundreds of thousands of workers and to force half of the government to justify why it should even be part of the government.

Past administrations' attempts to control the growth of government have been piecemeal—defunding programs, or consolidating or eliminating agencies. Almost all have foundered on Capitol Hill, where committee chairmen derive power from the size of the bureaucracies they oversee. Significantly, Bush can put his plan into place through policy changes, without a moment of debate in Congress.

Lawmakers are obviously concerned—with most, but not all, of the dissent coming from the Democratic side of the aisle. A group of House Democrats has attached a rider to an appropriations bill to stop the competitive bidding process at the Interior Department, presenting Bush with a potential veto dilemma. In the Senate, the confirmation of Clay Johnson as deputy director for management at the Office of Management and Budget was held up for five months over senators' objections to the administration's use of numerical goals to increase the number of employees competing for their jobs.

Federal employee unions are also fighting the changes. Last month, the union representing Treasury Department employees filed a lawsuit seeking to invalidate recent regulatory changes that the union says will be used to vastly increase the number of federal jobs slated for competition. Colleen Kelley, president of the National Treasury Employees Union, said the Bush administration wants to whittle down the number of workers whose jobs are off-limits to competition and privatization. In particular, she said, the White House has targeted the perennially unpopular Internal Revenue Service.

Some critics say the idea of competition is simply a ruse, arguing that the administration fully intends to shift as many of those 850,000 jobs as possible to the private sector. Kelley charges that the White House will use a regulatory "streamlining" process to deprive employees of due process in evaluating whether their jobs should be opened up to competition.

BACK TO BUSINESS SCHOOL

To learn more about the Bush initiative, go to a Web site created by the White House, *www.results.gov*. It's the home page for something called the President's Management Agenda, a five-part plan for improving management in government. The agenda was the baby of Mitchell E. Daniels Jr., the recently departed director of OMB.

Every president proposes some kind of plan (or sometimes several plans) to improve the day-to-day running of the executive branch, but it is fair to say that Bush's agenda is more ambitious than most. The plan unmistakably bears the imprint of the first president to hold an M.B.A. The management agenda contains a lot of meat, but it is also replete with business school jargon. Government employees are "human capital," and just about everyone gets to be a "strategic partner." There is "knowledge management," which is somehow distinct from "information management," and then there is something called "results-oriented performance management."

The language is a giveaway that the Bush team is trying to transplant into government successful ideas from the business world, an effort that almost every administration makes—and then abandons when the bureaucracy fights back. But all signs show that this administration is more committed to these reforms than others have been, and that its goals are more ambitious. Under one of the management agenda initiatives, "Budget and Performance Integration," the administration has proposed to strip funding from agencies if they don't perform a particular service well. The "Improving Financial Performance" initiative calls for more frequent and more-thorough financial audits, and requires agencies to improve their performance from audit to audit.

Some parts of the management agenda are a little fluffy—"human capital transformation" seems to involve techniques such as mentoring and performance bonuses that have been tried before. But the overall approach is to regularly and unflinchingly grade performance on the five initiatives, and then broadcast those results on a multicolored "scorecard" that reports whether a department or agency is succeeding (green), losing ground (yellow), or failing (red). To see how the various parts of the executive branch are doing as of June 30, check the Web site. The White House isn't pulling punches—most are getting failing grades in most areas.

The management agenda is not really revolutionary, but one of the five initiatives—"Competitive Sourcing"—potentially is. It takes another tried-and-true idea from the business world: designating some in-house work for "contracting out" or "outsourcing," and inviting outside companies to compete for it. Outsourcing has been one of the great revolutions in business over the last few decades. It has enabled corporations to slim down workforces that had swelled to cover all of the tasks a company needed done, and has led to huge gains in productivity. Think of IBM 25 years ago, with employees making every piece of every computer, from the microprocessor to the plastic housing. Now think of Dell Computer, which doesn't make a single component of its products, but is the leading supplier of computers in the country.

Competitive sourcing is a refinement of outsourcing because it lets government employees and managers compete to keep the work that is being offered to the private sector. As something of a gimmick, OMB demonstrated how this would work at the one time of year when Washington is paying a lot of attention to the budget office—in February, when OMB released the administration's proposed budget. Months before, OMB had quietly organized a competition for printing the multivolume budget, and helped workers at the Government Printing Office put together their own bid. The GPO won, and the result was a 23 percent savings in printing costs over the year before, which the GPO achieved by using fewer workers, working fewer hours, to print the budget—in other words, figuring out how to get the work done more productively.

OMB officials say that competition lowers the cost of government services by more than 30 percent when a private contractor wins the bid and by more than 20 percent when government workers win. But these numbers are based on a single study by the Center for Naval Analyses that looked at 16 of the 550 competitions held by the Pentagon since 1955. By any standard, this seems an inadequate basis for assuming that government can achieve similar levels of savings across the board.

Even tougher to assess is whether moving many functions of government into the private sector comes with other, less-quantifiable costs. Charles Goodsell, author of *The Case for Bureaucracy*, said the Bush initiative seems inspired by a conviction that most government bureaucrats are inefficient, and inferior to private-sector workers. The problem with contracting out, he said, is that once employees lose a competition, they are reassigned to other jobs, and their expertise is lost to the government forever.

REVIVING AN OLD IDEA

So is this idea of using competitive sourcing in the federal government really so new and revolutionary? Not exactly. As it happens, it is based on a policy that was adopted in 1955 by what was then the Bureau of the Budget. Before President Eisenhower started worrying about military contractors' influence on the government, he promulgated a simple principle intended to help control the growth of government: If a service is commercially available, the government should buy it instead of hiring someone to perform it and thus competing with the private sector. Circular A-76, as it was called, has been broadened several times over the years and assumed its current form in 1983.

But bureaucrats, aided by their patrons on Capitol Hill, by government employee unions, and even sometimes by top political appointees, prevented most government departments and agencies from ever taking A-76 seriously. A-76 competitions took place almost exclusively at the Pentagon, where the self-contained nature of the armed services and of military-base life had contributed to a pattern in which Defense Department personnel performed many tasks for which they were obviously ill-suited. Since 2000, the Pentagon has used A-76 to bid out services provided by 72,000 federal workers.

The Clinton administration made some late efforts to reinvigorate the competitive process, but ardent opposition by federal employee unions and Democrats in Congress stalled the attempts. In 1998, the Republican-controlled Congress passed the Federal Activities Inventory Reform Act, which for the first time called for every federal agency to count its jobs that are "commercial" in nature, distinguishing them from jobs deemed "inherently governmental." The legislation could have been a takeoff point for competitive sourcing, but after Clinton signed it into law, his administration did nothing with the information that was collected. Morley Winograd, who directed Clinton's "Reinventing Government" initiative, said that the data on savings from competitive sourcing was "flawed" and that the law, and Circular A-76 before it, did a poor job of distinguishing between the kind of work that could be outsourced and the kind that shouldn't be.

As a presidential candidate, Bush embraced the idea of using the FAIR Act to effect a government-wide move toward competition. Once elected, he settled on a goal of holding competitions for half of the 850,000 federal jobs now deemed commercial in nature, out of a full-time civilian workforce of 1.8 million. Then he set a shorter-term goal of designating a government-wide average of 15 percent of "commercial" jobs for competition by the end of 2003. That explicit goal led to the hold on Clay Johnson's nomination. Lawmakers assumed that the administration would require every executive branch body to meet the 15 percent goal, but OMB officials insist that that will not be the case.

In a related move, earlier this year the administration revamped A-76. At the urging of government employee unions, it closed some loopholes that had been used to privatize jobs without competitions, but it also narrowed the definition of "inherently governmental" jobs that can be protected from competition. The effect won't be clear till next year, but Kelley of the Treasury employees' union says the new rules could greatly increase the number of "commercially available" jobs in the federal workforce.

The administration insists that the new rules are not intended to force privatization and instead are designed to strengthen government by making it more useful. "We don't care who wins the competition," said Angela Styles, administrator of the Office of Federal Procurement Policy at OMB. "What matters is that everyone competes and that the taxpayers get the service performed in the most efficient way." Styles pointed out that at the Pentagon, government workers have won 60 percent of the competitions.

Styles and other OMB officials meet with representatives of all the departments and agencies to discuss their progress in achieving the competitive-sourcing goals. In another bow to a business practice in vogue, department officials sign a contract embracing agreed-upon goals for increasing employee competition.

SINGULARLY FOCUSED

Styles has been a patient overseer. She conceded that Competitive Sourcing will fall far short of the government-wide goal of 15 percent in 2003, and even admitted that only a handful of departments or agencies would meet that mark. She said she'd like to get to 15 percent by next summer, but her tone indicated that she isn't betting her house on it.

But the administration might just be taking a strategic pause in its march to inject competition into government. Talk to the officials responsible for implementing the sourcing initiative, and you get a portrait of OMB as singularly focused on getting to that 50 percent goal. At the Education Department, for example, about 1,000 out of its 5,000 jobs have been designated as commercial in nature. Competitions for 25 percent of those 1,000 jobs will be completed by September 1, according to Bill Leidinger, assistant secretary for management. That's better than the 20 percent goal that Education pledged to reach last year, and way ahead of the government-wide standard of 15 percent—but that hasn't satisfied Styles. For its achievement in competitive sourcing, Education earned an upgrade from red to yellow on its management scorecard. What will it take to get to green? "I think we're not going to get green until we're at 50 percent," said Leidinger.

Leidinger noted that the competitions involved Education Department employees from human resources and payment processing, two categories of government jobs that are often designated for competition. That is also the case at the Energy Department, where 1,180 jobs are slated for competitions, about 18 percent of its commercial inventory of 6,600, according to Dennis O'Brien, director of the office of competitive sourcing. Most departments and agencies are organizing competitions bureau by bureau, but Energy is planning to put jobs up for department-wide competition, something that has

OMB officials pretty interested. "At DOD, it would be like holding a competition across all the different services," said Jack Kalavritinos, OMB's associate administrator for competitive sourcing.

Despite union leaders' fears, department and agency officials appear to be helping employees compete effectively for their jobs. In fact, the time and resources devoted to these efforts make one wonder if any real savings will result. In most cases, outside consultants are helping employees prepare their bids, and employees are putting aside their regular work to participate in the competitions. Leidinger said the Education Department has spent about $1.5 million on procurement consultants from Booz Allen Hamilton. Employees worked full-time on their bids for about a month, he said, and their normal responsibilities were farmed out to others. Leidinger acknowledged that operations might have suffered a little, but said, "We're doing something really groundbreaking here, and we're going to be fair to our employees and do it the best that we can."

At least one prominent critic of the administration wonders whether the competitive-sourcing initiative will really reduce the size of government, even if it achieves all its aims. Paul Light of the Brookings Institution has long argued that contracting out for services merely hides the true size of government. One example is the Agency for International Development, where a Republican attack on the agency in the late 1990s coincided with a surge in demand for new specialists to help in the transition to democracy in Eastern Europe. Faced with a freeze on new hires, but with ample money to assist the former Eastern Bloc, USAID hired hundreds of outside contractors. Many departments and agencies are doing the same, to avoid attention-getting increases in their headcounts of full-time employees. Light says that competition can lower costs for some services, but that merely shifting jobs from government employees to private contractors does nothing to limit the size or reach of government.

And what if competitive sourcing creates a new class of special interests that will eventually subvert any efficiencies gained from competition? OMB officials point out that most competitive-sourcing contractors are won by small and medium-sized businesses, but it is not hard to imagine a giant accounting firm (like, say, Booz Allen) sewing up contracts for most of those financial jobs heading for competition.

Styles and the other competitive-sourcing officials have to walk a fine line between competing interests, showing a benign and reassuring face to federal employees and their supporters while maintaining the drive and focus to push forward such a fundamental change in government. Styles is well aware that slipping timetables are one of the first signs of a loss of political will for reform, but she says she is sustained by the commitment to reform she perceives at the top.

"Let me tell you, to the very highest levels, this administration is committed to this idea. And I know personally that no one is more committed than the president."

UNIT 3

Process of American Politics

Unit Selections

Key Points to Consider

- How "democratic" is the American political system compared with others?

- How do the political views and behavior of young Americans compare and contrast with those of their parents?

- Do you think that our current procedures for choosing the president are good ones? In light of the Florida controversy in the 2000 presidential election, do you think that electoral reforms are necessary? Explain your answer.

 **Links: www.dushkin.com/online/**
These sites are annotated in the World Wide Web pages.

The Henry L. Stimson Center
http://www.stimson.org

Influence at Work
http://www.influenceatwork.com

LSU Department of Political Science Resources
http://www.artsci.lsu.edu/poli/

NationalJournal.com
http://nationaljournal.com

Poynter Online
http://www.poynter.org

RAND
http://www.rand.org

According to many political scientists, what distinguishes more democratic political systems from less democratic ones is the degree of control that citizens exercise over government. This unit focuses on the institutions, groups, and processes that are supposed to serve as links between Americans and their government.

Political parties, elections, pressure groups, and media are all thought to play important roles in communications between people and government in the American political system. Changes that are occurring today in some of these areas may affect American politics for decades to come, and these changes are the focus of many of the readings in this unit.

The first three sections focus on politicians, parties, interest groups, money, and elections. Violence and controversy relating to the 1968 Democratic nominating convention led to a series of changes in the procedures that both parties use to select their presidential candidates. And one of the legacies of the Watergate scandal of the early 1970s was the passage of laws to regulate campaign financing, which was followed by extensive debate about the impact of those reforms.

In the 1980s, candidates increasingly used focus groups, political consultants, and public opinion polling to shape expensive advertising campaigns, and many observers thought that negative television advertisements played a particularly prominent role in the 1988 presidential campaign. In 1992 more changes in campaign tactics and techniques appeared, including numerous appearances by presidential candidates on television talk shows and a half dozen or so 30-minute paid "infomercials" by third-party candidate Ross Perot. In the 1994 congressional elections, Republicans were generally successful in "nationalizing" the

competition for 435 House and 30-odd Senate seats, apparently belying the adage that "all politics is local" and winning control of both houses of Congress for the first time since 1954. In 1996, apparently unprecedented amounts of "soft" money from questionable sources fueled President Clinton's reelection campaign, and campaign finance practices became the target of more and more criticism. The 2000 presidential election, of course, will long be remembered for the unprecedented 5-week controversy over which candidate had won Florida and had, in turn, secured an Electoral College majority. In early 2002, Congress passed a major campaign finance reform law long championed by Senators John McCain and Russ Feingold. Scheduled to take effect after the congressional elections in November 2002, the new law's impact will become clearer during the course of the 2004 elections for the presidency and Congress. All these events and more underlie the selections in this unit.

This unit also treats the roles of interest groups in the American political process and their impact on what government can and cannot do. While "gridlock" is a term usually applied to inaction resulting from "divided government," in which neither major party controls the presidency and both houses of Congress, it seems that "gridlock"—and perhaps favoritism in policy-making—also results from the interaction of interest groups and various government policymakers. The weakness of parties in the United States, compared to parties in other Western democracies, is almost certainly responsible for the unusually strong place of interest groups in the American political system. In turn, one can wonder whether a possible new era of stronger, more disciplined parties in government will eventually contribute to the weakening of interest groups.

The fourth section addresses news and other media, which probably play a more important role in the American political system than their counterparts do in any other political system. Television news broadcasts and newspapers are not merely passive transmitters of information. They inevitably shape—or distort—what they report to their audiences. They also greatly affect the behavior of people and organizations in politics. As already noted, less traditional media forums have played bigger roles in recent years, especially during the 1992 and 1996 presidential campaigns. Radio and television talk shows and 30-minute "infomercials" have entered the political landscape with considerable effect. Selections in the fourth section provide coverage of how media shape or distort both political communication and the behavior of political actors.

The Chieftains and the Church

An intellectual audit of the Democrats and the Republicans

BY TED HALSTEAD

This year marks the 150th anniversary of the rivalry between the Democratic and Republican Parties. Ever since 1854, when the implosion of the Whigs paved the way for the birth of the Republican Party (twenty-six years after the emergence of the Democrats), this rivalry has dominated and even defined American politics. Although the reign of these two parties has endured for well over half the life of our republic, it would be a mistake to assume that either party has remained consistent—or even recognizable.

Quick—which party stands for small government, states' rights, and laissez-faire economics? Which favors an activist federal government, public infrastructure projects, and expanded civil rights? Today the answers would be Republican and Democratic, respectively. Yet each party was founded on precisely the principles now associated with the other. And consider that the South, originally a stronghold of the Democrats, is now the anchor of the Republicans. But the most dramatic inversion in partisan identity is this: the Republicans in recent years have emerged as revolutionaries, while the Democrats have relegated themselves to defending tradition and the status quo.

The 150th anniversary of their rivalry provides an occasion for an intellectual audit of these two ever changing parties.

THE PARTY OF THE CHURCH

Let's begin with the Republicans, who under President George W. Bush have become the party of big ideas. There is no denying the range and boldness of their initiatives, from privatizing Social Security to institutionalizing a doctrine of preventive warfare; from eliminating taxes on capital gains and dividends to pulling out of numerous international treaties; from encouraging school choice to remaking the Middle East. This boldness is in itself an anomaly for a party that in past decades has tended to revere inherited norms and institutions, but it is just one of the signs that this is not the Republican Party of George W.'s father. Indeed, its identity seems to have no clear lineage.

The modern Republican tradition is usually thought to have originated with the firebrand rhetoric of Barry Goldwater, which ultimately paved the way for the two-term presidency of Ronald Reagan. The Reagan revolution was built on three unifying principles: anti-communism, social conservatism, and limited government. The sudden end of the Cold War left the Republicans with only two of these principles around which to organize. But most Americans let it be known that they were not particularly interested in fighting domestic culture wars, much less in turning back the clock on newfound personal freedoms. The Republican

Party's anti-government agenda, meanwhile, culminated in the Gingrich revolution of 1994, which sought to downsize all sorts of federal programs. To Newt Gingrich's surprise, the majority of Americans didn't really want a dramatic cutback in government programs and perceived his agenda as extremist.

George W. Bush is the first Republican President to recognize that the constituency for the Goldwater-Reagan-Gingrich anti-government crusade is dwindling—inspiring him to try to reposition his party. Although Bush calls his new and improved governing philosophy "compassionate conservatism," a more accurate description might be "big-spending conservatism."

Unlike Reagan, who shrank nondefense spending considerably and vetoed a number of spending bills in his first three years, Bush has so far increased total federal spending by a dizzying 20.4 percent and has yet to veto a single spending bill. The contrast is all the more dramatic when Bush is compared with Bill Clinton, who declared the end of big government, who in his first three years increased total government spending by only 3.5 percent, and who actually reduced discretionary spending by 8.8 percent. Clinton's Republican successor is quietly reversing course with a vengeance, leading the libertarian Cato Institute to accuse Bush of "governing like a Frenchman."

The President's reason for engineering this reversal, apparently, is to overcome the budgetary obstacles to parts of his agenda. For example, he seeks to privatize public services and enhance individual choice—school choice, retirement choice (through private Social Security accounts), and medical choice (through private health insurance instead of government-run programs). But moving from one-size-fits-all government programs to more-flexible privatized ones may require more public outlay, not less, than simply preserving the status quo. As the price for bringing competition into Medicare, for instance, Bush enacted a prescription-drug benefit that represents the largest expansion in entitlements since Lyndon Johnson's Great Society. And moving to private Social Security accounts would entail funding two entirely separate systems during the transition period.

Fighting the war on terrorism, too, is expensive. But rather than adjusting his agenda accordingly, Bush has pushed through three huge tax cuts in as many years. In the process he has fatally undermined the coherence of his overall program. Fusing vast new spending with deep tax cuts, Bush is locking into place long-term structural deficits whose costs to both our nation and the Republican Party would be difficult to overstate.

To understand why the Republican majority in Congress is playing along with the President, it helps to think of today's Republican Party as a theocracy; call it the Party of the Church. Under Bush the party is guided by a core ideology that it pursues with a near religious fervor, regardless of countervailing facts, changing circumstances, or even opposition among the conservative ranks. The President and his inner circle not only set the canon but demand—and usually get—strict compliance from Republican legislators in both houses of Congress. The two central tenets of Bush's orthodoxy are tax cuts and regime change in Iraq. He has staked the success of his presidency on them.

In the Party of the Church the theologians' role is played by hundreds of conservative scholars in think tanks, at publications, and on radio talk shows. That the academy is missing from this list is not

an accident: conservative scholars could not find comfortable perches within university settings. But being banished from the academy served the Republican theologians remarkably well, because it enabled them to cultivate a style of argument and writing far better suited to reaching—and converting—both the public and politicians. The infrastructure of conservative thought is as well financed as it is complex; it includes seminaries in which to train conservative young scholars (the Heritage Foundation even has special dormitories for its interns), and what might be thought of as separate "orders," each upholding a slightly different school of thought—from the libertarians to the social conservatives to the neoconservatives. This sprawling idea machine produces not only policy innovations but also the language ("welfare queens," "the death tax") with which to sell the party's agenda.

Not surprisingly, the Party of the Church is highly moralistic. President Bush tends to frame issues in terms of ethical absolutes: good and evil, right and wrong. Moralism may or may not make for good politics, but it rarely makes for good policy, because it substitutes wishful and parochial thinking for careful analysis. Its ascendancy reflects a broader shift in the Republican Party—a shift away from an identity that was secular, pragmatic, and northeastern toward one that, like the President himself, is more evangelical and southern. Nowhere is this more evident than in foreign policy, where Bush—reviving what the historian Walter Russell Mead calls the Jacksonian tradition—is turning his back on both the realpolitik of Richard Nixon and the conservative internationalism of Reagan and his own father, making preemption rather than containment the central organizing principle and favoring unilateral action over multilateral diplomacy. In doing so Bush has discarded hundreds of years of international law and decades of American tradition. The most immediate cost is that the United States has alienated much of the world in the name of making it safe.

"SUPPLY-SIDE KEYNESIANISM"

When it comes to economic orthodoxy, the Party of the Church is no more con-

sistent with traditional Republican principles. Although the Republicans claim to be devoted to free markets, most of the big economic interests identified with the party are surprisingly dependent on federal subsidies, protectionism, or both. The most obvious examples are southern growers of cotton, sugar, oranges, and peanuts, and midwestern producers of grain. The Administration is so committed to shielding these interests from global competition that it elected to let the Cancún round of trade negotiations collapse—dealing a significant blow to the prospects for expanded free trade—rather than pressure Congress to reduce U.S. agricultural subsidies. In similar fashion, the Bush Administration supports lavish federal subsidies for a wide range of extractive industries (including oil, gas, and coal) and for cattle ranching.

No assessment of the modern Republican Party would be complete without a discussion of the elaborate mythology of supply-side economics, whose logic has been strained to the breaking point under Bush's watch. The basic supply-side argument is that tax cuts increase the incentive to work, save, and invest, which boosts economic growth. During the Reagan years such logic was used to argue that slashing tax rates would actually increase tax revenues, by producing additional growth—but this has long since been dismissed by mainstream economists and shown false by the record of history. The party also uses supply-side economics to justify tax cuts that are disproportionately skewed in favor of the well-to-do, on the grounds that they are the most likely to save and invest. This argument has always been suspect, and it is even less credible in the aftermath of the technology bubble; the economic woes of the past few years have been due not to lack of investment but, rather, to an excess of capacity.

By sticking with the old supply-side formula—cut taxes as often as possible, especially for the wealthy—Bush has delivered a particularly costly and inefficient stimulus package to help the nation out of its economic downturn. And the Administration seems to recognize as much, given that it has hedged its bets by marrying large supply-side tax cuts with equally large demand-side spending increases, yielding an odd hybrid that might be called "supply-side Keynesianism." This contradictory policy suggests that not even Republicans still believe in the magic of their standard fix. Yet they are not about to abandon the myth. It is far too sacrosanct and convenient an article of faith in the Republican canon.

A major risk in combining moralism and policy, evidently, is that dogma often trumps intellectual honesty. This is particularly clear in the case of official claims that the Administration's overall economic agenda is aimed at helping middle-class families. A more candid articulation of its domestic-policy vision appeared in a June 2003 *Washington Post* op-ed article by Grover Norquist, one of the most influential of conservative strategists. "The new Republican policy is an annual tax cut," Norquist wrote; he predicted that Bush would proceed step by step to abolish estate and capital-gains taxes altogether, to exempt all savings from taxation, and to move the nation to a flat tax on wages only. Implicit in this vision is not only a grand contradiction—cutting taxes while raising spending is unsustainable—but also a significant shift in the burden of taxation from the wealthy to the working class and the poor. Apparently the contemporary Republican Party does remain faithful to at least one old conservative belief, which Clinton Rossiter, in his book *Conservatism in America*, described nearly fifty years ago as "the inevitability and necessity of social classes."

THE PARTY OF THE CHIEFTAINS

For its part, the Democratic Party suffers from a different sort of incoherence: plagued by constant squabbling among the interest groups that make up its base, it cannot agree on a clear message or purpose. The sheer breadth of the Democratic coalition is remarkable: it includes organized labor, teachers' and other public employees' unions, environmentalists, racial minorities (especially African-Americans), Hollywood, trial lawyers, the gray lobby, the gay lobby, civil libertarians, pro-choice activists, and a good bit of Wall Street. Although this breadth might seem to be an asset for

the Democrats, all these groups are veto-wielding factions when it comes to their respective chunks of the policy turf. This can be downright paralyzing.

If the Republicans are now the Party of the Church, then the Democrats are the Party of the Chieftains. They treat an election almost like a parade: groups that otherwise have little in common come together every year or two, only to return to their niches afterward. The multiplicity of purpose is all the more evident when the party is out of office. During his eight-year presidency Clinton relied on his political skill and charisma—and the benefits of a growing economy—to keep most Democratic factions happy and essentially reading from the same playbook.

When Bush took office, however, the deep tensions among the Democrats resurfaced. For instance, take the relationship between Wall Street and Main Street. Under the New Deal, when U.S. industry was little challenged by competition from abroad, workers and owners of capital managed to reach common ground on a number of issues, from workers' rights to basic benefits. But the subsequent globalization of manufacturing and services led to the collapse of this alliance. Thus whereas Wall Street and some high-tech firms favor financial liberalization, copyright protection, balanced budgets, and a strong dollar (to make imported goods less expensive), working-class Americans want curbs on job flight, tougher international labor standards, strengthened safety nets, and a weaker dollar (to boost exports of the goods they manufacture). The fiercer the global competition, the fiercer the tension between these traditional Democratic camps. The party is just as torn on social issues: Hollywood, members of minorities, and civil libertarians favor identity politics, social liberalism, and political correctness, whereas this agenda tends to offend the sensibilities of working-class white men.

In the run-up to this year's primaries, the tensions among the Democratic Chieftains have culminated in an all-out struggle for their party's soul, with one camp claiming to represent the "Democratic wing" and another claiming to represent the "electable wing." Although

the feuding is over style as well as substance, at least three issues clearly divide left and center: the left is resolutely against the war in Iraq, whereas the center defends it (though averring that it should have been conducted in a more multilateral fashion); the left wants to repeal all Bush's tax cuts, whereas the center favors repealing only some; and the left is wary of unregulated free trade, whereas the center embraces free trade and globalization. In many ways this is a battle over the Clinton legacy. Clintonian centrists fear that the party's new image on welfare, crime, free trade, foreign policy, and fiscal policy—which they worked so hard to establish—will be undermined by a nominee from the party's left.

Fiscal responsibility is another major source of tension within the Democratic Party. Ever since Clinton salvaged the party's credibility in this area, Democrats have tried to build on that new reputation. But those efforts produced two serious problems for the party, one short-term and one longer-term. Over the past three years, while the economy was weak, it may have been a mistake for the Democrats to hew to a policy of fiscal rectitude—especially when it prevented them from thinking creatively about a temporary stimulus package. Maintaining fiscal discipline over the longer term, however, is truly important. Yet it is unclear whether the Democrats will be able to do so given all the programs the various Chieftains are demanding. The race for the Democratic presidential nomination has thrown this conflict into sharp relief. All the contenders cite fiscal prudence as grounds for repealing some or all of Bush's tax cuts—but all then propose to spend the money thus recouped on everything from expanding health insurance to improving schools. From a budgetary perspective there is no difference between decreasing public revenue through tax cuts and increasing public spending through new programs. The Democrats could argue that theirs is a more compassionate form of fiscal irresponsibility (it's better to have health insurance for children than tax cuts for the rich), but they can't argue that they're being any more fiscally responsible than George Bush.

Regardless of who emerges as the Democratic nominee or which camp he hails from, the bulk of his agenda may be disturbingly predictable and backward-looking. Given the power of the Chieftains, it is almost a certainty that the Democratic candidate in 2004 will be against school choice (to appease teachers' unions) and Social Security reform (the gray lobby), and in favor of affirmative action (minorities) and employer-based health care (organized labor). In these and other ways he will be a defender of the status quo. As Al Sharpton recently put it, approvingly, the Democrats are now the true conservatives.

TRAPPED IN THE PAST

In its legitimate desire to preserve the achievements of the New Deal and the Great Society, the Democratic Party has become trapped in the past, routinely defending antiquated industrial-era programs even when these no longer serve their original ends. George Santayana once defined fanaticism as redoubling your efforts when you have forgotten your aim. Democrats are no fanatics, but they are increasingly guilty of confusing ends and means. Consider employer-based health insurance. The link between health insurance and employment was an accident of history, devised in a bygone era when spending one's working lifetime with a single company was the norm. Now that most Americans change employers every couple of years, does it make sense to rely on a system that forces one to change insurers—or, worse, risk losing coverage—every time? And when it comes to protecting Social Security, the Democrats are waging a battle against immutable demographic forces: a program that originated when working-age Americans far outnumbered retirees cannot remain essentially unchanged in a rapidly aging society.

Underlying this abdication of new thinking is a still more troubling liability: the Party of the Chieftains does not trust the American people to make responsible choices for themselves. Although the Democrats are known as the "pro-choice" party, the kinds of choice they are most eager to defend are in the private realm—reproduction and lifestyle. When it comes to the public sphere

(where your child goes to school, or how to invest your Social Security contributions), the Democrats tend to oppose expanding individual choice, largely because some of the leading Chieftains fear that it would weaken their own influence. The Chieftains' reluctance also derives in part from a fear that public programs with more options would undermine equity; but it's possible to devise creative new programs to enhance flexibility and fairness at the same time. Regardless of their reasons, in resisting the expansion of individual choice, a sine qua non of any successful information-age politics, the Democrats have positioned themselves on the wrong side of history.

This inability to advance creative policy solutions hints at yet another problem for the Democrats: the Party of the Chieftains is so busy playing defense that it has forgotten how to play offense. When the Republicans were in the minority during the early Clinton years, they introduced one bold proposal after another—never expecting that these would pass in the short run, but hoping to galvanize the party and set precedents for the future. To a considerable degree this worked. In contrast, the Democrats have spent the past three years turning timidity into an art form, allowing President Bush to set the terms of the debate and confining themselves to criticizing his agenda rather than venturing one of their own. This is the case even in the foreign-policy arena: other than vague calls for multilateralism and diplomacy, it's unclear how a Democratic grand strategy would differ from the President's.

In short, the Democrats have failed utterly to replenish the intellectual capital on which any party's success ultimately hinges. Whereas the Republicans can turn to large, multi-issue think tanks for guidance and inspiration, the Democrats have mainly single-issue groups—environmentalists, civil-rights activists, women's-rights activists—with neither the capacity nor the incentive to forge a greater whole. The flimsiness and Balkanization of the Democratic intellectual infrastructure owes much to the proclivities of progressive philanthropies, which are far more likely to invest in grassroots demonstration programs than in the war of ideas, and which tend to

award grants that are strictly limited to particular subject areas, thereby discouraging cross-pollination. Lacking other options, most liberal scholars therefore gravitate to the academy—which actually inhibits them from shaping the public debate. As academic disciplines become ever more specialized, professors are encouraged to publish in esoteric journals—whose only audience is other professors—rather than in the popular press. Whereas conservative scholars have influence far out of proportion to their numbers, liberal scholars have numbers far out of proportion to their influence.

Not only is the Party of the Chieftains at a loss for new ideas, but it lacks a language for defending its core values. In part this is because the Chieftains like to describe their respective constituencies as victims in order to secure concessions from a party that tends to root for the underdog. Republicans, in contrast, are likely to address citizens as if they were all just around the corner from becoming millionaires. This creates a perception that the Republicans are the party of winners and the Democrats the party of losers.

During the Great Depression, when it was painfully obvious that citizens were vulnerable to forces beyond their control, it was easier for a Democratic leader such as FDR to craft a message of collective well-being—that all Americans would be better off if each American were given a helping hand by the government. Nowadays American culture increasingly emphasizes the opposite message: that individuals are to blame for their own problems. Yet the profound dislocations caused by globalization and technological change make the need for an overarching vision of a better society just as urgent as it was in FDR's time.

"The success of a party," Woodrow Wilson claimed, "means little except when the nation is using that party for a large and definite purpose." By this standard both the Party of the Church and the Party of the Chieftains are failures. The Republicans are handicapped by an ideology holding that it is somehow possible to pursue big-spending conservatism at home and an interventionist military program abroad while cutting taxes repeatedly. The Democrats, meanwhile, are paralyzed by the micro-agendas of numerous feuding factions. Both parties wear straitjackets of their own design.

The American people deserve better— and they know it, to judge by the legions of self-described "independents." Fortunately, our major parties are mere vessels; the principles, agendas, and coalitions they contain can vary dramatically from decade to decade. It is just a matter of time, history suggests, until both parties are reinvented. Let us hope they will improve.

Ted Halstead is the founding president and CEO of the New America Foundation.

America as a One-Party State

Today's hard right seeks total dominion. It's packing the courts and rigging the rules. The target is not the Democrats but democracy itself.

By Robert Kuttner

AMERICA HAS HAD PERIODS OF SINGLE-PARTY DOMINANCE before. It happened under FDR's New Deal, in the Republican 1920s and in the early 19th-century "Era of Good Feeling." But if President Bush is re-elected, we will be close to a tipping point of fundamental change in the political system itself. The United States could become a nation in which the dominant party rules for a prolonged period, marginalizes a token opposition and is extremely difficult to dislodge because democracy itself is rigged. This would be unprecedented in U.S. history.

In past single-party eras, the majority party earned its preeminence with broad popular support. Today the electorate remains closely divided, and actually prefers more Democratic policy positions than Republican ones. Yet the drift toward an engineered one-party Republican state has aroused little press scrutiny or widespread popular protest.

We are at risk of becoming an autocracy in three key respects. First, Republican parliamentary gimmickry has emasculated legislative opposition in the House of Representatives (the Senate has other problems). House Majority Leader Tom DeLay of Texas has both intimidated moderate Republicans and reduced the minority party to window dressing, rather like the token opposition parties in Mexico during the six-decade dominance of the PRI.

Second, electoral rules have been rigged to make it increasingly difficult for the incumbent party to be ejected by the voters, absent a Depression-scale disaster, Watergate-class scandal or Teddy Roosevelt-style ruling party split. After two decades of bipartisan collusion in the creation of safe House seats, there are now perhaps just 25 truly contestable House seats in any given election year (and that's before the recent Republican super gerrymandering). What once was a slender and precarious majority—229 Republicans to 205 Democrats (including Bernie Sanders of Vermont, an independent who votes with Democrats)—now looks like a Republican lock. In the Senate, the dynamics are different but equally daunting for Democrats. As the Florida debacle of 2000 showed, the Republicans are also able to hold down the number of opposition votes, with complicity from Republican courts. Reform legislation, the 2002 Help America Vote Act (HAVA), may actually facilitate Republican intimidation of minority voters and reduce Democratic turnout. And the latest money-and-politics regime, nominally a reform, may give the right more of a financial advantage than ever.

Third, the federal courts, which have slowed some executive-branch efforts to destroy liberties, will be a complete rubber stamp if the right wins one more presidential election.

Taken together, these several forces could well enable the Republicans to become the permanent party of autocratic government for at least a generation. Am I exaggerating? Take a close look at the particulars.

I. Legislative Dictatorship

Political scientists used to describe America's Congress as a de facto four-party system. There were national Democrats, mostly liberals; "Dixiecrats," who often voted with Republicans (*Congressional Quarterly* called this the conservative coalition and tabulated its frequent wins); conservative Republicans; and moderate-to-liberal "gypsy moth" Republicans, who selectively voted with Democrats.

Ad hoc coalitions shifted with issues. Back-benchers and committee chairs alike often defied both the leadership and the party caucus. Party loyalty was guaranteed only in the biennial election of the speaker, to give the dominant party formal majority status and perquisites. Only at rare moments, such as the New Deal's first six years and Lyndon Johnson's storied 89th Congress of 1965–67 (295 Democrats, 140 Republicans), were majorities so large that one party had effective parliamentary discipline. Infrequently, there were other moments of centralized leadership and relative party unity, among them the 100th Congress (1987–89) under Democratic Speaker Jim Wright and the tenures of two autocratic Republican speakers, Thomas Reed and Joe Cannon, back in the Gilded Age. But the usual complaint, dating from political scientist Woodrow Wilson's 1885 text on Congress, was that the congressional party system was an unaccountable stew of freelancers. A famous 1950 report by the American Political Science Association argued that more responsible parties would make for more effective democracy.

Along with shifting coalitions and weak party discipline, there was usually reasonable comity between majority and minority party. Major legislation was the product of lengthy committee hearings. Both parties could call witnesses. On most bills (except tax legislation in the House) there could be floor amendments, with extensive debate. Recorded floor amendments allowed members to be held accountable by constituents. House-Senate conference committees included majority and minority party conferees, and their final product was a compromise between the House and Senate bills. Go to the official congressional Web site (http://thomas.loc.gov/home/lawsmade.bysec/lawsnew.tst) and you will learn that this is supposedly how a bill becomes a law.

ALL THAT HAS RADICALLY CHANGED. Seeds of the change began appearing during the speakerships of both Democrat Jim Wright (1987–89) and Republican Newt Gingrich (1995–99), which produced more centralized leadership and party discipline. But the more radical changes, at the expense of democracy itself, have occurred since 2002 under Tom DeLay. Here are the key mechanisms of DeLay's dictatorship:

Extreme Centralization. The power to write legislation has been centralized in the House Republican leadership. Concretely, that means DeLay and House Speaker Dennis Hastert's chief of staff, Scott Palmer, working with the House Committee on Rules. (Hastert is seen in some quarters as a figurehead, but his man Palmer is as powerful as DeLay.) Drastic revisions to bills approved by committee are characteristically added by the leadership, often late in the evening. Under the House rules, 48 hours are supposed to elapse before floor action. But in 2003, the leadership, 57 percent of the time, wrote rules declaring bills to be "emergency" measures, allowing them to be considered with as little as 30 minutes notice. On several measures, members literally did not know what they were voting for.

Sorry, No Amendments. DeLay has used the rules process both to write new legislation that circumvents the hearing process and to all but eliminate floor amendments for Republicans and Democrats alike. The Rules Committee, controlled by the Republican leadership, writes a rule specifying the terms of debate for every bill that reaches the House floor. When Democrats controlled the House, Republicans complained bitterly when the occasional bill did not allow for open floor amendments. In 1995, Republicans pledged reform. Gerald Solomon, the new Republican chairman of the committee, explicitly promised that at least 70 percent of bills would come to the floor with rules permitting amendments. Instead, the proportion of bills prohibiting amendments has steadily increased, from 56 percent during the 104th Congress (1995–97) to 76 percent in 2003. This comparison actually understates the shift, because virtually all major bills now come to the floor with rules prohibiting amendments.

By eliminating floor amendments, Tom DeLay gets the bill that the leadership wrote.

DeLay has elevated votes on these rules into rigid tests of party loyalty, on a par with election of the speaker. A Republican House member who votes against a rule structuring floor debate will lose committee assignments and campaign funds, and can expect DeLay to sponsor a primary opponent.

How does this undermine democracy? As the recent Medicare bill was coming to a vote, a majority of House members were sympathetic to amendments allowing drug imports from Canada and empowering the federal government to negotiate wholesale drug prices. But by prohibiting floor amendments, DeLay made sure that the bill passed as written by the leadership, and that members were spared the embarrassment (or accountability) of voting against amendments popular with constituents.

The Republican House Whip Organization uses "catch and release" to allow moderates to take turns voting for bills they oppose.

One-Party Conferences. The Senate still allows floor amendments, but Senate-passed bills must go to conference with the House. Democratic House and Senate conferees are increasingly barred from attending conference committees, unless they are known turncoats. On the Medicare bill, liberal Democratic Senate conferees Tom Daschle and Jay Rockefeller were excluded. The more malleable Democrats John Breaux and Max Baucus, however, were allowed in. [See Matthew Yglesias, "Bad Max," page 11.] All four House Democratic conferees were excluded. Republican House and Senate conferees work out their intraparty differences, work their respective caucuses and send the (nonamendable) bill back to each house for a quick up-or-down vote. On the Medicare bill, members had one day to study a measure of more than 1,000 pages, much of it written from scratch in conference.

Legislation Without Hearings. Before the DeLay revolution, drafting new legislation in conference committee was almost unknown. But under DeLay, major provisions of the Medicare bill sprang fully grown from a conference committee. Republicans got a conference to include a weakened media-concentration standard that had been explicitly voted down by each house separately. Though both chambers had voted to block an administration measure watering down overtime-pay protections for workers, the provision was tacked onto a must-pass bill in conference. The official summary of House procedures, written by the (Republican-appointed) House parliamentarian and updated in June 2003, notes: "The House conferees are strictly limited in their consideration to matters in disagreement between the two Houses. Consequently, they may not strike out or amend any portion of the bill that was not amended by the other House. Furthermore, they may not insert new matter that is not germane to or that is beyond the scope of the differences between the two Houses." Like the rights guaranteed in the Soviet constitution, these rules are routinely waived.

Appropriations Abuses. Appropriations bills are must-pass affairs, otherwise the government eventually shuts down. Traditionally, substantive legislation is enacted in the usual way, then the appropriations process approves all or part of the funding. There has long been modest abuse in the form of earmarked money for pet pork-barrel projects and substantive riders being tacked onto appropriations bills. But since Gingrich, a lot of substantive bill drafting has been centralized in House leadership task forces appointed by the majority leader. And under DeLay, Appropriations subcommittee chairs must now be approved by the leadership, as well as by the Appropriations chairman.

BUT DIDN'T THE DEMOCRATS COMMIT THE SAME ABUSES during their 40-year House majority? Basically, no. The legislation written by stealth in the Rules Committee and in conference, and the exclusion of the minority party from conferences, are new. In 1987–89, Speaker Jim Wright occasionally used closed rules restricting floor amendments, but DeLay has made the railroading systematic.

Before 1975, conservative Democratic committee chairs often blocked liberal legislation, despite nominal Democratic House majorities. In 1975, rules changes supported by the large and idealistic "Watergate class" allowed the caucus to elect committee chairs, overturning the system of seniority. During the speakerships of Tip O'Neill (1977–86) and Wright, the caucus gradually strengthened both the leadership and itself at the expense of committee chairs. As speaker, Wright gained control of the Rules Committee and occasionally used his powers to frustrate floor amendments. He devised complex rules that permitted nonbinding preliminary votes to be overridden by the final vote. This maneuver, bitterly criticized by Republicans at the time, was the germ of the rules abuses that DeLay has taken to dictatorial levels.

To enforce party discipline, the DeLay operation has also perfected a technique known as "catch and release." On close pending votes, the House Republican Whip Organization, with dozens of regional whips, will target, say, the 20 to 30 Republican members known to oppose the legislation. When the leadership gets a final head count and determines just how many votes are needed, some will be reeled in and others let off the hook and given permission to vote "no." According to Michigan Republican Nick Smith, the leadership threatened to oppose his son's campaign to succeed him unless he voted for the Medicare bill. Basically, Republican moderates are allowed to take turns voting against bills they either oppose on principle or know to be unpopular in their districts. On the Medicare bill, 13 Republican House members voted one way on the House-passed bill and the other way on the conference bill. That way they could tell constituents whatever they needed to. As one longtime House staffer observes, "They can say, 'I would have voted to amend it, but I didn't get the opportunity.'"

Here again, some previous House and Senate leaders were adept at squeezing wavering members with rewards or punishments. The difference is that today's tight caucus discipline is used to enforce broader anti-democratic abuse. On the Medicare bill, the final roll-call vote was held open a full three hours well after midnight so that the leadership could keep pressuring Republican legislators who wanted to vote "no." Back in 1987, Republicans went ballistic when then-Speaker Wright held a vote open for a then-record extra 15 minutes. Dick Cheney, at the time a Wyoming representative, termed the move "the most arrogant, heavy-handed abuse of power I've ever seen in the 10 years that I've been here."

IN SHORT, SOME OF THESE MANEUVERS HAD EMBRYONIC antecedents, but under DeLay differences in degree have mutated into an alarming difference in kind. Wright's regime lasted just one congressional session. It ended unceremoniously when a minor ethics breach (Wright's bulk sales of his book) was bootstrapped into a major scandal by a Republican back-bencher named Gingrich, leading to Wright's resignation and his replacement by the far less partisan Tom Foley, and then to the Democrats' loss of the House in 1994. DeLay's regime shows every sign of going on and on and on—with abuses of which the Democrats never dreamed.

Why is there no revolt of the Republican moderates? They are split along issue lines, too intimidated and too few to mount a serious challenge, and almost never vote as a bloc. The only House Republicans who openly challenge DeLay as a group are those to his *right*, almost all of whom voted against the Medicare bill as too expensive.

And why has this anti-democratic revolution aroused so little general attention or indignation? First, Democrats are ambivalent about taking this issue to the country or to the press because many are convinced that nobody cares about "process" issues. The whole thing sounds like inside baseball, or worse, like losers whining. If they complain that big bad Tom DeLay keeps marginalizing them, as one senior House staffer puts it, "It just makes us look weak." But when Joe Cannon, the Republican House speaker a century ago, played similar games, it was a very big deal indeed. Press investigation and popular outrage toppled him. Today's abuses are hidden in plain view, but the press doesn't connect the dots.

In the Senate, Democrats still have the filibuster as a weapon of last resort, though the Republicans want to abolish it for judicial nominations. The Senate also continues to permit recorded floor amendments. But there is far less unity among Senate Democrats than among House Democrats, and Senate Republicans are learning anti-democratic tactics from the House. Most notably, they are complicit in the abuse of conference committees.

II. A Permanent Legislative Majority

It may feel like an eternity, but wall-to-wall one-party government has been in place only since Republicans took control of the Senate briefly during 2001—they lost it when Vermont Senator Jim Jeffords quit the party that May—and again since January 2003. During Bill Clinton's first term, Democrats nominally controlled Congress, though with weak discipline. Clinton himself practiced bipartisan "triangulation," which further weakened the Democrats. Bush's presidency, by contrast, has produced a near parliamentary government, based on intense party discipline both within Congress and between Congress and the White House. It helps that Senate Majority Leader Bill Frist literally owes his job to Karl Rove.

In one sense, parliamentary discipline is good for democracy: It enables voters to hold the party of government accountable. If they don't like the results, they can throw the rascals out. But today, it has become far more difficult to oust the congressional in-party. One big reason is the vanishing swing district.

If the current abuse of parliamentary processes were operating in ordinary times, the opposition party would soon be returned to power and a cycle of reform would ensue. The 1903–11 dictatorship of the aforementioned Joe Cannon abruptly ended when widespread outrage produced an alliance between Democrats and Progressive Republicans to weaken the speaker's powers in 1910, and then a landslide repudiation that November in which Republicans lost 57 seats and Democrats took control for the first time since 1895.

But since the early 1980s, the number of contestable House seats has come down and down. It's not that voter preferences have become more stable; there are actually more registered independent voters than ever. Rather, in state legislatures both parties have worked to create unprecedented numbers of safe congressional seats. Sometimes the two parties have cut deals, redrawing district lines to make Republican House seats more Republican and Democratic ones more Democratic. In other cases, a state party with a legislative majority—Republicans in Texas today, Democrats in California in 1981—will redraw district lines that create the maximum number of safe seats for their party. Both courses are profoundly undemocratic because each leaves most members with little to fear from voters and reinforces the underlying pro-incumbent bias of Congress.

Both parties are partly to blame, but as the recent supergerrymandering caper in Texas illustrates, Republicans have played dirtier. Historically, districts are redrawn only after each decennial census. The unprecedented gerrymandering between censuses, carried out by the Texas legislature but orchestrated by Rove and DeLay, will likely shift seven seats from Democrats to Republicans. (The press paid far more attention to the jollity of Texas Democratic state representatives fleeing to Oklahoma and New Mexico to temporarily deny Republican legislators a quorum than to the deadly serious consequences when Republicans eventually prevailed.) A three-judge federal appeals court panel has upheld this caper, which will eventually come before the same Supreme Court that wrote *Bush* v. *Gore*.

Many Democrats thought themselves clever to collude in the safe-seat game. But this particular bout of musical chairs has ended with a nearly frozen House that is structurally tilted Republican. In combination with the DeLay parliamentary dictatorship, the consequence is a near permanent partisan lock. So today's Republican Party is more disciplined and accountable to party leaders but far less accountable to voters.

Here are the numbers: With 229 Republicans and 205 Democrats (counting Sanders), it would take a net Democratic pickup of just 13 seats (that's 13 Democratic gains equaling 13 Republican losses for a net swing of 26 seats) for the House to change control. Historically, that's a small swing. In the nine elections between 1968 and 1984, the median swing was 42

seats. In the nine elections since 1986, the opposition party enjoyed a swing of 26 or more only once (the Gingrich landslide of 1994), and the median swing was just 10 seats. So normally the current Republican majority would be vulnerable to a below-average election-year swing. Today, however, with only about 25 effectively contestable seats, Democrats would have to win about three-quarters of the contestable races to take control, i.e., 19 Democratic wins to just six Republican wins, which in turn would require a tidal shift of public opinion.

All told, there are as many as 60 swing seats. But many potentially competitive seats become contestable only after the current incumbent retires or dies. Conversely, swing seats often become safe seats once an incumbent is re-elected and entrenched. Because not all incumbents retire at once, at any given time the number of effective contestable seats does not exceed about 25.

Note also the interplay between the legislative dictatorship and the dwindling number of swing districts. In previous eras, a majority leader with a margin of just 26 seats would have to carefully broker compromises both with his own moderates and with the opposition party. But the DeLay dictatorship and the ever fewer swing districts have combined to produce the opposite result. Individual legislators with safe seats needn't worry about swing voters, and DeLay needn't worry about losing swing districts because so few are left. Accordingly, the congressional Republican Party has become more militantly conservative. Like Bush, who also had no real mandate for radical change, DeLay is governing as if his party had won by a landslide. The country may be narrowly divided, but precious few citizens can make their votes for Congress count. A slender majority, defying gravity (and democracy), is producing not moderation but a shift to the extremes.

HERE AGAIN THE SENATE IS A VARIATION ON THE THEME, but with the same essential consequence: long-term one-party control. Senators are of course elected statewide. By definition, there is no gerrymandering of the Senate. (The republic's Founders achieved that in advance by giving big states and small ones the same number of senators.) But for a variety of other reasons, Democrats are unlikely to retake the Senate anytime soon.

One reason is the increasingly solid Republican South, something that New Democrats hoped their centrist formula could stave off. In the 1980s and early '90s, several southern Democrats did get elected as pro-development, pro-defense, racial moderates. But this trend has now collapsed. Lately, Democrats have lost Senate seats they held in Georgia, Tennessee and Virginia. In 2004 they will very likely lose seats held by retiring incumbents in North Carolina, South Carolina and Georgia, and could also lose closer races in Louisiana and Florida. Democrats do have a couple of pickup opportunities elsewhere. But the likely southern losses make it almost a statistical impossibility for Democrats to take back the Senate in 2004. These losses are not the result of any direct Republican assaults on democracy per se, though holding down black southern turnout could be considered a kind of assault. But the consequences of such losses will reinforce one-party government.

III. Thumbs on the Electoral Scale

In the aftermath of the Republican theft of Florida's electoral votes and the 2000 presidential election, Congress passed the Help America Vote Act. Many states are using HAVA funds to shift from now-prohibited punch cards or old-fashioned voting machine systems to ATM-type computer terminals. However, the three biggest makers of such computerized voting systems have financial ties to the Republican Party, and there is already evidence that the biggest manufacturer, Diebold, has had trouble designing tamper-proof systems. Some Democrats, led by Rep. Rush Holt of New Jersey, have proposed that all such machines be backed up by "verifiable paper trails," but this suggestion has gotten almost no Republican support. Moreover, millions of the poorest Americans have no experience with ATMs, and could well be deterred from voting.

A second potential for mischief is the provision put into HAVA, at Republican insistence, requiring voters who register by mail to show a government ID at the polls. This sounds innocent enough. Republicans, however, have a long and sordid history of "ballot security" programs intended to intimidate minority voters by threatening them with criminal prosecution if their papers are not technically in order. Chief Justice William Rehnquist got his political start running a ballot-security program for the Republicans in the 1962 elections in Arizona. Many civil-rights groups see the new federal ID provision of HAVA as an invitation to more such harassment. The Department of Justice's rights division was once a bulwark against these tactics, but that division currently reports to an attorney general named John Ashcroft.

The latest semi-reform of our system of money and politics could also backfire. The Supreme Court recently upheld the McCain-Feingold law, which prohibits unlimited donations to political parties. Democrats have taken comfort from the ability of Howard Dean to raise large sums of small money, while major liberal donors like George Soros can donate vast funds to voter-registration, get-out-the-vote and issue-advocacy organizations. But McCain-Feingold also dramatically raised the ceiling on permissible hard-money donations and allowed unlimited sums for independent groups and state parties. The Democrats have one George Soros; the Republicans have dozens, and many thousands more donors capable of reaching the new $2,000 hard-money ceiling than the Democrats have.

Money also goes disproportionately to incumbents. For a generation Democrats offset Republican financial dominance by inviting wealthy donors to invest in their incumbency. When they didn't have Congress, Democrats had the presidency, and vice versa. No more. Now the Republicans can combine their natural financial dominance with wall-to-wall incumbency. This financial superiority further helps cement the Republican lock on Congress by dissuading challenges and also discourages potentially strong Democratic candidates from running.

When you add it all up, there is still far more conservative money than progressive money. The fewer the firewalls between big money and the electoral process, the more systematic advantage the right has in maintaining a permanent lock.

IV. Rubber-Stamp Courts

Recently, several close court decisions have defended democracy and due process. In December, a federal appeals panel in New York ruled that President Bush lacked the authority to define an American citizen arrested in the United States as an "enemy combatant" and to deny him or her due process. Another appeals court, in San Francisco, held that the indefinite imprisonment of 660 noncitizens at Guantanamo Bay, Cuba, violated both the U.S. Constitution and international law. A three-judge panel of the U.S. Court of Appeals for the District of Columbia Circuit blocked, at least temporarily, the Bush administration's efforts to gut major portions of the Clean Air Act by administrative fiat.

> ## By the end of a second term, Bush would likely have at least three more Supreme Court justices in the mold of Scalia and Thomas.

However, if George W. Bush is re-elected, a Republican president will have controlled judicial appointments for 20 of the 28 years from 1981 to 2008. And Bush, in contrast to both his father and Clinton, is appointing increasingly extremist judges. By the end of a second term, he would likely have appointed at least three more Supreme Court justices in the mold of Antonin Scalia and Clarence Thomas, and locked in militantly conservative majorities in every federal appellate circuit.

How would such a Supreme Court change American democracy? We already know from *Bush* v. *Gore* that even the current high court is a partisan rubber stamp for contested elections. A Scalia-Thomas court would narrow rights and liberties, including the rights of criminal suspects, the right to vote, disability rights, and sexual privacy and reproductive choice. It would countenance an unprecedented expansion of police powers, and a reversal of the protection of the rights of women, gays and racial, religious and ethnic minorities. An analysis of Scalia's and Thomas' rulings and dissents suggests that a Scalia-Thomas majority would also overturn countless protections of the environment, workers and consumers, as well as weaken guarantees of the separation of church and state, privacy, and the right of states or Congress to regulate in the public interest. (For a full and thoroughly chilling account, see "Courting Disaster II: How a Scalia-Thomas Court Would Endanger Our Rights and Freedoms," People for the American Way, June 2003, http://www.pfaw.org/pfaw/general/default.aspx?oid=11111.)

THE MOST PREDICTABLE PUBLIC-POLICY RESULT OF extended one-party rule would be the completion of the Bush/radical-right project: the dismantling of social investment, regulation, progressive taxation, separation of church and state, racial justice and trade unionism. The administration's opportunistic version of federalism would continue to preempt the ability of states and localities to enact progressive policies of their own.

Even more insidiously, the radical right would likely use its wall-to-wall control of government to reduce liberties, narrow electoral democracy and thereby minimize the risk that it would ever lose power. Republican one-party rule would also strategically target progressive habitats, changing laws that currently tolerate or incubate oases of progressive political power and build liberal coalitions, such as the labor movement, universal social insurance, and an effective and valued public sector.

IS THIS ONE-PARTY SCENARIO INEVITABLE? FOR A VARIETY of structural reasons noted above, Democrats are unlikely to take back Congress this decade, absent a national crisis or massive scandal that overwhelms the governing party. But, contrary to the views of some of my colleagues, I think a Democrat could well win the White House in 2004. The Democratic base is aroused in a fashion that it has not been in decades, and swing voters may yet have second thoughts about George W. Bush. It's not at all clear what the economy and the foreign-policy scene will look like next fall, or what scandals will ripen.

Democrats have also begun fighting back against legislative dictatorship, and this may yet become a public issue. When the Republican Senate leadership unveiled rules changes to make it effectively impossible for Democrats to block extremist judicial nominees with a filibuster, the Democratic leadership threatened to use parliamentary tactics to shut the place down. House Democrats are now almost as unified as their Republican counterparts, and, if anything, even angrier. Tom DeLay may be sowing a whirlwind. And if a variation of the 2000 Florida theft is attempted in 2004, it is inconceivable that Democratic leaders and activists would show the same docility that Al Gore displayed.

We've seen divided government before, with a Democratic president and a fiercely partisan Republican Congress. It is not pretty. But it is much more attractive than a one-party state.

Benjamin Franklin, leaving the Constitutional Convention in Philadelphia, was asked by a bystander what kind of government the Founders had bestowed. "A republic," he famously replied, "if you can keep it." There have been moments in American history when we kept our republic only by the slenderest of margins. This year is one of those times.

Republicans, Democrats, and Race: An Uneasy History

In 1948, Southern Democrats rebelled against their party's civil rights agenda. Many of them later joined the Party of Lincoln.

By Robin Toner

In July 1948, the liberal mayor of Minneapolis, Hubert Humphrey, rose at the Democratic National Convention and urged his party to embrace the cause of civil rights for black Americans.

In a fiery speech that would echo through American politics for the next 50 years, he urged Democrats to "get out of the shadow of states' rights and walk forthrightly into the bright sunshine of human rights."

It was not a politically easy position for the Democrats to take. In fact, it tore the party asunder. Almost immediately, a group of Southerners opposed to the party's new civil-rights platform broke away and formed a new party known as the Dixicrats. Ultimately, in the decades that followed, the Democrats' decision to push for civil-rights legislation cost them the support of many white Southerners and was a key factor in the Republican Party's growing dominance in the region.

The issue of how America's two main political parties have dealt with race is still a potent one, as Republican Senator Trent Lott of Mississippi discovered. He resigned under pressure from his leadership post in December after appearing to praise the Dixicrats and their 1948 presidential candidate, Strom Thurmond.

THE SOUTHERN WAY

In 1948, blacks and whites were segregated across the South—kept apart in schools, hotels, restaurants, and other public places. Some of the staunchest defenders of segregation in the South were Democrats, many of them members of Congress.

They asserted that segregation was simply the Southern way of life, protected by "states' rights." The federal government, these Southern Democrats maintained, had no right to dismantle it.

Still, spurred on by Humphrey and other Northern liberals, the delegates to the 1948 Democratic Convention adopted a platform that called for equal opportunity in the workplace, in politics, and in the military. The reaction from Southern Democrats was fast and furious.

Within days, some of them met in Birmingham, Alabama, to form their own party and mount their own presidential campaign. They called themselves the States' Rights Democratic Party, or the Dixicrats, and their presidential nominee was a prominent Governor from the region, Strom Thurmond of South Carolina.

DEFIANT CAMPAIGN

Thurmond was even more defiant on the campaign trail. "I want to tell you that there's not enough troops in the Army to force the Southern people to break down segregation and admit the Negro race into our theaters, into our swimming pools, into our homes and churches," he declared.

Representative John Lewis, a black Congressman from Atlanta, Georgia, and a civil-rights veteran, was a child in Alabama when the Dixicrats launched their campaign. He describes that era of white resistance as a time of "tremendous fear" for blacks.

Though he received only 2.4 percent of the vote nationwide, Thurmond carried four of the five Deep South states—Mississippi, Louisiana, South Carolina, and Alabama (and came in second in the fifth state, Georgia). He won an estimated 92 percent of the white vote in Mississippi, and 84 percent in Alabama, according to political scientists Merle Black and Earl Black, who described the campaign in their book The Vital South.

The Dixiecrats had hoped to show the Democratic Party that it could not win the White House without the South on board. Despite that, the Democrats' nominee, President Harry Truman, was re-elected. But the Dixiecrats' rebellion marked the beginning of a deep schism between the south and the Democratic Party, which traced its origins to the Democratic-Republican Party led by Thomas Jefferson of Virginia.

Before the party's embrace of civil rights, the "Solid South" had been one of the most reliable features of American politics. For generations, the region had delivered huge majorities for Democratic presidential nominees. The Republicans, whose party originated in the antislavery movement of the 1850s, were still widely hated as the party of the triumphant North, which had defeated and humiliated the South in the Civil War.

But the alliance between rural Southern whites and the Democrats grew increasingly strained over the race issue, Merle Black says. By 1964, when Democratic President Lyndon B. Johnson pushed through the Civil Rights Act that desegregated the South, the political implications were clear. After signing the law, Johnson told an aide, "I think we just delivered the South to the Republican Party for a long time to come."

That year, Thurmond (who had rejoined the Democrats and had been elected to the Senate) became a Republican. That same year, Barry Goldwater, a Republican presidential candidate who opposed the civil-rights bill, carried all five Deep South states, winning an estimated 71 percent of the votes cast by whites there, according to *The Vital South.* By contrast, four years earlier, another Republican presidential candidate, Richard Nixon, had done half as well in the region.

While many Southern whites now backed Republicans, the Democrats could count on heavy support from black voters, who after the Voting Rights Act of 1965 were finally able to fully participate in politics. Their influence, however, was often outweighed by the larger numbers of white voters.

Modern Republicans—who often call themselves "The Party of Abraham Lincoln"—resent the idea that their party has benefitted from a white backlash to the civil-rights movement. Indeed, many other factors besides race played a role in the Republican realignment, historians and political scientists say. Ken Connor, president of the Family Research Council, a conservative group, and a Southerner himself, says, "Southerners by nature tend to be more conservative fiscally. They tend to look less toward the federal government as the source of all blessings and the solution to all problems, and

place a greater emphasis on the role of the states." But the Democrats clearly paid a price for their stand on civil-rights.

SHADOW OF THE PAST

The tortured history of race in American politics helps explain the firestorm that erupted after Lott, at a party for Thurmond in December, declared that he was proud that Mississippi had voted for Thurmond in 1948. He also suggested the country would have been better off had other states done the same.

Lott insisted that he was merely praising an old colleague, not segregation. But the storm grew until he relinquished his Republican leadership job. The events of 1948 still echoed.

ROBIN TONER is a national correspondent in the Washington bureau of *The New York Times.*

From the *New York Times Upfront,* February 21, 2003, p. 26-28. © 2003 by Scholastic Inc. and The New York Times Company. Reprinted by permission of Scholastic Inc.

RUNNING SCARED

Painfully often the legislation our politicians pass is designed less to solve problems than to protect the politicians from defeat in our never-ending election campaigns. They are, in short, too frightened of us to govern

by ANTHONY KING

To an extent that astonishes a foreigner, modern America is *about* the holding of elections. Americans do not merely have elections on the first Tuesday after the first Monday of November in every year divisible by four. They have elections on the first Tuesday after the first Monday of November in every year divisible by two. In addition, five states have elections in odd-numbered years. Indeed, there is no year in the United States—ever—when a major statewide election is not being held somewhere. To this catalogue of general elections has of course to be added an equally long catalogue of primary elections (for example, forty-three presidential primaries last year). Moreover, not only do elections occur very frequently in the United States but the number of jobs legally required to be filled by them is enormous—from the presidency of the United States to the post of local consumer advocate in New York. It has been estimated that no fewer than half a million elective offices are filled or waiting to be filled in the United States today.

Americans take the existence of their never-ending election campaign for granted. Some like it, some dislike it, and most are simply bored by it. But they are all conscious of it, in the same way that they are conscious of Mobil, McDonald's, *Larry King Live*, Oprah Winfrey, the Dallas Cowboys, the Ford Motor Company, and all other symbols and institutions that make up the rich tapestry of American life.

INDIVIDUALLY AND COLLECTIVELY AMERICAN POLITICIANS ARE MORE VULNERABLE, MORE OF THE TIME, TO THE VICISSITUDES OF ELECTORAL POLITICS THAN ARE THE POLITICIANS OF ANY OTHER DEMOCRATIC COUNTRY.

To a visitor to America's shores, however, the never-ending campaign presents a largely unfamiliar spectacle. In other countries election campaigns have both beginnings and ends, and there are even periods, often prolonged periods, when no campaigns take place at all. Other features of American elections are also unfamiliar. In few countries do elections and campaigns cost as much as they do in the United States. In no other country is the role of organized political parties so limited.

America's permanent election campaign, together with other aspects of American electoral politics, has one crucial consequence, little noticed but vitally important for the functioning of American democracy. Quite simply, the American electoral system places politicians in a highly vulnerable position. Individually and collectively they are more vulnerable, more of the time, to the vicissitudes of electoral politics than are the politicians of any other democratic country. Because they are more vulnerable, they devote more of their time to electioneering, and their conduct in office is more continuously governed by electoral considerations. I will argue that American politicians' constant and unremitting electoral preoccupations have deleterious consequences for the functioning of the American system. They consume time and scarce resources. Worse, they make it harder than it would otherwise be for the system as a whole to deal with some of America's most pressing problems. Americans often complain that their system is not sufficiently democratic. I will argue that, on the contrary, there is a sense in which the system is too democratic and ought to be made less so.

Although this article is written by a foreigner, a Canadian citizen who happens to live in Great Britain, it is not written in any spirit of moral or intellectual superiority. Americans over the years have had quite enough of Brits and others telling them how to run their affairs. I have no wish to prolong their irritation. What follows is the reflections of a candid friend.

FEAR AND TREMBLING

POLITICS and government in the United States are marked by the fact that U.S. elected officials in many cases have very short terms of office *and* face the prospect of being defeated in primary elections *and* have to run for office more as individuals than as standard-bearers for their party *and* have continually to raise large sums of money in order to finance their own election campaigns. Some of these factors operate in other countries. There is no other country, however, in which all of them operate, and operate simultaneously. The cumulative consequences, as we shall see, are both pervasive and profound.

The U.S. Constitution sets out in one of its very first sentences that "the House of Representatives shall be composed of members chosen every second year by the people of the several states." When the Founding Fathers decided on such a short term of office for House members, they were setting a precedent that has been followed by no other major democratic country. In Great Britain, France, Italy, and Canada the constitutional or legal maximum for the duration of the lower house of the national legislature is five years. In Germany and Japan the equivalent term is four years. Only in Australia and New Zealand, whose institutions are in some limited respects modeled on those of the United States, are the legal maximums as short as three years. In having two-year terms the United States stands alone.

Members of the Senate are, of course, in a quite different position. Their constitutionally prescribed term of office, six years, is long by anyone's standards. But senators' six-year terms are not all they seem. In the first place, so pervasive is the electioneering atmosphere that even newly elected senators begin almost at once to lay plans for their re-election campaigns. Senator Daniel Patrick Moynihan, of New York, recalls that when he first came to the Senate, in 1977, his colleagues when they met over lunch or a drink usually talked about politics and policy. Now they talk about almost nothing but the latest opinion polls. In the second place, the fact that under the Constitution the terms of a third of the Senate end every two years means that even if individual senators do not feel themselves to be under continuing electoral pressure, the Senate as a whole does. Despite the Founders' intentions, the Senate's collective electoral sensibilities increasingly resemble those of the House.

Most Americans seem unaware of the fact, but the direct primary—a government-organized popular election to nominate candidates for public office—is, for better or worse, an institution peculiar to the United States. Neither primary elections nor their functional equivalents exist anywhere else in the democratic world. It goes without saying that their effect is to add a further dimension of uncertainty and unpredictability to the world of American elective politicians.

In most other countries the individual holder of public office, so long as he or she is reasonably conscientious and does not gratuitously offend local or regional party opinion, has no real need to worry about renomination. To be sure, cases of parties refusing to renominate incumbent legislators are not unknown in countries such as France, Germany, and Canada, but they are relatively rare and tend to occur under unusual circumstances. The victims are for the most part old, idle, or alcoholic.

The contrast between the rest of the world and the United States could hardly be more striking. In 1978 no fewer than 104 of the 382 incumbent members of the House of Representatives who sought re-election faced primary opposition. In the following three elections the figures were ninety-three out of 398 (1980), ninety-eight out of 393 (1982), and 130 out of 409 (1984). More recently, in 1994, nearly a third of all House incumbents seeking re-election, 121 out of 386, had to face pri-

mary opposition, and in the Senate the proportion was even higher: eleven out of twenty-six. Even those incumbents who did not face opposition could seldom be certain in advance that they were not going to. The influence—and the possibility—of primaries is pervasive. As we shall see, the fact that incumbents usually win is neither here nor there.

To frequent elections and primary elections must be added another factor that contributes powerfully to increasing the electoral vulnerability of U.S. politicians: the relative lack of what we might call "party cover." In most democratic countries the fate of most politicians depends not primarily on their own endeavors but on the fate—locally, regionally, or nationally—of their party. If their party does well in an election, so do they. If not, not. The individual politician's interests and those of his party are bound together.

In contrast, America's elective politicians are on their own—not only in relation to politicians in most other countries but also in absolute terms. Party is still a factor in U.S. electoral politics, but it is less so than anywhere else in the democratic world. As a result, American legislators seeking re-election are forced to raise their own profiles, to make their own records, and to fight their own re-election campaigns.

If politicians are so vulnerable electorally, it may be protested, why aren't more of them defeated? In particular, why aren't more incumbent congressmen and senators defeated? The analysis here would seem to imply a very high rate of turnover in Congress, but in fact the rate—at least among incumbents seeking re-election—is notoriously low. How can this argument and the facts of congressional incumbents' electoral success be reconciled?

This objection has to be taken seriously, because the facts on which it is based are substantially correct. The number of incumbent congressmen and senators defeated in either primary or general elections *is* low. But to say that because incumbent members of Congress are seldom defeated, they are not really vulnerable electorally is to miss two crucial points. The first is that precisely because they are vulnerable, they go to prodigious lengths to protect themselves. Like workers in nuclear-power stations, they take the most extreme safety precautions, and the fact that the precautions are almost entirely successful does not make them any less necessary.

Second, congressmen and senators go to inordinate lengths to secure re-election because, although they may objectively be safe (in the view of journalists and academic political scientists), they do not know they are safe—and even if they think they are, the price of being wrong is enormous. The probability that anything will go seriously wrong with a nuclear-power station may approach zero, but the stations tend nevertheless to be built away from the centers of large cities. A congressman or a senator may believe that he is reasonably safe, but if he wants to be re-elected, he would be a fool to act on that belief.

HOW THEY CAME TO BE VULNERABLE

AMERICAN politicians run scared—and are right to do so. And they run more scared than the politicians of any other democratic country—again rightly. How did this come to be so?

The short answer is that the American people like it that way. They are, and have been for a very long time, the Western world's hyperdemocrats. They are keener on democracy than almost anyone else and are more determined that democratic norms and practices should pervade every aspect of national life. To explore the implications of this central fact about the United States, and to see how it came to be, we need to examine two different interpretations of the term "democracy." Both have been discussed from time to time by political philosophers, but they have never been codified and they certainly cannot be found written down in a constitution or any other formal statement of political principles. Nevertheless, one or the other underpins the political practice of every democratic country—even if, inevitably, the abstract conception and the day-to-day practice are never perfectly matched.

One of these interpretations might be labeled "division of labor." In this view, there are in any democracy two classes of people—the governors and the governed. The function of the governors is to take decisions on the basis of what they believe to be in the country's best interests and to act on those decisions. If public opinion broadly supports the decisions, that is a welcome bonus. If not, too bad. The views of the people at large are merely one datum among a large number of data that need to be considered. They are not accorded any special status. Politicians in countries that operate within this view can frequently be heard using phrases like "the need for strong leadership" and "the need to take tough decisions." They often take a certain pride in doing what they believe to be right even if the opinion of the majority is opposed to it.

The function of the governed in such a system, if it is a genuine democracy, is very important but strictly limited. It is not to determine public policy or to decide what is the right thing to do. Rather, it is to go to the polls from time to time to choose those who will determine public policy and decide what the right thing is: namely, the governors. The deciding of issues by the electorate is secondary to the election of the individuals who are to do the deciding. The analogy is with choosing a doctor. The patient certainly chooses which doctor to see but does not normally decide (or even try to decide) on the detailed course of treatment. The division of labor is informal but clearly understood.

It is probably fair to say that most of the world's major democracies—Great Britain, France, Germany, Japan—operate on this basis. The voters go to the polls every few years, and in between times it is up to the government of the day to get on with governing. Electing a government and governing are two different businesses. Electioneering is, if anything, to be deplored if it gets in the way of governing.

This is a simplified picture, of course. Democratically elected politicians are ultimately dependent on the electorate, and if at the end of the day the electorate does not like what they are doing, they are dead. Nevertheless, the central point remains. The existing division of labor is broadly accepted.

The other interpretation of democracy, the one dominant in America, might be called the "agency" view, and it is wholly different. According to this view, those who govern a country should function as no more than the agents of the people. The job of the governors is not to act independently and to take whatever decisions they believe to be in the national interest but, rather, to reflect in all their actions the views of the majority of the people, whatever those views may be. Governors are not really governors at all; they are representatives, in the very narrow sense of being in office solely to represent the views of those who sent them there.

In the agency view, representative government of the kind common throughout the democratic world can only be second-best. The ideal system would be one in which there were no politicians or middlemen of any kind and the people governed themselves directly; the political system would take the form of more or less continuous town meetings or referenda, perhaps conducted by means of interactive television. Most Americans, at bottom, would still like to see their country governed by a town meeting.

WHY THEIR VULNERABILITY MATTERS

IN this political ethos, finding themselves inhabiting a turbulent and torrid electoral environment, most American elective officials respond as might be expected: in an almost Darwinian way. They adapt their behavior—their roll-call votes, their introduction of bills, their committee assignments, their phone calls, their direct-mail letters, their speeches, their press releases, their sound bites, whom they see, how they spend their time, their trips abroad, their trips back home, and frequently their private and family lives—to their environment: that is, to their primary and overriding need for electoral survival. The effects are felt not only in the lives of individual officeholders and their staffs but also in America's political institutions as a whole and the shape and content of U.S. public policy.

It all begins with officeholders' immediate physical environment: with bricks, mortar, leather, and wood paneling. The number of congressional buildings and the size of congressional staffs have ballooned in recent decades. At the start of the 1960s most members of the House of Representatives contented themselves with a small inner office and an outer office; senators' office suites were not significantly larger. Apart from the Capitol itself, Congress was reasonably comfortably housed in four buildings, known to Washington taxi drivers as the Old and New House and Senate Office Buildings. The designations Old and New cannot be used any longer, however, because there are now so many even newer congressional buildings.

Congressional staffs have grown at roughly the same rate, the new buildings having been built mainly to house the staffs. In 1957 the total number of people employed by members of the House and Senate as personal staff was 3,556. By 1991 the figure had grown to 11,572—a more than threefold increase within the political lifetime of many long-serving members. Last year the total number of people employed by Congress in all capacities, including committee staffs and the staffs of support agencies like the Congressional Research Service, was 32,820, making Congress by far the most heavily staffed legislative branch in the world.

Much of the growth of staff in recent decades has been in response to the growth of national government, to Congress's insistence on strengthening its policymaking role in the aftermath of

Vietnam and Watergate, and to decentralization within Congress, which has led subcommittee chairmen and the subcommittees themselves to acquire their own staffs. But there is no doubt that the increase is also in response to congressional incumbents' ever-increasing electoral exposure. Congress itself has become an integral part of America's veritable "elections industry."

One useful measure of the changes that have taken place—and also an important consequence of the changes—is the increased proportion of staff and staff time devoted to constituent service. As recently as 1972 only 1,189 House employees—22.5 percent of House members' personal staffs—were based in home-district offices. By 1992 the number had more than doubled, to 3,128, and the proportion had nearly doubled, to 42.1 percent. On the Senate side there were only 303 state-based staffers in 1972, making up 12.5 percent of senators' personal staffs, but the number had more than quadrupled by 1992 to 1,368, for fully 31.6 percent of the total. Since a significant proportion of the time of Washington-based congressional staffs is also devoted to constituent service, it is a fair guess that more than half of the time of all congressional staffs is now given over to nursing the district or state rather than to legislation and policymaking.

Much constituent service is undoubtedly altruistic, inspired by politicians' sense of duty (and constituents' understandable frustration with an unresponsive bureaucracy); but at the same time nobody doubts that a large proportion of it is aimed at securing re-election. The statistics on the outgoing mail of members of Congress and their use of the franking privilege point in that direction too. Congressional mailings grew enormously in volume from some 100 million pieces a year in the early 1960s to more than 900 million in 1984—nearly five pieces of congressional mail for every adult American. New restrictions on franking introduced in the 1990s have made substantial inroads into that figure, but not surprisingly the volume of mail emanating from both houses of Congress is still invariably higher in election years.

The monetary costs of these increases in voter-oriented congressional activities are high: in addition to being the most heavily staffed legislative branch in the world, Congress is also the most expensive. But there is another, non-monetary cost: the staffs themselves become one of the congressman's or senator's constituencies, requiring management, taking up time, and always being tempted to go into business for themselves. American scholars who have studied the burgeoning of congressional staffs express concern about their cumulative impact on Congress as a deliberative body in which face-to-face communication between members, and between members and their constituents, facilitates both mutual understanding and an understanding of the issues. Largely in response to the requirements of electioneering, more and more congressional business is conducted through dense networks of staffers.

One familiar effect of American politicians' vulnerability is the power it accords to lobbyists and special-interest groups, especially those that can muster large numbers of votes or have large amounts of money to spend on campaigns. Members of Congress walk the electoral world alone. They can be picked off one by one, they know it, and they adjust their behavior accordingly. The power of the American Association of Retired Persons, the National Rifle Association, the banking industry, and

the various veterans' lobbies is well known. It derives partly from their routine contributions to campaign funds and the quality of their lobbying activities in Washington, but far more from the votes that the organizations may be able to deliver and from congressmen's and senators' calculations of how the positions they take in the present may affect their chances of re-election in the future—a future that rarely is distant. Might a future challenger be able to use that speech against me? Might I be targeted for defeat by one of the powerful lobbying groups?

A second effect is that American politicians are even more likely than those in other countries to engage in symbolic politics: to use words masquerading as deeds, to take actions that purport to be instrumental but are in fact purely rhetorical. A problem exists; the people demand that it be solved; the politicians cannot solve it and know so; they engage in an elaborate pretense of trying to solve it nevertheless, often at great expense to the taxpayers and almost invariably at a high cost in terms of both the truth and the politicians' own reputations for integrity and effectiveness. The politicians lie in most cases not because they are liars or approve of lying but because the potential electoral costs of not lying are too great.

At one extreme, symbolic politics consists of speechmaking and public position-taking in the absence of any real action or any intention of taking action; casting the right vote is more important than achieving the right outcome. At the other extreme, symbolic politics consists of whole government programs that are ostensibly designed to achieve one set of objectives but are actually designed to achieve other objectives (in some cases simply the re-election of the politicians who can claim credit for them).

Take as an example the crime bills passed by Congress in the 1980s and 1990s, with their mandatory-minimum sentences, their three-strikes-and-you're-out provisions, and their extension of the federal death penalty to fifty new crimes. The anti-drug and anti-crime legislation, by the testimony of judges and legal scholars, has been at best useless and at worst wholly pernicious in its effects, in that it has filled prison cells not with violent criminals but with drug users and low-level drug pushers. As for the death penalty, a simple measure of its sheer irrelevance to the federal government's war on crime is easily provided. The last federal offender to be put to death, Victor H. Feguer, a convicted kidnapper, was hanged in March of 1963. By the end of 1995 no federal offender had been executed for more than thirty years, and hardly any offenders were awaiting execution on death row. The ferocious-seeming federal statutes were almost entirely for show.

The way in which the wars on drugs and crime were fought cannot be understood without taking into account the incessant pressure that elected officeholders felt they were under from the electorate. As one former congressman puts it, "Voters were afraid of criminals, and politicians were afraid of voters." This fear reached panic proportions in election years. Seven of the years from 1981 to 1994 were election years nationwide; seven were not. During those fourteen years Congress passed no fewer than seven major crime bills. Of those seven, six were passed in election years (usually late in the year). That is, there was only one election year in which a major crime bill was *not* passed, and only one non-election year in which a major crime bill *was* passed.

Another effect of the extreme vulnerability of American politicians is that it is even harder for them than for democratically elected politicians in other countries to take tough decisions: to court unpopularity, to ask for sacrifices, to impose losses, to fly in the face of conventional wisdom—in short, to act in what they believe to be their constituents' interest and the national interest rather than in their own interest. Timothy J. Penny, a Democrat who left the House of Representatives in 1994, put the point starkly, perhaps even too harshly, in *Common Cents* (1995).

> Voters routinely punish lawmakers who try to do unpopular things, who challenge them to face unpleasant truths about the budget, crime, Social Security, or tax policy. Similarly, voters reward politicians for giving them what they want—more spending for popular programs—even if it means wounding the nation in the long run by creating more debt.

America's enduring budget deficit offers a vivid, almost textbook illustration. For nearly a generation—ever since the early 1980s—American politicians have bemoaned the deficit and exhorted themselves to do something about it. However, they have never done nearly enough, even in their own eyes. Why? Part of the answer undoubtedly lies in genuine ideological differences that make it hard for conservatives and liberals to compromise; but much of the answer also lies in the brute fact that every year in the United States is either an election year or a pre-election year, with primaries and threatened primaries intensifying politicians' electoral concerns. In 1985 Senator Warren Rudman, of New Hampshire, reckoned that he and other senators who had voted for a bold deficit-reduction package had flown a "kamikaze mission." One of his colleagues said they had "jumped off a cliff." Twelve years later, not surprisingly, the federal budget remains in deficit.

MORE DEMOCRACY, MORE DISSATISFACTION

NUMEROUS opinion polls show that millions of Americans are profoundly dissatisfied with the functioning of their political system. Consequently, there is a widespread disposition in the United States—at all levels of society, from the grass roots to the editorial conference and the company boardroom—to want to make American democracy "work better," and concrete proposals abound for achieving this goal.

The proposed reforms can be grouped loosely under four headings. First come those that if implemented would amount to the creation of electronic town meetings, taking advantage of technological developments such as CD-ROM, interactive cable systems, electronic mail, and the Internet. *The Wall Street Journal* referred in this general connection to "arranging a marriage of de Tocqueville and technology."

Second, and related, are proposals for promoting democratic deliberation and citizen participation. The Kettering Foundation and the Public Agenda Foundation already organize National Issues Forums that embrace some 3,000 educational and civic groups across America. David Mathews, the president of the Kettering Foundation, considers these modern forums to be directly linked to America's ancient "town meeting tradition." Benjamin R. Barber, a political philosopher at Rutgers University, would go further and create a nationwide network of neighborhood assemblies that could take actual decisions on strictly local matters and also debate and lobby on broader national questions. James S. Fishkin, a political scientist at the University of Texas, likewise seeks to leap the modern barriers to face-to-face democracy by means of what he calls "deliberative opinion polls" (which have been tried, with considerable success, in England).

The third group of proposed reforms is equally radical but more old-fashioned. This group seeks to complete the work of Progressive Era reformers by extending to the federal level the characteristic state-level reforms that were introduced in that period: the referendum, the initiative, and the recall. The political analyst Kevin Phillips, for example, suggests that "the United States should propose and ratify an amendment to the Constitution setting up a mechanism for holding nationwide referendums to permit the citizenry to supplant Congress and the president in making certain categories of national decisions." He would also like to see congressmen and senators be subject to popular recall once they have been in office for a year. Certainly proposals of this kind have broad public support. Depending on the precise wording of the question, more than 50 percent of Americans support the idea of national referenda and more than 80 percent support both the initiative and the recall.

Finally, many commentators—and the majority of the American public—strongly back the newest and most fashionable item on the "making democracy work better" agenda: the imposition of term limits on both state and federal elected officials, notably members of Congress. But the great majority of those who favor term limits, true to the American democratic tradition, are less concerned with good government and the public interest as such than with the present generation of politicians' alleged lack of responsiveness to the mass of ordinary people. At the center of this argument is the idea that the United States is now governed by an unresponsive, self-perpetuating, and increasingly remote class of professional politicians, a class that ought to be replaced as soon as possible by "citizen legislators"—men and women who will serve the people simply because they *are* the people. As one advocate of term limits puts it, ordinary people—the proposed citizen legislators of the future—"know things about life in America that people who have lived as very self-important figures in Washington for thirty years have no way of knowing or have forgotten."

Some of the items on this four-part shopping list of reforms are intrinsically attractive, or at least a good case can be made for them. Nevertheless, taken as a whole, the mainstream reformist agenda, with its traditional American emphasis on agency democracy and its view of politicians as mere servants of the people's will, rests on extremely tenuous conceptual foundations and, more important, is almost certainly inappropriate as a response to the practical needs of turn-of-the-century America. America's problem of governance is not insufficient responsiveness on the part of its elected leaders. On the contrary, America's problem is their hyper-responsiveness. Politicians do not need to be tied down still further, to be subjected to even more external pressures than they are already. Rather, they need to be given just a little more political leeway, just a little more room for policy maneuver. Reforms should seek to strengthen division-of-labor democracy, not to create a still purer form of American-style agency democracy.

THE USUAL SUSPECTS

IF the reformist prescriptions are bad ones, there may be something wrong with the reformist diagnoses on which they are based. What *are* the principal sources of dissatisfaction with the current state of American democracy?

Many commentators have gotten into the habit of blaming Americans' dissatisfaction, in an almost knee-jerk fashion, on "the Vietnam War and Watergate." It is certainly the case that evidence of widespread dissatisfaction began to appear during and shortly after Vietnam and Watergate. *Post hoc, ergo propter hoc?* Maybe. But in the first place, Vietnam and Watergate led to a flowering of idealism as well as cynicism (and to the election, in 1974, of the "Watergate babies," one of the most idealistic and public-spirited cohorts ever to be elected to Congress). And in the second place, it seems strange to attribute the dissatisfactions of the 1990s to events that took place in the 1960s and early 1970s. That distance in time is roughly that between the two world wars; most of today's college students were not yet born when President Richard Nixon resigned. To be sure, subsequent scandals have undoubtedly (and deservedly) damaged the reputations of the White House and Congress, but at least some of the sleaze of recent years has come about because politicians need such enormous sums to finance their re-election campaigns.

Two other hypotheses can be dismissed, or at least assigned little importance. One is that politicians today are a poor lot compared with the intellectual and moral giants of the past. It probably is the case that having to run scared all the time has tended to drive some able people out of politics and to discourage others from coming in. But the phenomenon is a relatively recent one, and for the time being there is no reason to think that the average congressman or senator is in any way inferior to his or her predecessors. The quality of America's existing political class is at most a small part of the problem.

The same is almost certainly true of the idea that divided government—in which one party controls one or both houses of Congress while the other controls the presidency—is to be preferred. Divided government has characterized America for most of the past thirty years, and it has been associated with some of the more spectacular political and policy failures of that period—the Iran-contra scandal of the 1980s (which arose out of a Republican Administration's desire to circumvent a Democratic Congress), and successive shutdowns of parts of the government as Presidents and Congress have failed to agree on timely taxing and spending measures. Other things being equal, divided government is probably to be regretted.

All the same, it is hard to credit the idea that Americans' disillusionment with their politics would be significantly less today if party control had been mainly undivided over the past thirty years. On the one hand, recent periods in which the government has not been divided (the Carter years, 1977–1980, and

the first two Clinton years, 1993–1994) were not notably successful (Carter never surmounted the energy crisis, and Clinton failed to reform America's healthcare system even though that reform had figured prominently in his campaign promises). On the other hand, as David R. Mayhew, a political scientist at Yale University, has shown, periods of divided government have often been extremely productive in legislative terms. On balance, divided government appears to be more of a nuisance and a distraction than a root cause of either the government's difficulties or the public's disillusionment.

The idea that the system suffers from the excessive power of interest groups, however, needs to be taken seriously. Jonathan Rauch, in his recent book *Demosclerosis*, argues persuasively that America's interest groups have become larger, more numerous, and more powerful over the past three decades, to the point that they now have the capacity to prevent the government from doing almost anything that would disadvantage or offend any of the clients they represent—taking in, as it happens, virtually the whole American population.

> **WHEN AMERICANS BECOME DISSATISFIED WITH GOVERNMENT, THEY CALL FOR MORE DEMOCRACY. THE MORE THEY CALL FOR MORE DEMOCRACY, THE MORE OF IT THEY GET. THE MORE THEY GET, THE MORE DISSATISFIED THEY BECOME.**

Rauch is probably right; but one needs to go on to ask, as he himself does, what the power of these pullulating and all-encompassing lobby groups is based on. The answer is straightforward: their power depends ultimately on their money, on their capacity to make trouble for elected officials, on the votes of their members (the AARP has more than 30 million members), and on elective politicians' fear of not being re-elected. The groups' power, in other words, depends on politicians' electoral vulnerability; and America's interest groups are peculiarly powerful in large measure because America's elective politicians are peculiarly vulnerable. It is not quite as simple as that—but almost.

It is also important to note the precise timing of the developments described by Rauch and by almost everyone else who has written on this subject. Nearly all these developments date, almost uncannily, from the past thirty years: the rise in the number of interest groups, the growth in their membership and power, the decline in the public's trust in government officials, and the increased sense among voters that who they are and what they think do not matter to politicians and officials in Washington. In other words, the origins of the present era of democratic discontent can be traced to the end of the 1960s and the beginning of the 1970s. It was then that people began to think something was wrong not with this or that aspect of the system but with the system itself.

THERE IS NO SPECIAL VIRTUE IN A SYSTEM THAT REQUIRES LARGE NUMBERS OF POLITICIANS TO RUN THE RISK OF MARTYRDOM IN ORDER TO ENSURE THAT TOUGH DECISIONS CAN BE TAKEN IN A TIMELY MANNER IN THE NATIONAL INTEREST.

What happened at that time? It is hard to escape the conclusion that the crucial developments, largely provoked by the Vietnam War and Watergate, were the attempts from 1968 onward to open up the American system, to make it more transparent, to make it more accessible, to make it, in a word, more "democratic." These attempts led an increase in the number of primary elections, to a further weakening of America's already weak political parties, to increases in the already high costs of electoral politics, and to the increasing isolation, in an increasingly hostile environment, of elective officials. In short, the post-Vietnam, post-Watergate reforms led, as they were meant to lead, to increased vulnerability to their electorates on the part of individual American officeholders.

The paradox that has resulted is obvious and easily stated. Recent history suggests that when large numbers of Americans become dissatisfied with the workings of their government, they call for more democracy. The more they call for more democracy, the more of it they get. The more of it they get, the more dissatisfied they become with the workings of their government. The more they become dissatisfied with the workings of their government, the more they call for more democracy. The cycle endlessly repeats itself.

WHAT, IF ANYTHING, MIGHT BE DONE?

PRECISELY because American politicians are so exposed electorally, they probably have to display—and do display—more political courage more often than the politicians of any other democratic country. The number of political saints and martyrs in the United States is unusually large.

There is, however, no special virtue in a political system that requires large numbers of politicians to run the risk of martyrdom in order to ensure that tough decisions can be taken in a timely manner in the national interest. The number of such decisions that need to be taken is always likely to be large; human nature being what it is, the supply of would-be martyrs is always likely to be small. On balance it would seem better not to try to eliminate the electoral risks (it can never be done in a democracy) but to reduce somewhat their scale and intensity. There is no reason why the risks run by American politicians should be so much greater than the risks run by elective politicians in other democratic countries.

How, then, might the risks be reduced? What can be done? A number of reforms to the existing system suggest themselves. It may be that none of them is politically feasible—Americans

hold tight to the idea of agency democracy—but in principle there should be no bar to any of them. One of the simplest would also be the most radical: to lengthen the terms of members of the House of Representatives from two years to four. The proposal is by no means a new one: at least 123 resolutions bearing on the subject were introduced in Congress in the eighty years from 1885 to 1965, and President Lyndon B. Johnson advocated the change in his State of the Union address in January of 1966.

A congressman participating in a Brookings Institution round table held at about the time of Johnson's message supported the change, saying, "I think that the four years would help you to be a braver congressman, and I think what you need is bravery. I think you need courage." Another congressman on the same occasion cited the example of another bill that he believed had the support of a majority in the House. "That bill is not going to come up this year. You know why it is not coming up?… Because four hundred and thirty-five of us have to face election.… If we had a four-year term, I am as confident as I can be the bill would have come to the floor and passed."

A similar case could be made for extending the term of senators to eight years, with half the Senate retiring or running for re-election every four years. If the terms of members of both houses were thus extended and made to coincide, the effect in reducing America's never-ending election campaign would be dramatic.

There is much to be said, too, for all the reasons mentioned so far, for scaling down the number of primary elections. They absorb extravagant amounts of time, energy, and money; they serve little democratic purpose; few people bother to vote in them; and they place additional and unnecessary pressure on incumbent officeholders. Since the main disadvantage of primaries is the adverse effect they have on incumbents, any reforms probably ought to be concerned with protecting incumbents' interests.

At the moment, the primary laws make no distinction between situations in which a seat in the House or the Senate is already occupied and situations in which the incumbent is, for whatever reason, standing down. The current laws provide for a primary to be held in either case. An incumbent is therefore treated as though the seat in question were open and he or she were merely one of the candidates for it. A relatively simple reform would be to distinguish between the two situations. If a seat was open, primaries would be held in both parties, as now; but if the incumbent announced that he or she intended to run for re-election, then a primary in his or her party would be held only if large numbers of party supporters were determined to have one—that is, were determined that the incumbent should be ousted. The obvious way to ascertain whether such determination existed would be by means of a petition supervised by the relevant state government and requiring a considerable number of signatures. The possibility of a primary would thus be left open, but those who wanted one would have to show that they were both numerous and serious. A primary would not be held simply because an ambitious, possibly demented, possibly wealthy individual decided to throw his or her hat into the ring.

Any steps to strengthen the parties as institutions would be desirable on the same grounds. Lack of party cover in the United States means that elective officeholders find it hard to take tough decisions partly because they lack safety in numbers. They can seldom, if ever, say to an aggrieved constituent or a political-action committee out for revenge, "I had to vote that way because my party told me to," or even "I had to vote that way because we in my party all agreed that we would." Lack of party cohesion, together with American voters' disposition to vote for the individual rather than the party, means that congressmen and senators are always in danger of being picked off one by one.

BALLOT FATIGUE

WHAT might be done to give both parties more backbone? Clearly, the parties would be strengthened—and elective office-holders would not need to raise so much money for their own campaigns—if each party organization became a major source of campaign funding. In the unlikely event (against the background of chronic budget deficits) that Congress ever gets around to authorizing the federal funding of congressional election campaigns, a strong case could be made for channeling as much of the money as possible through the parties, and setting aside some of it to cover their administrative and other ongoing costs.

The party organizations and the nexus between parties and their candidates would also be strengthened if it were made easier for ordinary citizens to give money to the parties and for the parties to give money to their candidates. Until 1986, when the program was abolished, tax credits were available for tax-payers who contributed small sums to the political parties. These credits could be restored. Larry J. Sabato, a political scientist at the University of Virginia, has similarly suggested that citizens entitled to a tax refund could be allowed to divert a small part of their refund to the party of their choice. Such measures would not, however, reduce candidates' dependence on donations from wealthy individuals and PACs unless they were accompanied by measures enabling the parties to contribute more generously to their candidates' campaigns. At the moment there are strict legal limits on the amount of money that national or state party organizations can contribute to the campaigns of individual candidates. The limits should be raised (and indexed to inflation). There is even a case for abolishing them altogether.

All that said, there is an even more straightforward way of reducing incumbents' dependence on campaign contributors. At present incumbents have to spend so much time raising funds because the campaigns themselves are so expensive. They could be made cheaper. This, of course, would be one of the effects of making U.S. elections less numerous and less frequent than they are now. Another way to lower the cost of elections would be to provide candidates and parties with free air time on television and radio.

THE CASE FOR SWANS

CLEARLY, the idea of term limits also needs to be taken seriously. After all, if American politicians are excessively vulnerable at the moment, one way of rendering them invulnerable would be to prevent them from running for re-election—no impending election contest, no need to worry overmuch about the voters.

As is evident, much of the actual campaigning in favor of term limits takes the form of ranting—against big government, against Washington, against "them," against taxes, against the deficit. Much of the rhetoric of term-limiters is sulfurous, and their principal motive often seems to be revenge. They claim that members of Congress are insufficiently responsive to their constituents, when the evidence suggests that, on the contrary, they are far too responsive. The term-limits movement is of a piece with previous outbursts of frustrated American populism, including the Know-Nothing movement of the 1850s—an essay, as one historian has put it, in "the politics of impatience."

Nevertheless, there is an alternate case for term limits, based not on American politicians' alleged lack of responsiveness to the voters but on their alleged overresponsiveness to the voters and interest groups in order to secure their own re-election. The most persuasive and subtle advocate of this line of argument is the political commentator George F. Will. His goal, Will says partway through his book *Restoration* (1992), "is deliberative democracy through representatives who function at a constitutional distance from the people." He reiterates the point about distance in his final paragraphs: "Americans must be less demanding of government. They must give to government more constitutional space in which to think, more social distance to facilitate deliberation about the future."

The case for giving American politicians more space and distance is undoubtedly a strong one, but assuming these objectives are desirable, it is still not clear that term limits are a suitable means for achieving them. Three questions arise. Would term limits achieve the desired objectives? Would they do so at an acceptable cost in terms of other American goals and values? Might the desired objectives not be better achieved by other means? The first question is strictly empirical. The other two mix the empirical and the moral.

One way in which term limits might promote deliberation is by causing some incumbent legislators—namely those serving out their final term under term limits—to think, speak, and vote differently from the way they would have thought, spoken, and voted if they had been eligible and running for re-election. In addition, for term limits to affect the behavior not just of certain individuals but of Congress as a whole, it would be necessary for any given Congress to contain a significant number of these final-term members. In other words, congressional lame ducks would have to quack differently from other ducks, and there would have to be a fair number of them on the pond.

It is impossible to be sure, but it seems unlikely that term limits would have significant effects along these lines. In the first place, existing research (along with most human experience) suggests that a final-term congressman or senator, after eleven or twelve years on Capitol Hill, would be unlikely to alter his pattern of behavior in any radical way. He might send out fewer pieces of franked mail and make fewer trips back home, but he would probably not execute many U-turns in the way he spoke and voted. In the second place, although the proportion of senators who would be in their final term under term limits would normally be large (possibly half if senators were restricted to two terms), the proportion of lame-duck congressmen would normally be much smaller (an average of sixty to seventy out of 435 if House members were limited to six terms). The cumulative impact of the lame ducks would thus be much greater in the Senate than in the House, and in both houses it would probably be felt mainly at the margins (though of course the margins can, on occasion, be important).

But those who advocate term limits in fact build very little of their case on the expected future behavior of lame ducks. Rather, they are seeking to create a wholly new class of elected representatives. George Will holds out the prospect that mandatory term limits would have the effect of replacing today's political careerists with noncareerists—in other words, of replacing today's ducks with creatures more closely resembling swans. The new legislators, because they were not careerists, would not be driven by the need to secure re-election, and for that reason they would be more likely to concern themselves with the national interest. Also because they were not political careerists, they would be more likely to have some personal, hands-on understanding of America and its real concerns.

The prospect is undoubtedly attractive. But is it realistic? Would term limits in fact diminish the number of careerists and produce legislators who were more national-minded and disinterested?

The most important difficulties with Will's hypothesis are twofold. One is that modern politics at all levels, local and state as well as national, is an immensely time-consuming, energy-consuming activity that demands enormous commitment from those who are attracted to it. Legislative sessions are long, constituents' demands are exigent, policy problems are increasingly complicated. As a result, politics all over the world, not just in the United States, is becoming professionalized. Men and women in all countries increasingly choose a political career at an early age and then stick with it. It seems likely that even under term limits the great majority of congressmen and senators would be drawn from this professional political class, which has not only the commitment to politics but also the requisite patience, skills, and contacts. To be sure, people's political careers would take a different shape; but they would still be political careers.

The other difficulty is the reverse of the first. Just as politics is becoming more professionalized, so is almost every other occupation. As many women in particular know to their cost, it is becoming harder and harder to take career breaks—those who jump off the ladder in any profession find it increasingly hard to jump back even to the level they were on when they left, let alone the level they would have attained had they stayed. For this reason it is hard to imagine that many upwardly mobile corporate executives or successful professionals or small-business owners would take time off to serve in Congress on a citizen-legislator basis. The citizens who sought to serve on this basis would probably be largely the rich and the old.

VOTER-PROOFING

DESPITE their differences, term limits and the proposals offered here have in common the fact that they seek major changes in America's political institutions—in some cases involving an amendment to the Constitution. But of course America's politicians are free to alter the way they behave in the context of the country's existing institutions. They can try to find alternative ways of insulating at least some aspects of policymaking from the intense campaigning and electioneering pressures they are now under.

Short of taking difficult issues out of electoral politics altogether, there are tactics that could be employed. Most of them are out of keeping with the contemporary American preferences for direct democracy, high levels of political participation, and the maximum exposure of all political processes to the public gaze; but that is precisely their strength. Bismarck is reputed to have said that there are two things one should never watch being made: sausages and laws. Both should be judged more by the end result than by the precise circumstances of their manufacture.

One available tactic might be called "the collusion of the elites." There may be occasions on which the great majority of America's politicians, in both the executive and legislative branches, are able to agree that an issue is of such overriding importance to the nation that it must be dealt with at almost any cost; that the politicians involved must therefore be prepared to set aside their ideological and other differences in the interests of finding a workable solution; and that having found a solution, they must stick together in presenting it to what may well be a disgruntled or even hostile electorate. In order to be successful, the collusion-of-elites tactic requires not only a substantial degree of bipartisanship (or, better still, nonpartisanship) but also unusually small teams of negotiators, complete secrecy (not a single ray of "sunshine" must penetrate the proceedings), and the presentation to Congress and the public of a comprehensive, all-or-nothing, take-it-or-leave-it proposal.

The number of occasions on which politicians will be prepared to set aside their ideological differences and pool their political risks in this fashion will inevitably be small. There were no signs that such a spirit might prevail when President Clinton and the Republican majorities in Congress wrangled over how to cut the budget deficit last winter. But there have been instances of the successful collusion of elites, even in relatively recent times.

One of them occurred in 1983, when representatives of President Reagan and the two party leaderships on Capitol Hill colluded to save the Social Security system, which at that time was in imminent danger of bankruptcy. Paul Light's classic account of the 1983 Social Security reform, *Artful Work* (1985), is in effect a case study of how to conduct collusion-of-elites politics and of the circumstances in which it may succeed. The so-called Gang of Seventeen that was originally put together to hammer out a deal (and was later reduced to a Gang of Nine) excluded all the more-extreme ideologues and met in circumstances of great secrecy, even using, according to one participant, "unmarked limos."

Of the Gang of Seventeen's activities, Light writes,

> The meetings seemed to inaugurate a new form of presidential-congressional government. The meetings were secret. There were no minutes or transcripts. All conversations were strictly off the record. The gang was free to discuss all of the options without fear of

political retaliation. It... [existed] completely outside of the constitutional system.

Ultimately, as Light relates, the "secret gang built a compromise, wrapped it in a bipartisan flag, and rammed it through Congress. There was no other way to move. It was government by fait accompli." It was also successful government—and none of the participants suffered electoral damage.

Another possible tactic, with many similarities to the collusion of elites, might be called "putting it into commission." If taking tough decisions is too risky politically, then get someone else to take them. If someone else cannot be found to take them, then make someone else *appear* to take them. The someone else need not be but usually will be a bipartisan or nonpartisan commission of some kind.

Such a commission, the National Commission on Social Security Reform, played a role in the passage of the 1983 act, but an even better example was the procedure adopted by Congress in 1990 for closing redundant military bases. Earlier practice had been almost a caricature of Congress's traditional decision-making process. The Secretary of Defense would propose a program of base closures. Senators and congressmen would immediately leap to the defense of targeted bases in their home states or districts. They of course had the support of their colleagues, who were threatened with or feared base closures in *their* home states or districts. Almost never did anyone manage to close any bases.

Realizing that the process was absurd and that huge sums of taxpayers' money were being wasted in keeping redundant bases open, Congress decided to protect itself from itself. It established the Defense Base Closure and Realignment Commission, which employed an extraordinarily simple formula. The Defense Secretary every two years published a list of the bases he proposed to close, together with a statement of criteria he had used in compiling his list. The commission then examined the list in light of the criteria, held public hearings, and recommended a modified list (with additions as well as deletions) to the President. The President was obliged to accept the commission's list as a whole or reject it as a whole. If, as invariably happened, he accepted it, Congress could intervene only if within forty-five legislative days it passed a bill overriding the President's decision and rejecting the whole list. This it never did.

The formula was a near miracle of voter-proofing. Members of Congress were left free to protest the closure of bases in their home districts or states, but the decision was ultimately taken by the President, who could nonetheless ascribe all blame to the commission, and all Congress had to do for the President's decision to take effect was to do nothing. In the event, hundreds of bases were closed and millions of dollars saved, but no member of Congress ever had to vote—and be seen by his constituents to be voting—in favor of closing a base near home. Beyond any question the results were in America's national interest.

It is not wholly fantastic to suppose that the President in odd-numbered years might, on the basis of advice received from a bipartisan commission, announce a list of "program eliminations," which Congress could countermand only by voting to reject the list as a whole. Presidents would probably prefer to put forward such lists at the beginning of their first term in office—or at any time during their second term—when they, at least, were not up for re-election.

A final tactic, which could also be adopted without major institutional change, might be described as "thinking big." Proposals that are put forward on a piecemeal basis can also be opposed, and in all probability defeated, on a piecemeal basis. In contrast, large-scale, broad-based proposals may have a better chance of success simply by virtue of their comprehensiveness. They can provide something for everyone—conservatives as well as liberals, deficit cutters as well as program defenders, residents of the Sun Belt as well as of the Rust Belt. Gains as well as losses can be broadcast widely. The 1983 Social Security reform and the 1986 tax reform were certainly "big thoughts" of this general type. So, in its way, was the recent base-closure program.

Tactics like these—the collusion of elites, putting issues into commission, and thinking big—all have their virtues, but they also suffer from being tactics in the pejorative as well as the descriptive sense. At bottom they are somewhat cynical devices for getting around the real difficulty, which is the hyper-responsiveness of American politicians that is induced by their having to run scared so much of the time. Although it would be harder, it would be better over the long term to confront this problem directly and try to bring about at least some of the fundamental institutional changes proposed here. The American people cannot govern themselves. They therefore need to find appropriate means of choosing representatives who can do a decent job of governing on their behalf, and that means giving the people's representatives space, time, and freedom in which to take decisions, knowing that if they get them wrong, they will be punished by the voters. In twentieth-century America the airy myths of agency democracy are precisely that: myths. What America needs today, though it does not seem to know it, is a more realistic and down-to-earth form of division-of-labor democracy.

Anthony King, a political scientist who teaches at the University of Essex, and an elections analyst for the British Broadcasting Corporation, is a regular contributor to *The Economist*.

From *The Atlantic Monthly*, January 1997, pp. 41-44, 46-48, 52-54, 56-58, 60-61. Adapted from *Running Scared: Why America's Politicians Campaign Too Much and Govern Too Little* by Anthony King. © 1997 by Free Press. Reprinted by permission of Simon & Schuster.

Leaders Should Not Follow
OPINION POLLS

"To maintain that the people, as haphazardly defined by a telephone-dialing machine and as interviewed by those beyond public accountability, should guide elected officials is nonsense."

BY ROBERT WEISSBERG

IN THE SPACE OF 50 YEARS, the public opinion poll has evolved from an occasional curiosity to a carefully heeded political force. "Bad poll numbers" can be disastrous. Nobody wants to champion unpopular schemes or seek public office when drawing single-digit name recognition in the latest survey. Even skeptical officials routinely monitor approval ratings lest tumbling figures embolden rivals. Poll-supplied numbers often shape momentous decisions. The Reagan White House spent $1,000,000 a year on polling. Pres. Bill Clinton's legislative agenda on spending the budget surplus, funding Social Security, and other key issues was shaped almost entirely by poll findings. When he discovered that his plan to make parents legally responsible for their children's crimes drew dismal numbers, it was quickly abandoned.

Is such homage to the polls wise? Pollsters certainly think so. They celebrate their accomplishments as promoting democracy, especially defending the "ordinary citizen" against the powerful. Telephone surveys, they maintain, allow once-unheard voices to force government responsiveness. Ordinary citizens seemingly echo pollsters' claims. One 1999 survey found that 80% believed the nation would benefit if leaders heeded poll results. Ninety percent expressed greater confidence in their own reasoning over what leaders believed. Two-thirds agreed with the pollsters that polls served the public interest.

We profoundly disagree—surveys *cannot* provide useful advice. It is not that numbers lie, analysts are dishonest, or people are secretive over the telephone, although these misrepresentations do occur. The surveys' shortcomings are more serious and, critically, these deficiencies are not curable under present-day conditions, if at all. What garden-variety advice solicitations uncover is generally politically irrelevant, even if respondents are absolutely honest and the highest technical standards are satisfied. The wrong opinions are being collected, and leaders following this guidance only invite trouble. Intuition or personal experiences provide a better course of action.

Let's begin by comparing polling with elections. An obvious point is that elections impose strict participatory standards. Laws about voting stipulate necessary age, citizenship, and residency qualifications plus standards of mental competence and criminal background for potential voters. Detailed registration requirements guard against fraud. These restrictive provisions are taken seriously, and violators are punished. Imagine an "Everybody welcome, no questions asked" sign on Election Day! Abolishing standards would insult democracy. Who would accept an outcome if illegal immigrants or foreign tourists cast millions of ballots?

The modern poll, by contrast, resembles a "you cannot be turned down" credit card offer. Who knows if the agreeable voice at the other end is really a citizen, over 18, or mentally competent? The interviewer can hardly verify fraudulent claims by checking proof of age, citizenship documents, or any other requirement prior to soliciting opinions. The opposite is possible as well. No doubt, millions of absolutely qualified voters are "disqualified" by interviewers if their English is limited or if they are uneasy about revealing guarded views to strangers.

The vote, unlike the survey response, is private, and this protection is legally guaranteed. The scientific pollster is absolutely correct that small samples can represent entire populations. This is beside the point, though. Random samples of people owning phones are not legally stipulated governing majorities. Governance is *only* by those legally permitted to participate, however we may draw the lines. It is bizarre to insist that *any* 1,000 people selected by a random number generator should authoritatively advise government.

The electoral process is also eminently accountable and transparent. *Everything* about it, from ballot layout to polling place location, must pass official approval. These critical details may be flawed—recall the famous Palm Beach, Fla., butterfly ballot confusion in the 2000 presidential election—but, for better or worse, these features are *publicly* controllable. If people, acting through elected officials, prefer old-style paper ballots, this can be done. Where disputes arise—again recall the Florida Circus—they are open to public inspection, even lawsuits. In fact, the disgruntled have endlessly petitioned legislatures and judges to act, and it is inconceivable that any U.S. election official would secretly try to gain advantage without risking public reprimand.

The contrast with polling is, again, enormous. Polling (with scant exception) is a private, commercial enterprise. Everything is negotiated between the paying client and the private firm, and is ultimately owned by the client. *Zero* public scrutiny attends this process, and, should the public peek behind the curtain, it still remains powerless. Pollster integrity is irrelevant: public control is the issue, not professional honesty or expertise. Analysts can make unwelcome results vanish or be quietly manipulated statistically, and everything would pass professional muster. Enraged citizens cannot demand to see the questionnaire or listen in on interviews.

What might happen to pollsters or clients "cooking" the results before passing them off as "the true popular democratic voice"? Absolutely nothing. Envision a Secretary of State who refused public oversight of absentee ballot validation or utilized a mysterious formula to "adjust" the final vote count. The uproar would be deafening, and the courts would instantly (and properly) intervene once a challenge came before them. Pollsters escape even the most minimal public regulation despite their lofty self-anointed public responsibility. Barbers and hairdressers are held to higher standards.

A different poll deficiency concerns the *quality* of this advice. Whether ordinary citizens are sufficiently wise to rule is a complicated subject, but even the most ardent popular sagacity defenders concur that the average person cannot respond intelligently when unexpectedly quizzed on dozens of issues long baffling experts. Learning about Social Security, educational testing, balancing the budgets, and untold other pollster repertory items is no small task, and to expect those suddenly picking up the telephone to be well-prepared is utter fantasy. Thoughtful survey firms should at least provide advance warning so information could be gathered, mail off some balanced background material, or offer on-the-spot tutorials. Alas, this vital service is almost never provided, and if some additional facts are supplied, they are merely gross simplifications of hugely complex issues.

Compounding this lack of preparation is that the questions themselves seldom permit informed respondents to render intelligent advice. By commercial necessity, modern polling must produce instant results by reducing complicated, multifaceted issues to a few crude alternatives. Queries about the military budget typically focus on "increasing/decreasing/or no change" spending choices. No room exists for more-sophisticated respondents who might want to cut some expenditures while expanding others. Nor does this typical question permit well-versed advice that reflects actual conditions—for example, increasing spending provided certain bellicose dictators remain in power, but otherwise seek reductions. Worse, this commonplace format *never* asks for specific dollar figures. Two people can agree on cutting Pentagon budgets, but one desires a modest $100,000,000 largely symbolic cut while the other prefers lopping off $200,000,000,000. This numerical difference is critical politically, but disappears when the public's "voice" is crudely transmitted via the poll.

What makes the pollsters' celebration of poll-solicited advice especially odd is that they certainly know the public's limitations. Surveys relentlessly confirm public ignorance beyond the most obvious. This is particularly true when wrestling with specific policies, even though these have long been newsworthy. Poll after poll reveals majorities poorly informed about tax rates, entitlement programs, and legislative proposals, although, to be sure, opinions on these topics are readily offered. This pessimistic assessment has less to do with innate cognitive capacity than the irrelevancy of most political debates from daily life. People pay attention to what matters and, for most of them, the topics raised by interviewers can safely be ignored.

Pollster ignorance

The poll's inadequacy of providing sound advice is made even worse by pollster ignorance. Poll question writers are expert in drafting questionnaires, not the policy at hand. To expect otherwise is unrealistic given commercial survey cost constraints. Not even Gallup could hire learned experts to consult on each of hundreds of questions. The upshot is that the array of permissible answers inevitably reflects the imperfect worldview of a policy amateur, and often an inadequate view at that. If the respondent rejects this imposed framework or these options have little to do with actual government choices, the re-

sults—no matter how honest and sincere—are politically meaningless. Irrelevant questions beget beside-the-point answers.

A particularly glaring, though hardly extreme, inappropriateness example comes from a professionally executed poll asking about ending world hunger. The question was framed in terms of increasing foreign aid to cut world hunger in half by 2014. The public's response was heartfelt support (83% favored it), and programs to assist children and women were particularly popular. Even though respondents usually expressed reservations about foreign aid, most still wanted sharp increases in national generosity (boosting outlays by a factor of 10, no less!). On its face, then, the poll's message is clear: Washington should be more bighearted in eliminating overseas famine. What could possibly be ambiguous about this message?

Plenty could be. For one, astute observers of world hunger might argue that the problem is not one of donating food for the famished. A more-daunting quandary may be convincing host governments to permit this humanitarian intervention or supplying the infrastructure necessary to promote self-sufficiency. There are also momentous political problems having little to do with airlifting wheat to famine-stricken regions—for instance, ending wars in which starvation is a military tactic. More telling, such generosity may make matters worse by destroying local agriculture and breeding permanent dependency. How can local farmers compete against free food? *Genuine* assistance might mean withholding foodstuff while demanding the necessary political and economic reforms to prevent future catastrophes. In other words, the question writer's off-the-top-of-the-head opinions to the contrary, starvation is not really a foreign aid issue, and those who grasp this fact are totally "lost" in this survey.

Our last qualm regarding poll-solicited public counsel concerns the fundamental disjunction between economic reality and the poll-supplied reality. Simply put, by rejecting economics, polls facilitate fantasy. Consider supermarket shopping. Certain absolutely inescapable facts attend this journey. First, acquiring food is not free, so better bring money, but not one's entire fortune, since there are also rent, car payments, etc. Second, though one might covet everything in the aisles, budgetary constraints may mandate picking and choosing—buying expensive T-bone steaks forgoes other essential edibles. Third, each additional item's marginal value must be calculated. Hamburger may be on sale for an incredible 69 cents a pound, but blowing every last nickel on 300 pounds of chopped beef is stupid. Finally, risk and liabilities must be appraised—skip rancid hamburger regardless of its cheap price.

Polls are oblivious to these clear economic limits. When shopping for government policies via the survey, consumers are wonderfully free. When offered government-provided health care, more schools, assistance to senior citizens, and/or cleaner environments, the entire menu is easily purchased. Unlike the prudent shopper, the survey respondent need not fret about costs (and no bill is sent). Nobody is forced to choose among competing benefits, nor are respondents told that buying more and more may mean progressively less value received. When embracing such skyrocketing government spending, nobody remembers that 300 pounds of hamburger can be a liability. To make this gluttony even more pleasurable, dangers are banished from the poll-created universe. Respondents are not told, for example, that Washington's bounteousness toward local education may load more red tape onto already overburdened schools or distort educational objectives. Nor is anybody informed that higher taxes mean less personal choice for acquiring identical benefits. Drug manufacturers should enjoy such freedom from listing potentially dangerous side effects in advertising their panaceas.

This obliviousness to inescapable economics is not a nefarious pollster plot to entice Americans to "buy" dubious government-supplied nostrums. Some analysts may welcome this benevolence given their liberal bents, but ideological bias is hardly the chief culprit. More relevant is that the modern poll, for all of its scientific paraphernalia and claims of exactitude, *cannot* insert credible economic checks into the standard telephone interview. Like any instrument, the poll can perform only so much. The interviewer is not the IRS, which can compel payment for desired government services. The brief telephone interview is also incapable of permitting respondents to make realistic trade-offs, calculating benefits vs. costs, and including all the other ingredients necessary for sensible decisionmaking. While, in principle, a policy's downside can be explained, this is often impractical given typical respondent attention spans. There is also the quandary of deciding what, exactly, constitute a proposal's genuine risks, no small matter given future uncertainties. All in all, then, to expect sound advice when polling citizens about what government should do is unreasonable.

Our argument has focused on a single aspect of polling—its use to solicit policy advice from ordinary citizens. Even though we believe that this invariably invites foolishness, we are *not* attacking polls per se. The debate concerns appropriateness. To maintain that the people, as haphazardly defined by a telephone-dialing machine and as interviewed by those beyond public unaccountability, should guide elected officials is nonsense. Moreover, no government, no matter how attentive to public opinion, can possibly satisfy people unencumbered by the most-elementary economic constraints. These poll-formulated solicitations invite bankruptcy. It would be the equivalent of turning the space program over to engineers who disbelieve the laws of physics.

The opinion poll's proper role is assessing public *opinion*. Opinions differ fundamentally from advice in their standards. Everyone has a valid opinion: not everyone can offer sound advice. If our doctor says that the Beatles were the best rock-and-roll group ever, who can argue, or even insist upon documentation? It is quite different, however, if one's physician counsels sacrificing chickens to cure pneumonia. The standards for advice are infinitely higher, and, by these tough standards, most Americans are ill-prepared to render expert snap judgments about matters of national significance beyond their expertise. Let us not confuse flattering popular wisdom with gaining something of value.

Robert Weissberg is professor of political science, University of Illinois at Urbana-Champaign.

From *USA Today* magazine (Society for the Advancement of Education), May 2002, pp. 10-11. © 2002 by the Society for the Advancement of Education.

Government's End

THE REFORMERS IN THE '80S AND '90S TRIED TO PULL THE FEDERAL GOVERNMENT TO THE RIGHT OR THE LEFT. BUT, IN THE END, THEY DID NOT REMAKE GOVERNMENT. IT REMADE THEM.

By Jonathan Rauch

Since 1980, three waves of reformers have sought to transform American government. None succeeded. What went wrong? And what does it mean? In his new book Government's End: Why Washington Stopped Working—*extensively revised since its first publication in 1994 as* Demosclerosis—*National Journal senior writer Jonathan Rauch suggests an answer: The American public, having accepted limits on government's ability to change society, must now also accept equally exacting limits on society's ability to change government. An adapted excerpt follows.*

To look back upon the 1980s and 1990s is to see what appears to be, at first blush, a period of quietude following the social and political storms of the 1960s and 1970s. The Reagan and Clinton years brought fiscal wars over deficits and culture wars over abortion and political correctness, but no Vietnam, no stagflation, no dogs and fire hoses in Alabama, and no chilling confrontations between democracy and totalitarianism. Intellectuals often complained that the Reagan period was complacent and vacuous, and that the Clinton years brought the abandonment of the activist spirit that once had energized American liberalism. The appearance, though, was partly deceiving. If American society was calmer after the 1970s, American government decidedly was not, for discontent with society had been displaced by discontent with government.

The era beginning in 1981 and ending, perhaps, in 1996 marks the most concentrated period of governmental reformism since the Progressives swept to power in Washington and in the cities nearly a century earlier. There was, however, a difference. The Progressives largely succeeded in breaking the old cronyist machines and replacing them with a class of professional administrators and a "clean government" ethic (with mixed effects, by the way). The reformers in the Reagan-to-Clinton years failed. They did not remake government; it remade them.

For the Progressives, the problem had been corruption and greed and the heavy hands of the bosses, who favored friends and shut out adversaries and thereby (in the view of the day) created political monopolies as damaging to the public good as were the great economic trusts. More openness, more access, and above all more professionalism were the answers. By 1981, when President Reagan took office, the Progressive formula had been turned on its head, although at that point few people realized the extent of the change. America's government was easily among the cleanest in the world or, indeed, in history. Endless safeguards of bureaucratic procedure and legal due process ensured that any decision that was deemed arbitrary or unfair could be challenged, first in administrative rulemaking, then in court, and finally in Congress. The civil service had been professionalized—and so, more recently and probably more importantly, had been the political class. It was now not only possible but common to be a full-time, professional lobbyist or political consultant.

And access? It was copious, redundant—so copious and redundant as to transform Washington itself into the site of a bidding war. With the old congressional seniority system weakened by the post-Watergate reformers of the 1970s, Congress now consisted of 535 individual entrepreneurs, each member chosen independently of party and president, each member a canny survivalist who could be asked to follow where the committee chairman or whip led but who could not be required to do so. For the (now) countless thousands of groups that professionally worked Washington, this meant that what you did not get from one member of Congress you could seek from another. The relationship worked the other way, too. When the politicians came calling on the lobbies for campaign money, as they did with growing brazenness, each group knew there were plenty of other lobbies, often competitors and adversaries, eager to help. If the Banking Committee chairman did not get what he wanted from the American Bankers Association, why, the credit union people or S&L people or insurance people or securities people were only too willing to step into the breach. The culture of government, by 1981, was honest and professional and astonishingly transparent; no one hid anything. But the economics of government, by then, was that of a piranha pool, with thousands of small but sharp-toothed and very strongly motivated actors determined not to be the loser at the end of the day. Every actor's activity, of course, drew in yet more actors. The Maryland state lottery, once ran an ad campaign on the theme "If you don't play, you can't win." By the 1980s, Washington had become a kind of demented casino, whose slogan was "If you don't play, you can't win—but boy, can you lose!" Not surprisingly, everybody played.

PUSH, PULL:
With his ambitious health reform plan, Bill Clinton tried to move government to the left. With his Contract With America, Newt Gingrich tried to move it to the right. Both failed.

The public, of course, was angry and disillusioned by 1981. The "trust in government" barometer had collapsed since the early 1960s. Confidence in government had been replaced with cynicism and suspicion. Among conservatives, a reform movement had arisen, in tandem with the change in the government itself. The movement was not progressivism so much as regressivism, but it was equipped with a powerful and sweeping critique of government and with a grand architecture of reform. Some liberals, too, dreamed of sweeping change. Ironically, however, although the liberal reformers and conservative reformers vied to pull Washington in opposite directions, they would soon discover they were trapped together like antagonistic prisoners thrown into the same cell. Both were mostly helpless.

If you view Washington's problems as superficial and transitory—the result of having elected this or that president, or of divided partisan control of government, or

what have you—then the answer should be to elect some new leader or to consolidate power. If you think the problem is that the politicians are all the same, all empty suits wedded to the status quo, then the solution should be to elect some revolutionaries who will shake things up. If you think the problem is that reform in one direction simply goes the wrong way, then the right approach should be to try reform in the opposite direction.

As it turned out, the era of reform proved to be a uniquely useful natural laboratory for diagnosing government's condition, because many of the available permutations were tried. First the Republicans enjoyed effective control of both Congress and the White House, then the Democrats controlled both branches, and then control was divided. Far from electing empty suits, the voters on three occasions brought in strikingly fresh and energetic leaders, leaders who fervently believed in reform and who spared no effort to make it happen. And far from standing pat in moderation, the reform efforts lurched in two opposite directions. Reagan and House Speaker Newt Gingrich had pulled to the right, and had mostly failed (with a few important exceptions, such as Reagan's tax reform and Gingrich's welfare reform); Bill Clinton, with his sweeping health-care reform, had pulled to the left, but fared no better.

Yet, by the end of the 1990s, the reform era had subsided into exhaustion. The voters seemed to have given up, and there was no viable reform movement anywhere in sight. The battlefield was empty, the Bastille untaken, and the adversary little more than inconvenienced. In fact, the Washington establishment was fatter and happier than ever.

A Revolutionary's Blueprint

Of the reformers, none showed more energy and promise than Newt Gingrich. In hindsight (always the most discerning kind of vision), Gingrich seems to have been an overweening idealist who pushed his luck too far. But defeat appears inevitable only after the war. Gingrich did not enter office as House speaker without a plan. He explained it in January 1995, and it was not a stupid plan.

Gingrich was no newcomer. He went in with his eyes wide open. The power structure on Capitol Hill, he told *The Washington Times* as he assumed the speakership, had "ossified into a straitjacket. That is not partisan or ideological—these guys and their staffs had networks of power and networks of relationships and habits and things that they weren't going to break for a mere president. They'd ignored Nixon, Ford, Carter. They had blocked Reagan and beaten Bush." Moreover, "every time you mention something which ought to be shrunk or zeroed, twenty-five people who are making money off of it jump up to explain why it is a wonderful institution and they should continue to make money off it."

Gingrich's response, his battle plan, is instructive, because on paper it was plausible. First, he would mobilize his supporters, the fiery voters who had demolished Democrats and tossed out a reigning House speaker to put Gingrich and his reformers in charge. "The point we're going to make to people is, you'd better call your representative and tell them you want them to help pass the constitutional amendment to require a balanced budget—with a tax-increase limit. We're going to use every bully pulpit we have…. And we're going to tell every conservative group in the country and every group that wants smaller government, you'd better talk to your representatives." The intensity of the government reformers was high, Gingrich knew, so they could mobilize some of the same merciless spot pressure as the interest groups.

As for the Democrats, the 1994 election had thrown them into disarray. The president sounded chagrined, humbled, the wind knocked out of him. "I agree with much of what the electorate said yesterday," he said the day after the election. "They still believe that government is more often the problem than the solution. They don't want any party to be the party of government. They don't want the presumption to be that people in Washington know what's best…. I accept responsibility for not delivering to whatever extent it's my fault we haven't delivered." This humbled president would still wield a veto, but he would be presented with a stream of bills passed on the Republicans' terms in the wake of an election that had given them a mandate. If he refused to deal, he would risk seeming obstructive and deaf to the voters' demands. Anyway (said the Republicans to themselves), this was not a president who had shown a lot of backbone.

The lobbies, of course, could be counted upon to try to block or emasculate everything. Gingrich's response: swamp them. Attack so many programs at once that the Democrats and liberals and establishmentarians would have to choose the programs they wanted to save. The rest, the Republicans would knock off. The Democrats would have to "figure out which fights to stay and fight," Gingrich said. Gingrich was hoping to invert the usual Washington pattern, in which reformers were required to focus their energies on a few programs and let the rest of their agenda slide away. By attacking on a broad front, he would force the *defenders* to concentrate their fire. The Republicans would not get everything, but they would get a great deal.

Finally, Gingrich knew that at each stage of the process—House deliberations, Senate deliberations, House-Senate conferences, negotiations with the White House, presidential vetoes—he would lose bits and pieces of his agenda. A month or a year wouldn't be enough, a point he went out of his way to emphasize. Instead, he would start in 1995, running a flying wedge through the Washington power structure, and then come back again and again after that, widening the breach. There could be no "Mao-style revolution," he said. "I want to get to a dramatically smaller federal government. I think you do that one step at a time, but you insist on steps every year…. The reason I keep telling people to study FDR is if you take fourteen steps successfully you're a lot farther down the road than this guy next to you if he's trying to get all fourteen steps in one jump."

The trouble was, of course, that he never got to the second step. Why?

The Paradox Of Particulars

Voters in the polling booth vote for "change" in the abstract. But presidents and members of Congress can't. "In Congress, we don't get to vote on the abstraction," Republican Rep. Vin Weber of Minnesota told Time Magazine in 1992, shortly before retiring from office. "We have to vote for or against actual programs." That means confronting actual constituencies. Gingrich's hope to invert this equation foundered on the fact that in the case of any *particular* program or subsidy or perquisite of whatever sort, there is almost always far more energy on the defensive side than on the offensive side.

Say someone in Gingrich's position as a House leader hoped to reform or abolish a thousand programs. No one of those programs is essential to his effort. If he must, he can always drop twenty or thirty or even a hundred or two. There is no overwhelming incentive to go after any particular constituency. To the defender of the subsidy for left-handed screwdrivers, however, only *one* program matters: his own. He will spare no effort. For that defender, and for each of the others, it's life or death.

TRUE TO FORM:
The public wants the government to be leaner, but not at the expense of students, farmers, bankers, workers, veterans, retirees.

Gingrich understood this but thought he could count on his zealous Republicans to hold the line across a broad front. The discipline he was expecting, however, was superhuman. The temptation to help out this one group, or that one, was not Democratic or liberal; it was universal. After all, the clients understood that if one congressman would not help them, another might. Every congressman understood this, too. Why let someone else do the rescuing and take the credit? And every congressman also understood that every other congressman understood. And so, at every stage in the process, Democrats *and* Republicans demanded that this or that program be let off the hook. "I'd love to support you, Mr. Speaker, but I tell you, I am just taking a beating from those left-handed screwdriver people in my district—you've got to cut me a break." Facing this inevitable onslaught, Gingrich found that it was he and his reformers, not the Democrats or liberals, who were swamped.

HARRY AND LOUISE:
With their narrow focus, lobbies are adept at defending themselves with "red alert" mailings and scary television ads.

David Stockman, Reagan's reformist budget director, had run into the same problem, and had reacted with contempt for the gutless Republicans who were all for cutting government except the bits they wanted to save. Stockman, however, missed the point: Given the calculus of the game, the gutless Republicans were doing the only rational thing. The same sort of calculus had wrecked Clinton's health-care package in 1994. In fact, what was remarkable in 1995, arguably, was not how much the reform package was watered down in Gingrich's House (with significant program terminations shrinking by a factor of ten) but how large a tattered remnant actually survived.

Gingrich understood the importance of public mobilization. He counted on it to push his program past the Democrats and Clinton. In Gingrich's case, and also in Stockman's and Clinton's, the reformers depended on the public to rally around when political hackery began to prevail over the spirit of reform. And, sure enough, the public always did rally—but *to the wrong side*.

It turns out to be surprisingly easy for the protectors of programs to spook the public by screaming bloody murder. The public wants the government to be leaner, but not at the expense of students, farmers, bankers, workers, veterans, retirees, homeowners, artists, teachers, train riders, or cats and dogs. The people cannot abide the ghoulish shrieks and moans that are heard the moment the reformers' scalpel comes out. The same narrow focus and intense commitment that make lobbies so adept at defending themselves on Capitol Hill also make them good at alarming the public with "red alert" mailings and scary television ads (as with "Harry and Louise"). When all else fails, there is the old "Don't hurt our children" ploy. In 1993, when Congress managed to abolish the wool and mohair subsidy, the reformers were all the more courageous for having faced down pleas like the one from Nelda Corbell, whose parents raised mohair in Texas: "I am eight years old and I want to know why the government wants to take away our living." What kind of monster would hurt little Nelda?

Now and then, politicians manage to turn public opinion against a particular lobby, or at least they manage to exploit a change in public opinion, as the tobacco lobby found out. But usually they can't even do that. In his 1996 presidential campaign, when Bob Dole tried to mobilize public sentiment against the teachers' unions, he was judged quixotic. The public is nervous, often rightly, when politicians try to demonize some faction or other. Public nervousness makes the climate of opinion flammable; all that remains is to light a spark.

CHOP, CHOP:
With the help of Stockman, Reagan tried to cut government programs, but encountered GOP resistance.

Rational Paranoia

In May 1981, President Reagan, on Stockman's advice, proposed a package of modest reductions in Social Security: reduced benefits for early retirees, a three-month delay in the cost-of-living adjustment, and so forth. The result was what Congressional Quarterly described as a "tempest in Congress." The Democrats until then had been helpless against Stockman, but they knew that this time he had stumbled onto vulnerable ground. The House Democratic caucus promptly and unanimously passed a resolution denouncing Reagan's "unconscionable breach of faith" and swearing not to "destroy the program or a generation of retirees." Democrats in the Senate promised to use "every rule in the book" to stop the proposal. "Democrats waged their assault with obvious glee," said Congressional Quarterly, and they kept waging it through the 1982 elections, when they gained twenty-six seats in the House and regained effective control there. Painting Reagan and the Republicans as scourges of Social Security received a good deal of the credit (the economic recession received most of the rest).

In 1995, Newt Gingrich's Republicans, responsibly and courageously, undertook to propose some modest but significant reforms of the Medicare program for the elderly. That the program's finances were in trouble, and that reductions would have to be made one way or another, were facts known to everybody in Washington, including President Clinton. He proposed reducing the growth of Medicare's costs from more than 4 percent a year for six years to 2.7 percent. The Republican plan, in not exactly sharp contrast, proposed reducing the growth path to 1.5 percent, with some larger structural reforms than Clinton preferred. In dollars, the difference between the plans was about 7 percent in the last year, 2002. But that was enough for the Democrats. Through the 1996 campaigns, they hammered the Republicans for "cutting" Medicare. "The Republicans are wrong to want to cut

Medicare benefits," a voice-over intoned in one Democratic ad, as the faces of Bob Dole and Newt Gingrich danced on the screen. "And President Clinton is right to protect Medicare, right to defend our decision as a nation to do what's moral, good, and right by our elderly." The campaign became known as Mediscare, and it was accounted a great success. The public was quite willing to believe that Gingrich and his crew were out to gut Medicare. Despite their pleas of innocence, the Republicans never recovered.

In 1993, Bill Clinton proposed his health-care reform package. In 1994 came the "Harry and Louise" ads and plenty of others like them. Again, opponents had little trouble arousing public hostility to reform. So the trick works for both parties.

It works, you may say, because the public is ignorant and easily frightened. That explanation is right, to some extent. But it fails to give the public quite enough credit, because the public's suspicions were rational in each case. When the Gingrichites tried to make changes in Medicare, they plausibly argued that the (small) pain they were imposing on one group would be more than offset by the benefits to everybody from lower deficits, lower taxes, and a solvent Medicare program. But at that stage, the Democrats and the lobbies, acting as a swing vote, did exactly as the playbook suggests. They recast the debate as group versus group rather than as group versus nation. They stood on a box with a megaphone and warned: "Don't believe those Republicans! They're not going to give anything back to you once they've cut Medicare. They're financing tax cuts for the rich! They're just taking from you to give to their friends!"

Most Americans will sacrifice for a larger public good, but few will sacrifice for a competing group. The larger public loses interest in reducing Medicare, or in reducing anything else, if it believes that the only result will be to shift resources from one group to another. By kindling suspicions that the Republicans were acting in the interests of their favorite clients rather than of the nation as a whole, the Democrats and their allied lobbies had no trouble sinking the Republicans' Medicare deal. On health reform, the Republicans and the plan's other opponents used the same tactic against Clinton and the Democrats. "This plan doesn't mean more care at lower prices," they said. "It means poorer care for you and better care for other people, with huge new bureaucracies in the bargain."

Alas, this trick of kindling mistrust can almost always be used by somebody, because the charges, though overdrawn and often misleading, are usually plausible and partly true. The Republicans *were* trying to cut Medicare while also reducing taxes for better-off citizens. The Democrats *were* relying on bureaucratic controls to constrain choices for the middle class and expand health access for the poor. In 1981, the Reagan administration *was* trying to use Social Security reductions to help pay for upper-class tax cuts. In a democracy, parties do not get things done

(or win elections) unless they favor their supporters, which means that the other side of any argument can always cry foul. And the voters' cynicism, which admittedly is often justified, makes them quick to believe charges that the system will double-cross them. The cynicism, of course, is self-fulfilling.

So here is the conundrum of collective political action. If you assume that everyone else will act in his rational self-interest, you have every reason to support politicians who put dollars or benefits or protections in your pocket, and little or no reason to support politicians who remove them. Although it is certainly possible to neutralize the opposition party and divide the lobbies and win the public's support, no sensible politician or voter ought to expect it to happen. Far more likely is the fate of the reformers of the 1980s and 1990s, who found themselves, after starting out well, suddenly staring at a coalition of opponents that comprised the opposition party, the lobbies, and the broad public. Against that array of forces, there is simply no hope. Reformers are crushed.

ON GUARD:
Lobbyists have been succesful in perpetuating a stalemate. The borders of the jungle are more or less set.

In the movie *The African Queen*, a famous scene has the protagonists' boat hopelessly stuck in a marsh—only a few yards, it turns out, from open water. Today's government is in a similar plight. Dissatisfaction ought, by rights, to open the path to comprehensive change. But it does not. The *African Queen* was lifted from the quagmire by the tide. But in the case of the American government, the boat cannot be lifted. The government is, of its nature, inseparable and inalienable from the million commitments it has made and the million interest groups it has spawned. They now form its environment. It cannot lift itself above them. With the replacement of Carter with Reagan, Bush with Clinton, and Clinton (for a while) with Gingrich, the restive electorate outside Washington showed that it could still radicalize politics, at least temporarily, and shake the very ground of the capital. Notwithstanding all the little gray groups and politicians and lobbyists and claques that occupy and ossify the government, the broad electorate proved more than able to coil itself and strike back. What was lacking in the system was not energy or leadership but the ability to focus reformist energy on any *particular* program of reform. Converting the electorate's shuddering waves of discontent into the hundreds or thousands of alterations to programs affecting specific groups is like converting earthquake energy into steam power: possible in theory but elusive in practice.

Borders of the Jungle

In ideological terms, conservatives see government as properly a guarantor of individual rights, and possibly also as a watchman for the interests of enterprise. For 150 years or so, American government conformed largely to their vision. By today's standards, it was very small and very weak, and the country's many associations were of the voluntary, nonlobbying kind that were familiar to Alexis de Tocqueville in the 1830s.

Liberals see government as properly a solver of national problems, and possibly also as a builder of a more nearly ideal society. For thirty or forty or fifty years, beginning around the time of the New Deal, the liberals had their day: The government was ambitious, undertook all sorts of commitments to pensioners and veterans and students and consumers, and seemed often successful in meeting them. But with the growth of the programs came the dense jungle of modern Washington, with all its burrowing and flying and stinging creatures; and with the growing perception of the failure—with farmers being paid not to grow food, the welfare culture expanding, the tax code becoming spaghetti, lawyers and lobbyists overrunning Washington, inflation, deficits, bureaucracies—came the backlash and the era of reform.

And now, at last, comes this, what you see around you: the perpetual stalemate of evolutionary equilibrium, in which the clients and the calculus of collective action will not allow the government to become much smaller or to reorganize its basic functions, while the taxpayers will not suffer it to grow much bigger. The borders of the jungle are more or less as they will be. From a distance, in macrocosm, the jungle seems an immovable mass, unchanging from year to year and impenetrably dense, whereas up very close, in microcosm, it is a constant turmoil of digging and scurrying and eating and mating. But it exists primarily to survive from year to year and to feed its clients. Its clients—we—draw sustenance from it but yield control.

In the end, it is not the conservative vision of government or the liberal vision that prevailed. It is no vision at all that prevailed. The client groups prevailed. And that is the end of government. To see the future, look around.

ASSOCIATIONS WITHOUT MEMBERS

BY THEDA SKOCPOL

In just a third of a century, Americans have dramatically changed their style of civic and political association. A civic world once centered in locally rooted and nationally active membership associations is a relic. Today, Americans volunteer for causes and projects, but only rarely as ongoing members. They send checks to service and advocacy groups run by professionals, often funded by foundations or professional fund-raisers. Prime-time airways echo with debates among their spokespersons: the National Abortion Rights Action League debates the National Right to Life Committee; the Concord Coalition takes on the American Association of Retired Persons; and the Environmental Defense Fund counters business groups. Entertained or bemused, disengaged viewers watch as polarized advocates debate.

The largest membership groups of the 1950s were old-line and well-established, with founding dates ranging from 1733 for the Masons to 1939 for the Woman's Division of Christian Service (a Methodist women's association formed from "missionary" societies with nineteenth-century roots). Like most large membership associations throughout American history, most 1950s associations recruited members across class lines. They held regular local meetings and convened periodic assemblies of elected leaders and delegates at the state, regional, or national levels. Engaged in multiple rather than narrowly specialized pursuits, many associations combined social or ritual activities with community service, mutual aid, and involvement in national affairs. Patriotism was a leitmotif; during and after World War II, a passionate and victorious national endeavor, these associations sharply expanded their memberships and renewed the vigor of their local and national activities.

To be sure, very large associations were not the only membership federations that mattered in postwar America. Also prominent were somewhat smaller, elite-dominated civic groups—including male service groups like Rotary, Lions, and Kiwanis, and longstanding female groups like the American Association of University Women and the League of Women Voters. Dozens of ethnically based fraternal and cultural associations flourished, as did African-American fraternal groups like the Prince Hall Masons and the Improved Benevolent and Protective Order of Elks of the World.

For many membership federations, this was a golden era of national as well as community impact. Popularly rooted membership federations rivaled professional and business associations for influence in policy debates. The AFL-CIO was in the thick of struggles about economic and social policies; the American Legion and the Veterans of Foreign Wars advanced veterans' programs; the American Farm Bureau Federation (AFBF) joined other farmers' associations to influence national and state agricultural policies; and the National Congress of Parents and Teachers (PTA) and the General Federation of Women's Clubs were influential on educational, health, and family issues. The results could be decisive, as exemplified by the pivotal role of the American Legion in drafting and lobbying for the GI Bill of 1944.

Then, suddenly, old-line membership federations seemed passé. Upheavals shook America during "the long 1960s," stretching from the mid-1950s through the mid-1970s. The southern Civil Rights movement challenged white racial domination and spurred legislation to enforce legal equality and voting rights for African Americans. Inspired by Civil Rights achievements, additional "rights" movements exploded, promoting equality for women, dignity for homosexuals, the unionization of farm workers, and the mobilization of other nonwhite ethnic minorities. Movements arose to oppose U.S. involvement in the war in Vietnam, champion a new environmentalism, and further other public causes. At the forefront of these groundswells were younger Americans, especially from the growing ranks of college students and university graduates.

The great social movements of the long 1960s were propelled by combinations of grassroots protest, activist radicalism, and professionally led efforts to lobby government and educate the public. Some older membership associations ended up participating and expanding their bases of support, yet the groups that sparked movements were more agile and flexibly structured than pre-existing membership federations.

> # The model of civic effectiveness has been upended since the 1960s. Activist groups no longer need actual members.

The upheavals of the 1960s could have left behind a reconfigured civic world, in which some old-line membership associations had declined but others had reoriented and reenergized themselves. Within each great social movement, memberships could have consolidated and groups coalesced into new omnibus federations able to link the grass roots to state, regional, and national leaderships, allowing longstanding American civic traditions to continue in new ways.

But this is not what happened. Instead, the 1960s, 1970s, and 1980s brought extraordinary organizational proliferation and professionalization. At the national level alone, the *Encyclopedia of Associations* listed approximately 6,500 associations in 1958. This total grew by 1990 to almost 23,000. Within the expanding group universe, moreover, new kinds of associations came to the fore: relatively centralized and professionally led organizations focused on policy lobbying and public education.

Another wave of the advocacy explosion involved "public interest" or "citizens'" groups seeking to shape public opinion and influence legislation. Citizens' advocacy groups espouse "causes" ranging from environmental protection (for example, the Sierra Club and the Environmental Defense Fund), to the well-being of poor children (the Children's Defense Fund), to reforming politics (Common Cause) and cutting public entitlements (the Concord Coalition).

THE FORTUNES OF MEMBERSHIP ASSOCIATIONS

As the associational explosions of 1960 to 1990 took off, America's once large and confident membership federations were not only bypassed in national politics; they also dwindled as locally rooted participant groups. To be sure, some membership associations have been founded or expanded in recent de-

cades. By far the largest is the American Association of Retired Persons (AARP), which now boasts more than 33 million adherents, about one-half of all Americans aged 50 or older. But AARP is not a democratically controlled organization. Launched in 1958 with backing from a teachers' retirement group and an insurance company, the AARP grew rapidly in the 1970s and 1980s by offering commercial discounts to members and establishing a Washington headquarters to monitor and lobby about federal legislation affecting seniors. The AARP has a legislative and policy staff of 165 people, 28 registered lobbyists, and more than 1,200 staff members in the field. After recent efforts to expand its regional and local infrastructure, the AARP involves about 5 to 10 percent of its members in (undemocratic) membership chapters. But for the most part, the AARP national office—covering an entire city block with its own zip code—deals with masses of individual adherents through the mail.

Four additional recently expanded membership associations use modern mass recruitment methods, yet are also rooted in local and state units. Interestingly, these groups are heavily involved in partisan electoral politics. Two recently launched groups are the National Right to Life Committee (founded in 1973) and the Christian Coalition (founded in 1989). They bridge from church congregations, through which they recruit members and activists, to the conservative wing of the Republican Party, through which they exercise political influence. Two old-line membership federations—the National Education Association (founded in 1857) and the National Rifle Association (founded in 1871)—experienced explosive growth after reorienting themselves to take part in partisan politics. The NRA expanded in the 1970s, when right-wing activists opposed to gun control changed what had traditionally been a network of marksmen's clubs into a conservative, Republican-leaning advocacy group fiercely opposed to gun control legislation. During the same period, the NEA burgeoned from a relatively elitist association of public educators into a quasi-union for public school teachers and a stalwart in local, state, and national Democratic Party politics.

Although they fall short of enrolling 1 percent of the adult population, some additional chapter-based membership associations were fueled by the social movements of the 1960s and 1970s. From 1960 to 1990, the Sierra Club (originally created in 1892) ballooned from some 15,000 members to 565,000 members meeting in 378 "local groups." And the National Audubon Society (founded in 1905) went from 30,000 members and 330 chapters in 1958 to about 600,000 members and more than 500 chapters in the 1990s. The National Organization for Women (NOW) reached 1,122 members and 14 chapters within a year of its founding in 1966, and spread across all 50 states with some 125,000 members meeting in 700 chapters by 1978. But notice that these "1960s" movement associations do not match the organizational scope of old-line membership federations. At its post-World War II high point in 1955, for example, the General Federation of Women's Clubs boasted more than 826,000 members meeting in 15,168 local clubs, themselves divided into representative networks within each of the 50 states plus the District of Columbia. By contrast, at its high point in 1993, NOW reported some 280,000 members and 800 chapters, with no intermediate tier of representative governance between the national center and local chapters. These membership associations certainly matter, but mainly as counterexamples to dominant associational trends—of organizations without members.

After nearly a century of civic life rooted in nation-spanning membership federations, why was America's associational universe so transformed? A variety of factors have contributed, including racial and gender change; shifts in the political opportunity structure; new techniques and models for building organizations; and recent transformations in U.S. class relations. Taken together, I suggest, these account for civic America's abrupt and momentous transition from membership to advocacy.

SOCIETY DECOMPARTMENTALIZED

Until recent times, most American membership associations enrolled business and professional people together with white-collar folks, farmers, and craft or industrial workers. There was a degree of fellowship across class lines—yet at the price of other kinds of exclusions. With only a few exceptions, old-line associations enrolled either men or women, not both together (although male-only fraternal and veterans' groups often had ties to ladies' auxiliaries). Racial separation was also the rule. Although African Americans did manage to create and greatly expand fraternal associations of their own, they unquestionably resented exclusion by the parallel white fraternals.

> # The styles of civic involvement have changed, especially for women—much to the disadvantage of associations trying to hold regular meetings.

Given the pervasiveness of gender and racial separation in classic civic America, established voluntary associations were bound to be shaken after the 1950s. Moreover, changing gender roles and identities blended with other changing values to undercut not just membership appeals but long-standing routes to associational leadership. For example, values of patriotism, brotherhood, and sacrifice had been celebrated by all fraternal groups. During and after each war, the Masons, Knights of Pythias, Elks, Knights of Columbus, Moose, Eagles, and scores of other fraternal groups celebrated and memorialized the contributions of their soldier-members. So did women's auxiliaries, not to mention men's service clubs and trade union "brotherhoods." But "manly" ideals of military service faded after the early 1960s as America's bitter experiences during the war in Vietnam disrupted the intergenerational continuity of male identification with martial brotherliness.

In the past third of a century, female civic leadership has changed as much or more than male leadership. Historically, U.S. women's associations—ranging from female auxiliaries of male groups to independent groups like the General Federation of Women's Clubs, the PTA, and church-connected associations—benefited from the activism of educated wives and mothers. Although a tiny fraction of all U.S. females, higher-educated women were a surprisingly substantial and widespread presence—because the United States was a pioneer in the schooling of girls and the higher education of women. By 1880, some 40,000 American women constituted a third of all students in U.S. institutions of higher learning; women's share rose to nearly half at the early twentieth-century peak in 1920, when some 283,000 women were enrolled in institutions of higher learning. Many higher-educated women of the late 1800s and early 1900s married immediately and stayed out of the paid labor force. Others taught for a time in primary and secondary schools, then got married and stopped teaching (either voluntarily or because school systems would not employ married women). Former teachers accumulated in every community. With skills to make connections within and across communities—and some time on their hands as their children grew older—former teachers and other educated women became mainstays of classic U.S. voluntary life.

Of course, more American women than ever before are now college-educated. But contemporary educated women face new opportunities and constraints. Paid work and family responsibilities are no longer separate spheres, and the occupational structure is less sex-segregated at all levels. Today, even married women with children are very likely to be employed, at least part-time. Despite new time pressures, educated and employed women have certainly not dropped out of civic life. Women employed part-time are more likely to be members of groups or volunteers than housewives; and fully employed women are often drawn into associations or civic projects through work. Yet styles of civic involvement have changed—much to the disadvantage of broad-gauged associations trying to hold regular meetings.

THE LURE OF WASHINGTON, D.C.

The centralization of political change in Washington, D.C. also affected the associational universe. Consider the odyssey of civil rights lawyer Marian Wright Edelman. Fresh from grass-roots struggles in Mississippi, she arrived in Washington, D.C. in the late 1960s to lobby for Mississippi's Head Start program. She soon realized that arguing on behalf of children might be the best way to influence legislation and sway public sympathy in favor of the poor, including African Americans. So between 1968 and 1973 Edelman obtained funding from major foundations and developed a new advocacy and policy research association, the Children's Defense Fund (CDF). With a skillful staff, a small national network of individual supporters, ties to social service agencies and foundations, and excellent relationships with the national media, the CDF has been a determined proponent of federal antipoverty programs ever since. The CDF has also worked with Democrats and other liberal advocacy groups to expand such efforts; and during periods of conservative Republican ascendancy, the CDF has been a fierce (if not always successful) defender of federal social programs.

Activists, in short, have gone where the action is. In this same period, congressional committees and their staffs subdivided and multiplied. During the later 1970s and 1980s, the process of group formation became self-reinforcing—not only because groups arose to counter other groups, but also because groups begot more groups. Because businesses and citizens use advocacy groups to influence government outside of parties and between elections, it is not surprising that the contemporary group explosion coincides with waning voter loyalty to the two major political parties. As late as the 1950s, U.S. political parties were networks of local and state organizations through which party officials often brokered nominations, cooperated with locally rooted membership associations, and sometimes directly mobilized voters. The party structure and the associational structure were mutually reinforcing.

> **In the new electoral arena, where political parties consist largely of direct mailings and fundraisers, advocacy groups can play an influential role.**

Then, demographic shifts, reapportionment struggles, and the social upheavals of the 1960s disrupted old party organizations; and changes in party rules led to nomination elections that favored activists and candidate-centered efforts over backroom brokering by party insiders. Such "reforms" were meant to enhance grassroots participation, but in practice have furthered oligarchical ways of running elections. No longer the preserve of party organizations, U.S. campaigns are now managed by coteries of media consultants, pollsters, direct mail specialists, and—above all—fundraisers. In this revamped electoral arena, advocacy groups have much to offer, hoping to get access to elected officials in return for helping candidates. In low-turnout battles to win party nominations, even groups with modest mail

memberships may be able to field enough (paid or unpaid) activists to make a difference. At all stages of the electoral process, advocacy groups with or without members can provide endorsements that may be useful in media or direct mail efforts. And PACs pushing business interests or public interest causes can help candidates raise the huge amounts of money they need to compete.

A NEW MODEL OF ASSOCIATION-BUILDING

Classic American association-builders took it for granted that the best way to gain national influence, moral or political, was to knit together national, state, and local groups that met regularly and engaged in a degree of representative governance. Leaders who desired to speak on behalf of masses of Americans found it natural to proceed by recruiting self-renewing mass memberships and spreading a network of interactive groups. After the start-up phase, associational budgets usually depended heavily on membership dues and on sales of newsletters or supplies to members and local groups. Supporters had to be continuously recruited through social networks and person-to-person contacts. And if leverage over government was desired, an association had to be able to influence legislators, citizens, and newspapers across many districts. For all of these reasons, classic civic entrepreneurs with national ambitions moved quickly to recruit activists and members in every state and across as many towns and cities as possible within each state.

Today, nationally ambitious civic entrepreneurs proceed in quite different ways. When Marian Wright Edelman launched a new advocacy and research group to lobby for the needs of children and the poor, she turned to private foundations for funding and then recruited an expert staff of researchers and lobbyists. In the early 1970s, when John Gardner launched Common Cause as a "national citizens lobby" demanding governmental reforms, he arranged for start-up contributions from several wealthy friends, contacted reporters in the national media, and purchased mailing lists to solicit masses of members giving modest monetary contributions. Patron grants, direct mail techniques, and the capacity to convey images and messages through the mass media have changed the realities of organization building and maintenance.

The very model of civic effectiveness has been upended since the 1960s. No longer do civic entrepreneurs think of constructing vast federations and recruiting interactive citizen-members. When a new cause (or tactic) arises, activists envisage opening a national office and managing association-building as well as national projects from the center. Even a group aiming to speak for large numbers of Americans does not absolutely need members. And if mass adherents are recruited through the mail, why hold meetings? From a managerial point of view, interactions with groups of members may be downright inefficient. In the old-time membership federations, annual elections of leaders and a modicum of representative governance went hand in hand with membership dues and interactive meetings. But for the professional executives of today's advocacy organizations, direct mail members can be more appealing because, as Kenneth Godwin and Robert Cameron Mitchell explain, "they contribute without 'meddling'" and "do not take part in leadership selection or policy discussions." This does not mean the new advocacy groups are malevolent; they are just responding rationally to the environment in which they find themselves.

ASSOCIATIONAL CHANGE AND DEMOCRACY

This brings us, finally, to what may be the most civically consequential change in late-twentieth-century America: the rise of a very large, highly educated upper middle class in which "expert" professionals are prominent along with businesspeople and managers. When U.S. professionals were a tiny, geographically dispersed stratum, they understood themselves as "trustees of community," in the terminology of Stephen Brint. Working closely with and for nonprofessional fellow citizens in thousands of towns and cities, lawyers, doctors, ministers, and teachers once found it quite natural to join—and eventually help to lead—locally rooted, cross-class voluntary associations. But today's professionals are more likely to see themselves as expert individuals who can best contribute to national well-being by working with other specialists to tackle complex technical or social problems.

Cause-oriented advocacy groups offer busy, privileged Americans a rich menu of opportunities to, in effect, hire other professionals and managers to represent their values and interests in public life. Why should highly trained and economically well-off elites spend years working their way up the leadership ladders of traditional membership federations when they can take leading staff roles at the top, or express their preferences by writing a check?

If America has experienced a great civic transformation from membership to advocacy—so what? Most traditional associations were racially exclusive and gender segregated; and their policy efforts were not always broad-minded. More than a few observers suggest that recent civic reorganizations may be for the best. American public life has been rejuvenated, say the optimists, by social movements and advocacy groups fighting for social rights and an enlarged understanding of the public good.

Local community organizations, neighborhood groups, and grassroots protest movements nowadays tap popular energies and involve people otherwise left out of organized politics. And social interchanges live on in small support groups and occasional volunteering. According to the research of Robert Wuthnow, about 75 million men and women, a remarkable 40 percent of the adult population, report taking part in "a small group that meets regularly and provides caring and support for those who participate in it." Wuthnow estimates that there may be some 3 million such groups, including Bible study groups, 12-step self-help groups, book discussion clubs, singles groups, hobby groups, and disease support groups. Individuals find community, spiritual connection, introspection, and personal gratification in small support groups. Meanwhile, people reach

out through volunteering. As many as half of all Americans give time to the community this way, their efforts often coordinated by paid social service professionals. Contemporary volunteering can be intermittent and flexibly structured, an intense one-shot effort or spending "an evening a week on an activity for a few months as time permits, rather than having to make a long-term commitment to an organization."

In the optimistic view, the good civic things Americans once did are still being done—in new ways and in new settings. But if we look at U.S. democracy in its entirety and bring issues of power and social leverage to the fore, then optimists are surely overlooking the downsides of our recently reorganized civic life. Too many valuable aspects of the old civic America are not being reproduced or reinvented in the new public world of memberless organizations.

Despite the multiplicity of voices raised within it, America's new civic universe is remarkably oligarchical. Because today's advocacy groups are staff-heavy and focused on lobbying, research, and media projects, they are managed from the top with few opportunities for member leverage from below. Even when they have hundreds of thousands of adherents, contemporary associations are heavily tilted toward upper-middle-class constituencies. Whether we are talking about memberless advocacy groups, advocacy groups with some chapters, mailing-list associations, or nonprofit institutions, it is hard to escape the conclusion that the wealthiest and best-educated Americans are much more privileged in the new civic world than their (less numerous) counterparts were in the pre-1960s civic world of cross-class membership federations.

Mostly, they involve people in "doing for" others—feeding the needy at a church soup kitchen; tutoring children at an after-school clinic; or guiding visitors at a museum exhibit—rather than in "doing with" fellow citizens. Important as such volunteering may be, it cannot substitute for the central citizenship functions that membership federations performed.

A top-heavy civic world not only encourages "doing for" rather than "doing with." It also distorts national politics and public policymaking. Imagine for a moment what might have happened if the GI Bill of 1944 had been debated and legislated in a civic world configured more like the one that prevailed during the 1993–1994 debates over the national health insurance proposal put forward by the first administration of President Bill Clinton. This is not an entirely fanciful comparison, because goals supported by the vast majority of Americans were at issue in both periods: in the 1940s, care and opportunity for millions of military veterans returning from World War II; in the 1990s, access for all Americans to a modicum of health insurance coverage. Back in the 1940s, moreover, there were elite actors—university presidents, liberal intellectuals, and conservative congressmen—who could have condemned the GI Bill to the same fate as the 1990s health security plan. University presidents and liberal New Dealers initially favored versions of the GI Bill that would have been bureaucratically complicated, niggardly with public expenditures, and extraordinarily limited in veterans' access to subsidized higher education.

But in the actual civic circumstances of the 1940s, elites did not retain control of public debates or legislative initiatives. Instead, a vast voluntary membership federation, the American Legion, stepped in and drafted a bill to guarantee every one of the returning veterans up to four years of post–high school education, along with family and employment benefits, business loans, and home mortgages. Not only did the Legion draft one of the most generous pieces of social legislation in American history, thousands of local Legion posts and dozens of state organizations mounted a massive public education and lobbying campaign to ensure that even conservative congressional representatives would vote for the new legislation.

Half a century later, the 1990s health security episode played out in a transformed civic universe dominated by advocacy groups, pollsters, and big-money media campaigns. Top-heavy advocacy groups did not mobilize mass support for a sensible reform plan. Hundreds of business and professional groups influenced the Clinton administration's complex policy schemes, and then used a combination of congressional lobbying and media campaigns to block new legislation. Both the artificial polarization and the elitism of today's organized civic universe may help to explain why increasing numbers of Americans are turned off by and pulling back from public life. Large majorities say that wealthy "special interests" dominate the federal government, and many Americans express cynicism about the chances for regular people to make a difference. People may be entertained by advocacy clashes on television, but they are also ignoring many public debates and withdrawing into privatism. Voting less and less, American citizens increasingly act—and claim to feel—like mere spectators in a polity where all the sig-

nificant action seems to go on above their heads, with their views ignored by pundits and clashing partisans.

From the nineteenth through the mid-twentieth century, American democracy flourished within a unique matrix of state and society. Not only was America the world's first manhood democracy and the first nation in the world to establish mass public education. It also had a uniquely balanced civic life, in which markets expanded but could not subsume civil society, in which governments at multiple levels deliberately and indirectly encouraged federated voluntary associations. National elites had to pay attention to the values and interests of millions of ordinary Americans.

Over the past third of a century, the old civic America has been bypassed and shoved to the side by a gaggle of professionally dominated advocacy groups and nonprofit institutions rarely attached to memberships worthy of the name. Ideals of shared citizenship and possibilities for democratic leverage have been compromised in the process. Since the 1960s, many good things have happened in America. New voices are now heard, and there have been invaluable gains in equality and liberty. But vital links in the nation's associational life have frayed, and we may need to find creative ways to repair those links if America is to avoid becoming a country of detached spectators. There is no going back to the civic world we have lost. But we Americans can and should look for ways to recreate the best of our civic past in new forms suited to a renewed democratic future.

The Redistricting Wars

THE REPUBLICAN DRIVE REPRESENTS A POWER GRAB UNPRECEDENTED IN SCALE AND TIMING.

SASHA ABRAMSKY

Traditionally, state legislatures and courts spend the year after the national Census redrawing Congressional maps to fit the new demographic realities. The party in control of the most state legislatures and governorships at that moment in time is able to muscle through federal Congressional redistricting maps tailored to benefit itself. And then, having spent a year maneuvering for advantage, the parties back off the issue and accept that the new maps will stay in place until the next Census. That, at least, is how things have worked in the past.

Recently, however, having gained control over more state legislatures than it's had since 1952 (twenty-one to the Democrats' sixteen, plus twenty-nine governorships), the GOP has not only redrawn the state electoral maps after the Census, it has broken with the decennial tradition and rammed through redistricting plans in mid-decade, most notably in Texas but also in Colorado, where the State Supreme Court recently tossed out the Republican legislature's new plan.

This aggressive Republican drive represents a Congressional power grab unprecedented in scale and timing. It is being executed with the encouragement of White House operatives from Karl Rove on down, with the full-throttle support of GOP House majority leader Tom DeLay. And its aim is to shore up the party's Congressional majorities for the next decade.

Amid the brouhaha over redistricting in Texas earlier this year, Representative Martin Frost's office requested that Library of Congress researchers investigate when the last mid-decade redistricting occurred. David Huckabee, specialist in American national government for the Congressional Research Service, wrote back that "there are no prohibitions for states to revisit the issue of redistricting during the decade following the census, but they appear not to have done so except in response to legal action during the past 50 years." In other words, actions like those undertaken by Texas Republicans have never in living memory been launched by either political party.

"There's been a gentlemen's agreement over time by both parties that you only do redistricting in a year ending in one," explains Representative Sherrod Brown, an Ohio Democrat. "If a party gains ascendancy later in the decade, it's unprecedented to do it at the next election." Redistricting, says Rob Richie of the Center for Voting and Democracy, "is a longstanding blood-sport. The Democrats traditionally had stuck it to Republicans because they ran so many more states. But they weren't creative enough to realize they could do it mid-decade."

The Texas redistricting fight, which featured Democrats fleeing to New Mexico and Oklahoma to prevent the legislature from having a quorum and federal law enforcement officials sent into action by Republican politicians to track down the absentee Donkeys, received by far the most publicity. Wrongly, much of the media portrayed it as a quirky Texas cowboy story with no wider ramifications. In reality, however, this was a power grab orchestrated by the national Republican Party and clearly intended to consolidate power nationally.

To recap the Texas saga in brief: State Republicans, goaded by Tom DeLay and supported by DeLay-sponsored political action committees (Americans for a Republican Majority and Texans for a Republican Majority), as well as the Republican Congressional Campaign Committee, successfully broke the Democratic resistance to mid-decade redistricting. On October 13, they managed to pass a redistricting plan that all concerned agreed would likely give the Republicans an additional seven seats in the House of Representatives.

'I talked to a number of Republican legislators and they said, "I've got to do this. I'm being forced to do this."'

—US Representative Diane DeGette

On many levels, it was a sleazy political power play. Supporters of redistricting were buoyed by having one of the country's top redistricting attorneys serving both the State of Texas and Republican lobbying groups most active in pushing for the state to implement a new Congressional map. Since May of this year, according to the Texas Attorney General's office, the State of Texas has paid three attorneys more than $200,000 to do legal work on the redistricting issue. One of them, Andy Taylor, is also being paid for his redistricting expertise by the avowedly partisan Texans for a

Republican Majority. (Taylor, along with DeLay, Rove and a number of state Republican politicians, did not return my calls requesting interviews.) TRM, largely bankrolled by a Republican front organization named the Texas Association of Business, has spent the past several years working to achieve Republican control of Texas's political machine, at least in part with the intent of parlaying this power into a redistricting advantage for federal Congressional elections.

While the attorneys and the political players argued that the redistricting was solely concerned with divvying up the Texas Congressional delegation to more accurately reflect party loyalties in the Lone Star State, opponents believe that they were attempting to nullify the impact of a large number of conservative voters who split their votes between Republicans in presidential and local elections and Democrats in Congressional races.

Texas was only one part of a national strategy. In Colorado, after the Republicans won control of the state legislature in 2002, they promptly redrew a redistricting map imposed by the courts a little more than a year before. On December 1, Colorado's Supreme Court stepped into the fray, ruling that the state's Constitution only permitted redistricting once per decade, and that since the districts had already been redrawn by the courts in 2001–02, the Republicans had acted illegally by instituting a fresh round of redistricting this year. The court's majority held that "the state constitution limits redistricting to once per census…. Having failed to redistrict when it should have, the General Assembly has lost its chance to redistrict until after the 2010 federal census."

This decision has given new hope to the Texas Democratic Party in its lawsuit seeking to overturn the Republican coup. While the Texas State Constitution does not, apparently, explicitly forbid multiple redistrictings within a single decade, opponents of the redistricting plan have argued that it violates the voting rights of minorities by reducing the number of seats effectively controlled by minority voters; they have also argued that politically motivated redistricting is inherently unlawful. A three-member panel of federal judges is slated to hear the case starting in mid-December. Already Tom DeLay and other top Republicans have been subpoenaed in the case.

Yet even as these lawsuits wend their way through the courts, there are rumors that Republicans elsewhere are planning similar power grabs. In Ohio, in particular, there are rumors that Republicans are planning mid-decade redistricting.

In each state where mid-decade redistricting has become a major issue, key Republican state representatives told the media that they had been telephoned about the redistricting issue by Karl Rove. *The Washington Post* reported that Rove even phoned one GOP state senator in Texas who was opposed to redistricting to indicate how important this issue was to President Bush. "It was the most unbelievable raw exercise of power," recalls US Representative Diane DeGette, a Colorado Democrat. "The leadership suspended rules and just rammed it through. I talked to a number of Republican legislators and they said, 'I've got to do this. I'm being forced to do this.'" Other White House confidantes, including ex-Bush spokeswoman Karen Hughes, are also known to have discussed the issue with Texas Governor Rick Perry.

While White House officials acknowledge that Rove talked with some state legislators about redistricting, the White House and the national Republican Party have repeatedly denied that the Administration has been orchestrating a redistricting power grab. They portray the Rove conversations as the innocuous musings of one lone individual. It's a point of view Democrats aren't buying. "Rove is the national Republican Party," asserts Representative Frost. "He's the President's chief political operative. He's not doing this on his own. It would be inconceivable for him to not be doing it for the Republican Party."

In addition to the machinations in Texas, Colorado and Ohio, a particularly robust round of routine post-Census redistricting had already occurred in 2001–02 in four crucial swing states where the Republicans had control of the state apparatus. In Michigan, in 2000 the Democrats had a 9-to-7 edge in Congressional representation; in 2002, despite the Democrats' polling 49 percent, as against 48 percent for the GOP, according to the Center for Voting and Democracy, the Republicans ended up with a 9-to-6 edge in Congressional seats. In Pennsylvania, Republicans created a 12-to-7 divide instead of the 11-to-10 split resulting from the previous election. In Florida, the Republicans expanded their majority from 15-to-8 to 18-to-7, "entirely due to redistricting," according to the center's Rob Richie. Similarly, in Ohio, even before the rumors about additional mid-decade changes, redistricting had already moved a seat into the GOP column.

The US Supreme Court heard arguments on December 10 in *Vieth v. Jubelirer*, a case challenging the constitutionality under the equal protection clause of Pennsylvania's newly gerrymandered Congressional boundaries. Several Democratic Congressmen, the ACLU and the NYU Brennan Center for Justice have all filed friend-of-the-court briefs in the case. In the meantime, however, the redistricting maps remain in place.

All told, assuming support for the two major parties remains roughly constant, and assuming the Supreme Court does not step into the fray too aggressively, the 2001 redistricting in newly GOP-controlled Florida, Michigan, Ohio and Pennsylvania, coupled with the ongoing power grab in Texas, Colorado and possibly Ohio, could give the Republicans up to twenty additional House seats in the next election. The cumulative impact of this change will make it far harder for the Democrats to secure a Congressional majority over the course of the next several election cycles.

Beyond controlling a historically exceptional number of state polities, the Republicans have also been aided in their plans by the advent of extraordinarily powerful redistricting software. In the decade-plus since the last round of redistricting following the 1990 Census, the technology of redistricting software has improved to the point where any organization can load sophisticated mapping programs onto their operatives' laptops, plug in demographic variables and generate devastatingly accurate redistricting maps designed to concentrate or diffuse party supporters in units tailor-made to benefit one party over another.

"The fact that the software's really affordable means a lot of these groups are using it. It's about $5,000 a copy," says Howard Simkowitz, product manager for Maptitude for Redistricting, a high-selling software package produced by the Caliper Corporation. Ten years ago, explains Simkowitz, "it would have been probably ten times as much. The price is way down. We got into the redistricting market in a big way this time around. It's become a lot easier to build districts that are lopsided districts, because people can understand the data so much better. You're able to really manipulate the data quickly, to try different scenarios, to move the boundaries around and see what that means."

Parties can now work out the most effective ways either to ghettoize their opponents' votes into a small number of extremely safe seats, or dilute their votes by redrawing Congressional boundaries so as to break up voting blocs into several different districts thought to be populated by a majority from the other party. Indeed, the power of this software is mentioned in the US Supreme Court briefs as one more bit of evidence indicating that those who draw the Congressional lines now effectively control the contours of Congress.

While in theory the redistricting technology that has recently come online is party-neutral, in practice the maps produced by the party in control of state legislatures at the time the software became widely available were implemented wholesale, while the maps produced by those affiliated with the minority party are essentially little more than whimsical wish lists. Because of the current state political landscape, the advent of this technology has further played to the Republicans' advantage.

In Texas, for example, the Republicans chose to concentrate Democratic votes into a handful of massively safe Democratic seats, in the process diluting the Democratic presence in many other seats that, until this year, were considered competitive for both parties. While such practices have a long history, the precision of the new software makes it that much easier to create boundaries that are virtually invulnerable to electoral surprises. Thus it makes those in control of the mapmaking that much more important within the political process. Many Democrats believe the Republican strategy in Texas ultimately involves creating a handful of ultrasafe Democratic seats based on the votes of African-Americans and Latinos, while ringing these seats with safe Republican districts dominated by conservative white voters.

Absent an extraordinary collapse in levels of public support for the GOP, or a comprehensive Supreme Court ruling against the practice of out-and-out political gerrymandering during redistricting battles, the result of all this maneuvering is likely to be a Republican stranglehold on the House of Representatives for the rest of the decade. And this is despite the fact that the electorate is split virtually down the middle in its support for the two main parties. "Not counting 2002," a year in which the Republicans polled better than in recent elections, helped by the coattails effect of the wartime popularity of President Bush, "the last three elections before that had less than 1 percent difference between Democrats and Republicans," says Steve Hill of the Center for Voting and Democracy. "That's only happened seven times in the past century. It's conceivable that [as a result of redistricting] you could see Democrats winning more of the popular vote nationwide than Republicans, yet winning less of the seats."

The Republicans are playing a very risky game. As with the 2000 presidential election and the California gubernatorial recall election, by undermining the traditional time constraints on redistricting, they have carried out an end run around the accepted parameters of political partisanship. In so doing, they are greatly diminishing the ability of the country's political structures to float above the debates and passions engendered by day-to-day politicking. By impinging on the structures themselves, the Republican machine may ultimately render stable governance a halcyon vision from the past. For what one party does, the other party is sure to follow up on.

Some strategists believe that the Democrats, when they still controlled the legislature and governorship in California, should have broken up the Republican voting bloc in conservative Orange County by extending the boundaries of overwhelmingly Democratic districts from Los Angeles southward. "The Democrats had the chance to do in California what Tom DeLay is doing in Texas," states Steve Hill. "The Democrats didn't leave themselves enough opportunities to retake the House. They're going to suffer that problem now throughout the rest of the decade. This is the winner-take-all system. That's the game." Now, in the states they still control, the Democrats will likely face tremendous pressure to try to counteract the Republican seat grab in Texas and Colorado. With both Democrats and Republicans scrambling to redraw Congressional lines after each election, a downward cycle of political one-upmanship has now become a virtual certainty.

Sasha Abramsky is the author of Hard Time Blues *(St. Martin's) and co-author of the recently published Human Rights Watch report* Ill Equipped: US Prisons and Offenders With Mental Illness.

A Better Way?

THE AUTHOR, A LONGTIME COLLEAGUE OF RALPH NADER'S, SUGGESTS A NEW METHOD FOR DECIDING PRESIDENTIAL ELECTIONS.

By ALAN B. MORRISON

The 2000 presidential election focused public attention on several serious and long-standing flaws in our election system. Since then, Congress has passed legislation to replace outdated voting machines and to curtail practices that prevented tens of thousands of voters from having their ballots counted. But three major problems remain.

First, every state except Maine and Nebraska employs a winner-take-all method of allocating Electoral College votes. In 2000 in Florida, because of that method, a few hundred votes out of more than 6 million determined who won all of the state's 25 electoral votes and thus became president.

Second, the current system results in third parties' playing what are often seen as spoiler roles, rather than constructive roles, in the presidential selection process. In almost every presidential election since 1980, third-party candidates have received enough popular votes that, had the votes gone exclusively or even largely to the runner-up, they would have changed the outcome. The 2000 election made the role of third-party candidates more visible than usual, but there is no reason to expect their influence to diminish.

NOT AGAIN:

The way to eliminate the possibility of another Florida is to eliminate the winner-take-all system of awarding electoral votes.

And third, under the present rules, if a presidential election fails to produce a majority in the Electoral College, then the House of Representatives chooses the president, in a most unrepresentative way. The rules call for one vote per state. In 2000, California, with its 52 House members, would have cast one vote, and so would each of eight states that had only on representative. However one defines democracy, there is simply no defense, in the

21st century, for picking a president on a "one-state, one-vote" basis.

ROADBLOCKS TO REMEDIES

It would be convenient if Congress could pass a law solving these problems. The Constitution makes that impossible, however, by placing the first two issues entirely within the control of the states. Unless all or most of the states agreed on solutions, the resulting confusion would be as bad as the current situation. But even the states can't improve the way we choose a president when no one wins a majority of the electoral vote, because the Constitution mandates the current procedure. Since only a constitutional amendment could address all three problems, we should think big and decide what we want.

The most obvious answer is to do what every state does: Elect the president by popular vote. That idea would have great appeal if we were starting from scratch—but we are not. The Electoral College, despite its flaws, does reflect notions of federalism that are the basis of our system of government and would be hard to overturn. Because the Electoral College adds two votes for each senator to the one for each member of the House, the small states have more power than they would have under a strict population-based system. And since 24 states will have five or fewer House members in the new Congress, there is no chance that the requisite three-fourths of the states (38) would agree to abolish the Electoral College.

Historian Arthur Schlesinger, writing in the March 25, 2002, issue of *The American Prospect,* proposed a system under which a presidential candidate would receive one electoral vote for each congressional district he or she won in a state and two electoral votes (corresponding to the number of senators) for winning the total vote in a state. Maine and Nebraska have chosen this method, but the fact that no other state has joined them suggests that it has little support. Moreover, such a system could work only if it were adopted nationally, and only a constitutional amendment could bring that about. If we are going that far, this kind of minimalist change hardly seems worth the effort.

LESS PIVOTAL:

Under a different system, the fight in Florida would have been over just one electoral vote.

NO MORE 'WINNER TAKE ALL'

The winner-take-all system should be changed, not just because of what happened in Florida, but because it effectively disenfranchises the millions of voters who cast their ballot for a candidate who did not finish first in their state. For example, the more than 4.5 million Californians who voted for George W. Bush, constituting nearly 42 percent of the state's electorate, might as well have stayed home, since they produced not a single electoral vote for their candidate. The same can be said for the 8.6 million Bush supporters in Illinois, Michigan, New York, and Pennsylvania and for the 4.6 million people who voted for Al Gore in Ohio and Texas. And in Florida, regardless of which candidate won, more than 2.9 million votes might just as well not have been cast or counted. In these eight states alone, the winner-take-all effect negated 20 million out of some 109 million votes cast nationwide. And it seems highly likely that a significant, if undeterminable, number of voters in states where the race was not close simply stayed away from the polls because their vote would have had no effect.

Second, the winner-take-all rule forces candidates to focus on the undecided voter in the middle, and to do that, candidates often fudge their positions to avoid offending voters and losing their support. The blurring of distinctions among candidates, not to mention their efforts to hide or at least soften their true views until after the election, is bad for democracy. The more the candidates sound alike, the less inclined the mildly apathetic voters—or those looking to shake up the status quo—will be to go to the polls.

Finally, and most dramatically, the current system results in situations such as the one in Florida, where a swing of fewer than 2,000 votes out of the 6 million cast determined how all of the state's 25 electoral votes were awarded. Given human errors and the inevitable failures of even the most sophisticated equipment, having an election turn on so few votes should be avoided whenever possible.

PROPORTIONATE ALLOCATION

The way to prevent another outcome like the one in Florida, and to reinvigorate presidential elections, is to institute a proportionate-allocation system. Under such a

system, each candidate would receive a percentage of a state's electoral votes matching his or her percentage of the popular votes. In 2000, in a race between just Gore and Bush, Bush would have received 13 of Florida's electoral votes and Gore 12, meaning that any post-election fight would have been over only one electoral vote. Thus, proportionate allocation would virtually eliminate the chance that any court, let alone the Supreme Court, would be in a position to decide the outcome of the election.

Ending the winner-take-all system would also significantly change the way candidates allocated their appearances and their expenditures, particularly for media advertising. Under the current system, once a state is seen as safe for one candidate, none of the candidates spends any significant time or money there. But proportionate voting would create an incentive to campaign everywhere, because even in the states with the fewest electoral votes, picking up at least one of them would be relatively easy. Exactly how presidential races would change is impossible to predict, but they would certainly not be the same, which we can hope would mean more interesting races and greater turnout.

A BACKUP PLAN:

Voters could indicate a backup choice for president in case no one got a majority of electoral votes. Third-party candidates, such as John Anderson, Ralph Nader, Ross Perot, and Patrick Buchanan, would thus play less of what some see as a spoiler role.

What would have happened if a system of allocating electoral votes proportionately had been in place in 2000? There can be no definitive answer, because analysis must rest on the unlikely assumption that all of the candidates would still have conducted their campaigns precisely as they did. In this theoretical exercise, however, when the Electoral College votes were allocated in accordance with the popular vote in each state, another problem surfaced that initially appeared to be a mathematical anomaly but turned out to have far deeper implications. Because more than two candidates received measurable percentages of the vote—Bush and Gore each received about 48 percent, while Ralph Nader had 2.7 percent and Patrick Buchanan had 0.4 percent—under a state-by-state proportionate-allocation system, neither Bush nor Gore would have achieved the required 270-vote majority. Bush would have had 265 votes, Gore 264, and Nader 9. This revelation raises the much more fundamental issue of what to do about third-party candidates—not just under a proportionate-allocation system, but under the winner-take-all system as well.

One choice would be to disregard the popular vote given to third parties and allocate electoral votes solely on the votes of the two major-party candidates—as is done, in effect, in a disguised manner, under the current winner-take-all system. But even that policy would not have resolved the election in 2000, because the result would have been a flat tie at 269 electoral votes each, assuming no challenges or recounts.

Even if disregarding Ralph Nader's 2.7 percent of the nationwide votes might have produced a winner in 2000, that approach would be much less palatable in years like 1992, when Ross Perot had 19 percent of the popular vote, and Bill Clinton and George Bush had 43 percent and 38 percent, respectively. Under the existing rules, Clinton garnered 370 electoral votes to Bush's 168, but under a proportionate-allocation system, the totals would have been Clinton 236, Bush 197, and Perot 105—again, no winner. Since Perot finished second in Maine and Utah, and he won more than 25 percent of the vote in six other states, eliminating his votes would not be a legitimate option under a proportionate-allocation system.

A presidential election in which a third-party candidate receives a significant number of votes can be resolved in many ways. But the fairest one, which would best reflect the will of the voters, is called "preference voting" or "instant-runoff voting" and has recently been adopted by the city of San Francisco for choosing its mayor, council members, and other high-ranking officers. Each voter marks a first choice and then has the option of indicating a "backup" choice—which is counted only if no candidate secures 270 of the 538 electoral votes (using proportionate voting). Had this two-prong system been in use in 2000, Nader and Buchanan voters who had made a backup selection would have added their votes to those whose first choice was Bush or Gore to determine the eventual winner. In this way, voters could have expressed their true preferences without fearing that their vote might help elect the person they most strongly opposed. It might also have meant that at least on the second round, the thousands of Floridians who mistakenly cast two votes for president might have had their votes counted, as long as at least one of their selections was Gore or Bush.

THIRD PARTIES CAN'T BE IGNORED

This inquiry has another important byproduct: It requires us to think more deeply about the role of third parties in presidential and perhaps other elections. The instinctive reaction of the leaders, and probably many members, of the two major parties will be to oppose anything that gives third parties greater legitimacy. For the major parties, proportionate voting and instant runoffs would only encourage third parties and thereby drain strength and money from the major parties.

The real basis of that opposition is the assumption that if the present system is retained, third parties will disappear. But it is the current system that has spawned alternative parties, even with all the barriers the major parties have placed in their way. Moreover, third parties are not a recent arrival, but have been a significant factor in pres-

idential elections for well over a century; in the 1912 election, Theodore Roosevelt ran as a third-party candidate.

The Constitution neither enshrines a two-party system nor implies that presidential elections should be between only two candidates. Thus, both the original version of Article II, Section 1, Clause 3, and the changes made to it in 1804 by the 12th Amendment, specifically contemplated that more than two people would run for president. After requiring a majority of the electoral vote to elect the president, the Constitution directs the House of Representatives to decide the election "from the persons having the highest numbers [of electoral votes] not exceeding three [originally five] on the list of those voted for as President." Although the Constitution may not mandate greater accommodations for third parties in presidential races, it surely refutes the commonly held notion that the two-party system is an essential part of our democracy and that candidates who run against the major-party nominees are somehow un-American.

But even if the major parties could continue the pretense that third parties don't (or shouldn't) exist and are therefore to be disregarded, they cannot hide from the fact that third parties do influence elections. Ralph Nader has been called a spoiler, a candidate who had no chance of winning but took enough votes from Al Gore in Florida (and in New Hampshire) to give the election to George W. Bush. Few observers have noted that if Gore had won Florida, the same "spoiler" charge could have been leveled against Patrick Buchanan, even though he gained only 0.44 percent of the popular vote nationwide. If all of Buchanan's supporters had gone instead for Bush in Iowa (7 electoral votes), New Mexico (5), Oregon (7), and Wisconsin (11), Bush would have received 30 additional electoral votes, and he would have become president even if Gore had won Florida. Indeed, the spoiler effect is not limited to presidential elections. As John J. Miller of the *National Review* recently observed, the Libertarian Party has quite likely cost the Republican Party a seat in the Senate in each of the last three elections—this time in South Dakota and previously in Nevada and Washington.

Whatever truth there may be to the claim that neither Nader or Buchanan was a spoiler in the 2000 election, there can be no doubt that in some situations, a third-party candidate who cannot win may draw enough votes from another candidate to change the result. And that is as true under the current regime as it would be under one based on proportionate allocation. But when that happens, the blame should be placed not on the third party, but on the system that opens the door for a spoiler effect. The proper question is not what to do about third parties, but what to do about the system so that third parties, which will inevitably exist, will play a constructive, not a spoiler, role. The solution is to stop letting the initial vote be the final vote if no candidate obtains a majority, and to use instant-runoff voting to resolve outcomes and eliminate speculation about which way votes for a third-party candidate *would* have gone.

POPULAR VS. ELECTORAL

Under the present system, presidential candidates often win a much larger percentage of electoral votes than popular votes.

	% OF POPULAR VOTE	% OF ELECTORAL VOTES
1980		
Reagan	50.8%	90.9%
Carter	41.0	9.1
Anderson	6.6	0
1984		
Reagan	58.8	97.6
Mondale	41.0	2.4
1988		
Bush	53.4	79.2
Dukakis	45.7	20.6
1992		
Clinton	43.0	68.8
Bush	37.5	31.2
Perot	18.9	0
1996		
Clinton	49.2	70.4
Dole	40.7	29.6
Perot	8.4	0
Nader	0.7	0
2000		
Bush	47.9	50.4
Gore	48.4	49.4
Nader	2.7	0
Buchanan	0.4	0

SOURCE: *Uselectionatlas.org*

RESOLVING WINNERLESS ELECTIONS

Finally, it is time to change the way we decide presidential elections in which no one garners a majority of electoral votes. Under the current system, if there is no winner, the election goes to the newly elected House of Representatives with each state having a single vote, whatever the size of its House delegation. This means that the 27 states with eight or fewer electoral votes could theoretically elect the president, even though they have only 24 percent of the *electoral* votes (and in 2000, their residents cast less than 18 percent of the popular vote). Instant runoffs would probably eliminate the need for a presidential election to be decided by the House. But until such a mechanism is in place, we should change the deadlock system to eliminate the disproportionate role for small states; for example, by giving one vote to each House member, instead of to each state.

Our system for electing a president may not be completely broken, but it is in serious need of repair. The winner-take-all outcome, the failure to account for the inevitable third parties, and an outmoded way of resolving disputed elections should be changed.

Let the debate begin.

Alan Morrison is the Irvine Visiting Fellow at Stanford Law School. This month, he will return to the Public Citizen Litigation Group, which he founded with Ralph Nader in 1972. He can be reached at amorrison@law.stanford.edu.

The Short, Unhappy Life
of Campaign Finance Reform

Everyone seems ready to bury the McCain-Feingold law—
including those responsible for enforcing it.

by Paul Taylor

Reform, reform, don't speak to me of reform.
We have enough problems already.
—LORD THOMAS MACAULAY, 19TH-CENTURY BRITISH POLITICIAN

SENATORS JOHN MCCAIN AND RUSSELL FEINGOLD needed all of seven years to nurse their campaign finance reform bill through a reluctant Congress. The bill's opponents needed all of three hours to start strangling it.

The McCain-Feingold law, which seeks to outlaw large political donations is nearly a year old now and still gasping for each breath it draws. It's under pitiless assault from every corner of the political universe—unions, corporations, right-to-lifers, civil libertarians, gun owners, broadcasters, Christians, fat cats, purists who think it doesn't go far enough, Democrats, Republicans, Congress, the White House, and even the regulators who are supposed to enforce it. Its fate is in the hands of the U.S. Supreme Court, which will rule this summer on a raft of constitutional challenges. But no matter what the court decides, the resistance mounted by the armies of the status quo has already made for a sobering spectacle—full of naked hypocrisies, petty vanities, low politics, high farce, and, yes, a vexingly difficult clash of core values in a democracy. It has also provided a useful reminder about the pitfalls of reform. Somewhere, surely, Lord Macaulay is grinning in his grave.

This is the saga of the long, hard "morning after" for McCain-Feingold. It begins on March 27, 2002, the day the bill was signed into law. The measure outlaws the half-billion dollars of unlimited checks—so-called soft money—that flood the coffers of the political parties each election cycle. (Contributions that go directly to individual candidates have been limited by law since Watergate.) As keeper of the world's thickest Rolodex of political donors, President Bush has little use for a ban on soft money, and even less for McCain, his tenacious rival for the GOP presidential nomination. In different circum-

stances, the president might well have vetoed McCain's bill. But in the spring of 2002 the Enron scandal was raging, and the $312,500 that the president's pal "Kenny Boy" Lay and other top Enron executives had given to Bush's gubernatorial campaigns in Texas had become a political embarrassment. It wasn't the best time for the White House to derail the most important campaign finance reform legislation Congress had passed in a generation. Besides, there were so many other willing executioners.

So Bush bit his lip, dispensed with the usual Rose Garden ceremony, and put his signature on the bill early that morning in the privacy of his office. McCain and Feingold only learned of the signing afterward. The one politician Bush's staff did tip off was Senator Mitch McConnell (R-Ky.), the self-styled Darth Vader of campaign finance reform. A pompous man even by the lofty standards of the U.S. Senate, McConnell immediately rushed into court to secure the "naming rights" to a lawsuit that he hopes will become both a landmark constitutional case and his own great political legacy.

McConnell v. Federal Election Commission is a consolidated case with 84 plaintiffs, running the gamut from the Chamber of Commerce to the AFL-CIO, from the California Democratic Party to the Republican National Committee, from the Christian Coalition to the ACLU. All contend that in one way or another, the bill infringes on their rights to free speech and association. The plaintiffs certainly make for strange bedfellows, but the grander irony of this lawsuit is the identity of the defendant— the Federal Election Commission. That's the agency charged with enforcing the law. It's also the agency that has spent the past year sabotaging it. Most egregiously, the FEC adopted a regulation that allows the Democratic and Republican parties to create new shell organizations that can continue to collect the unlimited soft money that the bill sets out to ban. Democrats wasted little time in setting up something called the Democratic State Parties Organization to funnel five-, six-, and seven-figure checks to candidates. Not to be outdone, political operatives closely identified with the National Republican Congressional Committee and GOP House Majority Leader Tom DeLay created the "Leadership Forum" as a "conduit" for soft money. As one longtime cop fundraiser boasts, "This is the way politics and campaigns will be run under the new law."

The shell organizations incensed McCain, who is suing to have the regulations overturned. The FEC, he fumed, "ignored the plain language of the law, the clear intent of Congress, the legislative history, and even the recommendations of the agency's own general counsel and professional staff."

No one who has watched the FEC operate over its 28-year history could be surprised by its most recent handiwork. It has always been a "captive agency"—one whose sympathies line up squarely with the institutions it regulates. In the case of the FEC, this is not an accident; it's by design. The agency has six appointed commissioners, all of whom serve at the pleasure of the political parties and elected officials whose behaviors they are supposed to constrain. By law, the commission is made up of three Democrats and three Republicans—and, by law, tie votes result in no action. (Guess what happens when the parties disagree?) But if the agency is toothless, it isn't harmless. In the late 1970s, it issued a series of rulings that gave rise to the soft money loophole in the first place. Now, a generation after opening the loophole, the FEC is leading the charge to keep reformers from closing it.

Democratic and Republican party leaders have been taking in the action at the FEC with the satisfied smirks of high school students greeting their favorite substitute teacher. Just before the bill was to take effect last fall, Democratic National Committee Chairman Terry McAuliffe summoned his party's 40 top fundraisers to a meeting to reassure them that campaign finance reform was "nothing but junk," according to one participant. Never mind that Democrats in Congress had provided the lion's share of the votes to pass the bill; never mind that the DNC was on record supporting it.

CAN MCCAIN-FEINGOLD survive all this hostile fire? Parts of it probably will. The bill's central plank, the ban on soft money to political parties, is in sync with a long line of U.S. Supreme Court decisions that have held that Congress can limit contributions to prevent the appearance or reality of political corruption. Among the most telling evidence the new law's defenders presented in court last year was a nationwide survey showing that 71 percent of adults believe that members of Congress will vote for a bill in order to please a campaign contributor, even when they believe the bill is not in the best interest of the country. It's hard to imagine a more sweeping indictment of our new Gilded Age of politics—or a more muscular argument

in favor of the ban on soft money. As the Supreme Court noted in a recent case, "The cynical assumption that large donors call the tune could jeopardize the willingness of citizens to take part in democratic governance." Even if the court follows its own precedent and upholds the soft-money ban, however, it will also need to outlaw the new shell organizations if it wants to break the unsavory link between large contributions, political parties, and legislation.

Another part of the new law is built on more fragile constitutional footing. It seeks to impose limits on contributions used to finance the so-called sham issue ads that air during political campaigns and that in the past three election cycles have become a favorite weapon of corporations, unions, and interest groups. These are the ads that close with a tag line that's some variant of "Call Congressman Smith and ask him why he voted 12 times to raise your taxes." It's easy to see why McCain and Feingold felt the need to regulate them; without restrictions on the financing of such ads, much of the soft money their bill bans from political parties would wind up paying for sham issue ads instead, where they would have the same potential to corrupt the political process. But it's also easy to see why groups from all points on the ideological spectrum are up in arms. They argue that the very essence of the First Amendment protects the right of individuals and groups to sound off against their government. That's essentially what most of these ads do: They say Congressman X is a bum because he voted against Legislation Y. So the court must find a way to balance two fundamental rights—the right of free speech versus the right of Congress to protect the integrity of the political process against corruption.

There's one final irony in all these firefights: The bill at the center of the action is really a rather modest stab at reform. It doesn't go anywhere near two bolder proposals: putting limits on campaign spending and providing public financing or free TV time for candidates. Instead, McCain-Feingold simply tries to close the loopholes that eviscerated the last major campaign finance bill, which was passed on the heels of the Watergate scandal. Campaign finance reform has always played out according to rhythms that Lord Macaulay would recognize: first scandal, then legislation, then loopholes; then a new scandal, followed by more legislation, then new loopholes; and so on. In the past century, each cycle has taken roughly a generation to complete, with key legislation enacted in 1907, 1947, 1974, and 2002. This time around, it took the opponents of reform only a matter of months to start creating new loopholes. If the courts allow their handiwork to stand, the new scandals won't be far behind.

Paul Taylor is director of the Alliance for Better Campaigns and a former Washington Post *political correspondent.*

From *Mother Jones*, March/April 2003, pp. 28-31. © 2003 by Foundation for National Progress. Reprinted by permission.

JOURNALISM & DEMOCRACY

ON THE IMPORTANCE OF BEING A 'PUBLIC NUISANCE'

by BILL MOYERS

Hi. My name is Bill, and I'm a recovering Unimpeachable Source. I understand "Unimpeachable Source" is now an oxymoron in Washington, as in "McCain Republican" or "Democratic Party." But once upon a time in a far away place—Washington in the 1960s—I was one. Deep Backgrounders and Unattributable Tips were my drugs of choice. Just go to Austin and listen to me on those tapes LBJ secretly recorded. That's the sound of a young man getting high… without inhaling. I swore off thirty-four years ago last month, and I'm here to tell you, it hasn't been easy to stay clean. I can't even watch *The West Wing* without breaking into a sweat. A C-SPAN briefing by Ari Fleischer pushes me right to the edge. But I know one shot—just one—and I could wind up like my friend David Gergen, in and out of revolving doors and needing to go on *The NewsHour* for a fix between Presidents.

But I'm not here to talk about my time in the White House. I haven't talked much about it at all, though I do plan to write about it someday soon. During the past three and a half decades, I have learned that the job of trying to tell the truth about people whose job it is to hide the truth is almost as complicated and difficult as trying to hide it in the first place. Unless you're willing to fight and refight the same battles until you go blue in the face, to drive the people you work with nuts going over every last detail to make certain you've got it right, and then to take hit after unfair hit accusing you of having a "bias," or these days even a point of view, there's no use even in trying. You have to love it, and I do.

I always have. Journalism is what I wanted to do since I was a kid. Fifty years ago, on my 16th birthday, I went to work at the *Marshall News Messenger*. The daily newspaper in a small Texas town seemed like the best place in the world to be a cub reporter. It was small enough to navigate but big enough to keep me busy, happy and learning something new every day. I was lucky. Some of the old-timers were out sick or on vacation and I got assigned to cover the Housewives' Rebellion. Fifteen women in Marshall refused to pay the new Social Security withholding tax for their domestic workers. The rebels argued that Social Security was unconstitutional, that imposing it was taxa-

tion without representation, and that—here's my favorite part—"requiring us to collect [the tax] is no different from requiring us to collect the garbage." They hired themselves a lawyer—Martin Dies, the ex-Congressman best known (or worst known) for his work as head of the House Committee on Un-American Activities in the 1930s and 1940s. Eventually the women wound up paying the tax—while holding their noses. The stories I wrote for the *News Messenger* were picked up and moved on the Associated Press wire. And I was hooked.

Two years later, as a sophomore in college, I decided I wanted to become a political journalist and figured experience in Washington would show me the ropes. I wrote a man I had never met, a United States senator named Lyndon Johnson, and asked him for a summer job. Lucky again, I got it. And at summer's end LBJ and Lady Bird offered me a job on their television station in Austin for $100 a week. Looking back on all that followed—seminary, the Peace Corps, the White House, *Newsday*, PBS, CBS and PBS again—I often think of what Joseph Lelyveld, the executive editor of the *New York Times*, told some aspiring young journalists. "You can never know how a life in journalism will turn out," he said.

It took me awhile to learn that what's important in journalism is not how close you are to power but how close you are to reality.

It took me awhile after the White House to learn that what's important in journalism is not how close you are to power but how close you are to reality. Journalism took me there: to famine in Africa, war in Central America, into the complex world of inner-city families in Newark and to working-class families in Milwaukee struggling to survive the good times. My life in journalism has been a continuing course in adult education. From colleagues—from producers like Sherry Jones—I keep learning about journalism as storytelling. Sherry and I have been collaborating off and on for a quarter of a century, from the time we did the very first documentary ever about political action committees. I can still see the final scene in that film—yard after yard of computer printout listing campaign contributions unfurled like toilet paper stretching all the way across the Capitol grounds.

That one infuriated just about everyone, including friends of public television. PBS took the heat and didn't melt. When Sherry and I reported the truth behind the news of the Iran/*contra* scandal for a *Frontline* documentary called "High Crimes and Misdemeanors," the right-wing Taliban in town went running to their ayatollahs in Congress, who decried the fact that public television was committing—horrors—journalism. The Clinton White House didn't like it a bit, either, when Sherry and I reported on Washington's Other Scandal, about the Democrats' unbridled and illegal fundraising of 1996.

If PBS didn't flinch, neither did my corporate underwriter for ten years now, Mutual of America Life Insurance Company. Before Mutual of America I had lost at least three corporate underwriters, who were happy as long as we didn't make anyone else unhappy. Losing your underwriting will keep the yellow light of caution flickering in a journalist's unconscious. I found myself—and I could kick myself for this—not even proposing controversial subjects to potential underwriters because I had told myself, convinced myself: "Nah, not a chance!" Then Mutual of America came along and the yellow light flickers no more. This confluence of good fortune and good colleagues has made it possible for us to do programs that the networks dare not contemplate.

Commercial television has changed since the days when I was hired as chief correspondent for CBS Reports, the documentary unit. A big part of the problem is ratings. It's not easy, as John Dewey said, to interest the public in the public interest. In fact, I'd say that apart from all the technology, the biggest change in my thirty years in broadcasting has been the shift of content from news about government to consumer-driven information and celebrity features. The Project for Excellence in Journalism conducted a study of the front pages of the *New York Times* and the *Los Angeles Times*, the nightly news programs of ABC, CBS and NBC, and *Time* and *Newsweek*. They found that from 1977 to 1997 the number of stories about government dropped from one in three to one in five, while the number of stories about celebrities rose from one in every fifty stories to one in every fourteen.

Does it matter? Well, as we learned in the 1960s but seem to have forgotten, government is about who wins and who loses in the vast bazaar of democracy. Government can send us to war, pick our pockets, slap us in jail, run a highway through our garden, look the other way as polluters do their dirty work, take care of the people who are already well cared for at the expense of those who can't afford lawyers, lobbyists or time to be vigilant. It matters who's pulling the strings. It also matters who de-

fines the news and decides what to cover. It matters whether we're over at the Puffy Combs trial, checking out what Jennifer Lopez was wearing the night she ditched him, or whether we're on the Hill, seeing who's writing the new bankruptcy law, or overturning workplace safety rules, or buying back standards for allowable levels of arsenic in our drinking water.

> *Big money and big business, corporations and commerce, are again the undisputed overlords of politics and government.*

I need to declare a bias here. It's true that I worked for two Democratic Presidents, John Kennedy and Lyndon Johnson. But I did so more for reasons of opportunity than ideology. My worldview was really shaped by Theodore Roosevelt, who got it right about power in America. Roosevelt thought the central fact of his era was that economic power had become so centralized and dominant it could chew up democracy and spit it out. The power of corporations, he said, had to be balanced in the interest of the general public. Otherwise, America would undergo a class war, the rich would win it, and we wouldn't recognize our country anymore. Shades of déjà vu. Big money and big business, corporations and commerce, are again the undisputed overlords of politics and government. The White House, the Congress and, increasingly, the judiciary reflect their interests. We appear to have a government run by remote control from the US Chamber of Commerce, the National Association of Manufacturers and the American Petroleum Institute. To hell with everyone else.

What's the role of journalism in all this? The founders of our nation were pretty explicit on this point. The First Amendment is the first for a reason. It's needed to keep our leaders honest and to arm the powerless with the information they need to protect themselves against the tyranny of the powerful, whether that tyranny is political or commercial. At least that's my bias. A college student once asked the journalist Richard Reeves to define "real news." He answered: "The news you and I need to keep our freedoms." Senator John McCain echoed this in an interview I did with him a couple of years ago for a documentary called "Free Speech for Sale." It was about the Telecommunications Act of 1996, when some of America's most powerful corporations were picking the taxpayers' pocket of $70 billion. That's the estimated value of the digital spectrum that Congress was giving away to the big media giants.

Senator McCain said on the Senate floor during the debate, referring to the major media, "You will not see this story on any television or hear it on any radio broadcast because it directly affects them." And, in our interview, he added, "The average American does not know what digital spectrum is. They just don't know. But here in Washington their assets that they own were being given away, and the coverage was minuscule." Sure enough, the Telecommunications Act was introduced around May of 1995 and was finally passed in early February of 1996. During those nine months, the three major network news shows aired a sum total of only nineteen minutes on the legislation, and none of the nineteen minutes included a single mention of debate over whether the broadcasters should pay for use of the digital spectrum.

The Founders didn't count on the rise of mega-media. They didn't count on huge private corporations that would own not only the means of journalism but also vast swaths of the territory that journalism should be covering. According to a recent study done by the Pew Research Center for the People and the Press for the *Columbia Journalism Review*, more than a quarter of journalists polled said they had avoided pursuing some newsworthy stories that might conflict with the financial interests of their news organizations or advertisers. And many thought that complexity or lack of audience appeal causes newsworthy stories not to be pursued in the first place.

I don't mean to suggest there was a Golden Age of journalism. I told you earlier about covering the Housewives' Rebellion in Marshall, Texas, fifty years ago. What I didn't tell you is that it was the white housewives who made news with their boycotts of Social Security, not the domestic workers themselves. They were black; I wasn't sent to interview them, and it didn't occur to me that I should have. Marshall was 50 percent black, 50 percent white, and the official view of reality was that only white people made news. I could kick myself for the half-blindness that has afflicted me through the years—from the times at the White House when I admonished journalists for going beyond the official view of reality in Vietnam to the times I have let the flickering yellow light turn red in my own mind on worthy journalistic projects.

I'm sure that growing up a Southerner and serving in the White House turned me into a fanatic—at least into a public nuisance—about what journalism should be doing in our democracy. In the South the truth about slavery was driven from our pulpits, our newsrooms and our classrooms, and it took the Civil War to bring the truth home. Then the truth about Jim Crow was censored, too, and it took another hundred years to produce the justice that should have followed Appomattox. In the White House we circled the wagons, grew intolerant of news that didn't comfort us and, if we could have, we would have declared illegal the sting of the bee. So I sympathize with my friends in commercial broadcasting who don't cover the ocean they're swimming in. But I don't envy them. Having all those resources—without the freedom to use them to do the kinds of stories that are begging to be done—seems to me more a curse than a blessing. It reminds me of Bruce Springsteen's great line, "It's like eating caviar and dirt."

But I am not here to hold myself up as some sort of beacon. I've made my own compromises and benefited from the special circumstances of my own good luck. But the fact that I have been so lucky shows that it can be done. All that is required is for journalists to act like journalists, and their sponsors—public or private—to back them up when the going gets a little rough.

Because when you are dealing with powerful interests, be they in government or private industry, and bringing to light what has been hidden, the going does—inevitably—get a little rough.

Let me give you a couple of examples of what I mean—why the battle is never-ending: Some years ago my colleague Marty Koughan was looking into the subject of pesticides and food when he learned about a National Academy of Sciences study in progress on the effects of pesticide residuals on children. With David Fanning of *Frontline* as an ally, we set about a documentary. Four to six weeks before we were finished the industry somehow purloined a copy of our rough script—we still aren't certain how—and mounted a sophisticated and expensive campaign to discredit the documentary before it aired. They flooded television reviewers and the editorial pages of newspapers with propaganda. A *Washington Post* columnist took a dig at the broadcast on the morning of the day it aired—without even having seen it—and later admitted to me that the dig had been supplied to him by a top lobbyist in town. Some station managers were so unnerved that they protested the documentary with letters that had been prepared by industry. Several station managers later apologized to me for having been suckered.

Here's what most perplexed us: Eight days before the broadcast, the American Cancer Society—a fine organization that in no way figured in our story—sent to its 3,000 local chapters a "critique" of the unfinished documentary claiming, wrongly, that it exaggerated the dangers of pesticides in food. We were puzzled: Why was the American Cancer Society taking the unusual step of criticizing a documentary that it hadn't seen, that hadn't aired and that didn't claim what the society alleged? An enterprising reporter in town named Sheila Kaplan later looked into this question for *Legal Times*, which headlined her story: "Porter/Novelli Plays All Sides." It turns out that the Porter/Novelli public relations firm, which has worked for several chemical companies, also did pro bono work for the American Cancer Society. Kaplan found that the firm was able to cash in some of the goodwill from that pro bono work to persuade the compliant communications staff at the society to distribute some harsh talking points about the documentary that had been supplied by, but not attributed to, Porter/Novelli.

Others used the society's good name to discredit the documentary, including the right-wing polemicist Reed Irvine. His screed against what he called "Junk Science on PBS" called on Congress to pull the plug on public broadcasting. PBS stood firm. The report aired, the journalism held up (in contrast to the disinformation about it) and the National Academy of Sciences was liberated to release the study that the industry had tried to cripple.

But there's always the next round. PBS broadcast our documentary on "Trade Secrets." It's a two-hour investigative special based on the chemical industry's own archives, on documents that make clear, in the industry's own words, what the industry didn't tell us about toxic chemicals, why they didn't tell us and why we still don't know what we have the right to know. These internal industry documents are a fact. They exist. They are not a matter of opinion or point of view.

They state what the industry knew, when they knew it and what they decided to do.

The public policy implications of our broadcast are profound. We live today under a regulatory system designed by the industry itself. The truth is, if the public, media, independent scientists and government regulators had known what the industry knew about the health risks of its products—when the industry knew it—America's laws and regulations governing chemical manufacturing would be far more protective of human health than they are today. But the industry didn't want us to know. That's the message of the documents. That's the story.

The spokesman for the American Chemistry Council assured me that contrary to rumors, the chemical industry was not pressuring stations to reject the broadcast. I believed him; the controversy would only have increased the audience. But I wasn't sure for a while. The first person to contact us from the industry was a public relations firm here in Washington noted for hiring private detectives and former CIA, FBI and drug enforcement officers to do investigations for corporations. One of the founders of the company is on record as saying that sometimes corporations need to resort to unconventional resources, and some of those resources "include using deceit." No wonder Sherry and I kept looking over our shoulders. To complicate things, the single biggest recipient of campaign contributions from the chemical industry over the past twenty years in the House has been the very member of Congress whose committee has responsibility for public broadcasting's appropriations. Now you know why we don't take public funds for reports like this!

For all the pressures, America, nonetheless, is a utopia for journalists. In many parts of the world assassins have learned that they can kill reporters with impunity; journalists are hunted down and murdered because of their reporting. Thirty-four in Colombia alone over the past decade. And here? Well, Don Hewitt of *60 Minutes* said to me recently that "the 1990s were a terrible time for journalism in this country but a wonderful time for journalists; we're living like [GE CEO] Jack Welch." Perhaps that's why we aren't asking tough questions of Jack Welch.

I don't want to claim too much for our craft, but I don't want to claim too little, either. The late Martha Gellhorn spent half a century observing war and politicians and journalists, too. By the end she had lost her faith that journalism could, by itself, change the world. But she had found a different sort of comfort. For journalists, she said, "victory and defeat are both passing moments. There is no end; there are only means. Journalism is a means, and I now think that the act of keeping the record straight is valuable in itself. Serious, careful, honest journalism is essential, not because it is a guiding light but because it is a form of honorable behavior, involving the reporter and the reader." And, one hopes, the viewer, too.

Editors' Postscript: This article is adapted from Moyers's speech to the National Press Club on March 22, hosted by PBS to observe his thirtieth year as a broadcast journalist. The chemical industry's trade association did attempt to discredit the March 26 documentary, "Trade Secrets" (see "The Times *v. Moyers," April 16), accusing Moyers and Jones of "journalistic malpractice" for inviting industry participation only during the last half-hour of the broadcast. Moyers replied that investigative journalism is not a collaboration between the journalist and the subject.*

Bill Moyers is executive editor of Public Affairs Television, the independent production company he founded in 1986.

THE MAKING OF A MOVEMENT:
GETTING SERIOUS ABOUT MEDIA REFORM

BY ROBERT W. McCHESNEY AND JOHN NICHOLS

No one should be surprised by the polls showing that close to 90 percent of Americans are satisfied with the performance of their selected President, or that close to 80 percent of the citizenry applaud his Administration's seat-of-the-pants management of an undeclared war. After all, most Americans get their information from media that have pledged to give the American people only the President's side of the story. CNN chief Walter Isaacson distributed a memo effectively instructing the network's domestic newscasts to be sugarcoated in order to maintain popular support for the President and his war. Fox News anchors got into a surreal competition to see who could wear the largest American flag lapel pin. Dan Rather, the man who occupies the seat Walter Cronkite once used to tell Lyndon Johnson the Vietnam War was unwinnable, now says, "George Bush is the President.... he wants me to line up, just tell me where."

No, we should not be surprised that a "just tell me where" press has managed to undermine debate at precisely the time America needs it most—but we should be angry. The role that US newsmedia have played in narrowing and warping the public discourse since September 11 provides dramatic evidence of the severe limitations of contemporary American journalism, and this nation's media system, when it comes to nurturing a viable democratic and humane society. It is now time to act upon that anger to forge a broader, bolder and more politically engaged movement to reform American media.

The base from which such a movement could spring has already been built. Indeed, the current crisis comes at a critical moment for media reform politics. Since the middle 1980s, when inept and disingenuous reporting on US interventions in Central America provoked tens of thousands of Americans to question the role media were playing in manufacturing consent,

media activism has had a small but respectable place on the progressive agenda. The critique has gone well beyond complaints about shoddy journalism to broad expressions of concern about hypercommercial, corporate-directed culture and the corruption of communications policy-making by special-interest lobbies and pliable legislators.

Crucial organizations such as Fairness & Accuracy In Reporting (FAIR), the Institute for Public Accuracy, the Media-Channel, Media Alliance and the Media Education Foundation have emerged over the past two decades. Acting as mainstream media watchdogs while pointing engaged Americans toward valuable alternative fare, these groups have raised awareness that any democratic reform in the United States must include media reform. Although it is hardly universal even among progressives, there is increasing recognition that media reform can no longer be dismissed as a "dependent variable" that will fall into place once the more important struggles have been won. People are beginning to understand that unless we make headway with the media, the more important struggles will never be won.

On the advocacy front, Citizens for Independent Public Broadcasting and People for Better TV are pushing to improve public broadcasting and to tighten regulation of commercial broadcasting. Commercial Alert organizes campaigns against the commercialization of culture, from sports and museums to literature and media. The Center for Digital Democracy and the Media Access Project both work the corridors of power in Washington to win recognition of public-interest values under extremely difficult circumstances. These groups have won some important battles, particularly on Internet privacy issues.

Something Old, Something New

Media Policy in the Digital Age

JEFFREY CHESTER AND GARY O. LARSON

It's become commonplace to divide the media into "old" and "new," neatly corresponding to analog and digital technology. Under this handy dichotomy the old media (print and broadcast especially) represent mass marketing and mediocrity; conglomerate ownership and economies of scale have produced mainstream, profit-driven programming. Variations occur at the margins, certainly, but even their collective impact pales before the market share of newspaper chains, publishing empires and the assorted television, cable and entertainment giants. In contrast to these old-media oligopolies, the new, digital media—fueled by desktop production and driven by global, networked distribution— seem wildly democratic. So out with the old and in with the new; the World Wide Web awaits!

If only it were that simple. First, the old media aren't going anywhere, and their dominance in our lives—radio and TV usage still outstrip the Internet by a factor of 20–1—will continue for years. Second, the old media giants have made their presence felt online, too, establishing digital beachheads that might not be making much money (yet) but that are certainly attracting their share of online traffic. This is particularly true of the hybrid (and hydra-headed) AOL Time Warner, whose multimedia reach extends to more than 70 percent of all online users in the United States, and fully a third of all time spent online. Thus, even if the long-touted media convergence has been slow in arriving, the distinction between old media and new—particularly with regard to the impact of conglomerate culture—is largely a false one.

That's why the public-policy battles now being waged to rein in the power of the old media (many of them last-ditch efforts to limit further ownership consolidation and to make the media more publicly accountable) are important to the future of the new media as well—particularly in the areas of ownership limits, spectrum management and noncommercial programming.

A combination of successful court challenges and the ascendant deregulatory spirit in Washington has put the existing cable-ownership limits—currently 30 percent of all cable households nationwide—at risk. As a result, we now face the specter of a single company controlling access to more than half of all households. Broadcast networks and station groups (two of which have already throttled commercial radio) are also poised to tighten their grip on key TV markets by acquiring more stations, far exceeding the current 35 percent national audience limit and further eroding local news and public-affairs programming. Perhaps most alarming, the old prohibitions against one company owning both a TV station and a newspaper, or a cable system and a TV station and a newspaper, or a cable system and a TV station, in the same community are also under threat. In all these instances, the public's fundamental right to "the widest possible dissemination of information from diverse and antagonistic sources" (in the words of the Supreme Court) will be jettisoned in favor of lowest-common-denominator shows assembled by the conglomerate multimedia stables.

There are more media outlets than ever before, but this numerical growth, as Consumers Union has pointed out, "has not been accompanied by a comparable growth of independent, diversely owned competitive communications services and media voices."

On one level, spectrum management—literally, the organization and oversight of the radio frequencies that make broadcast and other wireless transmissions possible—is dauntingly complex. But the current battle over spectrum is distressingly simple: In 1996, the nation's 1,600 TV stations were lent additional spectrum (a six-megahertz slice equal to that over which they've been transmitting analog signals for years). According to the FCC's original timetable, all stations were to be broadcasting digitally by 2003, and by 2006 they were to return their old spectrum (which could then be auctioned off by the government and used for other purposes). For a variety of reasons, the digital TV transition has progressed slowly; in the interim, industry lobbyists have been pressing for stations to be allowed to retain their additional spectrum and put it to various commercial uses, like data transmission, or auction it off themselves. As appalling as that may sound,, it is not such a farfetched scheme, given the lobby's clout and Washington's belief in finding "marketplace solutions."

But this kind of corporate welfare is no solution at all. Not only should the spectrum be returned in a timely fashion but a portion of the subsequent auction proceeds should be devoted to noncommercial, public-interest content. Such programming, largely entrusted in the past to the Corporation for Public Broadcasting and its PBS grantees, needs a much broader mandate in the digital future. And here, too, old and new media converge. For perhaps now, with the additional capacity that digital broadcasting affords, and with funding derived from the spectrum auctions, we can finally realize the original vision for public-service broadcasting, updated for the digital age. As the Carnegie Commission on Educational Television wrote back in 1967, "We seek for the artist, the technician, the journalist, the scholar, and the public servant freedom to create, freedom to innovate, freedom to be heard in this most far-reaching medium. We seek for the citizen freedom to view, to see programs that the present system, by its incompleteness, denies him."

The emerging broadband networks, which promise to bring broadcast and online technologies together in a platform that fosters interactivity and exchange, has the potential finally to realize that vision—but only if public-interest policies are in place insuring that the old-media giants won't be able to stifle competition and diversity in the new-media environment, too.

Jeffrey Chester is executive director of the Center for Digital Democracy (www.democraticmedia.org), a Washington-based nonprofit organization dedicated to maintaining the diversity and openness of the new broadband communications systems. Gary O. Larson manages CDD's "Dot-Commons" project.

In addition, local media watch groups have surfaced across the nation. Citizens' organizations do battle to limit billboards in public places and to combat the rise of advertising in schools—fighting often successfully to keep Channel One ads, corporate-sponsored texts and fast-food promotions out of classrooms and cafeterias. Innovative lawsuits challenging the worst excesses of media monopoly are being developed by regional groups such as Rocky Mountain Media Watch and a national consortium of civic organizations, lawyers and academics that has drawn support from Unitarian Universalist organizations. Media activists in Honolulu and San Francisco have joined with unions and community groups to prevent the closure of daily newspapers that provided a measure of competition and debate in those cities.

Despite its successes, the media reform movement is at something of a standstill. The sheer corruption of US politics is one obstacle.

Despite all these achievements, however, the media reform movement remains at something of a standstill. The sheer corruption of US politics is itself a daunting obstacle. The Center for Public Integrity in 2000 issued "Off the Record: What Media Corporations Don't Tell You About Their Legislative Agendas"—an alarming exposé of the huge lobbying machines employed by the largest communications corporations and their trade associations, as well as the considerable campaign contributions they make. According to the center, the fifty largest media companies and four of their trade associations spent $111.3 million between 1996 and mid-2000 to lobby Congress and the executive branch. Between 1993 and mid-2000, the center determined, media corporations and their employees have given $75 million in campaign contributions to candidates for federal office and to the two major political parties. Regulators and politicians tend therefore to be in the pockets of big-spending corporate communications lobbies, and—surprise, surprise—the corporate newsmedia rarely cover media policy debates. Notwithstanding all the good work by media activists, the "range" of communications policy debate in Washington still tends to run all the way from GE to GM, to borrow a line from FAIR's Jeff Cohen.

At this very moment, for example, the FCC is considering the elimination of the remaining restrictions on media consolidation, including bans on cross-ownership by a single firm of TV stations and newspapers in the same community, and limits on the number of TV stations and cable TV systems a single corporation may own nationwide. The corporate media lobbying superstars are putting a full-court press on the FCC—which, with George W. Bush's imprint now firmly on its membership, is now even more pro-corporate than during the Clinton years. The proposed scrapping of these regulations will increase the shareholder value of numerous media firms dramatically, and will undoubtedly inspire a massive wave of mergers and acquisitions. If the lessons of past ownership deregulation—particularly the 1996 relaxation of radio ownership rules—are any

guide, we can expect even less funding for journalism and more commercialism. All of this takes place without scrutiny from major media, and therefore is unknown to all but a handful of Americans.

The immensity of the economic and political barriers to democratic action has contributed to demoralization about the prospects for structural media reform and an understandable turn to that which progressives *can* hope to control: their own media. So it has been that much energy has gone into the struggle over the future of the Pacifica radio chain, which looks at long last to be heading toward a viable resolution. The Independent Press Association has grown dramatically to nurture scores of usually small, struggling nonprofit periodicals, which are mostly progressive in orientation. And dozens of local Independent Media Centers have mushroomed on the Internet over the past two years. These Indy Media Centers take advantage of new technology to provide dissident and alternative news stories and commentary; some, by focusing on local issues, have become a genuine alternative to established media at a level where that alternative can and does shift the dialogue. We have seen the positive impact of the IMC movement firsthand—in Seattle, in Washington, at the 2000 Democratic and Republican national conventions, at the three lamentable presidential debates later that year, during the Florida recount and in the aftermath of September 11 in New York and other cities. It is vital that this and other alternative media movements grow in scope and professionalism.

Yet, as important as this work is, there are inherent limits to what can be done with independent media, even with access to the Internet. Too often, the alternative media remain on the margins, seeming to confirm that the dominant structures are the natural domain of the massive media conglomerates that supposedly "give the people what they want."

The trouble with this disconnect between an engaged and vital alternative media and a disengaged and stenographic dominant media is that it suggests a natural order in which corporate media have mastered the marketplace on the basis of their wit and wisdom. In fact, our media system is not predominantly the result of free-market competition. Huge promotional budgets and continual rehashing of tried and true formulas play their role in drawing viewers, listeners and readers to dominant print and broadcast media. But their dominance is still made possible, in large part, by explicit government policies and subsidies that permit the creation of large and profitable conglomerates. When the government grants free monopoly rights to TV spectrum, for example, it is not setting the terms of competition; it is picking the winner of the competition. Such policies amount to an annual grant of corporate welfare that economist Dean Baker values in the tens of billions of dollars. These decisions have been made in the public's name, but without the public's informed consent. We must not accept such massive subsidies for wealthy corporations, nor should we content ourselves with the "freedom" to forge an alternative that occupies the margins. Our task is to return "informed consent" to media policy-making and to generate a diverse media system that serves our democratic needs.

Isolated and impoverished, groups are forced to defend against new corporate initiatives rather than advance positive proposals.

In our view, what's needed to begin the job is now crystal clear—a national media reform coalition that can play quarterback for the media reform movement. The necessity argument takes two forms.

First, the immense job of organizing media reform requires that our scarce resources be used efficiently, and that the various components of a media reform movement cooperate strategically. The problem is that the whole of the current media reform movement is significantly less than the sum of its parts. Isolated and impoverished, groups are forced to defend against new corporate initiatives rather than advance positive reform proposals. When they do get around to proposing reforms, activists have occasionally worked on competing agendas; such schisms dissipate energy, squander resources and guarantee defeat. More important, they are avoidable. Organizers of this new coalition could begin by convening a gathering of all the groups now struggling for reform, as well as the foundations and nonprofits willing to support their work. "All the issues we talk about are interlinked. We are fighting against a lot of the same corporations. The corporations, while they supposedly compete with one another, actually work together very well when it comes to lobbying," explains Jeffrey Chester of the Center for Digital Democracy. "We need to link up the activists and start to work together as well as the corporations do for the other side." Will every possible member organization get on the same media reform page? No. But after years of working with these groups in various settings, we have no doubt that most will.

Second, a coherent, focused and well-coordinated movement will be needed to launch a massive outreach effort to popularize the issue. That outreach can, and should, be guided by Saul Alinsky's maxim that the only way to beat organized money is with organized people. If the media reform movement stays within the Beltway, we know that we will always lose. Yet, so far, outreach beyond the core community of media activists has been done on a piecemeal basis by various reform groups and critics with very limited budgets. The results have, by and large, been predictably disappointing. As a result, says Representative Jesse Jackson Jr., "the case for media reform is not being heard in Washington now. It is not easy to make the case heard for any reform these days. That's why we need to do more. I hear people everywhere around the country complaining about the media, but we have yet to figure out how to translate those complaints into some kind of activist agenda that can begin to move Congress. There has to be more pressure from outside Washington for specific reforms. Members have to start hearing in their home districts that people want specific reforms of the media."

That will only happen if a concerted campaign organized around core democratic values takes the message of media reform to every college and university, every union hall, every convention and every church, synagogue and mosque in the land. To build a mass movement, the new coalition must link up with organized groups that currently engage in little activity in the way of media reform but that are seriously hampered by the current media system. Organized labor, educators, progressive religious groups, journalists, artists, feminists, environmental organizations and civil rights groups are obvious candidates.

These groups will not simply fall into place as coalition partners, however. Media corporations do not just lobby Congress; they lobby a lot of the groups that suffer under the current system. Some of those groups have been bought off by contributions from foundations associated with AOL, Verizon and other communications conglomerates; others—particularly large sections of organized labor—have been convinced that they have a vested interest in maintaining a status quo that consistently kicks them in the teeth. Building a broad coalition will require a tremendous amount of education and old-fashioned organizing that will inevitably involve pressure from the grassroots on major institutions and unions in order to get the national leadership of those organizations to engage. Movement-building will require that able organizers like Chester, Cohen, FAIR's Janine Jackson and Media Alliance executive director Jeff Perlstein—who have already been engaged in the struggle—be provided with the resources to travel, organize and educate.

All the organizing in the world won't amount to a hill of beans, however, unless there is something tangible to fight for, and to win. That's why we need reform proposals that can be advocated, promoted and discussed. Media reform needs its equivalent of the Voting Rights Act or the Equal Rights Amendment—simple, basic reforms that grassroots activists can understand, embrace and advocate in union halls, church basements and school assemblies. And there has to be legislation to give the activism a sense of focus and possibility.

Fortunately, there are several members of Congress who are already engaged on these issues: Senator Fritz Hollings has emerged as a thoughtful critic of many of the excesses of media monopolies; Senator John McCain has questioned the giveaway of public airwaves to communications conglomerates; Representative John Conyers Jr., the ranking Democrat on the House Judiciary Committee, has been outspoken in criticizing the loss of diversity in media ownership and the failure of the FCC to battle monopolization and homogenization; Representative Louise Slaughter has introduced legislation mandating free airtime for political candidates; Senator Paul Wellstone has expressed an interest in legislation that would reassert standards for children's programming and perhaps adopt the approaches of other countries that regulate advertising directed at young children; and Jesse Jackson Jr. has expressed a willingness to introduce legislation aimed at broadening access to diverse media, along with a wide range of other media reform proposals. If an organized movement demands it, there are people in Congress with the courage and the awareness to provide it with a legislative focus.

Ultimately, we believe, the movement's legislative agenda must include proposals to:

- Apply existing antimonopoly laws to the media and, where necessary, expand the reach of those laws to restrict ownership of radio stations to one or two per owner. Legislators should also consider steps to address monopolization of TV-station ownership and move to break the lock of newspaper chains on entire regions.
- Initiate a formal, federally funded study and hearings to identify reasonable media ownership regulations across all sectors.
- Establish a full tier of low-power, noncommercial radio and television stations across the nation.
- Revamp and invest in public broadcasting to eliminate commercial pressures, reduce immediate political pressures and serve communities without significant disposable incomes.
- Allow every taxpayer a $200 tax credit to apply to any nonprofit medium, as long as it meets IRS criteria.
- Lower mailing costs for nonprofit and significantly noncommercial publications.
- Eliminate political candidate advertising as a condition of a broadcast license, or require that if a station runs a paid political ad by a candidate it must run free ads of similar length from all the other candidates on the ballot immediately afterward.
- Reduce or eliminate TV advertising directed at children under 12.
- Decommercialize local TV news with regulations that require stations to grant journalists an hour daily of commercial-free news time, and set budget guidelines for those newscasts based on a percentage of the station's revenues.

We know from experience that many of these ideas are popular with Americans—when they get a chance to hear about them. Moreover, the enthusiasm tends to cross the political spectrum. Much of our optimism regarding a media reform movement is based on our research that shows how assiduously the corporate media lobbies work to keep their operations in Washington out of public view. They suspect the same thing we do: When people hear about the corruption of communications policy-making, they will be appalled. When people understand that it is their democratic right to reform this system, millions of them will be inclined to exercise that right.

A broad coalition could stand outside political parties and pressure all of them to take up the mantle of democratic media reform.

What media policy-making needs is to be bathed in democracy. The coalition we envision will have its similarities to the civil rights movement or the women's movement—as it should, since access to information ought to be seen as a fundamental human right. It will stand outside political parties and encourage all of them to take up the mantle of democratic media reform,

much as Britain's impressive Campaign for Press and Broadcasting Freedom has done. Although its initial funding may well come from large grants, this reform coalition ultimately must be broad-based and member-funded, like Greenpeace or, dare we say it, the National Rifle Association. Activists must feel a sense of ownership and attachment to a citizen lobby if it is to have real impact. We understand that success will depend, over the long term, upon a rejuvenation of popular politics and, accordingly, a decrease in corporate political and economic power. At the same time, we are certain that a movement that expands the range of legitimate debate will ultimately change not just the debate but the current system. "I am convinced that when people start talking about these big issues, these fundamental issues, when they start to understand that they have the power as citizens in a democracy to take on the powers that be and change how things are done, then change becomes inevitable," says Jackson. "The challenge, of course, is to get people to recognize that they have that power."

Even before it gets down to the serious business of reforming existing media systems, the coalition we propose can lead an organized resistance to corporate welfare schemes like the proposed FCC deregulation. And it might even be able to prevent the complete corporatization of the Internet [see Jeffrey Chester and Gary O. Larson, "Something Old, Something New," *The Nation,* January 7/14, 2002]. The key is to have a network of informed organizations and individuals who are already up to speed on media issues and can swing into action on short notice. Currently that network does not exist. The heroic public-interest groups that now lead the fight to oppose corporate domination of FCC policies find themselves without sufficient popular awareness or support, and therefore without the leverage they need to prevail. The movement we propose will be all about increasing leverage over the FCC and Congress in the near term, with an eye toward structural reform down the road.

But is it really possible that such a coalition can take shape in the months and years to come and begin to shift the debate? History tells us that the possibility is real. At times of popular political resurgence throughout the twentieth century, media activism surfaced as a significant force. It was most intense in the Progressive Era, when the rise of the modern capitalist media system was met with sustained Progressive and radical criticism from the likes of Upton Sinclair, Eugene Victor Debs and Robert La Follette. In the 1930s a heterogeneous movement arose to battle commercial broadcasting, and a feisty consumer movement organized to limit advertising in our society. In the postwar years, the Congress of Industrial Organizations attempted to establish a national FM radio network, one of the first casualties of the war on independent labor and the left that marked that period. In the 1960s and '70s the underground press provided vital underpinning for the civil rights, antiwar and feminist movements.

In short, we are building on a long tradition. And there is considerable momentum at present to coalesce. In November some thirty-five media activists from all over the nation met for a day in New York to begin coordinating some of their activities on a range of issues, from local and national policy matters to creating alternative media. Leading media scholars and educators are forming a new national progressive media literacy organization, one that will remain independent of the media conglomerates that bankroll existing groups. We are excited by speculation that Bill Moyers, who has done so much to drum up funding for reform initiatives, will in 2002 use his considerable influence to convince progressive foundations to make a genuine commitment to this fundamental democratic initiative.

The bottom line is clear. Until reformers come together, until we create a formal campaign to democratize our communications policy-making and to blast open our media system, we will continue to see special issues of *The Nation* like this one lamenting our situation. We need no more proof than the current moment to tell us that the time to build a broad coalition for media reform has arrived.

Robert W. McChesney, who teaches at the University of Illinois at Urbana, Champaign, is the author of Rich Media, Poor Democracy *(The New Press), and co-editor of* Monthly Review. *John Nichols is* The Nation's *Washington correspondent and the author of* Jews for Buchanan: Did You Hear the One About the Theft of the American Presidency? *(The New Press). Together, they are the authors of* It's the Media, Stupid! *(Seven Stories).*

From *The Nation,* January 7/14, 2002, pp. 11, 13, 16-17. © 2002 by The Nation. Reprinted by permission.

Politics after the Internet

YUVAL LEVIN

IT is no longer in vogue, as it was just a few years ago, to gush breathlessly about politics in the age of the Internet. In the late 1990s, many commentators were convinced that a new day had dawned in the life of our republic. Some said direct democracy was just around the corner, as tens of millions of Americans in "chat rooms" would form, in one author's words, "a committee of the whole, made up of all citizens online." Others predicted enormous increases in voter participation, the rise of a more informed and active populace, and a decline in the importance of money in politics. It seemed for a moment as though everything was about to change, and for the better. That moment has passed, and the subject seems to have been dropped. It may be too soon to pick it up again in full. The influence of information technologies on our politics has not been playing out as anyone quite expected, and to say that we now know the shape of the future would be to repeat the mistake of earlier prognosticators. But by understanding the source of the error committed by the forecasters of the 1990s, we may be able to see farther than they did, if only by a little.

The cyber-utopians

Cyber-politics prophecy reached its height between 1995 and 2000. Writers in the genre ranged from communitarian liberals, who viewed the World Wide Web as a source of civic energy and unity, to libertarian futurists, who foresaw the dawn of a new age of direct democracy and individual power. Most analysts combined some features of each.

To the first group, the Internet seemed like a tool for building community and promoting civic activity. By opening up new sources of information and new means of participation, it would energize an American political system suffering from citizen apathy and cynicism. Political scientist Anthony Corrado predicted in his 1997 book *Elections in Cyberspace* that the Internet would bring about "a revitalized democracy characterized by a more active informed citizenry." Daniel Weizner of the Center for Democracy and Technology saw in the Internet "a vast new forum for political discourse and activism which allows genuine interaction between voters and elected representatives." Others saw the Web as a means of organization, of drawing in the politically disaffected. In his book *Netactivism*, Edward Schwartz wrote that the Internet was simply "the most powerful tool for political organizing developed in the past 50 years.

One consequence of the new Internet-based political activism would be the end of the two-party system. The rise of the Web, according to Corrado, meant that "in the future, the political system may no longer be dominated by the Democratic and Republican parties," as countless new political actors entered the field. Howard Rheingold, a student of the culture of cyberspace, argued that "the political significance of computer mediated communication lies in its capacity to challenge the existing political hierarchy's monopoly on powerful communications media, and perhaps thus revitalize citizen based democracy."

Some, including high-tech guru Esther Dyson, believed that this citizen-based democracy would have the most impact at the local level, where, as *Newsweek's* Howard Fineman wrote in 1997, the Web would produce "an explosion of microdemocracy." But most analysts of Information Age democracy focused their attention on the federal government, where they foresaw a new era of citizen authority. In his 1997 book *Politics on the Nets*, technology expert Wayne Rash argued that in the age of the Web, "voters will have a voice that reaches directly to the highest levels of both parties and the government" and might have the ability to "bring accountability directly to bear on elected officials." British M.P. Graham Allen, writing in *Wired* magazine in 1995, expressed the same view, arguing that "new technology affords the possibility of cutting out the middle person and directly inputting our views into the national, regional and local electronic parliaments."

Indeed, direct democracy was a central theme of the cyberpolitics genre. The classic example is the 1996 book *The Electronic Republic*, written by Lawrence Grossman, a former president of NBC and PBS. Grossman argued that the Internet was "a modern day extension of Jeffersonian participatory democracy," and that through the Web, citizens "are increasingly involved in day-to-day decision-making alongside the president and Congress." Former Clinton advisor Dick Morris whole-heartedly agreed in his 1999 book *Vote.com*. "In the new era, Morris wrote, "Congress will have to listen to us."

For Morris, the fact that politicians would now be held to account by the people also meant that the power of big-money lobbyists in Washington would dwindle. As the public moves onto the Internet in greater numbers, Morris argued, "money will lose most of its power in our politics." Wayne Rash agreed in more sober tones, writing that the Internet "drops the price of entry onto the political stage to a level that nearly everyone can afford," making big money less of a factor.

But Morris and others also saw much more over the horizon. The Internet would not only energize and purify the American system of representation but would actually begin to replace it. Morris wrote that "the incredible speed and interactivity of the Internet will inevitably return our country to a de facto system of direct democracy by popular referendums." This view appealed especially to those with a libertarian bent. In 1995, *Reason* magazine's Washington editor Rick Henderson pointed to electronic citizen lobbying and announced that "a new form of activism is shaking the political establishment, and it may crumble congressional and regulatory fiefdoms." Futurists Alvin and Heidi Toffler also foresaw the decline of representative government, while Ted Becker and Christa Slayton predicted the rise of "televoting," electronic town meetings, and direct democracy.

Analysts all along this continuum—from those who saw the Web bringing new life to American representative politics to those who saw a modern rebirth of direct citizen rule—shared the general conviction that big change was in the works. And yet, somewhere toward the end of the 1990s, the flood of enthusiastic predictions dwindled down to a trickle, and the excitement over the age of cyber-politics began to subside. This drop in interest seems to have resulted from the fact that the great changes the enthusiasts had predicted were slow in starting, and seemed increasingly unlikely to come at all. In her 1996 book *Electronic Democracy*, Graeme Browning reported the then-common opinion that the Internet would play a decisive role in the 2000 presidential election. Few would now argue that it did, or even that it will in 2004. So what happened? How is it that these predictions have not been realized and that fewer and fewer analysts repeat them? Where did they go wrong?

Why the revolution did not come

On their face, the predictions of a new world of cyber-politics were not entirely ridiculous. After all, information technologies make information more widely available and communication easier, and almost everything in politics has to do with information and communication. A functioning democracy requires an informed electorate, and it seems sensible that a new means of providing access to information might greatly help citizens stay informed. An election campaign aims to convey ideas and

arguments, and it seems only reasonable that a new and more efficient way to communicate might radically reshape campaigning. Empowered by the Internet and the personal computer, citizens could now know more, participate more, and influence the system more directly and effectively.

They could, but would they want to? The failure to ask this simple question explains why the cyber-politics experts greatly overreached in their predictions. The proposition that information technologies would address what are generally seen to be some of the deepest problems of our politics (e.g., apathy, the power of special interests, "soft money," low participation and voter rates) assumes that these problems result from poor communication or lack of information. They do not. Most citizens know very little about politics not because such knowledge is hard to find but because they have no interest in finding it. Most constituents never contact their members of Congress not because contacting them would be too difficult but because they do not want to contact them. Voter turnout is low not because it is hard for people to vote but because they choose not to vote. For the Internet to change any of this, it would have to increase people's interest in politics, and there is little reason to think it will.

Indeed, rather than bring massive change, information technology is likely to further recent trends in political life. The Internet makes it easy to know more about whatever one is interested in, but by itself it does not change one's interests. Today, the people who actively participate in politics are those who are interested enough to do so. Information technologies will make it easier for these people to be involved, and will therefore likely make them even more so. For those people with little interest in politics, the Internet will make it easier for them to become more engaged in their own particular areas of interest, leaving them even less time for politics. The Internet does not simply offer us information, it offers us our choice of information. Most of us choose to become better informed about, and more active in, those areas that are already of interest to us. The Internet gives us the power to do more, but it does not of itself change what we want to do.

This suggests that for the political world, the age of the Internet means largely more of the same. But more of the same is not exactly the same. Some features of our government are certainly shaped by difficulties in communication, and these are likely to change. In some cases, the change will be for the good. The inefficiency of government agencies is partly caused by their complicated procedures for moving information. Already the Internet is making it easier to flatten these hierarchies and make them more efficient. Moreover, some elements of the bureaucracy exist exclusively to distribute or exchange information. The clerk at the Department of Motor Vehicles takes information that you write on a form and enters it into a computer. The mailman delivers information door to door. Once a few technical problems of authentication and security are resolved, these sorts of functionaries will become far less necessary, and the bureaucracies that surround them could become less cumbersome. Tracking down grandma's social security check will be easier in the age of cyber-government.

But these improvements have more to do with administrative services and the bureaucracy than with politics. They have few parallels in the realm of electoral politics and representation, because difficulties here are generally unrelated to exchanging and accessing information.

A common example will help make this point. Some analysts (most notably Dick Morris) have suggested that information technologies will help ease the problem of money in politics. Since it will be easier for candidates and voters to reach one another, they argue, expensive political advertising will become less necessary, and therefore the costs involved in campaigning will decline dramatically. This argument again misses the difference between changes in what we *can* do and changes in what we *choose* to do. Most campaign funds today are spent on television commercials. These commercials are necessary because many voters are not sufficiently interested in being informed about the election to seek out information on their own. To get their attention, a politician must interrupt their favorite television program with a campaign ad. Since the Internet will not make Americans more interested in politics, it will not diminish the need to reach voters who do not wish to be reached. Communicating with such voters is expensive, and the proliferation of sources of information will make this task not less expensive but more so. The money problem in politics is, at its heart, a result of political apathy, and the Internet will not cure this ailment.

Worlds of our own making

Strangely enough, while difficulties in communication and shortages of information do not cause many of the bad things about our politics, they are behind several of the good things. These may be undermined—though only in quite subtle ways—by the dynamics of the Information Age. It seems odd to say so. After all, how could greater access to information and greater ease of communication be detrimental to a democracy? Under what circumstances are difficulties in communication good? I will suggest three such circumstances.

The first has to do with the political consequences that come with an abundance of choice. Those who wanted to be informed about politics before the dawn of the Information Age had to work somewhat to obtain information. In the process, they were often exposed to influences they might not have actively sought, and these tended to enrich their experience and their knowledge. The difficulties involved in obtaining and communicating information thereby indirectly enriched our political discourse.

The Internet, however, allows us to access precisely and almost exclusively those influences that we wish to access. Indeed, this is one of the best things about it. Through the Internet we seek out information that we believe is important, rather than settling for what the editor of the evening news or the *New York Times* thinks is worthy of our attention. Vast amounts of information are available on the network, and users can search out exactly what they want—be it information, entertainment, opinion, statistics, or a chat with a stranger. But this greater control raises a new problem: How will we know what to want? If we are not exposed to things we did not seek out, how will we know what those unlike us are thinking, or what other options exist?

That question puts the matter too starkly, to be sure. Very few of us could be so insulated from outside influences that we would truly live in a world of our own making. But if we come to rely more and more on customized Internet sources for information, we do run the risk of subtly diminishing the number and types of ideas to which we are exposed, thereby limiting our experience of new and different ways of thinking. We might increasingly come to be swaddled in our own preferences.

Many users of the Internet would argue that this has not been their experience. The vast amounts of information on the Web and the ubiquity of hyperlinks instantly connecting readers to other sources and sites expose users to a broad range of opinion. Many of us have certainly learned things online that we would never have thought to inquire about. But we have done it all by our own direct selection, and so our pre-existing interests have still defined our range of exposures. The virtual world of the Internet does not force us into contact with others, and therefore does not force us to expand our horizons. Unsought exposure to new ideas does not occur only when we run across some interesting articles as we flip through the morning paper in search of our favorite subjects. It includes individuals and ideas we encounter on the street corner, on our way to mail a letter or to do any of the other things that the Internet will make unnecessary. The world of the network isolates us even as it connects us. While it brings us into contact with others in the virtual reality of cyberspace, it leaves us all sitting individually at our desks in the real world. Exposure to new ideas is often a byproduct of something else we are doing in the real world, and when we come to do less in that world, we will have less such exposure.

This problem was analyzed in *Republic.com*, another of the cyber-politics books of the past few years. Its author, University of Chicago law professor Cass Sunstein, wondered if the world of "see only what you want to see, hear only what you want to hear, read only what you want to read" could be good for our politics. Democracy, he argued, "depends on shared experiences and requires citizens to be exposed to topics and ideas they would not have chosen in advance." But Sunstein vastly exaggerates the magnitude of the problem and its consequences, and therefore ends up proposing solutions that range from the overbearing (mandatory "must carry" rules for partisan Web sites requiring them to link to political opponents) to the downright absurd (government-subsidized "deliberative domain" sites to encourage on-line discussion). The fact is that some degree of greater isolation of individuals into worlds of their own making will be unavoidable, given the enormous power to define one's own experience in cyberspace. It will not mean the end of deliberative politics, and it does not call for government action, but it may lead to a certain hardening of interests and a kind of overspecialization of the citizen. Our new ability to inform ourselves may, ironically, make us less informed about matters beyond the bounds of our most active interests.

The politics of size and place

A second way in which our politics may have benefited by difficulties in communication was noted by James Madison as among the greatest attributes of the American republic. Creating a single republic over a nation the size of the United States (even in 1787) was the true political miracle of the American Constitution. Such a feat had been, in no uncertain terms, declared to be impossible by the greatest political minds of Western civilization. Republics had worked only in small communities with simple, homogenous interests; a large republic, it was thought, would be too unwieldy. The multiplicity of interests would create a multiplicity of factions, and the nation would be too large to properly contain them. Such a republic, it was reasoned, would be subject to constant civil strife.

Madison turned this logic on its head. In *Federalist* 10, he argued that the vast size of the nation was precisely what would contain the power of factions. "The influence of factious leaders may kindle a flame within their particular States," Madison wrote, "but will be unable to spread a general conflagration through the other States." The nation would simply be too big for citizens to communicate adequately with one another across the country. Because communication would be difficult, nationwide factions would not form, and local factions would do little harm on a national scale.

This may seem like a terribly arcane and ancient problem to be bringing up in a discussion of the Information Age. After all, technologies of transportation and communication have been shrinking the distances between the states since the nation's earliest days. In 1833, Madison himself remarked that "the improvements already made in internal navigation by canals and steamboats, and in turnpikes and railroads, have virtually brought the most distant parts of the Union, in its present extent, much closer together than were the most distant parts of a much smaller Union at the date of the Federal Constitution of 1787." But information technologies will make cooperation across distances by relatively small groups far easier than it has ever been. We have already seen some examples of this. The often violent demonstrations that

now regularly accompany meetings of world leaders and financial institutions would not be possible without the organizing power of e-mail and the Internet. The F.B.I. has shown that white supremacist groups have also effectively used the Web to organize members nationwide. And, of course, less sinister interest groups have done the same, building up far more effective political organizations than they could have developed before the age of the Internet.

Moreover, the Information Age not only makes distances smaller, it also tends to make geography increasingly irrelevant. The federal system is founded on the assumption that place matters. It is designed to channel the interests of different states and regions into national consideration. But the logic of the Internet undermines that assumption.

Consider one small example of this problem. Members of Congress receive a great deal of mail. Generally, when a letter arrives, it is categorized based upon its geographic origin. If the return address or postmark identify it as having come from the member's district, it is opened and dealt with promptly. If it did not come from the district, it is put aside. It may be read later (or it may not be), but it will probably not receive a response. In this way, the system takes heed of geography, which after all is the organizing principle of the American system of representation. But what if there is no way to know if a piece of mail has come from the member's district? With regular mail, you can always tell where a message has come from by the postmark. But with e-mail, you can never know unless the writers choose to tell you, and even then you cannot be certain they are telling the truth. And indeed, interest groups and lobbyists use e-mail to overcome the geographic character of the system and bombard particular members of Congress with what seems like constituent pressure but often is not.

If more of our politics comes to take little heed of place, the structure of the representative system will be undermined. This, together with the ease of collaborating across great distances, may tend slowly to undo what Madison considered the most important safeguards in the federal system. These are subtle problems, which cannot be "fixed" by blunt government action. But they indicate how information technologies may over time alter the delicately nuanced balances that allow the American system to function.

Haste makes waste

A third way in which the Information Age may create difficulties relates to the pace of politics. Put simply, politics will largely be more of the same, but *faster*. Information technologies eliminate obstacles and reduce frictions in the various stages of political action, and this means that political action will tend to be more immediate. Political leaders may not be more decisive, but they will be subject to a more furious flow of information, interests, and pressures. Leaders and citizens alike will need to act with greater speed to keep up, and both will be forced to make hastier judgments.

There are certainly situations in which faster is better. A system quicker to react to pressure is more responsive and more representative. And since events in general now seem to move faster than ever, it may be good that our political system can keep up. But for most political deliberation and thoughtful policy making, faster is not better. The delays that occur at every step of the American political process give us time to think and rethink, to reason, consider, and decide. They allow time for opposing views to be raised, for research to be conducted and presented, for perspectives to change and true priorities to become clearer. By drastically diminishing the element of time in politics, the Internet will lead to careless decision-making. The shrinking "sound-bite," which tends to suck the content out of media coverage of political issues, has already given us a sense of what the loss of time can mean in politics, and the instantaneity of the Internet threatens to make this condition worse.

Consider one form of the instant decision: "instant polling dials." Voters are placed in a room and asked to move a dial in response to what they hear the candidates say. They must react instantly, and thus their responses are pure gut reactions. The results, displayed as lines upon the screen, are said to be indicative of voter attitudes. The assumption behind this method is that the instant reaction, not the reasoned judgment, is what counts. In the Information Age, this assumption may grow increasingly true.

Another example of the quickening of politics in the Information Age—and its mixed consequences—can be found in the first real new political institution of the Internet: the "blog." Many blogs—or "web logs," on-line diaries and sites of instant commentary and opinion—are homes for genuine political reflection. And in their interactions with one another, bloggers sometimes resemble a genuine community of citizens. However, this burgeoning institution embodies many of the Internet's deficiencies: It often has the feel of an echo-chamber; it is placeless; and it thrives on instant responses to the latest events. Above all, blogging is immediate. This is part of its charm, for both the writer and the reader. But it is also its greatest drawback as a forum for political discourse and action. Blogging is a new outlet for political opinion, but for the most part it is unreflective opinion. Insulated from refining influences and institutions and unconnected to the direct political life of any particular place, blogging is mere instantaneous reaction. But the institutions of political life exist, to a great extent, to mediate, and hopefully to elevate, public opinion. This is why their practical effect is often to slow things down, and why the rise of unmediated institutions like blogging is a mixed blessing at best.

The narrowing of interests and the shrinking of distances will further intensify the quickening of our politics. Those citizens who are interested in politics will

know just what they want and will demand it right away, and a system free of the shackles of distance and place will respond quickly to such demands.

The framers of the Constitution certainly perceived a need for dispatch and energy in government, and the system they designed reflects that concern in some respects, particularly in its relation to foreign nations. But at the same time, they understood the danger of too much speed in politics. In its internal operations, the American system seems designed to work at a snail's pace, to avoid, as Alexander Hamilton put it, "haste, inadvertence and a want of due deliberation." The politics of the Information Age will break down these barriers to haste.

An old solution

So what is to be done? The honest answer is not much. The new information technologies do not pose a mortal threat to our republic, and most of the usual clever political remedies would do more harm than good. Rather than outline detailed remedies, we should reflect upon the fact that the problems raised by the Internet—intellectual isolation, the demise of distance, and an undue haste in our politics—are not entirely new to America. All of them point us to the greatest teacher on the subject of American political life, Alexis de Tocqueville.

The isolation of the Internet-empowered individual carries with it echoes of Tocqueville's fears of a corrosive democratic individualism. It is the technological version of what Tocqueville describes as that "mature and calm feeling, which disposes each member of the community to sever himself from the mass of his fellows and to draw apart … so that after he has thus formed a little circle of his own, he willingly leaves society at large to itself." Internet-empowered citizens draw a circle not so much around those who are near but around those ideas and individuals they decide to seek out. This process can, to borrow more of Tocqueville's words, "throw him back forever upon himself alone and threatens in the end to confine him entirely" within himself.

Tocqueville's solution to the problem is the involvement of citizens in the political affairs of their communities, which can be achieved by enhancing the power and authority of local governments. This will draw individuals out of their isolation and into contact with one another to exercise that power. "It is important to understand," Tocqueville writes, "that, in general, men's affections are drawn only in directions where power exists … the New Englander is attached to his township not so much because he was born there as because he sees the township as a free, strong corporation of which he is part and often which is worth the trouble of trying to direct." Strong local government, with a genuine power to make decisions that affect the lives of its citizens, will in small, quiet ways encourage people to participate. In the process of participating, individuals will be increasingly exposed to the real political world. "Local institutions," Tocqueville further states, "bring men constantly into contact, despite the instincts which separate them, and force them to hear and to know and to help one another." Local government would be a subtle treatment for the subtle isolation of the Information Age citizen. By devolving greater authority to states and (especially) localities, for instance in matters of education or welfare, we might draw the politically engaged away from their desks and toward the town hall. There they will find themselves exposed to political and intellectual influences that they did not select in advance.

Local government is also, and much more obviously, a way to make place and geography newly relevant. If local governments were given more authority to make real decisions, the focus of those who are interested in politics would shift down to that level. Powerful special interests would find it more difficult to exercise their influence in countless local venues than in one capital city. And of course, anyone who has seen a town council debate knows that letting localities take over more of the work of government is a surefire way to slow down our politics. The rise of the Internet can only serve to remind us of the importance of devolving political power to states and localities.

The most disconcerting feature of the Information Age is its tendency to separate citizens from place—from real neighborhoods and communities where the hum and drum of daily life takes place. These communities are, after all, where politics must of necessity occur. This is the key to what should concern us about the age of cyber-politics: the replacement of some elements of the real political world with virtual substitutes that can tend to blind us to the connection between politics and polities, and therefore to the real purpose of politics, and to its most appropriate and most important uses.

I do not mean to paint too dark a picture of the future. The political difficulties introduced by the Information Age will not bring about the demise of democracy or the end of deliberative politics. Indeed, they will not bring all that much change, good or bad. The essential purposes of government, and the very basic social and cultural forces that shape the political system, will not be transformed in a flash of electricity. But in preparing for the future, anticipating difficulties is often the most vital task. In that spirit, the coming of the Information Age suggests to us several imperatives: to seek ways to avoid intellectual isolation, to contain powerful interest groups, to make location and place newly relevant, and above all to slow things down and think them through.

YUVAL LEVIN is a member of the staff of the President's Council on Bioethics and author of *Tyranny of Reason: The Origins and Consequences of the Social Scientific Outlook* (University Press of America, 2000).

Reprinted with permission of the authors from *The Public Interest*, Fall 2002, pp. 80-94. © 2002 by National Affairs, Inc.

UNIT 4
Products of American Politics

Unit Selections

Key Points to Consider

- What do you think is the single most important social welfare or economic policy issue facing the American political system today? The single most important national security or homeland security issue? What do you think ought to be done about them?

- What factors increasingly blur the distinction between foreign and domestic policy issues? How does "homeland security" fit into this context?

- How would you compare President George W. Bush's performance in the areas of social welfare and economic policies with the way he has handled national security and diplomatic affairs? What changes has he tried to make in each of these areas?

- What policy issues currently viewed as minor matters seem destined to develop into crisis situations?

- What do you think is the most significant policy failure of American national government today? The most significant policy success? Explain.

- What do you think about the idea of devolution, which means giving state and local governments *more* responsibility for policy making and policy implementation and the national government *less*? What reasons are there to expect that state and local governments will do a better—or worse—job than the national government in such areas as welfare and health care benefits for the old and the poor?

- What short-term and long-term effects did the events of September 11, 2001, have on the U.S. policy process and the direction of U.S. government policies?

 **Links: www.dushkin.com/online/**
These sites are annotated in the World Wide Web pages.

American Diplomacy
http://www.unc.edu/depts/diplomat/

Cato Institute
http://www.cato.org/research/ss_prjct.html

Foreign Affairs
http://www.foreignaffairs.org

The Gallup Organization
http://www.gallup.com

International Information Programs
http://usinfo.state.gov

STAT-USA
http://www.stat-usa.gov/stat-usa.html

Tax Foundation
http://www.taxfoundation.org/index.html

"**P**roducts" refers to the government policies that the American political system produces. The first three units of this book have paved the way for this fourth unit, because the products of American politics are very much the consequences of the rest of the political system.

The health of the American economy is almost always a prominent policy issue in the American political system. One of the most remarkable consequences of twelve years (1981–1993) under President Reagan and the first President Bush was enormous growth in budget deficits and in the national debt. During the Clinton presidency, the country enjoyed the longest period of continuous economic growth in U.S. history, accompanied by low unemployment and inflation rates. Continuing economic growth increased tax revenues to such an extent that the long-sought goal of a balanced budget was reached in 1998 amid predictions that the entire national debt would be eliminated within a decade or so. In the last months of the Clinton administration, however, some signs of an economic slowdown appeared; the country entered a recession in the second half of President George W. Bush's first year in office, and the September 11 terrorist attacks accelerated the economic downturn.

By early 2004, large budget deficits had returned and the national debt grew accordingly. Meanwhile, the retirement of the first Baby Boomers inevitably drew closer and their Social Security and Medicare entitlements were certain to further stress the national government's fiscal situation.

Domestic public policy usually involves "trade-offs" among competing uses of scarce resources. During his 1992 campaign, Bill Clinton called attention to many such trade-offs in the area of health care. As president, Clinton introduced a comprehensive health care reform proposal late in 1993. Congress never voted on that proposal, and, while various minor changes were made in the nation's health care delivery system during the Clinton administration, no comprehensive overhaul was ever achieved.

Other domestic policy areas also involve trade-offs. To what extent should we make the unemployed who are receiving welfare payments work, and what responsibility should the government take for preparing such citizens for work and for ensuring that jobs are available? How much are cleaner air and other environmental goals worth in terms of economic productivity, unemployment, and so forth? How much of a role should the national government play in financing and shaping elementary and secondary schooling?

For most of the last half of the twentieth century, the United States and the Soviet Union each had the capacity to end human existence as we know it. Not surprisingly, the threat of nuclear war often dominated American foreign policy and diplomacy. During that same period, however, the United States used conventional military forces in a number of places such as Korea, Vietnam, Grenada, Panama, the Persian Gulf area, and Afghanistan. The demise of the Soviet Union in 1991 left the United States as the world's sole superpower, profoundly affecting world politics and U.S. foreign policy ever since. Questions about the appropriateness of U.S. intervention in such disparate places as Bosnia-Herzegovina, Somalia, Haiti, Iraq, Kosovo, and even Russia were at the forefront of foreign policy concerns during the Clinton administration. The George W. Bush administration has, of course, been preoccupied with antiterrorism efforts and homeland and national security since the September 11 terrorist attacks. In 2003, American troops continued their presence in Afghanistan and also invaded Iraq and overthrew the regime of Saddam Hussein.

The foreign and defense policy process in the United States raises a host of related issues, including continuing struggle between legislative and executive branches for control. In 1991, Congress authorized war with Iraq, which was the first time since World War II that there has been explicit and formal congressional approval prior to commencement of U.S. military hostilities. In late 1995, President Clinton committed the United States to sending troops to Bosnia-Herzegovina as part of a multinational peacekeeping force. Despite some opposition, Congress passed resolutions supporting the troops. Toward the end of 1997, President Saddam Hussein of Iraq obstructed UN weapons inspection teams in his country and President Clinton responded by increasing the readiness of U.S. military forces in the Persian Gulf. In late 1998, several days of U.S. air strikes on Iraq followed what was viewed as further provocation. In the aftermath of the terrorist attacks in 2001, Congress supported President George W. Bush in pursuing the perpetrators and launching an assault on al Qaeda sites in Afghanistan. In the fall of 2002, Congress authorized President Bush to wage war against Iraq if he deemed it necessary to safeguard American security. Early the next year, U.S. forces invaded Iraq, although some critics in Congress and elsewhere suggested that President Bush had made insufficient attempts to gain widespread international support for the invasion.

The traditional distinction between domestic and foreign policy is becoming more and more difficult to maintain, since so many contemporary policy decisions have important implications on both fronts. President Clinton's emphasis on the connection between domestic and international economic issues in maintaining what he called national economic security reinforced this point. In turn, he worked hard to pass the NAFTA accord of 1993, which dramatically reduced trade barriers among Canada, Mexico, and the United States. Similarly, President George W. Bush has repeatedly noted the connection between, on the one hand, military and diplomatic activities with respect to faraway places like Afghanistan, Iraq, Iran, and North Korea and, on the other, homeland security in the post–September 11 era.

The Tax-Cut Con

By PAUL KRUGMAN

1. The Cartoon and the Reality

Bruce Tinsley's comic strip, "Mallard Fillmore," is, he says, "for the average person out there: the forgotten American taxpayer who's sick of the liberal media." In June, that forgotten taxpayer made an appearance in the strip, attacking his TV set with a baseball bat and yelling: "I can't afford to send my kids to college, or even take 'em out of their substandard public school, because the federal, state and local governments take more than 50 percent of my income in taxes. And then the guy on the news asks with a straight face whether or not we can 'afford' tax cuts."

But that's just a cartoon. Meanwhile, Bob Riley has to face the reality.

Riley knows all about substandard public schools. He's the governor of Alabama, which ranks near the bottom of the nation in both spending per pupil and educational achievement. The state has also neglected other public services—for example, 28,000 inmates are held in a prison system built for 12,000. And thanks in part to a lack of health care, it has the second-highest infant mortality in the nation.

When he was a member of Congress, Riley, a Republican, was a staunch supporter of tax cuts. Faced with a fiscal crisis in his state, however, he seems to have had an epiphany. He decided that it was impossible to balance Alabama's budget without a significant tax increase. And that, apparently, led him to reconsider everything. "The largest tax increase in state history just to maintain the status quo?" he asked. "I don't think so." Instead, Riley proposed a wholesale restructuring of the state's tax system: reducing taxes on the poor and middle class while raising them on corporations and the rich and increasing overall tax receipts enough to pay for a big increase in education spending. You might call it a New Deal for Alabama.

Nobody likes paying taxes, and no doubt some Americans are as angry about their taxes as Tinsley's imaginary character. But most Americans also care a lot about the things taxes pay for. All politicians say they're for public education; almost all of them also say they support a strong national defense, maintaining Social Security and, if anything, expanding the coverage of Medicare. When the "guy on the news" asks whether we can afford a tax cut, he's asking whether, after yet another tax cut goes through, there will be enough money to pay for those things. And the answer is no.

But it's very difficult to get that answer across in modern American politics, which has been dominated for 25 years by a crusade against taxes.

I don't use the word "crusade" lightly. The advocates of tax cuts are relentless, even fanatical. An indication of the movement's fervor—and of its political power—came during the Iraq war. War is expensive and is almost always accompanied by tax increases. But not in 2003. "Nothing is more important in the face of a war," declared Tom DeLay, the House majority leader, "than cutting taxes." And sure enough, taxes were cut, not just in a time of war but also in the face of record budget deficits. Nor will it be easy to reverse those tax cuts: the tax-cut movement has convinced many Americans—like Tinsley—that everybody still pays far too much in taxes.

A result of the tax-cut crusade is that there is now a fundamental mismatch between the benefits Americans expect to receive from the government and the revenues government collect. This mismatch is already having profound effects at the state and local levels: teachers and policemen are being laid off and children are being denied health insurance. The federal government can mask its problems for a while, by running huge budget deficits, but it, too, will eventually have to decide whether to cut services or raise taxes. And we are not talking about minor policy adjustments. If taxes stay as low as they are now, government as we know it cannot be maintained. In particular, Social Security will have to become far less generous; Medicare will no longer be able to guarantee comprehensive medical care to older Americans; Medicaid will no longer provide basic medical care to the poor.

How did we reach this point? What are the origins of the antitax crusade? And where is it taking us? To answer these questions, we will have to look both at who the antitax crusaders are and at the evidence on what tax cuts do to the budget and the economy. But first, let's set the stage by taking a look at the current state of taxation in America.

2. How High Are Our Taxes?

The reason Tinsley's comic strip about the angry taxpayer caught my eye was, of course, that the numbers were all wrong. Very few Americans pay as much as 50 percent of their income in taxes; on average, families near the middle of the income distribution pay only about half that percentage in federal, state and local taxes combined.

In fact, though most Americans feel that they pay too much in taxes, they get off quite lightly compared with the citizens of other advanced countries. Furthermore, for most Americans tax rates probably haven't risen for a generation. And a few Americans—namely those with high incomes—face much lower taxes than they did a generation ago.

To assess trends in the overall level of taxes and to compare taxation across countries, economists usually look first at the ratio of taxes to gross domestic product, the total value of output produced in the country. In the United States, all taxes—federal, state and local—reached a peak of 29.6 percent of G.D.P. in 2000. That number was, however, swollen by taxes on capital gains during the stock-market bubble.

By 2002, the tax take was down to 26.3 percent of G.D.P., and all indications are that it will be lower still this year and next.

This is a low number compared with almost every other advanced country. In 1999, Canada collected 38.2 percent of G.D.P. in taxes, France collected 45.8 percent and Sweden, 52.2 percent.

Still, aren't taxes much higher than they used to be? Not if we're looking back over the past 30 years. As a share of G.D.P., federal taxes are currently at their lowest point since the Eisenhower administration. State and local taxes rose substantially between 1960 and the early 1970's, but have been roughly stable since then. Aside from the capital gains taxes paid during the bubble years, the share of income Americans pay in taxes has been flat since Richard Nixon was president.

Of course, overall levels of taxation don't necessarily tell you how heavily particular individuals and families are taxed. As it turns out, however, middle-income Americans, like the country as a whole, haven't seen much change in their overall taxes over the past 30 years. On average, families in the middle of the income distribution find themselves paying about 26 percent of their income in taxes today. This number hasn't changed significantly since 1989, and though hard data are lacking, it probably hasn't changed much since 1970.

Meanwhile, wealthy Americans have seen a sharp drop in their tax burden. The top tax rate—the income-tax rate on the highest bracket—is now 35 percent, half what it was in the 1970's. With the exception of a brief period between 1988 and 1993, that's the lowest rate since 1932. Other taxes that, directly or indirectly, bear mainly on the very affluent have also been cut sharply. The effective tax rate on corporate profits has been cut in half since the 1960's. The 2001 tax cut phases out the inheritance tax, which is overwhelmingly a tax on the very wealthy: in 1999, only 2 percent of estates paid any tax, and half the tax was paid by only 3,300 estates worth more than $5 million. The 2003 tax act sharply cuts taxes on dividend income, another boon to the very well off. By the time the Bush tax cuts have taken full effect, people with really high incomes will face their lowest average tax rate since the Hoover administration.

So here's the picture: Americans pay low taxes by international standards. Most people's taxes haven't gone up in the past generation; the wealthy have had their taxes cut to levels not seen since before the New Deal. Even before the latest round of tax cuts, when compared with citizens of other advanced nations or compared with Americans a generation ago, we had nothing to complain about—and those with high incomes now have a lot to celebrate. Yet a significant number of Americans rage against taxes, and the party that controls all three branches of the federal government has made tax cuts its supreme priority. Why?

3. Supply-Siders, Starve-the-Beasters and Lucky Duckies

It is often hard to pin down what antitax crusaders are trying to achieve. The reason is not, or not only, that they are disingenuous about their motives—though as we will see, disingenuity has become a hallmark of the movement in recent years. Rather, the fuzziness comes from the fact that today's antitax movement moves back and forth between two doctrines. Both doctrines favor the same thing: big tax cuts for people with high incomes. But they favor it for different reasons.

One of those doctrines has become famous under the name "supply-side economics." It's the view that the government can cut taxes without severe cuts in public spending. The other doctrine is often referred to as "starving the beast," a phrase coined by David Stockman, Ronald Reagan's budget director. It's the view that taxes should be cut precisely in order to force severe cuts in public spending. Supply-side economics is the friendly, attractive face of the tax-cut movement. But starve-the-beast is where the power lies.

The starting point of supply-side economics is an assertion that no economist would dispute: taxes reduce the incentive to work, save and invest. A businessman who knows that 70 cents of every extra dollar he makes will go to the I.R.S. is less willing to make the effort to earn that extra dollar than if he knows that the I.R.S. will take only 35 cents. So reducing tax rates will, other things being the same, spur the economy.

This much isn't controversial. But the government must pay its bills. So the standard view of economists is that if you want to reduce the burden of taxes, you must explain what government programs you want to cut as part of the deal. There's no free lunch.

What the supply-siders argued, however, was that there was a free lunch. Cutting marginal rates, they insisted, would lead to such a large increase in gross domestic product that it wouldn't be necessary to come up with offsetting spending cuts. What supply-side economists say, in other words, is, "Don't worry, be happy and cut taxes." And when they say cut taxes, they mean taxes on the affluent: reducing the top marginal rate means that the biggest tax cuts go to people in the highest tax brackets.

The other camp in the tax-cut crusade actually welcomes the revenue losses from tax cuts. Its most visible spokesman today is Grover Norquist, president of Americans for Tax Reform, who once told National Public Radio: "I don't want to abolish government. I simply want to reduce it to the size where I can drag it into the bathroom and drown it in the bathtub." And the way to get it down to that size is to starve it of revenue. "The goal is reducing the size and scope of government by draining its lifeblood," Norquist told U.S. News & World Report.

What does "reducing the size and scope of government" mean? Tax-cut proponents are usually vague about the details. But the Heritage Foundation, ideological headquarters for the movement, has made it pretty clear. Edwin Feulner, the foundation's president, uses "New Deal" and "Great Society" as terms of abuse, implying that he and his organization want to do away with the institutions Franklin Roosevelt and Lyndon Johnson created. That means Social Security, Medicare, Medicaid—most of what gives citizens of the United States a safety net against economic misfortune.

The starve-the-beast doctrine is now firmly within the conservative mainstream. George W. Bush himself seemed to endorse the doctrine as the budget surplus evaporated: in August 2001 he called the disappearing surplus "incredibly positive news" because it would put Congress in a "fiscal straitjacket."

Like supply-siders, starve-the-beasters favor tax cuts mainly for people with high incomes. That is partly because, like supply-siders, they emphasize the incentive effects of cutting the top marginal rate; they just don't believe that those incentive effects are big enough that tax cuts pay for themselves. But they have another reason for cutting taxes mainly on the rich, which has become known as the "lucky ducky" argument.

Here's how the argument runs: to starve the beast, you must not only deny funds to the government; you must make voters hate the government. There's a danger that working-class families might see government as their friend: because their incomes are low, they don't pay much in taxes, while they benefit from public spending. So in starving the beast, you must take care not to cut taxes on these "lucky duckies." (Yes, that's what The Wall Street Journal called them in a famous editorial.) In fact, if possible, you must *raise* taxes on working-class Americans in order, as The Journal said, to get their "blood boiling with tax rage."

So the tax-cut crusade has two faces. Smiling supply-siders say that tax cuts are all gain, no pain; scowling starve-the-beasters believe that inflicting pain is not just necessary but also desirable. Is the alliance between these two groups a marriage of convenience? Not exactly. It would be more accurate to say that the starve-the-beasters hired the supply-siders—indeed, created them—because they found their naive optimism useful.

A look at who the supply-siders are and how they came to prominence tells the story.

The supply-side movement likes to present itself as a school of economic thought like Keynesianism or monetarism—that is, as a set of scholarly ideas that made their way, as such ideas do, into political discussion. But the reality is quite different. Supply-side economics was a political doctrine from Day 1; it emerged in the pages of political magazines, not professional economics journals.

That is not to deny that many professional economists favor tax cuts. But they almost always turn out to be starve-the-beasters, not supply-siders. And they often secretly—or sometimes not so secretly—hold supply-siders in contempt. N. Gregory Mankiw, now chairman of George W. Bush's Council of Economic Advisers, is definitely a friend to tax cuts; but in the first edition of his economic-principles textbook, he described Ronald Reagan's supply-side advisers as "charlatans and cranks."

It is not that the professionals refuse to consider supply-side ideas; rather, they have looked at them and found them wanting. A conspicuous example came earlier this year when the Congressional Budget Office tried to evaluate the growth effects of the Bush administration's proposed tax cuts. The budget office's new head, Douglas Holtz-Eakin, is a conservative economist who was handpicked for his job by the administration. But his conclusion was that unless the revenue losses from the proposed tax cuts were offset by spending cuts, the resulting deficits would be a drag on growth, quite likely to outweigh any supply-side effects.

But if the professionals regard the supply-siders with disdain, who employs these people? The answer is that since the 1970's almost all of the prominent supply-siders have been aides to conservative politicians, writers at conservative publications like National Review, fellows at conservative policy centers like Heritage or economists at private companies with strong Republican connections. Loosely speaking, that is, supply-siders work for the vast right-wing conspiracy. What gives supply-side economics influence is its connection with a powerful network of institutions that want to shrink the government and see tax cuts as a way to achieve that goal. Supply-side economics is a feel-good cover story for a political movement with a much harder-nosed agenda.

This isn't just speculation. Irving Kristol, in his role as co-editor of The Public Interest, was arguably the single most important proponent of supply-side economics. But years later, he suggested that he himself wasn't all that persuaded by the doctrine: "I was not certain of its economic merits but quickly saw its political possibilities." Writing in 1995, he explained that his real aim was to shrink the government and that tax cuts were a means to that end: "The task, as I saw it, was to create a new majority, which evidently would mean a conservative majority, which came to mean, in turn, a Republican majority—so political effectiveness was the priority, not the accounting deficiencies of government."

In effect, what Kristol said in 1995 was that he and his associates set out to deceive the American public. They sold tax cuts on the pretense that they would be painless, when they themselves believed that it would be necessary to slash public spending in order to make room for those cuts.

But one supposes that the response would be that the end justified the means—that the tax cuts did benefit all Americans because they led to faster economic growth. Did they?

4. From Reaganomics to Clintonomics

Ronald Reagan put supply-side theory into practice with his 1981 tax cut. The tax cuts were modest for middle-class families but very large for the well-off. Between 1979 and 1983, according to Congressional Budget Office estimates, the average federal tax rate on the top 1 percent of families fell from 37 to 27.7 percent.

So did the tax cuts promote economic growth? You might think that all we have to do is look at how the economy performed. But it's not that simple, because different observers read different things from Reagan's economic record.

Here's how tax-cut advocates look at it: after a deep slump between 1979 and 1982, the U.S. economy began growing rapidly. Between 1982 and 1989 (the first year of the first George Bush's presidency), the economy grew at an average annual rate of 4.2 percent. That's a lot better than the growth rate of the economy in the late 1970's, and supply-siders claim that these "Seven Fat Years" (the title of a book by Robert L. Bartley, the longtime editor of The Wall Street Journal's editorial page) prove the success of Reagan's 1981 tax cut.

But skeptics say that rapid growth after 1982 proves nothing: a severe recession is usually followed by a period of fast growth, as unemployed workers and factories are brought back on line. The test of tax cuts as a spur to economic growth is whether they produced more than an ordinary business cycle recovery. Once the economy was back to full employment, was it bigger than you would otherwise have expected? And there Reagan fails the test:

between 1979, when the big slump began, and 1989, when the economy finally achieved more or less full employment again, the growth rate was 3 percent, the same as the growth rate between the two previous business cycle peaks in 1973 and 1979. Or to put it another way, by the late 1980's the U.S. economy was about where you would have expected it to be, given the trend in the 1970's. Nothing in the data suggests a supply-side revolution.

Does this mean that the Reagan tax cuts had no effect? Of course not. Those tax cuts, combined with increased military spending, provided a good old-fashioned Keynesian boost to demand. And this boost was one factor in the rapid recovery from recession that developed at the end of 1982, though probably not as important as the rapid expansion of the money supply that began in the summer of that year. But the supposed supply-side effects are invisible in the data.

While the Reagan tax cuts didn't produce any visible supply-side gains, they did lead to large budget deficits. From the point of view of most economists, this was a bad thing. But for starve-the-beast tax-cutters, deficits are potentially a good thing, because they force the government to shrink. So did Reagan's deficits shrink the beast?

A casual glance at the data might suggest not: federal spending as a share of gross domestic product was actually slightly higher at the end of the 1980's than it was at the end of the 1970's. But that number includes both defense spending and "entitlements," mainly Social Security and Medicare, whose growth is automatic unless Congress votes to cut benefits. What's left is a grab bag known as domestic discretionary spending, including everything from courts and national parks to environmental cleanups and education. And domestic discretionary spending fell from 4.5 percent of G.D.P. in 1981 to 3.2 percent in 1988.

But that's probably about as far as any president can shrink domestic discretionary spending. And because Reagan couldn't shrink the belly of the beast, entitlements, he couldn't find enough domestic spending cuts to offset his military spending increases and tax cuts. The federal budget went into persistent, alarming, deficit. In response to these deficits, George Bush the elder went back on his "read my lips" pledge and raised taxes. Bill Clinton raised them further. And thereby hangs a tale.

For Clinton did exactly the opposite of what supply-side economics said you should do: he raised the marginal rate on high-income taxpayers. In 1989, the top 1 percent of families paid, on average, only 28.9 percent of their income in federal taxes; by 1995, that share was up to 36.1 percent.

Conservatives confidently awaited a disaster—but it failed to materialize. In fact, the economy grew at a reasonable pace through Clinton's first term, while the deficit and the unemployment rate went steadily down. And then the news got even better: unemployment fell to its lowest level in decades without causing inflation, while productivity growth accelerated to rates not seen since the 1960's. And the budget deficit turned into an impressive surplus.

Tax-cut advocates had claimed the Reagan years as proof of their doctrine's correctness; as we have seen, those claims wilt under close examination. But the Clinton years posed a much greater challenge: here was a president who sharply raised the marginal tax rate on high-income taxpayers, the very rate that the tax-cut movement cares most about. And instead of presiding over an economic disaster, he presided over an economic miracle.

Let's be clear: very few economists think that Clinton's policies were primarily responsible for that miracle. For the most part, the Clinton-era surge probably reflected the maturing of information technology: businesses finally figured out how to make effective use of computers, and the resulting surge in productivity drove the economy forward. But the fact that America's best growth in a generation took place after the government did exactly the opposite of what tax-cutters advocate was a body blow to their doctrine.

They tried to make the best of the situation. The good economy of the late 1990's, ardent tax-cutters insisted, was caused by the 1981 tax cut. Early in 2000, Lawrence Kudlow and Stephen Moore, prominent supply-siders, published an article titled "It's the Reagan Economy, Stupid."

But anyone who thought about the lags involved found this implausible—indeed, hilarious. If the tax-cut movement attributed the booming economy of 1999 to a tax cut Reagan pushed through 18 years earlier, why didn't they attribute the economic boom of 1983 and 1984—Reagan's "morning in America"—to whatever Lyndon Johnson was doing in 1965 and 1966?

By the end of the 1990's, in other words, supply-side economics had become something of a laughingstock, and the whole case for tax cuts as a route to economic growth was looking pretty shaky. But the tax-cut crusade was nonetheless, it turned out, poised for its biggest political victories yet. How did that happen?

5. Second Wind: The Bush Tax Cuts

As the economic success of the United States under Bill Clinton became impossible to deny, there was a gradual shift in the sales strategy for tax cuts. The supposed economic benefits of tax cuts received less emphasis; the populist rationale—you, personally, pay too much in taxes—was played up.

I began this article with an example of this campaign's success: the creator of Mallard Fillmore apparently believes that typical families pay twice as much in taxes as they in fact do. But the most striking example of what skillful marketing can accomplish is the campaign for repeal of the estate tax.

As demonstrated, the estate tax is a tax on the very, very well off. Yet advocates of repeal began portraying it as a terrible burden on the little guy. They renamed it the "death tax" and put out reports decrying its impact on struggling farmers and businessmen—reports that never provided real-world examples because actual cases of family farms or small businesses broken up to pay estate taxes are almost impossible to find. This campaign succeeded in creating a public perception that the estate tax falls broadly on the population. Earlier this year, a poll found that 49 percent of Americans believed that most families had to pay the estate tax, while only 33 percent gave the right answer that only a few families had to pay.

Still, while an insistent marketing campaign has convinced many Americans that they are overtaxed, it hasn't succeeded in making the issue a top priority with the public. Polls consistently show that voters regard safeguarding Social Security and Medicare as much more important than tax cuts.

Nonetheless, George W. Bush has pushed through tax cuts in each year of his presidency. Why did he push for these tax cuts, and how did he get them through?

You might think that you could turn to the administration's own pronouncements to learn why it has been so determined to cut taxes. But even if you try to take the administration at its word, there's a problem: the public rationale for tax cuts has shifted repeatedly over the past three years.

During the 2000 campaign and the initial selling of the 2001 tax cut, the Bush team insisted that the federal government was running an excessive budget surplus, which should be returned to taxpayers. By the summer of 2001, as it became clear that the projected budget surpluses would not materialize, the administration shifted to touting the tax cuts as a form of demand-side economic stimulus: by putting more money in consumers' pockets, the tax cuts would stimulate spending and help pull the economy out of recession. By 2003, the rationale had changed again: the administration argued that reducing taxes on dividend income, the core of its plan, would improve incentives and hence long-run growth—that is, it had turned to a supply-side argument.

These shifting rationales had one thing in common: none of them were credible. It was obvious to independent observers even in 2001 that the budget projections used to justify that year's tax cut exaggerated future revenues and understated future costs. It was similarly obvious that the 2001 tax cut was poorly designed as a demand stimulus. And we have already seen that the supply-side rationale for the 2003 tax cut was tested and found wanting by the Congressional Budget Office.

So what were the Bush tax cuts really about? The best answer seems to be that they were about securing a key part of the Republican base. Wealthy campaign contributors have a lot to gain from lower taxes, and since they aren't very likely to depend on Medicare, Social Security or Medicaid, they won't suffer if the beast gets starved. Equally important was the support of the party's intelligentsia, nurtured by policy centers like Heritage and professionally committed to the tax-cut crusade. The original

Bush tax-cut proposal was devised in late 1999 not to win votes in the national election but to fend off a primary challenge from the supply-sider Steve Forbes, the presumptive favorite of that part of the base.

This brings us to the next question: how have these cuts been sold?

At this point, one must be blunt: the selling of the tax cuts has depended heavily on chicanery. The administration has used accounting trickery to hide the true budget impact of its proposals, and it has used misleading presentations to conceal the extent to which its tax cuts are tilted toward families with very high income.

The most important tool of accounting trickery, though not the only one, is the use of "sunset clauses" to understate the long-term budget impact of tax cuts. To keep the official 10-year cost of the 2001 tax cut down, the administration's Congressional allies wrote the law so that tax rates revert to their 2000 levels in 2011. But, of course, nobody expects the sunset to occur: when 2011 rolls around, Congress will be under immense pressure to extend the tax cuts.

The same strategy was used to hide the cost of the 2003 tax cut. Thanks to sunset clauses, its headline cost over the next decade was only $350 billion, but if the sunsets are canceled—as the president proposed in a speech early this month—the cost will be at least $800 billion.

Meanwhile, the administration has carried out a very successful campaign to portray these tax cuts as mainly aimed at middle-class families. This campaign is similar in spirit to the selling of estate-tax repeal as a populist measure, but considerably more sophisticated.

The reality is that the core measures of both the 2001 and 2003 tax cuts mainly benefit the very affluent. The centerpieces of the 2001 act were a reduction in the top income-tax rate and elimination of the estate tax—the first, by definition, benefiting only people with high incomes; the second benefiting only heirs to large estates. The core of the 2003 tax cut was a reduction in the tax rate on dividend income. This benefit, too, is concentrated on very high-income families.

According to estimates by the Tax Policy Center—a liberal-oriented institution, but one with a reputation for scrupulous accuracy—the 2001 tax cut, once fully phased in, will deliver 42 percent of its benefits to the top 1 percent of the income distribution. (Roughly speaking, that means families earning more than $330,000 per year.) The 2003 tax cut delivers a somewhat smaller share to the top 1 percent, 29.1 percent, but within that concentrates its benefits on the really, really rich. Families with incomes over $1 million a year—a mere 0.13 percent of the population—will receive 17.3 percent of this year's tax cut, more than the total received by the bottom 70 percent of American families. Indeed, the 2003 tax cut has already proved a major boon to some of America's wealthiest people: corporations in which executives or a single family hold a large fraction of stocks are suddenly paying much bigger dividends, which are now taxed at only 15 percent no matter how high the income of their recipient.

It might seem impossible to put a populist gloss on tax cuts this skewed toward the rich, but the administration has been remarkably successful in doing just that.

One technique involves exploiting the public's lack of statistical sophistication. In the selling of the 2003 tax cut, the catch phrase used by administration spokesmen was "92 million Americans will receive an average tax cut of $1,083." That sounded, and was intended to sound, as if every American family would get $1,083. Needless to say, that wasn't true.

Yet the catch phrase wasn't technically a lie: the Tax Policy Center estimates that 89 million people will receive tax cuts this year and that the total tax cut will be $99 billion, or about $1,100 for each of those 89 million people. But this calculation carefully leaves out the 50 million taxpayers who received no tax cut at all. And even among those who did get a tax cut, most got a lot less than $1,000, a number inflated by the very big tax cuts received by a few wealthy people. About half of American families received a tax cut of less than $100; the great majority, a tax cut of less than $500.

But the most original, you might say brilliant, aspect of the Bush administration's approach to tax cuts has involved the way the tax cuts themselves are structured.

David Stockman famously admitted that Reagan's middle-class tax cuts were a "Trojan horse" that allowed him to smuggle in what he really wanted, a cut in the top marginal rate. The Bush administration similarly follows a Trojan horse strategy, but an even cleverer one. The core measures in Bush's tax cuts benefit only the wealthy, but there are additional features that provide significant benefits to some—but only some—middle-class families. For example, the 2001 tax cut included a $400 child credit and also created a new 10 percent tax bracket, the so-called cutout. These measures had the effect of creating a "sweet spot" that could be exploited for political purposes. If a couple had multiple children, if the children were all still under 18 and if the couple's income was just high enough to allow it to take full advantage of the child credit, it could get a tax cut of as much as 4 percent of pretax income. Hence the couple with two children and an income of $40,000, receiving a tax cut of $1,600, who played such a large role in the administration's rhetoric. But while most couples have children, at any given time only a small minority of families contains two or more children under 18—and many of these families have income too low to take full advantage of the child tax credit. So that "typical" family wasn't typical at all. Last year, the actual tax break for families in the middle of the income distribution averaged $469, not $1,600.

So that's the story of the tax-cut offensive under the Bush administration: through a combination of hardball politics, deceptive budget arithmetic and systematic misrepresentation of who benefits, Bush's team has achieved a major reduction of taxes, especially for people with very high incomes.

But where does that leave the country?

6. A Planned Crisis

Right now, much of the public discussion of the Bush tax cuts focuses on their short-run impact. Critics say that the 2.7 million jobs lost since March 2001 prove that the administration's policies have failed, while the administration says that things would have been even worse without the tax cuts and that a solid recovery is just around the corner.

But this is the wrong debate. Even in the short run, the right question to ask isn't whether the tax cuts were better than nothing; they probably were. The right question is whether some other economic-stimulus plan could have achieved better results at a lower budget cost. And it is hard to deny that, on a jobs-per-dollar basis, the Bush tax cuts have been extremely ineffective. According to the Congressional Budget Office, half of this year's $400 billion budget deficit is due to Bush tax cuts. Now $200 billion is a lot of money; it is equivalent to the salaries of four million average workers. Even the administration doesn't claim its policies have created four million jobs. Surely some other policy—aid to state and local governments, tax breaks for the poor and middle class rather than the rich, maybe even W.P.A.-style public works—would have been more successful at getting the country back to work.

Meanwhile, the tax cuts are designed to remain in place even after the economy has recovered. Where will they leave us?

Here's the basic fact: partly, though not entirely, as a result of the tax cuts of the last three years, the government of the United States faces a fundamental fiscal shortfall. That is, the revenue it collects falls well short of the sums it needs to pay for existing programs. Even the U.S. government must, eventually, pay its bills, so something will have to give.

The numbers tell the tale. This year and next, the federal government will run budget deficits of more than $400 billion. Deficits may fall a bit, at least as a share of gross domestic product, when the economy recovers. But the relief will be modest and temporary. As Peter Fisher, under secretary of the treasury for domestic finance, puts it, the federal government is "a gigantic insurance company with a sideline business in defense and homeland security." And about a decade from now, this insurance company's policyholders will begin making a lot of claims. As the baby boomers retire, spending on Social Security benefits and Medicare will steadily rise, as will spending on Medicaid (because of rising medical costs). Eventually, unless there are sharp cuts in benefits, these three programs alone will consume a larger share of G.D.P. than the federal government currently collects in taxes.

Alan Auerbach, William Gale and Peter Orszag, fiscal experts at the Brookings Institution, have estimated the size of the "fiscal gap"—the increase in revenues or reduction in spending that would be needed to make the nation's finances sustainable in the long run. If you define the long run as 75 years, this gap turns out to be 4.5 percent of G.D.P. Or to put it another way, the gap is equal to 30 percent of what the federal government spends on all domestic programs. Of that gap, about 60 percent is the result of the Bush tax cuts. We would have faced a serious fiscal problem even if those tax cuts had never happened. But we face a much nastier problem now that they are in place. And more broadly, the tax-cut crusade will make it very hard for any future politicians to raise taxes.

So how will this gap be closed? The crucial point is that it cannot be closed without either fundamentally redefining the role of government or sharply raising taxes.

Politicians will, of course, promise to eliminate wasteful spending. But take out Social Security, Medicare, defense, Medicaid, government pensions, homeland security, interest on the public debt and veterans' benefits—none of them what people who complain about waste usually have in mind—and you are left with spending equal to about 3 percent of gross domestic product. And most of that goes for courts, highways, education and other useful things. Any savings from elimination of waste and fraud will amount to little more than a rounding-off error.

So let's put a few things back on the table. Let's assume that interest on the public debt will be paid, that spending on defense and homeland security will not be compromised and that the regular operations of government will continue to be financed. What we are left with, then, are the New Deal and Great Society programs: Social Security, Medicare, Medicaid and unemployment insurance. And to close the fiscal gap, spending on these programs would have to be cut by around 40 percent.

It's impossible to know how such spending cuts might unfold, but cuts of that magnitude would require drastic changes in the system. It goes almost without saying that the age at which Americans become eligible for retirement benefits would rise, that Social Security payments would fall sharply compared with average incomes, that Medicare patients would be forced to pay much more of their expenses out of pocket—or do without. And that would be only a start.

All this sounds politically impossible. In fact, politicians of both parties have been scrambling to expand, not reduce, Medicare benefits by adding prescription drug coverage. It's hard to imagine a situation under which the entitlement programs would be rolled back sufficiently to close the fiscal gap.

Yet closing the fiscal gap by raising taxes would mean rolling back all of the Bush tax cuts, and then some. And that also sounds politically impossible.

For the time being, there is a third alternative: borrow the difference between what we insist on spending and what we're willing to collect in taxes. That works as long as lenders believe that someday, somehow, we're going to get our fiscal act together. But this can't go on indefinitely. Eventually—I think within a decade, though not everyone agrees—the bond market will tell us that we have to make a choice.

In short, everything is going according to plan.

For the looming fiscal crisis doesn't represent a defeat for the leaders of the tax-cut crusade or a miscalculation on their part. Some supporters of President Bush may have really believed that his tax cuts were consistent with his promises to protect Social Security and expand Medicare; some people may still believe that the wondrous supply-side effects of tax cuts will make the budget deficit disappear. But for starve-the-beast tax-cutters, the coming crunch is exactly what they had in mind.

7. What Kind of Country?

The astonishing political success of the antitax crusade has, more or less deliberately, set the United States up for a fiscal crisis. How we respond to that crisis will determine what kind of country we become.

If Grover Norquist is right—and he has been right about a lot—the coming crisis will allow conservatives to move the nation a long way back toward the kind of limited government we had before Franklin Roosevelt. Lack of revenue, he says, will make it possible for conservative politicians—in the name of fiscal necessity—to dismantle immensely popular government programs that would otherwise have been untouchable.

In Norquist's vision, America a couple of decades from now will be a place in which elderly people make up a disproportionate share of the poor, as they did before Social Security. It will also be a country in which even middle-class elderly Americans are, in many cases, unable to afford expensive medical procedures or prescription drugs and in which poor Americans generally go without even basic health care. And it may well be a place in which only those who can afford expensive private schools can give their children a decent education.

But as Governor Riley of Alabama reminds us, that's a choice, not a necessity. The tax-cut crusade has created a situation in which something must give. But what gives—whether we decide that the New Deal and the Great Society must go or that taxes aren't such a bad thing after all—is up to us. The American people must decide what kind of a country we want to be.

Paul Krugman is a Times columnist and a professor at Princeton. His new book is "The Great Unraveling: Losing Our Way in the New Century."

Liberal Lessons From Welfare Reform

Why welfare-to-work turned out better than we expected

BY CHRISTOPHER JENCKS

When Congress passed the Personal Responsibility and Work Opportunity Reconciliation Act (PRWORA) in 1996, the liberal community was almost unanimous in urging President Clinton to veto it. Even people like myself, who had supported Clinton's earlier efforts to "end welfare as we know it," thought that PRWORA went too far. Fortunately for the poor, the first five years of welfare reform inflicted far less economic pain than we had expected.

Now the Bush administration wants even tougher work requirements. Once again, most liberal Democrats think it is a mistake to worry about making every last single mother work when we have not yet ensured that those who already work can provide for their children. Once again, I agree: The administration's proposals are dreadful. But the people who claimed that PRWORA would cause a lot of suffering no longer have much credibility with middle-of-the-road legislators, who see welfare reform as an extraordinary success. If we want to regain credibility, we need to admit that welfare reform turned out better than we expected and figure out why that was the case. The usual explanation is simply that the economy did better than anyone expected, but that is only part of the story.

The traditional liberal position on single mothers was always "more is always better." More meant not only that the government should provide more resources but also that it should impose fewer restrictions on the recipients. The electorate has never accepted this view. Most Americans favor generous programs for people who are doing their best to help themselves. But when the government helps people who seem lazy or irresponsible, Americans tend to see this as rewarding vice. So the less a program asks of its beneficiaries, the less likely Americans are to support it. America's pre-1996 welfare program, Aid to Families with Dependent Children (AFDC), was a perfect example of how this logic plays out politically. It asked almost nothing of single mothers, and it gave them almost no money in return. As a result, everyone hated it.

Nonetheless, welfare-reform efforts achieved relatively little during the 1970s and 1980s. Welfare-rights groups were against requiring single mothers to work, and the liberal wing of the Democratic Party was reluctant to offend these groups, partly for fear of seeming racist. The labor market was soft, centrists feared that single mothers would not be able to find work in the private sector, and the right was against spending public money to provide jobs. Ambitious politicians came to see welfare reform as the Vietnam of domestic policy: a quagmire to be avoided at almost any cost. And because the welfare rolls were roughly constant from 1975 to 1989, the problem just simmered.

In 1991, with the welfare rolls rising rapidly, Bill Clinton decided that running against AFDC would be a good way to position himself as a "new" Democrat. As president, he set up a task force to propose a new system. By then the Democratic Party was deeply divided on welfare. Some supported a fundamental change, usually because they thought the only way to get more support for single mothers was to insist that the mother go to work. But many traditional liberals remained skeptical about serious work requirements. They saw the least-competent recipients as incapable of doing almost anything, and they could not imagine a system that drew a clear line between those who could work and those who could not. Clinton's 1994 proposals therefore needed Republican support to pass. By then the Republicans were more interested in humiliating Clinton than in reforming welfare, so his relatively generous version of welfare reform was stillborn.

After the Republicans gained control of Congress, they crafted a series of more draconian welfare-reform bills, which most liberals opposed. But after vetoing two such bills, Clinton signed the third. PRWORA replaced AFDC with Temporary Assistance for Needy Families (TANF). Under TANF, states could redesign welfare in almost any way they wanted, setting their own eligibility rules, work requirements, and time limits. TANF did establish federal time limits, but if states wanted to get around those limits they could do so by shuffling funds between programs.

The 1996 legislation was also a powerful symbolic statement. It made clear that America was no longer committed, even in principle, to supporting women who wanted to be full-time mothers. Anyone who wants to have children must either work or find a partner who will work. (The disabled are an exception, but "disability" is quite narrowly defined.) Single mothers judged capable of working can get short-term cash assistance from the government, but they cannot expect long-term assistance unless they have a job, and they cannot expect the government to find them one.

When this legislation was adopted, its opponents made four predictions:

- Many mothers would not be able to find jobs when they hit their TANF time limit;
- Even mothers who found jobs would seldom earn enough to support their family;
- Forcing unmarried mothers to work would not reduce unwed motherhood or discourage divorce; and
- There would not be enough good child care, so more children would be neglected.

What actually happened was rather different.

WORK When PRWORA passed, skeptics argued that there would not be enough jobs to go around. The proportion of single mothers who had worked at some point during the year rose from 73 percent in 1995 to 84 percent in 2000, while the proportion who had worked throughout the year rose from 48 percent to 60 percent. These were unprecedented increases: Nothing similar had happened during any earlier boom, and nothing similar happened among married mothers in the late 1990s.

PRWORA's critics often attribute these gains to the unusually tight labor market between mid-1997 and mid-2001. Some have suggested that unemployment among single mothers will rise sharply now that the labor market has gone soft. Some rise is inevitable in a recession, but the proportion of single mothers with jobs will not return to its 1995 level unless the recession gets much, much worse.

The unemployment rate for single mothers is normally about twice the rate for the labor force as a whole. In March 2001, for example, the overall unemployment rate was 4.3 percent but the rate for single mothers was 8.1 percent. The overall unemployment rate reached 6 percent in April 2002, so the rate for single mothers was probably just under 12 percent. That is surely causing a lot of suffering. But the fraction of single mothers with jobs is still far higher than it was before PRWORA.

The critics were right when they said that not all those who leave welfare would find work. Between 1994 and 2000, welfare receipt among single mothers fell from 32 percent to 15 percent, a 17-point drop; employment among single mothers, meanwhile, rose only 11 or 12 points. The question, though, is how many single mothers who *wanted* jobs failed to find them. The chart shows that the unemployment rate for single mothers fell between 1995 and 2000, which hardly suggests that the labor market was awash in single mothers unable to find work. Of course, workers only get counted as unemployed if they say they are currently looking for work. Some who left welfare presumably had looked earlier, found nothing, grown discouraged, and stopped looking.

INCOME When PRWORA was being debated, its opponents often argued that even if single mothers found work they would seldom earn enough to support themselves. If single mothers had to depend entirely on their own wages, this would often have been true. But most single mothers have multiple sources of income, and their economic status has clearly improved since 1996.

The official federal poverty rate among single mothers was 43 percent at the end of the 1980s expansion, 42 percent when PRWORA passed, and 33 percent in 2000. The drop among black single mothers was even larger. Poverty has probably risen over the past 18 months, but the rate for 2001 is almost certain to be lower than the rate for 1996. If the overall unemployment rate stays near 6 percent, single mothers are unlikely to experience as much material hardship in this recession as they did in the last one. A severe recession could be another story.

The critics were wrong because almost everyone underestimated how much government aid was being redirected from welfare support to work support. But will this continue?

Even before the current recession began, the Center on Budget and Policy Priorities had reported that the poorest single mothers were doing worse than they had before PRWORA passed. But census data on the poorest of the poor are problematic for a variety of technical reasons. Such data should never be trusted unless they are consistent with other evidence. If deep poverty had really increased between 1995 and 2000, for example, one would have expected more single mothers to move in with relatives. Census surveys showed no such increase. Likewise, an increase in deep poverty should have meant that more single mothers had trouble feeding their families. Yet the Agriculture Department's annual reports on its food-security surveys showed a fairly steady decline in the proportion of single mothers reporting food shortages, hunger, and related problems. My own work with Joseph Swingle and Scott Winship shows the same thing.

So why were the prophets of doom wrong? One answer is that almost everyone underestimated the extent to which government support for the poor was being redirected to people with jobs. Soon after Clinton took office in 1993, he persuaded Congress to expand the Earned Income Tax Credit (EITC). Today the EITC distributes more money to working parents than AFDC ever gave to mothers who stayed at home. For a minimum-wage worker with two children, the EITC means a 40 percent increase in annual earnings. More aggressive child-support enforcement has increased some working mothers' incomes even further. Extending Medicaid coverage to some of the working poor has also reduced some mothers' out-of-pocket medical spending, although much remains to be done in this regard.

TANF also gave states block grants that did not shrink as the welfare rolls shrank and allowed states to use these grants for child-care subsidies, which made it much easier for single mothers to survive on what they earned in low-wage jobs. Unfortunately, these subsidies are now in jeopardy, partly because the recession is putting pressure on state budgets and partly because the administration wants to force states to use their TANF money in other ways.

The net result of these changes is that the old "welfare state" is becoming what one might call a "wage-subsidy state," in which government assistance is tied to employment. By asking more of those who get government largesse, the new wage-subsidy system has substantially reduced political hostility to public spending on the poor. This is especially true at the state level. (In Washington the hard right is still riding high, and the Democrats remain reluctant to oppose the Bush administration even when it tries to limit states' ability to run welfare.)

But what about mothers who left welfare and did not find regular work? Many of these women are clearly struggling, but they are doing better than most of PRWORA's critics expected. They have not benefited from welfare reform, but it has been hard to find much evidence that their position deteriorated, at least prior to last September. One reason PRWORA's critics were too pessimistic about such mothers' prospects may have been that they were fooled by their own linguistic conventions. When we describe people as welfare mothers, we inevitably begin to see them mainly as people who get a check from the government every month. In reality, however, this check is hardly ever large enough to support the recipient's family. In their book *Making Ends Meet*, Kathryn Edin and Laura Lein reported that welfare checks typically covered about 40 percent of the recipient's expenses. Some of the rest came from food stamps; most of it came from relatives, boyfriends, and working off the books. Edin and Lein's data were gathered in the early 1990s, but the same pattern probably holds today.

When times are good, family members can be more generous and a mother has a better chance of finding off-the-books work. Boyfriends also earn more in good times, which may be one reason why more single mothers reported live-in boyfriends during the late 1990s. The value of an economic boom to a single mother depends, however, on current norms about how money should be spent. When incomes rose in the late 1980s, a lot of the money that flowed into poor neighborhoods ended up in drug dealers' pockets. When incomes rose in the late 1990s, expenditures on drugs were apparently falling, so more of the new money was available for food, rent, and fixing the TV.

MARRIAGE The idea that sending checks to unmarried mothers will encourage unwed motherhood and divorce has always seemed self-evident to most Americans. But back in 1996 it was hard to find much statistical evidence for this view. Single parenthood was becoming more common in all rich countries, regardless of how they organized their welfare system. And while welfare benefits varied a lot from one American state to the next, neither the proportion of children born out of wedlock nor the proportion of older children living with an unmarried mother appeared to correlate with benefit levels. When welfare reform was being debated in the mid-1990s, I do not recall hearing a single reputable scholar argue that changing the welfare system was likely to have much effect on marriage rates. I certainly expected no such effect. Even Charles Murray, who believed that welfare had played a role in the spread of single-parent families, felt that something more draconian than PRWORA would be needed to reverse the trend.

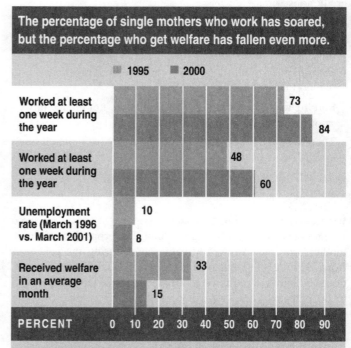

The percentage of single mothers who work has soared, but the percentage who get welfare has fallen even more.

	1995	2000
Worked at least one week during the year	73	84
Worked at least one week during the year	48	60
Unemployment rate (March 1996 vs. March 2001)	10	8
Received welfare in an average month	33	15

PERCENT 0 10 20 30 40 50 60 70 80 90

Sources: Welfare data are from the U.S. Department of Health and Human Services. Employment data and courts of single mothers are from tabulations by Joseph Swingle based on the March Current Population Surveys.

Since 1996 both the scholarly consensus and the facts on the ground have changed. Recent research suggests that welfare policy may, in fact, exert some effect on family structure. Furthermore, the spread of single-parent families has stopped. The proportion of mothers raising children without a husband had increased steadily between 1960 and 1996 (from 11 percent to 28 percent). But after March 1997, the proportion began to fall. By March 2001 it was down to 26.6 percent. That was hardly a revolution, but it cut the number of single mothers by half a million.

The proportion of children born to unmarried mothers is still inching up, but the increase since 1995 has been tiny. A study by Richard Bavier of the U.S. Office of Management and Budget suggests that women who have children out of wedlock are now marrying in greater numbers. We do not know whether these mothers are marrying their child's father or someone else. That is important, because children who grow up with a stepfather fare no better in adolescence or early adulthood than children who grow up with a single mother, even though the stepfather's presence substantially increases their family's income.

CHILDREN When PRWORA passed, its critics (including me) worried about how it would affect children. In material terms, children are now a little better off than they were in 1996. Children's psychological well-being is probably more important, but it is also harder to measure. A single mother who works full time obviously has less time for her children, and exhaustion may make her more irritable or more punitive. But the long-term effects of a single mother working remain uncertain and controversial. A lot probably depends on what the mother's job is really like, what it pays, and how flexible it is to family needs.

When mothers enter the labor market, however, their children's child-care arrangements become less stable. Government subsidies appear and disappear unpredictably. The women who provide child care for unskilled working mothers are often unreliable. Mothers often have to take either temporary jobs or jobs with unpredictable hours, and they usually have to change their child-care arrangements when their hours change. Children hate this kind of instability. Whether it causes long-term damage, however, remains unclear.

On balance, welfare reform has turned out far better than most liberals expected. Most Americans now see it as one of the great successes of the 1990s. Instead of remaining wedded to the idea that PRWORA was a bad idea because it was a supported by the lunatic right, liberals need to rethink. My own conclusions are three:

- Telling prospective parents that they would have to take primary responsibility for supporting themselves and their children was a good idea, because 60 years of experience showed that no other approach to reducing family poverty could win broad political support in America.

- Shifting government largesse toward those who work was a good idea, because it helped erase the stigma of single motherhood and made more resources available to single mothers and their children.

- Turning welfare over to the states was a really good idea, because most states currently take a less ideological view of single mothers' problems than does Congress.

Someday, of course, Congress may also show renewed interest in problem solving. At the moment, however, most states' approach to helping poor families is more pragmatic than Washington's, and the new emphasis on helping low-wage workers has created a significantly better system than we had in 1996.

CHRISTOPHER JENCKS *is the Malcom Wiener Professor at Harvard University's Kennedy School of Government and a founder of the* Prospect.

The O'Connor Project

Can we end racial discrimination without affirmative action? Here's what it will take.

By Lisbeth B. Schorr

JUSTICE SANDRA DAY O'CONNOR, SPEAKING FOR A MAJORITY of the U.S. Supreme Court in the University of Michigan affirmative-action case, declared, "We expect that 25 years from now, the use of racial preferences will no longer be necessary ...."

What would it take for that to become a reality?

In what we might call The O'Connor Project, we would have to commit ourselves to eliminating racial disparities at the starting line and at four subsequent crucial points, each of them involving changes that we already know how to make. By assembling existing knowledge, deepening it and scaling up from current isolated successes, our society could make a long-term commitment to action in each of these five arenas so that minority college applicants of 2028 would be educationally so well-equipped that they would not need the extra help of racial preferences.

Here are the concrete steps that would achieve that goal:

1. Eliminating racial disparities in birth outcomes. We could accomplish this by reducing the incidence of teen births and ensuring every pregnant woman high-quality prenatal care. Birth outcomes that predispose children to trouble at school, such as low birth weight (found twice as often among African American babies as among whites), are associated with serious cognitive impairments, behavioral and learning disorders, health problems and school failure.

2. Eliminating racial disparities in school readiness. By harnessing the tremendous growth in understanding of how parental support and early education (an essential part of high-quality child care) can equip young children for school learning, we could reduce by at least half the existing racial gap. A child's ability to reason and to master language and math depends on the stimulation, caring relationships and supports he or she experiences long before entering school. The founders of Head Start and other early childhood education programs knew this 40 years ago. Their successors are now proving it.

Because school readiness is more than a set of mechanical skills, the most effective ways to set children on a path to school success rely less on flash cards than on attention to emotional, social and health needs, and to the necessity of nurturing, supportive adults in settings that are language-rich and knowledge-centered. For families where parents are impaired by depression, substance abuse, personality disorders or domestic violence, programs must compensate by ensuring that all young children can grow up in environments that are safe, nurturing, stimulating and responsive.

3. Eliminating racial disparities in the opportunities offered by elementary, middle and high schools. Many individual schools have successfully broken the link between academic achievement and racial, economic and family background. Most recently, entire school districts have begun to shrink the race-based gaps that were once seen as immutable. Success has been most dramatic in the early grades. The latest results of nationwide testing among fourth-graders have shown universal improvement, and a significant narrowing in the gaps among racial groups.

Progress in middle schools has been slower and more sporadic, as broader reform efforts have collided with lesser capacity among front-line educators and greater chaos, indifference and hostility in the bureaucratic environment.

In high schools, the Bill and Melinda Gates Foundation is among those showing that we know enough to attack the gross inequities in preparing underserved young people for college. The foundation is successfully investing in the creation of smaller, more personalized learning environments, where every student is known by a school adult and held to high expectations.

Schools at every level and in every neighborhood must be able to attract, retain and support fully competent teachers, ending the scandal of children who need the most skilled instructors being taught by those least able to teach.

4. Eliminating racial disparities in the opportunities for adolescents to make a healthy transition into young adulthood. Here, too, our understanding of what works has taken a quantum leap in the last two decades. Local organizations like Big Brothers Big Sisters have been successful in matching at-risk young people with adult mentors. These trusting relationships produce measurable decreases in first-time drug use and improvements in school performance and behavior. Boys and Girls clubs, YMCAs, 4-H clubs, AmeriCorps and schools are running programs that are keeping youngsters constructively occupied during the hours when teens without such alternatives often get into trouble. In these ways, local communities are already well ahead of federal policy-makers in putting together the adults and resources that influence youth in a positive direction, complementing the work of schools in strengthening the capacity of adolescents to become competent and confident adults.

5. Eliminating racial disparities in the opportunities that families have to provide their children a good start in life. Most families share the same dreams for their children and would, if they could, provide them with safe neighborhoods, decent housing and good schools. Most would transmit to their children the security and optimism that usually comes to parents who work at jobs that pay a living wage. Most would provide the guidance that children need to grow into productive adults if they could command the resources to afford regular meals, books, computers and time. And yet large numbers of families, especially African American families in America's inner cities, cannot realize these dreams without help—from kin, from neighbors and from social institutions, including government. We know how to provide families with supports to enhance their economic well-being, the safety of their neighborhoods, the cohesiveness of their social environment and their parental abilities. We have work to do, though, before we are able to provide the needed supports at sufficient scale and in ways that a majority of Americans find compatible with their values. But that objective is also within our reach.

THE LEADERSHIP AND THE FINANCIAL AND INTELLECTUAL resources for such an ambitious undertaking as the O'Connor Project would have to come from a broad partnership, including government and public officials at all levels, philanthropy, the professional and academic communities, and the local groups throughout the country that are already working to make their communities a better place to live.

While we seek a wide base of support for committing the necessary resources, one model we could look to as a way to begin is the one now flourishing in Great Britain. When Prime Minister Tony Blair took office, the long-standing gap between the least and most advantaged populations was continuing to increase. He committed his government to eliminating poverty among children, to radically reducing income-based health disparities, and to narrowing the gap between deprived neighborhoods and the rest of the country—all within 20 years. Funding from both government and philanthropy has mobilized an extraordinary array of Britain's most daring and able individuals into the service of achieving these objectives. In the United States today, the challenge to embrace similarly lofty aspirations may seem particularly daunting, and even unrealistic. At a time of philanthropic retrenchment and fierce cuts in federal, state and local human-service budgets, how can the American public be expected to support an agenda as bold as the O'Connor Project contemplates?

First, we must be realistic about what works. We have already seen teen birth rates and juvenile violent crime decline in

Major Costs of "The O'Connor Project"	Estimated New Annual Costs
Eliminate racial disparities in birth outcomes	$3–6 billion
• Access for all teens to a variety of methods of preventing teen births • Outreach to provide all pregnant women with high-quality prenatal care	
Eliminate racial disparities in school readiness	$27–30 billion
• Expanded parental leave and family-support services • High-quality child care and pre-school education targeted to poor and minority children (including infants and toddlers) • Mental-health and social services for high-risk children and their families • Outreach to ensure that all young children receive high-quality health care	
Eliminate racial disparities in public schools	$40–45 billion
• Reform of schools and school districts; training, recruitment and retention of competent teachers • School construction and repairs in depleted neighborhoods	
Eliminate racial disparities in healthy transition into young adulthood	$5–6 billion
• After-school, school and community programs that support adolescent development and equip students for employment and post-secondary education • Outreach to ensure that all adolescents obtain high-quality health care	
Eliminate racial disparities in the opportunities for families to provide their children a good start in life	$35–40 billion
• Increased child allowance, tax credits and earnings supplements • Expanded support of decent housing in safe neighborhoods	

Source: These estimates are based primarily on calculations taken from One Percent for the Kids, edited by Isabel Sawhill (Brookings Institution Press, 2003); also from The Two Percent Solution: Fixing America's Problems in Ways Liberals and Conservatives Can Love, by Matthew Miller, (PublicAffairs Press, 2003).

response to initiatives of the last two decades, which incorporate some of the principles described above. But the most effective initiatives are typically underfunded and do not reach those most at-risk. And many well-intentioned efforts are not achieving their objectives. We must be prepared to move resources from less effective efforts to more effective ones—and to pay the costs of what it takes to understand the difference.

I calculate that the O'Connor Project would cost somewhere between $110 billion and $125 billion a year. (See table on previous page.) These estimates do not include the costs to universal health coverage for children, adolescents and pregnant women, which the nation seems gradually to be moving toward for reasons other than the elimination of racial disparities. This amount could be recouped by rescinding the portion of the 2001 tax cut allocated to the wealthiest 5 percent of U.S. families when fully phased in (about $88 billion a year), together with a modest increase in the gas tax or a 25 percent cut in "corporate welfare."

To bring the nation's actions in line with our best intentions, in just the ways that Justice O'Connor's decision implies, requires action on an agenda that is coherent, bold—and difficult. But don't let anybody tell you that it can't be done or that we don't know how to do it.

Lisbeth B. Schorr *directs the Pathways Mapping Initiatve of the Project on Effective Interventions at Harvard University, which is supported by the Annie E. Casey Foundation. She is the author of* Common Purpose: Strengthening Families and Neighborhoods to Rebuild America *and* Within Our Reach: Breaking the Cycle of Disadvantage.

By invitation: America's power

The new Rome meets the new barbarians

The United States is likely to be the world's top power for many years. This brings challenges that it should not try to face alone, writes Joseph Nye

CAMBRIDGE, MASSACHUSETTS

SHORTLY after September 11th, President Bush's father observed that

just as Pearl Harbor awakened this country from the notion that we could somehow avoid the call of duty to defend freedom in Europe and Asia in World War Two, so, too, should this most recent surprise attack erase the concept in some quarters that America can somehow go it alone in the fight against terrorism or in anything else for that matter.

But America's allies have begun to wonder whether that is the lesson that has been learned—or whether the Afghanistan campaign's apparent success shows that unilateralism works just fine. The United States, that argument goes, is so dominant that it can largely afford to go it alone.

It is true that no nation since Rome has loomed so large above the others, but even Rome eventually collapsed. Only a decade ago, the conventional wisdom lamented an America in decline. Bestseller lists featured books that described America's fall. Japan would soon become "Number One". That view was wrong at the time, and when I wrote "Bound to Lead" in 1989, I, like others, predicted the continuing rise of American power. But the new conventional wisdom that America is invincible is equally dangerous if it leads to a foreign policy that combines unilateralism, arrogance and parochialism.

A number of adherents of "realist" international-relations theory have also expressed concern about America's staying-power. Throughout history, coalitions of countries have arisen to balance dominant powers, and the search for traditional shifts in the balance of power and new state challengers is well under way. Some see China as the new enemy; others envisage a Russia-China-India coalition as the threat. But even if China maintains high growth rates of 6% while the United States achieves only 2%, it will not equal the United States in income per head (measured in purchasing-power parity) until the last half of the century.

Still others see a uniting Europe as a potential federation that will challenge the United States for primacy. But this forecast depends on a high degree of European political unity, and a low state of transatlantic relations. Although realists raise an important point about the levelling of power in the international arena, their quest for new cold-war-style challengers is largely barking up the wrong tree. They are ignoring deeper changes in the distribution and nature of power in the contemporary world.

Three kinds of power

At first glance, the disparity between American power and that of the rest of the world looks overwhelming. In terms of military power, the United States is the only country with both nuclear weapons and conventional forces with global reach. American military expenditures are greater than those of the next eight countries combined, and it leads in the information-based "revolution in military affairs". In economic size, America's 31% share of world product (at market prices) is equal to the next four countries combined (Japan, Germany, Britain and France). In terms of cultural prominence, the United States is far and away the number-one film and television exporter in the world. It also attracts the most foreign students each year to its colleges and universities.

After the collapse of the Soviet Union, some analysts described the resulting world as uni-polar, others as multi-polar. Both are wrong, because each refers to a different dimension of power that can no longer be assumed to be homogenised by military dominance. Uni-polarity exaggerates the degree to which the United States is able to get the results it wants in some dimensions of world politics, but multi-polarity implies, wrongly, several roughly equal countries.

Instead, power in a global information age is distributed among countries in a pattern that resembles a complex three-dimensional chess game. On the top chessboard, military power is largely uni-polar. To repeat, the United States is the only country with both intercontinental nuclear weapons and large state-of-the-art air, naval and ground forces capable of global deployment. But on the middle chessboard, economic power is multi-polar, with the United States, Europe and Japan representing two-thirds of world product, and with China's dramatic growth likely to make it the fourth big player. On this economic board, the United States is not a hegemon, and must often bargain as an equal with Europe.

The bottom chessboard is the realm of transnational relations that cross borders outside government control. This realm includes actors as diverse as bankers electronically transferring sums larger than most national budgets at one extreme, and terrorists transferring weapons or hackers disrupting Internet operations at the other. On this bottom board, power is widely dispersed, and it makes no sense to speak of uni-polarity, multi-polarity or hegemony. Those who recommend a hegemonic American foreign policy based on such traditional descriptions of American power are relying on woefully inadequate analysis. When you are in a three-dimensional game, you will lose if you focus only on the top board and fail to notice the other boards and the vertical connections among them.

A shrinking and merging world

Because of its leading position in the information revolution and its past investment in traditional power resources, the United States will probably remain the world's most powerful single country well into this new century. While potential coalitions to check American power could be created, it is unlikely that they would become firm alliances unless the United States handles its hard coercive power in an overbearing unilateral manner that undermines its soft or attractive power—the important ability to get others to want what you want.

As Josef Joffe, editor of *Die Zeit*, has written, "Unlike centuries past, when war was the great arbiter, today the most interesting types of power do not come out of the barrel of a gun." Today there is a much bigger payoff in "getting others to want what you want", and that has to do with cultural attraction and ideology, along with agenda-setting and economic incentives for co-operation. Soft power is particularly important in dealing with issues arising from the bottom chessboard of transnational relations.

The real challenges to American power are coming on cat's feet in the night and, ironically, the temptation to unilateralism may ultimately weaken the United States. The contemporary information revolution and the globalisation that goes with it are transforming and shrinking the world. At the beginning of this new century, these two forces have combined to increase American power. But, with time, technol-

ogy will spread to other countries and peoples, and America's relative pre-eminence will diminish.

For example, today the American twentieth of the global population represents more than half the Internet. In a decade or two, Chinese will probably be the dominant language of the Internet. It will not dethrone English as a *lingua franca*, but at some point in the future the Asian cyber-community and economy will loom larger than the American.

Even more important, the information revolution is creating virtual communities and networks that cut across national borders. Transnational corporations and non-governmental actors (terrorists included) will play larger roles. Many of these organisations will have soft power of their own as they attract citizens into coalitions that cut across national boundaries. It is worth noting that, in the 1990s, a coalition based on NGOs created a landmines treaty against the opposition of the strongest bureaucracy in the strongest country.

September 11th was a terrible symptom of the deeper changes that were already occurring in the world. Technology has been diffusing power away from governments, and empowering individuals and groups to play roles in world politics—including wreaking massive destruction—which were once reserved to governments. Privatisation has been increasing, and terrorism is the privatisation of war. Globalisation is shrinking distance, and events in faraway places, like Afghanistan, can have a great impact on American lives.

At the end of the cold war, many observers were haunted by the spectre of the return of American isolationism. But in addition to the historic debate between isolationists and internationalists, there was a split within the internationalist camp between unilateralists and multilateralists. Some, like the columnist Charles Krauthammer, urge a "new unilateralism" whereby the United States refuses to play the role of "docile international citizen" and unashamedly pursues its own ends. They speak of a uni-polar world because of America's unequalled military power. But military power alone cannot produce the outcomes Americans want on many of the issues that matter to their safety and prosperity.

As an assistant secretary of defence in 1994–95, I would be the last to deny the importance of military security. It is like oxygen. Without it, all else pales. America's military power is essential to global stability and an essential part of the re-

sponse to terrorism. But the metaphor of war should not blind us to the fact that suppressing terrorism will take years of patient, unspectacular civilian co-operation with other countries. The military success in Afghanistan dealt with the easiest part of the problem, and al-Qaeda retains cells in some 50 countries. Rather than proving the unilateralists' point, the partial nature of the success in Afghanistan illustrates the continuing need for co-operation.

The perils of going alone

The problem for Americans in the 21st century is that more and more things fall outside the control of even the most powerful state. Although the United States does well on the traditional measures, there is increasingly more going on in the world that those measures fail to capture. Under the influence of the information revolution and globalisation, world politics is changing in a way that means Americans cannot achieve all their international goals by acting alone. For example, international financial stability is vital to the prosperity of Americans, but the United States needs the co-operation of others to ensure it. Global climate change too will affect Americans' quality of life, but the United States cannot manage the problem alone. And in a world where borders are becoming more porous to everything from drugs to infectious diseases to terrorism, America must mobilise international coalitions to address shared threats and challenges.

The barbarian threat

In light of these new circumstances, how should the only superpower guide its foreign policy in a global information age? Some Americans are tempted to believe that the United States could reduce its vulnerability if it withdrew troops, curtailed alliances and followed a more isolationist foreign policy. But isolationism would not remove the vulnerability. The terrorists who struck on September 11th were not only dedicated to reducing American power, but wanted to break down what America stands for. Even if the United States had a weaker foreign policy, such groups would resent the power of the American economy which would still reach well beyond its shores. American corporations and citizens represent global capitalism, which some see as anathema.

Moreover, American popular culture has a global reach regardless of what the government does. There is no escaping the influence of Hollywood, CNN and the Internet. American films and television express freedom, individualism and change, but also sex and violence. Generally, the global reach of American culture helps to enhance America's soft power. But not, of course, with everyone. Individualism and liberties are attractive to many people but repulsive to some, particularly fundamentalists. American feminism, open sexuality and individual choices are profoundly subversive of patriarchal societies. But those hard nuggets of opposition are unlikely to catalyse broad hatred unless the United States abandons its values and pursues arrogant and overbearing policies that let the extremists appeal to the majority in the middle.

On the other hand, those who look at the American preponderance, see an empire, and urge unilateralism, risk an arrogance that alienates America's friends. Granted, there are few pure multilateralists in practice, and multilateralism can be used by smaller states to tie the United States down like Gulliver among the Lilliputians, but this does not mean that a multilateral approach is not generally in America's interests. By embedding its policies in a multilateral framework, the United States can make its disproportionate power more legitimate and acceptable to others. No large power can afford to be purely multilateralist, but that should be the starting point for policy. And when that great power defines its national interests broadly to include global interests, some degree of unilateralism is more likely to be acceptable. Such an approach will be crucial to the longevity of American power.

At the moment, the United States is unlikely to face a challenge to its pre-eminence from other states unless it acts so arrogantly that it helps the others to overcome their built-in limitations. The greater challenge for the United States will be to learn how to work with other countries to control more effectively the non-state actors that will increasingly share the stage with nation-states. How to control the bottom chessboard in a three-dimensional game, and how to make hard and soft power reinforce each other are the key foreign policy challenges. As Henry Kissinger has argued, the test of history for this generation of American leaders will be whether they can turn the current predominant power into an international consensus and widely-accepted norms that will be consistent with American values and interests as America's dominance ebbs later in the century. And that cannot be done unilaterally.

Rome succumbed not to the rise of a new empire, but to internal decay and a death of a thousand cuts from various barbarian groups. While internal decay is always possible, none of the commonly cited trends seem to point strongly in that direction at this time. Moreover, to the extent it pays attention, the American public is often realistic about the limits of their country's power. Nearly two-thirds of those polled oppose, in principle, the United States acting alone overseas without the support of other countries. The American public seems to have an intuitive sense for soft power, even if the term is unfamiliar.

On the other hand, it is harder to exclude the barbarians. The dramatically decreased cost of communication, the rise of transnational domains (including the Internet) that cut across borders, and the "democratisation" of technology that puts massive destructive power into the hands of groups and individuals, all suggest dimensions that are historically new. In the last century, Hitler, Stalin and Mao needed the power of the state to wreak great evil. As the Hart-Rudman Commission on National Security observed last year, "Such men and women in the 21st century will be less bound than those of the 20th by the limits of the state, and less obliged to gain industrial capabilities in order to wreak havoc... Clearly the threshold for small groups or even individuals to inflict massive damage on those they take to be their enemies is falling dramatically."

Since this is so, homeland defence takes on a new importance and a new meaning. If such groups were to obtain nuclear materials and produce a series of events involving great destruction or great disruption of society, American attitudes might change dramatically, though the direction of the change is difficult to predict. Faced with such a threat, a certain degree of unilateral action, such as the war in Afghanistan, is justified if it brings global benefits. After all, the British navy reduced the scourge of piracy well before international conventions were signed in the middle of the 19th century.

Number one, but...

The United States is well placed to remain the leading power in world politics well into the 21st century. This prognosis depends upon assumptions that can be spelled out. For example, it assumes that the American economy and society will remain robust and not decay; that the United States will maintain its military strength, but not become over-militarised; that Americans will not become so unilateral and arrogant in their strength that they squander the nation's considerable fund of soft power; that there will not be some catastrophic series of events that profoundly transforms American attitudes in an isolationist direction; and that Americans will define their national interest in a broad and far-sighted way that incorporates global interests. Each of these assumptions can be questioned, but they currently seem more plausible than their alternatives.

If the assumptions hold, America will remain number one. But number one "ain't gonna be what it used to be." The information revolution, technological change and globalisation will not replace the nation-state but will continue to complicate the actors and issues in world politics. The paradox of American power in the 21st century is that the largest power since Rome cannot achieve its objectives unilaterally in a global information age.

Joseph Nye is dean of Harvard's Kennedy School of Government and author of "The Paradox of American Power: Why the World's Only Superpower Can't Go It Alone" (Oxford University Press, 2002).

From *The Economist*, March 23, 2002, pp. 23-25. © 2002 by The Economist, Ltd. Distributed by the New York Times Special Features. Reprinted by permission.

The *Compulsive* Empire

Worried about the aggressive and unilateral exercise of U.S. power around the world today? Fine—just don't blame U.S. President George W. Bush, September 11, or some shadowy neoconservative cabal. Nations enjoying unrivaled global power have always defined their national interests in increasingly expansive terms. Resisting this historical mission creep is the greatest challenge the United States faces today.

By Robert Jervis

The United States today controls a greater share of world power than any other country since the emergence of the nation-state system. Nevertheless, recent U.S. presidents George H.W. Bush and Bill Clinton still cultivated allies and strove to maintain large coalitions. They considered such strategies the best way for the United States to secure desired behavior from others, minimize costs to the nation, and most smoothly manage a complex and contentious world.

By contrast, the fundamental objective of the current Bush doctrine—which seeks to universalize U.S. values and defend preventively against new, nontraditional threats—is the establishment of U.S. hegemony, primacy, or empire. This stance was precipitated both by the election of George W. Bush (who brought to the presidency a more unilateral outlook) and the terrorist attacks of September 11, 2001. Indeed, Bush's transformation after September 11 may parallel his earlier religious conversion: Just as coming to Christ gave meaning to his previously dissolute personal life, so the war on terrorism has become the defining characteristic of his foreign policy and his sacred mission. We can only speculate on what a President Al Gore would have done in the same situation; but while Gore probably would have invaded Afghanistan, he most likely would not have adopted anything like the Bush doctrine.

To some extent, then, the new assertiveness of U.S. hegemony is accidental, the product of a reaction of personalities and events. Yet deeper factors reveal that if this shift in policy was an accident, it was also an accident waiting to happen. The forceful and unilateral exercise of U.S. power is not simply the by-product of September 11, the Bush administration, or some shadowy neoconservative cabal—it is the logical outcome of the current unrivaled U.S. position in the international system.

> **It is not as if the Middle East has suddenly become more fertile ground for American ideals; it is just that the United States now has the means to impose its will.**

Put simply, power is checked most effectively by counterbalancing power, and a state that is not subject to severe external pressures tends to feel few restraints at all. Spreading democracy and liberalism throughout the world has always been a U.S. goal, but having so much power makes this aim a more realistic one. It is not as if the Middle East has suddenly become more fertile ground for American ideals; it's just that the United States now has the means to impose its will. The quick U.S. triumph in Afghanistan contributed to the expansion of Washington's goals, and the easy military victory in Iraq will encourage an even broader agenda. The Bush administration is not worried its new doctrine of preventive war will set a precedent for other nations, because U.S. officials believe the dictates that apply to others do not bind the United States. That is not a double standard, they argue; it is realistic leadership.

NIGHTMARES OF A HEGEMON

Great power also instills new fears in the dominant state. A hegemon tends to acquire an enormous stake in world order. As power expands, so does a state's definition of its own interests. Most countries are concerned mainly with what happens in their immediate neighborhoods; but for a hegemon, the world is its neighborhood, and it is not only hubris that leads lone superpowers to be concerned with anything that happens anywhere. However secure states are, they can never feel secure enough. If they are powerful, governments will have compelling reasons to act early and thus prevent others from harming them in the future. The historian John S. Galbraith identified the dynamic of the "turbulent frontier" that produced unintended colonial expansions. For instance, as European powers gained enclaves in Africa in the late 19th century, usually along a coast or river, they also gained unpacified boundaries that needed policing. That led to further expansion of influence and often of settlement, in turn producing new zones of threat and new areas requiring protection. This process encounters few natural limits.

Similarly, the recent wars in Afghanistan and Iraq led to the establishment of U.S. bases and security commitments in Central Asia—one of the last areas in the globe without them. It is not hard to imagine the United States being drawn further into regional politics, even to the point of deploying military force against terrorist or guerrilla movements that arise there, perhaps as a reaction to the hegemon's presence. (The same dynamic could easily play out in Colombia.)

The Bush administration's motives may not be selfish; rather, the combination of power, fear, and perceived opportunity lead it to seek to reshape global politics and various societies around the world. In the administration's eyes, the world cannot stand still. Without strong U.S. intervention, the international environment will become more menacing to the United States and its values, but strong action can help increase global security and produce a better world.

Such reasoning helps elucidate recent international disagreements about U.S. policy toward Iraq. Most of the explanations for the French-led opposition centered either on France's preoccupation with glory and its traditional disdain for the United States or on the peaceful European worldview induced by the continent's success in overcoming historical rivalries and submitting to the rule of law. Or, in neoconservative thinker Robert Kagan's terms, "Americans are from Mars, and Europeans are from Venus."

But are Europeans really so averse to force, so wedded to law? When facing terrorism, Germany and other European countries have not hesitated to employ unrestrained state power the likes of which U.S. Attorney General John Ashcroft would envy, and their current treatment of minorities, especially Muslims, hardly seems liberal. The French disregarded legal rulings against their ban of British beef; they also continue to intervene in Africa and to join other European states in flouting international laws requiring them to allow the import of genetically modified foods. Most European nations also favored the war in Kosovo. Finally, had Europeans suffered a direct attack like that of September 11, it's unlikely that they would have maintained their aversion to the use of force.

The claims of a deep transAtlantic cultural divide overlook the fundamental differences between the European and U.S. positions in the international system. U.S. hegemony has three long-term implications that were in high relief during the debate over U.S. action in Iraq. First, only the United States has the power to do anything about a problem like Iraq's Saddam Hussein; Europe faces obvious incentives to free ride in such situations. Second, the large European states have every reason to be concerned about U.S. hegemony and seek to constrain it; they understandably fear a world in which their values and interests are served only at Washington's sufferance. And third, the obsession of U.S. rivals with the role of the U.N. Security Council reflects less an abstract attachment to law and global governance than an appreciation of raw power. France especially, but also Russia and China (two countries that most certainly do not hail from Venus), would gain enormously by establishing the principle that large-scale force can be used only with the approval of the council, of which they are permanent members. Indeed, Security Council membership is one of the major resources at these countries' disposal. If the council were not central, France's influence would be reduced to its African protectorates.

Traditional power considerations also explain why many smaller European countries chose to support the United States on Iraq despite hostile public opinion. The dominance these nations fear most is not American but Franco-German. The United States is more powerful, but France and Germany are closer and more likely to overshadow them. Indeed, French and German resentment toward such nations is no more surprising than Washington's dismissal of "Old Europe." The irony is that even while France and Germany bitterly decried U.S. efforts to hustle them into line, these two nations disparaged and bullied the East European states that sided with Bush—not exactly Venus-like behavior.

The fate of the United States' design for world order lies in the hands of Washington's allies more than its adversaries.

Ultimately, the war against Saddam made clear the links between preventive war and hegemony. Bush's goals are extraordinarily ambitious, involving the remaking not only of international politics but also of recalcitrant societies, which is considered an end in itself as well as a means to U.S. security. The belief of Bush administration officials that Saddam's regime posed an unacceptable menace to the United States only underscores their extremely expansive definition of those interests. The war is hard to understand if its only purpose was to disarm Saddam or to remove him from power—the danger was simply too remote to justify the effort. But if U.S. officials expect regime change in Iraq to bring democracy to the Middle East, to discourage tyrants and energize reformers throughout the world, and to demonstrate the willingness of the

United States to ensure a good dose of what the Bush administration considers world order, then the war is a logical part of a larger project. Those who find such fears and hopes excessive would likely agree with the view of British statesman Lord Salisbury, when he opposed intervening against Russia in its conflict with Turkey in 1877–78. "It has generally been acknowledged to be madness to go to war for an idea," he maintained, "but if anything is more unsatisfactory, it is to go to war against a nightmare."

LEAD US NOT INTO INVASION

The United States is the strongest country in the world, yet its power remains subject to two familiar limitations: First, it is harder to build than to destroy. Second, success inevitably depends on others, because even a hegemon needs some external cooperation to achieve its objectives. Of course, countries like Syria and Iran cannot ignore U.S. military capabilities. They may well decide to limit their weapons of mass destruction programs and curtail support for terrorism, as Bush expects. But the prospects for long-run compliance are less bright. Although a frontal assault on U.S. interests is unlikely, highly motivated adversaries will not give up the quest to advance their own perceived interests. The war in Iraq has increased the risks of seeking nuclear weapons, for example, but it also has increased the rewards of obtaining them. Whatever else these weapons can do, they can deter all-out invasion, thus rendering them attractive to any state that fears it might be in the Pentagon's gun sights.

U.S. military strength matters less in relations with allies, and probably also with countries such as Russia, from whom the United States seeks support on a range of issues such as sharing highly sensitive information on terrorism, rebuilding failed states, and managing the international economy. The danger is not that Europe (or even "Old Europe") will counter the United States in the traditional balance-of-power sense, because such a dynamic is usually driven by fears that the dominant state will pose a military threat. Nevertheless, political resistance remains possible, and the fate of the U.S. design for world order lies in the hands of Washington's allies more than its adversaries. Although the United States governs many of the incentives that allies and prospective supporters face, Washington cannot coerce cooperation along the full range of U.S. interests. Perhaps weaker states will decide they are better off by permitting and encouraging assertive U.S. hegemony, which would allow them to reap the benefits from world order while being spared most of the costs. They may also conclude that any challenge to the United States would fail or could incite a dangerous new rivalry.

But the behavior of current and potential U.S. allies will depend on their judgments about several questions: Can the U.S. domestic political system sustain the Bush doctrine in the long run? Will Washington accept allied influence and values? Will it pressure Israel as well as the Palestinians to reach a final peace settlement? More generally, will the United States seek to advance the broad interests of the diverse countries and peoples of the world, or will it exploit its power for its own narrow political, economic, and social interests? Bush's worldview offers little place for other states—even democracies—beyond membership in a supporting cast. Conflating broad interests with narrow ones and believing one has a monopoly on wisdom is an obvious way for a hegemon to become widely regarded as a tyrant.

In his 2000 presidential campaign, Bush said the United States needed a "more humble foreign policy." But the objectives and conceptions of the Bush doctrine point to quite the opposite. Avoiding this imperial temptation will be the greatest challenge the United States faces.

Robert Jervis is the Adlai E. Stevenson professor of international politics at Columbia University and the former president of the American Political Science Association.

From *Foreign Policy*, July/August 2003, pp. 83-87. © 2003 by the Carnegie Endowment for International Peace. Reprinted by permission.

No, It's not Vietnam

The strategic context, the setting, the combatants, the size and scale—and America's national will—all make today's war in southwest Asia far different from the one 30 years ago in southeast Asia.

By James Kitield

ON MARCH 29, 1973, THE LAST OF THE KNOWN AMERICAN prisoners of war in Vietnam boarded C-141 transports and lifted off from Hanoi's Gia Lam Airport, bringing to a close one of the most painful chapters in modern American history. The Vietnam War had ripped at the fabric of American society for nearly a decade. With the return of the POWs, the entire sad tableau of the war—the violent campus protests and street demonstrations, the nightly images of fighting and atrocity, the napalm and the nattering inanities of the Saigon military briefings known as "The Five O' Clock Follies," the steady procession of flag-draped coffins—all of it could fade blessedly into the mists of history.

Or could it? From 1964 to 1973, 3 million American men and women served in Vietnam. Of that total, 304,000 were wounded and more than 58,000 would never return alive. After it was over, 1,280 American service members were still listed as missing in action, and more than 100 had died in captivity. Vietnam. Vietnam. Vietnam. For an entire generation, the name itself became a kind of shorthand for national folly, as evocative as the drumbeat of a funeral march.

Thirty years after the POWs left Hanoi, the Vietnam generation has taken its place at America's helm, and the U.S. military is once again engaged in a guerrilla war halfway around the world. Once again, the nation is deeply divided about the efficacy of war as a means of bringing democracy to a foreign land, and Americans are yet again transfixed by a mounting death toll. Perhaps not surprisingly, Vietnam, the familiar metaphor for quagmire and futility, has come to haunt much of the recent debate on Iraq.

"The ghosts of Vietnam are hovering around. For a generation that was seared by Vietnam, it's part of the mental furniture," said Eliot Cohen, professor of strategic studies at the John Hopkins University School of Advanced International Studies. At the mere mention of Vietnam, he said, "pretty awful pictures flash through your brain. The emotive content overwhelms the intellectual content." But the Vietnam-Iraq analogy "is profoundly misleading," Cohen asserts. "The circumstances are profoundly

different." From the broader nature of the conflict then and the ideological struggle it involved, to America's role in the world then versus now, to the strength of the U.S. military vis-à-vis the enemy then and now—the elements are all different. Cohen concludes: "Whatever this is, this is not like Vietnam."

In fact, many historians caution against any attempt to graft historical analogy onto new conflicts. Those who ignore history may be doomed to repeat it, but history rarely offers clear blueprints that can help us easily define or manage new events.

"When they figure in public discourse, historical analogies are really just akin to images" in an advertising campaign, said Andrew Bacevich, director of the Center for International Relations at Boston University. "By referring to the reconstruction of Germany and Japan after World War II, advocates of going to war attached a big smiley face to the prospect of liberating Iraq, even though circumstances in Iraq were radically different from postwar Germany and Japan. Likewise," he said, "when opponents of the war say that Iraq is like Vietnam, they make those comparisons to Vietnam because they want the interested public to turn away from the war and to oppose the re-election of President Bush. For people with their minds made up, pro-war or anti-war, the purpose is not to shed light on a complex problem. The purpose of the exercise is to attach the right labels, positive or negative."

SANCTUARY AND SUPPORT

Any careful comparison of the Vietnam War with Iraq has to begin with the very different strategic contexts. In the 1960s, Vietnam was viewed, by both the United States and a powerful bloc of Communist nations, as a key battleground in the decisive struggle between democracy and communism that was at the heart of the Cold War. The vast strategic stakes prompted the Soviet Union and China to funnel massive military and financial support to North Vietnam, giving it the stamina to continue the fight against superior U.S. forces far beyond what Hanoi could otherwise have mustered.

The determination of U.S. officials to avoid stumbling onto a nuclear tripwire with the Soviet Union, and to prevent drawing Chinese forces into the conflict as had happened in the Korean War, kept the United States from invading North Vietnam and decisively toppling the regime. For most of the war, U.S. officials were also unwilling to risk significantly escalating the conflict by interdicting North Vietnamese supply lines, the infamous Ho Chi Minh Trail, that ran along Vietnam's western border and through neighboring countries Laos and Cambodia.

The net result of that very complex strategic equation was that the North Vietnamese had two vital advantages that the insurgents in Iraq lack: a nearly inexhaustible wellspring of support from other nations, and nearby sanctuary. Yes, Baathist remnants in the Sunni Triangle are being reinforced by perhaps hundreds of Islamic terrorists who are crossing Iraq's porous borders with Iran, Saudi Arabia, and Syria. That influx of guerrilla fighters is hardly comparable, however, to the support and sanctuary the Vietcong received from North Vietnam and two major world powers.

"No matter how porous Iraq's borders are, or what assistance the Baathists and mercenaries are getting from Islamic terrorists, it is trivial compared to the support the North Vietnamese and Vietcong received from the Soviet Union and China," said Donald Kagan, Sterling professor of classics and history at Yale University. "That's not to say the Iraqi insurgents aren't a serious opponent, or that they might not have some external sources of money and support. But it's simply not on the same scale as Vietnam."

In addition to superpower support, the North Vietnamese had another strategic advantage in the person of their charismatic and widely respected leader, Ho Chi Minh. After leading the forces that ousted the French from Vietnam in the 1950s, Ho Chi Minh was a hero to many Vietnamese, and his message of nationalism and opposition to foreign occupiers resonated strongly throughout much of the divided country. Of course, a charismatic nationalist opposed to the U.S. occupation could still rise to unite Iraqis—a possibility that greatly concerns U.S. officials. But after suffering three decades of brutal tyranny, most Iraqis despise Baathist leader Saddam Hussein and his henchmen, and secular Iraq has relatively little sympathy for Islamic terrorists who come into the country to ignite suicide bombs that kill mostly Iraqis.

"The Iraqi insurgents don't have a Ho Chi Minh Trail to inexhaustible support, and they don't have a Ho Chi Minh," said retired U.S. Air Force Gen. Charles "Chuck" Horner, who served multiple tours in Vietnam and commanded American air forces during the 1991 war with Iraq. "America just saw Ho Chi Minh as a Communist, but to many of his countrymen he was a patriot, and there was something quite noble in his message of unification," Horner said. "In contrast, about the only people who want to return Saddam to power are the hardcore Baathists, and they are a small minority. Most Iraqis probably want us to go home, but not before we establish a certain level of security and help them open businesses and schools."

THE COMBATANTS

Any objective analysis of the relative strength of the U.S. military versus its chief opponents in Vietnam and in Iraq would have to conclude that the balance is tilted far more in the United States' favor today. America is now the lone superpower, operating without peer competitors—and that is largely because today's professional, all-volunteer U.S. military was purposefully reshaped by leaders who remembered the hard lessons learned in Vietnam.

Because ill-prepared troops were badly bloodied early in the Vietnam War, in fights such as the Battle of the Ia Drang Valley in 1965, today's U.S. military has trained relentlessly for high-intensity combat. "Mock war" training centers and exercises established after Vietnam include the Army's National Training Center in the California desert and the Air Force's "Red Flag" exercises at Nellis Air Force Base in Nevada. Many of the Army troops on the ground, including Special Forces units, have trained for guerrilla war and peacekeeping operations at the Joint Readiness Training Center at Fort Polk, La. Moreover, a majority of U.S. troops have served peacekeeping rotations in the Balkans over the past decade.

Because of discipline problems caused by rampant drug use in Vietnam, today's U.S. military is virtually drug-free, and soldiers are forbidden to drink alcohol while on deployment duty. And the Vietnam-era policy of rotating individual draftees into front-line combat units—a practice that dealt disruptive blows to unit cohesion—is long gone. Today, most soldiers will deploy to Iraq as part of a unit, and leave as part of that same unit.

The net outcome of these reforms, many experts say, is a U.S. military that today is better trained, more mature and disciplined, and more competently led and technically adept than the troops the United States fielded in Vietnam.

"I've been struck by how many soldiers who get wounded or return home from Iraq on [rest and relaxation] breaks say that they need to get back to their units because their buddies are counting on them. You didn't see that kind of cohesion in Vietnam," said retired Gen. Edward "Shy" Meyer, the former chief of staff of the Army who served multiple tours in Vietnam and instituted many of the post-Vietnam reforms. Because of conscription and rotation, Meyer said, his platoons in Vietnam would typically suffer 30 percent turnover every three months or so.

Meyer went on to list other differences between then and now. "As a brigade commander, I also had almost zero contact with the locals," he said. "Today, you can see that U.S. forces in Iraq are coordinating much closer with civil authorities and are much more sensitive to the challenge of winning hearts and minds. The Iraqi enemy is also focusing on soft targets because they are unwilling to confront U.S. forces head-on. That's very different than the North Vietnamese I fought in the Ia Drang Valley, who poured over the border in battalion-sized units looking for a fight."

Indeed, perhaps the most obvious contrast between Vietnam in the 1960s and Iraq in 2003 is the nature and size of the opposing force. The Vietnam War encompassed nearly a decade of high-intensity combat—at times, with half a million U.S. troops in the field—against battle-hardened North Vietnamese regular forces and determined, disciplined, and organized Vietcong insurgents. By contrast, the high-intensity phase of the Iraqi Freedom campaign, fought against poorly led and demoralized Republican Guard forces and loosely organized paramilitaries, lasted less than a month. The subsequent fight against a guerrilla insurgency by Baathist remnants, Islamic jihadists, and various mercenaries is now into its seventh month. Those differences explain why many experts say the Vietnam analogy is not applicable.

"In terms of the number of troops involved and level of effort, Vietnam was a major war, with both conventional and guerrilla phases and fronts," said retired Marine Lt. Gen. Bernard Trainer. "By contrast, Iraq is more akin to a policing action or trying to bring law and order to the Wild West…. In Iraq, I also don't sense that the enemy is particularly well organized or centrally commanded. They do not represent a cohesive ideology, and they don't seem to have a lot of popular support outside of a very finite area," he said. "Anybody who talks about that being another Vietnam is really pressing."

And another, often overlooked, factor makes Vietnam and Iraq very different narratives: terrain. Some experts doubt that the North Vietnamese and Vietcong could have persevered in their fight against the technologically far superior U.S. forces, whose aircraft owned the skies, without the cover of that country's thick jungles. "My answer to the question of whether Iraq is a quagmire is that I don't think you can have a quagmire in the desert," Kagan said. "The desert landscape in Iraq simply doesn't offer the kind of safe hiding places critical to sustaining a major and protracted guerrilla war."

NATIONAL WILL

Perhaps Iraq is most like Vietnam in this regard: U.S. troops dominate on the ground, but the enemy has identified the battle's center of gravity as the will of the American people. The turning point of the Vietnam War came in 1968, when the North Vietnamese and the Vietcong launched the Tet offensive—even while U.S. Gen. William Westmoreland was proclaiming that the light of victory was visible at the end of the war's long tunnel. At the time, the U.S. military portrayed the Tet offensive as a tactical disaster for the Vietcong and an act of desperation by a hopelessly outgunned enemy. That assessment, while true, eventually proved irrelevant.

The Tet offensive succeeded in changing the terms of the strategic debate. After Tet, everything hinged on how much pain the American people were willing to bear to prevail in a conflict with no clearly defined end in sight. With the recent Ramadan offensive of suicide bombings, rocket attacks, and ambushes, the Iraqi insurgents are clearly attempting to mimic that strategy.

In defining the Iraq conflict as a pre-emptive war and by failing to win United Nations, NATO, or widespread multinational support, the Bush administration disregarded one of the key lessons of Vietnam, one that is enshrined in the doctrine of former Joint Chiefs Chairman and now Secretary of State Colin Powell: Never again take the nation to war without the will of the American people fully behind you. Before the Iraq conflict,

83 percent of Americans supported military action if it were undertaken as part of a multilateral coalition, according to a September 2002 CNN/USA Today poll. But only 40 percent of the public said they supported a unilateral war. In going into Iraq virtually alone, the Bush administration committed U.S. troops to fighting a potentially protracted guerrilla war backed by an America of uncertain resolve.

Even when it comes to national will, however, the differences between Vietnam and Iraq are at least as striking as are the similarities. Whatever you believe about Iraq's connections to Al Qaeda before the war (and they seem to have been tenuous, at best, on September 11, 2001), Americans saw to their horror the repercussions of a failed state—in this case, Afghanistan—left to the untender mercies of Islamic terrorists bent on jihad against the United States. Many Americans understand that a similar nightmare could unfold in Iraq. Although Americans eventually lost the national will to "win" the Vietnam War, the 9/11 terrorist attacks remain a key factor in fortifying American resolve to stay the course in Iraq as a key front in the wider war against terrorism.

As has often been noted, the ending of the military draft after Vietnam cut one of the primary ties that bound the U.S. military to American society. The lack of conscription has insulated much of the American public from the direct pain of losing loved ones or being personally at risk in the Iraq war. "The major reason you don't see college campuses up in arms against the Iraq war is because we no longer have conscription," said Charles Moskos, a noted military sociologist at Northwestern University. "If you started drafting students again, you'd see the protests start up in a hurry."

Finally, while national resolve cannot be easily measured, this generation of Americans has yet to be tested on anything like the scale of Vietnam. At the height of the Vietnam War in 1967, more than 800 Americans a month were dying in action. More than 58,000 U.S. troops would ultimately perish, and more than 300,000 would be wounded. As of November 19, a total of 422 Americans had died in Iraq since the beginning of the war, and 2,387 had been wounded or injured.

"I still think the differences between Vietnam and Iraq are greater than the similarities," said Joseph Nye, dean of Harvard University's John F. Kennedy School of Government. "The casualties and body bags during Vietnam were just of a totally different magnitude, and we no longer have a draft that links U.S. troops at the front with 'Everyman' in a way that makes all Americans feel vulnerable," he said. "So in the final analysis, I still think we can prevail in Iraq and put down the insurgents in a way that defies the Vietnam analogy."

So perhaps the essential truth that links all wars is that every war is different. The Iraq conflict could still write its own dark chapter in American history, or it could prove to be the victory that future historians look back on as the turning point in the war on international terror. Whether it ends in victory or defeat, however, the Iraq war will play out according to its own unique and tragic rhythms, and it will take its place as an imperfect metaphor for all the wars yet to come.

From *National Journal*, November 22, 2003, pp. 3564-3567. Copyright © 2003 by National Journal. Reprinted by permission.

Index

Index

Test Your Knowledge Form

We encourage you to photocopy and use this page as a tool to assess how the articles in *Annual Editions* expand on the information in your textbook. By reflecting on the articles you will gain enhanced text information. You can also access this useful form on a product's book support Web site at *http://www.dushkin.com/online/*.

NAME:

DATE:

TITLE AND NUMBER OF ARTICLE:

BRIEFLY STATE THE MAIN IDEA OF THIS ARTICLE:

LIST THREE IMPORTANT FACTS THAT THE AUTHOR USES TO SUPPORT THE MAIN IDEA:

WHAT INFORMATION OR IDEAS DISCUSSED IN THIS ARTICLE ARE ALSO DISCUSSED IN YOUR TEXTBOOK OR OTHER READINGS THAT YOU HAVE DONE? LIST THE TEXTBOOK CHAPTERS AND PAGE NUMBERS:

LIST ANY EXAMPLES OF BIAS OR FAULTY REASONING THAT YOU FOUND IN THE ARTICLE:

LIST ANY NEW TERMS/CONCEPTS THAT WERE DISCUSSED IN THE ARTICLE, AND WRITE A SHORT DEFINITION:

We Want Your Advice

ANNUAL EDITIONS revisions depend on two major opinion sources: one is our Advisory Board, listed in the front of this volume, which works with us in scanning the thousands of articles published in the public press each year; the other is you—the person actually using the book. Please help us and the users of the next edition by completing the prepaid article rating form on this page and returning it to us. Thank you for your help!

ANNUAL EDITIONS: American Government 04/05

ARTICLE RATING FORM

Here is an opportunity for you to have direct input into the next revision of this volume.
We would like you to rate each of the articles listed below, using the following scale:

1. Excellent: should definitely be retained
2. Above average: should probably be retained
3. Below average: should probably be deleted
4. Poor: should definitely be deleted

Your ratings will play a vital part in the next revision.
Please mail this prepaid form to us as soon as possible.
Thanks for your help!

RATING	ARTICLE
	1. The Declaration of Independence, 1776
	2. The Constitution of the United States, 1787
	3. The Size and Variety of the Union as a Check on Faction
	4. Checks and Balances
	5. Why Don't They Like Us?
	6. The Death of Horatio Alger
	7. Coming Out Ahead: Why Gay Marriage is on the Way
	8. Party On, Dudes! Ignorance Is the Curse of the Information Age
	9. Federalism's Ups and Downs
	10. Rights, Liberties, and Security: Recalibrating the Balance After September 11
	11. Upon Further Review
	12. Winks, Nods, Disguises—and Racial Preference
	13. Guns and Tobacco: Government by Litigation
	14. The Return of the Imperial Presidency?
	15. The Accidental Radical
	16. Uncivil Liberties
	17. Packaging the President
	18. A Partner in Shaping an Assertive Foreign Policy
	19. The State of Congress
	20. The High Costs of Rising Incivility on Capitol Hill
	21. Legislative Season Drawn in Solid Party Lines
	22. On Their Own Terms
	23. The Price of Power
	24. John Dingell's Staying Power
	25. Sandra's Day
	26. A Judge Speaks Out
	27. One Branch Among Three
	28. Washington's Mega-Merger
	29. Turkey Farm
	30. Time for a Rethink
	31. Compete, or Else
	32. The Chieftains and the Church
	33. America as a One-Party State
	34. Republicans, Democrats, and Race: An Uneasy History

RATING	ARTICLE
	35. Running Scared
	36. Leaders Should Not Follow Opinion Polls
	37. Government's End
	38. Associations Without Members
	39. The Redistricting Wars
	40. A Better Way?
	41. The Short, Unhappy Life of Campaign Finance Reform
	42. Journalism and Democracy
	43. The Making of a Movement: Getting Serious About Media Reform
	44. Politics After the Internet
	45. The Tax-Cut Con
	46. Liberal Lessons From Welfare Reform
	47. The O'Connor Project
	48. The New Rome Meets the New Barbarians
	49. The Compulsive Empire
	50. No, It's Not Vietnam

(Continued on next page)

BUSINESS REPLY MAIL
FIRST CLASS MAIL PERMIT NO. 551 DUBUQUE IA

POSTAGE WILL BE PAID BY ADDRESEE

McGraw-Hill/Dushkin
2460 KERPER BLVD
DUBUQUE, IA 52001-9902

ABOUT YOU

Name _____   Date _____

Are you a teacher? ☐   A stud___
Your school's name _____

Department _____

Address _____   ___ e   Zip _____

School telephone # _____

YOUR COMMENTS A___

Please fill in the following inform___
For which course did you use thi___
_____

Did you use a text with this ANN___
What was the title of the text?
_____

What are your general reactions ___

Have you read any pertinent articles recently that you think should be included in the next edition? Explain.
_____

Are there any articles that you feel should be replaced in the next edition? Why?
_____

Are there any World Wide Web sites that you feel should be included in the next edition? Please annotate.
_____

May we contact you for editorial input?   ☐ yes ☐ no
May we quote your comments?   ☐ yes ☐ no